MW01038648

New Work on Speech Acts

New Work on Speech Acts

EDITED BY
Daniel Fogal, Daniel W. Harris,
and Matt Moss

Great Clarendon Street, Oxford, OX2 6DP,
United Kingdom

Oxford University Press is a department of the University of Oxford.
It furthers the University's objective of excellence in research, scholarship,
and education by publishing worldwide. Oxford is a registered trade mark of
Oxford University Press in the UK and in certain other countries

First Edition published in 2018

Impression: 2

Published in the United States of America by Oxford University Press
198 Madison Avenue, New York, NY 10016, United States of America

British Library Cataloguing in Publication Data
Data available

Library of Congress Control Number: 2017962126

ISBN 978-0-19-873883-1

Printed and bound by
CPI Group (UK) Ltd, Croydon, CR0 4YY

Contents

Preface and Acknowledgements   vii
Contributors   ix

1. Speech Acts: The Contemporary Theoretical Landscape   1
Daniel W. Harris, Daniel Fogal, and Matt Moss

2. Insinuation, Common Ground, and the Conversational Record   40
Elisabeth Camp

3. Clause-Type, Force, and Normative Judgment in the Semantics
of Imperatives   67
Nate Charlow

4. A Refinement and Defense of the Force/Content Distinction   99
Mitchell S. Green

5. Types of Speech Acts   123
Peter Hanks

6. Blocking as Counter-Speech   144
Rae Langton

7. Explicit Indirection   165
Ernie Lepore and Matthew Stone

8. On Covert Exercitives: Speech and the Social World   185
Mary Kate McGowan

9. Force and Conversational States   202
Sarah E. Murray and William B. Starr

10. The Social Life of Slurs   237
Geoff Nunberg

11. Commitment to Priorities   296
Paul Portner

12. Speech Acts in Discourse Context   317
Craige Roberts

13. Dogwhistles, Political Manipulation, and Philosophy of Language   360
Jennifer Saul

14. Dynamic Pragmatics, Static Semantics   384
Robert Stalnaker

15. Expressivism by Force   400
Seth Yalcin

Name Index   431
Term Index   435

Preface and Acknowledgements

In recent decades, speech-act theory has come to span many disciplines that would normally be disconnected. Foundational work in the philosophy of language continues unabated, but speech acts have also made notable appearances in formal semantics, pragmatics, sociolinguistics, computer science, epistemology, moral philosophy, social and political philosophy, feminist theory, gender theory, and the philosophy of law. What is particularly exciting is that these conversations have not been entirely siloed: new developments in each area have made their way into neighboring literatures, with the concepts of speech-act theory serving as vectors of intellectual exchange.

Our ambition has been to further this exchange, both by publishing papers that advance existing literatures and by bringing these literatures together for cross-pollination. We hope that readers who have come to learn about slurs, dogwhistles, and hate speech will stay for debates about the semantics and pragmatics of imperatives and the nature of the force/content distinction, for example. And we hope that those who have been drawn to the volume for work in formal semantics and pragmatics will be excited to find that their work intersects agenda-setting work in, for example, feminist philosophy. In short, we hope that the volume can provide a space in which to be drawn out of one's disciplinary comfort zone.

We have made a pair of editorial choices that bear mentioning. First, we present the papers in alphabetical order by author name, rather than splitting the volume into thematic sections. Our main reason for this is that—happily—many of the essays would span the relevant categories. Second, several of the papers deal with the semantics and pragmatics of slurs, one of whose characteristic features is that their derogatory effects are not cancellable under mention or direct quotation. There is consequently disagreement about whether and how their mention should be minimized or circumvented in talks and publications about slurs. We have left it to our authors' discretion whether to explicitly mention slurs or adopt strategies to avoid their mention, since the issue is a matter of substantive debate.

The project of this volume had its start in a conference held September 27–29 2013 at Columbia University, also named *New Work on Speech Acts*. We thank all the participants and the audience, as well as Columbia University, CUNY, and CUNY's Docotoral Students' Council for their support in making that event possible. We owe a special debt to the administration of the Columbia philosophy department, in particular Stacey Quartaro and Maia Bernstein, without whose efforts the conference could not have enjoyed the success it did. The conference extended our collaborative work on the research group we founded together in fall of 2011, the New York Philosophy of Language Workshop. That we felt inspired to organize the conference was due in large part to the workshop's speakers, attendees, and supporters, who made it the success it continues to be.

For suggesting that we edit this volume, and for a great deal of further guidance, we thank Peter Momtchiloff. Two anonymous referees for Oxford University Press gave us very useful suggestions that led us to add several papers. Leah Fortgang helped us with the index and with proofreading. Elmar Unnsteinsson gave us useful feedback on our introductory essay.

Contributors

ELISABETH CAMP, Rutgers University

NATE CHARLOW, University of Toronto

MITCHELL S. GREEN, University of Connecticut

PETER HANKS, University of Minnesota

RAE LANGTON, University of Cambridge

ERNIE LEPORE, Rutgers University

MARY KATE McGOWAN, Wellesley College

SARAH E. MURRAY, Cornell University

GEOFF NUNBERG, University of California, Berkeley

PAUL PORTNER, Georgetown University

CRAIGE ROBERTS, Ohio State University

JENNIFER SAUL, University of Sheffield

ROBERT STALNAKER, Massachusetts Institute of Technology

WILLIAM B. STARR, Cornell University

MATTHEW STONE, Rutgers University

SETH YALCIN, University of California, Berkeley

1

Speech Acts

The Contemporary Theoretical Landscape

Daniel W. Harris, Daniel Fogal, and Matt Moss

Speech-act theory was born of a central insight: language is a medium for many kinds of action, but its superficial uniformity tends to mask this fact.[1] Consider (1):

(1)   He should be here by now.

The point of uttering (1) could be to assert that someone should be here by now, to command someone else to get him, to assign blame for his lateness, to threaten, to act out a role in a play, to lodge a formal complaint, and so on. Without a clear understanding of these and other kinds of speech acts, we would have no hope of understanding how humans use language. Nor would we have much hope of understanding the many activities in which speech plays a central role. This is why speech-act theory has become essential to so many areas within philosophy and the cognitive and social sciences.

Unless we say otherwise, we will use 'speech act' to refer to *illocutionary* acts. This is a category first singled out by J. L. Austin (1962; 1970). There is no theory-neutral way of saying what makes for an illocutionary act, but it is relatively uncontroversial that paradigm cases include asserting, requesting, commanding, questioning, promising, testifying in court, pronouncing marriage, placing someone under arrest, and so on. In singling out illocutionary acts for theoretical attention, Austin distinguished them from *locutionary* acts, which are mere utterances of meaningful expressions, and *perlocutionary* acts, which are acts of producing effects that are causally downstream from illocutionary acts. Two utterances of (1) may be utterances of the very same sentence with the very same semantic properties. Yet, on one occasion, the utterance may constitute a complaint, on another, a mere observation. This raises the central question of speech-act theory: what makes it the case that an utterance constitutes an illocutionary act of a given kind? Answers to this question—i.e., theories of speech

---

[1] We find early articulations of this insight in Austin's discussion of the descriptive fallacy (1962, 1–3), in Grice's theories of speaker meaning and implicature (1957, 1961, 1975), in early versions of metaethical expressivism (Ayer, 1936; Hare, 1952; Stevenson, 1937), and in various guises in the work of Wittgenstein—most poetically, perhaps, in his comparison of linguistic expressions to a collection of handles whose functions are heterogeneous, but that "all [look] more or less alike. (This stands to reason, since they are all supposed to be handled.)" (Wittgenstein, 1953, §12).

acts—have proliferated. Our main goal in this paper is to clarify the logical space into which these different theories fit.

We begin, in §1.1, by dividing theories of speech acts into five families, each distinguished from the others by its account of the key ingredients in illocutionary acts. Are speech acts fundamentally a matter of convention or intention? Or should we instead think of them in terms of the psychological states they express, in terms of the effects that it is their function to produce, or in terms of the norms that govern them? In §1.2, we take up the highly influential idea that speech acts can be understood in terms of their effects on a conversation's context or "score". Part of why this idea has been so useful is that it allows speech-act theorists from the five families to engage at a level of abstraction that elides their foundational disagreements. In §1.3, we investigate some of the motivations for the traditional distinction between propositional content and illocutionary force, and some of the ways in which this distinction has been undermined by recent work. In §1.4, we survey some of the ways in which speech-act theory has been applied to issues outside semantics and pragmatics, narrowly construed.

1.1 What Makes for a Speech Act? The Five Families

1.1.1 Convention

One of the two theories of speech acts to be articulated in postwar Oxford is conventionalism, which originates in the work of J. L. Austin (1962; 1963; 1970). According to Austin, an illocutionary act is a "conventional procedure" whose performance is a matter of behaving in accordance with a collection of "felicity conditions", which are themselves a matter of localized social conventions. Violating some of these felicity conditions, as in making a promise that one doesn't intend to fulfill, results in an infelicitous act—i.e., a performance that is normatively defective in some way. Violating other felicity conditions, as one would do in attempting to pronounce a couple married without possessing the required status of an officiant, results in a "misfire"—i.e., nonperformance, a failed attempt to perform the act. In illustrating his theory, Austin focuses on highly ritualized examples of illocutionary acts, such as officiating a marriage ceremony, christening a ship, and willing property (1962, 5)— acts whose performance is impossible outside the context of established customs, social institutions, or legal frameworks. Nonetheless, his conventionalist analysis is intended to apply to all illocutionary acts. To perform an illocutionary act, according to Austin, requires first being in a context in which the convention is in effect, and then acting in accordance with it.

Although conventionalism makes sense of ritualized and institutionalized acts like marriage, it struggles with the illocutionary acts that make up our basic communicative repertoire, including asserting, asking questions, and making requests. Unlike marriage, asserting, asking, and requesting needn't be performed relative to the "jurisdiction" of any particular set of institutions or conventions: it is possible to assert and ask questions across international borders, but not to marry or testify in court, for example. And whereas the nature of marriage varies widely between societies, so that marriage is, at best, a loose cluster concept, asserting, asking, and requesting seem to be part of humans' cross-cultural toolkit for social interaction (even if the means of performing them vary between languages). It is also striking that every known human language includes clause-types whose function is to perform assertion-like, question-like, and request-like acts (Zanuttini et al., 2012), suggesting that their presence in our illocutionary repertoire is not itself a matter of convention. And whereas there are societies in which marriage ceremonies last years and involve complex exchanges of property, it is difficult to imagine rituals of this kind being necessary to, say, ask what the weather is like. It is therefore tempting to recognize a category of *communicative* illocutionary acts that function in a different, and less conventional, way than the essentially conventional illocutionary acts on which Austin focused (Bach and Harnish, 1979, chs. 6–7).

Considerations like these have led most contemporary conventionalists to hold that the conventions that define acts like asserting, questioning, and requesting are *linguistic* conventions, rather than social conventions of the kind emphasized by Austin. To assert *p*, on this view, is to produce an utterance that conforms to the linguistic conventions for asserting *p* in the language being used; *mutatis mutandis* for asking, requesting, and so on. A view of this kind seems to be widely assumed, though it has less often been explicitly defended. An influential defense of linguistic conventionalism—albeit a version that incorporates elements from various competing views to be described below—can be found in Searle's 1969 book, *Speech Acts*. The most notable recent defense can be found in Ernie Lepore and Matthew Stone's 2015 book, *Imagination and Convention*, which tackles many of the standard objections that have been raised against Searle and other earlier conventionalists.

Linguistic conventionalism faces a variety of serious challenges.[2] One major challenge is to account for semantic underdetermination—the fact that the speech act one performs is rarely, if ever, fully determined by the linguistic meanings of the expressions one uses to perform it. Consider (2):

(2)   Can you lend me a hand tomorrow?

In uttering (2), for example, a speaker may be requesting the addressee's help, or merely asking whether it will be available. The content of (2) will vary depending on who the addressee is, the flavor of the modal 'can', and whether the speaker is using 'lend me a hand' with its idiomatic sense or (in the macabre case) with its unidiomatic, fully compositional sense. The linguistic conventions governing (2) would seem to be neutral between these forces and contents; if so, something other than conventions will have to do the work of determining particular answers on particular occasions. Analogous points can be made about a wide range of linguistic expressions, and all (or nearly all) natural-language sentences, even when they are being used to perform direct and literal speech acts. Many have therefore given the speaker's intentions a role to play in determining what is said with an utterance.[3] When indirect and

---

[2] For some objections to conventionalism, see Bach and Harnish (1979); Davidson (1979a); Harris (2016); Starr (2014); Strawson (1964); Unnsteinsson (2016).

[3] Bach (1987, 1992); Carston (2002); Heim (2008); Kaplan (1989); King (2013, 2014); Michaelson (2013); Neale (2004, 2005, 2007); Schiffer (1981, 2003); Sperber and Wilson (1995).

nonliteral speech acts are considered, the case against conventionalism seems even more pressing (Bach and Harnish, 1979).

Lepore and Stone mix two strategies for responding to these worries. First, they argue that many alleged instances of illocutionary acts, including those involving metaphor, insinuation, and many cases of indirect speech, should not be considered illocutionary acts at all, since there can be no well-defined conditions for successfully communicating by means of them. There is no clear proposition p such that communication would succeed if one were to take Romeo to be asserting p in uttering 'Juliet is the sun', for example, and many cases of indirect speech seem to face the same issue.[4] In effect, Lepore and Stone hold that these phenomena are better understood as perlocutionary acts rather than as illocutionary acts: the speaker's goal is not to communicate a specific content, but merely to cause an open-ended chain of thoughts in the addressee. Lepore and Stone's second strategy is to draw on recent work in dynamic semantics, discourse representation theory, and discourse coherence theory in order to argue that many purported instances of semantic underspecification and indirect speech actually arise from complex but convention-governed interactions between utterances and discourse contexts. Due to the hitherto-unappreciated complexity of contexts and linguistic conventions, Lepore and Stone argue, many more speech acts turn out to be amenable to conventionalist treatment than had previously been thought. Their contribution to this volume, which we will? discuss in §1.2, applies this strategy to indirect speech acts.

1.1.2 Intention

The other classical theory of speech acts is intentionalism, which Paul Grice began to develop in parallel to Austin's views while they were both at Oxford in the 1940s. The central claim of intentionalism is that performing a communicative illocutionary act is a matter of producing an utterance with a special sort of intention, normally called a 'communicative intention', a 'meaning intention', or an 'm-intention'. The nature of communicative intentions is a matter of debate, but the crucial idea is that performing a communicative act is a matter of producing an utterance intending both (a) for one's addressee to have a specified response, and (b) for one's addressee to recognize that this response is intended.

One virtue of this view is that it correctly predicts a three-way distinction among the success conditions for speech acts. To succeed in *performing* an illocutionary act requires merely producing an utterance with a communicative intention; nothing on the part of the addressee is required. To succeed in *communicating* via one's act requires that the addressee recognize what kind of response one is trying to produce. Actually *producing* this response, on the other hand, constitutes a further kind of perlocutionary success. According to a simple intentionalist account of assertion, for example, asserting p requires uttering something with a communicative intention for one's addressee to believe p. Communication happens when the addressee recognizes that this is what one intends. Actually convincing them of p is another matter.

---

[4] Lepore and Stone (2015). It is worth noting, however, that this issue arises for most literal and direct speech acts as well (Buchanan, 2010; Harris, 2016). This argument's prototype is given in Lepore and Stone (2010), which is influenced by Davidson (1979b).

Different kinds of communicative act are distinguished, on this view, by the different kinds of responses that they are intended to have. To direct someone to ϕ—to request or command that they ϕ, for example—is to communicatively intend for them to respond by ϕing (or by forming an intention to ϕ). Questions, according to most intentionalists, comprise a sub-category of directives whose aim is for the addressee to respond by answering. Although intentionalists have typically focused on these three categories, other kinds of communicatively intended responses are easy to think of, and Grice considered some others.

Most of this picture is already visible in Grice's early work on speaker meaning (1957; 1968; 1969), though Grice avoids most of the vocabulary of speech acts, which he seems to have regarded as proprietary to Austin's competitor view. Later intentionalists, including Strawson (1964), Schiffer (1972, ch.4), and Bach and Harnish (1979), show how to translate Grice's ideas into the standard terminology of speech-act theory, construct detailed taxonomies of illocutionary acts by carving up the different kinds of responses at which they're aimed, and extend Grice's views in some other ways.

No intentionalist claims that this view applies to all of what Austin called illocutionary acts. One can't get married or testify in court just by speaking with certain intentions, for example; various cultural or institutional background conditions must also obtain. Intentionalists typically argue that, unlike these constitutively conventional acts, communicative illocutionary acts needn't be performed relative to any particular cultural or institutional background (Bach and Harnish, 1979, chs.6–7). All that is required to perform an assertion or a request, or to successfully interpret one, on this view, is that one be a creature with an advanced capacity to represent other agents' mental states.[5] It is therefore open to intentionalists to hold that the categories of speech acts in which they're interested are natural kinds—defined in terms of cognitive endowments shared by nearly all humans—unlike the localized and contingent social kinds on which Austin focused. Partly for this reason, intentionalism has been an influential view among anthropologists, cognitive ethologists, and cognitive scientists who study the psychological underpinnings and evolutionary origins of language and communication.[6]

An influential kind of objection to intentionalism accuses it of being too unconstrained, in part because it minimizes the role of linguistic convention in limiting which speech acts can be performed. A simple worry of this kind stems from the accusation of Humpty Dumptyism: it seems to follow from intentionalism, as just

---

[5] The idea that communication requires advanced mindreading capacities is an empirical prediction that some have sought to falsify. For example, the fact that three-year-olds can use language but routinely fail explicit false-belief tasks was widely thought to pose a potential counterexample (e.g., Breheny, 2006) until new experimental methods suggested that infants detect others' goals and false beliefs much earlier (Carey, 2009; Carruthers, 2006; Onishi and Baillargeon, 2005; Tomasello, 2008). Some autistic adults pose a similar problem, and a similar dialectic has emerged (for a summary, see Goldman, 2012). On the other hand, some accounts of both the phylogenetic and ontogenetic development of human language hold that advanced mindreading capacities play a crucial role (Bloom, 2000; Hacquard, 2014; Scott-Phillips, 2014; Tomasello, 2008). These views sit nicely with intentionalism.

[6] Csibra (2010); Moore (2015, 2017); Scott-Phillips (2014); Sperber (2000); Sperber and Wilson (1995); Tomasello (2008).

stated, that any utterance can be used to perform any kind of speech act, so long as the speaker has the requisite intentions. But, according to the critics, we can't say anything we choose with any words we please; the conventions governing the expressions we use place strict constraints on what we can use them to mean (see, e.g., Searle, 1965; 1969). Intentionalists typically respond to this line of thought by pointing out that, at least if we are rational, what we intend is constrained by what we believe. You can't rationally intend to eat an entire herd of cattle today because the possibility of doing so is ruled out by your beliefs. Likewise, if you think it is impossible to communicate the entire content of the Pentagon Papers with a wink of an eye, you can't rationally form a communicative intention to do so. On this view, one's appreciation of linguistic conventions constrains which speech acts one can perform by constraining what one can rationally intend to get across by speaking.[7]

Of course, it does follow from intentionalism that speakers can sometimes perform speech acts that bear no conventional relationship to the expressions they utter. Given the existence of indirect and nonliteral speech acts, most intentionalists take this to be a welcome consequence of their view. The counterintuitive corollary is that it is also possible for a speaker to perform speech acts that bear no conventional relationship to the expressions they utter, even if they don't intend to speak indirectly or non-literally, provided that they are sufficiently delusional or irrational. If a speaker comes to mistakenly believe that 'it's warm in here' is, according to local conventions, a good way to assert that it's cold in here, then they can indeed do so. The best response available to the intentionalist may be that, although it is indeed unintuitive to say that such speakers are performing the predicted assertions, that *is* what a hearer would have to interpret them as doing in order for communication to take place. And, indeed, if the hearer is aware of the speaker's delusion, this may very well happen. Supposing that an illocutionary act is that which must be correctly interpreted in order for communication to succeed, intentionalism seems to make the right predictions in such cases.

A final noteworthy consequence of intentionalism is that that communicative illo-cutionary acts turn out not to be essentially linguistic in nature or form. Grice makes it clear that by 'utterance' he means any observable behavior, linguistic or otherwise, that can serve as a vehicle for speaker meaning. This includes linguistic utterances, but also various other kinds of behaviors, as several of his original case studies demonstrate. Consider Grice's example of drawing a "picture of Mr. Y [displaying undue familiarity to Mrs. X] and show[ing] it to Mr. X" in order to mean "that Mr. Y had been unduly familiar" (1989, 218). There is no convention at work here, but merely a loose iconic relationship between the picture and its subject matter, which the "speaker" exploits in order to guide Mr. X to a correct hypothesis about their communicative intention. But for an intentionalist, the speaker here is performing essentially the same kind of communicative act as they would have if they had said, 'Mr. Y has been unduly familiar with Mrs. X'. What distinguishes the two cases is merely the kind of evidence that the speaker offers of their communicative intentions. Semantics, on this view, can be thought of as the study of a system by which language users encode richly structured,

---

[7] On this response to Humpty-Dumpty worries, see Donnellan (1968); Grice (1969); Neale (2004).

but merely partial evidence of their communicative intentions (Neale, 2004, 2005; Schiffer, 2003; Sperber and Wilson, 1995). This view has interesting consequences for the nature of assertion, among other acts. For although we can continue to use 'assertion' to denote communicative acts performed with language, this would make the category somewhat theoretically uninteresting. If 'assertion' picks out a natural kind, then it is a kind that brings together both linguistic and nonlinguistic acts that are united by the sorts of intentions with which they're performed.

1.1.3 Function

The family of views we'll call 'functionalism' is easiest to understand as an alternative to intentionalism. Both perspectives maintain that a speech act is characterized by the effect that it is the act's purpose to have. But whereas intentionalists think that a communicative act's purpose derives from the intention with which it was performed, functionalists think that a speech act at least sometimes has a purpose that derives from some other, less agential source. For example, Millikan (1998) argues that, in at least some cases, the properties of a speech act are a matter of its *proper function*, and that a given kind of speech act acquires its proper function through a process akin to natural selection. Millikan holds that causing belief is the proper function of certain assertions. Assertions will have this function because prior iterations have caused similar beliefs, and, crucially, these past successes have played a crucial causal role in their reproduction. Millikan argues that these functions attach to grammatically individuated utterance-types, such as clause types:

Thus, a proper function of the imperative mood is to induce the action described, and a proper function of the indicative mood is to induce belief in the proposition expressed.   (2005, 157)

Millikan's view is complicated by the fact that she also bases her theory of convention around the notion of proper function. Her theory could therefore be categorized as a compromise between intentionalism and a version of conventionalism: what defines a speech act is its purpose, which may derive from either the intention or the convention (i.e., proper function) behind it, or perhaps some complex combination of the two. However, since Millikan leaves open the possibility that an act-type's proper function may have been selected for not just during the language-learning process but also during biological evolution—it may be, for example, that the functions of certain grammatical features are innate and universal to humans—her version of conventionalism differs from most of the others on the market.

Building on Millikan's influence, a related version of functionalism about communicative acts has developed around the study of signaling games in the theory of replicator dynamics.[8] As in both Grice's and Millikan's theories, this view takes communication to be a way of influencing others' thoughts or actions. We can think of each instance of potential communication as a signaling game in which a sender performs an action and a receiver responds in some way. By making minimal assumptions about agents' shared interests and capacities to replicate behaviors that

---

[8] Replicator dynamics is the study of evolutionary processes using the theory of iterated games. For an overview of applications to communication, see Harms (2004a) and Skyrms (2010).

have tended to serve those interests in the past, one can show, by means of precise game-theoretic models, that they will reach equilibria in which senders reliably produce advantageous responses in receivers. This can be seen as a theory of linguistic convention, and as a theory of how different kinds of illocutionary acts, which function to reliably produce different kinds of effects in addressees, could enter a population's repertoire. However, as in Millikan's theory, replicator-dynamic models abstract away from questions about whether the kind of replication in question is a kind of learning or a kind of biological evolution. For this reason, such models have become important tools in the study of animal communication (see, e.g., Bradbury and Vehrencamp, 2011, ch.1).

The fact that functionalist models of communication have been applied to organisms varying in sophistication from bacteria to humans gives rise to interesting questions. For example: what are the conditions in which signals with different kinds of illocutionary force can be said to exist in signaling systems of this kind? Millikan (1984; 2005) argues that simple organisms and their signaling systems (as well as, e.g., the human autonomic nervous system) should be understood in terms of "pushmi-pullyu representations", which "at the same time tell what the case is with some part of the world and direct what to do about it" (2005, 87). Similarly, Harms (2004b) argues that only a kind of "primitive meaning", with no differentiation between assertoric and directive force, can emerge in populations of psychologically unsophisticated organisms.[9]

Are bacteria communication and human communication really so similar that they can be modeled in the same way? There are some concrete reasons to think not. In order to have a certain communicative function, a signal-type must have a history of differential reproduction. But humans often communicate with novel signal types. Most linguistic utterances, which involve sentences never before uttered, give us one kind of example. It may be that this problem can be solved by showing how sentences' proper functions are determined compositionally from the proper functions of their sub-sentential parts.[10] However, nonlinguistic communicative acts, indirect speech acts, and speech acts performed with context-sensitive vocabulary seem to be improvisational and dependent on humans' rich cognitive capacities in ways that resist this treatment. In the right context, it is possible to use a sentence to implicate something that it has never been used to implicate before, for example, and a gradable adjective (e.g. 'tall') can be used in context to literally and directly express a novel property (tall, by the standards of the marathon runners in this race). This suggests that human communication is thoroughly infused with greater flexibility than functionalist models can account for.

In practice, many theorists have therefore sought to combine functionalist and intentionalist models, with the former accounting for animal communication and

---

[9] Criteria for distinguishing assertoric and directive force in iterated signaling models are proposed by Blume and Board (2013); Franke (2012); Huttegger (2007); Zollman (2011). Murray and Starr (this volume) use work in the functionalist tradition to draw fine-grained distinctions between kinds of illocutionary force.

[10] This is what Millikan suggests in her discussion of "semantic mapping functions" (Millikan, 2005, ch. 3).

perhaps some simple cases of human communication, and the latter accounting for flexible and cognitively demanding instances of human communication.[11]

1.1.4 Expression

We'll use the label 'expressionism' for another family of views that have often been advocated as less intellectually demanding alternatives to intentionalism.[12] Theories of this kind are based on the idea that performing a speech act is fundamentally a matter of expressing a state of mind, and that different kinds of illocutionary acts express states of different kinds. Expressionism is a close relative of intentionalism, since it grounds the properties of illocutionary acts in facts about speakers' mental states. Whereas intentionalists categorize speech acts in terms of the psychological responses they are intended to *produce* in addressees, however, expressionists categorize speech acts in terms of the different kinds of states in the speaker's mind that they express. So, for example, whereas a simple intentionalism will say that a speech act is an assertion because it is performed with the intention of getting the *addressee* to form a belief, a simple expressionism will say that an act counts as an assertion because it is an expression of the *speaker's* belief.

Several arguments for preferring expressionism over intentionalism rest on the premise that intentionalism over-intellectualizes the performance of speech acts by requiring speakers to have complex, higher-order thoughts. Some have doubted that such complex cognitive states are necessary for language use, or that they are present in many human language users. Others have argued that intentionalism's rich psychological commitments obscure important points of contact between speech acts and closely related categories of communicative action. Green (2007b) argues that expressionism makes better sense of the continuities between illocutionary acts, on one hand, and behaviors that are expressive of thought in less controlled or voluntary ways, on the other. In a similar vein, Bar-On (2013) argues that expressionism does better than intentionalism at explaining the continuities between human communication and the kinds of less cognitively sophisticated communication employed by our non-human ancestors.[13]

The crucial ingredient in any version of expressionism is the relation of *expressing a state of mind*. Different versions of expressionism cash out this relation in different ways. Some accounts of the expressing relation are epistemic. According to Davis's account (1992; 2003), to express a thought is to do something in order to *indicate*— i.e., to give strong but defeasible evidence—that one has the thought. Pagin (2011) articulates an alternative epistemic relation between assertions and thought contents that he calls 'prima facie informativeness'. Green (2007b) combines expressionism

---

[11] E.g., Green (2007b); Millikan (1998); Scott-Phillips (2014).

[12] Note that the term 'expressionism' should not be confused with 'expressivism'. Although some versions of expressivism assume that speech acts are individuated by the kinds of mental states they express, so that, for example, moral claims are distinguished from factual assertions by the fact that they express non-cognitive states of mind rather than beliefs, other versions of expressivism have been constructed to fit with other theories of illocutionary acts. We'll say more about this in §§1.2–1.3.

[13] For a rejoinder to Bar-On's line of thought, see Scott-Phillips (2014, §2.7), who argues that human communication is discontinuous with all known non-human communication precisely because of the role played by communicative intentions.

with intentionalism in holding that performing a speech act is a matter of intentionally and overtly making one's thoughts manifest, but argues that it is also possible to express mental states in ways that don't presuppose intentional control. Other expressionist accounts have been spelled out in terms of relations that are causal rather than epistemic in nature (Rosenthal, 1986; Turri, 2011), including some who have appealed to the idea that it is the proper function of certain behaviors to express certain kinds of thoughts, thus blurring the lines between functionalism and expressionism (Bar-On, 2013; Green, 2007b). More often, the idea that it is the role of speech to "express thought" has been presented as a platitude or as a pretheoretic datum, without a serious attempt to elucidate the notion of expressing involved (e.g. Devitt, 2006, §8.2; Fodor et al., 1974).

One additional challenge for expressionism is to find a different kind of thought to individuate each theoretically interesting kind of speech act. It is a commonplace among expressionists that assertions express beliefs (or, alternatively, knowledge; see Turri, 2011). But what about other kinds of speech acts? One methodological tactic for answering this question revolves around Moore's paradox. Assertions of sentences of the form ⌜p, but I don't [believe/know] that p⌝, such as (3) and (4), are always infelicitous in some way, although their contents are neither contradictory nor necessarily false.

(3)   I have two hands, but I don't believe that I have two hands.
(4)   I'm doing philosophy, but I don't know that I am doing philosophy.

Some have argued that infelicity of this kind arises because, for example, someone who uses (3) literally would be expressing a belief that they have two hands (with the first conjunct) while also reporting that they lack this belief (with the second conjunct).[14] So, although the content of a Moore-paradoxical assertion is not contradictory, there is clearly something irrational about performing such an assertion. The subsequent line of thought is that we may be able to use variations on Moore's paradox to diagnose the mental states expressed by other kinds of speech acts. For example, Condoravdi and Lauer (2012) argue that sentences of the form ⌜φ, but I don't want you to φ⌝, such as (5), are Moore-paradoxical.

(5)   Take the train, but I don't want you to take it.

Partly on the basis of this evidence, Condoravdi and Lauer conclude that the speech acts we canonically perform with imperatives are expressions of "effective preference", which they take to be a species of desire.

Expressionism is sometimes preferred to intentionalism on the grounds that, by removing the addressee from the picture, it can account for speech acts that lack an addressee (e.g. Davis, 1992, 239). However, this feature can also be a bug. Removing the addressee from the picture is problematic because a single utterance sometimes

---

[14] E.g. Black (1952); DeRose (1991, 2002); Green (2007a); Rosenthal (1986); Slote (1979); Turri (2011); Unger (1975); Williamson (2000). The origins of this way of thinking about Moore's paradox can be found in the late work of Wittgenstein (e.g. 1953, §§87ff.). Of course, proponents of each of the other families of views about speech acts have proposed alternative accounts of Moore's paradox as well, and so it is controversial whether Moore's paradox gives any support to expressionism as such.

seems to be used to perform two distinct speech acts with distinct addressees. To use a slightly silly example, imagine a harried Wall Street trader shouting, 'Sell!' while holding a phone to each side of his face—one connecting him to stockbroker A, who handles his Apple stock, and the other connecting him to stockbroker B, who handles his Google stock. A plausible description of what is going on here would be that the trader is telling A to sell his Apple stock and telling B to sell his Google stock—two distinct directives, aimed at different addressees, performed by means of a single utterance. Although this case is somewhat artificial, a variety of real-world analogues are possible. Egan (2009) considers distributed readings of multiple-addressee assertions and directives in which a different content is expressed relative to each addressee, for example. It is quite plausible that a similar phenomenon is at work when a political satirist manages to come across as endorsing a policy to a right-wing audience while simultaneously mocking that audience and the proposal to a left-wing audience. The same sort of phenomenon is frequently exhibited by politicians and other public figures when they employ dogwhistles—speech acts that communicate a literal meaning to the public while also communicating some more controversial message to a subset of the public who are in the know.

The most obvious accounts of these and other highly nuanced communicative phenomena draw on the resources of intentionalism: one can perform two speech acts addressed to two audiences with a single utterance because one can communicatively intend to affect two addressees in different ways at the same time. Jennifer Saul (this volume) gives roughly this kind of account of what she calls 'overt dogwhistles'. In a similar vein, Elisabeth Camp (this volume) argues that insinuation is a speech act that is made possible by communicators' highly nuanced appreciation of one another's beliefs, intentions, and commitments. Any version of expressionism or functionalism that wishes to avoid appealing to intentionalist resources will have to say what is going on in such cases. In practice, many expressionists and functionalists *do* appeal to speakers' intentions, if only to explain what makes such cases so much more sophisticated than run-of-the-mill speech (Green, 2007b; Millikan, 1998).

1.1.5 Norm

A final family of theories holds that speech acts are fundamentally *normative* phenomena. An influential version of this idea holds that the act of asserting is constitutively normative—that at least part of what makes an act an assertion is that the act is governed by a special norm. Although normative accounts of assertion have been around for decades (Dummett, 1973; Unger, 1975), the view has recently been revived and influentially defended by Timothy Williamson (2000), who argues that the knowledge norm is the constitutive norm of assertion.

(1) THE KNOWLEDGE NORM
     One must: assert p only if one knows that p.   (Williamson, 2000, 243)

It is important to separate out two claims here. First, it is relatively uncontroversial that assertion is governed by some epistemic norm or other. We subject speakers to warranted criticism for saying things that they don't believe, that aren't true, for which they lack evidence, or that they don't know. It is tempting to think that Moore-paradoxical claims of the form $\ulcorner p$, but I don't [believe/know/have evidence] that $p \urcorner$

are not merely infelicitous, but normatively defective—a point that Williamson uses to defend the knowledge norm. Much of the debate about norms of assertion has revolved around whether the norm of assertion should be formulated in terms of knowledge, belief, truth, justification, or some other notion.[15]

A second, much more controversial claim is that being subject to an epistemic norm of this kind is what *makes* an act an assertion—i.e., that there is a *constitutive* norm of assertion. Few of Williamson's arguments seem to bear on this issue, and few others in the literature on knowledge norms have taken it up either. But, for the purpose of understanding the nature of speech acts, this is the crucial issue. After all: an intentionalist, conventionalist, functionalist, or expressionist could agree that assertion is governed by an epistemic norm, but argue that this follows from their particular account of assertion together with broader facts about the norms governing social interaction more generally. Certain normative consequences follow from Searle's (1969) accounts of various speech acts, for example, but he holds that this is a consequence of the conventions governing speech acts' sincerity conditions. Likewise, an intentionalist might argue that assertion is governed by an epistemic norm because it is governed by the maxim of quality, which is just one manifestation of Grice's cooperative principle, which governs all cooperative activities. On this view, arguments over the formulation of the knowledge norm might best be understood as arguments over which formulation of the maxim of quality follows from the cooperative principle.[16]

A second worry about the idea that assertion is constituted by an epistemic norm is that it is hard to see how such an account would extend to other speech acts. How, for example, would we fill in the gaps in (2)–(4) in order to give constitutive accounts of questioning, requesting, and advising?

(2)   One must: ask someone whether q only if . . .
(3)   One must: request that someone ψ only if . . .
(4)   One must: advise someone to ψ only if . . .

No attempt has been made to answer these questions, or to say what would count as a general theory of speech acts in the spirit of an epistemic-norm account of assertion. However, the idea that we should treat assertion as theoretically disjoint from other speech acts is bizarre. As McGlynn puts the point, knowledge-norm accounts of assertion threaten to repeat the mistake that speech-act theory was founded in order to address, since they ignore "the worry that many philosophers had fetishized the

---

[15] Proponents of some version of the knowledge norm include Adler (2002); Benton (2011, 2012a,b); DeRose (2002); Engel (2008); Hawthorne (2004); Reynolds (2002); Schaffer (2008); Stanley (2005); Turri (2010, 2015); Unger (1975); Williamson (1996, 2000). Others have argued, instead, that knowledge is governed by norms of knowledge-transmissibility (García-Carpintero, 2004; Hinchman, 2013; Pelling, 2013), belief (Bach, 2008), rational belief (Douven, 2006, 2009), reasonable belief (Lackey, 2007), supportive reasons (McKinnon, 2015), justification (Kvanvig, 2009, 2011), evidence-responsiveness (Maitra and Weatherson, 2010), epistemic certainty (Stanley, 2008), and truth (MacFarlane, 2014; Weiner, 2005). For overviews of this literature, see Weiner (2005) and Pagin (2016, §6.2).

[16] The idea of reducing the norm of assertion to a Gricean maxim has been suggested by Cappelen (2011); Goldberg (2013); Montgomery (2014); Sosa (2009). Benton (2016) argues that this sort of reduction fails. Ball (2014) argues that the normative properties of speech acts follow from their naturalistic properties by giving an account that draws on both Grice's and Millikan's ideas about speech acts.

speech act of assertion, and ignored all the rest" (2014, 82). This presumably plays a role in explaining why interest in epistemic-norm accounts has been stronger among epistemologists than among philosophers of language or linguists.

A different kind of normative account is built around the idea that performing a speech act is, fundamentally, a matter of doing something that gives rise to certain rights (or entitlements) and obligations (or commitments). An influential defense of this idea is due to Brandom (1983; 1994; 2000), who argues that to assert p is to do something that entitles participants in the conversation to make a characteristic range of p-related inferences and responses, and that commits the speaker to justify p and related claims going forward.[17] MacFarlane (2011; 2014) defends a similar account, on which asserting p is understood in terms of a public commitment to p's truth as assessed in the context of utterance as well as a commitment to retract p should it come to light that p is not true relative to a new context of assessment.[18]

Although Brandom and MacFarlane ignore speech acts other than assertion, Kukla and Lance (2009) and Lance and Kukla (2013) have developed a related, normative treatment of a range of other illocutionary acts, and several authors have argued that normatively rich accounts of speech acts can help us to understand speech acts of urgent social concern. Kukla (2014) draws on an account of this kind in order to argue that a speaker's social status can contravene their intentions, altering their act's illocutionary force—for example, by demoting it from a command to a request. Lynn Tirrell has used a normative pragmatic framework to understand the hate speech that typifies the buildup to acts of genocide (2012). In a series of papers, Mary Kate McGowan has argued that a wide range of speech acts, including regular communicative acts but also pornography and hate speech, should be understood as having "covert exercitive force": they change what is permissible in a norm-governed social activity going forward (2003; 2004; 2009a; 2009b; 2012; this volume).

How should we understand the claim that speech acts of a given kind enact norms? This could be a fundamental fact about the speech act—part of what makes it the kind of speech act it is. Brandom, MacFarlane, and Kukla and Lance clearly wish to be understood in this way, and so their theories must be understood as competing with the other accounts of speech acts outlined here. A deflationary alternative would be to concede that the speech acts in question sometimes, normally, or even always have the effect of enacting normative facts, but to hold that this is a mere consequence of some not-essentially-normative account of the speech act itself, together with facts about the wider normative scene in which speech acts are situated. Promising, for example, would seem to be a norm-enacting speech act if any is, since a felicitous promise is characterized by the creation of what is often called a "promissory obligation"—the speaker's obligation to keep the promise. Theories that take speech acts to be fundamentally norm enacting would seem to have a head start on explaining this phenomenon. However, there are alternative options. In Searle's (1969, ch.3)

---

[17] Brandom says that his theory of assertion "is largely a footnote to Sellars' [1956] seminal discussion of . . . endorsement" (1983, fn.14). Sellars can also be seen as a major influence on functionalist theories. For an discussion of Sellars' differing influences on Millikan and Brandom, see Millikan (2005, ch.4).

[18] Krifka (2014) also endorses a commitment-theoretic account, of illocutionary force, but without fleshing out the foundational details.

influential account of promising, which serves as the template for his account of other illocutionary acts, enacting new commitments is indeed part of what it is to make a promise. However, for Searle, this outcome of promises is, like the rest of his theory of speech acts, ultimately a matter of linguistic convention. Likewise, an intentionalist, a functionalist, or an expressionist could hold that promissory obligation results from the expectations that tend to result from successfully coordinating one's intentions with others—a view that can be made to fit with a range of normative theories (see, e.g., Norcross, 2011; Scanlon, 1990; 1998, ch.7). Likewise, the commitments engendered by assertion might be understood as consequences of intentionalism plus Grice's cooperative principle: roughly, asserting p commits one to justify p, and to retract p should its falsity come to light, because it would be uncooperative to intend for one's actions to produce a belief in p if one did not undertake commitments of this kind.[19]

1.2 Discourse Context and Conversational Score

Much recent work on speech acts, including most of the work collected in this volume, is based on the idea that conversations are organized around *contexts*. In the technical sense at issue here, contexts are shared and evolving representations of the state of play in a conversation that both shape the qualities of speech acts and are in turn shaped by them.[20] Following Lewis (1979), it has become common to discuss context through the metaphor of "conversational score". Just as the activities in a baseball game are dictated by the current state of its score—the current inning and number of runs, outs, balls, strikes, etc.—a conversation's score dictates how context-sensitive expressions can be used and interpreted. And just as plays in a baseball game function to change one or more elements of the score, moves in a language game—i.e., speech acts—function to change the state of the context.

1.2.1 Score and the Five Families

Score-theoretic accounts of speech acts are sometimes treated as an alternative to the five families of theory discussed in §1.1. In fact, however, talk of context and conversational score has been variously interpreted so as to be compatible with theories of all five kinds. As a result, many debates in contemporary semantics and pragmatics appear to be framed in terms of shared assumptions about conversational score, but this framing often masks foundational disagreements.

According to one influential view, originating with Stalnaker (1978), the context of a conversation reduces to the shared propositional attitudes of its participants. To perform a speech act is to do something with an intention of changing these shared attitudes. This amounts to a version of intentionalism that substitutes shared, public mental states for the private ones that Grice took to be the targets of speech

---

[19] Several authors have defended similar lines of thought aimed at showing that the normativity of both speech acts (and, in some cases, also thoughts) is not among their fundamental features (Ball, 2014; Boghossian, 2003; Glüer, 2001; Glüer and Wikforss, 2009; Wikforss, 2001).
[20] Contexts, thus conceived, have traveled under various aliases: "common ground" and "context set" (Stalnaker, 1978, 2014), "discourse context" (Stalnaker, 1998), "scoreboard" (Lewis, 1979), "files" (Heim, 1982, §3.1.4), "conversational record" (Thomason, 1990), "information structure" (Roberts, 2012), "information state" (Veltman, 1996), "conversational state" (Starr, 2010, ms), and so on.

acts.[21] In her contribution to this volume, Craige Roberts articulates a detailed theory of this kind that accounts for assertions, questions, and directives. Roberts follows Stalnaker in taking assertions to be aimed at adding their content to the common ground—the set of propositions that the participants in a conversation commonly accept for the purposes of the conversation. Questions and directives aim to alter other components of the context, each of which reflects participants' publicly shared goals. A directive's aim is to add to the addressee's *domain goals*—the perhaps extra-conversational goals to whose satisfaction participants are publicly committed. The aim of a question is to make it the new *question under discussion* (QUD)—the question that it is currently the participants' conversational aim to answer. Roberts' version of intentionalism resembles Grice's, except that the roles he assigns to beliefs and intentions are, for her, played by the interlocutors' shared information and goals. At this level of abstraction, Roberts agrees with Portner (2004; 2007; 2012), who argues that assertions are proposals to change the common ground, questions are proposals to change the QUD, and directives are proposals to change the To-Do List, which he thinks of as the "public and interactional" counterpart to agents' desires or intentions, just as common ground is the public and interactional counterpart to their beliefs (2004, 242).

It's easy to see that a functionalist about speech acts can adopt a similar approach by positing the same components of context, grounded in the same way in agents' propositional attitudes. The difference would be that what makes it the case that an utterance of a certain kind is a speech act of a certain kind is that, in at least some cases, utterances of that kind have the proper function of changing the context in a given way.

Each of the foregoing views presupposes psychologism about context—the view that facts about context are somehow grounded in facts about the mental lives of the participants in a conversation. But there are several alternative conceptions of the metaphysics of conversational score. For example, Brandom argues that speech acts "alter the deontic score, they change what commitments and entitlements it is appropriate to attribute, not only to the one producing the speech act, but also to those to whom it is addressed" (Brandom, 1994, 142).[22] On this view, facts about score are deeply normative, and may float free of participants' opinions about what the score is. In their contributions to this volume, both McGowan and Camp argue that at least some components of the score must be objectively normative in this sense. McGowan's reason is that an objective notion of score is needed to make sense of covert exercitives—speech acts that change permissibility facts in ways that may go unacknowledged by the participants in a conversation. Camp argues that a normative

---

[21] Although Stalnaker often frames his view as a version of intentionalism—including in his piece for this volume—he sometimes instead refers to speech acts as "proposals" to change the context without further cashing out this talk of proposals in terms of the speaker's intentions. And in at least one place, he expresses doubt about whether every such proposal to change the context must be intended to change the context in the way proposed (1999, 87).

[22] For a lucid comparison of Brandom's views to those of orthodox dynamic semanticists, see Nickel (2013).

account of score is needed to make sense of the way in which insinuation can give rise to unacknowledged commitments on the part of the speaker.

Camp also argues that at least some aspects of the score are "essentially linguistic", in that "the kind of commitment one undertakes by an utterance depends in part on the language game in which it is generated" (this volume, p.63). This idea presents another sort of alternative to psychologism about context. On this conventionalist approach, conversational score is the product of the conventions governing either language use itself or social interaction more broadly. This way of thinking is suggested by Lewis's (1979) analogy with baseball score. The fact that baseball involves both balls and strikes is due to nothing deeper than the conventions of baseball. Perhaps the fact that contexts include both, say, a common ground and a To-Do List is similarly due to nothing deeper than the conventions governing our language games. Imagine that, halfway through a baseball game, everyone involved is overcome by a collective delusion: although the home team has scored only two runs, everyone comes to commonly believe that they have scored three. Nonetheless, this delusion would not make it the case that a third run has been scored. There are objective, mind-independent facts about what a baseball game's score is at a given moment. These facts are determined by the conventional rules governing the kinematics of baseball—the rules by which games may unfold over time—together with facts about what has already taken place in the game. In principle, everyone could be wrong about the score. According to DeVault and Stone (2006), we should understand conversational score as being "objective and normative" in just this sense. Conversational score is determined by the rules of language, together with the fact that certain other moves have been made up until now in the discourse. Although participants should attempt to track the score with their shared attitudes, the score is not just whatever interlocutors take it to be. The chief advantage of this conception of score, according to DeVault and Stone, is that it allows us to make better sense of discourses that turn on the participants' confusion about what has already taken place in a conversation.

A conventionalist approach to conversational score fits nicely with dynamic-semantic approaches to sentence meaning.[23] On views of this kind, the meaning of a sentence is its *context-change potential*—a function that determines a unique output context for every context in which the sentence can be felicitously uttered. On this view, provided that participants are speaking literally, the series of past conversational moves together with the semantics of the language being spoken would fully determine the score at a given moment.

This is the sort of system that DeVault and Stone (2006) present, and that Lepore and Stone (2015; this volume) defend. At the center of their approach is an attempt to respond to a serious problem for conventionalist approaches built

---

[23] Note, however, that the connection between dynamic semantics and conventionalism about conversational score is somewhat loose. An intentionalist could adopt dynamic semantics, taking each sentence's context-change potential to be evidence of how a speaker who used the sentence literally would be intending to affect the context. Likewise, conventionalism about context does not, strictly speaking, entail dynamic semantics: a static semantics could be paired with pragmatic rules governing the kinematics of score, but these pragmatic rules could be construed as ultimately a matter of social convention. The latter option would depend on some explanation of why we should distinguish the semantic conventions from the pragmatic conventions, but the position is a coherent one.

around conversational score, stemming from the observation that the context of a conversation often seems to evolve in ways that aren't wholly governed by convention. Some aspects of conversational score can be manipulated by means of indirect speech acts, whose content and force seemingly aren't a matter of convention. Lepore and Stone reply that these supposedly non-conventional speech acts fall into one of two categories. Some aren't really illocutionary acts at all: since it's impossible for interlocutors to agree on the precise way in which many indirect speech acts are intended to update the score, they mustn't be attempts to do so. On the other hand, some genuine examples of indirect speech acts should be understood as semantically encoded. In their paper for this volume, Lepore and Stone develop this approach by giving a dynamic-semantic treatment of the indirect-request reading of sentences like 'Can you pass the salt?'. On their view, this sentence has a reading on which its semantic value is a context-change potential that specifies two successive updates to the context, the first a question and the second a request. If an account of this kind can be generalized to make sense of other indirect speech acts, conventionalism will have answered one of its most significant objections.

Further challenges lurk, however. One way for it to become common ground that there is a goat in the room is for someone to assert that there is a goat in the room; another way is for a goat to wander into our midst and for us all to notice it (and notice each other noticing it, etc.). Importantly, each of these events can influence the future of the conversation in similar ways. For example, either event licenses the use of a pronoun ('it', or perhaps 'he' or 'she') to discuss the goat. Roberts (2002; 2003; 2005) argues that this is no coincidence: definite noun phrases are sensitive to facts about the context, but don't care whether the context got that way by linguistic or nonlinguistic means. Roberts thus advocates a kind of "dynamic pragmatics" on which the rules by which conversational score evolves is largely a matter of pragmatic, rather than semantic, factors. Other defenders of dynamic pragmatics include Karen Lewis (2011; 2012; 2014), Portner (2004; this volume), and Stalnaker (2014; this volume). Stalnaker's contribution to this volume, in particular, is aimed at challenging both conventionalist theories of context and dynamic approaches to semantics; he argues that we should "represent the structure of discourse in a way that is independent of the linguistic mechanisms by which the purposes of the practice of discourse are realized" (p.384).

1.2.2 Speech-Act Taxonomy and The Structure of Contexts

Theories of speech acts that are spelled out in terms of context or conversational score suggest the following approach to taxonomizing speech acts: identify the components of context (score) that we have reason to posit, identify the different ways in which those components can be manipulated by speaking, and individuate speech-act categories in terms of these different ways of manipulating the different components of score.[24] As we have already seen, Roberts and Portner each pursue a version of this strategy to account for the difference between assertions, questions, and directives.

---

[24] Influential early statements on of this idea include Carlson (1982); Cohen and Perrault (1979); Gazdar (1981); Hamblin (1971); Heim (1982, 1983); Kamp (1981); Lewis (1979); Stalnaker (1978). The idea is

But of course, these three aren't the only interesting categories of speech act. There are also various other categories, and there are apparently also sub-categories within these categories. The latter point is most obvious in the case of the speech acts that we tend to perform with imperative sentences, which include distinct sub-categories of directives, such as requests and commands, as well as weaker, non-directive acts, such as permissions, acquiescences, wishes, and disinterested advice.[25]

(5)	Bring me my scepter!	COMMAND/ORDER
(6)	Pass me the hammer.	REQUEST
(7)	Have a cookie.	PERMISSION/OFFER
(8)	(Go ahead:) Eat the rest of my sandwich.	ACQUIESCENCE
(9)	Get well soon!	WISH
(10)	Take the six train.	DISINTERESTED ADVICE/INSTRUCTION

Various strategies for drawing these distinctions have been pursued. One idea is that the different uses of imperatives involve different kinds of indirect speech acts either in addition to or instead of the main speech act. Condoravdi and Lauer (2012) defend a version of this view on which imperatives literally encode an expression of desire, and on which various flavors of directive force arise due to features of the context. Harris (2014) argues that imperatives encode neutral directive force, but follows Schiffer (1972) in thinking that both individual flavors of directive force and non-directive uses result from indirect speech acts that communicate the reason for which the speaker expects the addressee to act. von Fintel (1994) and Charlow (this volume) argue that *some* indirect-speech-act account must be correct, without supplying one.

Portner (2007; 2012) defends a different pragmatic account of imperatives' illocutionary variability. On his view, imperatives are always used to update the addressee's To-Do List, but each To-Do List contains different sub-lists corresponding to the different kinds of reasons that agents have for acting. Whereas a command proposes an update to the part of the To-Do List that corresponds to the addressee's duties, a request proposes an update to the part of the To-Do List that corresponds to the speaker's desires. In his contribution to this volume, Portner further elaborates this picture by distinguishing the To-Do Lists that represents interlocutors' mutual commitments from those that publicly represent their individual commitments. In effect, this gives Portner a way of modeling the idea that whereas directive acts (such as requests and commands) propose coordination on a new shared commitment on the basis of the speaker's preferences, weak uses of imperatives (e.g. permissions and acquiescences) propose coordination on a new shared commitment on the basis of the addressee's preferences.

---

now too widespread to comprehensively cite, though some influential recent contributions that focus on the nature of communicative acts include Beaver (2001); Condoravdi and Lauer (2012); Farkas and Bruce (2010); Ginzburg (2012); Gunlogson (2001); Murray (2014); Murray and Starr (ms); Portner (2004, 2007, 2012); Roberts (2004, 2012); Starr (ms, 2010, 2014); Thomason (1990); Veltman (1996); Yalcin (2007, 2012).

[25] Stalnaker (this volume) suggests that the same issues arise for declaratives, and that what many philosophers think of as assertions should be thought of as an epistemically distinctive sub-genre of what Stalnaker categorizes as assertions.

The most prominent semantic account of the illocutionary variability of imperatives has been defended by Kaufmann (2012), who argues that imperatives are deontic modals whose presuppositional contents force them to be used performatively.[26] Just as the flavor of a deontic modal depends on the ordering source relative to which it is interpreted, the kind of speech act one performs by uttering an imperative depends on the operative ordering source (and perhaps also on other contextual parameters as well). In her contribution to this volume, Roberts splits the difference between Portner's and Kaufmann's views: imperatives denote properties rather than modals, and they are used to propose shared goals (a view similar to Portner's), but, like deontic modals, imperatives' semantic values are parameterized to a modal base and ordering source, allowing them to be used with different forces.

In their contribution to this volume, Murray and Starr take a different kind of approach to the illocutionary variability of the three major clause types. They individuate speech acts at two distinct levels of abstraction and defend different kinds of theory about how individuation works at each level. At the more abstract level, Murray and Starr are conventionalists: each major clause type (declarative, interrogative, and imperative) is governed by a linguistic convention according to which uttering a clause of a given type results in a distinctive kind of context update. When it comes to finer-grained distinctions within each of these broad categories, Murray and Starr are functionalists. They argue that the particular illocutionary force of a speech act is a matter of how updating the context functions to affect interlocutors' private mental states. Although all literal speech acts performed using imperatives update the dimension of context that represents interlocutors' joint preferences, doing so may have the function of changing interlocutors' private mental states in different ways, and their illocutionary force is a matter of this function, which arises from a selection process akin to those posited by, e.g., Millikan (1998) and Skyrms (1996).

A wide range of different kinds of context update have been posited in the semantics and pragmatics literature, and it is an open question whether all of these should be thought of as illocutionary acts. There are several interesting borderline cases. For example: one early argument for extending Stalnaker's model of common ground came from Irene Heim (1982; 1983), who argues that a variety of data about anaphora motivates positing a stock of *discourse referents* in as a component of the context.[27] On Heim's view, the semantic values of definite noun phrases are determined, in part, by facts about the discourse referents currently on file in the context. On the other hand, part of the semantic role of indefinite noun phrases is to establish new discourse referents. In uttering, 'A dog ate my homework', for example, a speaker not only contributes some information about the fate of their homework; they also establish a new discourse referent that may help to determine the semantic value of

---

[26] The idea that imperatives are deontic modals in disguise has also been defended by Han (1998); Lewis (1975). Charlow (2010; 2014; this volume) also posits a close connection between deontic modals and imperatives, but with the twist that he is an expressivist about deontic modals, so that his view might better be described as one that uses the resources of a theory of imperatives to understand the nature of modals, rather than the other way around.

[27] Heim explicitly construes her theory of context as an extension of Stalnaker's in her dissertation (1982, ch.3, §§1.3–1.4). For related views, each of which can be understood as positing similar components of context, see Groenendijk and Stokhof (1989, 1991); Kamp (1981); Kamp and Reyle (1993); Karttunen (1976).

future definite noun phrases. From the fact that indefinites are, on this view, used to change the context in a distinctive kind of way, should we conclude that indefinites are used to perform a distinctive kind of illocutionary act? An affirmative answer would seem to follow from some versions of the idea that kinds of illocutionary act just are kinds of context update (e.g., Gazdar, 1981), but more nuanced ways of drawing principled distinctions between illocutionary updates and other kinds of updates may also be available (e.g., Murray, 2014).

A related set of questions arises from ways of conveying information that are unlike assertion in various respects. Take the following examples.

(11)   a. Tony, who is a linguist, often says 'ah ha' when listening to others.
      b. Tony is a linguist.

(12)   a. My sister is coming to town.
      b. I have a sister.

(13)   a. É-hó'tåhéva-Ø Sandy
        3-win-DIR Sandy
        'Sandy won (I witnessed).'   (Murray, 2014, 2:3)
      b. I have direct evidence that Sandy won.

(14)   a. I'm in a bit of a hurry. Is there any way we can settle this right now?
        [to a cop after being pulled over for speeding]   (Pinker et al., 2008)
      b. I am willing to bribe you not to write me a ticket.

In uttering (11)a, one normally *conventionally implicates* a proposition that could be paraphrased with (11)b. Conventionally implicating a proposition is normally a way of informing one's interlocutors about it (Potts, 2005, §2.5.3). In uttering (12)a, one normally *presupposes* a proposition that could be paraphrased with (12)b. Presupposition is often explicated by saying that an utterance that presupposes p is felicitous only if p is already in the common ground. However, presupposed contents that aren't already common ground are often accommodated (Lewis, 1979; Roberts, 2015a), so that (12)a can be a way of informing others that one has a sister. By virtue of the semantic rules governing evidential particles in Cheyenne, a speaker who utters (13)a would normally convey the content of (13)b. In uttering (14)a, one would normally be *insinuating* something that could be paraphrased as (14)b. However, each of these ways of informing differs from asserting in being less direct and harder to respond to in some ways. One can't disagree with any of these contributions by saying 'wrong' or 'that's false', for example, and they otherwise resist being referred to with propositional anaphora, as in 'that's very interesting'.

Some have tried to account for these phenomena by complicating their theories of conversational score in various ways. For example, Murray (2014) argues that, in addition to adding its content to the common ground, a successful assertion updates the score by establishing a propositional discourse referent for its content, allowing it to be anaphorically picked up by propositional anaphora. Not-at-issue contributions to common ground, such as those made via conventional implicatures, presuppositions, and evidentials, differ in that they fail to establish discourse referents.

Camp (this volume) pursues a similar account of insinuation and other communicative strategies that she describes as "off-record". She distinguishes between the common ground, which is roughly as Stalnaker describes it, and the conversational record, which is an objective record of prior conversational contributions, and whose state is (at least largely) determined by linguistic conventions. Whereas a normal, literal, direct, and linguistically encoded assertion, if successful, both adds its content to the common ground and registers itself on the conversational record, not-at-issue contributions such as (11)b–(13)b may be added to the common ground without making it onto the record, and insinuated contents like (14)b can be communicated via a roughly Gricean mechanism despite *neither* becoming common ground *nor* registering on the conversational record.[28] This not only explains why insinuated content can't be the target of propositional anaphora; it also explains why the speaker can often get away with denying that skillfully insinuated content was intended at all, even after having successfully communicated it to the addressee.

Another area where various novel ways of manipulating contexts have been posited is the literature on expressivism. One way of framing the project of expressivism is to say that when a speaker utters declarative sentences containing expressions of a certain kind—for example, normative expressions—the speech acts that they perform aren't normal assertions, but something else.[29] For example, Hare (1952) argues that declarative sentences containing moral terms are used to perform special kinds of acts of recommendation, commendation, and condemnation, rather than assertion. On the contemporary scene, the obvious move is to develop expressivism into the view that certain expressions are used to update contexts in ways that differ from regular (i.e. 'factual') assertions. Recent years have seen an explosion of theories of this kind.[30]

In his contribution to this volume, Seth Yalcin argues that it is a mistake to view these theories as trafficking in claims about illocutionary force, at least if 'illocutionary force' is understood in the same sense that speech-act theorists have traditionally been interested in. More broadly, Yalcin distinguishes the illocutionary force of a speech act from what he calls its *dynamic force*. By the latter, he means just the sort of force that we've been discussing in this section: the characteristic effect of an act on the context. But Yalcin argues that this notion of force is distinct from illocutionary force as traditionally conceived. The two notions belong to two kinds of theories that describe conversation at different levels of abstraction. Illocutionary force belongs to a level at which we aim to characterize the extra-linguistic uses to which speech is put. Dynamic force, on the other hand, characterizes conversation at a level of abstraction that "prescinds from the question what exactly the conversational state is taken by the interlocutors to be characterizing, and from the question what the speaker

[28] On the idea that some speech acts can be understood in terms of addressee-directed communicative intentions but not in terms of context-directed communicative intentions, see also Harris (2014, ch.3).

[29] Influential early statements on this idea can be found in Ayer (1936); Hare (1952); Stevenson (1937, 1944); Wittgenstein (1953). For an overview, see Schroeder (2010, ch.2). Austin alludes to these early noncognitivists as some of the main precursors to his development of speech-act theory (1962, 2–3).

[30] For treatments of deontic modals and other normative talk, see Charlow (2015, 2016); Ninan (2005); Pérez Carballo and Santorio (2016); Starr (2016b); Willer (2014). For treatments of epistemic and/or probability modals, see Swanson (2016); Veltman (1996); Willer (2013, 2015); Yalcin (2007, 2012, 2015). For treatments of indicative and counterfactual conditionals, see von Fintel (2001); Gillies (2007, 2010); Starr (2010).

might be aiming to do, extra-linguistically speaking, by adding certain information to that state" (p.405).

Yalcin's is a heterodox view; most proponents of context-change accounts of speech acts have taken their theories to be in competition with alternative theories of illocutionary force.[31] Moreover, several others have given rather different answers to the question of how facts about context relate to facts about interlocutors' beliefs, plans, and other private mental states. As we have seen, Murray and Starr (this volume) argue that changes to context have the function of causing changes to interlocutors' private mental states. Harris (2014, ch.3) argues for the more traditionally Gricean view that speech acts are aimed primarily at changing addressees' private mental states, with changes to the context being a downstream consequence in at most some special cases. And Camp (this volume) argues that a full appreciation of the range of speech acts we perform requires us to distinguish between those that change the objective context, those that change the intersubjective context, and those that change only interlocutors' private mental states. How best to understand the relationship between contexts and interlocutors' minds is thus an open and important theoretical question.

1.3 Force and Content

According to Austin, we should "distinguish *force* and meaning in the sense in which meaning is equivalent to sense and reference, just as it has become essential to distinguish sense and reference within meaning" (1962, 100). Similarly, Searle argues that we should distinguish between an illocutionary act and the act of expressing a proposition at its core. For Austin and Searle, these are distinctions between two levels of abstraction at which we may individuate speech acts. A locutionary or propositional act is a speech act individuated only in respect of its content, and illocutionary force is the extra ingredient bridging the gap from sense and reference to the full illocutionary act. Some distinction of this kind is now widely taken for granted, though different theories draw it in different ways.

There are two influential reasons for thinking of the illocutionary force of a speech act as something that can be abstracted away from its content. One is that the two components can apparently vary independently. Assertion is something that can be done with any proposition, and a given proposition can apparently serve as the content of various other illocutionary acts as well. For example, one can assert, suppose, deny, promise, and command that Fido will fetch his stick, and one can also ask whether Fido will fetch his stick. All of these acts plausibly have the same propositional content, but involve doing different things with this content.

In a similar vein, it has sometimes been claimed that trios of sentences such as the following can be used to perform literal and direct speech acts that have the same content but that differ only in force.[32]

---

[31] Roberts (this volume) is particularly explicit about this, as are Gazdar (1981) and Levinson (1983). Although Stalnaker admits that his theory of assertion characterizes a wider family of speech acts than some others have referred to as 'assertion', he has also said that his theory "is an account of the force of an assertion" (1999, 10–11).

[32] E.g. Katz (1981); Searle (1965, 1969, 1975); Searle and Vanderveken (1985).

(15)   Fido will fetch his stick.
(16)   Will Fido fetch his stick?
(17)   Fetch your stick. [addressed to Fido]

Some support for this idea comes from data about cross-force propositional anaphora. The following example is naturally described by saying that Ann asserts a proposition, Bob asks a polar question whose content is the same proposition, and Ann points this out.[33]

(18)   Ann: Fido will fetch his stick.
       Bob: Will Fido fetch his stick?
       Ann: That's what I just said.

Similar data suggest that the contents of speech acts can also serve as the contents of a variety of intentional mental states.

(19)   Ann: Dogs are better than cats.
       Bob: That's what I [think/believe/hope].

It is also sometimes possible to coordinate speech-act reports, suggesting that the speech acts being reported share contents.

(20)   Ann claimed, but Bob merely suggested, that dogs are better than cats.
(21)   Judy asked whether, and John confidently asserted, you will be at dinner tonight.

A second kind of argument for the force–content distinction stems from the idea that semantic composition acts only on contents, not on speech acts. This view originates with Frege (1879), whose *Begriffsschrift* notation separates force from content by representing force with the vertical judgment stroke '|' and content with the the horizontal content stroke '—', along with everything that follows it. Importantly, Frege's syntax allows for only one judgment stroke per sentence; it is only content-denoting expressions that can recursively combine. The idea that speech acts have a single force but arbitrarily complex contents has proven influential, as has the related idea that sentences can be factored, for the purposes of semantics, into a component that expresses their content (sometimes called a 'sentence radical') along with a component that determines the illocutionary force with which they can be literally uttered (a 'mood marker' or 'force indicator').[34]

Both of these arguments for the force–content distinction have recently faced challenges from a range of angles. An initial challenge comes from evidence about the semantics of non-declarative clauses, which purports to show that interrogative and imperative clauses don't express *propositional* contents at all. This is most intuitive in the case of wh-interrogatives, such as (22), for which there is no plausible propositional semantic value.

(22)   Who loves the funk?

---

[33] It is notably harder to find analogous data suggesting that directive acts can have the same contents as assertions or polar questions.

[34] Davidson (1979a); Grice (1968); Hare (1952); Lewis (1970); Sadock (1974); Searle (1965, 1968, 1969, 1975); Starr (ms, 2010).

Semanticists now widely believe that an interrogative's semantic content is a set of propositions (or a property that these propositions share). Intuitively, the propositions in question are the possible or actual answers to the question that the interrogative encodes.[35] For example, the semantic content of (22) might be identified with the set of propositions p such that, for some agent x, p is the proposition that x loves the funk. Similarly, several authors have argued that imperatives' semantic contents aren't propositions but some other kind of semantic object, such as addressee-restricted properties or actions.[36]

By undermining the idea that, for example, assertions, questions, and directives can have the same content, these views undermine one of the motivations for drawing a content–force distinction.[37] Still, a modified force–content distinction is viable. For example, Gazdar (1981) argues that whereas the (not-necessarily-propositional) content of a literal and direct speech act is just the semantic content of the sentence uttered, the speech act's illocutionary force is supplied by a pragmatic "force-assignment rule" that maps this content to a way of updating the context. In their contributions to this volume, Stalnaker, Roberts, and Portner defend views that incorporate versions of this dynamic-pragmatic take on the force–content distinction.

Further problems lurk, however. One is that, as Starr (ms; 2016a) has pointed out, imperatives can be conjoined and disjoined, both with other imperatives and with declaratives. Moreover, any such combination can be the consequent of a conditional.

(23)   Fix me a drink and make it a double.
(24)   Mow the lawn and I'll wash the car.
(25)   Play a waltz if the mood is right.
(26)   If you're an egalitarian, how come you're so rich?
(27)   If we only have enough money to buy one book, put back Naked Lunch or I'll put back Waverley.

Examples like these undermine the traditional force–content distinction in several ways. First, there seems to be no simple answer to the question of whether, in using a mixed imperative-declarative sentence literally, one would be performing an assertoric act or a directive act. Rather, the speech acts involved appear to be complex hybrids of the two. Second, and relatedly, there is seemingly no way to factor out the force-marking components of sentences like these from their content-expressing components. Both of these observations suggest that conjunction, disjunction, and conditionalization can act on speech acts' forces and not merely their contents. Third, several authors have argued that the speech acts we perform with conditional imperatives and conditional interrogatives, such as (25) and (26), must be thought of not as questions and directives with conditional contents, but as

---

[35]   See, e.g., Gazdar (1981); Groenendijk and Stokhof (1984); Hamblin (1958, 1973); Karttunen (1977); Roberts (2012).

[36]   Barker (2012); von Fintel and Iatridou (2017); Hausser (1980, 1983); Portner (2004, 2007, 2012); Roberts (2015b, 2017); Zanuttini et al. (2012). Even Frege (1892) argues that non-declarative sentences express non-propositional contents (i.e., incomplete thoughts that lack *Bedeutungen*).

[37]   There remain some interesting reasons to think that polar questions have propositional contents; see Farkas and Bruce (2010); Gunlogson (2001).

conditional questions and conditional directives.[38] In uttering (25), for example, one does not request for a conditional to be made true; rather, such a speech act would be satisfied only if the addressee enters a conditional state of mind—something like a contingency plan.[39]

These observations have led several theorists to adopt techniques from dynamic semantics. Some have taken clauses to be context-change potentials: the meaning of any clause is an operation on contexts, but clauses of different kinds manipulate different components within contexts. This is the view that both Murray and Starr and Lepore and Stone advocate in their contributions to this volume, for example.[40] Others have identified clausal semantic values with the cognitive instructions they give to addressees: the meaning of every clause is modeled as a condition on addressees' mental states, but clauses of different kinds instruct addressees to change mental states of different kinds.[41] Either of these views allows for complex meanings to be recursively defined out of simpler meanings without first separating out the parts responsible for force from those that encode content.

A modified force–content distinction may still be salvageable in light of these views. Speech acts of different kinds—and the meanings of the sentences that encode them—can be understood in terms of different kinds of effects that they have on either contexts or addressees' minds. Whereas the force of a speech act is a matter of which component of the context (or mind) it operates on, its content is a matter of the contribution that it makes there. For example, although Charlow (2014) represents the semantic values of both declarative and imperative clauses as properties of agents' minds, declaratives (and the assertions they encode) place conditions on the doxastic components of minds, whereas imperatives (and the directives they encode) place conditions on their planning components. Complex sentences that combine declarative and imperative clauses encode more complex properties of minds that may place conditions on both doxastic and planning components. So, some sentences encode speech acts whose forces are hybrids of assertion and direction, and whose contents are difficult to disentangle from their forces.[42]

In his contribution to this volume, Peter Hanks has defended a much more radical rejection of the force–content distinction than anything we've discussed so far.[43] On Hanks's view, the force of a speech act is determined by the very relation that unifies its propositional content. Recall (15)–(17):

[38] See, e.g., Edgington (1986, 1991, 1995); von Fintel (ms); Charlow (this volume); Krifka (2014).
[39] Charlow (this volume) and Starr (2016a, ms) argue that these data pose insurmountable challenges to views on which imperatives denote properties. Charlow (this volume) marshalls further evidence, in the form of sentences in which quantifiers outscope imperative operators (e.g., 'everyone take [his/her/their] seat'), to object to Kaufman's view that imperatives are deontic modals. Like Krifka's (2001) related argument that quantifiers sometimes outscope question operators, these data further undermine the standard, Fregean abstraction of force from content.
[40] See also Asher and Lascarides (2003); Condoravdi and Lauer (2012); Farkas and Bruce (2010); Gunlogson (2001); Krifka (2014); Murray (2014); Murray and Starr (forthcoming); Starr (ms, 2010).
[41] Charlow (2014, this volume); Harris (2014).
[42] For similar views, see Harris (2014); Murray (2014); Starr (ms, 2010).
[43] Hanks's paper builds on ideas that he has defended elsewhere—e.g., Hanks (2007, 2011, 2013, 2015).

(15)   Fido will fetch his stick.
(16)   Will Fido fetch his stick?
(17)   Fetch your stick. [addressed to Fido]

Bracketing tense and aspect, the contents of these sentences have the same components: Fido, the relation of fetching, and Fido's stick. But, Hanks points out, a
proposition is something over and above its components. A proposition must be
unified in some determinate way, and distinct propositions may consist of the same
parts unified in different ways; this is why the proposition that Fido fetches his stick is
distinct from the proposition that Fido is fetched by his stick. Hanks argues that the
differences in the speech acts we would perform with literal utterances of (15)–(17)
consists of differences in the ways in which their parts are unified. Assertions are acts
of *predicating* propositional components of one another; questions are acts of *asking
whether* the components of propositions are connected in certain ways; directives
are acts of *ordering* a propositional component (normally, the addressee) to have a
certain property. On this usage, predicating, asking, and ordering are different kinds
of *combinatory* acts—different ways of forming propositions from their components.
Hanks posits an analogous suite of combinatory mental acts to explain the difference
between believing a proposition, wondering whether it is true, and desiring for it to
be true. On this view, there is nothing like a force–content distinction: speech acts of
different kinds differ solely in having different kinds of content.

One challenge for Hanks is to draw more fine-grained distinctions between kinds
of speech acts within his three broad categories, such as the distinction between
requests and commands. Another important challenge to Hanks's view is developed
by Green (this volume), who argues that we can't do without at least some combinatory
acts—some forms of predication, say—that are force neutral.[44] In using a declarative
sentence in the context of pretense, or to suppose a proposition for the sake of
reductio, or as the antecedent of a conditional, for example, one doesn't assert the
proposition expressed, but one does express a unified proposition.

1.4 Applied Speech-Act Theory

Speech-act theory has always been driven by issues that extend beyond the study of
language and communication. Austin's earliest deployment of his theory of performative utterances took place in the context of a debate with John Wisdom about
the problem of other minds, for example Austin (1946). Work on expressivism—
early versions of which Austin (1962, 1970) mentions as a precursor to his theory
of speech acts—aims to solve big philosophical problems about the metaphysics and
epistemology of normativity. Grice's original pitch for his theory of implicature was
that it could be used as a tool for countering certain views put forward by ordinary-
language philosophers, both in the philosophy of perception (1961) and in semantics
and the philosophy of logic (1975). Debates between the five families of speech-act

---

[44] For related concerns, see Hom and Schwarz (2013); Reiland (2013, 2017); Stokke (2016).

theory have often turned on the question of which theory is best able to fit meaning and intentionality into a naturalistic worldview.[45]

Speech-act theory has continued to be a versatile philosophical tool, particularly in the philosophy of law and social and political philosophy.

Consider the philosophy of law.[46] It is tempting to think of the creation of laws as a kind of speech act. But several considerations have led philosophers to think that legislative speech acts are special, and, in particular, that their properties cannot be grounded in speakers' intentions: they are performed by legislatures rather than individual speakers, it is a democratic imperative that the law be public, and whereas the usual pragmatic mechanisms for interpreting speech acts depend on cooperativity, legal contexts are adversarial (Marmor, 2008; 2014; Poggi, 2011). These and other considerations have led some to conclude that we should avoid intentionalist accounts of legislative speech acts, opting instead for views on which the properties of these acts are determined by linguistic convention alone ("textualism") or by some combination of convention and legal principles or the purposes to which laws are put ("purposivism").[47] Others have argued that some role for speakers' intentions in fixing the properties of legislative speech acts is both workable and unavoidable.[48]

In social theory, speech acts have been of interest for the roles they play in the construction of various social entities and institutions. This idea is already present in the early work of Searle (1969, §2.7) and Bach and Harnish (1979, appendix), and Searle has developed some of the connections in his influential work on social construction (Searle, 1995; 2010). Austin's ideas have also been a significant influence on Judith Butler's influential view that gender is a performative social construct (1990; see also Salih, 2007).

Certain categories of speech act have also held special interest for ethicists and political philosophers. A large literature has grown up around the nature of lying, for example, and some have argued that the distinction between lying and misleading is not merely of normative interest, but is also a useful diagnostic for distinguishing what speakers say from what they merely implicate.[49] In a similar vein, much work has gone into understanding the nature of promises, not just because promises and other commitment-engendering speech acts are held to play a special role in normative ethics and political philosophy, but also because this role is sometimes held to demand a deeply normative theory of the speech act itself.[50]

---

[45] E.g., Bar-On (2013); Green (2007b); Lewis (1969); Schiffer (1982); Scott-Phillips (2014); Sellars (1954, 1956); Skyrms (1996, 2010); Tomasello (2008).

[46] H. L. A. Hart is one of only three philosophers whom Austin cites by name in *How to do Things with Words* (1962, 7n1), and was one of the earliest philosophers to apply Austin's ideas (Hart, 1949, 1954).

[47] Scalia (1998) influentially defends textualism. An influential version of purposivism has been defended by Dworkin (1986). For an overview of the space of options and related issues, see Marmor (2011).

[48] E.g., Elkins (2012); Marmor (1995, 2014); Neale (ms).

[49] On the idea that the lying–misleading distinction can serve as a guide to the saying–implicating distinction, see, e.g., Adler (1997); Michaelson (2016); Saul (2012). For overviews of the literature on lying, see Mahon (2016); Stokke (2013).

[50] For an overview of the literature on the nature of promises, see Habib (2014). Habermas (1984, 1998) and Raz (1986) defend deeply normative accounts of a variety of speech acts on the grounds that they play an essential role in democratic institutions.

A particularly rich application of speech-act theory has centered around a cluster of issues pertaining to freedom of speech. The central insight of this work is simple and compelling: many of the traditional defenses of liberal free-speech protections depend on the assumption that the function of speech is to express beliefs and share information. But the founding insight of speech-act theory is that speech does much besides this, sometimes in ways that are easy to miss. To varying extents, recognition of this point is already baked into most legal systems, which don't grant everyone an equal right to issue commands, for example, and which don't protect incitations to violence and disorder. But speech-act theorists have argued that the upshots of this line of thought have not been fully appreciated. For example, MacKinnon, Langton, Hornsby, and others have developed an influential case against free-speech protections for pornography, on the grounds that if we take seriously the idea of pornography as speech, this speech should be understood as constituting illocutionary acts of silencing and subordinating women.[51] Related considerations have been brought to bear on hate speech. McGowan's contribution to this volume builds on her previous arguments that certain forms of speech, including some hate speech, can change societal norms in pernicious ways as a matter of their illocutionary force.[52] Waldron (1999) argues, in effect, that publicly displayed hate speech works via a pair of indirect speech acts, issuing a threat aimed at its targets and a covert rallying cry to like-minded bigots.[53]

A closely related and rapidly expanding literature deals with slurs and other pejorative expressions. Here two debates converge. One debate, which dovetails with debates about hate speech, concerns the nature of the derogation or harm that seems to be consistently accomplished by the use of slurs. A second debate concerns the nature of the linguistic mechanisms by which slurs accomplish their derogative effects. Although some have argued that the derogative function of slurs can be understood as an aspect of their semantic contents, most have located the effect in some orthogonal semantic or pragmatic dimension of their use, invoking presupposition, conventional implicature, or some variety of expressive meaning.[54] Camp (2017) argues that slurs should be understood as devices for performing two speech acts at once—one neutral act of predicating a property of group membership, and another of casting their targets in a hateful perspective. In his contribution to this volume, Nunberg effectively agrees with this dual-speech-act view, but denies that we need to appeal to any special semantic mechanism in order to explain how these speech acts are performed. Slurs, he argues, are native to the dialects of hateful and oppressive groups; to use a slur is to mark oneself as hateful, either by virtue of belonging to one of these groups, or by means of a kind of manner implicature that affiliates one with the group.[55] Nunberg's

---

[51]   See, e.g., Hornsby (1993); Hornsby and Langton (1998); Langton (1993, 2009); MacKinnon (1987, 1993); Maitra (2012). See also Stanley (2011) for applications of the idea of silencing to political speech, and Murray and Starr (this volume) for a functionalist account of silencing.

[52]   McGowan (2003, 2004, 2009a,b, 2012). See also Tirrell's (2012) work on hate speech and the Rwandan Genocide.

[53]   For several other recent philosophical contributions to the literatures on free speech, censorship, hate speech, and related topics, see the papers in Maitra and McGowan (2012).

[54]   For overviews of the slurs literature, see Hom (2010) and Nunberg (this volume).

[55]   For a similar pragmatic account, see Bolinger (2015).

account is interesting not just as a purely pragmatic theory of slurs, but also as a case study in how the philosophy of language can benefit from some of the explanatory resources of sociolinguistics.

Another rich area of applied speech-act theory deals with speech that is less than fully cooperative—a genre that many theorists have idealized away. For example, McKinney (2016) argues that some false confessions constitute what she calls "extracted speech"—speech acts performed unintentionally and against the speaker's will, and that are made possible by felicity conditions that have been set up and exploited in ways that serve interrogators' interests. Stanley (2015) argues that some propaganda can be understood as involving a special kind of not-at-issue speech act, whereby the propagandist surreptitiously changes the conversational score in a way that bypasses interlocutors' consent. Several contributions to this volume develop related themes. Camp and McGowan both use uncooperative speech to build on contemporary theories of conversational score and not-at-issue content. Langton's contribution explores strategies for blocking pernicious not-at-issue contributions that have a tendency to be sneakily accommodated against some interlocutors' interests. In her contribution, Jennifer Saul argues that although some dogwhistles work by being understood in overtly different ways by different audiences, others are *covert*: they function by activating hearers' prejudices in ways that are outside their conscious awareness. And because these speech acts rely on unconscious, arational psychological mechanisms, they can be performed unintentionally—for example, when a newscaster unwittingly repeats a politician's covertly prejudiced buzzword. Each of these essays both highlights some of the ways in which speech-act theory can be applied to help us better understand kinds of speech that are of urgent social concern, while also showing how these applications can give us new reasons for revising or enriching our theoretical outlooks.

1.5 Speech-Act Theory as an Integrated Conversation

Speech-act theory has often proceeded as a series of separate conversations—one pertaining to foundational issues about the nature of communication and illocutionary force, another centered around technical and empirical issues in the semantics of non-declarative clauses, and another centered around social, moral, and political issues arising from normatively important or problematic kinds of speech. We believe that each of these conversations can succeed only when they are self-consciously taken to be strands within a single, broader conversation about the nature and uses of speech acts. Applied speech-act theory that is not grounded in current technical, empirical, and foundational developments deprives itself of new resources and datapoints. Work on the semantics of non-declaratives that floats free of both foundational underpinnings and practical applications risks superficiality. Work on foundational issues that proceeds independently of technical, empirical, and applied issues will be overly speculative. All three conversations must proceed in parallel and with attention to what is happening in the others if any of them can hope to get us closer to the truth. The papers collected here exemplify this integrative approach to speech-act theory, and we hope that they will inspire more work of a similar kind.

References

Adler, J. (1997). Lying, deceiving, or falsely implicating. *Journal of Philosophy*, 94(9): 435–452.

Adler, J. (2002). *Belief's Own Ethics*. MIT Press, Cambridge, MA.

Asher, N. and Lascarides, A. (2003). *Logics of Conversation*. Cambridge University Press, Cambridge, UK.

Austin, J. L. (1946). Other minds. *Proceedings of the Aristotelian Society, Supplementary Volume*, 20: 148–187.

Austin, J. L. (1962). *How to Do Things with Words*. The Clarendon Press, Oxford.

Austin, J. L. (1963). Performative-constative. In Caton, C. E., editor, *Philosophy and Ordinary Language*, pages 22–54. University of Illinois Press, Urbana.

Austin, J. L. (1970). Performative Utterances. In Urmson, J. O. and Warnock, G. J., editors, *Philosophical Papers*, chapter 10, pages 233–252. Oxford University Press, Oxford, second edition.

Ayer, A. J. (1936). *Language, Truth and Logic*. Gollancz, London.

Bach, K. (1987). *Thought and Reference*. Oxford University Press, Oxford.

Bach, K. (1992). Intentions and demonstrations. *Analysis*, 52: 140–146.

Bach, K. (2008). Applying pragmatics to epistemology. *Philosophical Issues*, 18: 68–88.

Bach, K. and Harnish, R. M. (1979). *Linguistic Communication and Speech Acts*. MIT Press, Cambridge, MA.

Ball, B. (2014). Speech acts: Natural or normative kinds. *Mind & Language*, 29(3): 336–350.

Bar-On, D. (2013). Origins of meaning: Must we 'go gricean'? *Mind and Language*, 28(3): 342–375.

Barker, C. (2012). Imperatives denote actions. In Guevara, A. A., Chernilovskaya, A., and Nouwen, R., editors, *Proceedings of Sinn and Bedeutung 16*, chapter 5. MIT Working Papers in Linguistics.

Beaver, D. (2001). *Presupposition and Assertion in Dynamic Semantics*. CSLI, Stanford, CA.

Benton, M. (2011). Two more for the knowledge account of assertion. *Analysis*, 72: 682–687.

Benton, M. (2012a). Assertion, knowledge, and predictions. *Analysis*, 72: 102–105.

Benton, M. (2012b). *Knowledge Norms: Assertion, Belief, and Action*. PhD thesis, Rutgers University, New Brunswick, NJ.

Benton, M. (2016). Gricean quality. *Noûs*, 50: 689–703.

Black, M. (1952). Saying and disbelieving. *Analysis*, 13(2): 25–33.

Bloom, P. (2000). *How Children Learn the Meanings of Words*. MIT Press, Cambridge, MA.

Blume, A. and Board, O. (2013). Language barriers. *Econometrica*, 81(2): 781–812.

Boghossian, P. (2003). The normativity of content. *Philosophical Issues*, 13: 31–45.

Bolinger, R. (2015). The pragmatics of slurs. *Noûs*, Online First.

Bradbury, J. W. and Vehrencamp, S. L. (2011). *Principles of Animal Communication*. Sinauer Associates, Sunderland, MA, second edition.

Brandom, R. (1983). Asserting. *Noûs*, 17(4): 637–650.

Brandom, R. (1994). *Making it Explicit: Reasoning, Representing, and Discursive Commitment*. Harvard University Press, Cambridge, MA.

Brandom, R. (2000). *Articulating Reasons*. Harvard University Press, Cambridge, MA.

Breheny, R. (2006). Communication and folk psychology. *Mind and Language*, 21(1): 74–107.

Buchanan, R. (2010). A puzzle about meaning and communication. *Noûs*, 44(2): 340–371.

Butler, J. (1990). *Gender Trouble*. Routledge, New York.

Camp, E. (2017). Slurs as dual-act expressions. In Sosa, D., editor, *Bad Words*. Oxford University Press, Oxford.

Cappelen, H. (2011). Against assertion. In Brown, J. and Cappelen, H., editors, *Assertion: New Philosophical Essays*, pages 21–48. Oxford University Press, Oxford.

Carey, S. (2009). *The Origin of Concepts*. Oxford University Press, Oxford.

Carlson, L. (1982). *Dialogue Games: An Approach to Discourse Analysis*. Number 17 in Synthese Language Library. D. Reidel, Dordrecht, The Netherlands.

Carruthers, P. (2006). *The Architecture of Mind: Massive Modularity and the Flexibility of Thought*. Oxford University Press, Oxford.

Carston, R. (2002). *Thoughts and Utterances: The Pragmatics of Explicit Communication*. Blackwell, Oxford.

Charlow, N. (2010). Restricting and embedding imperatives. In Aloni, M., Bastiaanse, H., de Jager, T., and Schulz, K., editors, *Logic, Language, and Meaning: Selected Papers from the 17th Amsterdam Colloquium*. Springer.

Charlow, N. (2014). Logic and semantics for imperatives. *Journal of Philosophical Logic*, 43: 617–664.

Charlow, N. (2015). Prospects for an expressivist theory of meaning. *Philosophers' Imprint*, 15(23): 1–43.

Charlow, N. (2016). Decision theory: Yes! truth conditions: No! In Charlow, N. and Chrisman, M., editors, *Deontic Modality*, pages 47–81. Oxford University Press, Oxford.

Cohen, P. R. and Perrault, C. R. (1979). Elements of a plan-based theory of speech acts. *Cognitive Science*, 3: 177–212.

Condoravdi, C. and Lauer, S. (2012). Imperatives: Meaning and illocutionary force. In Pinõn, C., editor, *Empirical Issues in Syntax and Semantics 9: Papers From the Colloque de Syntaxe et Sémantique à Paris 2011*, pages 37–58.

Csibra, G. (2010). Recognizing communicative intentions in infancy. *Mind and Language*, 25(2): 141–168.

Davidson, D. (1979a). Moods and performances. In Margalit, A., editor, *Meaning and Use*. D. Reidel, Dordrecht.

Davidson, D. (1979b). What metaphors mean. In Sacks, S., editor, *On Metaphor*, pages 29–45. University of Chicago Press, Chicago.

Davis, W. (1992). Speaker meaning. *Linguistics and Philosophy*, 15(3): 223–253.

Davis, W. (2003). *Meaning, Expression, and Thought*. Cambridge University Press, Cambridge, UK.

DeRose, K. (1991). Epistemic possibilities. *Philosophical Review*, 100: 581–605.

DeRose, K. (2002). Assertion, knowledge, and context. *Philosophical Review*, 111: 167–203.

DeVault, D. and Stone, M. (2006). Scorekeeping in an uncertain language game. In Schlangen, D. and Fernández, R., editors, *Brandial 2006: Proceedings of the 10th Workshop on the Semantics and Pragmatics of Dialogue*, volume 10, pages 139–146. SemDial, University of Potsdam.

Devitt, M. (2006). *Ignorance of Language*. Oxford University Press, Oxford.

Donnellan, K. S. (1968). Putting humpty dumpty together again. *Philosophical Review*, 77(2): 203–215.

Douven, I. (2006). Assertion, knowledge, and rational credibility. *Philosophical Review*, 115: 449–485.

Douven, I. (2009). Assertion, Bayes, and Moore. *Philosophical Studies*, 144: 361–375.

Dummett, M. (1973). *Frege: Philosophy of Language*. Duckworth.

Dworkin, R. (1986). *Law's Empire*. Harvard University Press, Cambridge, MA.

Edgington, D. (1986). Do conditionals have truth conditions? *Critica*, 18(52): 3–30.

Edgington, D. (1991). The mystery of the missing matter of fact. *Proceedings of the Aristotelian Society*, 65: 185–209.

Edgington, D. (1995). On conditionals. *Mind*, 104(414): 235–329.

Egan, A. (2009). Billboards, bombs, and shotgun weddings. *Synthese*, 166(2): 251–279.

Elkins, R. (2012). *The Nature of Legislative Intent*. Oxford University Press, Oxford.

Engel, P. (2008). In what sense is knowledge the norm of assertion? *Grazer Philosophische Studien*, 77: 45–59.

Farkas, D. F. and Bruce, K. B. (2010). On reacting to assertions and polar questions. *Journal of Semantics*, 27: 81–118.

von Fintel, K. (1994). *Restrictions on Quantifier Domains*. PhD thesis, University of Massachusetts, Amherst, Amherst, MA.

von Fintel, K. (2001). Counterfactuals in a dynamic context. In Kenstowicz, M., editor, *Ken Hale: A Life in Language*, pages 123–152. MIT Press, Cambridge, MA.

von Fintel, K. (ms). How to do conditional things with words. *Unpublished Manuscript*.

von Fintel, K. and Iatridou, S. (2017). A modest proposal for the meaning of imperatives. In Arregui, A., Rivero, M., and Salanova, A. P., editors, *Modality Across Semantic Categories*. Oxford University Press, Oxford.

Fodor, J. A., Bever, T. G., and Garrett, M. F. (1974). *The Psychology of Language: An Introduction to Psycholinguistics and Generative Grammar*. McGraw-Hill, New York.

Franke, M. (2012). On assertoric and directive signals and the evolution of dynamic meaning. *International Review of Pragmatics*, 4: 232–260.

Frege, G. (1879). *Begriffsschrift, eine der Arithmetischen Nachgebildete Formelsprache des Reinen Denkens*. Louis Nebert, Halle.

Frege, G. (1892). Über Sinn und Bedeutung. *Zeitschrift für Philosophie und philosophische Kritik*, 100: 25–50.

García-Carpintero, M. (2004). Assertion and the semantics of force-markers. In Bianchi, C., editor, *The Semantics/Pragmatics Distinction*, pages 133–166. CSLI, Stanford, CA.

Gazdar, G. (1981). Speech act assignment. In Joshi, A. K., Weber, B. L., and Sag, I. A., editors, *Elements of Discourse Understanding*, pages 64–83. Cambridge University Press, Cambridge, UK.

Gillies, A. S. (2007). Counterfactual scorekeeping. *Linguistics and Philosophy*, 30(3): 239–360.

Gillies, A. S. (2010). Iffiness. *Semantics and Pragmatics*, 3(4): 1–42.

Ginzburg, J. (2012). *The Interactive Stance: Meaning for Conversation*. Oxford University Press, Oxford.

Glüer, K. (2001). Dreams and nightmares: Conventions, norms, and meaning in Davidson's philosophy of language. In Kotatko, P., Pagin, P., and Segal, G., editors, *Interpreting Davidson*, pages 53–74. CSLI, Stanford, CA.

Glüer, K. and Wikforss, Å. (2009). Against content normativity. *Mind*, 118: 23–51.

Goldberg, S. (2013). Disagreement, defeat, and assertion. In Christensen, D. and Lackey, J., editors, *The Epistemology of Disagreement: New Essays*. Oxford University Press, Oxford.

Goldman, A. (2012). Theory of mind. In Margolis, E., Samuels, R., and Stich, S., editors, *Oxford Handbook of Philosophy and Cognitive Science*, pages 402–424. Oxford University Press, Oxford.

Green, M. (2007a). Moorean absurdity and showing what's within. In Green, M. and Williams, J. N., editors, *Moore's Paradox: New Essays on Belief, Rationality, and the First Person*, chapter 9, pages 189–216. Oxford University Press, Oxford.

Green, M. S. (2007b). *Self-Expression*. Oxford University Press, Oxford.

Grice, H. P. (1957). Meaning. *The Philosophical Review*, 66(3): 377–388.

Grice, H. P. (1961). The causal theory of perception. *Proceedings of the Aristotelian Society, Supplementary Volume*, 35: 121–153.

Grice, H. P. (1968). Utterer's meaning, sentence-meaning, and word-meaning. *Foundations of Language*, 4(3): 225–242.

Grice, H. P. (1969). Utterer's meaning and intention. *The Philosophical Review*, 78(2): 147–177.

Grice, H. P. (1975). Logic and conversation. In Cole, P., editor, *Syntax and Semantics 3: Pragmatics*. Academic Press, Cambridge, MA.

Grice, P. (1989). *Studies in the Way of Words*. Harvard University Press, Cambridge, MA.

Groenendijk, J. and Stokhof, M. (1984). *Studies on the Semantics of Questions and the Pragmatics of Answers*. PhD Dissertation, Institute for Logic, Language, and Computation (ILLC), University of Amsterdam.

Groenendijk, J. and Stokhof, M. (1989). Dynamic Montague grammar. In Kálmán, L. and Pólos, L., editors, *Logic and Language*. Akadémiai, Budapest.

Groenendijk, J. and Stokhof, M. (1991). Dynamic predicate logic. *Linguistics and Philosophy*, 14: 39–100.

Gunlogson, C. (2001). *True to Form: Rising and Falling Declaratives as Questions in English*. Routledge.

Habermas, J. (1984). *Theorie des Kommunikativen Handelns, Band I: Handlungsrationalität und Gesellschaftliche Rationalisierung*. Suhrkamp Verlag, Frankfurt am Main.

Habermas, J. (1998). *On the Pragmatics of Communication*. MIT Press, Cambridge, MA.

Habib, A. (2014). Promises. In Zalta, E. N., editor, *Stanford Encyclopedia of Philosophy (Spring 2014 Edition)*. <https://plato.stanford.edu/archives/spr2014/entries/promises/>.

Hacquard, V. (2014). Bootstrapping attitudes. In Snider, T., editor, *Proceedings of SALT 24*, pages 330–352.

Hamblin, C. (1958). Questions. *Australasian Journal of Philosophy*, 36: 159–168.

Hamblin, C. L. (1971). Mathematical models of dialogue. *Theoria*, 37: 130–155.

Hamblin, C. L. (1973). Questions in Montague English. *Foundations of Language: International Journal*, 10(1): 41–53.

Han, C. (1998). *The Structure and Interpretation of Imperatives: Mood and Force in Universal Grammar*. PhD thesis, University of Pennsylvania.

Hanks, P. (2007). The content-force distinction. *Philosophical Studies*, 134: 141–164.

Hanks, P. W. (2011). Structured propositions as types. *Mind*, 120: 11–52.

Hanks, P. W. (2013). First-person propositions. *Philosophy and Phenomenological Research*, 86: 155–182.

Hanks, P. W. (2015). *Propositional Content*. Oxford University Press.

Hare, R. M. (1952). *The Language of Morals*. Oxford University Press, Oxford.

Harms, W. F. (2004a). *Information and Meaning in Evolutionary Processes*. Cambridge University Press, Cambridge, UK.

Harms, W. F. (2004b). Primitive content, translation, and the emergence of meaning in animal communication. In Oller, D. K. and Griebel, U., editors, *Evolution of Communication Systems: A Comparative Approach*, The Vienna Series in Theoretical Biology, chapter 3, pages 31–48. MIT Press, Cambridge, MA.

Harris, D. W. (2014). *Speech Act Theoretic Semantics*. PhD Dissertation, City University of New York Graduate Center.

Harris, D. W. (2016). Intentionalism versus the new conventionalism. *Croatian Journal of Philosophy*, 16(47): 173–201.

Hart, H. L. A. (1949). The ascription of responsibility and rights. *Proceedings of the Aristotelian Society*, 49: 171–194.

Hart, H. L. A. (1954). Definition and theory in jurisprudence. *The Law Quarterly Review*, 70: 37–60.

Hausser, R. (1980). Surface compositionality and the semantics of mood. In Searle, J., Kiefer, F., and Bierwisch, M., editors, *Speech Act Theory and Pragmatics*, pages 71–96. Reidel, Dordrecht.

Hausser, R. (1983). The syntax and semantics of english mood. In Kiefer, F., editor, *Questions and Answers*, pages 97–158. Reidel, Dordrecht.

Hawthorne, J. (2004). *Knowledge and Lotteries*. Oxford University Press, Oxford.

Heim, I. (1982). *The Semantics of Definite and Indefinite Noun Phrases*. PhD Dissertation, University of Massachusetts at Amherst.

Heim, I. (1983). File change semantics and the familiarity theory of definiteness. In Bäuerle, R., Schwarze, C., and von Stechow, A., editors, *Meaning, Use and Interpretation of Language*, pages 164–189. de Gruyter, Berlin.

Heim, I. (2008). Features on bound pronouns. In Harbour, D., Adger, D., and Bejar, S., editors, *Phi-Theory: Phi-Features across Modules and Interfaces*. Oxford University Press, Oxford, UK.

Hinchman, E. (2013). Assertion, sincerity, and knowledge. *Noûs*, 47: 613–646.

Hom, C. (2010). Pejoratives. *Philosophy Compass*, 5(2): 164–185.

Hom, C. and Schwarz, J. (2013). Unity and the Frege–Geach problem. *Philosophical Studies*, 163(1): 15–24.

Hornsby, J. (1993). Speech acts and pornography. *Women's Philosophical Review*, 10: 38–45.

Hornsby, J. and Langton, R. (1998). Free speech and illocution. *Legal Theory*, 4(1): 21–37.

Huttegger, S. M. (2007). Evolutionary explanations of indicatives and imperatives. *Erkenntnis*, 66: 409–436.

Kamp, H. (1981). A theory of truth and semantic representation. In Groenendijk, J., Janssen, T., and Stokhof, M., editors, *Formal Methods in the Study of Language, Part 1*, volume 135, pages 277–322. Mathematical Centre Tracts, Amsterdam.

Kamp, H. and Reyle, U. (1993). *From Discourse to Logic*. Kluwer, Dordrecht.

Kaplan, D. (1989). Afterthoughts. In Almog, J., Perry, J., and Wettstein, H., editors, *Themes from Kaplan*, pages 565–614. Oxford University Press, New York, NY.

Karttunen, L. (1976). Discourse referents. In McCawley, J. D., editor, *Syntax and Semantics 7: Notes from the Linguistic Underground*, pages 363–385. Academic Press, New York, NY.

Karttunen, L. (1977). Syntax and semantics of questions. *Linguistics and Philosophy*, 1: 3–44.

Katz, J. J. (1981). *Language and Other Abstract Objects*. Rowman & Littlefield, Totowa, NJ.

Kaufmann, M. (2012). *Interpreting Imperatives*. Springer.

King, J. C. (2013). Supplementives, the coordination account, and conflicting intentions. *Philosophical Perspectives*, 27.

King, J. C. (2014). Speaker intentions in context. *Noûs*, 48(2): 219–237.

Krifka, M. (2001). Quantifying into question acts. *Natural Language Semantics*, 9: 1–40.

Krifka, M. (2014). Embedding illocutionary acts. In Roeper, T. and Speas, M., editors, *Recursion: Complexity in Cognition*, Studies in Theoretical Psycholinguistics, chapter 4, pages 59–87. Springer.

Kukla, R. (2014). Performative force, convention, and discursive injustice. *Hypatia*, 29(2).

Kukla, R. and Lance, M. (2009). *'Yo!' and 'Lo!': The Pragmatic Topography of the Space of Reasons*. Harvard University Press, Cambridge, MA.

Kvanvig, J. L. (2009). Assertion, knowledge, and lotteries. In Greenough, P. and Pritchard, D., editors, *Williamson on Knowledge*, chapter 9, pages 140–160. Oxford University Press, Oxford.

Kvanvig, J. L. (2011). Norms of assertion. In Brown, J. and Cappelen, H., editors, *Assertion: New Philosophical Essays*, pages 233–250. Oxford University Press, Oxford.

Lackey, J. (2007). Norms of assertion. *Noûs*, 41(4): 594–626.

Lance, M. and Kukla, R. (2013). 'Leave the gun; take the cannoli': The pragmatic topography of second-person calls. *Ethics*, 123(3): 456–478.

Langton, R. (1993). Speech acts and unspeakable acts. *Philosophy and Public Affairs*, 22: 305–330.

Langton, R. (2009). *Sexual Solipsism*. Oxford University Press, Oxford.

Lepore, E. and Stone, M. (2010). Against metaphorical meaning. *Topoi.*

Lepore, E. and Stone, M. (2015). *Imagination and Convention.* Oxford University Press, Oxford.

Levinson, S. (1983). *Pragmatics.* Cambridge University Press, Cambridge, UK.

Lewis, D. K. (1969). *Convention: A Philosophical Study.* Harvard University Press, Cambridge, MA.

Lewis, D. K. (1970). General semantics. *Synthese,* 22(1/2): 18–67.

Lewis, D. K. (1975). A problem about permission. In Saarinen, E., et. al., editors, *Essays in Honour of Jakko Hintikka.* D. Reidel, Dordrecht, The Netherlands.

Lewis, D. K. (1979). Scorekeeping in a language game. *Journal of Philosophical Logic,* 8(3): 339–359.

Lewis, K. (2011). *Understanding Dynamic Discourse.* PhD Dissertation, Rutgers University.

Lewis, K. (2012). Discourse dynamics, pragmatics, and indefinites. *Philosophical Studies,* 158(2): 313–342.

Lewis, K. (2014). Do we need dynamic semantics? In Burgess, A. and Sherman, B., editors, *Metasemantics.* Oxford University Press, Oxford.

MacFarlane, J. (2011). What is assertion? In Brown, J. and Cappelen, H., editors, *Assertion,* pages 79–96. Oxford University Press, Oxford.

MacFarlane, J. (2014). *Assessment Sensitivity: Relative Truth and its Applications.* Oxford University Press, Oxford.

MacKinnon, C. (1987). *Francis Biddle's Sister: Pornography, Civil Rights, and Speech,* chapter 14. Harvard University Press, Cambridge, MA.

MacKinnon, C. (1993). *Only Words.* Harvard University Press, Cambridge, MA.

Mahon, J. E. (2016). The definition of lying and deception. In Zalta, E. N., editor, *Stanford Encyclopedia of Philosophy (Winter 2016 Edition).* <https://plato.stanford.edu/archives/win2016/entries/lying-definition/>.

Maitra, I. (2012). Subordinating speech. In Maitra, I. and McGowan, M. K., editors, *Speech and Harm,* pages 94–120. Oxford University Press, Oxford.

Maitra, I. and McGowan, M. K., editors (2012). *Speech and Harm: Controversies over Free Speech.* Oxford University Press, Oxford.

Maitra, I. and Weatherson, B. (2010). Assertion, knowledge, and action. *Philosophical Studies,* 149(1): 99–118.

Marmor, A. (1995). *Interpretation and Legal Theory.* Oxford University Press, Oxford.

Marmor, A. (2008). The pragmatics of legal language. *Ratio Juris,* 21: 423–452.

Marmor, A. (2011). Introduction. In Marmor, A. and Soames, S., editors, *Philosophical Foundations of Language in the Law.* Oxford University Press, Oxford.

Marmor, A. (2014). *The Language of Law.* Oxford University Press, Oxford.

McGlynn, A. (2014). *Knowledge First?* Palgrave Macmillan, London and New York.

McGowan, M. K. (2003). Conversational exercitives and the force of pornography. *Philosophy & Public Affairs,* 31(2): 155–189.

McGowan, M. K. (2004). Conversational exercitives: Something else we do with our words. *Linguistics and Philosophy,* 27(1): 93–111.

McGowan, M. K. (2009a). On silencing and sexual refusal. *Journal of Political Philosophy,* 17(4): 487–494.

McGowan, M. K. (2009b). Oppressive speech. *Australasian Journal of Philosophy,* 87(3): 389–407.

McGowan, M. K. (2012). On 'whites only' signs and racist hate speech: Verbal acts of racial discrimination. In Maitra, I. and McGowan, M. K., editors, *Speech and Harm,* pages 121–147. Oxford University Press, Oxford.

McKinney, R. (2016). Extracted speech. *Social Theory and Practice,* 42(2): 258–284.

McKinnon, R. (2015). *The Norms of Assertion: Truth, Lies, and Warrant*. Palgrave Macmillan, London.

Michaelson, E. (2013). *This and That: On the Semantics and Pragmatics of Highly Context-Sensitive Terms*. PhD thesis, University of California, Los Angeles.

Michaelson, E. (2016). The lying test. *Mind and Language*, 31(4): 470–499.

Millikan, R. G. (1984). *Language, Thought, and Other Biological Categories*. MIT Press, Cambridge, MA.

Millikan, R. G. (1998). Proper function and convention in speech acts. In Hahn, L. E., editor, *The Philosophy of Peter F. Strawson*, The Library of Living Philosophers, pages 25–43. Open Court, LaSalle, Illinois.

Millikan, R. G. (2005). *Language: A Biological Model*. Oxford University Press, Oxford.

Montgomery, B. (2014). In defense of assertion. *Philosophical Studies*, 171(2): 313–326.

Moore, R. (2015). Meaning and ostension in great ape gestural communication. *Animal Cognition*, 19(1): 223–231.

Moore, R. (2017). Gricean communication and cognitive development. *The Philosophical Quarterly*, 67(267): 303–326.

Murray, S. E. (2014). Varieties of update. *Semantics and Pragmatics*, 7(2): 1–53.

Murray, S. E. and Starr, W. B. (forthcoming). The structure of communicative acts. *Linguistics and Philosophy*.

Neale, S. (2004). This, that, and the other. In Bezuidenhout, A. and Reimer, M., editors, *Descriptions and Beyond*, pages 68–182. Oxford University Press, Oxford.

Neale, S. (2005). Pragmatism and binding. In Szabó, Z. G., editor, *Semantics versus Pragmatics*, pages 165–285. Oxford University Press, Oxford.

Neale, S. (2007). Heavy hands, magic, and scene-reading traps. *European Journal of Analytic Philosophy*, 3(2): 77–132.

Neale, S. (ms). Textualism with intent. *Unpublished Manuscript*.

Nickel, B. (2013). Dynamics, brandom-style. *Philosophical Studies*, 162(2): 333–354.

Ninan, D. (2005). Two puzzles about deontic necessity. In Nickel, B., Yalcin, S., Gajewski, J., and Hacquard, V., editors, *New Work on Modality*, pages 149–178. MIT Working Papers in Linguistics.

Norcross, A. (2011). Act-utilitarianism and promissory obligation. In Scheinman, H., editor, *Promises and Agreements: Philosophical Essays*. Oxford University Press, Oxford.

Onishi, K. and Baillargeon, R. (2005). Do 15-month-olds understand false beliefs? *Science*, 308: 255–258.

Pagin, P. (2011). Information and assertoric force. In Brown, J. and Cappelen, H., editors, *Assertion*, pages 97–136. Oxford University Press, Oxford.

Pagin, P. (2016). Assertion. In Zalta, E. N., editor, *Stanford Encyclopedia of Philosophy (Winter 2016 Edition)*. URL = <https://plato.stanford.edu/archives/win2016/entries/assertion/>.

Pelling, C. (2013). Assertion and the provision of knowledge. *Philosophical Quarterly*, 63: 293–312.

Pérez Carballo, A. and Santorio, P. (2016). Communication for expressivists. *Ethics*, 126(3): 607–635.

Pinker, S., Nowak, M., and Lee, J. (2008). The logic of indirect speech. *Proceedings of the National Academy of Sciences*, 105(3): 833–838.

Poggi, F. (2011). Law and conversational implicature. *International Journal for the Semiotics of Law*, 24: 21–40.

Portner, P. (2004). The semantics of imperatives within a theory of clause-types. In Watanabe, K. and Young, R., editors, *Proceedings of SALT 14*. CLC Publications.

Portner, P. (2007). Imperatives and modals. *Natural Language Semantics*, 15: 351–383.

Portner, P. (2012). Permission and choice. In Grewendorf, G. and Zimmermann, T., editors, *Discourse and Grammar: From Sentence Types to Lexical Categories*. Mouton de Gruyter, Berlin.

Potts, C. (2005). *The Logic of Conventional Implicatures*. Oxford University Press, Oxford.

Raz, J. (1986). *The Morality of Freedom*. Oxford University Press, Oxford.

Reiland, I. (2013). Propositional attitudes and mental acts. *Thought*, 1: 239–245.

Reiland, I. (2017). review of propositional content by peter hanks. *Philosophical Review*, 126: 132–136.

Reynolds, S. L. (2002). Testimony, knowledge, and epistemic goals. *Philosophical Studies*, 110(2): 139–161.

Roberts, C. (2002). Demonstratives as definites. In van Deemyer, K. and Kibble, R., editors, *Information Sharing*, pages 1–48. CSLI.

Roberts, C. (2003). Uniqueness in definite noun phrases. *Linguistics and Philosophy*, 26: 287–350.

Roberts, C. (2004). Context in dynamic interpretation. In Horn, L. and Ward, G., editors, *The Handbook of Pragmatics*, pages 197–220. Blackwell, Oxford.

Roberts, C. (2005). Pronouns as definites. In Reimer, M. and Bezuidenhout, A., editors, *Descriptions and Beyond*, pages 503–543. Oxford University Press, Oxford.

Roberts, C. (2012). Information structure in discourse: Toward an integrated formal theory of pragmatics. *Semantics and Pragmatics*, 5: 1–69.

Roberts, C. (2015a). Accommodation in a language game. In Loewer, B. and Schaffer, J., editors, *A Companion to David Lewis*, pages 345–366. Wiley-Blackwell, Oxford.

Roberts, C. (2015b). Conditional plans and imperatives: A semantics and pragmatics for imperative mood. In Brochhagen, T., Roelofsen, F., and Theiler, N., editors, *Proceedings of the 20th Amsterdam Colloquium*, pages 353–362.

Roberts, C. (2017). Speech acts in discourse context. In Fogal, D., Harris, D., and Moss, M., editors, *New Work on Speech Acts*, Oxford University Press, Oxford.

Rosenthal, D. M. (1986). Intentionality. *Midwest Studies in Philosophy*, 10: 151–184.

Sadock, J. (1974). *Toward a Linguistic Theory of Speech Acts*. Academic Press.

Salih, S. (2007). On Judith Butler and performativity. In Lovaas, K. E. and Jenkins, M. M., editors, *Sexualities and Communication in Everyday Life*, chapter 3, pages 55–68. Sage.

Saul, J. (2012). *Lying, Misleading, and What is Said: An Exploration in Philosophy of Language and in Ethics*. Oxford University Press, Oxford.

Scalia, A. (1998). *A Matter of Interpretation: Federal Courts and the Law*. Princeton University Press, Princeton, NJ.

Scanlon, T. M. (1990). Promises and practices. *Philosophy and Public Affairs*, 19(3): 199–226.

Scanlon, T. M. (1998). *What We Owe Each Other*. Cambridge University Press, Cambridge, UK.

Schaffer, J. (2008). Knowledge in the image of assertion. *Philosophical Issues*, 18: 1–19.

Schiffer, S. (1972). *Meaning*. Oxford University Press, Oxford.

Schiffer, S. (1981). Indexicals and the theory of reference. *Synthese*, 49(1): 43–100.

Schiffer, S. (1982). Intention-based semantics. *Notre Dame Journal of Formal Logic*, 23(2): 119–156.

Schiffer, S. (2003). *The Things We Mean*. Oxford University Press, Oxford.

Schroeder, M. (2010). *Noncognitivism in Ethics*. Routledge, Oxford and New York.

Scott-Phillips, T. (2014). *Speaking Our Minds: Why Human Communication is Different, and How Language Evolved to Make it Special*. Palgrave Macmillan.

Searle, J. (1965). What is a speech act? In Black, M., editor, *Philosophy in America*, pages 221–239. Allen and Unwin, London.

Searle, J. (1968). Austin on locutionary and illocutionary acts. *The Philosophical Review*, 77(4): 405–424.

Searle, J. (1969). *Speech Acts*. Cambridge University Press, London.

Searle, J. (1975). A taxonomy of illocutionary acts. In Gunderson, K., editor, *Language, Mind, and Knowledge*, volume VII of *Minnesota Studies in the Philosophy of Science*, pages 344–369. University of Minnesota Press, Minneapolis.

Searle, J. (1995). *The Construction of Social Reality*. The Free Press, New York.

Searle, J. (2010). *Making the Social World*. Oxford University Press, Oxford.

Searle, J. and Vanderveken, D. (1985). *Foundations of Illocutionary Logic*. Cambridge University Press.

Sellars, W. (1954). Some reflections on language games. *Philosophy of Science*, 21(3): 204–228.

Sellars, W. (1956). Empiricism and the philosophy of mind. In Feigl, H. and Scriven, M., editors, *The Foundations of Science and the Concepts of Psychology and Psychoanalysis*, volume 1 of *Minnesota Studies in the Philosophy of Science*, pages 253–329. University of Minnesota Press, Minneapolis.

Skyrms, B. (1996). *Evolution of the Social Contract*. Cambridge University Press.

Skyrms, B. (2010). *Signals*. Oxford University Press, Oxford.

Slote, M. (1979). Assertion and belief. In Dancy, J., editor, *Papers on Logic and Language*, pages 177–190. Keele University Library, Keele.

Sosa, D. (2009). Dubious assertions. *Philosophical Studies*, 146: 269–272.

Sperber, D. (2000). Metarepresentations in an evolutionary perspective. In Sperber, D., editor, *Metarepresentations: A Multidisciplinary Perspective*, pages 117–137. Oxford University Press, Oxford.

Sperber, D. and Wilson, D. (1995). *Relevance: Communication and Cognition*. Blackwell, Oxford, second edition.

Stalnaker, R. (1978). Assertion. In Cole, P., editor, *Syntax and Semantics 9*, pages 315–332. Academic Press, New York.

Stalnaker, R. (1998). On the representation of context. *Journal of Logic, Language, and Information*, 7(1): 3–19.

Stalnaker, R. (1999). *Context and Content*. Oxford University Press, Oxford.

Stalnaker, R. (2014). *Context*. Context and Content. Oxford University Press, Oxford.

Stanley, J. (2005). *Knowledge and Practical Interests*. Oxford University Press, Oxford.

Stanley, J. (2008). Knowledge and certainty. *Philosophical Issues*, 18: 35–57.

Stanley, J. (2011). The ways of silencing. *The New York Times*, June 25.

Stanley, J. (2015). *How Propaganda Works*. Princeton University Press, Princeton, NJ.

Starr, W. B. (2010). *Conditionals, Meaning and Mood*. PhD thesis, Rutgers University.

Starr, W. B. (2014). Mood, force, and truth. *Protosociology*, 31: 160–180.

Starr, W. (2016a). Conjoined imperatives and declaratives. In *Proceedings from Sinn and Bedeutung 21*. University of Edinburgh, Edinburgh.

Starr, W. B. (2016b). Dynamic expressivism about deontic modality. In Charlow, N. and Chrisman, M., editors, *Deontic Modality*. Oxford University Press, Oxford.

Starr, W. (ms). A preference semantics for imperatives. *Unpublished Manuscript*.

Stevenson, C. L. (1937). The emotive meaning of ethical terms. *Mind*, 46(181): 14–31.

Stevenson, C. L. (1944). *Ethics and Language*. Yale University Press, New Haven, CT.

Stokke, A. (2013). Lying, deceiving, and misleading. *Philosophy Compass*, 8(4): 348–359.

Stokke, A. (2016). Review of *Propositional Content* by Peter Hanks. *Notre Dame Philosophical Reviews*.

Strawson, P. F. (1964). Intention and convention in speech acts. *The Philosophical Review*, 73(4): 439–460.

Swanson, E. (2016). The application of constraint semantics to the language of subjective uncertainty. *Journal of Philosophical Logic*, 45(2): 121–146.

Thomason, R. H. (1990). Accommodation, meaning, and implicature: Interdisciplinary foundations for pragmatics. In Philip, R., Cohen, J. M., and Pollack, M. E., editors, *Intentions in Communication*, chapter 16, pages 325–364. MIT Press, Cambridge, MA.

Tirrell, L. (2012). Genocidal language games. In Maitra, I. and McGowan, M. K., editors, *Speech and Harm*, pages 174–221. Oxford University Press, Oxford.

Tomasello, M. (2008). *Origins of Human Communication*. MIT Press, Cambridge, MA.

Turri, J. (2010). Epistemic invariantism and speech act contextualism. *Philosophical Review*, 119: 77–95.

Turri, J. (2011). The express knowledge account of assertion. *Australasian Journal of Philosophy*, 89(1): 37–45.

Turri, J. (2015). Knowledge and the norm of assertion. *Synthese*, 192: 385–392.

Unger, P. (1975). *Ignorance: A Case for Skepticism*. Oxford University Press.

Unnsteinsson, E. (2016). A Gricean theory of malaprops. *Mind and Language*, forthcoming.

Veltman, F. (1996). Defaults in update semantics. *Journal of Philosophical Logic*, 25(3): 221–261.

Waldron, J. (1999). *Law and Disagreement*. Oxford University Press, Oxford, UK.

Weiner, M. (2005). Must we know what we say? *Philosophical Review*, 114: 227–251.

Wikforss, Å. (2001). Semantic normativity. *Philosophical Studies*, 102: 203–226.

Willer, M. (2013). Dynamics of epistemic modality. *Philosophical Review*, 122(1): 45–92.

Willer, M. (2014). Dynamic thoughts on ifs and oughts. *Philosophers' Imprint*, 14(28): 1–30.

Willer, M. (2015). 'An Update on Epistemic Modals', *Journal of Philosophical Logic*, 44/6: 835–849.

Williamson, T. (1996). Knowing and asserting. *Philosophical Review*, 105: 489–523.

Williamson, T. (2000). *Knowledge and its Limits*. Oxford University Press, Oxford.

Wittgenstein, L. (1953). *Philosophical Investigations*. Blackwell, Oxford.

Yalcin, S. (2007). Epistemic modals. *Mind*, 116(464): 983–1026.

Yalcin, S. (2012). Bayesian expressivism. *Proceedings of the Aristotelian Society*, 112(2): 123–160.

Yalcin, S. (2015). Epistemic modality de re. *Ergo*, 2(19): 475–527.

Zanuttini, R., Pak, M., and Portner, P. (2012). A syntactic analysis of interpretive restrictions on imperative, promissive, and exhortative subjects. *Natural Language & Linguistic Theory*, 30(4): 1231–1274.

Zollman, K. J. S. (2011). Separating directives and assertions using simple signaling games. *The Journal of Philosophy*, 108(3): 158–169.

2

Insinuation, Common Ground, and the Conversational Record

Elisabeth Camp

2.1 Cooperation and Conflict

Most theorizing about linguistic communication assumes that conversation is a cooperative enterprise—specifically, one in which parties contribute information to a joint project of figuring out how the world is.[1,2] There are many reasons to adopt an assumption of cooperativity. First, simply as an empirical generalization, many conversations are cooperative; and it's methodologically wise to start with common, simple cases. Second, the fundamental nature of language as a conventional representational system requires a significant degree of cooperation for linguistic communication to occur at all. As Locke says, because the association between linguistic sign and signified is voluntary and arbitrary, each person has an "inviolable liberty to make words stand for what ideas he pleases"; it is only a desire to be understood that produces a "tacit consent" to go along with "common use" (1689, III.2). These features, of voluntariness and arbitrariness, render it very natural to model linguistic meaning as a set of conventions for solving a coordination problem, which builds in cooperativity (Lewis 1969, Skyrms 2010). Third, the fundamental nature of conversation involves coordination on and joint contributions to a common topic (Clark and Brennan 1991, Roberts 1996). Finally, much communicated is not explicitly articulated; to determine these contents, whether they are triggered by specific expressions or by the overall utterance in context, a hearer must consider what would make the utterance a cooperative contribution to the conversation (Grice 1975).

[1] Thanks to audiences at Cambridge University, the Columbia-CUNY conference 'New Work on Speech Acts', MIT, the New Mexico Texas Philosophical Society, Notre Dame University, the 2013 Rutgers Semantics Workshop, Tufts University, Université Libre de Bruxelles, University of Michigan, University of Pittsburgh, University of Texas Austin, and Yale University for very helpful discussion. Special thanks to Kent Bach, David Beaver, Daniel Harris, Claire Horisk, Jeff King, Eliot Michaelson, Andy Rogers, and Lynne Tirrell for extensive comments and discussion.
[2] Many conversations also aim to achieve agreement about practical, evaluative, and interpretive matters, and it is not obvious that these are appropriately analyzed in informational terms I largely leave this concern aside for current purposes; see Camp 2017c for general discussion, and Camp 2017b for discussion of non-information-driven conversational contributions within Stalnaker's model.

So the cooperative model is highly intuitive and theoretically fruitful. However, its plausibility has led theorists to largely ignore the range of cases and ways in which communication is less than fully cooperative. Many, even most conversations involve only partial alignment in interlocutors' interests, either in ultimate goals or in which information they prefer to share. The most obvious examples of non-aligned conversations are formally antagonistic interactions, such as courtroom cross-examination, or insurance contracts and settlements. But a wide range of business negotiations and personal interactions—including between intimate partners—are at least somewhat conflictual. In other cases, the parties' interests do align, at least in relevant respects; but there is some significant uncertainty about the degree of alignment. And in yet other cases, such as political speech, the speaker directs their utterance at, or knows it may be received by, multiple hearers with divergent assumptions and goals.

In all such contexts, an actual or epistemically possible conflict motivates at least one interlocutor to be *strategic* about their conversational contributions, by minimizing their overall commitments and/or by directing the conversation toward some contents and away from others. (In the structurally analogous case of badinage or witty banter, there is no substantive conflict, but a positive pleasure in interpretive strategy as an aesthetic end.) Further, at least in the cases I'll be discussing, both parties are, or should be, aware that the conversation is partially and/or potentially strategic in this way.[3]

Strategic conversations are not pure coordination problems in Lewis's (1969) sense. But they are still substantively cooperative enterprises, characterized by the same basic discourse structure and semantic and pragmatic principles as fully cooperative conversations. Interlocutors still employ linguistic conventions to undertake speech acts in a joint project of establishing a consistent set of claims and other commitments; and they still take turns and obey basic conversational principles. Irrelevant non-sequiturs, false statements, and 'Humpty Dumptyism'—unmarked abrogations of the 'tacit consent' to use words in their conventional sense—are all treated by participants as transgressing the conversational norms in a way that merely guarded or potentially misleading utterances are not.

The key difference from more standard conversations is that at least one party takes themselves to be bound only to *minimal* standards of cooperation. That is, rather than aiming to produce utterances that are maximally informative given minimal interpretive effort (Sperber and Wilson 1995), speakers may aim to ensure only that there is *some* accessible interpretation of their utterance which makes *some* relevant, true contribution to the question(s) under discussion. Correlatively, hearers may aim only to recover *some* interpretation that *some* audience might reasonably take the speaker to have intended. As we might put it, at least one side is prepared to 'work to conversational rule'—to refuse to go above and beyond the minimal norms of conversational duty. Thus, I take it that in addition to their practical importance, such conversations are theoretically interesting, because they reveal the conversational

---

[3] In this respect, the cases I'm concerned with differ importantly from at least many cases of propaganda as discussed by Stanley (2015) and of dogwhistles as discussed by Saul (this volume).

gears and cogs whose operations can be occluded when they are immersed in a sludge of charitable good-feeling and fully collaborative effort.

Some theorists have recently attended to strategic contexts, exploring the ways in which mutual awareness of conflictual or risky communication drives the production of phenomena like politeness (Brown and Levinson 1987), vagueness (Blume and Board 2013) and scalar implicature (Jäger 2013). Here, I focus on *insinuation*: the communication of beliefs, requests, and other attitudes 'off-record', so that the speaker's main communicative point remains unstated.[4]

Before delving into more theoretical discussion, it will be useful to have some concrete examples in hand. A paradigmatic example of implicature from Grice (1975) also provides an elegant illustration of insinuation. Thus, when a professor writes:

(1)   Mr. X's command of English is excellent, and his attendance at tutorials has been regular.

as the entirety of a letter of recommendation, their reticence effectively communicates that Mr. X is a poor candidate, even though the letter's explicit content is innocuous. In some cases, such as insinuating 'telling details', the speaker may overtly disavow the intention to communicate anything more than this uncontroversial explicit content. For instance, by uttering:

(2)   You know that Obama's middle name is Hussein. I'm just saying.

the speaker conjures up a host of associated but unarticulated images and ideas in a way that shifts responsibility for recovering them onto the hearer, or perhaps onto the broader culture (Camp 2008).

While the insinuation in (2) is quite open-ended, the message in other cases is more specific. Thus, consider (3), uttered by George W. Bush during the second debate with Al Gore in the 2004 presidential election, when asked about his criteria for Supreme Court appointees:

(3)   I would pick somebody who would not allow their personal opinion to get in the way of the law. . . . Another example would be the Dred Scott case, which is where judges, years ago, said that the Constitution allowed slavery because of personal property rights. That's a personal opinion. That's not what the Constitution says. It doesn't speak to the equality of America.

Here, as in (1), the explicit claim is uncontroversial, even banal. However, where the main communicative work of the explicit content in (1) was simply *not* being more relevantly substantive, the specific content in (3) plays a more specific role in generating the insinuated meaning. By explicitly criticizing a judicial decision that turned on 'personal rights', Bush implicitly rejects other judicial decisions that have likewise invoked 'personal rights' in order to deny rights to other persons—thereby insinuating the intention to appoint a Justice who would vote to overturn the legalization of abortion effected by Roe v. Wade. For Bush, (3) thus functions as

---

[4] For other discussions of insinuation, see especially Solan and Tiersma 2005, Pinker et al. 2008, Lee and Pinker 2010, Terkourafi 2011, Fricker 2012, and Asher and Lascarides 2013. Godfrey-Smith and Martinez (2013) argue that honest informational signaling can arise in cases of limited common interest, including zero common interest, and even when dishonesty is cheap rather than costly.

a 'dogwhistle' (Saul, this volume) to those with the ears to hear, while explicitly he rejects any "litmus test" on abortion for judicial appointees.

The utterances in (1) through (3) are directed toward a public audience, so that the speaker either cannot know who will receive it, or knows that its recipients will have divergent perspectives. We'll see in in §2.2 that there is a sense in which hearer multiplicity is indeed a key ingredient in insinuation more generally. However, many insinuations are addressed to specific audiences. Thus, consider (4), addressed to potential buyers from a different racial or religious background or sexual orientation than the local majority:

(4)   Perhaps you would feel more comfortable locating in a more . . . transitional neighborhood, like Ashwood?

Here although the (nearly) explicit suggestion is just that the hearers themselves would be more comfortable elsewhere, the implicit imputation is that the hearers should feel uncomfortable in the current locale, by virtue of not 'belonging' to the majority group. The utterance is thereby intended to *make* its addressees uncomfortable; but the Realtor carefully avoids liability for discriminatory housing practices by framing her utterance as a perky, positive suggestion. Although in this case the interlocutors are relative strangers, insinuations can also arise between intimates. Thus, a spouse who utters:

(5)   Wow, it's late! The party must have been really fun, huh?

to their tipsy partner ostensibly returning from an obligatory annual office party might thereby insinuate a suspicion that their partner has been engaged in illicit post-party gallivanting.

Finally, we should note that insinuations can communicate contents with various types of attitude or force. Thus, while (1) is overtly a statement and (4) is a question, both generate implicit directives; and (2) undertakes an implicit commitment to action. Other insinuations produce implicit requests. Thus, a driver stopped for speeding might utter (6) in order to suggest a bribe (Pinker et al. 2008, Lee and Pinker 2010):

(6)   I'm in a bit of a hurry. Is there any way we can settle this right now?

Similarly, Henry II is reputed to have uttered something like (7) as a veiled command to assassinate Thomas Becket (thanks to Barry Smith for having suggested this example):[5]

(7)   What miserable drones and traitors have I nourished and brought up in my household, who let their Lord be treated with such shameful contempt by a low-born cleric?

In sum, these examples are diverse along multiple dimensions: the specificity of their implicit message and/or their intended audience; their communicative force; the conversational stakes; and the degree of common background and shared interest between interlocutors. What they share is that the speaker has crafted their utterance in a way that minimizes conversational risk: their explicit, on-record content is unobjectionable, and their riskier conversational point or move is implicit.

---

[5] Thanks to Barry Smith for the example.

Mitigating communicative risk by leaving contents unstated is a distinctive rhetorical advantage of insinuation. Specifically, it allows speakers to get contents and commitments across while preserving *deniability* about those contents, shifting responsibility for those contents away from themselves, onto either the hearer or else a more amorphous, putative collective intentionality—what 'people say'.

Risk-mitigation is far from the only reason for speaking indirectly; and insinuation is far from the only way to depart from fully explicit articulation.[6] Just as there are importantly different ways to be indirect and/or inexplicit, including implicature, figurative speech, loose talk, explicature, and ellipsis, there are also importantly different reasons why speakers choose not to be fully direct and explicit, including politeness (Brown and Levinson 1987); efficiency in transmitting complex contents through the 'articulatory bottleneck' of language's linear format (Levinson 2000, 28); preservation of vagueness and indeterminacy in the attitudes the speaker wants to communicate (Dennett 1981); and transcendence of expressive limitations, especially in referring to experiential states (Pugmire 1998, Camp 2006a).

However, risk-mitigation is indeed *a* key reason for communicative indirection, and one that insinuation is especially effective at achieving. In §2.2, I explain how insinuation can exhibit the crucial but puzzling feature of deniability, given the obvious fact that communication does succeed in these cases. In §2.3, I offer a theoretical characterization of insinuation and explore its consequences for our theoretical understanding the speaker's meaning, common ground and the conversational record.

2.2 Deniability and Its Limits

2.2.1 How Insinuation Works

Although the basic phenomenon of insinuation is familiar enough, its workings are more theoretically puzzling. To see why, and how it works, we need a slightly more general characterization of cases like (1)–(7) above.

In these cases, a speaker S produces an utterance U of a sentence L whose conventional function is to present a proposition P with illocutionary force F. (U might also have the conventional function of committing the speaker to a non-cognitive attitude. Although such utterances may be used to insinuate, I ignore them here.) S locutes $F(P)$: they intend to be recognized as producing an utterance with that conventional function. Further, S illocutes $F(P)$: they intend to be recognized as asserting, or asking, or commanding, or promising P. (In other cases, such as figurative speech and loose talk, S intends to be recognized as illocuting a proposition P' not conventionally associated with L. Although such utterances may be used to insinuate, I ignore them here.) In addition, S also intends to be recognized as presenting a distinct proposition, Q, in a mode M: as a contribution of information, a query, a directive, etc. (That is, these 'modes' have the same "essential effect" (Stalnaker 1978, 86) as assertions, questions,

---

[6] Pinker and colleagues present risk-mitigation as a general explanation for communicative indirection; specifically, they claim that speakers employ indirection in order to mitigate the risk involved in renegotiating the type of relationship operative between speaker and hearer: in switching among communal sharing, authority ranking, and equality matching (Lee and Pinker 2010, 794).

and commands, though they may differ from them in detail.) Finally, in all of these cases, communication is successful in the sense that the hearer H recognizes all of these intentions. Indeed, in many (though not all) cases, communication succeeds in the more robust sense that H doesn't merely come to believe that S intended to communicate $M(Q)$, or that S believes, desires, or intends Q, but themselves come to believe, desire, or intend Q (or an appropriate correlate thereof).

So far, nothing distinguishes U from standard cases of implicature, as in (8):

> (8) A (standing by car on the side of the road): I'm out of gas.
> B: There's a service station two blocks up State Street.

where B implicates, but does not say or assert, that the closest gas station is two blocks away, and that it is currently open, sells gas, and will otherwise address A's obvious but unstated needs. What is distinctive of insinuation is that if H, or someone else who overhears the conversation or hears an indirect report of U, explicitly attributes $M(Q)$ to S, then S is prepared and able to coherently *deny* $M(Q)$.

The most straightforward and minimal such denial merely insists on a narrow literal construal of L. Thus, in response to an accusation like:

> (1.1)   Hey wait a minute! Do you mean that Mr. X is a bad philosopher?

or a report like:

> (1.2)   George told us Mr. X is a bad philosopher.

the writer of the pallid letter in (1) might utter something like:

> (1.3)   I didn't say that.
> (1.4)   All I said was that Mr. X is punctual and has good handwriting. And that he does!

So long as $F(P)$ on its own would constitute at least a minimally cooperative contribution to the conversation, narrowly focusing on $F(P)$ may suffice as a rebuttal of the attribution of $M(Q)$. (Indeed, given this, S may need to rely on non-verbal cues like body language, along with verbal cues like tone and manner, to get H to recognize that they intended more than $F(P)$, but in a way that preserves deniability.)[7] However, in many cases of insinuation, $F(P)$ is so anodyne that it does not meet even minimal standards of conversational relevance. Especially in such cases, the denying speaker may offer an alternative content $M(Q)'$ as their putatively intended communicative contribution, which would render U cooperative.

---

[7] The need to provide an additional positive indication of the speaker's intention to communicate something more or other than the conventional meaning $F(P)$ in cases where $F(P)$ suffices as a minimally cooperative conversational contribution also arises in non-insinuating cases, especially with manner implicatures. Thus, the proposition expressed by 'She produced a series of notes closely corresponding to the Star Spangled Banner' suffices informationally as a response to 'What did Jane sing?', but implicates that she did a bad job of it. 'Twice-apt' metaphors, like 'Jesus was a carpenter' or 'There are storm clouds on the horizon', may be conversationally appropriate on their literal interpretation; it may only be their occurrence within a poem, or their accompaniment by an arched eyebrow, which indicates an additional layer of meaning (Searle 1979).

Of course, these claims by S about their communicative intentions, in the face of an explicit attribution of $M(Q)$, would be disingenuous. Further, in most successful cases of insinuation, H realizes this (and S realizes that H realizes this). Nonetheless, when an insinuation is properly executed, the denial sticks: H lacks the resources to rebut S's denial of having meant $M(Q)$. I am hesitant to offer a definition of insinuation, partly because it is by its nature a murky phenomenon that pushes the boundaries of communication. But this phenomenon of *implicature with deniability* clearly lies at its core: it is what makes insinuation practically useful for speakers, and theoretically interesting for philosophers and linguists.[8]

Not all cases of insinuation involve the speaker insidiously attempting to further their own goals at the hearer's expense, although it is obviously ripe for this. Some insinuations probe the extent of alignment between speaker and hearer; while others aim to protect the hearer, or a third party, from the shame of explicit accusation or the pain of explicit acknowledgment. Given this variety, not all hearers will always want to resist the speaker's conversational move. However, a speaker's use of insinuation puts a hearer who *does* want to resist in a frustrating position, insofar as a commitment they want to reject has been thrust into the conversation, but in a way that escapes easy response. That is, a direct negation, along the lines of:

(1.5)   That's not true.
(1.6)   No, he doesn't.

will target U's explicit, anodyne content, and leave the troublesome message untouched. But an explicit query or accusation about the speaker's insinuated message, as in (1.1), both disrupts the ordinary conversational flow and invites speaker denial of having meant this. The same difficulties beset an explicit retort such as:

(1.7)   I believe that Mr. X is an excellent philosopher.

Worse, in at least some cases an explicit query, accusation or response, like:

(2.1)   Are you suggesting that Barack Obama is a radical Islamist?

can actually lend credence to Q, by demonstrating that Q is something someone might plausibly think on the basis of P, thereby inviting S to respond with a follow-up like:

(2.2)   You said it, not me; but now that you mention it…

---

[8] In introducing insinuation in §2.1, I said that the explicit literal content is 'designedly' uncontentious; and in the previous paragraph, I described deniability in terms of a speaker's being 'prepared' to deny having meant $M(Q)$. How much explicit foresight does insinuation require? Most of the time, insinuating speakers presumably hope communication goes smoothly, so that the need for denial never arises. Nonetheless, in many cases of insinuation, especially with high stakes, speakers do formulate their words carefully, planning for downstream conversational contingencies. In other cases, speakers minimize their conversational commitments with a merely intuitive feel for the possible conversational openings they could duck into. Finally, in still other cases, a speaker may initially intend to straightforwardly implicate $M(Q)$, and realize its conversational costliness and the availability of a conversational out only when challenged. I am unsure whether to count these last cases as insinuations. I take clarifying the commonalities and differences in operative interpretive mechanisms to be more important than taxonomizing the range of cases for its own sake.

At the same time, even as insinuations do place resistant hearers in a rhetorically frustrating position, it's not as if speakers hold all the communicative cards. Insinuation constitutes a kind of communicative bluff: an attempt to make a conversational move without paying the conversational cost. An explicit attribution of $M(Q)$ attempts to call that bluff; and a speaker denial doubles down on it. However, the speaker's use of insinuation also renders them vulnerable to a commensurate form of interpretive foot-dragging by the hearer, in the form of *pedantry*: a refusal by H to pick up on and respond to $M(Q)$ despite recognizing it as having been intended.[9]

Hearer pedantry takes two main forms. In *flat-footed pedantry*—especially beloved of philosophers—H insists on construing U as simply meaning $F(P)$, and balks at $F(P)$'s conversational insufficiency. Thus, H might respond to (1), not with an explicit attribution as in (1.1), but with something like:

(1.8)   Why should we care about Mr. X's elocutionary abilities? We want to know how he is as a philosopher.

Alternatively, in *cunning pedantry*, H twists U to serve their own conversational ends; thus, H might respond to (1) with something like:

(1.9)   Well, people always say that anyone who can speak clearly can think clearly, so I guess you're saying that we should hire him.

With both forms of pedantry, H's refusal to pick up the conversational ball at the point where S had hoped to roll it forces S to either shoulder the responsibility for introducing $M(Q)$ overtly, or else abandon the attempt to make $M(Q)$ as a conversational move altogether. The accompanying risk is that with both speaker and hearer dragging their interpretive feet, conversation slows to an unproductive literalistic crawl.

2.2.2 Plausible Deniability and Its Limits

Deniability and pedantry are flip sides of a common conversational coin, which interlocutors can deploy to achieve their respective conversational aims with minimal conversational liability. It is, I take it, an empirical fact that insinuated speech is often deniable, and that hearers sometimes retaliate with pedantry. We observe both denial and pedantry in operation in political speech, courtroom testimony, business negotiations, and conversations among intimates. They often provide grist for witty banter in romcoms, and for intrigue in spy flicks. Even the plots in children's books—for instance, *Pippi Longstocking, Winnie the Pooh,* and *A Bargain for Frances*—sometimes hinge on insinuation, denial, and pedantry. But how is deniability even possible? After all, S intends to communicate $M(Q)$ by getting H to recognize this communicative intention, and H successfully recognizes this. Further, if S does claim to have meant $M(Q)'$ instead of $M(Q)$, she lies about her communicative intentions; and that lie is often a bald-faced one. How does the speaker get away with it? It's clear enough why speakers would *want* to communicate without assuming conversational liability; but why would hearers go along?

---

[9] I discuss deniability and pedantry in connection with figurative speech in Camp 2006b, 2007, 2008, 2012, and 2017b.

Insinuation is not a fully uniform phenomenon. It comes in degrees of obscurity; and speakers vary in their brazenness. But even highly transparent insinuations still admit at least some deniability. Thus, for instance, Lee and Pinker (2010) found that subjects estimated the probability that a speaker meant to offer a bribe with the obvious insinuation:

(6.1)   I'm very sorry, officer. But I'm actually in the middle of something right now, sort of an emergency. So maybe the best thing would be to take care of this here . . . without going to court or doing any paperwork.

as extremely high, but still short of full certainty, while they did report certainty about the overt statement:

(6.2)   I'm very sorry, officer. If I give you a fifty, will you just let me go?

(Lee and Pinker 2010, 800).[10] As Pinker et al. (2008, 836) put it, "Any 'deniability' in these cases is really not so plausible after all." And yet—it is *possible*. 'Plausible deniability' is usually quite *im*plausible; but it is an all-too-familiar feature of strategic communicative contexts.

The contrast between (6.1) and (6.2) might suggest that the crucial difference is between explicit, primary messages and implicit, secondary ones. Thus, Lee and Pinker (2010, 801) suggest that "there is a qualitative psychological difference between a direct proposition and even the most obvious indirect one . . . with direct speech, no uncertainty exists in any direction: Present and absent parties are both completely certain of the intent, and the speaker knows it." Similarly, Elizabeth Fricker claims that "a speaker can never be incontrovertibly nailed with commitment to a mere conversational implication E of what she stated" (2012, 89)—in effect, that it is in the nature of conversational implicature in general that denial is *always* possible. But this can't be right. For one thing, even (6.2) is not fully explicit as a bribe. Indeed, most "direct" speech involves context-sensitive expressions and other determinants of meaning that are not fully explicit and determinate, which also produce some degree of deniability (Hawthorne 2012, King 2014).

More importantly for current purposes, deniability does have its limits. Sometimes a politician's, or a spouse's, denial falls flat: his intended meaning was just too obvious, and his proffered alternative just too ridiculous. Thus, we need to understand both how deniability is possible even when it's not plausible, and also what its limits are.

The key feature of denial, I think, is that it trades on the gap between what is in fact mutually obvious to the speaker and hearer, on the one hand, and what both parties are prepared to *acknowledge* as mutually obvious, on the other.[11] In cases like (1) through (7), S intends for H to take the fact that she uttered U in C as evidence that she means $M(Q)$. Further, S intends H to arrive at $M(Q)$ by relying on a set

[10] "Whereas the direct bribe was judged by all the participants but one as 100% certain, the thinly veiled bribe was judged by most of them as exactly one percentage point less certain: The mode, median, and 75th percentile of responses were at exactly 99%." They also found that subjects preferred more indirect statements for communicating riskier contents in higher-stakes contexts.

[11] Although it differs in some important details, and although we disagree significantly about the theoretical upshot, my explanation in this section is largely compatible with that in Fricker (2012), and overlaps in important ways with that of Lee and Pinker (2010).

of interpretive presuppositions, I, that are in fact mutually salient to S and H in C. Finally, in cases of successful insinuation, H recovers all of these intentions. The crucial feature exploited by speaker denial is that the presuppositions I that generate $M(Q)$ on the basis of U are context-specific and merely implicit. In actual fact, these presuppositions really are mutually obvious to S and H. But when S is challenged about what she meant, she pretends that this is not the case. In effect, she pretends to be in a slightly different conversational context C', governed by an alternative set of interpretive assumptions I', which differ from I in crucial but relatively intangible ways, such as the relative ranking of salience among features or objects, or the relative probabilities of various counterfactual possibilities. Given these differences, the calculation of U plus I' delivers $M(Q)'$ rather than $M(Q)$ as U's implicated content.

Thus, for instance, if the Realtor who uttered (4) were accused bigotry, she might respond with a denial like:

(4.1)   Oh dear me, I didn't mean to suggest anything like that. I only meant that with so many families with young children here, you might not find as many people to socialize with as in a more up-and-coming neighborhood.

In (4.1), S suggests that the 'comfort' the addressees might not feel in the local neighborhood derives from being childless rather than from racial or other demographic difference, and that Ashwood's being 'transitional' consists in its being on an upward trajectory, rather than from its being further from amenities like parks and museums. While these are indeed factors that someone might consider in deciding where to live, by fixing on them S conveniently pretends to ignore other factors which are in fact more obvious to both parties.

Speaker denials are so annoying because it is obvious to H not just that I constitutes the actually operative set of presuppositions, but also that S is in fact exploiting I in communicating—indeed, S may have constituted I *as* presupposed by uttering U. But speaker denial is still possible because those presuppositions are merely implicit, and because identifying them requires a nuanced sensitivity to interpretive salience and relevance. Most of us are in fact remarkably sensitive to such interpretive nuances. We effortlessly, even automatically pick up on fine-grained conversational cues, including a host of non-verbal and quasi-verbal signals like bodily stance, gesture, facial expression, discourse speed, prosody, register, and tone; and we fluidly adjust our mindsets to match the speaker's in light of these cues. From a theoretical perspective, though, our ability to coordinate on these highly specific conversational details often appears miraculous: it involves abductive identification of just the right premises at just the right moment, in a way that makes many Gricean appeals to 'calculability' look like *post hoc* rationalizations, and confounds much computational AI processing of natural discourse. More importantly, insofar as the resulting presuppositions aren't mandated either by direct anaphoric reference to previous linguistic context or by explicit appeal to concrete, objective, discrete features of the extralinguistic conversational context, S can pretend to be relying on slightly but crucially different presuppositions without overtly violating basic communicative principles.

Hearer pedantry is underwritten by this same gap between in-fact mutually obvious interpretive presuppositions and mutually acknowledged presuppositions. Faced with an insinuation, H can pretend either to have failed to identify any plausible set of unstated interpretive assumptions that could render U conversationally cooperative, as in flat-footed pedantry; or else invoke an alternative set of unarticulated assumptions I'' to derive Q'' as the purported implicature, as in cunning pedantry.

The gap between interpretive assumptions that are in fact mutually obvious and those that are mutually acknowledged as being obvious also explains the *limits* of deniability. That is, in all cases, a speaker who exploits deniability 'plays to a virtual audience' (Goffman 1967; Lee and Pinker 2010, 7896), pretending to address U to a possible hearer H_P who would sincerely employ the alternative assumptions I' to derive $M(Q)'$. For the alternative interpretation $M(Q)'$ to be *admissible*—or above the threshold of 'plausible deniability'—it must be *reasonable* to calculate $M(Q)'$ on the basis of the uttered sentence's conventional meaning $F(P)$, the commitments undertaken in the conversation to this point, and some set I' of epistemically accessible presuppositions consistent with those commitments, in a way that renders U at least minimally conversationally cooperative.

Fricker is correct that what she aptly calls the "dodgy epistemics" of pragmatic interpretation (2012, 89) guarantees that there will virtually always be at least some leeway among admissible interpretations. However, the range of presuppositions that are accessible, and the stringency of what counts as reasonable, varies by context. Both Lee and Pinker and Fricker assume a cross-contextually stable—and universally high—standard for deniability. But an interpretation $M(Q)'$ might be grudgingly admissible in one context and not in another, depending on which interpretive assumptions are epistemically accessible and reasonably relevant in that context.

One factor affecting admissability is how wide a range of alternative assumptions can be ruled out as not actually *accessible* in C. A speaker's denial of $M(Q)$ may be directed either at the original interlocutor H, or at a third party who overhears U or who makes or hears an indirect report of U. Often, speakers directing denials at third parties will be able to invoke a wider range of possible alternatives: because the third party lacks full access to the immediate context C, they don't know what spoken and unspoken assumptions were actually operative in C. By contrast, H is more likely to be in a position to invoke a richer body of explicit and implicit commitments, which S would not be prepared to repudiate if pressed directly, and which could militate in favor of $M(Q)$ over $M(Q)'$.

However, even a denial directed at the actual hearer in a conversation between long-term intimates about familiar topics may still be able to exploit significant latitude in accessible presuppositions. For instance, while the imagined speaker of:

(5)   Wow, it's late! The party must have been really fun, huh?

actually insinuated that their tipsy spouse was out gallivanting after a party they both know to have been dreary, the stay-at-home partner might respond to an accusation of having meant this by offering specific reasons that they are purportedly happy that the party-goer is apparently forging better collegial ties. In the imagined scenario, such an innocent expression of optimism is in fact less plausible than resentful accusation. But the putative optimistic interpretation impersonates a sunnier incarnation of the speaker, one he might still manage to instantiate on his better days, and that the hearer might have to admit could have been actual on this occasion.

In addition to variability in the accessibility of alternative interpretive assumptions, conversations also vary in the stringency of the operative standard of *reasonableness*, in at least two ways. First, the more there is a known likelihood of conflict or other motivation for strategic interpretation, the more reasonable it is to be actively on one's interpretive guard. And this in turn widens the scope of deniability (and cunning pedantry), by increasing the range of alternative assumptions one must be able to rule out to eliminate a putative alternative interpretation. Second, interlocutors' willingness to push the bounds of reasonable reinterpretation depends on their willingness to bear larger social costs. A speaker who expects future interactions with H to be quite limited may be more prepared to offer an alternative interpretation $M(Q)'$ at the outer bounds of admissibility; while a speaker who is concerned to preserve the relationship, or their own reputation going forward, may be less inclined to invoke minimally credible reinterpretations. Thus, a tourist trying to avoid paying the fine for having failed to pre-purchase a metro ticket may be more likely to double down on insisting that they didn't intend a bribe by (6) than a driver stopped by a cop in their hometown; and the resentful stay at home partner who utters (5) will be more or less likely to admit his insinuated suspicions when challenged, depending on whether he hopes that the relationship can be still salvaged.

We can observe all these factors in operation, in sometimes cross-cutting ways, in public discussions of what speakers have insinuated and the legitimacy of their attempted denials, for instance in talk-show debates about a politician's latest controversial tweet and attempted 'walk-back'. Speakers do regularly push the bounds of deniability, claiming to have been quoted out of context and insisting that their utterance was innocuous, or just a joke. And often they do get away with denying something they obviously did mean: the recipients of the denial roll their eyes but acquiesce. But speakers are also sometimes held legally, administratively and politically responsible for content they have merely insinuated, on the ground that any reasonable person would have taken them to have meant $M(Q)$, or something else equally damning, given what else is known about the conversation and surrounding context.

One particularly fraught class of cases concern sexual harassment. The Equal Employment Opportunity Commission includes merely implicit threats to continued employment within the scope of "Quid pro quo" sexual harassment.[12] Many employers' HR policies follow suit, prohibiting the "direct or indirect request" for sexual favors, as well as repeated suggestions of sexual interest, whether direct or indirect, after the subordinate has "shown," again either directly or indirectly, lack of interest in a sexual relationship.[13] Thus, legal and administrative standards recognize that even indirect, insinuated contents can be genuinely meant, and that speakers can sometimes be held liable even for statements designed to be deniable—so long as the plaintiff can demonstrate that the relevant suggestions and refusals were in fact made. At the same time, in applying these clauses, the operative standard is not how the actual supervisor or subordinate actually interpreted the utterance, but how a

---

[12] See https://www.eeoc.gov/eeoc/publications/upload/currentissues.pdf

[13] See e.g. Muse (1996, 79). Pinker et al. (2008, 785) cite the 2008 arrest of Massachusetts State Senator Dianne Wilkerson, whose acceptance of $2,000 "in appreciation of her efforts" to obtain a liquor license for a client was treated as a case of bribery; and the 2009 arrest of Robert Halderman for attempted blackmail after he attempted to "sell a screenplay" to David Letterman depicting Letterman's sexual relationships with staffers.

"reasonable person" would have, or could only have, interpreted that utterance in that context. And demonstrating this requires establishing, to a sufficiently robust degree, the limits of reasonable interpretation in that particular conversational context— something that is often difficult to do in practice. Thus, these policies confirm simultaneously that insinuation affords a significant degree of protection against conversational liability and consequent testimonial report; but also that it does not confer blanket immunity. Sometimes speakers are "nailed" for what they insinuate, because their proffered reinterpretations fail to meet a standard of reasonableness.

2.3 Common Ground, Mutual Knowledge, and the Conversational Record

In §2.2, I described the workings of insinuation, focusing on the twin interpretive weapons of speaker deniability and hearer pedantry, and explaining the puzzling phenomenon of implausible "plausible deniability" as exploitation of the interpretive leeway generated by the "dodgy epistemics" of pragmatics. In this section, I explore the theoretical implications of insinuation, deniability and pedantry for our under-standing of meaning and communication more generally.

I began §2.1 by alluding to an intuitive, informally assumed model of communi-cation in terms of cooperative contributions to a common epistemic (and sometimes practical) enterprise. A maximally straightforward implementation of that model is represented in Figure 2.1.

On this simple version, a speaker S who produces an utterance U thereby *says* or *asserts* the content P that is compositionally determined by the conventional meanings of the words they utter. Saying/asserting is a proposal to add the proposition P

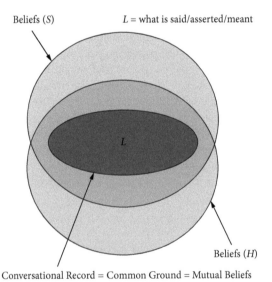

Figure 2.1 Intuitive, simplistic model of cooperative communication.

conventionally associated with the uttered sentence L to the *conversational score* or *common ground*, where saying is equivalent to asserting and the conversational score is a record of contributions to the common ground, which is in turn a matter of what is mutually believed. If the hearer H does not object, S's utterance makes P common ground between S and H; the overall goal of communication is to enlarge the common ground until the set of possibilities that could be actual is reduced to a singleton, or at least a relevantly sufficiently restricted set.

This simplistic version of the cooperative model is a mash-up of three strands of contemporary theorizing about linguistic communication. It implements the basic outlines of a broadly Gricean story about speaker's meaning, as the attempt to change another's mind by giving them a reason to do so, within a broadly Stalnakerian framework, of conversation as an evolving pool of mutual information, by employing a broadly Lewisian (1979) notion of conversational score to track the evolution of that common ground, and a broadly Lewisian (1969) notion of convention to fix the contents of speakers' contributions to it.

I doubt any theorist accepts this simple version in its entirety. For one thing, some theorists deny the existence or theoretical relevance of some of the relevant terms. To take just one recent lively debate, Lepore and Stone (2015) argue for a thoroughly conventionalist, neo-Lewisian view of meaning, while Bach and Harnish (1979), Neale (2005), and Harris (2016), among others, argue for the neo-Gricean view that meaning is always ultimately a matter of speakers' intention, with Davidson (1986) rejecting any substantive theoretical role for convention in theories of communication and meaning. More relevantly, many theorists already insist on refinements and distinctions among the various terms equated in Figure 2.1. However, many of these same theorists also appear to accept the simple model as a decent starting point, and frequently employ it in practice. In this section, I aim to remind them, and to convince others, of the need to distinguish its various terms. Specifically, I use insinuation to argue that Gricean speaker's meaning, contributions to the Stalnakerian common ground, and updates to the Lewisian score are all distinct. (Indeed, we will find reason to distinguish conversational record from conversational score.) One can successfully mean, and communicate, something without entering it onto the score or even the common ground.

2.3.1 Speaker's Meaning

Why should we think that in successful cases of insinuation, $M(Q)$ is part of what S means by U? Although an impeccable appeal to authority is available, given that our initial example is both a paradigmatic case of Gricean implicature and a paradigmatic case of insinuation, it is not very satisfying. The core of Grice's notion of non-natural meaning is that it is an attitude that H comes to entertain at least partly in virtue of recognizing S's intention that H recognize S as intending that H entertain it. This entails two features: first, that S have an intention which plays a significant role in getting H to entertain that attitude; and second, that S's intention to get H to entertain it be open and overt. I'll take the two conditions in turn.

First, why think an insinuating speaker S intends to get H to entertain some content, such that this intention is not just a cause but a reason for H's entertaining it? One might deny this, as Lepore and Stone (2010, 2015) do for hints and innuendos; instead, they think, hints are cases of merely natural meaning, akin to one parent leaving a vase broken by their child out for the other to see (Grice 1957, 440). One thread of their complaint is that a hinting speaker S lacks an appropriately determinate communicative intention. I think we should reject any determinacy requirement on meaning. As Grice pointed out (1975, 58), most implicatures are indeterminate; indeed, this can be an important expressive advantage, even in fully cooperative contexts. Further, many straightforwardly literal utterances lack determinate communicative contents (Camp 2006a, Buchanan 2010). But in any case, a requirement of determinacy can't be wielded against insinuation as a class of speaker's meaning. It is true that some insinuations, like (2), are determinedly indeterminate, conjuring up an amorphous cloud of unspecified associations; perhaps most or all hints and innuendoes are like this. But in many other cases of insinuation, the range of what S means is just as bounded as in uncontroversial cases of meaning. Thus, within their respective imagined contexts, the speaker's actual insinuated messages in (1), (3), (4), (6), and (7) are close to the following:

(1.10)   Mr. X is not a good candidate for a job in philosophy.

(3.1)   I will appoint a Supreme Court Justice who will vote to overturn Roe v. Wade.

(4.2)   People like you aren't welcome here.

(6.3)   Can I pay you to let me off the hook?

(7.1)   Kill Thomas Becket.

A second part of Lepore and Stone's complaint against counting hints and innuendos as speaker's meaning is that recognition of S's intention fails to play a sufficiently central role in H's identification of $M(Q)$. When Salome showed Herod the head of St. John the Baptist on a charger, this communicated that John was dead, but by *showing* this rather than telling it (Grice 1957, 382). Perhaps likewise in (1) through (7), S simply 'lets it be known,' or 'puts it out there' that $F(P)$, while leaving the hearer to arrive at the insinuated attitude $M(Q)$ on their own.

This is indeed the avowed strategy in (2). But even in this case, the connection between explicit and insinuated content depends on recognition of the speaker's intentions, in at least two ways. First, as we saw in §2.2, the connection is underwritten by a rich set of assumptions I about how the world is, and about how objective facts and interpretive opinions are connected—assumptions the hearer may otherwise fail to entertain, and may actively reject. Even for 'telling details' like (2), the connection between $F(P)$ and $M(Q)$ only takes on a semblance of 'naturalness' relative to a certain cognitive perspective. This is illustrated by the fact that although the literal content of a telling detail, as in (2), is assumed to be uncontroversially true, the insinuated content Q may be false—and H may know this. But a *sine qua non* of natural meaning is that if P obtains, then Q does too: P merely 'indicates' or 'shows' Q.

Second, even if we include the interpretive assumptions I as part of the 'natural environment' of U, typically $M(Q)$ still does not follow 'naturally' from $F(P)$, or even from the fact that S believes or desires P; instead, it follows from the fact that S has uttered L, with $F(P)$ as its conventional content, to H in this context C. Simply overhearing S enunciating any of (1) through (7), or knowing that S was entertaining (1) through (7), would not suffice to lead H to (1.10) through (7.1). The fact that S is not simply manifesting a state of the world or of her own mind, which H then picks up on, is especially obvious when we recall that the insinuations in (1) through (7) involve suggestions, commissions, and directives: that is, contents presented in a certain mode, and not just bare propositions.

Thus, it appears that insinuating speakers do intend to produce cognitive effects in their hearers, and that these intentions play some sort of important role in getting the hearer to entertain $M(Q)$. What about the second condition for speaker's meaning: that S's intentions be overt and open rather than duplicitous? Communicative signals that lack this feature—such as Iago's surreptitiously leaving Desdemona's handkerchief in Cassio's apartment, or a man M who is playing bridge with his boss B, and who smiles in an almost-natural way, because M wants B to think that he wants B to recognize that M is bluffing, but not for B to recognize that M wants B to recognize this intention (Strawson 1964, Grice 1969, Schiffer 1972)—are classic counterexamples to Grice's original analysis. And it might seem that communication that is 'off-record' or 'under the table' must not be overt and open in the relevant way. Thus, Bach and Harnish (1979, 101) hold that "devious acts" of "innuendo, deliberate ambiguity, and sneaky presupposition" do not count as cases of speaker's meaning, precisely because they are designed to preserve deniability. The only way to achieve deniability, they think, is for S to intend that her intention that H entertain Q should fail to be recognized by H as S's communicative intention—in which case the intention would lack the appropriate reflexive Gricean structure.[14]

Clearly, some "devious acts" of idea transmission, such as subliminal advertising and covert dogwhistles (Saul, this volume), do lack the right sort of reflexive intentions. Perhaps some of these cases might intuitively be called 'insinuations'. However, in cases like (1) through (7) and other typical cases of insinuation, S does intend for their communicative intention to be *manifest* to H, in the sense of being "obviously evident" to both of them (Stalnaker 2014, 47). That is, S does want H to recognize, by means of this utterance, that she intends for him to take her to be suggesting Q (or suggesting that she, or the hearer, will, or should Q), just as in standard cases of meaning. Furthermore, H does recognize this intention, and S knows this. S's deviousness consists only in being unwilling to own up to those intentions explicitly, whether directly to H or to some third party. This is the sense in which the speaker is engaged in a communicative bluff. But there are no veiled higher-order intentions. Indeed, an insinuating speaker typically intends H to recognize their intention that $M(Q)$ be off-record, and that they are prepared to deny having meant $M(Q)$ if challenged. If and when S does deny having meant $M(Q)$, they don't typically expect H to believe that they actually meant $M(Q)'$ rather than $M(Q)$; they merely hope to avoid conversational liability for it.

Thus, paradigmatic cases of insinuation involve at least as much determinacy, dependency, and clarity in the speaker's communicative intentions as standard cases

---

[14] Similarly, Strawson (1964, 454) denies that insinuation is an illocutionary act, because "overtness" is "an essential feature of the intentions which make up the illocutionary complex . . . They have, one might say, essential avowability."

of communication—including not just implicature but also many cases involving the pragmatic determination and modulation of literal content (Hawthorne 2012, King 2014). If we raise the standard for what counts as successful intention-recognition to rule out insinuation as a case of speaker's meaning, we thereby rule out many ordinary, intuitively successful cases of communication as well.

2.3.2 Common Ground

If insinuations are a form of speaker's meaning, in which a speaker makes their communicative intentions manifest to their hearer, it might seem to follow directly that insinuated attitudes must become part of the common ground, in Stalnaker's sense of "common background knowledge shared by the participants in a conversation" (2014, 36). After all, if H recognizes S's intention to communicate $M(Q)$, how can it not become mutual knowledge that S meant this? Of course H always has the option of rejecting $M(Q)$ itself, but surely at a minimum, if it is manifest to both parties that S meant $M(Q)$, then this fact becomes part of what is mutually assumed in C. And on many natural continuations of (1) through (7), H does actually acquiesce in $M(Q)$ or an appropriate correlative of it: H decides that it's not worth buying a house in an unwelcoming neighborhood, or to go kill Thomas Becket. Communication then succeeds in the strong sense that the speaker's illocutionary and perlocutionary aims are not just recognized but achieved. How could the common ground not be altered accordingly?

The notion of common ground is closely connected to mutual belief or knowledge, and some theorists do sometimes use them interchangeably. But Stalnaker is consistently careful to distinguish them (e.g., 1978, 321; 2002, 704; 2014, 45). Mutual belief is defined in terms of the transitive closure of accessibility relations among the belief states of the relevant individuals, where individual beliefs are themselves defined in terms of epistemically accessible possibilities (2014, 44). Common ground is defined in a way that is structurally parallel, but based on mutual *acceptance*, for which actual belief is neither necessary nor sufficient.

Stalnaker's primary motivation for grounding common ground in acceptance rather than belief is to allow assumptions that are not believed but merely conjectured, or pretended, or otherwise adopted for the purposes of conversation, into the common ground. I think insinuation demonstrates the need to distinguish them in the opposite direction as well.[15] That is, I argued in §2.2 that deniability trades on the gap between what is actually manifest to both parties and what one or the other party is willing to acknowledge as manifest; but this is precisely the difference between mutual belief and acceptance.

Not all insinuating speakers aim to exclude communicated contents from the common ground. Often, S is willing for $M(Q)$ to become an established assumption; their motivation for insinuating is just to avoid assuming liability for defending or executing it themselves. Many cases of insinuated bigotry work like this: thus, in (2), S would be delighted for H to follow up by enumerating some of the many

---

[15] Stalnaker (2014, 46) agrees.

sinister features purportedly possessed by people named 'Hussein', and by Barack Obama in particular. Such insinuations function as probes of perspectival alignment; as interpretive harmony becomes more firmly established, S may feel increasingly free to overtly assert claims that would be controversial or repugnant in other contexts. But again, similar dynamics can also obtain even among intimates: thus, the resentful stay-at-home partner who utters (5) might be relieved if his utterance prompted H to own up to his after-party gallivanting, followed either by an apology or a final blow-out argument.

In these cases, if H does explicitly articulate $M(Q)$ in response to U, S will then grant its truth or desirability—perhaps prefaced by a cautionary 'You said it, not me.' In other cases, neither interlocutor may want to assume liability for $M(Q)$ themselves, but at least one party still wants the conversation to include an indefeasible commitment to $M(Q)$. If so, each participant may frame their contribution in a way that comes increasingly close to entailing $M(Q)$, hoping that the other party will tip over into explicit avowal. Thus, the speeding driver and the patrol officer may employ increasingly obvious winks, nudges, and euphemisms to inch toward open acknowledgment that they are exchanging a bribe, even as each also tries to lob the hot potato of conversational responsibility back at the other.

Both of these classes of cases involve jockeying over how $M(Q)$ enters the common ground, rather than whether it enters at all. For especially volatile contents, however, S may be unwilling even to allow H to avow $M(Q)$, or to make a conversational move that entails it. In such cases, it may still become mutually believed between S and H not just that S meant $M(Q)$, but that Q itself is true or desirable. But even so, S may insist on keeping Q in 'deep shadow'—while simultaneously seeking confirmation from the way H crafts their response that they have indeed picked up on, and tacitly accepted, $M(Q)$. The insinuated command to kill Thomas Becket in (7) seems likely to have taken this form. But again, conversations between intimates can follow this pattern as well. Thus, the party-attending addressee of (5) might respond to the insinuation of having been out gallivanting with:

(5.1)   Oh, I just got a quick drink with John after the party to discuss a killer presentation we have next week.

H might thereby implicitly admit to socializing with John while overtly retaining the excuse of engaging in professional business. As the relationship deteriorates, and such putative business meetings become more frequent, it may become increasingly manifest that H is having an affair, although neither H nor S are willing to openly admit as much, because such direct face-to-face acknowledgment would be too painful. (Even their final separation might be couched in terms of H's needing a *pied-a-terre* to "minimize the commute.") In effect, in such cases a shadow conversation emerges, with overt claims serving as proxies for a series of commitments that one or both parties are unwilling to bring into the conversational light.

The phenomenon of refusing to overtly acknowledge assumptions about facts that are actually manifest to all parties isn't limited to insinuation. Many conversations, even healthy ones, occur against the background of various sorts of 'unmentionables', including differences in social status, and bodily and other handicaps, challenges, and realities. What's distinctive about 'deep' insinuation is that it doesn't merely navigate around or depend upon manifest facts that one or both parties would prefer to avoid mentioning, or even would strenuously deny if made explicit. Rather, 'deep' insinuation is designed to *make* a fact, desire, or commitment manifest, and actively guides communication and action going forward, while still remaining unacknowledgable.

2.3.3 Conversational Record

The final notion I want to use insinuation to clarify is that of the conversational record or score, based on Lewis's (1979) metaphor of conversation as a language game. Lewis analogizes conversation, not to the looser-form games invoked by Wittgenstein (1953), but to the highly structured, conventionalized game of baseball, in which certain moves are permissible at certain points and the effect of a move depends on the score to that point. Because, as we saw in §2.3.2, the common ground is defined in terms of acceptance rather than mutual belief, it might seem that we could simply identify the common ground with the conversational score or record. The intuitive characterization of insinuation as 'off-record' speech would then be a reflection of the central point of §2.3.2, that insinuation can successfully communicate contents while keeping them out of the common ground. Both Lee and Pinker (2010) and Asher and Lascarides (2013) in effect treat the phenomenon of deniability through indirect speech as demonstrating just this.

A simple equation between common ground and conversational record cannot be right. The common ground encompasses an indefinitely large class of substantive empirical and evaluative assumptions that are so deeply engrained and/or so obvious that they don't require or perhaps even permit articulation. By contrast, the record or score is highly structured. Most obviously, it specifies the claims, questions, promises and instructions issued by each interlocutor. But these are not merely listed in temporal sequence: they are embedded within a more complex discourse structure, which guides and constrains interpretation. This discourse structure includes, most notably, the Question Under Discussion, often along with a stack of sub-questions (Roberts 1996/2012). There are also various discourse referents and accessible possibilities (Heim 1990), ranked in salience, which play a crucial role in phenomena like resolution of ellipsis and anaphora, presupposition projection, and prosodic focus (Roberts 2015). Further, utterances of sentences and sub-clauses are linked to one another and to the QUD by rhetorical relations like explanation, elaboration, and contrast (Hobbs 1985, Kehler 2002, Asher and Lascarides 2003).

These differences in structure and content don't yet force a fundamental distinction between conversational record or score and common ground, though. Depending on one's theoretical proclivities, one might subsume the common ground as an element within the record or score (e.g. Roberts 2015), or else subsume the score as a subset of discourse-related assumptions within the common ground (Stalnaker 2014). However, a deeper difference lurks.

Lewis (1979) worried about whether to define conversational 'kinematics' and score in objective or subjective terms. On the one hand, the score needs to provide a norm governing the evolution of conversations, specifying what moves can be made and their constitutive effects at any given point. On the other hand, it also needs to track and describe conversations as they actually evolve; and if all parties take a certain move to have been made, or to have been permissible, then at a certain point it seems that the move *has* been made or was permissible. To reconcile this tension, Lewis proposes a "middle way" on which the conversational score is causally guided and normatively governed by the rules that specify the scoreboard's functional role, but where the actual conversational score is, "by definition, whatever the mental scoreboards say it is" (1979).

Whatever the merits of this compromise in resolving the tension that worried Lewis, I think insinuation pushes us toward a more objective, normatively constrained view of the record or score than Lewis wants because it shows us that there is a substantive difference between the commitments the interlocutors have actually made themselves liable for defending, on the one hand, and either the sets of attitudes they attribute to themselves and the other, or the pool of assumptions they mutually take to be conversationally available, on the other.[16]

Better, I think it pushes us to distinguish the record from the score in a way that most theorists don't explicitly do. Many aspects of the score as usually understood, including the relative salience of potential discourse referents and relative accessibility of possibilities, are transient states that evolve continuously through a conversation. And often enough, a given conversational move matters only because and to the extent that it affects the conversation going forward. For these purposes, it makes sense to treat these dimensions of the conversation in terms of their dynamic effects, and specifically as updates to the common ground.

But the current context, with its particular common ground, is not the only factor to be explained. Stalnaker (2014, 162) resists thoroughly dynamic analyses of phenomena like modals and conditionals on the ground that they express contents which are "detachable" from their current contexts. He is primarily thinking of cases where a hearer acquires a belief from an utterance and then deploys it in some other context. As we saw in §2.3.1, most insinuations are detachable or cross-contextually stable in this sense: that is, S successfully communicates $M(Q)$, in the fullest sense of producing in H a belief, desire, or intention that appropriately correlates to $M(Q)$, and which H can use in their own reasoning elsewhere. But insinuation aims to achieve this sort of coordination while avoiding the distinctive species of cross-contextual stability that is generated by on-record speech, in the form of indirect reports. And such reports matter, most obviously because they play a central role in the testimonial acquisition of knowledge (Fricker 2012, Lackey 2008).

Our theory of meaning thus needs a way to track and explain commitments that interlocutors undertake in conversations which they are liable for defending or executing in other contexts. Interpreting the conversational record as the record of public speech acts, along the pragmatist lines articulated by Peirce (1934), Brandom (1983), and MacFarlane (2011), is a promising way to do this. Of course, in actual fact hearers and reporters often lack the evidentiary basis that would enable them to hold speakers responsible for their on-record conversational commitments, just as they lack the evidentiary basis to hold them responsible for off-record insinuations. But this doesn't undermine the fact that certain aspects of utterances do function to undertake such indefeasible commitments, in such a way *if* a transcription or video footage were available, then they *would* undeniably be liable for them, in a way they are not for insinuated attitudes.

One might think that such a restricted notion of the conversational record will be theoretically otiose because it will end up being purely disquotational—in the case

---

[16] Cf. Langton (this volume) for discussion of distinct but related reasons to distinguish common ground from conversational score.

of assertion, amounting to the claim that S commits themselves to the attitude $F(P)$ determined by the conventional compositional meaning of the uttered sentence L. This is emphatically not the case, for multiple reasons. First, a speaker who utters L may commit, with the force of assertion, question, or directive, to some content $F(R)$ *other* than, and not merely in addition, to $F(P)$, most obviously by speaking figuratively (Camp 2008, 2012, 2017a) or by other forms of meaning modulation. Second, a speaker may undertake an on-record commitment to $F(R)$ without any direct articulation, literal or figurative, of $F(R)$, for instance in response to an explicit question or as a result of enrichment. Third, a speaker who asserts or otherwise illocutes $F(P)$ also thereby commits herself to a host of other contents. These include (at least some) logical, nomological, and material consequences of $F(P)$ (Stalnaker 1978, Soames 2008). But they also include presuppositions and implicatures that are generated, not by $F(P)$ in isolation, but by the fact that S has committed to $F(P)$ at this point in this context C—and specifically by the location of the uttered sentence L, and its sub-sentential elements, within the overall discourse structure (Asher and Lascarides 2013). Thus, while direct, explicit articulation is the simplest, most reliable and forceful way to place contents on the record, it is far from the only one. What matters for on-record status is not the mechanism by which an attitude is contributed, but its status as a commitment the speaker is liable for defending or executing.

If we understand the conversational *record* in this cross-contextually stable way, then we might want to reserve the notion of conversational *score* for those evolving assumptions which govern the permissibility, relevance, and interpretation of sentences within the dynamic discourse structure: for features like the partitioning and relative accessibility of possibilities, and the existence and relative salience of discourse referents. I won't press this distinction further here. More importantly for current purposes, as noted in §2.2.2, many of these context-local features of the score have the same sort of unarticulated, nuanced, but in-fact-coordinated character as the interpretive assumptions that drive the interpretation of implicature in general and insinuation in particular. Aspects of on-record speech that depend upon these features, such as domain restriction and anaphora resolution, also engage the "dodgy epistemics" of pragmatic interpretation. This means that even contextually-determined semantic contents can exhibit some degree of deniability, as when Athanasius purportedly answered the question "Where is Athanasius?" with:

(8)   The man you seek is not far from here.

or Bill Clinton said:

(9)   There is no sexual relationship.

when asked whether he had had an affair with Monica Lewinsky (Saul 2000, 2013).

The pervasive role of epistemically dodgy interpretation in communication renders the distinction between explicit on-record commitments and implicit off-record communication less sharp than Lee and Pinker (2010) and Fricker (2012), among others, assume, insofar as not all apparently on-record content is 'safe' for contextual exportation. At the same time, there are still important differences in the way those dodgy epistemics play out in negotiations over meaning. Although a full discussion is beyond our current scope, deniability appears to be significantly more restricted, and pedantry to be nearly eliminated, in on-record speech like (8) and (9) as compared to implicature.

So far in this section, I have focused on distinguishing the conversational record from the common ground in terms of contextual relativity and stability. We saw in §2.3.2 that insinuation can at least sometimes achieve coordination between interlocutors without entering the insinuated attitude into the common ground. And of course, insinuation is designed to be off-record. Thus, we might think that despite the differences just surveyed in cross-contextual stability, the common ground and conversational record are still on a par in having a public status that successful Gricean communication lacks. And if that is right, then perhaps insinuation as a private, off-record form of communication, *always* falls outside the common ground, as Lee and Pinker (2010) and Asher and Lascarides (2013) maintain. Or more radically, perhaps the notion of common ground falls away as otiose, its explanatory work divvied up between a public conversational record and a private Gricean exchange of attitudes.

All three of these conclusions are unwarranted. First, while the common ground is indeed an essentially social phenomenon, it is not a public one. Publicity just is a matter of being available to a range of audiences, across a range of contexts, and this is precisely the feature that the conversational common ground lacks. As we just saw, publicity matters, most obviously in the form of testimonial reports. But the common ground matters too. Its dual functions—as a set of background assumptions which interlocutors draw on in framing and interpreting utterances, and as a set of possibilities among which they navigate as the conversation evolves (Stalnaker 2014, 36)—are theoretically powerful, especially in explaining the intimate interplay between semantics and pragmatics. But beyond this, one lesson not just of insinuation but also of exploratory conjecture and polite chat, is that conversation often involves performing a role or inhabiting a persona that does not fully reflect one's private attitudes. The contributions and commitments of such conversational personae are restricted to the current context in a way that neither public on-record commitments nor private Gricean coordination are. We need a mechanism for tracking and explaining this level of communication, in just the way the common ground does.

Finally, and most importantly for current purposes, insinuations do often function to alter the common ground. As I noted in §2.3.2, speakers are often happy for $M(Q)$ to enter the common ground; they simply want to avoid the risk and liability of introducing it themselves. Cases of 'deeply shadowed' insinuation are an extreme, if theoretically and practically important, subclass of the more general phenomenon. We can hold on to the claim that insinuated content always falls outside the common ground only if we exclude all attitudes that are not explicitly articulated or mandated in connection with on-record contents. But this would dramatically distort the actual function and usual theoretical understanding of the common ground. It would also impose a sharper dichotomy between insinuation and other forms of implicature than is warranted—especially given that insinuating speakers have not always determined in advance just how staunchly they will resist acknowledging $M(Q)$ as the conversation evolves. Instead, we should accept that the boundaries between both on-record and off-record content, and between common ground and mutually obvious but unacknowledged assumptions, are blurry. Deniability straddles both boundaries. But those boundaries do matter, both for explaining how insinuation and deniability play out in actual conversations, and for making sense of communication more generally.

2.4 Conclusion

I have argued that understanding the ways in which ordinary speakers and hearers employ insinuation to navigate the strategic communication of risky contents pushes us to refine theoretical notions that it is easy to run together in more fully cooperative contexts. In particular, I argued in §2.2 that insinuation's twin characteristics of deniability and pedantry exploit a gap between interpretive assumptions that are mutually obvious and those that are mutually acknowledged as such. The "dodgy epistemics" of pragmatic interpretation guarantee that there will typically be at least some such gap; but this gap is limited, insofar as a 'plausible' denial of having meant $M(Q)$ must be supportable by a reasonable interpretation based on accessible interpretive assumptions. In §2.3 I used this gap to argue that each of Gricean speaker's meaning, Stalnakerian common ground, and Lewisian scoreboard—or better, conversational record and score—carve out distinct categories of meaning and serve distinct explanatory functions.

Thus, in lieu of the simple set of relations in Figure 2.1, we now have the multi-layered convolution of Figure 2.2. We retain the basic contrast between overlapping beliefs and mutual beliefs. (In the interest of simplicity, I suppress attitudes other than belief here.) But mutual beliefs and common ground are now also distinct though overlapping. In a well-formed conversation, all elements of the conversational record are in the common ground; but contents can enter the common ground without going on the record. What a speaker actually says—their semantically encoded content—may differ both from what they assert and from what they otherwise mean. And they

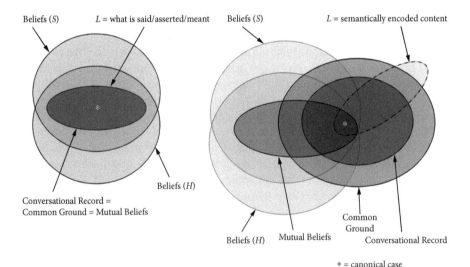

Figure 2.2 Multi-layered sets of attitudes and meanings.

may mean, and successfully communicate, contents without entering them into either the record or the common ground.

This picture is complex. But as we've seen, the distinctions it encodes are accessible to and exploited by ordinary speakers in everyday conversations. In one-off exchanges with strangers, in tussles and tender moments between intimates and colleagues, and in depositions and political speeches, speakers regularly frame their own utterances and respond to others in ways that display a nuanced sensitivity to these distinct varieties of meaning and the different norms they entail. I have focused on insinuation here, because it throws those differences in to especially sharp relief. But we see them at work in other ways as well, including in more fully cooperative contexts.

Both speaker's meaning and contributions to the common ground are fundamentally medium-neutral, non-conventional modes of communication: ways of coordinating on common attitudes by exploiting and creating manifest facts in the environment (Stalnaker 2014). One key difference is that speaker's meaning can be private, in the sense of coordinating between two individual persons, while the common ground is constructed by personae, who may not directly reflect their enactors' actual attitudes. (Of course, speaker's meaning is also operative in contexts where the utterer's actual intentions are inaccessible or irrelevant. The most obvious example is literature, where the narrator or author is best understood as a character postulated in the course of interpretation (Nehamas 1987, Camp 2015).) While the private coordination of attitudes and the performative coordination of assumptions often coincide, they can also come apart—again, not just in insinuation, but also in exploratory conjecture and polite chat.

By contrast, the conversational record is essentially public, and essentially linguistic. It is public insofar as it involves a cross-contextual liability for the commitments it records. And it is linguistic insofar as the kind of commitment one undertakes by an utterance depends in part on the language game in which it is generated. Utterance-types, such as assertion, presupposition, and conventional implicature, can have the same "essential effect" on the common ground but differ in their specific on-record status, in ways that are indicated by specific sub-sentential structures. And some utterance-types, such as promises and conditional commands, arguably cannot be undertaken without some conventional way of marking their status (Camp 2017b).

The conversational record is also the species of meaning most closely connected to conventional semantic meaning. Conventional semantic meaning, in virtue of its public status, provides a stable common explanatory and justificatory factor which reporters can cite and interpreters can employ across contexts (Camp 2016). As we've seen, deniability and pedantry often trade on the difference between narrow semantic meaning and various species of looser, enriched pragmatic meaning. However, we've also seen that there is no easy equation between semantic contents and on-record commitments: commitments can enter the record without being semantically articulated, and semantic articulation need not generate an on-record commitment. In typical conversations between interlocutors who share a language, all three varieties of meaning—speaker's meaning, common ground, and conversational record— exploit both linguistic conventions and reflexive intention-recognition in order to coordinate on attitudes toward contents. Where the varieties of meaning differ is not the mechanisms by which they are generated, or the types of attitudes they communicate, but in the status of the commitments they entail: in when and how they are liable to be defended.

References

Asher, Nicholas and Alex Lascarides (2003): *Logics of Conversation* (Cambridge: Cambridge University Press).

Asher, Nicholas and Alex Lascarides (2013): "Strategic Conversation," *Semantics & Pragmatics* 6: 1–62.

Bach, Kent and Robert Harnish (1979): *Linguistic Communication and Speech Acts* (Cambridge, MA: MIT Press).

Blume, Andreas and Oliver Board (2013): "Intentional Vagueness," *Erkenntnis* 79 (S4):1–45.

Brandom, Robert (1983): "Asserting," *Noûs* 17, 637–50.

Brown, Penelope and Stephen Levinson (1987): *Politeness* (Cambridge: Cambridge University Press).

Buchanan, Ray (2010): "A Puzzle about Meaning and Communication," *Noûs* 44(2): 340–71.

Camp, Elisabeth (2006a): "Metaphor and That Certain 'Je Ne Sais Quoi'," *Philosophical Studies* 129(1) (May 2006): 1–25.

Camp, Elisabeth (2006b): "Contextualism, Metaphor, and What is Said," *Mind and Language* 21(3): 280–309.

Camp, Elisabeth (2007): "Prudent Semantics Meets Wanton Speech Act Pluralism," in *Context-Sensitivity and Semantic Minimalism: New Essays on Semantics and Pragmatics*, eds. G. Preyer and G. Peter (Oxford: Oxford University Press), 194–213.

Camp, Elisabeth (2008): "Showing, Telling, and Seeing: Metaphor and 'Poetic' Language," in *The Baltic International Yearbook of Cognition, Logic, and Communication*, vol. 3: *A Figure of Speech: Metaphor*, (Lawrence, KS: New Prairie Press), 1–24.

Camp, Elisabeth (2012): "Sarcasm, Pretense, and the Semantics/Pragmatics Distinction," *Noûs* 46(4): 587–634.

Camp, Elisabeth (2015): "Metaphors in Literature," in *The Routledge Companion to Philosophy of Literature*, ed. Noël Carroll and John Gibson (London: Routledge Press), 334–46.

Camp, Elisabeth (2016): "Conventions' Revenge: Davidson, Derangement, and Dormativity," *Inquiry* 59(1): 113–38.

Camp, Elisabeth (2017a): "Why Metaphors Make Good Insults: Perspectives, Presupposition, and Pragmatics," *Philosophical Studies* 174: 1, 47–64.

Camp, Elisabeth (2017b): "Pragmatic Force in Semantic Context," *Philosophical Studies* 174: 6, 1617–1627.

Camp, Elisabeth (2017c): "Expressivism," in *Routledge Handbook of Metaethics*, eds. D. Plunkett and T. McPherson (Oxford: Routledge), 87–101.

Clark, Herb and Susan Brennan (1991): "Grounding in Communication," in *Perspectives on Socially Shared Cognition*, eds. L. B. Resnick, J. M. Levine, and S. D. Teasley (Washington: APA Books), 127–49.

Davidson, Donald (1986): "A Nice Derangement of Epitaphs," in *Truth and Interpretation: Perspectives on the Philosophy of Donald Davidson*, ed. Ernie Lepore (New York: Blackwell), 433–46.

Dennett, Daniel (1981): "True Believers: The Intentional Strategy and Why It Works," in *Scientific Explanation: Papers Based on Herbert Spencer Lectures Given in the University of Oxford*, ed. A. F. Heath (Oxford: Clarendon Press), 150–67.

Fricker, Elizabeth (2012): "Stating and Insinuating," *Proceedings of the Aristotelian Society* S86(1): 61–94.

Godfrey-Smith, Peter and Manolo Martínez (2013): "Communication and Common Interest," *PLOS Computational Biology* 9(11): 1–6.

Goffman, Erving (1967): "On Face Work," in *Interaction Ritual: Essays in Face-to-Face Behavior* (Chicago: Aldine), 5–45.

Grice, H. P. (1957): "Meaning," *Philosophical Review* 66(3): 377–88.

Grice, H. P. (1969): "Utterer's Meaning and Intention," *Philosophical Review* 78(2): 147–77.

Grice, H. P. (1975): "Logic and Conversation," in *Syntax and Semantics 3: Speech Acts*, eds. Peter Cole and Jerry L. Morgan (New York: Academic Press), 187–210.

Harris, Daniel (2016): "Intentionalism versus The New Conventionalism," *Croatian Journal of Philosophy* 16(2): 173–201.

Hawthorne, John (2012): "Some Comments on Fricker's 'Stating and Insinuating,'" *Proceedings of the Aristotelian Society* S86(1): 95–108.

Heim, Irene (1990): "E-type Pronouns and Donkey Anaphora," *Linguistics and Philosophy* 13: 137–78.

Hobbs, Jerry (1985): *On the Coherence and Structure of Discourse* (Palo Alto, CA: CSLI Publications).

Jäger, Gerhard (2013): "Rationalizable Signalling," *Erkenntnis* 79: 1–34.

Kehler, Andrew (2002): *Coherence, Reference, and the Theory of Grammar* (Palo Alto, CA: CSLI Publications).

King, Jeffrey (2014): "Speaker Intentions in Context," *Noûs* 48(2): 219–37.

Lackey, Jennifer (2008): *Learning from Words: Testimony as a Source of Knowledge* (Oxford: Oxford University Press).

Lee, James and Steven Pinker (2010): "Rationales for Indirect Speech: The theory of the strategic speaker," *Psychological Review* 117: 785–807.

Lepore, Ernie and Matthew Stone (2010): "Against Metaphorical Meaning," *Topoi* 29(2):165–80.

Lepore, Ernie and Matthew Stone (2015): *Imagination and Convention: Distinguishing Grammar and Inference in Language* (Oxford: Oxford University Press).

Levinson, Stephen (2000): *Presumptive Meanings: The Theory of Generalized Conversational Implicature* (Cambridge, MA: MIT Press).

Lewis, David (1969): *Convention: A Philosophical Study* (Cambridge, MA: Harvard University Press).

Lewis, David (1979): "Scorekeeping in a Language Game," *Journal of Philosophical Logic* 8: 339–59.

Locke, John (1689): *An Essay Concerning Human Understanding* (London: Thomas Bassett).

MacFarlane, John (2011): "What is Assertion?," in *Assertion*, eds. Jessica Brown and Herman Cappelen (Oxford: Oxford University Press), 79–96.

Muse, Ivan (1996): *Oral and Nonverbal Expression* (Larchmont, NY: Eye on Education).

Neale, Stephen (2005): "Pragmatism and Binding," in *Semantics versus Pragmatics*, ed. Zoltan Szabó (Oxford: Oxford University Press), 165–285.

Nehamas, Alexander (1987): "Writer, Text, Work, Author," in *Literature and the Question of Philosophy* ed. A. Cascardi (Baltimore: Johns Hopkins University Press), 265–91.

Peirce, Charles S. (1934): *Belief and Judgment* (Cambridge, MA: Harvard University Press).

Pinker, Steven, Martin Nowak, and James Lee (2008): "The Logic of Indirect Speech," *Proceedings of the National Academy of Sciences* 105(3): 833–38.

Pugmire, David (1998): *Rediscovering Emotion: Emotion and the Claims of Feeling* (Edinburgh: Edinburgh University Press).

Roberts, Craige (1996/2012): "Information Structure in Discourse: Toward an Integrated Formal Theory of Pragmatics. *Semantics and Pragmatics* 5, 1–69.

Roberts, Craige (2004): "Discourse Context in Dynamic Interpretation," in *Handbook of Contemporary Pragmatic Theory*, eds. Laurence Horn and Gregory Ward, (Oxford: Blackwell), 197–220.

Roberts, Craige (2015): "Accommodation in a Language Game," in *A Companion to David Lewis*, eds. Barry Loewer and Jonathan Schaffer (Oxford, UK: John Wiley & Sons, Ltd.), 345–66.

Saul, Jennifer (2000): "Did Clinton Say Something False?" *Analysis* 60(267): 219–95.

Saul, Jennifer (2013): *Lying, Misleading, and The Role of What is Said* (Oxford: Oxford University Press).

Schiffer, Stephen (1972): *Meaning* (Oxford: Oxford University Press).

Searle, J. (1979): "Metaphor," in *Expression and Meaning: Studies in the Theory of Speech Acts*, Cambridge: Cambridge University Press, 76–116.

Skyrms, Brian (2010): *Signals: Evolution, Learning, and Information* (Oxford: Oxford University Press).

Soames, Scott (2008): "The Gap Between Meaning and Assertion: Why What We Literally Say Often Differs from What Our Words Literally Mean," *Philosophical Papers* Vol. 1: *Natural Language: What It Means and How We Use It* (Princeton: Princeton University Press), 278–97.

Solan, Lawrence and Peter Tiersma (2005): *Speaking of Crime: The Language of Criminal Justice* (Chicago, IL: University of Chicago Press).

Sperber, Dan and Deidre Wilson (1995): *Relevance: Communication and Cognition, 2nd edn.* (Oxford: Blackwell).

Stalnaker, Robert (1978): "Assertion," in *Syntax and Semantics 9: Pragmatics*, ed. P. Cole (New York: Academic Press), 315–22.

Stalnaker, Robert (2002): "Common Ground," *Linguistics and Philosophy* 25: 701–21.

Stalnaker, Robert (2014): *Context* (Oxford: Oxford University Press).

Stanley, Jason (2015): *How Propaganda Works* (Princeton NJ: Princeton University Press).

Strawson, Peter F. (1964): "Intention and Convention in Speech Acts," *Philosophical Review* 73: 439–60.

Terkourafi, Marina (2011): "The Puzzle of Indirect Speech," *Journal of Pragmatics* 43: 2861–5.

Wittgenstein, Ludwig (1953): *Philosophical Investigations*, trans. G. E. M. Anscombe (Oxford: Blackwell).

3

Clause-Type, Force, and Normative Judgment in the Semantics of Imperatives

Nate Charlow

3.1 Introduction

Semantic theorizing about *clause-types* proceeds by identifying a *canonical discourse role* displayed by sentences of clause-type T, then assigning sentences of type T semantic values that—perhaps together with independent pragmatic principles linking semantic values to discourse functions—allow them to play their canonical discourse role.[†] Declaratives are assigned propositions as their semantic values to account, inter alia, for the canonical link between declaratives and the speech act of assertion. Interrogatives are assigned partitions as their semantic values to account, inter alia, for the canonical link between interrogatives and the speech act of questioning. In such theorizing, the *canonical cognitive role* displayed by sentences of type T—e.g., the mental state canonically involved in accepting a sentence of type T—does not figure centrally in accounting for their meaning, though it may be derived as a kind of "downstream" (e.g., perlocutionary) effect of the canonical discourse role that is identified for T-sentences.

This is a successful and widely accepted methodology for semantic theorizing about clause-types, which recent work on imperatives takes largely for granted. Portner's theory of imperatives is a well-known example (Portner 2004, 2007, 2012, this volume). The major competitor account to Portner's—the modal theory of imperatives championed most persuasively by Kaufmann, on which imperatives are assigned modal *propositions* as their semantic values (Schwager 2007; Kaufmann & Schwager 2011; Kaufmann 2012)—is another.

[†] For discussion and feedback I am grateful to Nick Asher, Chris Barker, Simon Charlow, Kit Fine, Daniel Fogal, Arno Goebel, Daniel Harris, Benj Hellie, Magda Kaufmann, Phil Kremer, Sven Lauer, Barbara Partee, Paul Portner, Jim Pryor, Mandy Simons, Eric Swanson, Rich Thomason, and Will Starr. The material in this paper has benefited from feedback from audiences at Carnegie Mellon, Cornell, Göttingen, Konstanz, New York University (several times), and Sinn und Bedeutung 17. The support of the Social Sciences and Humanities Research Council of Canada (Insight Grant #435-2015-0423) is gratefully acknowledged.

This paper will describe an alternative methodology for theorizing about the semantics of imperatives—and clause-types more generally—on which their canonical cognitive role is treated as semantically fundamental—and encoded in the semantic value of an imperative—and their canonical discourse role is derived as a kind of "downstream" effect of their canonical cognitive role. It is worth mentioning upfront why this sort of methodology might be reasonably regarded as a non-starter in the case of imperatives. Strikingly, unlike declaratives and interrogatives, imperatives *strongly* resist embedding as the complements of attitude verbs.[1]

(1)   a.   Bernie knows that Hillary shut the door
       b.   Bernie knows whether Hillary shut the door
       c.   *Bernie knows [*that] shut the door, Hillary

Since there are precious few, if any, grammatical attitude constructions embedding imperatives as their complements, it would seem difficult to approach the semantics of imperatives by asking after the semantics of such constructions.[2] Indeed, the difficulty of locating a canonical way of ascribing a psychological relation between an agent and an imperative sentence might be taken to suggest that imperatives lack anything like a canonical cognitive role at all.

I nevertheless will argue that this alternative methodology is worth pursuing in the case of imperatives (though not, of course, via the semantics of uninterpretable constructions like (1c)). The argument in this paper will be somewhat indirect, but the general idea is as follows. Accounts of imperative meaning like Portner's seem to suffer from explanatory deficits vis-à-vis imperatives embedded in conditionals and under quantifiers. A modal account like Kaufmann's offers an appealing alternative, but has its own explanatory deficits (owing mainly to its assignment of a proposition as the semantic content of an imperative). These latter deficits are most clear when one considers the canonical cognitive role for an imperative—a role that, while somewhat difficult to access via attitude ascription, is easier to access via philosophical psychology and cognitive science—to which a propositional account of the imperative seems to be committed.

This paper will motivate an alternative paradigm for theorizing about the semantics and pragmatics of imperatives. On the analysis advanced here, imperatives express contents that are both cognitively and semantically related to, but nevertheless distinct from, modal propositions (compare the position defended in Charlow (2014a)). Imperatives, on this analysis, semantically encode *features of planning that are modally specified*. Uttering an imperative amounts to tokening this feature in discourse, and thereby proffering it for adoption by the audience. This analysis deals

---

[1] In many languages (English included), imperatives appear to embed under speech act verbs (e.g. 'say') (see, e.g., Crnic & Trinh 2008; Kaufmann and Poschmann 2013). This does not vitiate the observation in the main text.

[2] The classic discussion of the relation between the semantics of interrogatives and the semantics of attitude ascriptions embedding interrogatives is Karttunen (1977). Cremers & Chemla (2016) offer an updated assessment, proposing a revision to the standard semantics of interrogatives motivated by considerations involving the semantics of attitude ascriptions embedding interrogatives.

smoothly with the problems afflicting the accounts of Portner and Kaufmann. It also suggests an (in my view) appealing reorientation of clause-type theorizing, in which the cognitive act of updating on a typed sentence plays a central role in theorizing about both its semantics and role in discourse.

3.2 Clause-Type Analysis: A Very Short Overview

Three major clause-types appear to be attested across natural languages: declarative, interrogative, and imperative.[3]

(2) a. Hillary shut the door. [*Type*: DEC]
     b. Did Hillary shut the door? [*Type*: INT]
     c. Shut the door, Hillary! [*Type*: IMP]

Clause-types tend to be seen as broadly conventional encodings of the clause's "force" (in a sense to be precisified). Conversely, the major types of "force" are presumed to have dedicated linguistic devices for their expression—a fact that suggests at least a partial explanation of the universality of the three major clause-types (see esp. Sadock & Zwicky 1985; Portner 2004).

3.2.1 Force

In what sense is "force" encoded in a sentence's clause-type? The most natural reading of "force" would be Austin's (1975) notion of *illocutionary* force.[4] Portner (2004), however, rejects the idea that illocutionary force could be encoded at the level of clause-type, citing examples of sentences that exhibit an apparent mismatch of clause-type and illocutionary force, like:

(3) Can you pass the salt?
     [*Type*: INT; *Illocutionary Force*: REQUEST]

But this would be premature. The literature is replete with analyses on which a speaker uttering a sentence like (3) performs a request *by asking a question* (Searle 1975; Asher & Lascarides 2001; Charlow 2011: Ch. 3). On such analyses, the (primary) illocutionary act of asking a question may well be encoded in the clause-type of (3), while the (secondary, or, more commonly, *indirect*) illocutionary act of making a

---

[3] An overview of clause-typing and its role in semantic and pragmatic theorizing is provided by Portner (2004), which in turns draws on Sadock & Zwicky (1985); Ginzburg & Sag (2001), among others. Universally attested clause-types are here labeled as "major". Non-universally attested clause-types (like the Korean promissive) are generally assumed to derive their core semantic features from universally attested clause-types (like the imperative); from a semantic perspective, then, the Korean promissive, may be (and typically is) regarded as a sub-type of the imperative (see, e.g., Portner 2004: §4).

[4] This paper mostly elides the distinction between *illocutionary force*—a notion tied to speaker meaning in context—and what has been termed *dynamic force*—a notion tied to the informational change induced by updating a context or cognitive state on a sentence (Yalcin forthcoming). It is more accurate to say that clause-type analyses associate sentences—in virtue of associating them with canonical discourse roles—with a canonical dynamic (or para-illocutionary; see note 5) force, rather than illocutionary force proper. The account I go on to develop will be in this spirit.

request may be derived from the primary illocutionary act, together with some form of conversational (e.g. Gricean) reasoning.[5]

This is important to appreciate, since many influential objections to specific clause-type analyses of the imperative begin with the observation that imperatives are well-suited for a wide range of illocutionary ends, beyond what we might call *directive* ends. Here are some standard examples (some borrowed from Wilson & Sperber 1988).

(4) Come earlier (if you like) [PERMISSION]
(5) Have an apple! [INVITATION]
(6) Take the A-Train (to get to Harlem) [INSTRUCTION]
(7) Get well soon! [WELL-WISH]
(8) Throw it, I dare you! [DARE/THREAT]

Following Condoravdi & Lauer (2012), we can provisionally understand an utterance of an imperative with a directive end as one that "(I) expresses a certain content related to the addressee's future actions; (II) conveys that the speaker wants the content to become reality; and (III) acts as an inducement for the addressee to bring about the content" (38).[6] It is clear that none of the above examples are naturally counted as directive uses of the imperative, in this sense.

It is sometimes alleged that, in light of such examples, any analysis of the imperative which conventionalizes its directive "force" cannot be correct.[7] But this objection loses a great deal of its appeal, once a satisfying treatment of, e.g., (3) under the rubric of *indirect speech acts* is in view. Like (3), any of these sentences might naturally receive the indicated illocutionary interpretation, despite a conventional association with an altogether distinct illocutionary force.

3.2.2 Individuating Types

It is similarly important to emphasize the various shapes an account of the clause-type/force link might take. One (unappealing) option is that clause-type is an abstraction from force, clause-type being simply a way of categorizing sentences according to an independently attested canonical discourse role or force. But this risks conflating two sentences of manifestly different clause-types that share a discourse role, like (2b) and its performative analogue (9):

(9) I hereby query whether Hillary shut the door

[5] Asher & Lascarides (2001) include the question expressed by (3) as part of what is meant, by the speaker, with an utterance of (3): the speaker literally performs *both* the illocutionary act of questioning and the illocutionary act of questioning with such an utterance (compare also Lepore & Stone forthcoming). This idea has some limitations; I prefer, instead, to think of the question interpretation of (3) as being defeated, in a typical context, at some stage of conversational reasoning, with the request interpretation being supplied in its stead by abduction (Charlow 2011: Ch. 3). Whether the question survives as a bona fide *illocutionary act*, on my own analysis—or as a kind of para-illocutionary act—is a question of terminology.

[6] I say "provisionally" because there are clearly directive uses of imperatives that do not convey that "the speaker wants the content to become reality," a point of which Condoravdi and Lauer are aware. (Consider a speaker known to have been coerced, against her own desires, to deliver an order to an addressee, and who does so with an imperative.) I suggest a different, more or less Gricean, understanding of direction in §3.5.3.

[7] Representative statements may be found at Schwager (2007: 241); Condoravdi & Lauer (2012: 40).

More plausibly, instantiation of a clause-type T is the feature *in virtue of which* sentences of type T are associated by the grammar with a canonical discourse role or force. What type of feature would this be—morphosyntactic or semantic? Perhaps sentences of type T are so-typed in virtue of containing a silent force marker in their syntax (e.g., Han 1998), in which case clausal typing falls plausibly within the domain of Universal Grammar. Perhaps sentences of type T are so-typed according to language-specific morphosyntactic properties (like *wh*-movement or a null subject and uninflected verb), in which case clausal typing falls plausibly within the domain of the language-specific grammar. Finally, perhaps sentences of type T are so-typed according to features of their *semantic values*—perhaps according to the model-theoretic type of semantic value, or something more fine-grained still.

Clause-type analysis, *per se*, requires none of these options. The common meta-linguistic representation of a typed clause with a sentential operator scoping over an untyped clause—e.g., representing the sentences in (2) using "force operators" (like the Fregean assertion operator ⊢, a question operator ?, or an imperative operator !) scoping over untyped "sentence radicals"—is, in fact, *neutral* between the understandings of clause-typological individuation just described. In particular, such a representation—in a regimented formal metalanguage, à la Montague (1973)—need not (and generally does not) purport to realistically represent the actual syntax of the corresponding sentence in natural language.

This a well-appreciated point in the literature. A related, but somewhat less well-appreciated, point is that distinct clause-types might be represented in the metalan-guage as varying, not along the force operator dimension, but rather along another dimension altogether. It is, for instance, open to us to represent one clause-type as somehow parasitic or dependent on another clause-type. Imperatives, for example, might be represented in the metalanguage as being derived from related (e.g., modal) declaratives—perhaps, as I will ultimately suggest, by some type-shifting operation—without object-language imperatives being actually derived from modal declaratives, or in fact *containing a modal* in their morphosyntax at all.

This flexibility allows a certain kind of theorist (mine) to prescind from many of the questions that have lately animated the linguistic literature on imperatives. Do imperatives contain modals?[8] Are there force operators in syntax? I do not propose to answer these questions here. Can the semantics of imperatives be theorized about, under the rubric of clause-type analysis, while availing ourselves of the tools of our best theories of linguistic modality? Could imperatives have a "modal semantics"— even while failing to display some of the hallmarks of linguistic modality? That will mostly depend on the explanatory attractions of the semantics. I will later suggest that there are enough for us to respond to these questions with a cautious *yes*.[9]

---

[8] Kaufmann argues *yes* (see esp. Kaufmann 2012). Portner argues *no* (see esp. Portner 2007). von Fintel & Iatridou (2009, 2017) side tentatively with Portner.

[9] Roberts (2015) represents another account in this general vein.

3.2.3 Semantic Value and Content

Since clause-type analysis aspires to provide a semantics for—or at least a rubric for theorizing about the semantics of—typed clauses, it is important to know *what type of semantic theory* is supposed to be on offer. There are at least two options. The program of modern Generative Semantics is generally understood as providing a compositional characterization of a sentence's semantic value, with an eye to revealing what *semantic competence* with respect to that sentence consists in. Semantic theorizing in more philosophical circles tends to aim at something different: a (possibly noncompositional) characterization of the (typically propositional) *content conventionally proffered* by a sincere utterance of a sentence.[10] What type of semantic theorizing is clause-type analysis engaged in?

Clause-type analyses—like that of Portner, as well as, for example, Roberts (1996, 2015, forthcoming)—should generally be read as offering a semantic analysis in the second sense (which is, of course, not to say that they involve any sort of rejection of the Generative program). Portner describes a tight relationship between (i) model-theoretic type of semantic value and (ii) canonical discourse role. The semantic values of declaratives—propositions—are fit for the illocutionary act of assertion (and when tokened in discourse are added by default to the Common Ground); the semantic values of interrogatives—questions—are fit for the illocutionary act of questioning (and when tokened in discourse are added by default to the list of Questions under Discussion, à la Roberts (1996)). It is well-understood that assertoric content often diverges from compositional semantic value; indeed for many purposes it does not make much sense to say that the compositional semantic value of a declarative is a proposition, in the ordinary sense—i.e., a thing fit for the content of assertion and belief, and the object of credence—at all (Lewis 1980; Ninan 2010). Portner (and Roberts) thus seem to be giving analyses that link conventionally proffered contents to canonical discourse roles.

Clause-type theorizing, so understood, does place constraints on compositional semantic theorizing—and vice versa—since there is assumed to be some sort of *deter-minative relation* holding between compositional semantic value and conventionally proffered content. But the constraints are plausibly looser than is ordinarily assumed in the literature on imperatives. Consider the possibility that (i) the conventionally proffered content of an imperative is modeled with a modal operator, (ii) no corresponding modal operator is witnessed in our representation of the imperative's compositional semantic value.[11] Such a proposal would free the clause-type theorist to explore the conventionally proffered content of an imperative via a modally loaded

---

[10] On the distinction, see Lewis (1980); Ninan (2010); Yalcin (2014). Though notions like 'content' have unclear purchase in certain (e.g., dynamic) frameworks, such frameworks do traffic in notions like conventionally proffered meanings (in dynamic frameworks, these tend to be modeled as update instructions).

[11] Such a proposal might raise the suspicion that the imperative's conventionally proffered content stands in an obscure relationship to its compositional semantic value. The alleged obscurity might be remedied with, for example, an account of the determinative relation that holds between these entities, which does not amount to simple *identity*. I can provide no such account here, since I take basic questions regarding the compositional semantic contribution of the imperative to be unsettled.

account of its canonical discourse role—or better, as I will ultimately suggest, a modally loaded account of its canonical cognitive role—while sidestepping definite commitments in the realm of compositional semantics.

3.2.4 Canonical Cognitive Role

We've seen that clause-type analysis is naturally understood as offering a rubric for theorizing about the content conventionally proffered by an utterance of a typed clause. Conventionally proffered contents are posited to explain, inter alia, *what is said* by an utterance in a standard context of utterance. Conventionally proffered contents are, in other words, things proffered by speakers for addition to the Common Ground, for cognitive adoption—acceptance—by conversational participants, and so on.

(What is acceptance? I understand *update* and *acceptance* as loosely interdefinable: acceptance of content C may be understood in terms of redundant update on C, while updating on C is a state that generally induces acceptance of C. *Acceptance* of an interrogative is, roughly, the sort of state in which updating on that interrogative would be *redundant*.[12])

Clause-type analysis suggests a link between the *semantic content* of a typed clause and the *attitude* typically induced by an utterance of that clause. As the content of a typed clause determines a canonical discourse role—whatever discourse role is associated, by default, with the absorption of such a content into the context— it also determines a canonical cognitive role—whatever cognitive role is associated, by default, with *update on* that content. Declaratives, as devices for expressing propositions, are linked to *propositional attitudes*—attitudes taking embedded declaratives as their complements, and which paradigmatically (in, e.g., the case of belief) ascribe acceptance of the declarative's content to the attitude-ascription's subject. Interrogatives, as devices for expressing questions, are linked to *question-directed attitudes*—attitudes taking embedded interrogatives as their complements, and which paradigmatically (in, e.g., the case of wondering) ascribe acceptance of an interrogative content to the attitude ascription's subject.

The link between an analysis of clause-type T and attitudes taking sentences of type T as complements must be stated with care, since (i) propositional attitude-ascriptions (e.g., desire-ascriptions) need not ascribe acceptance of a propositional content to their subjects; (ii) interrogative attitude-ascriptions (e.g., certain forms of knowledge-*wh*-ascription) need not ascribe acceptance of an interrogative content, in the just-described sense, to their subjects.[13]

---

[12] A useful comparison is with Stalnaker (2002). Stalnaker uses 'acceptance' to delimit "a category of propositional attitudes and methodological stances toward a proposition, a category that includes belief, but also some attitudes (presumption, assumption, acceptance for the purposes of an argument or an inquiry) that contrast with belief, and with each other" (716). Like Stalnaker's notion, my notion of acceptance is broader than belief: one might accept that *p* (in the context of, say, a supposition), without believing that *p*; in my idiom, this means that, in the context of the relevant supposition, updating on *p* would be redundant. Unlike Stalnaker's notion, my notion of acceptance encompasses attitudes (like wondering) whose functional role is not to be understood as serving up a *propositional content* for the sake of some cognitive activity.

[13] Point (i) is obvious. On point (ii), I do *not* mean that, since knowledge-*wh* ascriptions ascribe knowledge to their subjects, they do not ascribe uncertainty, hence do not ascribe acceptance of an interrogative content. Acceptance of an interrogative content is to be sharply distinguished from *uncertainty*

Such attitudes are *not* linked in the envisioned way to the posited canonical discourse role for declaratives or interrogatives. Instead, clause-type analysis suggests an understanding of the attitudes that are induced, *by default*, when an agent updates on the conventionally proffered content of a typed clause: a "core" propositional attitude, like belief (or something close, like conditionalization of one's probabilities on a propositional content), in the case of declaratives; a "core" interrogative attitude, like issue-sensitivity (or something close, like wondering wh-), in the case of inter-rogatives. In this way, a sentence's *canonical cognitive role* may be derived from its canonical discourse role *via* its conventionally proffered content.

3.3 Portner

This section and the next will situate the accounts of imperatives developed by Paul Portner and Magdalena Kaufmann within the understanding of clause-type analysis sketched in this section. I will raise some (more or less) empirical doubts about both types of account.

3.3.1 Dynamic Pragmatics

Portner develops his analysis of the imperative within the framework of what he terms Dynamic Pragmatics.[14] His description of the program's key tenets:

Dynamic Pragmatics

  i. Sentences have standard static semantic values.
 ii. The communicative effect of utterances in discourse is modeled as the effect they have on the discourse context.
iii. The effect of a particular sentence is determined by pragmatic principles on the basis of the sentence's form or semantics. (Portner this volume, pp. 297–8)

He links Dynamic Pragmatics to clause-type analysis as follows:

Semantic Values

  i. The semantic value of a declarative sentence is a proposition.
 ii. The semantic value of an interrogative sentence is a set of propositions.

---

about how to answer the question expressed by the interrogative: uncertainty about some proposition does not imply acceptance of a corresponding interrogative content, nor does acceptance of an interrogative content imply uncertainty about its propositional answers. A subject can recognize the issue expressed by the embedded interrogative—can partition her information along the lines suggested by the interrogative—even when she is not uncertain about how to resolve it; example (1b) is naturally read in this manner. Consider, however, non-exhaustive (e.g., mention-some) readings of embedded interrogatives.

    (10)   Maria knows where to buy an Italian newspaper
    (11)   Maria knows how to play guitar

It is enough for the truth of (10) that when Maria wants an Italian newspaper, she *reliably will go* to a place where an Italian newspaper is available for purchase. Similarly a sufficient condition for (11) is that Maria *is able* to play guitar. Asking Maria where to buy an Italian newspaper, or how to play guitar, is liable to raise cognitively novel issues for her. Thanks here to Simon Charlow.

[14]   This exposition draws from Portner (2004, 2007, 2012, this volume).

iii. The semantic value of an imperative sentence is a property restricted to one individual (the addressee). (Portner forthcoming a)

Force Assignment
The force of a root sentence S is a function updating the discourse context by adding $[\![S]\!]$ to the component of the context which is a set of objects from the same semantic domain as $[\![S]\!]$ (Portner forthcoming a)

Dynamic Pragmatics, as pursued by Portner, involves a specific form of clause-type analysis, in the sense we have sketched. Sentences are assigned a clause-type representation according to the model-theoretic type of their conventionally proffered content. A sentence's canonical discourse role is derived from its clause-type representation: given an utterance of a sentence at a context, a parameter of that context is selected for update according to the *semantic type* of its conventionally proffered content. The canonical discourse role of a sentence (with conventionally proffered content of semantic type τ) is the addition of its conventionally proffered content to a contextual parameter that records the conventionally proffered contents of utterances—when, but only when, that content is of type τ.

It is important to remember that Portner does *not* encode illocutionary force at the level of clause-type: addition of a content of propositional type to a contextual parameter that records contents of propositional type—i.e., a set of propositions— may correspond to assertion (when the relevant contextual parameter is *the Common Ground*), but to a distinct illocutionary act as well (when the relevant set of propositions is distinguished from the Common Ground). More generally, the illocutionary force of an utterance of a typed clause with conventionally proffered content of semantic type τ is, for Portner, a function, not only of its clause-type, but also *which record* (or records) of τ-type contents the utterance targets for update.

3.3.2 Many To-Do Lists

The semantic value of an imperative is, for Portner, an addressee-restricted property:

$$[\![\text{shut the door!}]\!]^c = \lambda x : x = addressee_c . x \text{ shuts the door}$$

By the Force Assignment principle, the force of uttering an imperative is to add the utterance's semantic value to a dedicated contextual record: a set of entities of the same semantic type. Portner dubs such sets "To-Do Lists," and introduces a To-Do List function—typed, roughly, as a function from individuals into their To-Do Lists—as a novel parameter of the context (Portner 2004, 2007, 2012).[15] Within this framework, Portner attempts to account for the wide varieties in illocutionary force associated with imperative utterances by appeal to one of the following:

---

[15] The conceptual foundations for a To-Do List account—in particular, the functional role of the To-Do List in a general account of practical rationality and conversation—seem to merit further consideration. Portner (this volume) writes that "the to-do list defines a pre-order over the context set and an action by participant p is deemed rational and cooperative if it tends to make it the case that the actual world is maximally highly ranked according to p's to-do list" (303, see also Portner 2007: 358). Rationality, as I understand it, is tied to an agent's maximization of subjective expected utility, which has little—as best I can see—to do with her To-Do List.

- The existence of different species of commitment *within* an individual's To-Do List (e.g., deontic, legal, bouletic, teleological). Commands interpretations, perhaps, involve updates to an agent's *deontic To-Do's*. Suggestion interpretations, perhaps, involve updates to her *bouletic To-Do's*. (Portner 2007)
- Contextual factors. A permission interpretation of an imperative, for example, is claimed to arise in contexts where a property that is inconsistent with the property expressed by the imperative is already present on the addressee's To-Do List. (Portner 2012)

A signal attraction of the account is what we might call its illocutionary "flexibility"—its broad structural adaptability to uses of imperatives that have stymied competitor accounts. As illustration of this adaptability, Portner (this volume) jettisons the assumption that there is a single To-Do List for each individual. The objective here is to account for a further aspect of variability in imperative usage: variability in imperative *strength*, of the sort attested in the following minimal pair:

(12)   a. Take a seat$^\Uparrow$ [WEAK]
       b. Take a seat$^\Downarrow$ [STRONG]

Rising imperatives are naturally associated with invitations or suggestions, falling imperatives with orders or directives.[16]

Portner's strategy here will seem familiar: illocutionary variability is variation in *which* To-Do List(s) are selected for update, as a function of the imperative's intonational profile.

- Rising imperatives propose to add their content to a To-Do List that represents the addressee's representation of her own commitments.
- Falling imperatives propose to add their content to a To-Do List that represents the speaker's representation of the addressee's commitments.

Portner's account achieves a remarkable degree of coverage—a degree that is, in principle, indefinitely extensible, through the further proliferation of To-Do Lists—over the wide range of illocutionary variety attested in imperative utterances. But, I will now argue, it has prima facie difficulty accounting, even in principle, for two kinds of embeddings of the imperative: as the matrix clause of a conditional, and under apparently quantificational operators.[17]

3.3.3 Conditional Imperatives

Conditional imperatives like (13) exhibit the familiar characteristics of ordinary, or unconditional, imperatives (for a helpful catalogue, see Roberts 2015).

(13)   If it starts to rain, shut the door

In particular, conditional imperatives, like ordinary imperatives, tend strongly to have a directive function in discourse (which can, as ever, be modulated by contextual

---

[16] The association is not conventional. Rising imperatives can, for example, receive extremely strong interpretations (*don't you dare*$^\Uparrow$). Portner need not commit himself to any such conventional association in order to display the illocutionary flexibility of the clause-type analysis he favors.

[17] For earlier discussion of this type of data for quantified imperatives, see Charlow (2010: 230–2; 2011: §4.4.7). On conditional imperatives, see Charlow (2011: §4.5; 2014a: 652ff; 2014b: 546ff).

variation, intonation, and so on). We can "operationalize" this directive function by noticing that utterances of imperatives of any type tend to *make true* (or else *be grounded in the truth of*) a corresponding modal statement like (14).[18]

(14)   If it starts to rain, you [should/must] shut the door

From the perspective of clause-type analysis, the shared characteristics of conditional and ordinary imperatives might seem unremarkable. Indicative conditionals are standardly assigned a clause-type as a function of the clause type of their *main clause* (i.e., consequent) (Bhatt and Pancheva 2006), while indicative antecedents are surmised to express a kind of restrictive operation on the semantic value of the main clause (à la Kratzer 1981, 1991).[19] From this perspective, conditional imperatives are nothing special: conditional imperatives are *imperatives*, and propose some sort of property—restricted in some fashion or other by their antecedents—for addition to the addressee's To-Do List(s).

In fact, however, Portner's Dynamic Pragmatic account sits uneasily with these pieces of orthodoxy. If a sentence like (13) is typed as imperative, its semantic value will be given by a logical form of roughly the shape in (15):

(15)   [if it starts to rain]$[\lambda x_{addressee}[x$ shuts the door]]

Such a logical form is, however, problematic: there is apparently no operator present for the *if*-clause to restrict.[20] If this is how conditional imperatives are represented at logical form, conditional imperatives are semantically ill-formed.

But let us bracket this worry, and assume that a logical form of the right type is computable for (13). This property will have roughly the shape in (16):

(16) $\lambda x_{addressee}[x$ shuts the door if it starts to rain]

Such a content, being of the semantic type *addressee-restricted property*, is predicted, in Portner's Dynamic Pragmatics, to have the discourse profile typical of other property-type semantic values: its canonical discourse function is to be added to some set of property-type semantic values, i.e., one or more of the To-Do Lists made available by the context of utterance.

---

[18] The connection between imperatives and corresponding modal statements is perhaps their most carefully studied property. A chronological sampling of references that treat this connection as theoretically central: Åqvist (1964); Han (1998); Aloni (2007); Schwager (2007); Portner (2007); Charlow (2011); Kaufmann (2012); Charlow (2014a); Starr (forthcoming). Portner (this volume) makes the very interesting observation that a judgment of the truth of (14) can both *justify* and *be justified* by a speaker's utterance of (13), which I have taken on here.

[19] Kaufmann (2012) argues convincingly that examples like (13) are *bona fide* "hypothetical" indicative conditionals, i.e., not relevance (biscuit) conditionals or factual (echoic) conditionals. On my possibly idiosyncratic understanding of the hypothetical/non-hypothetical contrast, the antecedents of hypothetical conditionals contribute their semantic values to the computation of the semantic value of the entire conditional structure, while the antecedents of non-hypothetical conditionals perform some other non-semantic function (e.g., signaling relevance).

[20] Ordinarily, Kratzer (1991) suggests, we may posit an unpronounced epistemic necessity modal so that the compositional function of the *if*-clause may be fulfilled. This suggestion is a non-starter for conditional imperatives: quite unlike ordinary imperatives, this would wrongly construe directive uses of conditional imperatives as directives concerning features of an *epistemic state*, rather than the addressee's actions (*vis-à-vis*, say, the door).

This prediction is incorrect.[21] Directive uses of conditional imperatives, as noted above, tend to *make true* (or else *be grounded in the truth of*) corresponding modal statements. But the truth condition of a modalized conditional like (14) is *not* the presence of the property in (16)—or of a proposition derived from that property, to the effect that the addressee shuts the door if it starts to rain—on the ordering source relevant for the interpretation of the matrix modal of (14). According to the basic analysis of Kratzer (1981), the truth condition of (14) is that the most highly ranked (according to the ordering source) contextually relevant possibilities are ones in which you shut the door. The mere *presence* of the property in (16) on an ordering source is not sufficient for this (if, for example, an incompatible property is already present in the ordering source, so that the ordering source, once updated with the relevant property, is *indifferent* or *lacks a preference* between shutting and not shutting the door in the event of rain) (a point also noted in Charlow (2011: 15ff); Condoravdi & Lauer (2012: 56)).[22]

But let us bracket this worry, too, and ask simply *what sort of property is (16) supposed to be?* Trivially, the property of making a conditional true. What kind of conditional? I know of no option other than the material conditional.[23] Now consider the sequence in (17):

(17)   a. Don't rob me. $\lambda x[x$ does not rob *speaker*]
         b. If you do, leave my phone. $\lambda x[x$ leaves *speaker*'s phone if x robs *speaker*]

This is as unremarkable a sequence of imperatives as one is likely to find.

Interpreted as the property of making a material conditional true, however, the addressee's satisfaction of the property in (17b) is *logically guaranteed* by the addressee's satisfaction of the property in (17a). In other words, (17b) adds a *weaker*

---

[21] Portner (forthcoming b) has pondered the adoption of a dynamic account of conditional imperatives, like the ones defended in Charlow (2011); Starr (forthcoming). A dynamic account would, indeed, be well-positioned to accommodate the data presented in this section. This option is, however, foreclosed to Portner, given his broader programmatic commitments to the shape of clause-type theorizing (cf. Charlow 2014a: 653). For the Dynamic Pragmaticist, "sentences have standard static semantic values"; dynamic or discourse-level meanings must be derived by application of the Force Assignment principle. More generally, a Portnerian Dynamic Pragmatic account is distinguished by assigning sentences theoretically "minimal" semantic values: imperatives denote properties because they are null-subject VPs, and null-subject VPs denote properties. If conditional imperatives turn out not to denote properties—something that would be required for Portner to avoid the argument I am making here—it would seem that the Dynamic Pragmatic program, as presented by Portner, is untenable after all.

[22] Thus Portner predicts the possible coherence—in at least one sense of coherence—of a discourse sequence that involves an imperative requiring p and an expression of permission allowing $\neg p$. There is, I argue elsewhere, strong evidence that such sequences are *semantically disallowed*—literally contradictory (see, e.g., Charlow 2014a: 653–4). It is possible for Portner to avoid this, by incorporating a *revision procedure* into his account, so that updating a To-Do List *tdl* on an imperative requiring p makes it the case that *tdl* requires p, as in Starr (forthcoming). Such a revision procedure, in my view, takes us beyond the subject-matter of semantic/pragmatic theorizing (Charlow 2014a: 654–6).

[23] As I mentioned in note 20, construing directive uses of conditional imperatives as directives concerning an epistemic state misconstrues what we might call their "subject-matter". Indicative conditionals are, it is now widely accepted, semantically evaluated relative to epistemic—or, more neutrally, informational—states. It follows that we cannot construe the conditional embedded in (16) as an indicative conditional.

demand to the relevant To-Do List(s) than (17a) (Charlow 2014a: 625–6). Such a discourse move is, however, ordinarily quite marked:[24]

(18)   Leave my phone . . . #If you rob me, leave my phone.
(19)   Don't take my possessions . . . #Don't take my phone.

The reason for this seems clear enough (at least in broad outline): conditional on having expressed an expectation that someone see to it that ϕ, expressing a weakened expectation (i.e., expressing the expectation that someone see to it that ψ when ϕ strictly entails ψ) is pragmatically unavailable (except, perhaps, given explicit or implicit retraction of the earlier-expressed stronger expectation). But if this holds true for (18) and (19), why would it not hold true for (17)?

I did not, of course, invent this sort of case—it is borrowed from the literature on Contrary-To-Duty (or Second-Best) Obligations, which recent sophisticated treatments have analyzed utilizing the *information-sensitivity* of expressions like deontic modals (and the ability of indicative antecedents to shift the information against which information-sensitive material in their main clauses is evaluated) (see, e.g., Willer 2014). Conditional imperatives, it is worth noting, apparently display a sort of information-sensitivity similar to that exhibited by deontic conditionals.[25] Consider the following example (from Charlow 2014a: 625):[26]

(20)   a. If it's going to rain, take the umbrella (but leave the sunglasses)
       b. If it's not going to rain, take the sunglasses (but leave the umbrella)
       c. Bring both (. . . since we don't know)

Sequence (20) is, to my ear, unremarkable: (20a) and (20b) can be offered as conditional advice the day before the referenced outing; (20c) can be offered as additional advice the day of the outing, without any sense that the speaker is changing her mind or retracting her conditional advice. (Notice that if, subsequent to the utterance of (20c), it begins to look as if it's going to rain, the speaker's advice to take the umbrella will *still apply* to the addressee.) However, the properties expressed by these three imperatives, on my understanding of a Portnerian analysis of conditional imperatives, are *known by a competent speaker* to be inconsistent—jointly logically unsatisfiable by any agent. It is mysterious how a speaker could—without manifest incoherence—propose such inconsistent properties for addition to the same To-Do List.

---

[24] Examples of allegedly "valid imperative inferences" adduced in the literature (in, e.g., Vranas 2008, 2010; Parsons 2013) are, for this very reason, generally quite marked.

[25] For my own understanding of information-sensitivity in deontic conditionals, see Charlow (2013a). A hallmark of information-sensitivity, on this sort of view, as noted by Willer (2012) (see also Yalcin 2012b), is the apparent failure of *modus tollens* for natural language indicatives with information-sensitive consequents: rejection of the consequent of such a conditional does not commit one to rejection of its antecedent (as seems clear from sequence (20)).

[26] It is also worth mentioning that it is possible to recreate Kolodny & MacFarlane (2010)'s Miner Paradox—a core data point in the case for information-sensitivity (see, among many others, Charlow 2013b; Cariani et al. 2013; Carr 2015)—with (weak) imperative, rather than deontic, conditionals. For the case, see Charlow (2010: 227).

3.3.4 Quantified Imperatives

Quantified imperatives like (21) also exhibit familiar characteristics of ordinary imperatives.

(21)   Everyone$_i$ take [his/her/their]$_i$ seat

In particular, quantified imperatives tend strongly to have a directive function in discourse (subject to the usual caveats). As before, one way of "operationalizing" this directive function is to notice that utterances of quantified imperatives tend to *make true* (or else *be grounded in the truth of*) a corresponding modal statement like (22).

(22)   Everyone$_i$ [should/must] take [his/her/their]$_i$ seat

A logical form of the right type would seem to be computable for (21):

(23) $\lambda x_{addressee}[x$ takes x's seat]

Such a property would then be added, as indicated by the quantifier phrase, to each (relevant) $tdl(x)$, for each addressee x.

This is a prima facie satisfactory story about the canonical discourse role for (21).[27] But there is something curious about it: such a logical form involves the (unexplained) deletion of the quantifier phrase *everyone*, which is subsequently treated as a discourse-level signal regarding which To-Do Lists to select for update—the relevant $tdl(x)$'s, *for each addressee x*.

There is, to be clear, nothing mysterious about this sort of deletion when the deleted noun phrase is vocative—serving to explicitly indicate the addressee, but obviously not part of the relevant sentence's logical form:

(24)   Bernie, take your seat $\lambda x : x =$ Bernie[x takes x's seat]

The fact that the quantifier phrase in (21) binds a pronoun seems, however, to indicate that it cannot be considered vocative.[28]

There is another option for a Portnerian analysis to try out here: leave the quantifier phrase in place, and (vacuously) λ-abstract over the entire sentence.

(25) $\lambda x_{addressee}$[everyone$_i$ takes [his/her/their]$_i$ seat]

The logical form in (25), though equivalent to a proposition, is nevertheless a property, and so is fit for addition to the relevant To-Do List(s). Suppose, as seems forced, that this property is added to each (relevant) $tdl(x)$, for each addressee x. Ordinarily, this will have the effect of making it required, of each addressee x, that x see to it that *everyone takes their seat*. In other words, we have the makings of an explanation of

---

[27] Though it does face the problem, mentioned in the previous section, that the mere presence of a property on a To-Do List is consistent with that To-Do List being indifferent between its agent taking a seat or not; see note 22.

[28] See earlier discussion in Mauck et al. (2005); Charlow (2010). Second-person pronouns are, for some speakers, preferred to third-person pronouns in examples like (21). So it is worth noting that there is strong reason to regard treat second-person pronouns as being anaphorically bound in such examples (Mauck et al. 2005).

why an imperative like (21) would tend to make true, or else be grounded in the truth of, a modal statement like (26).

(26)   Everyone [should/must] see to it that everyone$_i$ takes [his/her/their]$_i$ seat

The difficulty is that imperative (21) simply lacks the envisioned connection to modal statement (26). (21) tends to make true, or else be grounded in the truth of, a modal statement like (22). (22) describes an *individual-level* obligation concerning each person's position relative to their own chair. It does not describe a "state-level" obligation, as (26) seems to do, regarding each person's obligation to bring about a world that is preferred from the standpoint of the speaker—a world in which everyone takes their seat.[29]

A final option is the introduction of a To-Do List indexed to a collective addressee— roughly, the To-Do List for everyone.

(27) $\lambda x : x =$ everyone[x takes x's seat]

This is not necessarily *ad hoc*: collective addressees are required for understanding imperative utterances that target *group actions* (Charlow 2010: 231).

(28)   Play Beethoven's Fifth $\lambda x : x =$ the orchestra[x plays Beethoven's Fifth]

A group action is, however, clearly not the target of (21), any more than it is the target of (22). (In any case, while there is such a thing as the playing of Beethoven's Fifth by the orchestra, there is no such *thing* as *everyone's seat*, and so there can be no action that involves the taking of it by everyone.) As with conditional imperatives, the prospects for explaining the discourse role of quantified imperatives in a Portnerian clause-type analysis are unclear.

3.4 Kaufmann

Our discussion of Portner has highlighted the following three features of imperatives:

- The tight discourse-level links—of somewhat indeterminate shape—between imperatives and corresponding modal statements
- The information-sensitivity of imperatives (witnessed in conditional imperatives)
- The ability of quantifier phrases to take non-vacuous "scope" over imperative "force"

Impressively, there is an account of imperatives that would seem to get all of these features *for free*: the modal account, championed most comprehensively by Magdalena Kaufmann.

3.4.1 *Imperatives as Performative Modals*

Kaufmann (see Schwager 2007; Kaufmann & Schwager 2011; Kaufmann 2012) ana- lyzes imperative statements *as* modal statements. There are two theses to distinguish

---

[29] Compare the distinction between *evaluative* (state-level) and *deliberative* (individual-level) readings of prioritizing modals advocated in Schroeder (2011).

here: one about the compositional semantics of imperatives—which Kaufmann supports with a wide range of linguistic data—another about their conventionally proffered contents.

Imperatives Contain Modal Quantifiers
Imperatives contain prioritizing necessity modals in their compositional semantics

Imperatives Express Modal Propositions
The conventionally proffered content of an imperative is a modal proposition

Since my interest here is confined to clause-type analysis of the imperative, I will here confine my attention to the second of these theses (recall §3.2.3).[30]

The notion that Imperatives Express Modal Propositions invites an incredulous stare (as Kaufmann appreciates). The behavior of imperatives in discourse is altogether distinct from that of declaratives; indeed, this is one of the insights around which clause-type analysis is built. Imperative utterances strikingly resist characterization as true or false—indeed, attempts at such characterization are, in every case of which I am aware, *ungrammatical*—and, relatedly, seem not to warrant the sorts of downstream discourse moves we normally take assertions to warrant—affirmation (on grounds of truth), rejection (on grounds of falsity), and so on.[31] In other words, imperative utterances, quite unlike modal utterances, cannot be used to *report or state* standing modal facts. This is quite surprising, if the conventionally proffered content of an imperative is in fact a modal proposition.

The insight on which Kaufmann builds her account is that the striking differences between imperatives and modal declaratives might be accounted for by appeal to the alleged *performativity* of imperative utterances. Imperative utterances, Kaufmann suggests, are performative in exactly the way that performative uses of their corresponding modals are performative. Like imperatives, performative utterances lack a reportative or descriptive function.

(29)   A: I promise to be at your party
       B: #No you don't/#That's false!

(30)   Louis XIV decrees: You may not execute this peasant!
       Executioner: #Yes, I may

---

[30] von Fintel & Iatridou (2009, 2017) adduce interesting data from Imperative-and-Declarative (IaD) constructions (constructions like *drink another beer and you'll lose your lunch*) that seems to suggest that (i) imperatives do not contain prioritizing necessity modals in their compositional semantics; (ii) such constructions are best thought of under the rubric of conditional conjunction (≈*if you drink another beer, you'll lose your lunch*) (cf. Culicover & Jackendoff 1997; Klinedinst & Rothschild 2012); (iii) for such constructions to function as conditional conjunctions, imperatives must have the sort of "minimal" compositional semantics suggested by Portner. I am inclined to agree with them, at least in part, but nothing here will turn on this, as I will explain.

[31] Additionally, imperatives, as we have already seen, resist embedding in environments that ordinarily take propositional arguments: indicative antecedents, as the complements of propositional attitude verbs, etc. I here focus on Kaufmann's attempt to account for the diverse behavior of imperatives and modal declaratives in discourse. Differences in embeddability are plausibly due to the distinctive syntax of the imperative.

Thus, if imperative utterances are a species of (obligatorily) performative modal utterances, we can straightforwardly explain why imperatives cannot be used to report standing modal facts (and hence, for example, cannot be targeted by the sorts of downstream discourse moves that such reports tend to warrant).

What feature might make imperative utterances *obligatorily* performative and thus "shield the truth value [of an imperative] from being conversationally accessible" (Kaufmann 2012: 57)? Example (30) is suggestive here. A performative interpretation of a modal utterance is *forced* in a context in which it is generally known that the modal facts are at the discretion, or under the authority, of the speaker. The central idea here is voiced by another target of the incredulous stare:

There is a certain symbol ! that may be prefixed to any sentence ϕ to make a new sentence !ϕ, called an imperative sentence, that is true at t at w iff ϕ is true at t at every world that is both accessible and permissible at t at w...The [imperative] may be used to command: the Master says it to the Slave, his purpose is to control the Slave's actions by changing the sphere of permissibility, and truthfulness is automatic *because the sphere adjusts so that saying so makes it so.*   (Lewis 1979: 164–6, my emphasis)

A pressing question is whether actual conversations share the features of Lewis's "little language game" (Lewis 1979: 164)? Plausibly, they do, provided that we understand the flavor of modality expressed by the imperative in a sufficiently subtle manner—something like *in view of what the speaker says is X-necessary*, where X may be any of the familiar flavors of modality: deontic, legal, bouletic, teleological, and so forth (see esp. Kaufmann 2012: Ch. 4). Command uses of imperatives may be associated with an *in view of what the speaker says she commands*-flavor, suggestion uses with an *in view of what the speaker says is necessary for the addressee to fulfill her desires*-flavor, and so on. While Portner achieves variability in illocutionary force by appeal to differences in which To-Do Lists are targeted for update by an imperative utterance, Kaufmann achieves variability in illocutionary force by appeal to differences in which flavor of modality is expressed by the imperative utterance's modal logical form.[32]

3.4.2 Explanations

A modal account seems *immediately* well-positioned to explain the links in discourse between imperatives and corresponding modal statements. These are, on my understanding of Kaufmann's account, akin to the links between the following two statements of deontic necessity:

(31)   [Given what I say is X-necessary] you [should/must] shut the door

(32)   [Given what is X-necessary] you [should/must] shut the door

These links might appear initially mysterious—what do the addressee's actual obligations (given X) have to do with what the speaker *says* is necessary (given X)?

---

[32] I have reservations regarding Kaufmann's use of authority to achieve performative force, which she implements via what she terms an *Epistemic Authority Presupposition*. This presupposition roughly enforces the speaker's *infallibility* with respect to the truth of the modal proposition expressed by the imperative (Kaufmann 2012: Ch. 4). The conceptual and explanatory role of Epistemic Authority is difficult to understand in Kaufmann's analysis (for skeptical discussions, see Charlow 2010, 2011). I pass over it here.

Kaufmann suggests that the gap here is filled by the following principle, connecting sentences of the imperative clause-type to *affirmative speech acts*:[33]

Ordering Source Affirmation
The speaker of an imperative utterance affirms the ordering source that determines the flavor of modality expressed by the imperative as the correct ordering source to use in practical deliberation for the addressee.

Suppose (32) expresses the verdict of an episode of practical deliberation, concerning what to do relative to a decision problem that is salient in the context of utterance (Kaufmann 2012: 162). The speaker's affirmation of the ordering source for her own imperative utterance as the ordering source to consult in deliberation about what to do in the salient decision problem—*if accepted at the context*—will reliably explain the truth of (32) in a context in which the imperative utterance has been made. (If the affirmation is rejected, the suggested connection will fail, but this is just what we would expect—a rejected imperative has no reliable effect on the truth of a corresponding deontic modal.)

On information-sensitivity and quantification, we can be very brief. Modals are the *paradigmatic* information-sensitive expression; if imperatives are modals, the information-sensitivity attested in conditional imperatives follows directly. On quantification, any good theory of natural language modality must identify a sense in which a sentence like (22) reports an individual-level obligation concerning each person's position relative to their own chair. Once such a theory is in hand, a theory of how a quantified imperative like (21) tends to generate this sort of individual-level obligation would *seem* to be close behind.

3.4.3 Criticisms

This section briefly advances two criticisms of Kaufmann's approach, both of which I take to stem from her account's more or less orthodox understanding of the shape of clause-type theorizing. The first criticism is that, perhaps contrary to appearances, Kaufmann, like Portner, lacks any clear explanation of the canonical discourse role of quantified imperatives like (21), repeated here as (33):

(33) Everyone$_i$ take [his/her/their]$_i$ seat

From the discussion of Portner's difficulties with quantified imperatives (§3.3.4), it is already fairly clear that the relationship between (i) the ordering source constructed to verify the truth of the performatively used imperative modal, (ii) the ordering source used in the interpretation of descriptions of addressee-obligations like (22), repeated here as (34), is not as transparent as the Ordering Source Affirmation principle would seem to suggest.

(34) Everyone$_i$ [should/must] take [his/her/their]$_i$ seat

---

[33] This principle receives various formulations in Schwager (2007); Kaufmann & Schwager (2011); Kaufmann (2012). The formulation here aims to capture a common thread between them. One might worry that this principle is stipulated to make the account work. Kaufmann argues (see, e.g., Schwager 2007: note 13) that the principle is independently motivated by the badness of sequences like #*go to Kyoto, although I don't think you should.*

The most plausible representation of the ordering source for (33) contains the proposition *that everyone takes his/her/their seat* (or else a collection of propositions that together entail this one). But if *this* is the ordering source affirmed by the speaker for use in practical deliberation by the imperative's addressees, Kaufmann apparently predicts a relationship, not between (33) and the modal statement in (34), but rather between (33) and the modal statement in (26), repeated here as (35):

(35)   Everyone [should/must] see to it that everyone$_i$ takes [his/her/their]$_i$ seat

This is, I have already argued, the wrong relationship to predict. Kaufmann's coarse-grained Ordering Source Affirmation principle, like Portner's suggested coarse-grained link between imperatives and To-Do Lists, apparently gets the wrong proposition into the ordering source(s) relevant for the evaluation of the corresponding modal declarative.

This sort of worry might be somehow finessed. My other worry is more serious. Kaufmann endeavors to explain the factors that might "shield the truth value [of an imperative] from being *conversationally accessible*" (my emphasis). Even if this explanation succeeds it would not explain why the modal proposition expressed, on her account, by an imperative would be, as it clearly is, *inaccessible to propositional cognition*, by which I mean that it apparently *cannot* function as the object of a propositional cognitive state (like belief or desire), or as the argument to a mathematical device (like, e.g., a probability function) that takes propositional arguments. Even if Kaufmann has explained why imperative utterances resist characterization as true or false *in discourse*, she has yet to explain why, roughly speaking, imperative *thoughts* resist characterization as true or false/likely or unlikely/desirable or undesirable, and so on.[34]

Somewhat less roughly, according to the account of canonical cognitive roles sketched in §3.2.4, canonical cognitive roles for sentences are related to their canonical discourse roles, via their conventionally proffered contents. According to Kaufmann, the conventionally proffered content of an imperative is a *modal proposition*. When that proposition is tokened in discourse using an imperative, the utterance is assigned a performative interpretation. But when that same proposition is tokened in thought with an imperative, it is hard to know what to say. While performativity might explain why the modal proposition expressed, by Kaufmann's lights, by the imperative is conversationally inaccessible, the notion of performativity has no clear purchase when theorizing about an agent's cognitive system: performativity seems unable to explain why the modal proposition expressed, by Kaufmann's lights, by the imperative is inaccessible to cognitive environments that select for *inputs of propositional type*.

Here is a possible line of reply. As we have observed, attitude-ascriptions embedding imperatives are ungrammatical; thus, it might be suggested that the reason agents cannot have desires with imperative contents is that there are no grammatical sentences reporting such attitudes. In reply: the nonexistence of a grammatical way

---

[34] Compare the critique of Kratzer's stipulation that probability judgments cannot be directed to the proposition expressed by a conditional (see, e.g., Kratzer 2012: 107) pursued by Rothschild (2012: 54) and Charlow (2016b).

of reporting a state of affairs S has basically no bearing on whether S is possible. The theorist has (and ought to have) complete freedom to define a metalanguage unencumbered by the grammatical limitations of natural language. The probability calculus, to take one obvious example, is such a metalanguage: the only restriction on applying a probability function Pr to a sentence ϕ is that ϕ's semantic value is an element of the Boolean algebra over which Pr is defined. If we are resistant to the notion that an imperative could have a probability (as seems correct), we cannot countenance the notion that imperatives have proposition-type semantic values. Similar observations will hold for metalanguages that contain a truth-predicate or attitude-predicate that is stipulated to select for arguments of propositional type.

3.5 Cognition First

On the view I will outline here, tokening an imperative content in thought is a mundane occurrence. A speaker tokens such a content when forming the *normative judgment* that is expressed by a sincere imperative utterance, and an addressee does it when updating on the content that is expressed by such an utterance, and thereby coordinating with the speaker on the normative judgment that her utterance expressed. (A normative judgment, in the intended sense, is a particular kind of judgment—what kind of judgment, I'll say more about below—about what the addressee should or must do.) This section will sketch an analysis of imperatives that attempts to build on these (admittedly somewhat cryptic) suggestions.[35]

It remains true that natural languages lack a canonical form for ascribing cognitive states with imperative contents to agents. That is to say, they lack a form which embeds a clause of the appropriate type under an attitude verb. In this respect, imperatives are unlike declaratives and interrogatives; recall example (1). Nevertheless, I will argue, the suggestion that a sincere imperative utterance tends strongly[36] to express a speaker's normative judgment concerning the actions of her addressees[37] is both sensible and explanatory.

If this is right, the cognitive role of contents of imperative type will be accessible via attitude-ascriptions that attribute normative judgments to agents. (Indeed, even if it is not right, consideration of normative attitude-ascriptions is, I will argue, a productive way to begin theorizing about the cognitive role of the imperative.) This appears, at

---

[35] The view I defend here descends from Charlow (2011, 2014a) (which also offer a fuller defense of the view than I am able to undertake here). I take Condoravdi & Lauer (2012); Harris (2014); Starr (forthcoming) to be in agreement on much of what I say in this final section. Harris, in particular, describes a cognitive approach to semantic and pragmatic theorizing (generally, but also specifically for imperatives) that has many affinities with the view I lay out here. My own view has been influenced in many ways by their work (and, more recently, by Roberts (2015)). A full comparison is, alas, beyond the purview of this paper.

[36] The tendency is imperfect, as can be seen from, e.g., well-wish imperatives like (7). More on this below.

[37] Probably within a salient decision problem. Kaufmann, we noted, makes use of the notion of a decision problem in her unpacking of the Ordering Source Affirmation principle. I have argued elsewhere for the representation of decision problems (as well as decision theories) in the semantics of prioritizing deliberative modals (see, e.g., Charlow 2016a, forthcoming).

first blush anyway, to be a plausible prediction. Consider the unremarkable (if tedious) narrative in (36).

(36) a. Bernie thinks Hillary should shut the door
      b. So, Bernie plans for Hillary to shut the door
      c. So, Bernie tells Hillary to shut the door
      d. Hillary accepts Bernie's utterance
      e. So, Hillary comes to think that she should shut the door
      f. So, Hillary plans to shut the door

As this narrative illustrates, normative judgment—of the sort routinely attributed by sentences like (36a) and (36e)—is plausibly implicated in both the *production* of a paradigmatic imperative utterance, as well as its *perlocutionary force*.

3.5.1 Internal and External Attitudes

If normative judgment, of the sort attributed by (36a) and (36e), were simply a *propositional* attitude, the suggestion to treat such normative judgments as a guide in theorizing about the semantics of imperatives would get us nowhere fast. Very plausibly, however, normative judgment is not univocally propositional. As others have noticed, it is possible to read (36a) in both what I will call *internal* and *external* senses.[38] The external reading of (36a) attributes to Bernie belief in a propositional content representing the proposition that Hillary shuts the door as required *relative to* a salient body of law, preference, regulation, etc. (The propositional complement, in the case of the external reading of (36a), is analogous to the above-mentioned "reportative" reading of the prioritizing modal.) The internal reading of (36a), however, attributes to Bernie roughly the *possession of a plan*[39] *according to which it is required that Hillary shut the door*. I will take it as obvious that the state of having a plan that requires x and the state of believing that x is required, relative to a salient body of law, preference, regulation, etc., are distinct.

How could these two readings of normative judgment-ascriptions exist? How are these two readings related? Here is one possibility, which would explain both the *existence* of these readings, as well as the *systematic semantic relationship* that seems to hold between them:

Imperatives Characterize Modal Propositions
Imperative contents are functions mapping some kind of argument into a modal truth condition.

The suggestion is to think of (metalinguistic representations of) imperative contents as derived from (metalinguistic representations of) modal propositions through some ordinary compositional mechanism, like λ-abstraction (Heim & Kratzer 1998, Chapter 5).

---

[38] This is an old, if disputed, observation in the meta-ethical literature on *judgment internalism*. The Expressivist Allan Gibbard has developed a "plan-laden" semantics for normative attitude-ascriptions around it (see esp. Gibbard 1990, 2003). For more recent discussion, see Charlow (2015); Cariani (2016); Yalcin (forthcoming).

[39] Or preference, or desire, or whatever (though I will generally default to 'plan').

As illustration, consider the following (extensional) representation of a modal logical form:

$$\Box_{f,g}(Restrictor)(Scope)$$

This representation follows Kratzer (1981): modals are generalized quantifiers expressing a relation between (i) a domain of quantification jointly characterized by the Modal Base f, the Ordering Source g, and a (explicitly or implicitly provided) Restrictor, and (ii) a set of possibilities characterized by the Scope. Provided we assume that there are finitely many worlds compatible with f, the domain of quantification is simply the set of possibilities compatible with f and the Restrictor that are minimal in the ordering characterized by g. The relationship expressed between this domain and the set of possibilities characterized by the modal's Scope is simply $\subseteq$.

A logical form of this shape is tailor-made to account for external (reportative) readings of modal expressions. Such a logical form expresses the proposition that *all* possibilities in the domain of quantification (jointly characterized by f, g, and the Restrictor) witness the truth of the Scopal proposition. If an agent stands in a cognitive relationship to this logical form—e.g., belief—then we may say that the agent believes *that the Scopal proposition is required by the domain of quantification jointly characterized by f, g, and the Restrictor.*

A logical form of closely related shape is, I suggest, tailor-made to account for internal readings of modal expressions:

$$\lambda g[\Box_{f,g}(Restrictor)(Scope)]$$

Such a logical form expresses the *property an ordering source g has* iff the Scopal proposition is required by the domain of quantification jointly characterized by f, g, and the Restrictor. As a convenient shorthand, we may say that this is the property g has when g requires the Scopal proposition (relative to the relevant Modal Base and Restrictor). Obviously this is not a truth condition: it is a (modally specified) *property* of the ordering source. Thus, unlike Kaufmann's account, our account is at no risk of misconstruing the canonical cognitive role of imperative contents as akin to the canonical cognitive roles of propositions.[40]

---

[40] What of the earlier-mentioned criticisms of Kaufmann's account that target the claim that the *compositional semantics of an imperative is modal* (e.g., von Fintel & Iatridou 2009, 2017)? Such criticisms do not apply to the account I have given—I stress that I have not given a compositional semantics for the imperative. Which is to say: I have not, in this paper, given any account of what an imperative contributes to an environment like the following.

(37)   Drink another beer, and you'll lose your lunch
(38)   Stop drinking beer, or you're grounded

These sorts of "Imperative-and/or-Declarative" constructions are, in my view, probably just equivalent to ordinary conditionals (cf. Culicover & Jackendoff 1997; Klinedinst & Rothschild 2012). I do not see the proposal I have suggested here as contributing to the analysis of such constructions as conditional in meaning. For all I have said here, the *compositional semantic contribution* of an embedded imperative is exhausted by what I have called the Scopal proposition—in the case of *shut the door, Hillary*, the proposition that Hillary shuts the door—and the conventionally proffered content of an imperative is derived from the Scopal proposition at a distinct level of semantic representation.

There is no antecedent reason to think that an agent could not stand in a cognitive relationship to this sort of logical form. If, for example, an agent's plans *are representable* with g, then we may say that the agent *cognitively instantiates* the property expressed by this logical form.[41] My present suggestion is that we may refer to the adverted sort of cognitive relationship as a *belief*—and, more specifically, as an *internal normative judgment*).

The overarching suggestions of this section have been these:

- External readings of normative judgment-ascriptions ascribe a relationship between an agent and a propositional content.
- Internal readings of normative judgment-ascriptions ascribe a relationship between an agent and an imperative content.
- Imperative contents characterize properties of the semantic parameter responsible for the action-guiding/normative flavor of prioritizing modalities—the ordering source.
- The propositional content that is the object of an external normative judgment-ascription is related to the imperative content that is the object of an internal normative judgment-ascription by λ-abstraction.

(36a) (on its internal reading) and (36b) ascribe a relationship between Bernie and an imperative content (which Bernie instantiates just if he has a plan representable with an ordering source satisfying the property characterized by this imperative content). Bernie tokens this content in discourse when he utters the imperative *shut the door, Hillary*. In accepting Bernie's utterance, Hillary comes to bear a cognitive relationship to this same imperative content. As with Bernie, this amounts to her adopting a plan that is representable as an ordering source satisfying the property characterized by this imperative content.

3.5.2 Embeddings

This section will extend the foregoing analysis to the two embeddings of imperatives that have featured in this paper: *conditional* and *quantified* imperatives. Let us again begin by considering normative judgment-ascriptions:

(39) Bernie thinks Hillary should shut the door if it starts to rain
(40) Bernie thinks everyone$_i$ should take [his/her/their]$_i$ seat

On its internal reading, I suggest that (39) asserts a cognitive relation—here termed *Bel*—between Bernie and an imperative content:

$$Bel(Bernie, \lambda g[\Box_{f,g}(it\ starts\ to\ rain)(Hillary\ shuts\ the\ door)])$$

If imperatives conventionally proffer the property an ordering source has when it requires the Scopal proposition, conditional imperatives conventionally proffer the

---

[41] I provide an account of the relationship between a formal semantic object constructed out of possibilia (like an *ordering*) and the actual *plans* or *preferences* of an agent in Charlow (2015: §5). Neither that account nor the account presented here is intended as a compositional semantics for belief-ascriptions. Since, however, they are intended as accounts of the truth conditions of internal and external readings of belief-ascriptions, they should be compositionally implementable. I see no reason to think they would not be.

property an ordering source has when it requires the Scopal proposition, *against a restriction* to possibilities compatible with their antecedents. Indicative antecedents play an ordinary compositional restrictive function—albeit at the level of convention-ally proffered content.[42] I note in passing that, so long as the ordering characterized by g depends on the information expressed by the restrictor clause, this account is well-positioned to account for the information-sensitivity outlined in §3.3.3.[43]

On its internal reading, I suggest that (40) asserts the *Bel*-relation, not between Bernie and a single imperative content, rather between Bernie and a constellation of imperative contents:[44]

$$\forall x : Bel(Bernie, \lambda g[\Box_{f,g}(\top)(x \ takes \ x\text{'s} \ seat)])$$

Universal quantifiers play an ordinary quantificational function when they take scope over the imperative—when, roughly speaking, they take scope over an imperative force operator in the metalanguage. (When they do so, their semantic function is anal-ogous to conjunction of substitution instances.) If, then, imperatives conventionally proffer the property an ordering source has when it requires the Scopal proposition, universally quantified imperatives conventionally proffer a constellation of properties: for each addressee x, the property an ordering source has when it requires x to realize the Scopal proposition. And this is exactly the sort of story for quantified imperatives I have suggested is needed.

3.5.3 *Illocution via Cognition*

Imperative utterances, on the proposal I have outlined here, conventionally proffer the contents of (internal readings of) normative judgment-ascriptions. Trivially, they proffer these contents *for acceptance*. But *how* do addressees (or contexts) that accept an imperative utterance update on an imperative content? I have been speaking in a rough-and-ready way about this issue above. In this section, I will try to be more precise.

First, a necessary formal refinement. Following Portner, we *index ordering sources to agents* (since, intuitively, the considerations that bear on a judgment of what an agent x should do—the ordering source relevant for evaluating a modal judgment

---

[42] I am not a proponent of Kratzer's restrictor analysis of the conditional (see Charlow 2016b), but explaining why (and how to modify the account to deal with this) would take me too far afield. I will note that I—like most other folks of the "dynamic" persuasion—think of indicative antecedents (as well as quantifier phrases) as, roughly speaking, devices for expressing *context change* or *discourse operations*. From this perspective, the notion that indicative antecedents (and quantifier phrases) play their main semantic role at the level of conventionally proffered content (and that quantifier phrases can nevertheless bind downstream pronouns) is expected. A useful formalism for modeling this level of semantic representation is Segmented Discourse Representation Theory (see esp. Asher & Lascarides 2003).

[43] For varying accounts of this dependence—which goes by the name of "serious informational depen-dence" in the literature—see Kolodny & MacFarlane (2010); Charlow (2013b); Cariani et al. (2013); Carr (2015).

[44] Since the imperative in question is unconditional, its logical form is vacuously restricted, to $\top$. A more realistic analysis, pursued in Charlow (2011: Ch. 4), would treat the modal's restriction as jointly determined by (i) a variable tracking contextually imposed restrictions, (ii) explicitly introduced restrictions (if the imperative is conditional). On the character of modal subordination for imperatives, see Charlow (2011: 184ff).

of this form—can vary with x). The conventionally proffered content of an ordinary imperative can thus be represented by the following schematic logical form:

$$\lambda x \lambda g[\Box_{f,g(x)}(Restrictor)(Scope)]$$

This function's individual argument may be associated with a definite individual, provided either implicitly (e.g., demonstratively) or explicitly (as with an explicit addressee imperative like *if it starts to rain, shut the door, Hillary*).

$$\lambda g[\Box_{f,g(Hillary)}(it\ starts\ to\ rain)(Hillary\ shuts\ the\ door)]$$

Or the variable can be bound by the universal quantifier, in which case we have the following constellation of contents:

$$\bigcup_{x}\{\lambda g[\Box_{f,g(x)}(Restrictor)(Scope)]\}$$

This is the constellation of contents that results from *collating each content* of the form $\lambda g[\Box_{f,g(x)}(Restrictor)(Scope)]$ (for each addressee x in the quantifier's domain).

This refinement in place, we are in a position to state a schematic recipe for determining how an addressee x (likewise, a context c) updates on an imperative accepted by x (likewise, updates on an imperative accepted at c). Step One is a formal assignment of imperative contents.

Step One: Semantics for Imperatives

The imperative interpretation function $||\cdot||$ is a function mapping imperatives to their contents, where:

$$||(if\ X)(a!Y)|| = \{\lambda g[\Box_{f,g(a)}(X)(Y)]\}$$

$$||\forall x(if\ X)(x!Y)|| = \bigcup_{x}\{\lambda g[\Box_{f,g(x)}(X)(Y)]\}$$

Of note: (i) I treat all imperative contents as *sets of properties of ordering sources*. (In the case of unquantified imperatives, this set is a singleton.) (ii) I represent a contextually disambiguated imperative of the form *see to it that X, a* with the abbreviation *a!X*. (iii) An ordinary imperative is treated as a conditional imperative with a restriction to ⊤.[45]

Step Two: we state a principle linking imperative contents to illocutionary forces or discourse moves. Because imperative contents are, in a manner of speaking, properties that can be instantiated by psychological concreta (e.g., an agent's plans), the force of an imperative Φ_{IMP} is, very simply, to propose that a range of selected states come to "believe" (in the internal sense) $||\Phi_{IMP}||$.[46] If $||\Phi_{IMP}||$ contains a property of the ordering source for agent x—a property of the form $\lambda g[\Box_{f,g(x)}(X)(Y)]$—the

---

[45] This is not intended as a final or complete statement of the view. It ignores context-sensitivity (and plays fast-and-loose with use and mention in, e.g., its handling of variables), for one. For two, it does not account for existential quantification that takes scope over imperative "force". On existential quantification see Charlow (2011: 155ff).

[46] The range of states to which such an update is proposed may include the context. "Belief" by a context is analogous to presupposition: a context c believes that p iff p is presupposed at c. On the account suggested here, if a speaker attempts to update the context with an imperative—I stress that I take no stand on whether

imperative proposes that the state that $g(x)$ represents come to "believe" (in the internal sense) $\lambda g[\Box_{f,g(x)}(X)(Y)]$.

Step Two: Force Assignment for Imperatives

Consider an utterance of the imperative Φ_{IMP}, where:

$$||\Phi_{IMP}|| = \{\lambda g[\Box_{f,g(x_1)}(X)(Y)], \ldots, \lambda g[\Box_{f,g(x_n)}(X)(Y)]\}$$

The force of Φ_{IMP} is to propose that the salient ordering source for x_i satisfy $\lambda g[\Box_{f,g(x_i)}(X)(Y)]$ (for each i).

An imperative utterance, directed at a single addressee x, proposes that x's plans (equally, the context's representation of x's plans) come to be representable with an ordering source that *requires* the imperative's prejacent. This follows from the fact that, if $g(x)$ is the salient ordering source for x, and $g(x)$ gives a set of things x plans on, then changing the value of $g(x)$ so that it comes to satisfy the specified modal property must involve a corresponding change in x's plans. An imperative utterance, directed at multiple addressees $x_1, \ldots, x_n$, proposes, for each i, that x_i's plans (equally, the context's representation of x_i's plans) come to be representable with an ordering source that requires the imperative's prejacent. In a slogan: *imperative utterances are conventionally associated with attempts to get their addressees to plan on realizing their prejacents.* In an even briefer slogan: *imperatives conventionally express directive speech acts.*

How might the manifold illocutionary forces associated with standard imperative utterances be accounted for on this proposal? Here I must be brief (while pointing my reader to earlier work). Speaking broadly, command, suggestion, invitation, etc., interpretations will be construed as determinates of the determinable DIRECTIVE. Since an agent's plans (and the ordering sources that represent her plans) come in many varieties—plans for pursuing what duty requires, plans for pursuing what her desires require, and so on—and are, additionally, represented in various *loci*—by the agent, by the context, and by agents distinct from the agent—this account's degree of illocutionary flexibility compares favorably with the degree of illocutionary flexibility one finds in both Portner's accounts: so far as I can see, all the maneuvers that Portner exploits to account for illocutionary variability are open to the account stated here. A suggestion or invitation, for instance, may be construed as a proposed update to what an addressee plans for the sake of pursuing her own desires. A command may be construed as a proposed update to what an addressee plans for the sake of doing her duty (or perhaps to what an addressee plans *sans phrase*). And so on.[47]

---

speakers should generally be understood as attempting to do such a thing—the speaker makes a discourse move whose intended effect is to make an internal normative judgment *presupposed.*

[47] For further details, including how to derive non-directive (permission, instruction) interpretations of imperatives under the rubric of indirect speech acts (cf. §3.2.1), see Charlow (2011: Ch. 3). A brief summary: permission interpretations are supplied by abduction in contexts where a directive interpretation cannot be attributed to a rational speaker. Instruction interpretations (e.g., 'to get to Union Square, walk along 14th') are generated by combining an imperative content—a function from an ordering source into a modal proposition—with an ordering source (expressing the designated goal—in this case, getting to Union Square) by a version of Functional Application. The instruction imperative is thus interpreted as

3.5.4 Extensions

If imperatives are linked to canonical discourse/cognitive roles by the Force Assignment principle, how are declaratives and interrogatives linked to canonical discourse/cognitive roles? Supposing we are in fact after a unified account here, my suggestion will be simple and fairly conservative. The standard proffered contents of both declaratives and interrogatives—propositions and questions, respectively—provide recipes for characterizing the cognitive properties one instantiates when one accepts a declarative and accepts an interrogative (in the special sense of §3.2.4). The Force Assignment principle may be extended to these properties, and the canonical discourse roles of declaratives and interrogatives subsumed within it.[48]

A proposition—to fix ideas, let this be a set of possible worlds—determines the property of self-locating in one of those possible worlds. A question—to fix ideas, let this be a way of partitioning a set of possible worlds—determines the property of partitioning the set of worlds in which one self-locates along the lines of that partition. A declarative that expresses a proposition p proposes that a salient representation of location in modal space represent the location as falling within p. An interrogative that expresses a partition $\{p, \bar{p}\}$ proposes that a salient representation of issues-under-discussion come to partition its information into p-regions and $\bar{p}$-regions.

I pitch this as a "conservative" way of extending Force Assignment to cover the other major clause types. That said, notice that if the interpretation function $\| \cdot \|$ maps sentences into their conventionally proffered contents, the conventionally proffered contents of declaratives and interrogatives, like those of imperatives, are just characteristics of abstract entities representing, in the first instance, a cognitive state of an agent. Semantic theorizing, at this level anyway, is cognitively loaded in a way that may be startling to some practitioners. Startling or not, the analysis underlying this understanding should be given the chance to earn its linguistic keep.

3.6 Conclusion

This paper developed a clause-type analysis of the imperative that improved, I argued, on the major extant clause-type analyses of the imperative: the Dynamic Pragmatic account of Portner, and the Modal account of Kaufmann.

Portner's analysis typed clauses in virtue of the semantic types of their proffered contents, and assigned them a particular force—addition of a proffered content to a set (or sets) of objects of the same semantic type—in virtue of this type. This analysis ran into difficulty with conditional and quantified imperatives, both of which seem to lack proffered contents of the sort that would allow conditional and quantified

---

proffering a modal content: that the addressee should/must perform the relevant action (walking along 14th) in order to achieve the designated goal (getting to Union Square).

[48] For approaches to semantic and pragmatic theorizing that are broadly in this vein (though developed specifically in the context of a nonpropositional semantics and pragmatics of epistemic and probabilistic operators in declarative sentences), see Swanson (2006, forthcoming); Yalcin (2011, 2012a); Rothschild (2012); Moss (2015). An important question that I do not address here is how to fit declaratives that express cognitive properties that are not equivalent to propositional belief (e.g. epistemic and normative uses of modals) into the broader project of clause-type theorizing.

imperatives to play the sort of role in discourse that they seem, in fact, to play. Portner's understanding of clause-type theorizing—an understanding which compels him to identify proffered contents for conditional and quantified imperatives of a type fit for addition to a To-Do List—limited his options for dealing with these difficulties.

Seen from the vantage of this (admittedly focused) range of explananda, Kaufmann's analysis appeared to represent an improvement over Portner's. By introducing modality into the analysis of the imperative—via the suggestions that imperatives (i) contain modal quantifiers in their compositional semantics and (ii) conventionally proffer modal propositions when uttered in discourse—Kaufmann was able to exploit the flexibility of modal expressions, with respect to their information-sensitivity, their ability to take scope under quantificational operators, and their ability to receive performative interpretations. This last ability, impressively, rendered the imperative's alleged propositional content inaccessible in discourse *and* seemed to offer an appealing account of the discourse role of imperatives of basically any type.

The utility of modal performativity was, however, limited. Clause-type analysis aspires to offer a theory of *proffered content*. One therefore expects a clause-type analysis to explain the sorts of changes in both common and individual attitudes that result when the proffered content of an imperative is tokened in thought (for, e.g., the sake of being updated on). A propositional analysis of the imperative could not explain why, for example, an imperative could not be entertained as likely, true, or desirable.

A common feature of these accounts was their attempt to exploit coarse-grained discourse principles—Portner's *Force Assignment*, Kaufmann's *Ordering Source Affirmation*—connecting utterances of typed clauses to (para-)illocutionary forces—To-Do List addition, for Portner, and affirmation of the ordering source, for Kaufmann. In both cases, any connection of an imperative to the truth of a corresponding modal sentence was *indirect* or *derived*—resulting from the application of the relevant discourse principle to the utterance's claimed proffered content.

On the "Cognition First" account advanced in this paper, the connection between imperatives and corresponding modal sentences was not indirect in this fashion. On this account, the content of an imperative may be simply *read off* the content of a corresponding normative judgment-ascription (on what I called its internal reading). An utterance proffering this content in discourse is associated with a very natural discourse role: a proposal, roughly, that an addressee *x come to share the speaker's view of what x should do*.

Like Kaufmann's account, my account exploited the scope-taking abilities and information-sensitivity of modal expressions in accounting for quantified and conditional imperatives. Unlike Kaufmann's account, I required neither that modal expressions figure in the compositional semantics of imperatives, nor that imperatives proffer modal propositional contents that are, quite exceptionally, *inaccessible* in conversation or cognition. An imperative, on my analysis, expresses a characteristic of a plan (by expressing a characteristic of an ordering source). Such characteristics are not evaluable for truth, in conversation *or* cognition. To adopt such a characteristic is to come to have a certain kind of plan, not to commit oneself to representing the world in any sort of fashion.

References

Aloni, Maria. (2007). Free choice, modals, and imperatives. *Natural Language Semantics* 15: 65–94. doi:10.1007/s11050-007-9010-2.

Åqvist, Lennart (1964). Interpretations of deontic logic. *Mind* 73: 246–253. doi:10.1093/mind/LXXIII.290.246.

Asher, Nicholas & Alex Lascarides. (2001). Indirect speech acts. *Synthese* 128: 183–228. doi:10.1023/A:1010340508140.

Asher, Nicholas & Alex Lascarides. (2003). *Logics of Conversation*. Cambridge: Cambridge University Press.

Austin, J. L. (1975). *How to Do Things with Words*. Cambridge: Harvard University Press.

Bhatt, Rajesh & Roumyana Pancheva. (2006). Conditionals. In M. Everaert & H. van Riemsdijk (eds.) *The Blackwell Companion to Syntax*, vol. 1, 638–687. Malden: Blackwell.

Cariani, Fabrizio (2016). Deontic modals and probabilities: One theory to rule them all? In N. Charlow & M. Chrisman (eds.) *Deontic Modality*. Oxford: Oxford University Press.

Cariani, Fabrizio, Magdalena Kaufmann & Stefan Kaufmann. (2013). Deliberative modality under epistemic uncertainty. *Linguistics and Philosophy* 36: 225–259. doi:10.1007/s10988-013-9134-4.

Carr, Jennifer (2015). Subjective *Ought*. *Ergo* 2: 678–710. doi:10.3998/ergo.12405314.0002.027.

Charlow, Nate. (2010). Restricting and embedding imperatives. In Aloni, M., Bastiaanse, T. de Jager & Schulz (eds.) *Logic, Language, and Meaning: Selected Papers from the 17th Amsterdam Colloquium*. ILLC. doi:10.1007/978-3-642-14287-1_23.

Charlow, Nate. (2011). Practical language: Its meaning and use. http://www.natecharlow.com/work/dissertation.pdf. Ph.D. Dissertation, University of Michigan.

Charlow, Nate (2013a). Conditional preferences and practical conditionals. *Linguistics and Philosophy* 36: 463–511. doi:10.1007/s10988-013-9143-3.

Charlow, Nate (2013b). What we know and what to do. *Synthese* 190: 2291–2323. doi:10.1007/s11229-011-9974-9.

Charlow, Nate (2014a). Logic and semantics for imperatives. *Journal of Philosophical Logic* 43: 617–664. doi:10.1007/s10992-013-9284-4.

Charlow, Nate. (2014b). The meaning of imperatives. *Philosophy Compass* 9: 540–555. doi:10.1007/s10992-013-9284-4.

Charlow, Nate. (2015). Prospects for an expressivist theory of meaning. *Philosophers' Imprint* 15: 1–43.

Charlow, Nate. (2016a). Decision theory: Yes! Truth conditions: No! In Charlow & M. Chrisman (eds.) *Deontic Modality*, 47–81. Oxford: Oxford University Press.

Charlow, Nate. (2016b). Triviality for restrictor conditionals. *Noûs* 50: 533–564. doi:10.1111/nous.12111.

Charlow, Nate (forthcoming). Decision-theoretic relativity in deontic modality. *Linguistics and Philosophy*, doi: 10.1007/s10988-017-9211-1.

Condoravdi, Cleo & Sven Lauer. (2012). Imperatives: meaning and illocutionary force. In C. Piñón (ed.) *Empirical Issues in Syntax and Semantics*, vol. 9, 37–58. CSSP, Paris.

Cremers, Alexandre & Emmanuel Chemla. (2016). A psycholinguistic study of the exhaustive readings of embedded questions. *Journal of Semantics* 33: 49–85. doi:10.1093/jos/ffu014.

Crnic, Luka and Tue Trinh. (2008). Embedding imperatives in English. In Riester & T. Solstad (eds.) *Proceedings of Sinn und Bedeutung 13*. Stuttgart. http://www.ims.uni-stuttgart.de/projekte/sfb-732/sinspec/sub13/crnicTrinh.pdf.

Culicover, Peter W. & Ray Jackendoff. (1997). Semantic subordination despite syntactic coordination. *Linguistic Inquiry* 28: 195–217. http://www.jstor.org/stable/4178974.

von Fintel, K. & Sabine Iatridou. (2009). Covert modals? One particular case. http://web. mit.edu/fintel/lsa220-class-6-handout.pdf. Lecture delivered at LSA 2009, Berkeley.

von Fintel, Kai & Sabine Iatridou. (2017). A modest proposal for the meaning of imperatives. In A. Arregui, M. Rivero & A. Pablo Salanova (eds.) *Modality across syntactic categories.* Oxford: Oxford University Press.

Gibbard, Allan. (1990). *Wise Choices, Apt Feelings.* Cambridge: Harvard University Press.

Gibbard, Allan. (2003). *Thinking How to Live.* Cambridge: Harvard University Press.

Ginzburg, Jonathan & Ivan A. Sag. (2001). *Interrogative Investigations: the form, meaning, and use of English interrogatives.* Stanford: CSLI Publications.

Han, Chung-hye. (1998). The structure and interpretation of imperatives: Mood and force in universal grammar. http://www.sfu.ca/~chunghye/papers/dissertation.pdf. Ph.D. Dissertation, University of Pennsylvania.

Harris, Daniel W. (2014). Speech act theoretic semantics. http://danielwharris. com/dissertation.pdf. Ph.D. Dissertation, CUNY.

Heim, Irene & Angelika Kratzer. (1998). *Semantics in Generative Grammar.* OXford: Blackwell.

Karttunen, Lauri. (1977). Syntax and semantics of questions. *Linguistics and Philosophy* 1: 3–44. doi:10.1007/BF00351935.

Kaufmann, Magdalena (2012). *Interpreting Imperatives.* Dordrecht: Springer.

Kaufmann, Magdalena & Claudia Poschmann. (2013). Embedded imperatives: Empirical evidence from colloquial German. *Language* 89: 619–637. doi:10.1353/lan.2013.0050.

Kaufmann, Stefan & Magdalena Schwager. (2011). A unified analysis of conditional imperatives. In E. Cormany, S. Ito & D. Lutz (eds.) *Proceedings of SALT 19,* 239–259. Ithaca: CLC Publications. semanticsarchive.net/Archive/TYzZWYyM/.

Klinedinst, Nathan & Daniel Rothschild. (2012). Connectives without truth tables. *Natural Language Semantics* 20: 137–175. doi:10.1007/s11050-011-9079-5.

Kolodny, Niko & John MacFarlane. (2010). Ifs and oughts. *Journal of Philosophy* 107: 115–143. doi:10.5840/jphil2010107310.

Kratzer, Angelika. (1981). The notional category of modality. In H. Eikmeyer & H. Rieser (eds.) *Words, Worlds, and Contexts,* 38–74. Berlin: De Gruyter.

Kratzer, Angelika. (1991). Conditionals. In A. von Stechow & D. Wunderlich (eds.), *Semantics: An International Handbook of Contemporary Research,* 651–656. Berlin: De Gruyter.

Kratzer, Angelika. (2012). *Modals and Conditionals.* Oxford: Oxford University Press.

Lewis, David. (1979). A problem about permission. In E. Saarinen, R. Hilpinen, I. Niiniluoto & M. B. Provence Hintikka (eds.) *Essays in Honour of Jaakko Hintikka,* 163–179. Dordrecht: D. Reidel.

Lewis, David. (1980). Index, context, and content. In S. Kanger & S.Ohman (eds.) *Philosophy and Grammar,* 79–100. Holland: D. Reidel.

Mauck, Simon, Miok Pak, Paul Portner & Raffaella Zanuttini (2005). Imperative subjects: A cross-linguistic perspective. In C. Brandstetter & D. Rus (eds.) *Georgetown University Working Papers in Theoretical Linguistics,* 135–152. http://faculty.georgetown.edu/portnerp/ nsfsite/MPPZ.pdf.

Montague, Richard. (1973). The proper treatment of quantification in ordinary English. In Jaakko Hintikka, Julius Moravcsik & Patrick Suppes (eds.) *Approaches to Natural Language: Proceedings of the 1970 Stanford Workshop on Grammar and Semantics,* 221–242. Dordrecht: D. Reidel. Reprinted in *Formal Philosophy,* by Richard Montague, Yale University Press, New Haven, 1974, pages 247–270.

Moss, Sarah. (2015). On the semantics and pragmatics of epistemic modals. *Semantics and Pragmatics* 8:1–81.

Ninan, Dilip. (2010). Semantics and the objects of assertion. *Linguistics and Philosophy* 33: 355–380.

Parsons, Josh. (2013). Command and consequence. *Philosophical Studies* 164: 61–92. doi:10.1007/s11098-013-0094-x.

Portner, Paul. (2004). The semantics of imperatives within a theory of clause types. In Robert B. Young (ed.) *Proceedings of SALT 14*, 235–252. CLC Publications. http://semanticsarchive. net/Archive/mJlZGQ4N/.

Portner, Paul. (2007). Imperatives and modals. *Natural Language Semantics* 15: 351–383. doi:10.1007/s11050-007-9022-y.

Portner, Paul. (2012). Permission and choice. In Grewendorf & T. Zimmermann (eds.) *Discourse and Grammar: From Sentence Types to Lexical Categories*. Studies in Generative Grammar. Mouton de Gruyter. http://semanticsarchive.net/Archive/jI1YjMyY/.

Portner, Paul. (forthcoming). Imperatives. In M. Aloni & P. Dekker (eds.) *Cambridge Handbook of Formal Semantics*. Cambridge University Press. http://www.semanticsarchive. net/Archive/jgzNDdhM/.

Roberts, Craige. (1996). Information structure in discourse: Towards an integrated formal theory of pragmatics. In *OSU Working Papers in Linguistics, Vol 49: Papers in Semantics*. Ohio State University. http://semanticsarchive.net/Archive/WYzOTRkO/.

Roberts, Craige. (2015). Conditional plans and imperatives: A semantics and pragmatics for imperative mood. In T. Brochhagen, F. Roelofsen & N. Theiler (eds.) *Proceedings of the 20th Amsterdam Colloquium*, 353–362. University of Amsterdam: Institute for Logic, Language, and Computation.

Rothschild, Daniel. (2012). Expressing credences. *Proceedings of the Aristotelian Society* CXII, Part 1:99–114. doi:10.1111/j.1467-9264.2012.00327.x.

Sadock, Jerrold M. & Arnold M. Zwicky. (1985). Speech act distinctions in syntax. In T. Shopen (ed.) *Language typology and syntactic description: Clause structure*. Cambridge: Cambridge University Press.

Schroeder, Mark. (2011). *Ought*, agents, and actions. *The Philosophical Review* 120: 1–41. doi:10.1215/00318108-2010-017.

Schwager, Magdalena. (2007). Conditionalized imperatives. In M. Gibson & J. Howell (eds.) *Proceedings of SALT 16*, 241–258. Ithaca: CLC Publications.

Searle, John R. (1975). Indirect speech acts. In P. Cole & J. Morgan (eds.) *Syntax and Semantics Volume 3: Speech Acts*, 59–82. New York: Academic Press.

Stalnaker, Robert. (2002). Common ground. *Linguistics and Philosophy* 25: 701–721. doi:10.1023/A:1020867916902.

Starr, William B. (forthcoming). A preference semantics for imperatives. *Semantics and Pragmatics*.

Swanson, Eric. (2006). Interactions with context. http://www-personal.umich.edu/~ericsw/ Swanson,%20Interactions%20with%20Context.pdf. Ph.D. Dissertation, MIT.

Swanson, Eric (forthcoming). The application of constraint semantics to the language of subjective uncertainty. *Journal of Philosophical Logic*. doi:10.1007/s10992-015-9367-5.

Vranas, Peter B. M. (2008). New foundations for imperative logic I: Logical connectives, consistency, and quantifiers. *Noûs* 42: 529–572.

Vranas, Peter B. M. (2010). In defense of imperative inference. *Journal of Philosophical Logic* 39: 59–71. doi:10.1007/s10992-009-9108-8.

Willer, Malte. (2012). A remark on iffy oughts. *Journal of Philosophy* 109: 449–461. doi:10.5840/jphil2012109719.

Willer, Malte. (2014). Dynamic thoughts on ifs and oughts. *Philosophers' Imprint* 14: 1–30.

Wilson, Deirdre & Dan Sperber. (1988). Mood and the analysis of non-declarative sentences. In J. Dancy, J. Moravcsik & C. Taylor (eds.) *Human agency: Language, duty and value*, 77–101. Stanford: Stanford University Press.

Yalcin, Seth. (2011). Nonfactualism about epistemic modality. In Andy Egan & Brian Weatherson (eds.) *Epistemic Modality*, 295–332. Oxford: Oxford University Press.

Yalcin, Seth. (2012a). Bayesian expressivism. *Proceedings of the Aristotelian Society* CXII, Part 2: 123–160. doi:10.1111/j.1467-9264.2012.00329.x.

Yalcin, Seth. (2012b). A counterexample to modus tollens. *Journal of Philosophical Logic* 41: 1001–1024. doi:10.1007/s10992-012-9228-4.

Yalcin, Seth. (2014). Semantics and metasemantics in the context of generative grammar. In A. Burgess & B. Sherman (eds.) *Metasemantics: New Essays on the Foundations of Meaning*, 17–54. Oxford University Press.

4

A Refinement and Defense of the Force/Content Distinction

Mitchell S. Green

4.1 Benchmarks and Concepts for an Adequate Theory

A familiar tool in the philosophical study of language for over a century has been the distinction between semantic content and illocutionary force: a distinction, roughly, between what is said (or at least communicated) by a speaker, and how she says (communicates) it.[1] Actions generally permit a distinction between what an agent does and the way in which she does that action. Some harms, for instance, are done inadvertently while others are done with malice, and one farewell might be made ruefully while another is done with relief. Yet among communicative acts, it is often epistemically, and sometimes even ethically significant to distinguish between what a speaker is committing herself to, and the way in which she is doing so. This allows us to determine whether that speaker is vindicated or not as more information comes to light, as well as to discern what would count as a disagreement with that speaker or a change of position on her part, and, if so, what kind of change.

In a number of well-known passages, Frege advocated adherence to this distinction between the force and content of an utterance. In 'The Thought: A Logical Inquiry' for instance, he writes:

> Consequently two things must be distinguished in an assertoric sentence: the content, which it has in common with the corresponding propositional question; and assertion. The former is the thought or at least contains the thought. So it is possible to express a thought without laying it down as true. The two things are so closely conjoined in an assertoric sentence that it is possible to overlook their separability. Consequently we distinguish:
>
> (1) the grasp of a thought—thinking.
> (2) the acknowledgment of the truth of a thought—the act of judgment.
> (3) the manifestation of this judgment—assertion.[2]

---

[1] An earlier draft of this paper was presented at the *New Work on Speech Acts* conference, Columbia University, September 2013. I am grateful to comments from the audience on that occasion, as well as to the editors of this volume for their astute suggestions for improvement of that draft.

[2] Frege 1976. By 'assertoric sentence' here, Frege means what would now be called an indicative sentence: 'Snow is white,' 'Grass is green,' etc. By a 'propositional question' Frege means a yes/no question, such as, 'Is snow white?' See Green 2002 for references and further discussion.

Given what he says in the text before the three items he wishes to distinguish, Frege would evidently add a fourth, namely:

(4)   the thing that is grasped in an act of thinking, acknowledged to be true in an act of judgment, and asserted to be true in a manifestation of that judgment—the thought.

In what follows we will use 'thought' and 'proposition' interchangeably. However, literature subsequent to Frege has adopted a generalized notion—content—that includes thoughts (propositions) but that also includes what is expressed by sentences of other grammatical moods. If, as we will suggest in Section 4.2, other grammatical moods do express things different from propositions, then there will be sentential contents that are not propositions, even if all propositions are contents.

Frege and those writing in his tradition invoke the force/content distinction to account for a range of phenomena, among the most prominent of which are perhaps the following:

1. *Predication and Assertion* It is possible for a thinker to express a thought, such as that cucumbers are fruits, without asserting it or otherwise committing herself to its truth. This observation is sometimes expressed as the admonition not to confuse predication with assertion. One can "apply" a property to an object, for instance in the course of supposing a thought for the sake of argument or asking whether that thought is true. In so doing, one need not also be judging or asserting that this thought is true, or otherwise committing oneself to its truth.[3]

2. *Agreement and Disagreement* One person might make a statement that another denies. In so doing, these two interlocutors seem to be expressing different attitudes toward one and the same thought. Likewise, it seems possible for one person to agree with another's remark, as well as for a single individual to change her position on an issue. She might, for instance, go from asserting that a certain suspect is guilty of the crime she is investigating, to putting forth that claim instead as a conjecture now that further evidence has come to light. Such phenomena as these seem to mandate holding that there is a common thought that two interlocutors may agree or disagree about, and about which a single thinker may change her position.

---

[3] In order to avoid confusion stemming from the well-known ing/ed ambiguity of the term 'thought', in what follows I use it to refer to what an individual thinks rather than her thinking of it. Also, on the current usage one can suppose a thought to be true either in one's private musings, or publicly, say by leading a class through a *reductio ad absurdum* argument. See Green 2000a for discussion of different facets of supposition. Also, in a recent sustained discussion of the force/content distinction, Hanks 2015 distinguishes between what he terms its *taxonomic* and *constitutive* versions. According to the former view, Hanks writes, ". . . there is a single kind of propositional content, with truth conditions, running through all the different kinds of attitudes and speech acts." (2015, p. 9) We shall see in a moment that a proponent of the force/content distinction does well to abjure this version of the distinction. In characterizing the constitutive version, Hanks writes "The constitutive version of the content-force distinction . . . is the idea that there is nothing essentially assertive about the propositional contents of assertions." (2015, p. 19) As we will see in Section 4.2, this formulation is ambiguous, and is plausible on one disambiguation and dubious on another.

3. *Cogent Inference* A single thought may in the course of a valid argument occur asserted at one point and occur without being asserted at another. In a typical application of *modus ponens*, for instance, (if P, then Q; P; therefore Q), P is asserted in the second premise but not in the first. This will not prevent the argument from being valid. Since the validity of an argument depends on the absence of equivocation, this means that the presence or absence of assertoric force need not make a difference to the thought that occurs at more than one point in that argument. As we will see below, force is an aspect of what is meant, and only in special cases an aspect of what is said.

Another dimension of cogency of inference requires attention to the force with which contents are put forth. Observe first of all that force is not in general deductively closed: if A asserts P, and asserts that if P, then Q, it does not follow that she has asserted Q. She is, however, committed to Q. It may, further, be important in some cases to keep track of the manner in which she is committed to Q. Had A asserted P, while *conjecturing* that if P then Q, she would still be committed to Q but in a different manner from the way in which she had been when she asserted that if P, then Q. For instance, after pointing out this commitment to Q, it would be inappropriate to challenge her with the question, "How do you know that Q?" Instead, an appropriate response would be to provide good reasons for doubting Q's truth. Let us call this phenomenon in virtue of which one illocution commits a speaker to another, *illocutionary commitment*.

The above three—Predication and Assertion, Agreement and Disagreement, and Cogent Inference (of which illocutionary commitment is a special case)—are phenomena that an adequate semantic and pragmatic theory of language and communication would seem to need to respect, either by accounting for them or explaining them away by showing how the appearance of their truth rests on a confusion. A well-known means of adopting the former strategy is with the help of a distinction between illocutionary force and semantic content. To develop a parsimonious but still adequately explanatory formulation of this distinction, I will need to say a bit about some concepts that are intimately connected to it.

4.1.1 Speaker meaning

In what follows I will distinguish between meaning as a property that words, and phrases built out of them have, and the way in which agents mean things in using words or, more generally, in their behavior. The latter notion—usually called speaker meaning—is often conceptualized, following Grice 1957, 1989, as an agent's doing something with an intention to produce a psychological effect on another by means of the other's recognition of the agent's intention. This intention is known as a reflexive communicative intention. However, as Davis 2003 argues, it is doubtful that reflexive communicative intentions, or even communicative intentions, are required for speaker meaning. An agent can speaker-mean something in the course of talking to a newborn baby or non-human animal; yet it would be unreasonable in such cases to expect that agent to intend to produce a psychological effect on their addressee by means of their recognition of agent's intention. In fact, we may even doubt that the speaker needs to intend to produce a psychological effect on their audience at all. So too I might think out loud, meaning what I say, without intending to produce an effect on anyone, including myself or any imaginary interlocutors.[4]

A more accurate conceptualization of speaker meaning preserves the overtness that it requires while jettisoning the further condition that an agent intend to produce a psychological effect on any audience. Accordingly, Green 2007, 2016a offers an alternative notion of speaker meaning whose core requirement is intending to make some aspect of one's psychological state manifest, while also intending that this very intention be manifest. (I make my psychological state manifest when I make it readily knowable, by virtue either of their perceptible or their inferential capacities, to appropriate others such as conspecifics.) However, intending to make an aspect of my psychological state manifest does not require intending that anyone become aware of it; instead I need only intend that it be there for the grasping by appropriate others. Further, an overt manifestation of my psychological state can take the form of an utterance, a gesture, or a willed facial expression. In those cases in which a speaker uses a sentence in the course of (speaker-) meaning something, it would seem natural to ask not just what she means (that there will be a storm tomorrow, say) but also how she means it: as a guess, as a conjecture, an assertion, or as something she insists or swears is the case. As we will see below, the notion of illocutionary force may be seen as a way of describing how agents mean what they do.

4.1.2 Acts of speech, speech acts, and expressive acts

An act of speech is simply an act of uttering a meaningful word, phrase or sentence; it is the same as what Austin 1962 called a locutionary act. One performs acts of speech while testing a microphone or rehearsing lines for a play. By contrast 'speech act' is a quasi-technical term referring to any act that can be performed by speaker meaning—that is, overtly manifesting—one's intention to perform that act (Green 2014). Promising, asserting, commanding, and excommunicating are all speech acts on this criterion; insulting, convincing, and screaming are not. One can perform an act of speech without performing a speech act. The converse is also true: among Japanese gangsters known as Yakuza, cutting off a finger in front of a superior is a way of apologizing for an infraction. A sufficiently stoic gangster can issue an apology in this manner without making a sound. Also, speech acts can be performed by saying that one is doing so, but need not be. One can assert that the window is open by saying, "I assert that the window is open." But one also can simply say, "The window is open,"

---

[4] It might be replied that speaker meaning is a quasi-technical notion that is a building block in a larger theory of communication. As such, while it may be granted that in the cases imagined in the text, the speaker means something, he is neither communicating nor intending to do so. As a result, the critic may point out, such a speaker does not mean anything in the quasi-technical sense of that term. I of course cannot prevent anyone who chooses to do so from stipulating a technical sense of a term. However, although I cannot argue for the claim here, I hold that my notion of speaker meaning as overt manifestation of a psychological state can do the explanatory work that the mooted quasi-technical notion can do, while also being closer to our commonsense usage of that notion. (Observe also that Grice's own writings over three decades strongly suggest a desire to develop a notion of speaker meaning that corresponds to one of our commonsense notions of meaning; otherwise he would not have revised that notion in light of counterexamples.)

and if one does so with the appropriate intentions and in the right context, one has still made an assertion.[5]

Another feature distinguishing speech acts from acts of speech is that the former may be retracted but the latter may not be. As Sbisà 2007 observes, I can take back an assertion, declaration, promise, or conjecture, but I cannot take back an act of speech. Of course, I cannot on Wednesday change the fact that on Tuesday I made a claim, promise, or threat. However, on Wednesday I can retract Tuesday's claim with the result that I am no longer at risk of being shown wrong, and no longer obliged to answer such challenges as, "How do you know?" This pattern recurs with other speech acts such as compliments, threats, warnings, questions, and objections. By contrast, with speech acts whose original felicitousness required uptake on the part of an addressee, subsequent retraction mandates that addressee's cooperation. I cannot retract a bet with the house without the house's cooperation, and I cannot take back a promise to Shaikha without her releasing me from the obligation that the promise incurred.

Between speech acts and acts of speech are expressive acts: acts and behaviors designed to manifest a speaker's psychological state. In some cases, such as inadvertent facial expressions of basic emotions, the designer in question is natural selection (Green 2016b). In other cases, some of which include language use, the designer in question may be cultural evolution. A speaker may acquire from her social milieu an intonational pattern such as that associated with upspeak without being aware of doing so, but nevertheless use it in a way that enables her to manifest an affiliative or non-aggressive sensibility. In other language-involving cases, the designer is an intelligent, sentient agent. But while an agent may intend with her act to manifest some aspect of her psychological state, her act need not be overt: expressive utterances are not thereby speaker-meanings. In a presupposition-generating construction such as a genitive—'Clarissa's cat'—for instance, Jordan willingly but non-overtly manifests his belief that Clarissa has at least one cat. Taking him to be reliable, Jordan's interlocutors may enter that proposition into their conversational common ground without his having made any assertion concerning the number of Clarissa's pets. Similarly, one who asserts P expresses the belief that P (and expresses *her* belief that P if she is also sincere) but need not thereby speaker mean that she believes P.[6]

4.1.3 Propositional and other contents

Discussions of the force/content distinction often assume that content is identical with propositional content, that is, that insofar as a speech act has any content at all, that

---

[5] Failure to keep in view a distinction between speech acts and acts of speech invites confusion. For instance, Langton 1993 begins as follows, "Pornography is speech. So the courts declared in judging it protected by the First Amendment. Pornography is a kind of act. So Catharine MacKinnon declared in arguing for laws against it. Put these together and we have: pornography is a kind of speech act." Although Langton's conclusion may be correct, the reasoning she uses to arrive at it is fallacious: the most that her premises establish is that pornography is an act of speech.

[6] Green 2007 offers an account of self-expression that is refined in Green 2011 and generalized in Green 2016b; Green 2017, building on Stalnaker 2015, develops in more detail a conception of sub-illocutionary acts that situates them relative to pragmatic presupposition as well as conversational dynamics.

content must be a proposition.[7] However, useful conceptions of content associated with each of the three major grammatical moods are available. The interrogative mood is associated with the speech act of asking a question. The imperatival mood is associated with the speech act of issuing a directive.[8] One strategy for the semantics of interrogatives is to construe them as expressing sets of propositions rather than a single proposition, where each element of the putative set is a complete answer to the question at issue (Bell 1975, Karttunen 1977, Pendlebury 1986). Thus the content expressed by, 'How many apples are in the bowl?' will be {<No apples are in the bowl>, <One apple is in the bowl>, ...} where the ellipsis will be filled by as many other propositions as it is reasonable to interpret the questioner as asking after. Call such a set an *Interrogative*. A complete answer to an Interrogative is an element of the set by which it is defined; a partial answer is a subset of that set containing more than one member, as in, 'Between two and four apples are in the bowl.' On the present conceptualization, just as we may distinguish between expressing and asserting a propositional content, we may also distinguish between expressing an Interrogative and asking a question. One expresses an Interrogative, but does not ask a question, in such an utterance as, 'John wonders how many apples are in the bowl.' A single utterance may indeed express two Interrogatives while asking nothing, as in, 'How many apples are in the bowl will depend on how many lunches have been served.'

Asking a question is no less substantial a conversational move than is making an assertion. One influential conceptualization of the latter treats it as *inter alia* a proposal to update conversational common ground (that set of propositions that are mutually accepted among interlocutors) with the content of that assertion (Stalnaker 2015). If the proposal is accepted among other interlocutors, the result will be a new set of propositions that constitute the updated common ground. (This set may be equally well expressed as a *context set*, namely that set of possible worlds compatible with the conjunction of all the accepted propositions.) Asking a question fits into this framework as well: one who asks a question in a conversation proposes that others join her in undertaking the task of answering it. If others agree, then interlocutors are to pool their information in aid of answering the question. Formally, the act of accepting a question partitions the context set into a set of sets: each set of sets will be a complete answer to the question that has been posed. (The set corresponding to the answer, 'There are four apples in the bowl,' will be a set of worlds in which the bowl in question contains four apples.) Discussion aimed at answering the question that now partitions our conversational common ground continues until that conversational project is achieved in full (by narrowing our context set into one of the partitions), in part (by mutual recognition that the best we can do is settle on a partial answer), or abandoned.

---

[7] Barker and Popa-Wyatt 2015 for instance write, "Central to modern semantics is Frege's distinction between force and sense. According to that distinction, the content of an illocutionary act – a self-standing utterance of a sentence S–can be divided into two components. One is the proposition P that S's linguistic meaning and context associates with it. The other is S's illocutionary force." See also Barker 2007, Searle 1965, Searle 1969, and Stenius 1967. Curiously, Frege himself seemed open to the possibility that non-indicative sentences express contents other than propositions. See for instance his 1948, p. 220.

[8] Recanati 2013 argues that Austin would likely have been open to the possibility of semantic contents other than propositional contents.

Imperatives play a role in this common-ground framework as well. For instance, construing agency from within a temporal framework, we may understand common ground not just as a set of worlds, but as a set of temporally extended worlds, that is, as histories. Two such histories might overlap until a certain time and then diverge. That divergence might represent an indeterministic event such as an instance of radioactive decay; alternatively it might represent an agent's choice.[9] A plan is then a function from such choice-points to histories; it selects a distinguished set of histories as "what is to be done." Accordingly, an imperative may be given as its semantic value such a function. (Adopting a plan does not itself narrow the context set: we may plan a course of action that we hope, but do not yet believe, we will be able to carry out.)

The foregoing are proposals for the semantics of interrogatives and imperatives. Other proposals are available for both types of content[10], and we need not decide here which of them is the strongest. What matters for present purposes is that propositions are not the only type of viable semantic content for non-indicative sentences, and thus, commitment to the force/content distinction does not mandate exclusive reliance on propositions beyond the realm of the indicative.

4.1.4 *"Objects" of attitudes and illocutions*

Proponents of a distinction between force and content are sometimes thought thereby to be committed to the claim that propositional attitudes and the speech acts expressing them place thinkers (speakers) in relation to propositions; this is sometimes also expressed as the thought that one to whom we ascribe a propositional attitude has a proposition as the object of her thought. Neither such commitment is mandatory, however. An empirically adequate theory of interpretation for an agent's words and actions might ascribe to that agent the belief that P. However, this by itself is insufficient to show that she stands in the belief relation to this proposition. The reason is as follows. A system of measurement for a group of physical objects is only accurate up to admissible transformations; beyond that, specifics of a particular system are artifactual. A person's weighing 180 pounds, for instance, is equivalent to his weighing 81.65 kilos. But a measurement system places that person in relation neither to the number 180 nor to the number 81.65. So too, considerations about the indeterminacy of translation suggest that if one system of attitudes and speech-act ascriptions is empirically adequate, then there will be at least one other distinct such system that is as well. The first system might ascribe to an agent the belief that P, while another does not do so but instead ascribes the belief that P'. The only fact either system of ascription captures is what is held in common between them as well as any other admissible transforms. But bearing the belief relation to P is not one of those preserved features; similarly for P'. Insofar as a force/content distinction employs devices of attitude and speech act ascription, then, this does not imply commitment to a view of agents as standing in relations to propositions or as having those propositions as objects of their thought. Instead, propositions are systems of abstracta that we use to rationalize

---

[9] Belnap, Perloff, and Xu 2001 provide detailed formal semantics underwriting such an approach.

[10] Portner 2004, drawing on Hausser 1980, construes imperatives as expressing properties. Kaufmann 2012 instead analyzes them as expressing modalized propositions, but which carry presuppositions of such a kind as to block their standard use as assertions.

certain forms of intelligent action, including language use. Paradigm cases of such application are adumbrated in Agreement and Disagreement, and Cogent Inference in Section 4.1: we use abstract systems of propositions to assess when two agents agree or disagree, when a single agent has changed her mind about an issue, and whether agents are reasoning cogently.[11]

4.1.5 Three kinds of speech act norms: liability, frankness, and fidelity

It is widely acknowledged that speech acts are subject to norms, and such norms are sometimes cast in terms of the notion of commitment. Yet commitment as it is adduced in theorizing about speech acts has multiple dimensions that it will be helpful to distinguish here. First of all, many speech acts once performed and not rescinded make the agent producing them liable to being either correct or mistaken depending on how things are. If I assert that cucumbers are fruits, this implies that I am correct or not, depending on whether they in fact are fruits. So too for predictions and retrodictions. We may express this norm governing speech acts as liability to being correct or incorrect, or *liability* for short. Commission of a speech act that is a member of what I elsewhere (Green 2013, 2016a) term the *assertive family* (which includes assertion proper, as well as conjectures and guesses among others), carries this liability. By contrast, some speech acts, such as supposing a content for the sake of argument, do not make one liable to being either correct or incorrect. If, for instance, I suppose P for *reductio*, it would betray a misunderstanding of my enterprise to respond, "No, you're mistaken, since P is not true."[12]

Another norm governing speech acts flows from the fact that some of them demand that their producer be in a certain psychological state. An assertion (proper) that P demands belief that P, and a promise to do Q mandates that the agent making the promise intend to do Q. Not all speech acts place such psychological demands on their producers: it is doubtful that one performing a speech act of appointing another to a certain post needs to be in any particular state of mind other than intending to do what she is doing. To follow Austin's terminology, if an agent produces a psychological-state demanding illocution, without being in that state, her act is an abuse rather than a misfire. (By contrast, in a misfire, one purports to perform a speech act but produces at most an act of speech: in saying, in all sincerity, "I bequeath the Taj Mahal to my niece Tatiana," I will bequeath nothing.) Accordingly, this *frankness* condition is different from liability, whose absence will cause a misfire in that an act of speech but no speech act will be performed.

Finally, particular speech acts are associated with conversational proprieties. *Fidelity* to one's assertion (proper) demands that one be prepared to back it up in response to a 'how do you know?' challenge. One making a guess or even a conjecture is not so obliged. Fidelity to one's question requires readiness to defend against challenges that might be raised to any presuppositions it may have, while fidelity to one's own advice requires being able to explain why the proposed course of action

---

[11] Green 1999 discusses the relation between attitude ascription and measurement in greater detail.

[12] Liability applies beyond the assertive family. Questions may be apt or not depending on whether the project of answering them furthers goals that we share, and imperatives are apt or not depending on whether conforming to them furthers our goals.

is reasonable for the addressee. Even when two speech acts share a content (one agent asserts that P while another conjectures that P), they may place their producers under different fidelity demands.

4.1.6 Force as an aspect of speaker meaning

An illocution's content underdetermines its force, and yet the force of an utterance is an aspect of what a speaker means in producing it. Whether an utterance is an assertion, conjecture, or wild guess will depend not just on the indicative sentence used in its performance, but also on the intentions with which that sentence is uttered. We observed above that speaker meaning is a matter of overtly signaling one's psychological state, and an intention to undertake a particular set of commitments is one such state. Thus if I utter, 'Cucumbers are fruits' with the overt intention to undertake the set of commitments appropriate to a conjecture, then I speaker-mean this proposition as a conjecture; and so on for other illocutionary forces.[13]

4.1.7 Illocutionary commitment redux

In support of a notion of commitment that tracks illocutionary force, we may first define the notion of illocutionary validity. Let S be an arbitrary speaker, and $<\Delta_1 A_1, \ldots, \Delta_n A_n, \Delta B>$ a sequence of force/content pairs; then:

$<\Delta_1 A_1, \ldots, \Delta_n A_n, \Delta_B>$ is illocutionarily valid iff speaker S is committed to each A_i under mode Δ_i, then S is committed to B under mode Δ.

This notion will piggyback on whatever is one's favored notion of validity at the semantic level. It also requires reference to a partial ordering of illocutionary forces in terms of strength. Assertion is, in this sense, stronger than a guess, and a command stronger than a suggestion. Illocutionary validity is closed only under the weakest force occurring in the inference. (This comports with our earlier observation that one who asserts P, and conjectures that if P, then Q, is committed to Q but only in a way appropriate to conjectures.) Vanderveken 1990 provides tableaux for various families of forces that help elucidate the sense in which one force may be stronger or weaker than another.

4.2 Force and Content Refined

Our question is whether the, or a, force/content distinction can be sustained, and that question may be further refined as the question whether the distinction earns its explanatory keep. It might for instance be that while there is a difference between force and content, it is not one that we need to invoke in order to account for linguistic phenomena falling within the purview of pragmatics or philosophy of language. After all, we might distinguish between the semantic content and the decibel level of an utterance, but also doubt that such a distinction will shed much light on issues of meaning, use, truth, reference, interpretation, and like notions. Earning its explanatory

---

[13] Green 2013, 2016a develops an account of members of the assertive family of speech acts (of which assertion, conjecture, presumption, and guesses are members) on which these speech acts differ from one another in terms of the various conversational proprieties that their production generates.

keep is not, however, the same thing as being self-evident. Although the force/content distinction is so familiar to many that it may appear a truth of reason, this may just be a case of familiarity breeding contentment. I will look only at the questions whether the distinction is the best available account of Predication and Assertion, Agreement and Disagreement, and Cogent Inference. One way of supporting a negative answer to these questions would be to show how we may eschew the force/content distinction, and account for the above benchmarks with an approach that is otherwise simple, coherent, consistent with other things we know, and explanatorily fecund.

A standard formulation of the force/content distinction may be found in Searle 1969, 1983, who uses the notation, F(P) where 'F' refers to an illocutionary force and 'P' to a propositional content.[14] Let us assume that not only are F and P distinct, but also that a particular value for either term does not determine the value of the other. Then the distinction as drawn by Searle is compatible with, and helps to account for, the above two benchmarks of Predication and Assertion, and Agreement and Disagreement. It also accounts for that part of Cogent Inference stating that the occurrence of a content with one illocutionary force at one point in an argument, and its recurrence at another with a different, or no force, need not undermine that argument's validity.[15] However, it implies that contents of speech acts are always propositional, whereas we have seen reason to find this assumption unduly restrictive. What is more, the formulation leaves the status of the 'F' component of a speech act unclear: it does not tell us whether the force component of a force/content pair is an aspect of what an agent speaker-means, nor whether the force component is, or can be, an aspect of what an agent says—if in fact she says anything in the course of her speech act.[16]

Concerning the first question, we have suggested that illocutionary force provides an answer to the question *how* an agent speaker-means the content that she does: as an assertion or conjecture, for propositional contents, a request or command for imperatival contents, and so forth. Concerning the second question, no doubt the force component of a speech act *need* not be part of what an speaker says: I may simply assert that P without saying that I am doing so. But *can* a force component

[14] Searle also allows that some of what he calls speech acts have no content, citing such examples as "Ouch!' and "Hooray!" According to the conceptualization of speech acts used in this paper, however, these would more likely be used to perform expressive acts than illocutionary acts. Less-common grammatical moods, such as the optative, may also be amenable to similar treatment: "If only I hadn't missed the bus!" may be a conventionalized means of expressing a rueful attitude toward one's having missed the bus.

[15] Searle's original formulation of speech-act theory did not address illocutionary commitment. However, his joint work with Vanderveken (Searle and Vanderveken 1985) and Vanderveken's later work (his 1990) does so without departing dramatically from any of the original tenets of speech-act theory.

[16] I treat what a speaker says as reasonably measured by what would be reported in indirect discourse. *Pace* Grice's idiosyncratic understanding of saying as a species of speaker meaning, one can say something without illocuting. Also, asking and suggesting are typically ways of saying; as a result, we report what a person said with such words as, "She asked him to shut the door," and "I told him not to be late." Also, tethering what is said to indirect discourse reports does not mandate as strict adherence to the speaker's words as is sometimes thought. When Shaikha assertively utters, "Joe kicked the bucket," meaning that Joe died, we may accurately report her as having said that Joe died. Similarly, when Shaikha assertively utters, "Joe was poor but honest," she may well have said the same thing as if she had assertively uttered the words, "Joe was poor and honest," the difference being that in the former, but not the latter, she expressed a conviction of a contrast or tension between honesty and poverty.

be part of what a speaker says? It is sometimes suggested that constructions such as 'I assert that . . .', and 'I promise to . . .' are force indicators—the first of assertoric force and the second of promissory force. When this is meant as the modest claim that such expressions help speakers to indicate what speech act they are performing, the point is not controversial. But more is sometimes meant.[17] In an examination of Austin's distinction between locutionary meaning and illocutionary force, Strawson 1973 contends that there are sentences whose very meaning requires that their utterance guarantees the performance of a speech act. He has in mind examples of "performative" sentences such as, 'I hereby promise to pay you $5 by next Tuesday.' Cohen 1964 had made a similar point, and in a like spirit Searle 1968 writes,

> . . . though the sentence "I am going to do it" can be seriously uttered with its literal meaning in any number of illocutionary acts, what about the sentence "I hereby promise that I am going to do it"? Its serious and literal utterance must be a promise.

Claims such as those of Strawson, Cohen, and Searle at the very least need more refinement before being made defensible. For a speaker might utter, 'I hereby promise to pay you $5 by next Tuesday,' using her words literally and seriously, without making any promise. For instance, she may utter that sentence in the antecedent of a conditional that she is asserting without making a promise. Likewise, she may seriously and literally utter that sentence unembedded but within the scope of a supposition and yet not make a promise. She might for example use the tools of natural deduction systems in order to flag the fact that this sentence is being put forth as a supposition, and in so doing indicate that she is not making any promise but rather aiming to determine what this sentence logically entails.[18]

A more formalist tradition inspired by Frege's practice in the *Begriffschrift,* and followed by Reichenbach, Hare, Stenius, and Dummett, imagines a logically purified notation distinct from any extant natural language, and containing expressions whose use guarantees that the sentences to which they are appended must be being put forth with a certain illocutionary force. The so-called assertion sign ('⊢') is a case in point: on the formalist tradition, to token '⊢p' in an appropriate notation is, at the very least, to assert p. This tradition provoked a challenge from Davidson 1979, who argued that no conventionally significant linguistic device could guarantee that what follows it is being used with a certain force. Call such a device a *strong illocutionary force indicating device (strong ifid)*: an expression any utterance of which guarantees that an associated content is being put forth with a certain force. Davidson's point is that we need only imagine a joker or actor using a putative strong ifid with no, or some other illocutionary force, to belie the putative force-indicator's indicating role. From this observation, Davidson drew the following moral:

---

[17] Adding to the difficulty of settling these issues is that 'force indicator' is used in a variety of ways. In some uses the term refers to any linguistic or paralinguistic entity that a hearer may use to determine a speech act's force: these will include a sentence's grammatical mood, a speaker's intonation, her gaze, and aspects of conversational context such as whether the speaker is responding to the request to make a promise, or instead just a prediction about her plans. Calling any or all of these items force indicators is a roundabout way of saying that we have means by which we indicate the illocutionary force of our speech acts.

[18] Green 2000a discusses the use of natural deduction techniques in everyday reasoning.

Autonomy of Linguistic Meaning: Once a bit of language has been imbued with meaning, it can then be used for any of a variety of extralinguistic purposes.

The Autonomy thesis implies that it can be no part of a word's, phrase's or sentence's meaning that it can only be used to commend, denigrate, or perform some other kind of speech act; it is also often taken to imply that no strong ifid can have semantic content. However, in my 1997 I proposed, and then further developed (see my 2000b), a middle ground between Davidson's and the formalist positions to which he was responding, arguing that the former's considerations are compatible with the possibility of sentences that can be used for any of a variety of extralinguistic acts, but such that if they are used in a speech act at all, there is at least one further illocutionary act that they must also be performing. Further, some natural languages may realize this possibility. Consider:

(1)   If, as is the case, snow is white, then grass is green.

Consistent with the Autonomy Thesis, the conditional in which the as-parenthetical is embedded may be used in an assertion, conjecture, or any of a variety of other speech acts. However, if the sentence is used in a speech act, then the speaker performing that act is also undertaking assertoric commitment to the proposition that snow is white. We may thus call constructions such as the as-parenthetical in (1) *weak ifids*: let "$\Delta\_\_$" be, syntactically, a function from sentences into sentences, chosen from a set of connectives each element of which is in the domain of a function IF, whose range comprises illocutionary forces. This allows us to speak of "the force associated with connective '$\Delta\_\_$'". Let f_Δ denote that force. Then we may say that "$\Delta\_\_$" is a *weak illocutionary force indicating* device (hereafter *weak ifid*) just in case for all illocutionary forces f' and sentences A, the inference

$$f' \ldots \Delta(A) \ldots$$
$$\text{---------------}$$
$$f_\Delta A$$

is illocutionarily valid.[19]

The existence of weak ifids is noteworthy because it not only suggests a qualification of the Autonomy Thesis, it also shows that a doctrine commonly adduced as part of the force/content distinction is not mandatory. That doctrine is:

---

[19] Potts 2002 provides a detailed analysis of as-parentheticals on which they are Prepositional Phrases and thus embed in larger syntactic structures as other PPs would be expected to do. His syntactic analysis is detailed, supported with cross-linguistic evidence, and overall compelling. However, Potts also contends that as-parentheticals (or their semantic values) make no contribution to the truth conditions of the sentences in which they occur, and further that they are devices of conventional implicature. Thus the difference between (1) and that same sentence stripped of its as-parenthetical is like the difference between 'A but B' and 'A and B'. However, while conventionally implicating expressions are not normally thought of as contributing to what is said, surely as-parentheticals do contribute to what is said. One who uses the following in a speech act, that is, says, *inter alia*, that she believes that snow is white:

(1') If, as I believe, snow is white, then grass is green.

This is why it is more accurate to place as-parentheticals in the category of weak ifids than that of conventional implicature.

Embedded Force Exclusion: Illocutionary force indicating devices do not embed within sentences, but instead always take widest scope.

(1) puts pressure on EFE by being an example in which an indicator of force occurs within the antecedent of a conditional.[20] But we may still maintain a force/content distinction while acknowledging cases such as (1) and eschewing EFE. To do so, we need only replace EFE with:

Illocutionary Tolerance of Force Indicators: If φ is either a part of speech or a sentence, and φ contains some indicator f of illocutionary force, then if φ occurs embedded in sentence S then φ does not constrain the variety of forces with which S (or its semantic value) may be put forth.

A refined force/content distinction will enable us to see that explicit performatives such as 'I promise to r', 'I assert that P', and the like, are merely sentences whose normal use is one in which a speaker is describing herself as performing a type of illocutionary act. Further, on the plausible assumption that in some cases, committing oneself to the truth of a proposition is a very good, though not infallible way of making that proposition true, we may see that what are sometimes called performative prefixes are not force-indicators at all but are perfectly banal verb phrases. They are thus also part of what an agent says, and help determine what she speaker-means when she uses one of them in a speech act. What is more, when an agent speaker-means that she asserts that P (perhaps by uttering the sentence, 'I assert that P' with the appropriate intentions), she not only expresses and undertakes commitment to the proposition that she asserts that P; she also undertakes assertoric commitment to the proposition P.

A refined force/content distinction also encourages clarity about what are sometimes referred to as forceless semantic contents. In discussing the distinction between force and content, Hanks characterizes it as committed to what he calls a constitutive version, writing, "The constitutive version of the content-force distinction . . . is the idea that there is nothing essentially assertive about the propositional contents of assertions." (2015, p. 19) This formulation is evidently unduly narrow, and would require generalization to apply across the range of speech acts. At the same time, and just restricted to the case of assertion, the formulation is also ambiguous between two readings:

---

[20] We could define the notion of force indicator adduced here as an expression such that if it is used in a speech act, then there is as at least one further commitment that the speaker is undertaking. For a more precise account of a *weak ifid*, see Green 2000b. Also, it is natural to resist the suggestion that an as-parenthetical such as the above genuinely embeds in the antecedent of a conditional: we immediately wish to reconstrue (1) as a conjunction. Brief reflection shows that taking the conjunction as having narrow scope ('If snow is white and I believe that snow is white, then grass is green') will not do. Instead taking it to have widest scope is more plausible. A reconstrual of a sentence's apparent grammatical structure should preserve its semantic and, if it has any, pragmatic properties as well. But taking (1) to have the logical form of a conjunction will provide no explanation of the fact that any use of it in a speech act will commit the speaker to the proposition that she believes that snow is white. By contrast, taking '. . . , as is the case,' as a weak ifid enables us both to preserve grammatical appearances and to account for (1)'s pragmatic properties. (I take these considerations about conjunctive readings of as-parentheticals to carry over to the suggestion that they should be read as entirely separate sentences. Heim and Kratzer 1998, p. 88, advocate a "two separate sentences" view of non-restrictive relative clauses that has a natural analogue for as-parentheticals.)

Const1.   All assertions contain propositional contents that are not essentially assertive.

Const2.   Some assertions contain propositional contents that are not essentially assertive.

Our refined force/content distinction implies Const2. However, it is not committed to Const1. The reason is that some assertoric speech acts contain propositional contents that are essentially assertive by virtue of containing weak ifids.

Just as a refined force/content distinction does well not to insist on an absolute bifurcation between those expressions that indicate force and those that contribute to what is said, so too, it does well to abjure other naïve characterizations of its significance. For one, just as it would be simplistic to assume that in judgment, first a thinker grasps a content, and then judges it to be true, false, probable, or improbable as the case may be; so too, it would be naïve to characterize the force/content distinction as requiring that a speaker first present a content for consideration and then manifest the nature of her commitment to it. This *may* happen, but in the more typical case we would expect little temporal distinction between content expression and force assignment.[21]

Similarly, we would not expect that content determination will occur independently of force assignment. Instead, it may happen that reference assignment, resolution of lexical or structural ambiguity, or other aspects of contextual determination of what is said will depend on whether we take the speaker to be making a command, a comment, or a criticism, and likewise depend on the kind of conversation in which she is engaging.[22]

Gathering these strands together, we can offer a refined force/content distinction that is more permissive than the one that is commonly invoked, but that is still up to the explanatory task for which the distinction was originally formulated:

1. The content dimension of the force/content distinction may be propositional, interrogative, or imperatival.
2. Force is an aspect of speaker meaning: an utterance's illocutionary force is always part of what its producer speaker-means.
3. Force is in some cases an aspect of what is said in the sense that a weak ifid may have conventional, verbalizable content; in other cases, force is no part of what is said.
4. Speech-act norms, often lumped in the category of commitment, divide into liability, frankness, and fidelity.
5. Not only contents, but also forces may stand in inferential relations to one another as codified by the notion of illocutionary validity.

---

[21] Hanks is thus criticizing a straw version of the force/content distinction in writing: "Predicating a property of an object does not require any sort of neutral, non-committal preliminary. Suppose Obama enters a room, sees Clinton sitting in a chair and judges that Clinton is sitting. There is no neutral act of entertainment that precedes this judgment, whether conscious or unconscious." (Hanks 2015, p. 21) A properly formulated force/content distinction will abjure any commitment to an interpretation of its core notions in terms of a temporal sequence.

[22] I develop point this point in Green 2017 in the course of offering a taxonomy of conversation-types.

4.3 Challenges to the Force/Content Distinction

In this section I consider some direct challenges to the force/content distinction. (In Section 4.4 I will consider challenges that are indirect in that they propose to account for our benchmark phenomena in a way that is more parsimonious than ours.) Some have contended that the arguments for the force/content distinction are inconclusive (Hanks 2007). This should immediately give us pause: the considerations above were not meant to be conclusive, but to support the force/content distinction by means of inference to the best explanation. So the question is not whether Predication and Assertion, Agreement and Disagreement, and Cogent Inference logically imply some version of the force/content distinction. The question is whether an approach that does not distinguish between force and content can do a better job either in accounting for these phenomena, or in showing one or more of them to be illusory. At the very least we would expect an alternative approach to be internally coherent, consistent with other established views, and no less simple than its rivals.

We will consider such an alternative in the next section. In the meantime it will be instructive to consider two direct challenges to the force/content distinction that accuse it of incoherence or commitment to a false conclusion. Making the incoherence charge, the first challenge focuses on the possibility, espoused by any reasonable version of the force/content distinction, of an agent entertaining a propositional content without asserting or judging it to be true. Following Hanks 2015, let us call the act of predicating a of F while prescinding from commitment to the question whether or not a is F, an act of *neutral predication*. Then, it might be contended, neutral predication is incoherent. For suppose that S performs an act of neutral predication that a is F, and suppose furthermore that a is not F. Then, we might reason as follows:

1. S's act of predication is false.
2. S's act of predication is incorrect.
3. S made a mistake.
4. S must have taken a position about whether a is F.
5. S's act of predication was not neutral.[23]

From the above line of reasoning one might conclude that no act of predication can be both truth-evaluable and neutral. The reasoning, however, is unsound. For the inference to (3) from (2) is fallacious. Let us grant that acts can have truth conditions, and that when an act of predication is false, that act is also incorrect. It does not follow that the agent performing that act has made any mistake. We have already seen why in our discussion of the applicability of the liability condition to members of the assertive family. For if S's act had been an assertion proper, a conjecture, an educated guess, or other member of the assertive family, her act would have been incorrect if P is false. However, we also saw that if S's act is a supposition for the sake of argument (such as occurs in a *reductio* argument), she would not have been liable to being either correct or incorrect depending on the truth of P. Evidence for this may be found in the fact

---

[23] Hanks gave this argument in his presentation to the *New Work on Speech Acts* conference, Columbia University, September 2013. He reproduces it in his 2015, p. 37.

that we do not accuse a person supposing P for the sake of *reductio*, of having made a mistake if P is false.

Hanks is aware of this point. In a later discussion in the same book in which the above argument occurs, he considers the case of suppositions for *reductio*, and has this to say:

> When the math teacher says, 'Suppose that 2 has a rational square root,' . . . she and her students can predicate the property of having a rational square root of the number 2, and they can draw inferences from this predication, without being held accountable for these acts of predication. If you suppose that a is F for the sake of an inference or argument you do not break any rules if a is not F, or if you do not believe or know or have reasons for a's being F.   (2015, p. 111)

Hanks also considers an objection to the above-displayed argument that denies that acts can have truth conditions. Such an objection will call into doubt that argument's first premise. However, Hanks sees that this argument may be reformulated with no such commitment:

1′. S inaccurately represented a as F.
2′. S made a mistake.
3′. S must have taken a position about whether a is F.
4′. S's act of predication was not neutral.

This argument does not presuppose that token acts can be truth evaluable, but its fallaciousness is still patent. The reason is that there is no reason to think that inaccurate representations bring it about that those who produce them are in error. We have already seen this in the case of *reductio* arguments. Similarly, imagine a cartoonist who draws a caricature that obviously distorts the physical features of a political candidate to achieve comic effect. Such an inaccurate representation would not put the cartoonist in error. (Consider the cartoonist's likely attitude to a critic who remarks, "Ma'am, you've made a mistake. The candidate's nose is nowhere near this long!") So too, even if we agree that the aforementioned math teacher inaccurately represents 2 as having a rational square root, this fact should give no succor whatever to the idea that she has made a mistake.

Hanks' own discussion, quoted above, of the math teacher, suggests that he himself acknowledges the possibility of neutral predication in spite of inveighing earlier in the same book against its coherence. Hanks seems to be sensitive to this, for he remarks (2015, p. 39) that the context in which the math teacher makes her supposition is not one of "pure predication." This suggests a distinction between pure and impure (or non-pure) predication, on the basis of which the reader would expect to see an explanation of how impure predications are not neutral predications. No such explanation is offered in Hanks 2015, and likewise one searches in vain for it in his other work such as Hanks, this volume. In the absence of any such explanation, we are free to continue to suggest that supposing a content for *reductio*, for instance, is a case of neutral predication, and thus that Hanks has failed to challenge this aspect of the force/content distinction.

Barker and Popa-Wyatt 2015 also attack the force/content distinction. In the course of this attack they assume (p. 9) that this distinction mandates a treatment of content as propositional. These authors aim to rebut a doctrine that they take to be implied by the force/content distinction. If they can rebut this doctrine, their hope is that this will in turn undermine the distinction. This doctrine they call:

T-C Embedding: if a sentence S is embedded in a compound sentence (... S ...), then the speech act performed with S is a *propositional act*: an act that involves uttering S with a propositional (true-false assessable) content and no other content.   (2015, p. 9)

Barker and Popa-Wyatt tell us that T-C Embedding follows from the force/content distinction together with, "... plausible background assumptions and the fact that forces don't seem to embed." (2015, p. 9). These authors nowhere specify what these other assumptions are. Note also that if we adhere to a distinction between speech acts and acts of speech as advocated above, we will not generally call the tokening of an embedded sentence a speech act. In addition, illocutionary forces are not words or phrases, and as a result talk of forces embedding is a category mistake.

We have, however, suggested a sense in which some kinds of force indicator may occur embedded within sentences. Moreover, both the original and the refined force/content distinction are neutral on the question how utterances of sentences help to produce the contents of speech acts. In some cases, an utterance of a sentence contributes that sentence's literal meaning, and no other content, to the speech act in which it occurs. In other cases, an utterance of a sentence might contribute that sentence's literal meaning together with something like a generalized conversational implicature to the speech act in which it occurs. ("If you've broken a finger, you'd best get yourself to the nearest emergency room to have it checked out!")[24] In yet other cases, an utterance of a sentence might contribute none of its literal content, but rather only the speaker-meaning that its utterance generates in the pertinent context of utterance. Misspeaking, misuses, and irony are cases of this kind. Barker and Popa-Wyatt focus on the case of irony, discussing one reading of:

(BPW) Max believes that George is a real genius.   (2015, p. 10)

On one reading, this ascribes to Max a dim view of George's intellect. This is pertinent to the force/content distinction, these authors hold, because they (a) take it to show that irony is a pragmatic rather than a semantic phenomenon, but (b) contend that BPW shows that in some sense, irony embeds.

Even if we revert to an unrefined force/content distinction and insist that all sentential content is propositional, Barker and Popa-Wyatt's objections to that distinction will miss their mark. The complement of the attitudinative in BPW, 'George is a real genius' is not being used in that sentence to contribute its literal meaning to that attitudinative. Instead, it is being used to contribute something like the negation of that literal meaning. That, however, does not imply that it is contributing something other than a content, or even a propositional content to BPW. Compare: in the sentence,

If you broke a finger, you'd better get yourself to a hospital,

the embedded sentence ("you broke a finger") is most naturally read as contributing its generalized conversational implicatum (that the finger in question was one of

---

[24] Green 1998 discusses cases of this kind.

your own rather than someone else's) to the antecedent of the conditional. This is perfectly consistent with T-C Embedding, which insists that an embedded sentence contributes only a propositional content to the matrix in which it embeds, but is silent on whether that content must be identical with or otherwise closely correspond to that sentence's literal meaning. Accordingly, both the original and the refined versions of the force/content distinction may accept T-C embedding as well as Barker and Popa-Wyatt's examples of "embedded irony." (The refined version of the force/content distinction would of course prefer that T-C Embedding be restricted to apply only to indicative sentences.) It follows that Barker's and Popa-Wyatt's attacks on the force/content distinction do not succeed.

Finally, one may worry that if the force/content distinction permits that conversational implicata embed (as in the case of generalized implicature as discussed above), then its rejection of T-C Embedding will come at too high a price. For will not allowing conversational implicata to embed within larger sentential contexts compromise compositionality? (Similar worries might arise for other cases in which sentences contribute something other than their literal content to the larger sentential contents in which they occur.) Doing so will not compromise compositionality so long as we distinguish between a stronger and a weaker formulation of that principle: the strong formulation says that the semantic value of a complex expression is a function of the semantic values of its parts together with their mode of composition. The weaker version of compositionality holds that the semantic value of a complex expression depends systematically on the semantic values of its parts together with any other contents that may be contributed in the course of the speech act in which they are used. The latter version of compositionality is sufficient to account for the core phenomenon for which compositionality is normally invoked to explain, namely our ability to comprehend a potentially unlimited stock of novel sentences. What is more, this latter version is compatible with the embedding of implicata. A refined force/content distinction accordingly need rely on no stronger doctrine than this.

4.4 Two Alternative Approaches

In this section, I consider two different attempts (by one author) to develop an alternative to the force/content distinction purporting to be explanatory of the relevant phenomena, internally coherent, and consistent with other established theories. As we know from Predication and Assertion, representations are not inherently commissive. I can represent myself as believing in miracles without committing myself to the claim that there are miracles, or that I believe in such things. (A drawing of me with a face full of awe as I observe the sea being parted, for instance, will do the trick.) And there would seem no reason that the particular kind of representation known as a proposition should be any different. But Hanks adopts a contrary approach. More precisely, he adopts two different positions, the first in Hanks 2007 and 2011, and the second, developed in response to criticisms of the position he advocates in those two articles,[25] in Hanks 2015. For ease of reference I will term these positions Phase I and Phase II.

---

[25] Reiland 2013, and Hom and Schwartz 2013 criticize Hanks' first position, as did I in a presentation of an earlier draft of the present paper at the *New Work on Speech Acts* conference in 2013. In response to my

Phase I

Hanks sees propositions as types of act, writing:

The proposition expressed by the sentence 'George is clever,' is...a type of action a speaker performs when she asserts that George is clever.   (2011, p. 11)

Next, Hanks conceptualizes assertive force in the following way: the assertion sign represents predication (which is an act of applying a property to an object), a word in bold represents a type of act of referring to an object, and an underlined word represents a type of act of expressing a property. A formula like the following, then,

⊢<**George**, <u>clever</u>>

represents a proposition, which for Hanks is a type of action in which, in this case, a subject refers to George, expresses the property of being clever, and predicates this property of George (2007, p. 153; 2011, p. 41). For Hanks, then, no propositions without predication.

What happens under embedding, or when an indicative sentence is uttered in an act of speech but no speech act, or when I put forth a sentence so that we may contemplate its consequences, say for the sake of *reductio*? Those of us inured to a force/content distinction will say that force will be absent in such cases, and that what is left is a bare propositional content. Hanks comes tantalizingly close to saying this when he introduces the notion of *force-cancellation*. As a first delineation of his notion of force-cancellation, Hanks tells us that cancellation is not retraction, which is what occurs in:

George is clever. No, wait, I take it back!

Hanks writes:

This is not the kind of cancellation involved when a sentence is uttered as the antecedent or consequent of a conditional . . . At no point in the utterance of a conditional does a speaker assert either the antecedent or consequent. The kind of cancellation involved in conditionals is semantic; it is a feature of the meaning of "if . . . then . . ." that it cancels the assertive force of the contents of indicative sentences embedded inside it.   (2007, p. 154)

One might have thought the most that can plausibly be said on this issue is that a speaker who asserts a conditional is not *thereby* asserting either its antecedent or its consequent. But this does not mean that she cannot be undertaking assertoric commitment to one or both of these: as we observed in Section 4.3, natural languages contain constructions permitting just this. Consider the following:

(2)   Either George is clever or, as is the case, Karla is foolish.

Here the speaker is *inter alia* undertaking assertoric commitment to the proposition that Karla is foolish in spite of the fact that the indicative sentence expressing that thought is embedded. But Hanks tells us that it is a feature of the meaning of "if . . . then . . ." that it cancels the assertive force of the sentences embedded inside of

presentation, Hanks acknowledged that my criticisms showed an error in his position. He does the same in response to Reiland, and to Hom and Schwartz in his 2015, p. 99, n. 3.

it. So in the parenthetical-containing conditional, the speaker both cancels assertoric force and, at the same time, undertakes assertoric commitment.

So, Hanks' position on how embedding constructions "cancel" assertoric force yields some odd results. Matters get worse. For we also need to get clear on how embedded indicative sentences possess the right sort of content to provide something for logical constants to operate on. What happens in such cases? Our refinement of the force/content distinction offered in Section 4.3 will tell us that in such cases the sentence expresses a forceless content for operators to operate on. But Hanks can't say that, on pain of reinstating the force/content distinction. Instead he writes:

> Finally, there are simple disjunctions, conjunctions, and conditionals. We can start with 'George is clever or Karla is foolish'. When a speaker assertively utters this sentence she neither asserts that George is clever nor that Karla is foolish, and *she neither predicates cleverness of George nor foolishness of Karla.*   (2011, p. 20; italics mine)

This should raise a concern about how for instance in a disjunction, 'or' can have anything like propositional contents to operate on. Let's look at disjunction as an illustration. Hanks represents an assertion that either George is clever or Carla is foolish as:

(3) $\vdash<<\sim\vdash<$**George**, <u>clever</u>$>, \sim\vdash<$ **Karla**, <u>foolish</u>$>>,$ OR$>$

The tilde is supposed to represent illocutionary cancellation. But (3) still involves a kind of assertion. The reason is that Hanks tells us that here the speaker predicates disjunction of the propositions that George is clever and Karla is foolish:

> This is the proposition expressed by 'George is clever or Karla is foolish'. The tildes in (3) are not negation signs. Rather, they indicate that the two internal predication operators in (3) have been cancelled, which means that in a token of (3) a speaker neither predicates cleverness of George nor foolishness of Karla. Along with OR, the two tildes are the semantic contribution of 'or' to (3). The outermost, uncancelled predication operator in (3) corresponds to the act of predication by which a subject predicates disjunction of the two propositions contained inside (3). The result is that a token of (3) is true if and only if George is clever or Karla is foolish. [Numbering of target sentence changed to fit the text]   (2011, p. 21)

The last claim of this quotation is made without any explicit definition of truth conditions for disjunctions or any other logical operators. As a result it does not follow from what came before it.

Let us ignore this lacuna however. More important, notice the reference in the penultimate sentence to "the two propositions contained in (3)." Hanks has gone to great lengths to abjure force-less propositions: he tells us that propositions are inherently illocutionary (2011, p. 13): the sentence 'George is clever' expresses a proposition containing an act of predication, which as we have seen requires a commitment to George's cleverness. Accordingly, there are no unasserted propositions. Thus, since the assertive force in the sentences 'George is clever,' and 'Karla is foolish' is canceled in (10), Hanks is committed to two claims:

(a) There are propositions contained inside (3).
(b) There are no propositions contained inside (3).

I will take a position's yielding an explicit contradiction to be a decisive strike against it.

Phase II

Might Phase II of Hanks' position fare any better? Acknowledging the error of his earlier position (2015, p. 99), Hanks shifts to a new position in his 2015 and his paper in this volume. In this phase, Hanks grants the possibility of predication occurring in unasserted contexts. For instance, he offers the example of an actor on stage making as if to assert that Russell is a philosopher (this volume, p. 137). Hanks tells us that the actor does predicate the property of being a philosopher of Russell. However, he continues, this act of predication is canceled, which for Hanks now means that the actor does not assert that Russell is a philosopher.

So far, so good: the actor predicates the property of being a philosopher of Russell, but does not assert that Russell is a philosopher; analogous patterns emerge for speakers who utter conditionals and who suppose contents for the sake of *reductio* arguments. All this is precisely what our refined version of the force/content distinction would endorse, and we should have no qualm about calling these cases of neutral predication. We might expect that Hanks would now explain why appearances are misleading, and that such predications are not neutral after all. However, in spite of strenuously denying the coherence of neutral predication (2015, pp. 35–6, 40, 60), Hanks also seems to grant that it can occur. In discussing unasserted occurrences of indicative sentences, Hanks writes:

A pure act of predication is an isolated act of predication in an ordinary context. No *pure* act can be both truth-evaluable and neutral, but that does not mean that the act cannot become neutral when it occurs in a wider, impure environment . . . [A]n act of predication, which is fully committal when it occurs in isolation, becomes non-committal when it occurs in the right sort of context.   (2015, p. 40)

Whether such acts of predication are pure or non-pure is beside the point. For here Hanks is conceding that some acts of predication are non-committal. In the absence of an explanation of how an act of predication's being non-committal does not entail that it is neutral, these remarks commit him to conceding the possibility of neutral predication. This is in spite of his frequent animadversions against this notion, such as:

I do not understand what it would be to attribute a property to an object while remaining completely neutral about whether the object has that property.   (2015, p. 36)

Fortunately, Hanks cannot be speaking the truth here, since he understands quite well how to carry out a *reductio* argument, for instance. What he has failed to appreciate is the significance of this understanding, which neutralizes his criticism of the force/content distinction.

Hanks' project was to develop an account of speech acts that eschews any commitment to a distinction between force and content. That project is, however, forced to choose between two horns of a dilemma, itself formed by two possible answers to the question, Do unasserted occurrences of indicative sentences involve predication?

Horn 1 (No):   Hanks might deny that indicative sentences occurring non-assertively (as pronounced by actors on stage, or in antecedents of conditionals, or as suppositions for *reductio* arguments) involve predication. However, Hanks is forced to acknowledge that such occurrences contain predication in order to explain how compositional processes work. Hence, Hanks' position both denies, and implies, that unasserted occurrences of indicative sentences involve predication.

Horn 2 (Yes):   Hanks might accept that indicative sentences occurring non-assertively do involve predication, but deny that such occurrences are cases of neutral predication. However, in spite of his frequent animadversions against the coherence of neutral predication, the above-quoted commitment to "non-committal predication" appears to be precisely an admission of this very phenomenon under a different guise. In the absence of an account of how the non-purity of unasserted occurrences of indicative sentences disqualifies them from neutrality, Hanks' position both implies, and denies, that these occurrences are neutral.

Regardless of the horn grasped, then, Hanks' position is impaled by a contradiction. By contrast, the refined force/content distinction offered here can answer the question (Do unasserted occurrences of indicative sentences involve predication?) with no danger of mutilation: to this question it offers a resounding Yes, while agreeing that such cases are also instances of neutral predication, *modulo* the qualification required by the phenomenon of weak ifids. Accordingly, while Hanks' challenge provides a welcome stress-test for the force/content distinction, the failure of that challenge to provide a coherent alternative suggests that this distinction continues in robust health and may be expected to be with us for many years to come.

References

Austin, J. L. (1962) *How To Do Things With Words*, 2nd Edition, edited by J. O. Urmson and M. Sbisá. Cambridge, MA: Harvard University Press.

Barker, S. (2003) 'Truth and Conventional Implicature,' *Mind* 112: 1–33.

Barker, S. (2007) 'Semantics without the Distinction between Sense and Force,' in S. Tsohatzidis (ed.) *John Searle's Philosophy of Language: Force, Meaning and Mind* (Cambridge: Cambridge University Press), 190–210.

Barker, S. and M. Popa-Wyatt (2015) 'Irony and the Dogma of Force and Sense,' *Analysis* 75: 9–16.

Bell, M. (1975) 'Questioning,' *The Philosophical Quarterly* 25: 193–212.

Belnap, N., M. Perloff, and M. Xu (2001) *Facing the Future: Agents and Choices in Our Indeterministic World* (Oxford: Oxford University Press).

Cohen, L. J. (1964) 'Do Illocutionary Forces Exist?' *The Philosophical Quarterly* 14: 118–37.

Davidson, D. (1979) 'Moods and Performances,' in *Inquiries into Truth and Interpretation* (Oxford: Clarendon), 109–23.

Davis, W. (2003) *Meaning, Expression and Thought* (Cambridge: Cambridge University Press).

Frege, G. (1948) 'Sense and Reference,' *The Philosophical Review* 57: 209–30.

Frege, G. (1976) 'The Thought: A Logical Inquiry,' in P. Strawson (ed.) *Philosophical Logic* (Oxford: Oxford University Press), 17–38.

Green, M. (1997) 'On the Autonomy of Linguistic Meaning,' *Mind* 106: 217–44.

Green, M. (1998) 'Direct Reference and Implicature,' *Philosophical Studies* 91: 61–90.

Green, M. (1999) 'Attitude Ascription's Affinity to Measurement,' *International Journal of Philosophical Studies* 7: 323–48.

Green, M. (2000a) 'The Status of Supposition,' *Noûs* 34: 376–99.

Green, M. (2000b) 'Illocutionary Force and Semantic Content,' *Linguistics and Philosophy* 23: 435–73.

Green, M. (2002) 'The Inferential Significance of Frege's Assertion Sign,' *Facta Philosophica* 4: 201–29.

Green, M. (2007) *Self-Expression* (Oxford: Oxford University Press).

Green, M. (2011) 'How to Express Yourself: Challenges, Refinements, and Elaborations on the Central Ideas of *Self-Expression*,' *Protosociology: Articles and Lectures on Contemporary Philosophy* (accessed at http://www.protosociology.de/on-philosophy.htm).

Green, M. (2013) 'Assertions,' in M. Sbisà and K. Turner (eds.) *Handbook of Pragmatics, Vol. II: Pragmatics of Speech Actions* (Berlin: de Gruyter-Mouton), 387–410.

Green, M. (2014) 'Speech Acts,' in E. Zalta (ed.) *Stanford Encyclopedia of Philosophy*. (The Metaphysics Research Lab, Center for the Study of Language and Information, Stanford University). Available online at https://plato.stanford.edu/archives/win2017/entries/speech-acts/

Green, M. (2016a) 'Assertion,' *Oxford Handbooks Online* (Oxford: Oxford University Press).

Green, M. (2016b) 'Expressing, Showing, and Representing,' in C. Abell and J. Smith (eds.) *The Expression of Emotion: Philosophical, Psychological, and Legal Perspectives* (Cambridge: Cambridge University Press), 25–45.

Green, M. (2017) 'Conversation and Common Ground,' *Philosophical Studies* 174: 1587–604.

Grice, H. P. (1957) 'Meaning,' *Philosophical Review* 66(3): 377–88.

Grice, H. P. (1989) *Studies in the Way of Words.* (Cambridge: Harvard University Press.)

Hanks, P. (2007) 'The Content-Force Distinction,' *Philosophical Studies* 134: 141–64.

Hanks, P. (2011) 'Structured Propositions as Types,' *Mind* 120: 11–52.

Hanks, P. (2015) *Propositional Content* (Oxford: Oxford University Press).

Hausser, R. (1980) 'Surface Compositionality and the Semantics of Mood,' in J. Searle, F. Keifer, and M. Bierwisch (eds.) *Speech Act Theory and Pragmatics* (Dordrecht: D. Reidel), 71–95.

Heim, I. and A. Kratzer (1998) *Semantics in Generative Grammar* (Oxford: Blackwell).

Hom, C., and J. Schwartz (2013) 'Unity and the Frege-Geach Problem,' *Philosophical Studies* 163: 15–24.

Karttunen, L. (1977) 'Syntax and Semantics of Questions,' *Linguistics & Philosophy* 1: 3–44.

Kaufmann, M. (2012) *Interpreting Imperatives* (Berlin: Springer).

Langton, R. (1993) 'Speech Acts and Unspeakable Acts,' *Philosophy and Public Affairs* 22: 293–330.

Pendlebury, M. (1986) 'Against the Power of Force: Remarks on the Meaning of Mood,' *Mind* 95: 361–72.

Portner, P. (2004) 'Semantics of Imperatives within a Theory of Clause Types,' SALT XIV (Ithaca: Cornell University), 235–52.

Potts, C. (2002) 'The Syntax and Semantics of As-Parentheticals,' *Natural Language and Linguistic Theory* 20: 623–89.

Recanati, F. (2013) 'Content, Mood, and Force,' *Philosophy Compass* 8: 622–32.

Reiland, I. (2013) 'Propositional Attitudes and Mental Acts,' *Thought* 1: 239–45.

Sbisà, M. (2007) 'How to Read Austin,' *Pragmatics* 17: 461–73.

Searle, J. (1965) 'What is a Speech Act?' in M. Black (ed.) *Philosophy in America* (London: Allen and Unwin), 221–39.

Searle, J. (1968) 'Austin on Locutionary and Illocutionary Acts,' *Philosophical Review* 77: 405–24.

Searle, J. (1969) *Speech Acts* (Cambridge: Cambridge University Press).

Searle, J. and D. Vanderveken (1985) *Foundations of Illocutionary Logic* (Cambridge: Cambridge University Press).

Searle, J. (1983) *Intentionality* (Cambridge: Cambridge University Press).

Stalnaker, R. (2015) *Context* (Oxford: Oxford University Press).

Stenius, E. (1967) 'Mood and Language-Game,' *Synthese* 17: 254–74.

Strawson, P. F. (1973) 'Austin and "Locutionary Meaning",' in I. Berlin (ed.) *Essays on Austin* (Oxford: Oxford University Press), 46–68.

Vanderveken, D. (1990) *Meaning and Speech Acts, Vol. I: Principles of Language Use* (Cambridge: Cambridge University Press).

5

Types of Speech Acts

Peter Hanks

5.1 Austin-Searle speech act theory

Let's start with some central and familiar elements of the prevailing theory of speech acts, as initiated by Austin (1975) and developed by Searle (1969, 1979). Perhaps the most basic element of the theory is the distinction between illocutionary force and propositional content. This is codified on page one of Searle's 'A Taxonomy of Illocutionary Acts' in the form of the '$F(p)$' schema, with 'F' for force and 'p' for propositional content (Searle 1979, ch.1). The idea is that every speech act can be factored into these two components, force and content, each of which can vary independently of the other. For example, an assertion that you will close the door and an order to you to close the door share the same propositional content (that you will close the door), but differ in illocutionary force. Conversely, an assertion that you will close the door and an assertion that you will open the door share the same illocutionary force (assertion), but differ in propositional content. With the illocutionary force/propositional content distinction in hand, the theory of speech acts is conceived of as the project of giving theoretical descriptions of the various kinds of illocutionary forces. As Searle puts it in the taxonomy paper, "the aim of this paper then is to classify the different types of F," (1979, 1).

These classifications are made along three primary lines: illocutionary point, direction of fit, and expressed psychological state. Illocutionary point captures the speaker's primary purpose in performing the speech act. The illocutionary point of an assertion is to commit the speaker to something's being the case.[1] The illocutionary point of an order is to attempt to get the hearer to do something. The illocutionary point of a promise is to commit the speaker to some future course of action.

Direction of fit is an abstract way of capturing differences in the satisfaction conditions of different kinds of speech acts. Assertions are satisfied when they are true, i.e. when they correctly describe the way things are. Assertions therefore have word-to-world direction of fit; an assertion has to match the world in order to be satisfied. Orders and promises, by contrast, require a change in the world, in the form

---

[1] This is how Searle puts it in (Searle 1979, 12). Elsewhere Searle writes that the point of an assertion is "to say how things are," (Searle and Vanderveken 1985, 87).

of an action by the hearer or speaker, in order to be satisfied. Orders and promises have world-to-word direction of fit.

The third dimension of classification is expressed psychological state. In making assertions speakers express beliefs, in giving orders they express desires, and in making promises they express intentions. A speech act's expressed psychological state is closely related to its sincerity conditions. A speech act is sincere if and only if the speaker actually possesses the psychological state that she expresses in the performance of that act.

Using these three dimensions of classification, along with differences in propositional content, Searle classifies speech acts into five broad categories: Assertives, Directives, Commissives, Expressives, and Declarations. I will use Searle's notation in giving this taxonomy:

Assertives: $\vdash \downarrow B\,(p)$

Examples: assert, state, predict, conclude, deduce, guess, hypothesize, suggest

'$\vdash$' stands for the illocutionary point of assertives, which is to commit the speaker to something's being the case. '$\downarrow$' stands for word-to-world direction of fit (words are above, the world is below). 'B' stands for belief, the expressed psychological state of assertives. '(p)' is a variable ranging over propositional contents. This indicates that there are no restrictions on the propositional contents of assertives.

Directives: $! \uparrow W\,(H$ does $A)$

Examples: order, command, request, ask, beg, plead, pray, entreat, invite, permit, advise

Special case: interrogatives

The illocutionary point of a directive (!) is to attempt to get the hearer to do something. The direction of fit for directives is world-to-word ($\uparrow$), and the expressed psychological state is desire, or want (W). The propositional contents of directives can only be to the effect that the hearer, H, will perform some future action, A. Note that interrogative speech acts are classified as a special case of directives. Like many other philosophers, Searle regards the act of asking a question as a request for an answer from the hearer.[2] (I'll argue below that this is a mistake.)

Commissives: $C \uparrow I\,(S$ does $A)$

Examples: promise, pledge, vow, swear, guarantee

'C' stands for the illocutionary point of commissives, which is to commit the speaker to a future course of action. Commissives have world-to-word direction of fit ($\uparrow$), and their expressed psychological state is intention (I). The propositional contents of commissives are always to the effect that the speaker, S, performs a future action, A.

Expressives: $E \oslash (P)\,(S/H+$ action/property$)$

Examples: thank, apologize, congratulate, condole, deplore, welcome

---

[2] Others include (Hare 1949), (Hintikka 1974), (Lewis 1969, 186), and (Schiffer 1972, 85).

The illocutionary point of an expressive, E, is to give voice to a psychological state about an action or property of the speaker or hearer. For example, if I thank you for opening the door, I express a state of gratitude about your act of opening the door. Expressives have no satisfaction conditions—they are not true or false or fulfilled or unfulfilled—and hence have no direction of fit (Ø). The expressed psychological states of expressives vary from one example to another, hence the variable '(p)'. The propositional contents of expressives always attribute an action or property to either the speaker or hearer.

> Declarations: $D \updownarrow Ø\,(p)$
>
> Examples: pronouncing two people man and wife, christening a ship, terminating someone's employment, adjourning a meeting, appointing someone chairman

Declarations are speech acts in which the speaker brings about a new state of affairs by declaring that that state of affairs is the case. For example, if I am your boss and I say, 'You're fired' then I make it the case that you are fired. Typically, declarations require a background institution or conventional practice, and the new states of affairs they bring into existence are within these institutions or practices. The illocutionary point of a declaration, D, is thus to bring about a new state of affairs by way of the successful performance of the declaration. According to Searle, declarations have both word-to-world and world-to-word direction of fit ($\updownarrow$). They are statements to the effect that things are thus-and-so (word-to-world), and at the same time attempts to make the world thus-and-so (world-to-word). Declarations lack sincerity conditions and consequently have no associated expressed psychological states (Ø). Finally, the propositional contents of declarations concern the new states of affairs that are brought into existence by their performance, hence the variable '(p)'.

The only speech acts left out of this taxonomy are those lacking propositional content, such as greetings ('Hello', 'So long') and exclamations ('Ouch', 'Damn'). Because they lack propositional contents these speech acts do not fit into the $F(p)$ schema. Otherwise, the taxonomy is meant to be exhaustive.

I have been belaboring all of this in order to set it up as a target. In the remainder of this paper I am going to argue that this approach to speech acts is all wrong, and not just in the details but in its fundamentals. The basic problem for Searle's theory of speech acts is that it is wedded to a conception of propositional content that is explanatorily empty and unsustainable. This conception has had a distorting influence on the classification of speech acts—in particular, it has led Searle to find propositional content in places where there isn't any. Replacing this conception of content with one that is more viable leads to a different view of the nature of speech acts and a different taxonomy.

5.2 The Fregean picture of propositional content

Let's now step back in order to get a clearer sense of the conception or picture of propositional content operating in the background of Austin-Searle speech act theory. This picture of content is largely due to Frege (in particular, Frege 1918a), although Russell is also a major influence. (Russell, however, abandoned the picture when he adopted his multiple-relation theory of judgment.[3] For that reason I prefer to leave Russell out of it and call it the Fregean picture of content.) It should be kept in mind, though, that nothing in the Fregean picture, as I will use the term, depends on or involves Fregean senses or modes of presentation. The picture operates at one remove from debates between Fregeans and Millians about the nature of the constituents of propositions. It is a framework in which those debates are conducted.

There are three major elements of the Fregean picture of content. The first is that propositions are regarded as the original or primary bearers of truth conditions. Other things that have truth conditions, such as beliefs, assertions, and declarative sentences, derive their truth conditions from propositions. An assertion that the door is closed, for example, is true iff the door is closed because this assertion has as its content the proposition that the door is closed, and this proposition is true iff the door is closed. The possession of these truth conditions by the proposition is primary; the assertion inherits its truth conditions from its propositional content. The same goes for non-truth-conditional speech acts. Orders and promises also derive their satisfaction conditions from their propositional contents, although in these cases the truth conditions of a proposition have to be converted into fulfillment conditions. If I order you to close the door my order is fulfilled iff you close the door. The order has these fulfillment conditions because its content is the proposition that you will close the door, and in giving the order I put this proposition forward with the force of an order. When that happens, the truth conditions of the proposition are converted into fulfillment conditions.

The claim that propositions are the *original* or *primary* bearers of truth conditions is thus explanatory in nature. It signals an explanatory order in which propositions are primary and speech acts are secondary. The nature of the explanation here is constitutive. Facts about the satisfaction conditions of speech acts are grounded in or (partly) constituted by facts about the truth conditions of propositions. To accept this element of the Fregean picture is to regard propositions as a source of truth conditions. That is their role in the theory— to serve as a repository of truth conditions, which we put to use in thought and speech. To explain why our thoughts and utterances have the satisfaction conditions that they have we must always look to the propositions that are deployed in their performance. This theory helps us understand how our thoughts and speech acts have satisfaction conditions only to the extent that we can understand how propositions have truth conditions.

The second major element of the Fregean picture is the distinction between content and force, crisply captured in Searle's $F(p)$ schema. In fact, the $F(p)$ schema combines two different ways of understanding the content–force distinction. The first, which I call the *taxonomic* version of the distinction, is the idea that there is a single kind of propositional content, which is truth conditional, and which is shared across all varieties of speech acts. On this form of the content–force distinction it is possible for an assertion and an order, for example, to share the same proposition as content. The contrasting view would be one on which the contents of assertions are different in kind from the contents of orders, where these differences consist at least in part in

---

[3] See (Hanks 2007) for the historical details.

differences in satisfaction conditions. On this view, an assertion that you will close the door and an order to you to close the door would not share the same truth-conditional proposition as content. Rather, the order would have a distinct type of entity as content, where this entity has fulfillment conditions instead of truth conditions. It is now standard in semantics to distinguish the contents of interrogative sentences, questions, from the contents of declaratives, and a similar view about imperative sentences is gaining currency.[4] Abandoning the taxonomic form of the content–force distinction involves making the same sorts of distinctions for speech acts.

The second form of the content–force distinction, the *constitutive* form, is the idea that propositional contents are entirely devoid of any elements of force. In particular, there are no assertoric elements in propositions. One way to put this is to say that in characterizing the nature of propositional contents we do not need to use any concepts of force, assertive or otherwise. Concepts of force characterize the actions that we perform with propositions. Propositions have their natures prior to and independently of these actions. This version of the content–force distinction goes to the heart of the conception of speech acts given to us by Austin-Searle speech act theory. To put it crudely, on this conception a speech act is something you do with a proposition.

The third major element of the Fregean picture is the view that any thought or speech act with propositional content can be factored into neutral and non-neutral components. In the case of mental acts or states, the neutral components are acts or states of *entertaining* a proposition. To perform a judgment, for example, is to entertain a proposition (neutral) while endorsing or accepting that proposition (non-neutral). To form a desire is to entertain a proposition (neutral) while wanting that proposition to be true (non-neutral). In general, to adopt a propositional attitude requires singling out or entertaining a proposition and taking a non-neutral attitude toward that proposition. These need not be conceived of as separate and freestanding mental acts, but rather as abstractions from the overall act of forming a judgment or desire, which we can distinguish as theorists. In the case of speech acts, the factoring idea is prefigured in a dark way by Austin's distinction between locutionary and illocutionary acts, which gets replaced and clarified in the form of Searle's distinction between propositional acts and illocutionary acts.[5] The thought is that every speech act can be factored into an act of *expressing a proposition* (neutral), while putting that proposition forward with a certain illocutionary force (non-neutral). As in the mental case, we do not have to view these as separate, individual acts but rather as theoretically distinguishable components of the overall act.

These three elements of the Fregean picture are all closely related, and it may be artificial to separate them out as distinct ideas. In fact, it is natural to see the second and third elements of the picture as reflexes of the first. Viewing propositions as the primary bearers of truth conditions involves regarding them as mind and language

---

[4] See (Groenendijk and Stokhof 1997) on interrogatives, and (Portner 2004) on imperatives. (Charlow 2014a) is a useful survey of approaches to imperatives. Charlow develops his own account of imperatives in (Charlow 2014b).

[5] See (Searle 1968) for his criticisms of Austin's concept of locutionary acts, and (Recanati 2013) for discussion and an attempt to rehabilitate Austinian locutionary acts.

independent entities that have their truth conditions prior to and independently of what people do when they are thinking or speaking. Propositions are already there, with their truth conditions, waiting for us to latch onto them and put them to use in thought and speech. This leads directly to the conception of speech acts given by the $F(p)$ schema and to the factoring idea captured by the concepts of entertainment and propositional acts. The three elements of the picture hang together in a coherent and elegant whole, which continues to exert considerable influence over philosophy of language and mind. The main difficulty for the picture, which Frege and Russell felt keenly, has only recently resurfaced.

5.3 The problem of the unity of the proposition

As I mentioned earlier, the Fregean picture of propositional content sheds light on how our thoughts and speech acts have satisfaction conditions only to the extent that we can understand how propositions themselves have truth conditions. This question—"How do propositions have truth conditions?"—goes to the heart of what is commonly known as the problem of the unity of the proposition. Given the explanatory structure of the Fregean picture, whatever answer we give cannot appeal to what people do when they are forming thoughts or performing speech acts. Propositions must have their truth conditions prior to those actions, and hence these acts are closed off from us in trying to explain how propositions are capable of being true or false. The natural reaction is to look to a proposition's internal components (if it has any) and their relations to one another to explain how it has truth conditions. This is why it makes sense to call this a "unity problem". The hope is that by understanding how the components of a proposition are bound together into a unified whole we will understand how the proposition represents the world as being a certain way and is truth-evaluable. The problem remains even if we give up the assumption that propositions are structured things with parts or constituents, although in that case the label "unity problem" looks inappropriate. It is still possible to ask how a simple, structureless entity is capable of representing things as being a certain way and having certain truth conditions.

Both Frege and Russell saw the problem clearly. Although they differed over the nature of the constituents, both held that propositions have constituents and structure and both felt the need to say something about how these constituents are unified together. Frege's solution bottoms out in a relation of saturation, whereby a saturated sense completes an unsaturated one (Frege 1918c, 390). This solves the problem only by positing an unexplained relation that has the power to generate contents with truth conditions. This is like introducing a primitive "propositional" relation, which has the ability to combine propositional constituents into unified, representational wholes. This is not a satisfying way of solving the unity problem. The question we are trying to answer is about how propositions are capable of representing the world and having truth conditions. It is altogether facile and unilluminating to be told that there is a primitive relation that does all the work.[6]

---

[6] See (Hanks 2015, ch.2) for more on Frege's account of propositional unity and the appeal to a primitive propositional relation.

Russell's solution is even worse. His 1903 theory assimilates propositions to states of affairs or facts in which objects are joined together by relations-that-relate (Russell 1903). This has the notorious consequence that there are no false propositions. If the objects are not related by the relevant relation then there's no fact available to serve as the proposition. Even if we put this problem aside, there are reasons to doubt the viability of Russell's solution. On Russell's view, the proposition that my computer is on my desk is the actual, concrete state of affairs consisting of my computer being on top of my desk. But that state of affairs does not have truth conditions. It makes no sense to say that this arrangement of objects is true (or false). Even allowing for non-existent false propositions, Russell's 1903 theory fails to identify entities that are capable of being true or false. Russell was sensitive to these problems, of course. It wasn't merely the problem of non-existent false propositions that led him to abandon propositions in favor of the multiple-relation theory of judgment. He was also concerned to reinstate a correspondence theory of truth, on which the bearers of truth and falsity are recognizably representational entities that may or may not correspond to how things are.[7]

A natural reaction to the difficulties faced by Frege and Russell is to reject the question with which they began. Perhaps there is no need to explain how propositions have truth conditions. Maybe this is just a brute, unexplainable, primitive fact about propositions. Perhaps propositions are, by nature, entities that are true or false, in which case it is a mistake to think that we need to give an account of how this is so.

This is a tempting thought. Accepting it, however, generates pressure to take on additional metaphysical commitments about the nature of propositions. In particular, it leads to the view that propositions are simple, unstructured entities that are the primitive and primary bearers of truth conditions. Presumably, if a proposition were composite, then we could use its constituents and their relations to one another to explain why it has its truth conditions. But on the present proposal there is no such explanation to be had. Furthermore, as Trenton Merricks has recently pointed out (Merricks 2015, 201–4), if propositions have constituents and are also primitive bearers of truth conditions then there would be an unexplained correlation between the constituents of a proposition and its truth conditions. Suppose the proposition that Russell is a philosopher has Russell and the property of being a philosopher as constituents. In addition, this proposition is true iff Russell is a philosopher, and primitively so. There is then a correlation between the constituents of the proposition, Russell and the property of being a philosopher, and the truth conditions of the proposition, Russell's possessing this property. But this correlation is coincidental and mysterious, since facts about the constituents of a proposition and its truth conditions are explanatorily independent. The fact that a proposition has its constituents cannot explain why it has its truth conditions, since by hypothesis there is no explanation for the latter. Conversely, the fact that a proposition has its truth conditions cannot explain why it has certain constituents, at least not in any robust sense of constituency. A robust sense of constituency would be one on which constituency is identified with something like set-membership or mereological part-hood—a relation on which

---

[7] See (Russell 1913, ch.5). I elaborate on these problems for Russell in (Hanks 2015, ch.2).

the proposition is literally composed out of and contains its constituents.[8] If that is how propositional constituency works then the explanation for why a proposition has its constituents wouldn't need to appeal to anything about the truth conditions of the proposition. All the explanatory work would be done by the compositional machinery that goes into constructing the proposition. Alternatively, we could take constituency in a non-robust sense, in which case to be a constituent of a proposition is nothing more than to figure in the right way in the truth conditions of the proposition (see McGlone 2012). That would use facts about the truth conditions of a proposition to explain why it has its constituents, but the proposition still wouldn't be composed out of these constituents in any literal sense. Once again, the most natural view to take here would be that propositions are simple and unstructured.

The lesson is that if we decline to answer the question about how propositions have truth conditions then there is considerable pressure to regard propositions as non-composite and metaphysically primitive. But one cannot stop there. If propositions lack constituents then entertaining a proposition cannot be understood as some kind of mental operation performed on its constituents. What would it be to entertain a simple, structure-less proposition? It looks as though we will also have to regard this as primitive. The same goes for the act of judging a proposition. Again, judgment cannot be construed as an operation performed on the constituents of a proposition, since propositions lack constituents. Nor can judgment be analyzed as an act of taking a proposition to be true, since to take a proposition to be true is just to judge it to be true. This would analyze judging that p in terms of judging that p is true, which sets off a vicious regress: to judge that p is to judge that p is true, which is judging that <that p is true>is true, which is judging that <<that p is true> is true>is true, and so on. So the act of judging a proposition will also have to be regarded as primitive.[9] Rejecting the need to explain how propositions have truth conditions leads to a creeping primitivism in which more and more has to be taken as brute and unexplainable. Here is where we end up: there are simple, metaphysically primitive entities that are the primary and primitive bearers of truth conditions. We latch onto these entities via a primitive relation of entertainment, and then judge them via a

---

[8] This distinction between robust and non-robust senses of propositional constituency is closely related to Jeff Speaks's distinction between "lightweight" and "heavyweight" senses of the claim that propositions are structured. See (King et al. 2014, 221–5).

[9] What about a functionalist analysis of entertainment and judgment, on which to entertain or judge that p is to be in possession of a mental state with a certain functional role? This is not an option for someone who accepts the Fregean picture of propositional content, with its commitment to the idea that propositions are the primary bearers of truth conditions. Part of what it means to say that propositions are the primary bearers of truth conditions is that beliefs and other propositional attitudes *derive* their representational features and truth conditions from propositions—truth conditions are *transmitted* from propositions to beliefs through the relations that believers bear to propositions. If that's right then any constitutive account of what it is to believe that p will have to make reference to a proposition, since without mentioning the proposition we won't be able to explain how a belief has the representational features and truth conditions that it has. On a functionalist account, however, we explain what it is to believe that p in terms of a mental state that bears causal connections to various sensory stimuli, other mental states, behavior, and so on. There's no mention here of the proposition that p. The picture offered by functionalism is not one on which a belief derives its truth conditions from a proposition, but rather one on which the representational features and truth conditions of a belief can be accounted for directly in terms of its functional role. See (Hanks 2017).

primitive act of judgment. The resulting judgments take on the truth conditions of the propositions that are entertained and judged. As a philosophical account of how we represent the world in thought this whole story seems empty, unsatisfying, and faintly bizarre.

Stepping back a bit, there is something dissatisfying about the very idea that propositions are the primary bearers of truth conditions. As we saw earlier, to view propositions in this way is to regard them as a source of representation and truth conditions for our thoughts and utterances. This goes counter to the intuitive thought that we are the source of representation, not some abstract entities in another dimension. Representation and truth conditions originate with us, in our acts of thinking and speaking about the world. We are producers of representations, not consumers of them. But making good on this intuitive thought leads to a very different view about propositions and a very different conception of the nature of speech acts.

5.4 The classificatory picture of propositional content

Instead of treating propositions as a source of truth conditions let's view them as classificatory entities, which we use for identifying, individuating, and classifying our mental and spoken actions. The primary bearers of truth and satisfaction conditions are the particular mental and spoken actions that people perform when they are thinking or speaking about the world. Propositions are devices for distinguishing and classifying these actions. More precisely, they are *types* of these actions, which derive their satisfaction conditions from their tokens. To give the propositional content of a speech act is, on this view, to classify that speech act under a type and thereby individuate it from other speech acts. This reverses the order of explanation of the Fregean picture. On the classificatory picture, token speech acts are the explanatorily basic bearers of satisfaction conditions. Propositions are abstractions from these actions that inherit their satisfaction conditions from their tokens.

This leads to a very different conception of the nature of speech acts. Consider a simple, atomic assertion, e.g. an assertion that Russell is a philosopher. On the Fregean picture, to perform this assertion is to put a proposition forward as true— but we've now moved beyond that. So what does the speaker do in asserting that Russell is a philosopher? She does three things. She *refers* to Russell, *expresses* the property of being a philosopher, and *predicates* this property of Russell. To predicate the property of Russell is to attribute or apply this property to Russell; it is to positively affirm that he has this property. Think of the act of predication as an act of sorting or categorizing. To predicate the property of being a philosopher of Russell is to sort Russell into a group with other philosophers.[10] Compare this with an act of *asking* whether Russell is a philosopher. In asking that question the speaker does not attribute

---

[10] The sorting metaphor also helps clarify what it is to express a property. Sorting an object into a group with other objects requires a rule or principle for sorting, where the rule determines whether any particular act of sorting is correct or incorrect. Suppose I'm sorting a pile of marbles into two groups, the green ones and the others. My rule for sorting is given by the property of being green, and an act of sorting an object into the green group is correct iff the object has this property. To express a property, then, is to give yourself a rule that determines whether your acts of predication with that property are correct or incorrect.

the property of being a philosopher to Russell. She doesn't sort Russell into the group of philosophers. Rather, she asks whether Russell belongs in this group. This is a different way of combining the property of being a philosopher with Russell. Unlike acts of predication, it does not make sense to say that this act of asking is true or false. Rather, an act of asking whether Russell is a philosopher is satisfied when it is *answered*. Whereas acts of predication have truth conditions, acts of asking have answerhood conditions.

To *order* Russell to be a philosopher is a third kind of act. In giving this order the speaker neither predicates nor asks whether Russell has the property of being a philosopher. Rather, she tries to bring it about that Russell this property. Let's call this *ordering*, or the imperative mode of combination. Acts of ordering have neither truth conditions nor answerhood conditions—they have *fulfillment* conditions.

By abstracting away from these token speech acts we can arrive at three different types, i.e. three different propositions:

1. ⊢ <**Russell**, PHILOSOPHER>
2. ? <**Russell**, PHILOSOPHER>
3. ! <**Russell**, PHILOSOPHER>

(1) stands for a type of act in which someone refers to Russell (**Russell**), expresses the property of being a philosopher (PHILOSOPHER), and predicates this property of Russell (⊢). Read the notation here as a description of a complex type, which is composed of a type of reference act, **Russell**, a type of act of property expression, PHILOSOPHER, and predication, ⊢. (Note that I've redeployed the single turnstile to stand for the act of predication. This is not how Searle uses it in his taxonomy.) Token acts of this type are particular assertions that Russell is a philosopher. These tokens are the primary bearers of truth conditions; the type (1) gets its truth conditions from these tokens. Similarly, (2) represents a type of act of referring to Russell, expressing the property of being a philosopher, and asking whether Russell has this property. Tokens of this type are particular cases in which someone asks whether Russell is a philosopher. Finally, (3) is a type of act like (1) and (2) except that it involves ordering Russell to have the property of being a philosopher. Tokens of this type are particular orders or commands to Russell to be a philosopher, which are fulfilled iff Russell obeys and is a philosopher. (The tokens of (3) are in fact more diverse than this and include, among other things, promises by Russell to be a philosopher. More on this below.)

This approach to propositional content and its attendant conception of speech acts abandons all three features of the Fregean picture. Propositions are not the primary bearers of truth conditions, nor do they serve as a source of truth conditions. Their role in the theory is classificatory; they are types that we use for making distinctions between speech acts. Furthermore, this approach gives up the content–force distinction, in both its taxonomic and constitutive forms. There is no single kind of propositional content running through all the varieties of speech acts. Rather, there are three kinds of contents, each with its own style of satisfaction conditions, which are the contents of speech acts with these respective satisfaction conditions. Furthermore, each kind of content has an element of force built into it, in the form of ⊢, ?, or !. In characterizing these different types we have to mention these three kinds of combinatory acts, and the concepts of these combinatory acts are concepts of force.

This leads to an entirely different understanding of the concept of force than the one given to us by Austin-Searle speech act theory. On that theory, the concept of an illocutionary force is the concept of something you do with a proposition. On the present classificatory alternative, at least in simple atomic cases, concepts of force are concepts of things you do with an object and property. Finally, this approach abandons the notions of entertainment and propositional acts. There is no factoring of mental states and speech acts into neutral and non-neutral components. To perform a judgment or assertion, on this view, is to predicate a property of an object. We cannot isolate within these acts any neutral core of entertaining or expressing a proposition.

Unlike the Fregean picture of content, which provides a single, all-purpose kind of proposition, the classificatory conception makes a three-way distinction between predicative, interrogative, and imperative propositions. This three-way distinction lines up with the three-way distinction in language between declarative, interrogative, and imperative sentences. This three-way distinction in sentences is, as it turns out, a linguistic universal (König and Siemund 2007).[11]

The three-way distinction in contents also lines up with a three-way distinction between embedded clauses. English has that-clauses, e.g. 'Frege said that Russell is a philosopher', whether and wh-clauses, e.g. 'Frege asked whether Russell is a philosopher', and non-finite clauses, e.g. 'Frege told Russell to be a philosopher'. In English, non-finite clauses are used to report not just orders and commands, but entreaties, promises, desires and intentions:

Frege told/ordered/commanded Russell to be a philosopher.
Frege begged Russell to be a philosopher.
Frege wants Russell to be a philosopher.
Russell promised to be a philosopher.
Russell intends to be a philosopher.

All of the speech acts and mental states listed here have fulfillment conditions with world-to-word or world-to-mind direction of fit. This is a unified category of acts and states, all of which have what I am calling imperative propositional content. The terms I used to characterize this kind of content, e.g. 'ordering' and 'imperative mode of combination', are thus misleading—although I am at a loss for coming up with something better. (A neologism might be called for, but I prefer to be suggestive, if potentially misleading.) The type of act of ordering, symbolized by '!', has to be understood at a high enough level of generality to cover not just orders and commands, but all the other acts and states on this list. To *order* an object to have a property is thus to perform an act that can be fulfilled or unfulfilled and which has world-to-word/mind direction of fit. 'Ordering' is, I admit, a misnomer for this kind of act.

---

[11] That is, every language has *at least* these three kinds of sentences, declarative, interrogative, and imperative. Many languages, such as English, have more, e.g. the optative mood, as in 'Would that Russell were a philosopher'. On the classificatory approach the contents of optatives are grouped together with imperatives, since they have fulfillment conditions and world-to-word direction of fit.

In fact all three kinds of combinatorial acts, predication, asking, and ordering, should be understood at this high level of generality. The type of act of predicating a property of an object admits of many different sub-types corresponding to the various species of assertion. Acts of predication can be statements, predictions, conclusions, deductions, guesses, explanations, confessions, warnings, conjectures, hypotheses, suggestions, etc. The type of act of asking whether an object has a property can be pointed, rhetorical, an examination question, mention-all or mention-some, open or confirmation.[12] The three kinds of propositional contents are coarsely grained types that serve to make broad distinctions between three kinds of speech acts, where these broad distinctions are keyed to things like variety of satisfaction conditions and sentential mood. Fine-grained distinctions between types of speech acts show up as finely grained distinctions within these three broad types. For example, a request to Russell to be a philosopher and a command to Russell to be a philosopher fall under distinct sub-types of the more coarsely grained imperative type, !<**Russell**, PHILOSOPHER>. We can represent these sub-types as follows:

4.   a. !$_{request}$ <**Russell**, PHILOSOPHER>
     b. !$_{command}$ <**Russell**, PHILOSOPHER>

The difference between these types is a difference in sub-types of !, one corresponding to acts of requesting and another to acts of commanding. I see no reason not to call these more finely grained types propositions. Insofar as the request and order fall under the coarsely grained type ! <**Russell**, PHILOSOPHER> they share a propositional content. Insofar as they fall under the distinct sub-types (4a) and (4b) they have different propositional contents. Remember that on this approach propositions play a classificatory role. Their job is to help us identify and individuate our mental states and speech acts. The identification of propositions with types allows us to make classificatory distinctions at many levels of fineness of grain. This captures another difference between the classificatory picture and the Fregean picture. On the latter, for any pair of speech acts there will be a single, univocal verdict about whether they share a propositional content. On the classificatory picture, the issue of whether two speech acts have the same propositional content will be informed by our classificatory interests and purposes. In some cases it will be useful or productive to classify a request and a command under the same propositional content and in others not.

Like the three-way distinction between satisfaction conditions (truth, answerhood, and fulfillment) there is also a three-way distinction between directions of fit, although saying this requires bringing to light a heretofore unrecognized third direction of fit. Predicative propositions have word-to-world direction of fit. Imperative propositions have world-to-word direction of fit. What about interrogative

---

[12] In a mention-all question, e.g. 'Who is coming to dinner?', a speaker is looking for a complete list of all the things that satisfy a certain predicate. By contrast, in a mention-some question, e.g. 'Where can I buy an Italian newspaper?', a speaker is only looking for some of the things that satisfy the predicate. See (Groenendijk and Stokhof 1997, 1111). The distinction between open and confirmation questions is due to (Fiengo 2007). In an open question a speaker is genuinely ignorant about the answer to the question and is seeking new information. In a confirmation question, e.g. I see you enter the room soaking wet and ask, 'Is it raining?', the speaker is seeking confirmation for something she already believes (Fiengo 2007, 11).

propositions? These have what I call *word-to-word* direction of fit (more generally, *representation-to-representation* direction of fit). An interrogative speech act is satisfied when it is answered, and to answer a question you have to make an assertion. The words in an interrogative speech act are thus satisfied by more words.[13] This draws out why it is a mistake to classify interrogative speech acts as a variety of directive, i.e. as requests for an answer from the hearer. For a request to be satisfied, the hearer has to perform the required action. If I ask you to open the door and someone else opens the door then I got what I wanted but my request was not fulfilled. By contrast, if I ask you whether the door is open and someone else says 'yes', then my question was answered even though you didn't answer it. Requests can be satisfied only by the person to whom the request is given. Questions aren't like that. The answer to a question can come from anywhere, even if the question is addressed to a specific person.

Summing this up, on the classificatory picture of propositional content we have three different kinds of propositions, which correspond to three-way distinctions in satisfaction conditions, direction of fit, sentence mood, and embedded clauses:

Type	Satisfaction conditions	Direction of fit	Sentence mood	Embedded clauses
⊢	truth conditions	word-to-world	declarative	that-clauses
?	answerhood conditions	word-to-world	interrogative	whether and wh-clauses
!	fulfillment conditions	world-to-word	imperative	non-finite clauses

In the last part of this paper I am going to use this approach to content to give a new taxonomy of speech acts. First, however, I need to remove the main obstacle in its way.

5.5 Cancellation

Accepting the classificatory conception of propositional content as I've articulated it here requires giving up the content–force distinction in both of its forms.[14] In particular, it requires giving up the constitutive form of this distinction. On the classificatory account, propositions are constitutively characterized by elements of force. The proposition that Russell is a philosopher is a type of act of predicating the property of being a philosopher of Russell, where the kind of predication involved is inherently assertoric in nature.

This runs headlong into Frege's forceful argument for keeping assertion out of propositional content (see Frege 1918b and Geach 1965). Frege's argument is based on the fact that in many practical and linguistic contexts it is possible to use a sentence,

---

[13] See (Hanks 2015, §9.2) for a semi-formal account of the relationship between an interrogative speech act and its answers.

[14] As we saw earlier (note 4), the taxonomic version of the distinction has largely been abandoned in semantics. The constitutive form of the distinction is still alive and well among philosophers and semanticists, although (Barker 2004) is an exception.

without any change in meaning or content, without asserting the content of that sentence. This occurs when actors use sentences on stage, or when poets write lines in poetry, or when someone utters a sentence inside a conditional or disjunction. In all of these cases speakers uses sentences with their normal meanings without in any way committing themselves to the propositional contents of those sentences. How could that be possible if these contents were inherently assertoric? Frege concluded that propositions must be devoid of any judgmental or assertoric components. This line of thought is central to the constitutive version of the content–force distinction and to the wider Fregean picture of propositional content in which it is embedded.

Here is a different way of thinking about it. Let's focus on the actor. When a person utters a declarative sentence as part of a play she is in a special sort of context in which performing an act of predication does not have its usual requirements or consequences. The actor says 'Russell is a philosopher' and predicates being a philosopher of Russell, but the actor need not believe this, nor is she committed to its truth. In other words, the actor performs an act of predication in a context in which that act does not have the status of an assertion. Call this sort of context a *cancellation* context, and an act of predication performed within it an act of *cancelled predication*. The reason that the actor's utterances are not assertions, then, is that they take place in a cancellation context. Similarly, when you utter a sentence inside a conditional, your use of 'if' creates a cancellation context for the acts of predication you perform with the antecedent and consequent.[15] So you do perform acts of predication with these embedded sentences, but these acts of predication are cancelled.[16] That's why your utterances of the antecedent and consequent are not assertions. It's not that there is *less* going on when you utter a sentence inside a conditional, e.g. the expression of a proposition without assertion. Rather, there is *more* going on. You have performed an act of predication in a special sort of context generated by your use of 'if', and in that kind of context acts of predication do not count as assertions.

There are reasons for thinking that cancellation does a better job of accounting for these cases than the Fregean approach. On Frege's view, the reason the actor's utterances are not assertions is that they lack assertoric force—the actor is not putting propositions forward as true:

When playing his part the actor is not asserting anything; nor is he lying, even if he says something of whose falsehood he is convinced. In poetry we have the case of thoughts being expressed without being actually put forward as true, in spite of the assertoric form of the sentence.   (Frege 1918a, 330)

[15] I think this is part of the meaning of the word 'if' (or, at least, some kinds of English conditionals). This is an instance of a general semantic distinction between sentence-embedding expressions. Sentence-embedding expressions come in two varieties: those that create cancellation contexts and those that do not. Examples of the former include 'or', 'not', and 'possibly', examples of the latter include 'and', 'true', and 'necessarily'. See (Hanks 2015, ch.4; 2016) for discussion.

[16] In a discussion of cancellation and disjunction I once wrote that in an utterance of 'George is clever or Karla is foolish', "a speaker neither predicates cleverness of George nor foolishness of Karla," (Hanks 2011, 21). That was a mistake. I did not understand my own concept of cancellation when I wrote that paper. The speaker *does* perform these acts of predication—it's just that these acts do not count as assertions. Green (this volume) argues that my account of cancellation in (Hanks 2011) is inconsistent, and he is right to do so.

If this were right then the actor's utterances would count as assertions if the actor were to supply the missing assertoric element. So, suppose the actor intends to put her utterances forward as true. Give her whatever intentions or beliefs or mental states you like. The problem is that nothing will suffice for turning her utterances into assertions. As long as she is acting her role in the play nothing she says counts as her own assertion. The only way for the actor to make assertions for herself is to leave the play—to get herself out of the fictional context of the play. This provides a strong indication that it is the special context of the play, and not any missing intentions or actions on the part of the actor, which explains why the actor's utterances are not assertions. The cancellation context generated by the play makes it impossible for her to perform assertions for herself. Something similar can be said about 'if', although here the situation is more complex because of the enormous complications surrounding conditionals in English.

I find the following analogy to be helpful in thinking about cancellation contexts and cancelled predication. In football (the American kind), when the defense commits a penalty the referees allow the play to continue, which typically results in a free play for the offense. Suppose this happens, e.g. a defensive player commits a holding penalty. Suppose also that after the penalty a defensive player does something good for the defense, e.g. tackles the opposing quarterback in the endzone. Normally this would count as a safety and the defense would get two points. However, because of the penalty, the play is called back and run over again. The defense has not scored a safety and does not get two points. Notice, though, that in this scenario the defense did exactly the same sort of thing they would normally do to score a safety. A defensive player actually tackled the quarterback in the endzone. But because of the penalty the act of tackling the quarterback does not count as a safety. This act of tackling the quarterback does not have the status of a safety within the game.

We have something similar in our language game. Predication is to tackling the quarterback as assertion is to scoring a safety. In an act of cancelled predication a speaker does exactly what she normally does when she performs an act of predication. Absent the cancellation context this act would count as an assertion with all of its usual requirements and commitments. But because the act of predication is performed on stage, or as part of a poem, or after the use of 'if', or inside a disjunction, this act of predication does not count as an assertion.[17] Acts of predication are inherently assertoric in the sense that to perform a stand-alone act of predication in a normal context is to perform an assertion. The fact that there are embedded acts of predication that are not assertions, or acts of predication in special environments that are not acts of predication, just shows that the assertoric character of predication can be overridden by the use of certain words or in special contexts.

---

[17] If the acts of predication found in antecedents and consequents and disjuncts are cancelled and non-assertoric then what accounts for their unity, and how do we still have truth-evaluable inputs for conditionals and disjunctions? (Jespersen 2012), (Reiland 2013), and (Hom and Schwartz 2013) all press these questions. I don't have the space to answer them here, but see the account of target-shifting in (Hanks 2015, ch.4 and Hanks 2016).

Frege's argument for the constitutive form of the content–force distinction is therefore not compelling.[18] The concept of cancellation provides us with a better way of understanding why we do not assert the antecedents or consequents of conditionals, which is consistent with acknowledging an assertoric element in the contents of declarative sentences. This removes, I think, the main barrier in the way of the classificatory conception of content.

5.6 A new taxonomy

The first major distinction in the taxonomy is between speech acts that have propositional contents and those that don't. On the non-propositional side we have acts like greetings ('Hello') and exclamations ('Ouch'). On the propositional side we have a three-way distinction between speech acts with assertive, interrogative, and imperative content.

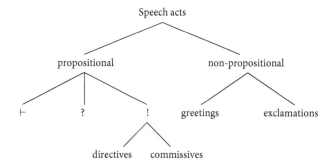

This is incomplete, since we still need to find places for Searle's categories of expressives and declaration. But before doing that I would like to highlight two aspects of the taxonomy as it currently stands. First, interrogatives are treated as a separate category all to themselves, not as a special case of directives. This reflects the fact that interrogatives have their own distinctive kind of satisfaction conditions and direction of fit. Second, Searle's categories of directives and commissives show up as sub-types of the wider category of speech acts with imperative content. Remember that the term 'imperative content' is a misnomer. The imperative kind of content has to be understood at a level of generality high enough to cover any speech acts with fulfillment conditions and world-to-word direction of fit. Both orders and promises fall into this category. Searle's taxonomy, by contrast, treats directives and commissives as two independent taxonomic categories, despite the fact that they have the same direction of fit. Searle was unhappy with this aspect of his taxonomy. As he put it, he could not avoid the "inelegant solution of two separate categories with the same direction of fit," (Searle 1979, 15).

---

[18] That said, I don't think there is anything *incoherent* about Frege's content–force distinction. Green (this volume) takes an argument I have given for the incoherence of Soames's concept of predication to be a general argument for the incoherence of the content–force distinction. I never intended to give such a general argument. See (Soames 2010; King et al. 2014) for Soames's account of predication, and (Hanks 2015, ch.1) for the argument against it that Green criticizes.

Where do Searle's categories of expressives and declarations fit in? They belong on the *non*-propositional side of the taxonomy, alongside greetings and exclamations. It is a mistake to think that expressives and declarations have propositional content. This is what I meant earlier when I said that the Fregean picture of content led Searle to find propositional content where there isn't any.

Let's start with declarations. The first clue that declarations lack propositional content comes from looking at the kinds of sentences we use to report declarations.

5. a. He pronounced them man and wife.
    b. She christened the ship the S.S. Minnow.
    c. I fired him.
    d. The chairman adjourned the meeting.
    e. The board appointed her chairman.

There are no embedded content clauses in these sentences, which is a strong indication that the actions they report lack propositional contents. The verbs in these sentences express simple relations between people and other people, or people and things like ships or meetings. To pronounce two people man and wife is not to do something with a proposition. It is to do something to the bride and groom (or to the social institution of marriage of which they are now participants).

Perhaps an even more telling fact about declarations is that they lack satisfaction conditions. Declarations are not true or false, nor are they fulfilled or unfulfilled. It makes no sense to say that an act of pronouncing two people man and wife is *true*, or that it was *fulfilled*. It is crucial here to distinguish between satisfaction conditions and *success* conditions. An act of marrying two people can, of course, be successful or unsuccessful. If the bride or groom is already married, or if the person doing the pronouncing is not in a position to do so, or if any number of other things have gone wrong, then the act of marrying has not gone off successfully. Like all speech acts, declarations have conditions for their successful performance. But success conditions are not the same as satisfaction conditions. Declarations have the former but not the latter. This draws out another mistake in Searle's taxonomy. According to Searle, declarations have *both* word-to-world and world-to-word direction of fit. If that were so then we should expect declarations to be *both* true or false and fulfilled or unfulfilled. But neither of these distinctions applies to declarations. Declarations have no direction of fit because they lack satisfaction conditions altogether.

One might try to resist this by pointing to examples of declarations that clearly can be evaluated for truth and falsity, e.g. when an umpire in a baseball game says, 'You're out', or a judge says to the defendant, 'You are guilty'. These are examples of what Searle calls "assertive declarations," cases in which an authority figure performs a declaration by asserting that something is the case (Searle 1979, 19–20).[19] Given that the authority figure can get the facts wrong (the runner beat the throw, the defendant didn't do it), it seems like these kinds of declarations can be assessed for truth and falsity. But this doesn't threaten my claim that declarations lack satisfaction conditions. The categories

---

[19] See also Bach and Harnish's distinction between effectives and verdictives (Bach and Harnish 1979, ch.6).

of assertives and declarations are just types of speech acts, and any particular token speech act can fall under multiple types. When the umpire says, 'You're out', he does two things at once: he asserts that you are out, and he makes a declaration to the effect that you are out. Only the former has truth conditions. Note the different ways of reporting the umpire's utterance:

6. a. The umpire said/asserted/stated that the runner was out.
    b. The umpire called the runner out.

(6a) has an embedded clause, (6b) does not. This reflects the fact that (6a) reports the umpire's utterance as an assertion with propositional content and truth conditions, whereas (6b) reports it as a declaration with neither.[20] The umpire's utterance *qua* assertion was true or false, but *qua* declaration it was neither. In terms of our new taxonomy, then, declarations belong on the non-propositional side along with greetings, exclamations, and other speech acts that lack satisfaction conditions.

The same goes for expressives, although here the case is a bit harder to make. The sentences we use to report expressives do contain embedded sentences, in the form of gerundive clauses:

7. a. He thanked her for opening the door.
    b. She apologized for stepping on his toe.
    c. He congratulated her for finishing her dissertation.

Like infinitive clauses, gerundive clauses, such as 'for opening the door' and 'for stepping on his toe', are thought to contain a null pronoun, PRO, in subject position (Haegeman 1994, 275–6). So, for example, the form of (7a) is held to be, 'He thanked her$_i$ for PRO$_i$ opening the door'. We have something fully clausal, then, in the complement positions of these reports. On Searle's account, these clausal complements express the propositional contents of the reported expressives. But now compare the examples in (7a–c) with the ones in (8a–c):

8. a. He hugged her for opening the door.
    b. They punished her for stepping on his toe.
    c. He paid her for finishing her dissertation.

No one thinks that acts of hugging, punishing, or paying have propositional contents. The gerundive clauses in (8a–c) are not being used to express the propositional contents of the acts they report. They are being used to give reasons or explanations for why these acts were performed. The *reason* he hugged her is that she opened the door. The same goes for the gerundive clauses in (7a–c). The gerundive clause in (7a) does not give the content of his act of thanking; it gives a reason for that act of thanking. It is a mistake, then, to think that the embedded clauses in reports of expressive speech acts give the propositional contents of those speech acts.

Another giveaway that expressives lack propositional contents can be found in Searle's own description of them. According to Searle, expressives have no direction

---

[20] Of course (6a) can also be used (indirectly, I would say) as a report of a declaration. The point is that (6a), unlike (6b), attributes propositional content and truth conditions to the umpire's speech act.

of fit. This means that they lack satisfaction conditions. Like all speech acts, an expressive speech act can be successful or unsuccessful (which in this case is largely a matter of being sincere or insincere). But they are not true or false or fulfilled or unfulfilled. Given this fact about expressives, it would be surprising to find that they had propositional contents. The role for propositional content in Austin-Searle speech act theory is to determine satisfaction conditions. Attributing propositional content to a speech act that lacks satisfaction conditions looks entirely otiose.

Here, then, is the completed taxonomy, with declarations and expressives filled in on the non-propositional side.

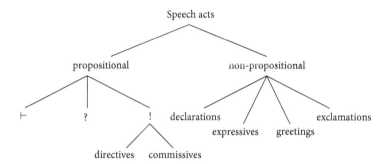

Expressives and declarations provide a good illustration of the way in which the Fregean picture of content and the $F(p)$ schema have had a distorting influence on our philosophical understanding of speech acts. Only by rejecting this Fregean picture can we come to have a clearer view of the nature of speech acts, a clearer view of the nature of force, and a proper scheme for categorizing speech acts into types.[21]

References

Austin, J. L. 1975: *How to Do Things with Words*. Second edition. Cambridge, MA: Harvard University Press.

Bach, Kent and Robert Harnish 1979: *Linguistic Communication and Speech Acts*. Cambridge, MA: MIT Press.

Barker, Stephen 2004: *Renewing Meaning: A Speech-Act Theoretic Approach*. Oxford: Oxford University Press.

Beaney, Michael (ed.) 1997: *The Frege Reader*. Oxford: Blackwell.

Charlow, Nate 2014a: "The Meaning of Imperatives". *Philosophy Compass*, 9/8: 540–55.

Charlow, Nate 2014b: "Logic and Semantics for Imperatives". *Journal of Philosophical Logic*, 43: 617–64.

Fiengo, Robert 2007: *Asking Questions: Using Meaningful Structures to Imply Ignorance*. Oxford: Oxford University Press.

Frege, Gottlob 1918a: "Thought". In Beaney 1997, pp. 325–46.

Frege, Gottlob 1918b: "Negation". In Beaney 1997, pp. 346–62.

[21] I presented earlier versions of this paper at the *New Work on Speech Acts* conference at Columbia University in September 2013, Ohio State in February 2014, Manitoba in October 2014, and St. Cloud State in November 2015. Thanks to the audiences at these events, with special thanks to Ben Caplan, Dan Harris, Bjørn Jespersen, and Chris Tillman. My greatest debt is, of course, to John Searle.

Frege, Gottlob 1918c: "Compound Thoughts". In Frege 1984, pp. 390–406.

Frege, Gottlob 1984: *Collected Papers on Mathematics, Logic, and Philosophy*. Edited by Brian McGuinness. Translated by Max Black, V. H. Dudman, Peter Geach, Hans Kaal, E. H. W. Kluge, Brian McGuinness, and R. H. Stoothoff. Oxford: Blackwell Publishers.

Geach, P. T. 1965: "Assertion". *The Philosophical Review*, 74: 449–65.

Groenendijk, Jeroen and Martin Stokhof 1997: "Questions". In van Benthem and ter Meulen 1997, pp. 1055–124.

Haegeman, Liliane (1994): *Introduction to Government and Binding*, Second edition. Oxford: Blackwell.

Hanks, Peter 2007: "How Wittgenstein Defeated Russell's Multiple Relation Theory of Judgment". *Synthese*, 154: 121–46.

Hanks, Peter 2011: "Structured Propositions as Types," *Mind*, 120: 11–52.

Hanks, Peter 2015: *Propositional Content*. Oxford: Oxford University Press.

Hanks, Peter 2016: "On Cancellation". *Synthese*. Online access: https://doi.org/10.1007/s11229-016-1260-4.

Hanks, Peter 2017: "The Explanatory Role of Propositions". *Analysis*, 77: 359–70.

Hare, R. M. 1949: "Imperative Sentences". *Mind*, 58: 21–39.

Hintikka, Jaakko 1974: "Questions about Questions". In Munitz and Unger 1974, pp. 103–58.

Hom, Christopher and Jeremy Schwartz 2013: "Unity and the Frege-Geach Problem". *Philosophical Studies*, 163: 15–24.

Jespersen, Bjørn 2012: "Recent Work on Structured Meaning and Propositional Unity". *Philosophy Compass*, 7/9: 620–30.

King, Jeffrey, Scott Soames, and Jeff Speaks 2014: *New Thinking About Propositions*. Oxford: Oxford University Press.

König, Ekkehard and Peter Siemund 2007: "Speech Act Distinctions in Grammar". In Shopen 2007, pp. 276–324.

Lewis, David 1969: *Convention: A Philosophical Study*. Cambridge, MA: Harvard University Press.

McGlone, Michael 2012: "Propositional Structure and Truth Conditions". *Philosophical Studies*, 157: 211–25.

Merricks, Trenton 2015: *Propositions*. Oxford: Oxford University Press.

Munitz, Milton and Peter Unger (eds) 1974: *Semantics and Philosophy*. New York: New York University Press.

Portner, Paul 2004: "The Semantics of Imperatives within a Theory of Clause Types". In Young 2004, pp. 235–52.

Recanati, François 2013: "Content, Mood, and Force". *Philosophy Compass*, 8/7: 622–32.

Reiland, Indrek 2013: "Propositional Attitudes and Mental Acts". *Thought*, 1: 239–45.

Russell, Bertrand 1903: *Principles of Mathematics*. New York: Norton.

Russell, Bertrand 1913: *Theory of Knowledge, The Collected Papers of Bertrand Russell, Volume 7*. Edited by Elizabeth Eames. London: George Allen & Unwin.

Schiffer, Stephen 1972: *Meaning*. Oxford: Oxford University Press.

Searle, John 1968: "Austin on Locutionary and Illocutionary Acts". *The Philosophical Review*, 77: 405–24.

Searle, John 1969: *Speech Acts*. Cambridge: Cambridge University Press.

Searle, John 1979: *Expression and Meaning*. Cambridge: Cambridge University Press.

Searle, John and Daniel Vanderveken 1985: *Foundations of Illocutionary Logic*. Cambridge: Cambridge University Press.

Shopen, Timothy (ed.) 2007: *Language Typology and Syntactic Description, Volume I, Clause Structure*. Second edition. Cambridge: Cambridge University Press.

Soames, Scott 2010: *What is Meaning?* Princeton: Princeton University Press.
Van Benthem, Johann and Alice ter Meulen (eds) 1997: *Handbook of Logic and Language.* Cambridge, MA: MIT Press.
Young, Robert (ed.) 2004: *Proceedings of Semantics and Linguistic Theory 14.* Ithaca, NY: CLC Publications.

6

Blocking as Counter-Speech

Rae Langton

6.1 Introduction

What is the remedy for 'evil' speech? Louis Brandeis had a famous answer.

If there be time to expose through discussion the falsehood and fallacies, to avert the evil by the processes of education, the remedy to be applied is more speech, not enforced silence.[1]

There should be no enforced silence of false, or fallacious, or otherwise 'evil' speech, because it can be remedied by more speech, said Brandeis. *Truth will out.* 'Let [Truth] and Falsehood grapple', said John Milton, for 'who ever knew Truth put to the worse in a free and open encounter?'[2]

That hope is inspiring but implausible, given limits on capacities to fight bad speech with good. 'Truth will out' is an empirical hypothesis disguised as a principle, and it deserves a skeptical eye. Speakers are threatened into silence, drowned out by heckling, or by the megaphone of money, which amplifies some voices, and gags others. Tribalism walls off one group from another, in online echo-chambers that exclude dissent.[3] Deliberation is policed by trolls, as well as by state agents. Attempts to squash rumors can backfire, giving falsehoods more credence than they had before.[4] Words that wound, hate speech scrawled on walls and side-walks—these are not invitations to conversation, but instructions to *get out*.[5] Click-bait, fake news, flood the marketplace of 'ideas', in a system where money trumps truth.

The 'more speech' doctrine deserves a skeptical eye, and it deserves a philosophical eye as well. Handicaps on speech are handicaps on *doing things with words*, when we bear in mind J. L. Austin's insight that saying is doing.[6]

From this viewpoint, there is more to 'evil' speech than 'falsehood and fallacies', as Brandeis put it. Speech can sometimes hurt people, without hurting truth. 'Colored' was a short-hand for 'Colored passengers are required to sit here'. That was *true*, but its truth did not improve it. When Rosa Parks responded by sitting where only whites were permitted, she didn't refute a false assertion. She disobeyed a true rule. We should expect counter-speech to look different, when evil speech is not lacking in truth.

---

[1] Brandeis 1927, 377. [2] Milton 1644. [3] Sunstein 2001. [4] Berinsky 2015.
[5] Waldron suggests the message of hate speech is 'get out, be afraid', 2012; see also Matsuda *et al.* 1993 on words that wound; Nielsen 2012 on *escape* as a response to hate speech; Langton 2014, and forthcoming a, b.
[6] Austin 1962.

When falsehoods are the problem, they do not always 'grapple' with truth in an 'open encounter', as Milton imagined. Often, they are not asserted, but merely presupposed. They creep into the stadium through back doors, keeping a low profile, steering clear of the official combatants, and then ascend the podium un-bloodied and untested, winners by default. We should expect counter-speech to look different, when evil speech is not open.

Could the 'exposure' Brandeis recommends address such problems? I want to take this seriously. I have two chief goals: first, to identify *blocking* as a distinctive form of counter-speech; and second, to identify some *handicaps* on its operation. Besides the barriers just described, there are others that need closer philosophical attention. Sometimes blocking is impossible. Sometimes blocking is possible, but difficult, given epistemic, structural and normative barriers: the 'evil speech' can be hard to see, or seem wrong to disrupt.

This is part of a wider project about the 'accommodation of injustice' (in my John Locke Lectures 2015).[7] Speech acts can build unjust norms and authority patterns, helped along by hearers who do not block them. The process follows what David Lewis called a 'rule of accommodation': a default adjustment, that tends to make a 'move in a language game' count as 'correct play', when certain conditions hold.[8] Blocking can prevent that default adjustment.

I set no store by the word 'evil', with its air of fairytale melodrama. My topics will range from subordinating law, to mundane speech acts that are barely noticed. Attempts to block can be equally mundane, like this light-hearted and high-decibel exchange I witnessed in 1990, at a Melbourne football game:

St. Kilda supporter to sluggish player: 'Get *on* with it, Laurie, you *great girl!*'
Alert bystander: 'Hey, what's wrong with a girl?'
St. Kilda supporter: 'It's got *no balls*, that's what's wrong with it!'

In case of doubt, the sluggish player is a man, and 'great' is an intensifier, not a compliment.[9] We shall return to this cameo in a moment.

To 'block' something is to 'hinder the passage, progress, or accomplishment' of something 'by, or as if by, interposing an obstruction', says the dictionary.[10] When you block something, you don't 'accommodate' it—you don't adjust to it, or help it along. Those ordinary senses of blocking and accommodation are alive in philosophical work on presupposition.

A hearer who blocks what is presupposed, also blocks the *speech act* to which the presupposition contributes, I shall argue. The success of a speech act can depend on its presuppositions, and on hearers accommodating those presuppositions. That is why blocking a presupposition can make the speech act fail. Blocking can disable, rather than refute, evil speech. It can make speech *misfire,* to use Austin's label for a speech act gone wrong. It offers a way of 'undoing' things with words (to twist his title)— and this 'undoing' has, I shall suggest, a *retroactive* character, which Austin himself

---

[7] Langton forthcoming b.   [8] Lewis 1979.
[9] Contrary to a hopeful but misguided interpretation of an audience member in the Netherlands, who had not come across this usage of 'great'.
[10] Merriam-Webster, http://www.merriam-webster.com/

described. It offers a ticket to a modest time machine, available to anyone willing and able to use it.[11]

Patterns of misfire are more familiar in a negative guise of *unjust* silencing, 'illocutionary disablement', and 'discursive injustice'.[12] Our question here is turning the tables. We are asking whether evil speech could itself misfire, could itself be disabled, when hearers exploit blocking, as counter-speech. I shall suggest a special role for blocking as a response to 'back-door' speech acts, as we might call them: low profile speech acts, enabled by presuppositions and their ilk, that tend to win by default.[13]

I give 'back-door' speech acts a metaphorical label, since familiar ones don't quite fit. 'Not-at-issue content' is close, but doesn't capture our interest in speech acts.[14] Sneaky 'conversational exercitives' (described by Mary Kate McGowan) covertly alter facts about what is permissible, but I have a wider range of act types in mind, including back-door testimony.[15] Many speech acts are achievable by back-door methods, and there is scope for philosophy of language to shed light on this. Mark Richard wrote of slurs, 'what makes a word a slur is that it is used to *do* certain things, that it has . . . a certain illocutionary potential'. His point generalizes from slurs to a larger toolkit of words and linguistic items: what matters is their 'illocutionary potential', their potential for *doing* certain things.[16]

Several back-door speech acts were performed, in the utterance of, 'Get on with it, you great girl!' The speaker's main 'front-door' purpose was presumably to *urge* a sluggish player, and *express* frustration. But regardless of his aims, there were several back-door speech acts achieved by 'great girl', and what it presupposed in that context.[17] The utterance implicitly *ranked* women, a verdictive speech act, in Austin's scheme. It implicitly *testified* that there is something wrong with a girl, in

---

[11] The unpublished notes are discussed in Sbisà 2007.

[12] 'Illocutionary disablement': see Langton 1993, 2009. The argument here bears on illocutionary disablement, which would have the same retroactive character. 'Discursive injustice': see Kukla 2014. She describes a systematic pattern of misfire, emphasizing the twisting of one force into another. There have been many related discussions of silencing; for a sample see Hornsby 1995, 2011, Hornsby and Langton 1998, Jacobson 1995, Butler 1997, Green 1998, Schwartzman 2002, West 2003, Saul 2006, Bianchi 2008, Maitra 2009, McGowan 2004, 2009, and this volume, Mikkola 2011, Dotson 2011, Simpson 2013, Davies 2016.

[13] 'And their ilk'—this hand-waving phrase expresses a hunch that back-door speech acts can be achieved via implicature and other mechanisms as well. I do not do justice to this, and ask the reader's forbearance for riding roughshod over distinctions often regarded, for other purposes, as crucial.

[14] Stanley 2015, especially ch. 5. 'Insinuation' doesn't quite fit either, implying deliberateness, see e.g. Camp this volume; Pinker *et al.* 2008; nor 'indirect speech act' for a similar reason (though this needs more attention).

[15] See McGowan 2004, and this volume.

[16] Richard 2008, 1. The thesis that presupposition contributes to force is implicit in Langton and West 1999, Langton 2012. It has a persuasive function, Sbisà 1999, Simon-Vandenbergen *et al.* 2007. Propaganda conveys subtle, not-at-issue content that threatens the democratic process, Stanley 2015. Insinuation can be antagonistic, Camp this volume. Speech enacts conversational exercitives, covertly enacting norms, McGowan 2004, and this volume. Political 'dog-whistles' convey specific messages via covert mechanisms, Saul, this volume. Generics add implicit ideological content to 'common ground', Haslanger 2011 and 2014, cf. Anderson *et al.* 2012. Racial slurs harm through their implicatures, Tirrell 2012, and 'cue' ideologies, Swanson forthcoming. Subtexts can be identified and thwarted through deconstruction, Butler 1997.

[17] I say the speech act did these, and perhaps the speaker, but either way I do not assume he did them deliberately.

that context, using potentially informative presupposition. It implicitly *legitimated* broader *norms* that say e.g., 'men take charge, women are gentle and obliging'.[18] The bystander was among the hearers, though not a 'hearer' in the usual sense: he was not being addressed, and the speaker hardly knew he was there. But, through his intervention, he became a proper hearer, a recognized party to the conversation. The bystander tried to block what was presupposed, by means of what Marina Sbisà has called 'explicitation': he spelled it out, and challenged it.[19] The bystander succeeded in one respect. He blocked them as *back-door* speech acts. They were no longer sneaked through, unattended. But he did not succeed, *tout court*.

The initial speech acts were shored up by the supporter's lively riposte, and creative use of loaded language: embracing what was spelled out, namely that there is indeed something wrong with a girl; twisting the bystander's rhetorical question into a request for information; adding more back-door speech acts, via the neutered pronoun 'it', and the literal-plus-metaphorical use of 'balls' to explain, so conveniently, what exactly is lacking in a girl.[20] The bystander did not succeed. But he might have succeeded, had the supporter been less quick-witted, or the tool-kit of metaphor less handy. And if he had succeeded, he might have made those back-door speech acts misfire.

A speech act misfires when its 'felicity conditions' are not satisfied, and Austin had some delightfully surreal examples. A 'low type' fails to name a ship *The Generalissimo Stalin*, despite rushing up with the right words, and smashing the right bottle on the prow. Two individuals fail to marry, when a would-be spouse turns out to be a monkey. A short-sighted saint fails to baptize the penguins, notwithstanding his pious intentions.[21] Something has in each case gone wrong. The right words are said, but the relevant speech act's felicity conditions are not fulfilled: in these examples, conditions requiring an authorized namer (not a low type), a human spouse (not a monkey), and a creature with a soul (not a penguin), respectively.[22]

A speech act can misfire when its *felicity conditions* are not satisfied, says Austin; and when its *presuppositions* encounter a problem, say I. What is the relation between these? Austin himself saw a 'similarity, perhaps even an identity' between presuppositions and felicity conditions. He went so far as to compare reference failure to an unhappy marriage, as cognoscenti may recall. ('Unhappy' in a technical sense, of course.) When a statement's referential 'presupposition' is unfulfilled, a felicity condition is unfulfilled, and the statement misfires. When a marriage's felicity condition is unfulfilled, a 'presupposition' for it is unfulfilled, and the marriage misfires.[23]

---

[18] Compare Langton and West 1999, Langton 2012, and forthcoming a and b; McGowan this volume, Leslie 2015, Murray and Starr this volume; Swanson forthcoming, on how slurs 'cue' ideologies. 'Girl' is being used as a slur; but slurs are just one of many tools used in back–door speech acts, and I shall not here address the substantial debate on this topic.

[19] Sbisà 1999.

[20] Compare Leslie 2015, Greer 1970. He could more charitably have been interpreted as indicating there is something 'wrong with a girl' *in that context*, as one might insult a heavy-weight by calling them a bantam-weight, and vice versa; but his riposte rules that out.

[21] Austin 1962, 24, and 1946, alluding to France 1909. The alert reader may wonder how even a fictional French saint could have encountered Antarctic penguins: they were Arctic Great Auks, see Preface to France 1909 for disputed nomenclature. Thanks to Richard Holton for this scholarly note.

[22] Those conditions are specified perhaps by convention, though that is a large topic I shall leave aside.

[23] Austin 1962, 51.

Austin's association of presupposition with felicity needs more disentangling, but in the meantime: if presupposition can contribute to felicity, and a problem with presupposition to infelicity, it would be no surprise if blocking a presupposition might contribute to infelicity, or misfire.

In what follows, I want to look at blocking as a linguistic and political maneuver, preventing default accommodation and undermining force (6.2). I shall consider whether authority might be presupposed by speakers, and blocked by hearers and bystanders (6.3). I shall look at the blocking of back-door speech acts, putting Austin together with Lewis to explain how blocking can disrupt accommodation, and make an associated speech act misfire (6.4). This amounts to a retroactive undoing of illocutionary force, I shall argue (6.5).

Blocking, thus understood, is a distinctive and under-appreciated form of counter-speech. But there are handicaps on blocking, as on speech acts generally (6.6). When a speech act cannot be undone that way at all, by a given hearer, blocking is impossible. When there are epistemic, structural and normative barriers, blocking might be possible, but difficult. Inattention, norms of cooperation, and other factors, place handicaps on the use of blocking, as counter-speech.

My conclusion will be no glib injunction to fight bad speech with good. That would be too much, given the handicaps described. Hearers and bystanders may need to acquire new skills, pick their battles, or use guerrilla tactics.[24] Background norms, institutions, and meanings, may need to alter. There are doubts for a 'more speech' solution, in the world as it stands. Would that leave 'enforced silence' of evil speech as the only alternative, as Brandeis implied? Not necessarily. The enabling conditions for speech cannot be taken for granted, but they can, perhaps, be built.[25]

6.2 Blocking: a first look

'Blocking' is a label for a hearer's resistance to what a speaker, or a speech act, presupposes: 'Wait a minute—' says the hearer, or 'Whaddya mean—*even* George could win?' A hearer who blocks, does not accommodate what is presupposed; in this instance, that George is an unpromising candidate.[26]

Blocking interferes with the evolving information taken for granted among participants in a conversation, and many have noted its political significance. Exposure *can* be a partial remedy, as Brandeis said. 'Revealing [problematic] implications or presuppositions and blocking them is a crucial part of ideology critique', says Sally Haslanger.[27] Presupposition 'can be used to smuggle in content that one would not necessarily accept if it was presented as the content asserted', says Jason Stanley—and if the problem is a smuggler, a spotlight could help.[28] Presupposition, says Sbisà,

[24] As Jonathan Elvin has reminded me (personal correspondence).
[25] On the substantial enabling conditions for free speech and counter-speech, see Brison 1998, Gelber 2012, Langton forthcoming b.
[26] Lewis 1979. The 'George' was Lakoff, in Lewis's teasing example, but let us take it as an arbitrary George.
[27] Haslanger 2011, 179. I shall not address the larger topic of ideology here.
[28] Stanley 2015, 150, concurring with Langton and West 1999. His argument about not-at-issue content in propaganda offers powerful resources for understanding back-door speech acts and their political use.

is suitable for transmitting a kind of content which might be called ideological: assumptions, not necessarily conscious but liable to be brought to consciousness, about how our human world is and how it should be. By the same token, criticism of ideology may avail itself of a knowledge of linguistic presupposition inducers and of their communicative dynamics.[29]

Sbisà recommends the spotlight of 'explicitation', demonstrated by the bystander in my example: the explicit exposure of implicit presuppositions. The skill of explicitation can be learned, she says, and linguists can help to teach it.[30] That skill can be urgently needed in contexts like political debate, and courtroom interrogation, where blind accommodation can hide evidence, and punish the innocent.[31]

If a hearer wants to block, there are alternatives to explicitation. Sometimes a rephrasing, a raised eyebrow, or a joke, might work better than a 'Wait a minute!' or a righteous calling out. A hearer might reframe, with a 'thank you for *asking*', in response to a rude demand.[32] Here is Tina Fey, explaining in 2011 why she wrote *Bossypants*:

Ever since I became an executive producer of *30 Rock*, people have asked, 'Is it hard for you, being the boss?' and 'Is it uncomfortable for you to be the person in charge? You know, in that same way they say, 'Gosh, Mr. Trump, is it awkward for you to be the boss of all these people?' I can't answer for Mr. Trump, but in my case it is not.[33]

Fey's absurd (and prescient) comparison exposes to attention the presupposed gender norms, and without spelling them out, skewers them.

Blocking can be an important resource for counter-speech, exposing 'falsehood and fallacies' that would otherwise persuade. But blocking can do more than reduce harmful effects. Besides interfering with persuasion—with 'perlocutionary' success, in Austin's terms—blocking can interfere with the speech act itself, its 'illocutionary' success.

Austin distinguished the meaning or content of an utterance, from its effects, and from the speech act itself. 'Shoot her!' might be a locutionary act, meaning by 'shoot' to shoot with a gun, and referring by 'her' to a salient woman; it might be a perlocutionary act of causing the woman's death; and it might be an illocutionary act, of ordering someone to shoot.[34] A hearer could disobey the order, or condemn it. But what if a hearer could, somehow, stop it *being* an order? We are making space for that theoretical possibility.

[29] Sbisà 1999, 493.
[30] See Sbisà 1999 for an empirical study of readers acquiring improved skill in identifying presupposition triggers (with help from linguists).
[31] Ehrlich and Sidnell 2006, Davies 2016.
[32] A silence might sometimes be *un*accommodating: for example, a stony silence in response to a racist joke. For the purpose of this paper, though, I shall take blocking to involve an active intervention. (For the illocutionary force of silence, in different contexts, see Langton 2007.)
[33] Fey 2011, 9. For more examples of ingenious blocking, see Ehrlich and Sidnell 2006, and Camp this volume.
[34] Austin 1962, 101–2.

6.3 Accommodating and blocking authority

Attempts to block bad speech can be mundane, or heroic. Rosa Parks acted heroically, but she did not say: 'No, that sign is a lie!' She did not use counter-speech of the sort imagined by advocates of the 'more speech' doctrine. She did not treat a true rule as a false assertion, by contradicting it. Instead, she challenged the *authority* the rule presupposed, in her actions, and her words, when she said, 'I don't think I should have to stand up', to the arresting officer.[35]

That was more than disobedience: it was an attempt to block the authority presupposed by the sign. She might have done so more explicitly, as 15-year-old Claudette Colvin did a year beforehand, loudly affirming her 'constitutional right' to remain seated.[36] As a strategy, this has more promise: to block an assumption of authority is to challenge a crucial felicity condition for directives, and sometimes this can work.[37]

A speaker's informal authority often depends on whether hearers go along with it, or block it. Richmond Thomason describes a familiar situation:

> There is a moment of indecision and then someone takes charge, asks for suggestions about restaurants, decides on one, and asks someone to get two cabs while she calls to make reservations. When no one objects to this arrangement, she became the group leader, and obtained a certain authority. She did this by acting as if she had the authority.[38]

The informal group leader *obtained* a certain authority by presupposing she had it, and getting it via a process of accommodation. 'Unless we believe in magic, the inanimate world is not accommodating', remarks Thomason—

> But *people* can be accommodating, and in fact there are many social situations in which the best way to get what we want is to act as if we already had it.[39]

This acquisition of informal authority follows what Lewis called a rule of accommodation: it emerges in a process of adjustment that tends to make what a speaker does count as 'correct play', when certain conditions hold—conditions which often include the acts and omissions of hearers.

A hearer could block the authority that was presupposed:

> Someone could have objected, saying *Who do you think you are, deciding where to go for us?* And the objection would have had a certain force.[40]

The would-be leader would not in that case obtain the authority she presupposed, and her attempted directives would misfire.

---

[35] Heffernan 2015, 125. Here the authority is practical. Authority may in general be practical or epistemic, and these interact in distinctive ways. Authority may also be relative to a domain, a jurisdiction, and a contrast class. I do not do justice to all these factors here, but see Langton 2017 and forthcoming a and b.

[36] Adler 2009.

[37] I treat directives as exercitive-like in requiring some degree of authority, see e.g. Langton 1993, 2004, 2017.

[38] Thomason 1990, 342, compare von Fintel 2008.

[39] Thomason 1990, 342. As noted above, accommodation does not involve *only* the co-operative adjustment of hearers, if it applies also to the creation of institutional facts (such as marriage) whose felicity conditions are very different.

[40] Thomason 1990, his italics.

The state of Alabama did not, of course, 'obtain' authority by presupposing they had it, and getting it on the fly. They had it already. And this difference in kind, degree, and origin of authority explains the different vulnerability to blocking. For Parks, the attempt to challenge authority could not succeed, not just like that. It would not help to follow Thomason's observation that often 'the best way to get what we want is to act as if we already had it'—that cheerful tenet of positive psychology, celebrated by William James.[41] Her attempt to act 'as if' she 'already had' what she wanted—as if the sign lacked authority—could not, on its own, undo the rule, or undermine its force. It would be no answer to the arresting officer who said 'The law's the law', and cited Chapter 6, Section 11 of the Montgomery City Code. But her challenge could do something significant with words. It was a protest, and part of a movement, a cumulative series of acts done with other speakers and actors—including, in the end, the authoritative speech of a greater law, which overturned the sign's authority, and ensured that from then on, all such signs would misfire.

Austin drew a contrast between institutional and informal authority, describing only the former as genuine:

> On a desert island you may say to me 'Go and pick up wood' and I may say 'I don't take orders from you' or 'you're not entitled to give me orders'—I do not take orders from you when you try to 'assert your authority' (which I myself fall in with but may not) on a desert island, as opposed to the case when you are the captain on a ship and therefore genuinely have authority.[42]

But what if I do 'fall in' and co-operate? If a hearer treats it as a felicitous binding order, it *is* a felicitous binding order: the speaker genuinely has authority, and 'obtains' it if he lacked it before. This can be spelled out in Lewisian terms, as Maciej Witek has argued. The speaker's 'illocutionary power'—

> is produced by a mechanism akin to what Lewis calls presupposition accommodation: a rule-governed process whose function is to adjust the context of an act to make it appropriate . . . the adjustment in question is triggered off and motivated by the hearer's default and tacit assumption to the effect that the speaker's utterance is a felicitous order.[43]

Authority may be gained via this mechanism, and it may be lost as well. Rebecca Kukla imagines a female employer who is granted institutional authority, but finds her directives treated by her sexist employees as mere requests: in which case they genuinely *are* mere requests, says Kukla, and the employer encounters 'discursive injustice'.[44]

---

[41] James 1896.

[42] Austin 1962, 28. Authority in this example is not strictly 'asserted', but presupposed.

[43] Witek 2013, 151–2. My first John Locke lecture argued that authority follows a rule of accommodation, and I was delighted to learn then of partly comparable work by Sbisà and Witek. I am not doing justice here to Witek's proposal about the relationship between Austinian (objective) 'presuppositions', i.e. felicity conditions, and Stalnakerian (subjective) pragmatic presuppositions.

[44] Kukla 2014. I am not doing justice to her account of the relation between uptake and the context of performatives. There are limits to what hearers can do, in my view. A hearer may weaken what would have been an order into a mere request, if an order requires a certain hearer-dependent felicity condition. But a hearer cannot e.g. twist sexual refusal into sexual consent, since consent requires a certain speaker-dependent felicity condition—the speaker's decision or intention to consent (see Hornsby and Langton 1998). This needs more discussion, but I shall not here be looking at the vast range of speech act types,

Hate speech itself may acquire authority from what hearers do, or fail to do.[45] Ishani Maitra has investigated this possibility, arguing that authority, thus acquired, can enable hate speech to *subordinate* its targets.[46] She begins with a range of examples comparable to those just considered. A teacher turns a blind eye to a bossy pupil—whose bossing obtains authority when the teacher does not object. Drivers accept direction around a crash-site from a fellow motorist—whose directives obtain authority when the drivers do not object. And she identifies a comparable pattern in the dynamics of hate speech. A city council turns a blind eye to a Klan cross-burning—which obtains authority when the council does not object. Subway passengers watch, as an Arab woman is a target of a racist tirade—which obtains authority when passengers do not object. Hearers do not block the authority presupposed by the speech acts of bossy pupil, cross burner, traffic director, racist abuser, and so they obtain authority. In this way, hate speech acquires an authority that is a felicity condition for subordination: enabling it to rank a group as inferior, legitimate discrimination against them, and deprive them of powers and rights.[47]

Speech acts, including directives generally, and hate speech specifically, can acquire authority by an everyday piece of social magic: authority gets presupposed, and hearers let it go through, following a rule of accommodation.

6.4 Blocking back-door speech acts

Lewis used Austinian performatives to illustrate his rule of accommodation, as 'moves in a language game' that tend to count as 'correct play' provided 'certain conditions' hold.[48] 'With this ring I thee wed', says a bridegroom in the presence of a proper celebrant. 'You are now permitted to cross the white line', says a master to a slave. 'This ship is named *The Generalissimo Stalin*', says an authorized ship-namer.[49]

Play can be 'correct' because it is true, e.g. 'You are now permitted to cross the white line.' Play can be 'correct' because it is acceptable for the purposes of the conversation, e.g. 'George is an unpromising candidate.'[50] We should add that play can be 'correct' because it is *felicitous*, in Austin's sense, if we are to take these examples seriously.

Unlike Austin, Lewis took these performatives to have truth-values, and to be self-verifying. But if they are true, that is because they are felicitous. Permissions

and their different (and disputed) patterns of hearer-dependent, speaker-dependent and background-dependent felicity conditions.

[45] Langton forthcoming a.

[46] Maitra 2012. She makes an important distinction between the responses of authoritative and non-authoritative bystanders, which I take up in Langton forthcoming a. She does not accept my 'accommodation' reading of the phenomenon.

[47] Maitra 2012, cf. Langton 1993, forthcoming a, b.

[48] Lewis's performatives are often forgotten, but see Roberts 2015 for a reminder. This means that 'accommodation' applies not only to a certain co-operative adjustment by hearers—which could satisfy one kind of felicity condition—but also to the creation of institutional facts, e.g. marriage, to which the attitudes of hearers might not contribute. (So I argue, in my 2015 Locke Lectures, forthcoming b.)

[49] Lewis 1979. A sly piece of mischief perhaps: Lewis twists Austin's example, making a felicity of the low type's misfire.

[50] Lewis does not consider the accommodation of authority, but it has philosophical as well as political interest, if presupposed authority can become genuine, and not just acceptable, as just argued.

might be regarded as true, and his rule of accommodation for permissibility is indeed formulated in terms of truth. But suppose the master had said to the slave, 'Don't cross the white line!' That, when felicitous, would *not* be true. (Or not without fancy footwork translating it into an indicative).[51] But the bounds of permissibility would again shift, following a rule of accommodation.

A rule for the accommodation of permissibility can be formulated in terms of felicity, a kind of 'correct play' that may, but need not, coincide with truth. There is no need to convert directives to indicatives to get accommodation's point. A speech act's felicity is in this sense more fundamental than its truth: it partly explains its truth, when it is true; and when it cannot be true (or false), its felicity is what follows accommodation's rule.

In short, the lesson to take from Lewis is that a move in a language game can earn, through accommodation, different kinds of success or correctness. It can earn not only the truth, or acceptability, of what is done with words, but also its force; in these performative cases, the force of marriage, permission, and naming. In considering how speech acts are accommodated, there is no need to confine our attention to truth-evaluable performatives.

Marriage, permission, and naming, are not back-door speech acts (or not as he describes them), but they remind us that accommodation applies to illocutionary acts, as well as to presupposition.[52] We get to back-door speech acts by putting these together.

'Even George could win' explicitly asserts that George could win, and performs a back-door speech act (perhaps several). The difference between 'George could win' and 'Even George could win', is partly a matter of force. They have much in common: both are assertions, and verdictives ranking George. But one ranks George as a somewhat promising candidate, the other as a somewhat unpromising candidate. One praises him, to a degree, while the other somewhat disparages him. The presupposition introduced by 'even' contributes to the difference in force, whatever else it may do.

If the hearer does not block by saying 'Whaddya mean, *even*?' the back-door speech act counts as 'correct play'. The presupposition counts as acceptable, and its associated speech act counts as felicitous: as a verdictive ranking; as testimony, if the speaker *conveys*, using potentially informative presupposition, that George is an unpromising candidate; as a back-door enactment of norms, if it alters permissibility facts about how George should be treated.[53] The back-door speech acts of informing, ranking, and norm-enacting contribute to the score of the conversation, which adjusts accordingly, making it appropriate for participants to go on as if George were an unpromising candidate.

When a speech act counts as 'correct play', following a rule of accommodation, it adjusts the score, just as hitting a run adjusts the score of a baseball game. 'Score' is an abstract and normative structure, which tracks the state of play in a conversation, and

---

[51] Lewis 1970, Section VIII.

[52] On the relation of performatives and presupposition, see also Langton and West 1999, Langton 2012, cf. Witek 2013, 2015.

[53] On informal norm enactment, see Langton and West 1999, Langton forthcoming a, b; McGowan 2004, 2009, this volume, and forthcoming; cf. Murray and Starr, this volume.

determines what is appropriate for players to do next. (Incorrect play might adjust score too, as a baseball score would include mere strikes on Lewis's expansive sense of 'score'.) The score accommodates what is done, altering what is appropriate for participants to do next, so that it is appropriate to go on as if George is an unpromising candidate, or as if girls lack 'balls' in the relevant sense.

Something is added to the score, and *also* to the 'common ground', a set of attitudes shared by the conversational participants.[54] Common ground consists, roughly, of the psychological states of participants, responding to what has been done. Speakers and hearers alter their beliefs and other attitudes, and go on with shared assumptions in place, for example believing that George is an unpromising candidate, and treating that as shared knowledge. There is a distinction between the accommodation of a speech act (and its associated norms), and the accommodation of common ground (and its associated states of mind).

What I am distinguishing as 'score' and 'common ground', Lewis describes as two alternative ways of understanding 'score'. He compares a normative understanding of score, which includes constitutive and regulative rules, with an alternative 'operationalism' about score, according which the scoreboard might be identified with certain attitudes—'maybe the invisible scoreboard in the head umpire's head, maybe the many scoreboards in many heads to the extent that they agree'.[55]

What Lewis sees as two ways of understanding the score, we can see as complementary. We need both. A change in attitudes is a downstream effect of what is done with a ball, or with words, in the 'game' itself. Aiming to fulfill certain regulative rules (about winning the game), the batter scores a home run, as defined by certain constitutive rules (about what counts as a home run). As Lewis puts it, the score 'straightway' changes—which means at that very time. The attitudes 'in many heads' change thereafter, as a causal consequence. The home run is comparable to an illocutionary speech act; the attitudes to some especially salient perlocutionary acts. Score tracks illocutionary acts (*inter alia*). Common ground tracks (some) perlocutionary acts. To identify normative score with psychological common ground would be to risk psychologism.[56]

When the hearer blocks with explicitation, forcing the speaker's cards onto the table, the back-door speech acts fail, at least as *back-door* speech acts. What was implicit is brought out into the open, where it has to be treated, and defended, as an explicit assertion.[57] It will *not* be normatively appropriate for participants simply to go on as if George is an unpromising candidate. The back-door speech

---

[54] Stalnaker 2002. The attitudes may be acceptance rather than belief, but I set this aside for present purposes. I argue elsewhere that common ground needs to include, besides cognitive attitudes, conative and emotional ones, in order to make sense of the dynamics of advertising, pornography, and hate speech (Langton 2012).

[55] Lewis 1979, 344.

[56] For this distinction between score and common ground, see Langton 2012 and forthcoming b, and a similar distinction in McGowan, this volume. See Witek 2013, 2015 for a partly comparable proposal about the relation between Austin, Lewis, and Stalnaker, contrasting 'objective' vs. 'subjective' accommodation. For a normative account of 'score' see Langton and West 1993, McGowan 2004, 2009, and this volume. See Sbisà 1999 for a normative account of 'common ground', which I would call 'score'; and compare Camp this volume, on relationship between score and public record.

[57] Sbisà 1999.

acts of informing, ranking, and norm-enacting would not then simply go through without more ado (though they may be registered as attempts). Blocking prevents illocutionary accommodation, tracked by score, *and* perlocutionary accommodation, tracked by common ground, achieving the latter, because it achieves the former.

The misfire of interest to us here—the misfire wrought by blocking—is both like, and unlike, Austin's amusing ceremonial examples. The likeness is in the failure of felicity conditions. But there is an important difference: they are failures of *hearer-dependent* felicity conditions, which were not the problem in those ceremonial infelicities. A comparison might be made with *uptake*, on Austin's picture. An attempted warning, which the hearer does not *take* to be a warning is not, according to Austin, a felicitous warning. He regarded uptake as a condition of success for most, perhaps all, speech acts.

For Austin, many factors contribute to force: a speaker's intentions; background social practices and conventions; background social structures and hierarchies; and the attitudes of hearers, who actively take a speaker to be performing some speech act. Uptake, for Austin, is a hearer's 'understanding of the meaning and the force', their *active* take on what the speaker is doing.[58] Uptake may be a take on the speaker's intention, and has been regarded as such by many; but it need not be that, or only that. It may be a take on whether other salient felicity conditions are satisfied, including authority—as on Austin's desert island, where shipwreck survivors are picking up wood.

Can uptake be passive, rather than active? This, in effect, is what we have been exploring. We can extend Austin's account of uptake to include a *default* or *tacit* uptake, which does not require an active state of the hearer's mind. And Lewis helps us to see it in just this light—when he added a role for mere *omissions* of hearers, occurring when a presupposition is not blocked, but allowed to pass. His rule of accommodation does not require active or conscious uptake on the part of hearers, an active recognition of what the speaker is doing with words. Omissions, failures to block, even unwitting or oblivious ones, function as default uptake, allowing what a speaker does to go through.

When authority is what is presupposed, default uptake allows it to go through, and the speaker actually obtains authority, empowering the speaker to perform speech acts whose felicity requires authority—directives of permission, command, and more.[59] Their felicity depends on a presupposed authority that becomes real, when passive hearers let it through. Observe here a difference between presupposed authority, and other presuppositions. Unblocked presuppositions tend to become acceptable rather than true: 'George is an unpromising candidate' may become acceptable, if unblocked, but that would not make it true. Authority is different. A presupposition of authority can become not just acceptable, but true, because its existence, not only its acceptability, depends in part on what hearers do or fail to do.

---

[58] Austin 1962, 117.

[59] As described in Witek 2013, who also explains why a presupposition of authority can become true rather than just acceptable.

6.5 Blocking as retroactive undoing

Austin wrote that speech acts could be *made undone* when, contrary to initial appear-ances, they turn out to have misfired. (Here we are indebted to Sbisà's illuminating discussion of Austin's unpublished notes.)[60]

This 'undoing' of speech acts is retroactive, according to Austin: it makes 'undone' something in the past. On Sbisà's account,

> Austin refers more than once to Aristotle's remark that since what is past is not capable of not having taken place, nobody can *make undone what has been done*: on this view, the effects of our actions are irreversible. But, Austin notices, the acts performed by means of performative utterances (therefore, illocutionary acts) appear to be an exception, since they may turn out to be null and void if certain conditions are found not to be satisfied.[61]

Illocutionary speech acts, Austin says, can in principle be *made undone*.

How can a speech act be made 'undone'? Austin's point can look epistemic, as if felicity conditions, required in the past, were later 'found' not to be satisfied: for example, if the bridegroom were later discovered to be a monkey; or the creatures baptized by the myopic saint were later discovered to be penguins. In like vein our understanding of a past speech act could 'shift over time', as Lisa Schwartzman says, so that 'what we once thought meant one thing can actually later be *discovered* to have meant something else'.[62]

We could see Austin's point as evidential, but it is better read as constitutive. It is not about future knowledge of past (absent) conditions, but future (absent) conditions themselves. Austin's point is that when it comes to speech acts, the future can shape the past, and 'undo' the past.

'Undo' is Austin's word, but it suggests a number of ideas that are not quite right. It can suggest altering the present, like shoe-laces that are made 'undone'—laces which are not, but *were once*, done. A better comparison, perhaps, is with a job that is left 'undone'—a job which is not, and *never was*, done.

'Undo' can also suggest altering the past, as if two competing histories were actual. That is not right either, although 'changing the past' is a tempting description, and adequate if we are careful. The past is 'undone' in the following sense only: it is made different to how it would *otherwise* have been.

What Lewis says about time travel is surprisingly apt in this context. The time traveller, he says, 'changes the past from the unactualized way it would have been . . . to the one and only way it actually is'.[63] The blocker, I suggest, does just the same. A successful blocker changes a past utterance from the unactualized way it would have been, to the way it actually is. If a speaker's presupposed authority is blocked by a hearer, as Thomason describes, that blocking changes the past, in the way a time traveller changes the past: for example, from the unactualized *order* it would have been, to something weaker—the mere *request* it actually is.

---

[60] Sbisà 2007.   [61] Sbisà 2007: my italics.
[62] Schwartzman 2002, 430, emphasis added. She has illocution, rather than locution, in mind—i.e. what was 'meant', as a speech act.
[63] Lewis 1976, 76.

Austin finds this retroactivity unique to illocution, but it occurs in many domains. Science fiction aside, the motion of a ball may be a goal, a stabbing may be a killing, and a belief about tomorrow's sunrise may be knowledge, partly in virtue of what happens later.[64] This does not require magic, or backwards causation, or changing the past, nor does it require a speech act to persist through to the relevant future.[65] There is no speech act, at a given time, *unless* a future condition holds, but that doesn't mean there is no speech act, at that time, *until* it holds.[66]

The possibility of retroactive undoing, for speech acts, is a consequence of the fact that felicity conditions for a speech act can be supplied, or not, in the future, relative to the time of utterance. This is in harmony with the familiar thought that a speech act's success may depend on factors extrinsic in time and space to the utterance. For 'I do' to count as a marriage may require felicity conditions in the past, e.g. the prior reading of banns in church, the prior absence of a different marriage. It may require felicity conditions in the present, e.g. the prospective spouse is a human being, not a monkey. And it may require felicity conditions in the future, e.g. the consummation of the marriage. We need not dwell on what sad events, or non-events, might retroactively 'undo' a marriage, readers will be relieved to hear. Our interest is in those special felicity conditions supplied, or removed, by what hearers and bystanders do later. Our interest is in a positive role for illocutionary undoing, achievable in part by those who hear and stand by.

This has something in common with a hope expressed by Judith Butler, that hearers might later 'resignify' oppressive speech:

The gap that separates the speech act from its future effects has its auspicious implications...[it] not only makes the repetition and resignification of the utterance possible, but shows how words might, through time, become disjoined from their power to injure.[67]

She sees this, it seems, as a *perlocutionary* resistance, arising from the 'gap' between a speech act and its future effects. These effects include later change to locution, for example, in reclamation projects that, over time, change what can be done with words like 'queer', that in earlier usage were injurious in their effects.[68] My interest, by contrast, is in an *illocutionary* resistance, enabled by the different 'gap' that separates an utterance from its future felicity conditions.

To block a presupposition can be to block the speech act to whose force it contributes, on this picture; and it is time to return to Austin's hunch about a connection—the supposed 'similarity, perhaps even an identity' between

---

[64] See Langton forthcoming b, for a range of retroactive phenomena. Compare e.g. moral luck; the 'Actual Futures' principle for the status of a fetus, Harman 1999; and for dissent on time of a killing, Thomson 1971.

[65] For response to accusations of 'magic' in the process of accommodation, see von Fintel 2008. For a performative's persistence through hearer responses, see Kukla 2014. For a claim that something like this involves changing the past, see Barlassina and del Prete 2015, who say it was true, at some past time, that Lance Armstrong won the Tour de France, but a later disqualification altered a past fact. There is no need for this, and my view is in harmony with the response given by Iacona 2016.

[66] For 'unless' vs. 'until', see White 1970, compare Lewis 1976, Langton forthcoming b, and thanks also to Lloyd Humberstone (personal correspondence).

[67] Butler 1997, 15.

[68] Butler 1997, my response to Butler in Langton 2009, ch. 5, compare Schwartzman 2002.

presupposition and felicity condition, and the comparison between reference failure and unhappy marriage.

A 'statement' depends on 'what has been called "presupposition"', he said. He compared this,

with our infelicity when we say, 'I name ...', but some of the conditions are not satisfied [...] Here we might have used the 'presuppose' formula: we might say that the formula 'I do' presupposes lots of things: if these are not satisfied the formula is unhappy, void.[69]

A statement misfires, when its 'presupposition', which is its felicity condition, is unful-filled. A marriage misfires, when its felicity condition, which is its 'presupposition', is unfulfilled.

There are two ideas to distinguish here. First, what has been called 'presupposition' is a felicity condition for statements—'presupposition', in a narrow sense used by philosophers talking about reference. Second, a felicity condition for marriage is its 'presupposition'—in some other sense, in which 'I do', said in the context of a marriage, 'presupposes' e.g. a human spouse, not a monkey.

I have, in effect, been extending the first of these two ideas. I have been ignoring the second, for present purposes. To take up the second would be to use 'presupposition' as a label for felicity conditions in general; we might want to call them 'Austinian presuppositions' as Witek suggests.[70] When Austin claims that referential presup-position contributes to the felicity of 'statements', he claims that presupposition in the first sense, i.e. requiring reference, is also presupposition in the second sense, i.e. a felicity condition. Put another way: semantic presuppositions are among the 'Austinian presuppositions' for 'statements'.

I have been extending the first idea, that presupposition contributes to felicity. Austin said that a statement's felicity conditions include 'what has been called "presup-position"', and we are taking this further. Many speech acts depend, for their felicity, 'on what has been called "presupposition"', but (I am suggesting) not just referential presupposition. Many speech acts depend, for their felicity, on presupposition con-strued more broadly, to include a presupposition that a speaker has authority or that George is an unpromising candidate. Put another way: pragmatic presuppositions are among the 'Austinian presuppositions' for many speech acts.

Presuppositions count as 'correct play' when hearers actively recognize and accept them, or passively let them pass. And this response, active or passive, also functions as the uptake, or default uptake, for the relevant *speech act* to count as 'correct play'. A presupposition of authority will go through, if nobody blocks it, whether because the hearer actively takes the speaker to have authority, or passively lets that presupposition pass; in either case, supplying uptake, active or passive.

It will not go through if somebody blocks it: 'Who do you think you are?' Such a hearer withholds acceptance of the presupposition. This blocks the obtaining of a salient felicity condition, namely authority, and withholds uptake from the speech act that would otherwise have occurred. In the absence of authority, and of uptake, active or passive, that speech act misfires.

---

[69] Austin 1962, 51.   [70] See Witek 2015; and for discussion, Sbisà forthcoming.

The retroactivity in Austin's picture is implicit in Lewis, though this has not to my knowledge been remarked upon. Lewis insists that the 'score' of a conversation alters 'straightway' at the time of the utterance. It is 'correct play' *at that time*: the bounds of permissibility straightway change, the ship is straightway named, the presupposition is straightway acceptable, and so forth. This holds, even though the alteration in score 'straightway' is partly hostage to later fortune, requiring later acts or omissions on the part of the hearer or bystander: for example, the absence of a later blocking that would stop it counting as correct play, at the earlier time referred to by 'straightway'.

This presents a further point of analogy with Lewis's guiding model of a sports game. A certain movement of a ball is a goal 'straightway', even though partly hostage to later fortune—requiring later acts or omissions on the part of the umpire, whose 'Out' would retroactively make it 'undone'. The umpire and the blocker alike would be able to change the past 'from the unactualized way it would have been...to the one and only way it actually is'.[71] The retroactive power Lewis ascribes to the time traveller applies equally to participants in a conversational language game, just as he describes them.

6.6 Handicaps on blocking

What hinders a hearer who might otherwise 'undo' bad speech? Some handicaps make blocking altogether impossible, because they make blocking itself misfire, the predicament faced by Claudette Colvin and Rosa Parks. Would-be blockers may encounter unjust illocutionary disablement, which thwarts an attempted blocking.[72]

Some handicaps can make blocking difficult, rather than impossible. A range of epistemological, structural, and normative barriers, apply especially to blocking.[73] Whether blocking is impossible or difficult may depend on not only the kind of 'evil' speech act, but also the kind of speaker, and the kind of hearer—that is to say, on social features, as well as linguistic ones, which contribute to the force of an utterance in a speech situation, and to the handicaps faced by potential speakers.

First, *epistemological* barriers place handicaps on blocking. Many back-door speech acts are hard to notice. When someone says 'Even George could win', attention is on 'George could win', not on 'even', still less on 'George is an unpromising candidate'. When someone says, 'Get on with it, Laurie, you great girl', the focus is on 'Get on with it', not on his being a girl, still less on what's wrong with a girl.

Back-door speech acts can have an under-the-radar quality absent in assertion.[74] But they can still function as testimony, exploiting potentially informative presupposition. In one respect they are *stronger* than assertion, presenting information as uncontroversial and not at issue—as shared knowledge or received wisdom, to be

[71] Lewis 1976, 76. For more on the umpire, see Langton 2009, ch. 5.
[72] Langton 1993, 2009, and discussed in Section 6.1.
[73] Many of these will apply in some form to other kinds of counter-speech, but I do not investigate this here.
[74] See Langton and West 1999; Sbisà 1999 on presupposition and ideology; Stanley 2015 on not-at-issue content; McGowan on covert conversational exercitives, this volume; Saul on covert 'dogwhistles', this volume.

taken for granted.[75] Backdoor testimony can be a potent source of 'falsehoods and fallacies' conveyed without attention or defense on the part of speaker or hearer.

These epistemological barriers can make it hard to block back-door speech acts. A hearer is less likely to notice they are being performed. If the hearer does notice, she has little reason to block, unless she is confident the speaker is wrong. If she is confident the speaker is wrong, she still risks being the epistemic outlier—the odd one out, who disagrees not only with the speaker, but also with what everyone supposedly takes for granted.

Second, there are *structural* barriers, which put a would-be blocker at a disadvantage. Lewis observed that accommodation can be *asymmetrically pliable*, easier to push in one direction rather than another. He applied this to the semantics of e.g. 'flat', and 'knows', where it seems easier to raise the standards than lower them. We might wonder, though, whether the apparent ease of standard-*raising* is an artifact of our profession's habits of pedantry and precision, and our familiarity with certain philosophical conversations. Often, elsewhere, it can seem easier to *lower* standards—as witnessed by recent electioneering rhetoric, characterized by a race to the bottom. The asymmetric pliability of accommodation has unnoticed implications for oppressive speech, or so McGowan and Robert Simpson have argued: it can be like 'ringing a bell' that cannot then be un-rung, making salient what cannot then be made unsalient.[76]

There is a phenomenon of *leaky quotes*, as I have called it.[77] Philosophers expect quotation marks to insulate their contents, like bubble wrap, so that what was harmfully used can be harmlessly mentioned. But there can be leaks, as when the injurious illocutionary potential of a slur seeps through into reported speech.[78] This presents difficulties, when a blocker needs to quote what was injurious: if the initial words cannot bear repeating, even to challenge them, it can be especially hard to fight words with words.

Finally, there are *normative handicaps* on blocking. To block is to put an obstruction in someone's way. That is true of blocking someone's driveway, and of blocking someone's speech act. To block is to flout co-operative norms, violate regulative rules about conduct in good conversation. A hearer may do so, may e.g. flat-footedly refuse to fill in the gaps, and supply what the speaker presupposes. A hearer may 'work to rule' and do the bare minimum required.[79] But such an interlocutor is not doing her job. She is being a nuisance, or worse. Other things being equal, you don't block the presuppositions of your interlocutor, since that derails the conversation.[80]

[75] Compare Langton and West 1999, Langton 2012, and forthcoming b; Sbisà 1999 on common ground as what *ought* to be shared; Sbisà forthcoming, on norms governing speech acts.

[76] McGowan 2009, Simpson 2013.

[77] Mostly on lecture handouts quoting hate speech, where I give a 'manufacturer's warning' to dispose of the handout carefully.

[78] There is a substantial literature on the 'scoping out' of slurs, but see e.g. Richard 2008, Anderson *et al.* 2012. We are considering not the semantics, but the injurious speech acts that go with injurious illocutionary potential.

[79] Camp this volume.

[80] A comic artist like Tina Fey can get away with it, in part by satirically pretending she is co-operating— e.g. expressed by 'you know', in 'you know, just like they ask Donald Trump.'

Social location makes a normative difference, in addition to the other differences it makes. Social norms apply differently to different people. For example, asymmetric gender norms about risk-taking, initiative, politeness, and deference, all affect the feasibility and costs of blocking, and amplify the handicaps just described.

These are just a few of the barriers that constrain the potential of blocking as counter-speech: epistemic, structural and normative barriers that can make it difficult to block back-door speech acts. They are inherent to the dynamics of accommodation, in concrete speech situations, where speakers perform speech acts, and hearers help them, through what they do, and fail to do.

6.7 Conclusion

We have been investigating a normative dimension to a familiar process in which speech acts are accommodated, or not. We have been finding a positive role for misfire—a rosier side to illocutionary silencing.[81] Back-door speech acts can be made to misfire, through blocking. And this makes space for the idea of blocking as a political resource: a counter-speech that might sometimes 'undo' the force of 'evil' speech, rather than refuting it. We have been taking up the hope expressed by Brandeis, that 'exposure' could be a kind of counter-speech—though he did not have blocking in mind, let alone blocking as modest time travel.

There is an uncomfortable side to this, and a different twist on an old dictum. What it takes for evil to succeed is for others to 'look on and do nothing', said J. S. Mill.[82] This applies quite literally to evil speech, if it can acquire authority and force from the omissions of others. Hearers and bystanders who do not block will sometimes, through that omission, make a speech act more evil, whether they mean to or no. The silence of hearers and bystanders can sometimes function as default uptake. This matters, when it comes to hate speech on a train, or back-door speech acts that rank people as inferior, enact hierarchy, and uphold oppressive norms. There are questions, then, about the responsibilities of hearers and bystanders, keeping in mind the handicaps just described, and the cruder handicaps described at the outset.[83] Blocking might be impossible. It might be possible, but hard. It might be required, or supererogatory, depending on situation, and social circumstance. It might need a raft of Aristotelian virtues—wit and good judgment, discretion and solidarity. But that takes us to different questions.

Here I hope, at the very least, to have brought out a distinctive sense to the idea that blocking 'obstructs' the 'accomplishment' of evil speech. It does not 'fight words with words' in the usual way: it does not refute bad speech, provide counter-evidence against it, or force its retraction. Blocking can 'undo' bad speech, by retroactively depriving it of certain hearer-based felicity conditions. If that is so, then blocking might retroactively *prevent*, rather than cure, a speech harm. If harmful speech can be

---

[81] Langton 1993, 2009.

[82] Mill 1867, 36. Similar sayings have also been variously attributed to Edmund Burke, Abraham Lincoln and others.

[83] Cf. Ayala and Vasilyeva 2016, Langton forthcoming b. In the sixth of the Locke Lectures I explore the responsibility of hearers as a Kantian imperfect duty.

'words that wound', then extending that metaphor we might say: instead of staunching the wound, blocking deflects the bullet, or blunts the knife.[84] There is a power in the hands of hearers to do something special. But that does not mean it is easy.

References

Adler, Margot. 2009. 'Before Rosa Parks there was Claudette Colvin'. *Radio Diaries*, NPR. http://www.npr.org/sections/codeswitch/2015/02/27/389563788/before-rosa-parks-a-teenager-defied-segregation-on-an-alabama-bus (accessed 23 November 2017).

Anderson, Luvell, with Sally Haslanger and Rae Langton. 2012. 'Language and Race', in *Routledge Companion to the Philosophy of Language*, eds. Gillian Russell and Delia Graff Fara (New York: Routledge), 753–67.

Austin, J. L. 1946. 'Other Minds', *Proceedings of the Aristotelian Society*, Supplementary Volume 20, 148–87, reprinted in *Philosophical Papers* (Oxford: Oxford University Press, 1979).

Austin, J. L. 1962. *How to Do Things with Words* (Oxford: Oxford University Press).

Ayala, Saray and Nadya Vasilyeva. 2016. 'Responsibility for Silence', *Journal of Social Philosophy* 47, 256–72.

Barlassina, L. and del Prete, F. 2015. 'The Puzzle of Changing the Past', *Analysis* 75, 59–67.

Berinsky, Adam. 2015. 'Rumors and Health Care Reform: Experiments in Political Misinformation,' *The British Journal of Political Science* 47, 241–262.

Bianchi, Claudia. 2008. 'Indexicals, Speech Acts and Pornography', *Analysis* 68, 310–16.

Brandeis, Louis. 1927. Opinion in *Whitney v. California*, 274 U. S. 357.

Brison, Susan. 1998. 'The Autonomy Defense of Free Speech', *Ethics* 108, 312–39.

Butler, Judith, 1997. *Excitable Speech: A Politics of the Performative* (New York and London: Routledge).

Davies, Alexander. 2016. 'How to Silence Content with Porn, Context and Loaded Questions', *European Journal of Philosophy* 24, 498–522.

Dotson, Kristie. 2011. 'Tracking Epistemic Violence, Tracking Practices of Silencing', *Hypatia* 26, 236–57.

Ehrlich, Susan and Jack Sidnell. 2006. ' "I Think That's Not an Assumption you Ought to Make": Challenging Presuppositions in Inquiry Testimony', *Language in Society* 35, 655–76.

France, Anatole. 1909. *Penguin Island*, trans. A.W. Evans (London and NY: J. Lane).

Gelber, Katharine. 2012. 'Hate Speech and the Australian Legal and Political Landscape', in *Speech and Harm*, eds. Maitra and McGowan, *q.v.*

Green, Leslie. 1998. 'Pornographizing, Subordinating, Silencing', in *Censorship and Silencing: Practices of Cultural Regulation*, ed. Robert Post (LA: Getty Research Institute), 285–312.

Greer, Germaine. 1970. *The Female Eunuch* (London: McGibbon and Kee).

Harman, Elizabeth. 1999. 'Creation Ethics: The Moral Status of Early Fetuses and the Ethics of Abortion', *Philosophy and Public Affairs* 28: 310–24.

Haslanger, Sally. 2011. 'Ideology, Generics, and Common Ground', in *Feminist Metaphysics*, ed. Charlotte Witt (Berlin: Springer Verlag), 179–207.

Haslanger, Sally. 2014. 'The Normal, the Natural and the Good: Generics and Ideology', *Politica e Societa* 3, 365–92.

Heffernan, William. 2015. *Dimensions of Justice: Ethical Issues in the Administration of Criminal Law* (Burlington MA: Jones and Bartlett).

Hornsby, Jennifer. 1995. 'Disempowered Speech'. *Philosophical Topics* 23, ed. Sally Haslanger, 127–47.

---

[84] Matsuda *et al.*, 1993.

Hornsby, Jennifer. 2011. 'Subordination, Silencing, and Two Ideas of Illocution', *Jurisprudence* 2, 379–85.

Hornsby, Jennifer and Rae Langton. 1998. 'Free Speech and Illocution', *Journal of Legal Theory* 4, 21–37.

Iacona, Andrea. 2016. 'On the Puzzle of Changing the Past', *Philosophia* 44, 137–42.

Jacobson, Daniel. 1995. 'Freedom of Speech Acts? A Response to Langton', *Philosophy and Public Affairs* 24, 64–79.

James, William. 1896. 'The Will to Believe', in *The Will to Believe and Other Essays in Popular Philosophy* (Norwood, MA: Plimpton Press).

Kukla, Rebecca. 2014. 'Performative Force, Convention, and Discursive Injustice', *Hypatia* 29, 440–57.

Langton, Rae. 1993. 'Speech Acts and Unspeakable Acts', *Philosophy and Public Affairs* 22, 305–30.

Langton, Rae. 2004. 'Projection and Objectification', in *The Future for Philosophy*, ed. Brian Leiter (Oxford: Oxford University Press), 285–303.

Langton, Rae. 2009. *Sexual Solipsism: Philosophical Essays on Pornography and Objectification* (Oxford: Oxford University Press).

Langton, Rae. 2012. 'Beyond Belief: Pragmatics in Hate Speech and Pornography', *Speech and Harm*, eds. Maitra and McGowan *q.v.*

Langton, Rae. 2014. 'Hate Speech and the Epistemology of Justice: Review of Jeremy Waldron, *The Harm in Hate Speech*'. *Criminal Law and Philosophy* 10(4), 865–73.

Langton, Rae. 2017. 'Is Pornography Like the Law?', in *Beyond Speech: Pornography and Analytic Feminist Philosophy*, ed. Mari Mikkola (Oxford: Oxford University Press), 23–8.

Langton, Rae, forthcoming a. 'The Authority of Hate Speech', Oxford Studies in Philosophy of Law Vol. 3, eds. John Gardner, Leslie Green and Brian Leiter.

Langton, Rae, forthcoming b. *Accommodating Injustice* (working title), The John Locke Lectures 2015 (Oxford: Oxford University Press).

Langton, Rae, with Caroline West. 1999. 'Scorekeeping in a Pornographic Language Game', *Australasian Journal of Philosophy* 77, 303–19.

Leslie, S. J. 2015. ' "Hillary Clinton is the Only Man in the Obama Administration": Dual Character Concepts, Generics, and Gender', *Analytic Philosophy* 56, 111–41.

Lewis, David. 1970. 'How to Define Theoretical Terms', *Journal of Philosophy* 67, 427–46.

Lewis, David. 1979. 'Scorekeeping in a Language Game', *Journal of Philosophical Logic* 8, 339–59, reprinted in *Philosophical Papers*, Vol. I (Oxford: Oxford University Press, 1983), 233–49.

Lewis, David. 1976. 'The Paradoxes of Time Travel'. *American Philosophical Quarterly* 13, 145–52, reprinted in *Philosophical Papers*, Vol. II (Oxford: Oxford University Press, 1986), 67–80.

Maitra, Ishani. 2009. 'Silencing Speech'. *Canadian Journal of Philosophy* 39, 309–38.

Maitra, Ishani. 2012. 'Subordinating Speech', in *Speech and Harm*, eds. Maitra and McGowan *q.v.*

Maitra, Ishani, with Mary Kate McGowan (eds.) 2012. *Speech and Harm* (Oxford: Oxford University Press).

Matsuda, Mari, with Charles R. Lawrence III, Richard Delgado, and Kimberlè Williams Crenshaw. 1993. *Words that Wound: Critical Race Theory, Assaultive Speech and the First Amendment* (Boulder, CO: Westview Press).

McGowan, Mary Kate. 2004. 'Conversational Exercitives: Something Else We Do With Our Words', *Linguistics and Philosophy* 27, 93–111.

McGowan, Mary Kate. 2009. 'Oppressive Speech', *Australasian Journal of Philosophy* 87, 389–407.

McGowan, Mary Kate, forthcoming. *Just Words: Speech and the Constitution of Harm*.

Mikkola, Mari. 2011. 'Illocution, Silencing and the Act of Refusal', *Pacific Philosophical Quarterly* 92, 415–37.

Mill, John Stuart. 1867. *Inaugural Address Delivered to the University of St. Andrews, Feb. 1st 1867* (London: Longmans, Green, Reader, and Dyer).

Milton, John. 1644. *The Areopagitica*. http://www.stlawrenceinstitute.org/vol14mit.html (accessed 23 November 2017).

Nielsen, Laura Beth. 2012. 'Power in Public: Reactions, Responses and Resistance to Offensive Public Speech', in *Speech and Harm*, eds. Maitra and McGowan *q.v.*

Pinker, Steven, with Martin Nowak and James Lee. 2008. 'The Logic of Indirect Speech', *Proceedings of the National Academy of Sciences* 105, 833–8.

Richard, Mark. 2008. *When Truth Gives Out* (Oxford: Oxford University Press).

Roberts, Craige. 2015. 'Accommodation in a Language Game', in *The Blackwell Companion to David Lewis*, eds. Barry Loewer and Jonathan Schaffer (Oxford: Blackwell), 345–366.

Saul, Jennifer M. 2006. 'Pornography, Speech Acts and Context', *Proceedings of the Aristotelian Society* 106, 229–48.

Sbisà, Marina. 1999. 'Ideology and the Persuasive Use of Presupposition', in *Language and Ideology: Selected Papers from the 6th International Pragmatics Conference* Vol. I., ed. J. Verschueren (Antwerp: International Pragmatics Association), 492–509.

Sbisà, Marina. 2007. 'How to Read Austin', *Pragmatics* 17, 461–73.

Sbisà, Marina, forthcoming. 'Varieties of Speech Act Norms', in Maciej Witek and Iwona Witczak-Plisiecka (eds.), *Dynamics and Varieties of Speech Actions*, a theme issue of Poznan Studies in the Philosophy of the Sciences and the Humanities (Brill).

Schwartzman, Lisa H. 2002. 'Hate Speech, Illocution, and Social Context: A Critique of Judith Butler', *Journal of Social Philosophy* 33, 421–41.

Simon-Vandenbergen, Anne-Marie, with Peter White and Karin Aijmer. 2007. 'Presupposition and "Taking-for-Granted" in Mass Communicated Political Argument', in *Political Discourse in the Media*, eds. Anita Fetzer and Gerda Lauerbach (Amsterdam and Philadelphia: John Benjamins), 31–74.

Simpson, Robert. 2013. 'Un-ringing the Bell: McGowan on Oppressive Speech and the Asymmetric Pliability of Conversations', *Australasian Journal of Philosophy* 91(3), 555–75.

Stalnaker, Robert. 2002. 'Common Ground', *Linguistics and Philosophy* 25, 701–21.

Stanley, Jason. 2015. *How Propaganda Works* (Princeton: Princeton University Press).

Sunstein, Cass. 2001. *Republic.com* (Princeton: Princeton University Press).

Swanson, Eric, forthcoming. 'Slurs and Ideologies', in R. Celikates, S. Haslanger, and J. Stanley (eds.), *Ideology* (Oxford: Oxford University Press).

Thomason, Richmond. 1990. 'Accommodation, meaning, and implicature: Interdisciplinary. foundations for pragmatics' in *Intentions in Communication,* eds. Philip R. Cohen, Jerry Morgan and Martha Pollack (Cambridge, MA: MIT Press), 325–63.

Thomson, Judith Jarvis. 1971. 'The Time of a Killing', *Journal of Philosophy* 68, 115–32.

Tirrell, Lynne. 2012. 'Genocidal Language Games', in *Speech and Harm*, eds. Maitra and McGowan, *q.v.*

von Fintel, Kai. 2008. 'What is Presupposition Accommodation Again?' *Philosophical Perspectives* 22, 137–70.

Waldron, Jeremy. 2012. *The Harm in Hate Speech* (Cambridge, MA: Harvard University Press).

West, Caroline. 2003. 'The Free Speech Argument Against Pornography', *Canadian Journal of Philosophy* 33, 391–422.

White, Alan. 1970. *Truth* (New York: Macmillan).

Witek, Maciej. 2013. 'How to Establish Authority with Words: Imperative Utterances and Presupposition Accommodation', in *Logic, Methodology and Philosophy of Science at Warsaw University*, ed. A. Brozżek (Warsaw: Warsaw University), 145–57.

Witek, Maciej. 2015. 'Mechanisms of Illocutionary Games'. *Language & Communication* 42, 11–22.

7

Explicit Indirection

Ernie Lepore and Matthew Stone

Introduction

It is tempting to regard our interpretive judgments about so-called "indirect speech acts" as a straightforward reflection of pragmatic reasoning. Take (1), the now stock example from Searle (1975), on its most plausible interpretation:

1. Can you pass the salt?

Literally, it seems that the speaker has asked a question, and it's likely that the hearer will go on to answer that question (Bach and Harnish 1979; Clark 1979), perhaps as in either (2) or (3).

2. No, sorry, I can't reach it.
3. Of course. Here it is.

But (1) is not just a question on its most plausible interpretation. It is also a request. The speaker expects the addressee to pass the salt, and an addressee who fails to realize this—who merely answers the literal question, for example—has not understood the speaker's utterance. In short, the traditional view of utterances such as (1) is that there is a literal meaning, for (1) a question, and simultaneously a further meaning, for (1) a request, which becomes obvious when the utterance is used in a context where the request would be expected and appropriate. When we describe our interpretive judgments in the traditional way, it can look as though it's part of the very data about such cases that they are examples of conversational implicature, in the sense of Grice (1975). In particular, on the traditional view, the interpretation of (1) as a request is not part of its literal meaning but something additional that's derived or "calculated" from that meaning on the assumption that the speaker's use of (1) is intended to advance the established purposes of the conversation. For recent defenses of the traditional view, see for example Bezuidenhout (2016). But you have felt the force of this perspective already if the title of this paper struck you as paradoxical.

As broadly accepted as it is, the view that the indirection involved in such utterances is a pragmatic phenomenon has far-reaching and, we think, problematic consequences. The fundamental difficulty is that there is overwhelming evidence that grammar governs indirect meanings. As Searle (1975) already noted, grammar distinguishes between utterances that regularly achieve indirect requests, such as (1), from apparently equivalent utterances that do not, such as (4):

4.   Are you capable of passing the salt?

Indirect but grammatically licensed directives permit the modifier "please", just like imperatives, but unlike creative hints intended to prompt an action on the part of the addressee (Horn 1989, Lakoff 1973, Sadock 1974). This leads, for example, to the contrast between (5), which sounds natural, and (6), which sounds odd (the sentences are 94 and 95 from Lepore and Stone 2015).

5.   I'd like a drink please.
6.   #I'm thirsty please.

Finally, the expressions that are assigned such indirect meanings exhibit substantial cross-linguistic variation (Wierzbicka 1985). To reconcile pragmatic accounts of indirection with these facts requires postulating new categories of pragmatic rules in grammar—customs (or conventions in the loose sense of Millikan's 1998 self-perpetuating patterns) that constrain the general rational purposes for which speakers can use language in communication but are integrated into the very architecture of the language faculty. Such rules challenge the view of language—common to both Grice (1975) and Chomsky (e.g., 2005)—as a neutral representational system whose use is whatever people make of it.

Our goal in this paper is to contest the traditional view of indirection in utterances such as (1) by developing a very different way of characterizing the interpretations involved. We argue that the felt "indirection" of such utterances reflects the kind of meaning the utterances have, rather than the way that meaning is derived. So understood, there is no presumption that indirect meanings involve the pragmatic derivation of enriched contents from a literal interpretation; rather, we argue that indirect meanings are explicitly encoded in grammar.

In particular, we argue that utterances such as (1) work by presenting a complex package of related meanings together as a single unit: on its usual interpretation, an utterance of (1) *first* raises the question whether the addressee can pass the salt and *second* expresses a preference, in the case that the answer is 'yes', that the addressee do so. This move feels indirect, we suggest, because of the weak commitment it imposes on the speaker and the flexible responses it affords the addressee. The move does not commit the speaker to a general preference for action on the part of the addressee; the preference is subject to the addressee's taking it on, by giving a 'yes' answer. Conversely, the preference itself does not even have to be addressed by the addressee for the request to be declined: a 'no' answer gives a coherent response to the open question, but simultaneously renders the speaker's conditional preference inert.

To make our ideas precise, we build on recent work on formalizing declarative, interrogative, and imperative meanings as distinct but compatible kinds of content for utterances (Charlow 2011, Starr 2010, to appear). In these frameworks, we can straightforwardly formalize our intuitive suggestion that (1) raises a question and then expresses a conditional preference. Moreover, we can formally analyze the information states that result from different potential responses on the part of the addressee: a 'yes' answer resolves the interaction to a directive followed by compliance, while a 'no' answer leads to a conversational state where the speaker is *not* committed to the directive and the addressee has *not* rejected it. These calculations substantiate our explanation of what felt indirection involves: the indirect utterance is formulated obliquely, in a way that respects both the speaker's authority and the addressee's autonomy (key aspects of Brown and Levinson's 1987 theory of politeness).

The resulting picture allows for straightforward statements of the semantic rules associating utterances like (1) with complex "indirect" interpretations and for a straightforward meta-semantics where these rules amount to conventions for committing to content, broadly in line with the ideas of Lewis (1969, 1979). Thus it is compatible not only with our interpretive intuitions, but with the ample evidence that these interpretations have their origins in the ordinary rules of language.

Background

Our view, then, is that apparently indirect utterances combine multiple semantic contributions. Not surprisingly, philosophers and linguists have developed many similar views over the years—going back at least to Sadock (1974) and perhaps even to Austin (1962). However, we find all the previous approaches problematic, and we find ourselves differing from them on key semantic and pragmatic issues. We therefore begin by acknowledging our debts to the past and highlighting what's distinctive about our view.

The key differences involve our take on meaning. We think of the content of a discourse in terms of changes to an abstract structure that records different kinds of contributions, following Lewis (1979) and Thomason (1990). We'll call this structure the conversational record. In order to capture the different contents of declarative, interrogative and imperative sentences, we model the conversational record as including not only the propositional information that is taken for granted in the discourse (Stalnaker 1978), but also the open issues that have been raised in the discourse (Ginzburg 2012, Roberts 2012) and the preferences that the discourse establishes (Charlow 2011, Portner 2005, Starr 2010, to appear). When we give the meaning of an utterance, then, we need to specify how the utterance changes each of these components of the conversational record. We'll use 'contributing propositions', 'raising questions', and 'establishing preferences' as terms of art that describe the particular semantic effects characteristically associated with declaratives, interrogatives and imperatives.

We think of the conversational record as a level of meaning that is public, determined by language users' deference to semantic conventions and shared practices of meaning making. See Lepore and Stone (2015) for an extended development and defense of this characterization. This gives teeth to the idea that updating the conversational record is a semantic notion. On our view, the updates associated with utterances are not simply a reflection of speakers' intentions for how the utterances should update the conversational record. Speakers can, for example, have mistaken assumptions about the meanings of utterances, and so they can inadvertently use utterances that contribute propositions, raise questions, or establish preferences that they did not intend. Cutting the familiar Gricean link between meaning and intention represents a deep disagreement with most research on speech acts (including Charlow 2011 and Harris 2014). Our view involves thinking of meaning not as psychological but as social, in the sense of Burge (1979), Kripke (1972), and Putnam (1975). We think this difference is important for making sense of our notion of explicit indirection. For example, we argue later that distinguishing meaning from intention recognition helps us explain the distinctive responses that interlocutors give to the contributions that utterances make explicitly, as distinguished from their engagement with information that other speakers merely make evident.

At the same time, the notion of the state of a discourse is underspecified in its import for the mental states of interlocutors. In particular, the commitments that speakers make in conversation cannot be reduced to such practical attitudes as belief and intention (Stalnaker 2002, Starr 2010, Thomason 1990). Contributing a proposition may commit the speaker to treat that proposition as true for the purposes of the conversation, but it does not commit the speaker either to believe the proposition herself or to intend her audience to believe it. Similarly, raising a question may commit the speaker to treat the question as open for the purposes of the conversation, but it does not commit her to need the answer or to expect one from her audience. An established preference, likewise, need not express the speaker's true desires or her actual intentions for her audience. Some philosophers think that this makes the idea of the conversational record counterintuitive (Harris 2014) or even empty (Bezuidenhout, to appear). By contrast, we argue below that our understanding of the conversational record dovetails with Brown and Levinson's (1987) influential theory of politeness. Politeness often seems to rely on serious utterances that nevertheless carry few consequences for interlocutors' attitudes—as illustrated by the ostensible but transparently insincere offers or the feigned and evidently bogus excuses that we use to smooth our interactions with one another. If this is the right way to think of politeness, then the flexibility of the conversational record must be something that speakers understand and exploit.

Finally, meaning itself is just the starting point for the effects speakers hope to bring about in using utterances. We see meaning as an input to a wide range of imaginative devices that exploit meaning but do not deliver meaning, including such practices as irony, sarcasm, and humor (Lepore and Stone 2015). On our view, such practices offer productive and general ways for speakers to use utterances whose meanings establish preferences without undertaking the commitments that come when they use those utterances seriously. And of course, directive utterances, including those with conventional indirect interpretations, can be used ironically, sarcastically, humorously, and so forth (Harris 2014).

Given the way we think of meaning, it should be clear that we do not think that the conventional meaning of an utterance can specify the speech act it performs, at least as speech acts are traditionally conceived. Searle (1969, 1975) characterizes speech acts in terms of preconditions and effects involving the mental states of the interlocutors. A request, for example, aims at getting the addressee to do something. In different ways, Charlow (2011) and Harris (2014) elaborate on this perspective to explain how philosophers might analyze directive meaning as a general constraint on the kinds of speech acts that utterances are generally used to perform. Harris in particular goes on to reject the notion of the conversational record and even the existence of conventions of meaning. This is not our view. We characterize the conventional meaning of utterances in terms of updates to the record, which do *not* entail specific preconditions or effects on the mental states of interlocutors and so do *not* accomplish specific *speech acts*, in Searle's or Harris's senses.

In particular, then, we do not suggest that (1) encodes a *request* as a matter of meaning. The directive content of (1) is simply to establish a preference. A speaker can sometimes make a request by using an utterance with such a meaning, but only when (among other conditions) the utterance is serious, the interlocutors have the right relationships, and they are interpreting the commitments of the conversational record in the right way. Since we think that indirection is a matter of semantics, we avoid talk of indirect speech acts or indirect requests, and will try to be explicit about the kinds of meanings we think are really involved. This may sometimes involve a certain amount of circumlocution.[1]

A corollary is that our view is not just a resurrection of the infamous performative hypothesis in grammar (Cresswell 1973, Lewis 1970, Ross 1970). The performative hypothesis is the idea that each main clause is embedded within a syntactically represented and semantically interpreted clause describing the speaker's speech act in using the utterance and involving a covert performative verb. Sadock (1974) is an extended development and defense of the performative hypothesis from a linguistic and philosophical point of view. Linguistically, it is controversial that the postulation of this covert structure explains the relevant syntactic and semantic phenomena as well as its proponents originally claimed (see McCawley 1985 for review). Philosophically, it leads to problems in answering which utterances are truth-evaluable and what their truth conditions are (Boër and Lycan 1980). At the same time, the performative hypothesis requires sentences to have logical forms that are inappropriately specific and that vary implausibly from one utterance of a sentence to the next (see Starr 2010 for discussion). These weaknesses of the performative hypothesis are well known (see Sadock 2004—we will not repeat the arguments). But it is also well-known that these weaknesses do not extend to current approaches to the semantics of mood, including those on which our account is based (see Harris 2014 and Starr 2010). The reason, of course, is that updates to the record may remain invariant even as the acts speakers accomplish with those updates vary.

Asher and Lascarides (2001) offer a different kind of formal development of the idea that utterances can conventionally combine a constellation of related speech acts. On their view, grammar assigns to conventionally indirect utterances semantic contents of mutually incompatible semantic types—for example, the content of a question and the content of a request. They assume that it is pragmatic reasoning that reconciles these incompatible meanings into a coherent whole, and that the result is in fact a series of related speech acts—for example, speech acts of questioning and of requesting. By contrast, we follow Starr's (2010) semantics, where declarative, interrogative, and imperative utterances all denote updates to the conversational record; the different updates just happen to affect different attributes of the record. Thus, we think there is no conflict or coercion involved in first raising a question and then establishing a conditional preference, so there is no obstacle to specifying an indirect meaning explicitly in grammar.

---

[1] Within semantics, there is a longstanding use of 'question' to name a semantic object, on a par with 'proposition', alongside uses naming a syntactic form and a kind of act. We think this terminology is unavoidable and will stick to it. Charitable readers should think of 'request', as used in Lepore and Stone's 2015 discussion of the meanings of indirect speech acts, in analogous terms, as a name for directive content, not a name for a kind of action.

Our differences with Asher and Lascarides (2001) are philosophical as well as formal. Asher and Lascarides insist that indirect readings are calculated and that cooperative reasoning is essential to this process. They therefore describe default rules that produce indirect readings and additional default rules that normally preempt the derivation of indirection outside of its conventional range. We deny that there are pragmatic processes of the sort that Asher and Lascarides envisage at work in conventionalized indirection. We think the generalizations that underwrite their default rules can be best explained, not as pragmatic principles, but rather as historical or meta-level generalizations about the kinds of meanings that a language tends to encode.

As we have already hinted, our technical approach follows Starr (2010, to appear). His formalism is compatible with a range of philosophical interpretations: his models can characterize individuals' private takes on the conversation (as in Ginzburg 2012), or individuals' occurrent mutual suppositions about the conversation (as in Thomason 1990). We do not claim that Starr subscribes to or would necessarily endorse exactly our understanding of the conversational record as a public social construct.

Most importantly, Starr himself makes no claims about indirect speech acts or about indirection in utterance interpretation more generally. In demonstrating how his formalism could handle conventionalized indirection, we think we are making a philosophical contribution that attests to the strength of his framework. But of course, his framework in no way precludes the exploration of other accounts of indirection (including accounts based on pragmatics).

Formal Model

We now review Starr's (2010, to appear) model and apply it to conventionalized indirection. We use the model, as formal semanticists commonly do, to make our empirical claims more precise. The formalism offers a specific realization that shows how propositional information, open issues, and established preferences can constitute an overarching record of the state of the conversation with substantive inferential and communicative dynamics. It lets us specify primitive meanings, compose them together into complex contributions, and explain what follows from them. In particular, we give a meaning for indirection that raises an issue and expresses a conditional preference; we show that the meaning allows for an answer, entails an ordinary directive if the answer is 'yes', and has no directive consequences if the answer is 'no'. (These inferences depend on some rather delicate definitions, so we proceed slowly, via worked examples.) Later, we will link these conversational properties to speakers' intuitions about the polite indirection of utterances such as (1). Thus, the model shows that our intuitive picture of conventionalized indirection is consistent in certain respects and allows us to substantiate our intuitive predictions about our view in a precise way.

Defining Content

We start by presenting the general picture of Starr's model, and giving (slightly streamlined) versions of the key definitions of the formal system. We refer the reader to Starr (2010, to appear) for the complete definitions.

To get the logic off the ground, we have a set of possible worlds Ω describing ways the world might be, and an interpretation function I that specifies the extensions of predicates across worlds and the reference of terms. We also need a relation of accessibility A among possible worlds, to interpret 'can' sentences: wAw' just in case w' represents a possible alternative for w. Formulas are constructed from atoms, negation, and possibility operators. An atomic formula $P(n_1 \ldots n_k)$ is true at world w if and only if $< I(n_1) \ldots I(n_k) > \in I(P)(w)$. Conversely, if ρ is a formula, then $\neg\rho$ is true at w if and only if ρ is not true at w. Finally, if ρ is a formula, then $\Diamond\rho$ is true at w if and only if there is some world w' with wAw' such that ρ is true at w'.

Starr models propositional information using sets of possible worlds. (This idea has been a standard tool since Stalnaker 1978.) The basic operation of contributing information is to start from a set of worlds and narrow the set down to just those where the information is true. If c is a set of worlds and ρ is a formula, we use the notation $c[\rho]$ for $\{w \in c \mid \rho$ is true at $w\}$.

The content of a discourse is not limited to propositional information, however. Discourse can also raise questions. Semantically, Starr proposes to model questions as sets of their possible answers; a question expresses an interest in establishing that one of the answer propositions is true, but which one, of course, remains to be determined. This is a familiar idea going back to Hamblin (1958). Now, by representing discourse content as a set of alternatives, we can capture both declarative meaning and interrogative meaning; see Ciardelli, Groenendijk, and Roelofsen (2015). The open questions of the discourse concern the differences among the alternative possibilities; its propositional content, meanwhile, consists in what all the alternatives have in common. We can record the contribution of new propositional information by selecting and refining the alternatives. We can record the raising of a new question by introducing additional alternatives to describe the possible ways the question could be resolved. Since many questions are normally on the table, these alternatives involve not only answering the question individually but also providing detailed answers that address this question in tandem with others.

Imperative meaning, for Starr, also involves alternatives. Imperatives involve a preference for one alternative over another. Starr models this with a binary relation R: given sets of possible worlds a and a' that are alternatives in the discourse, aRa' indicates that the content of the discourse establishes the preference that a is better than a'. This is naturally understood as a transitive, asymmetric relation (assuming that the preferences established by a discourse are consistent). It's also convenient to assume that the necessarily false proposition $\emptyset$ is always part of the domain of R and that consistent alternatives are always preferred to it. That way we can use R simply to identify a set of consistent alternatives, even when R establishes no substantive preferences among them.

In short, we can represent discourse content in terms of a binary preference relation R over propositions. The domain of R specifies the set of alternatives at issue in the discourse—encoding possible answers to the open questions raised in the discourse. The propositional content of the discourse is the disjunction of these propositions—giving the information that all the possible answers have in common.

Let's give a concrete example to illustrate the features of the formalism and motivate the definitions to follow. Consider a simple, idealized situation: there is an upcoming concert with four possible singers: Chris, Kim, Robin, and Sandy. This gives a model with sixteen possible worlds, each of which we can indicate by listing who will sing (they are: ckrs, ckr, cks, ck, crs, cr, cs, c, krs, kr, ks, k, s, r, –). Suppose that a discourse says that Chris will sing, asks whether Kim will sing, commands that Robin sing, and is silent about Sandy. Let's compose the relation R_1 that we will use to represent the content of the discourse.

First, let's consider the alternatives. The discourse has explicitly raised the question whether Kim will sing. It also needs alternatives for whether Robin will sing, since it prefers that Robin sing. And it needs alternatives that give answers to both questions simultaneously. All the alternatives must reflect the fact that Chris will sing. And they should all make no commitment about Sandy one way or the other. That gives eight propositions, to which we add the information that Chris will sing and the necessarily false proposition to get the roster in (7):

7. {ckrs, ckr, cks, ck, crs, cr, cs, c}—Chris will sing.
    {ckrs, ckr, cks, ck}—Will Kim sing? Yes.
    {crs, cr, cs, c}—Will Kim sing? No.
    {ckrs, ckr, crs, cr}—Will Robin sing? Yes.
    {cks, ck, cs, c}—Will Robin sing? No.
    {ckrs, ckr}—Which of Kim and Robin will sing? Both.
    {cks, ck}—Which of Kim and Robin will sing? Kim.
    {crs, cr}—Which of Kim and Robin will sing? Robin.
    {cs, c}—Which of Kim and Robin will sing? Neither.
    Ø—absurdity

We prefer that Robin sing, other things being equal: better Robin sings than not, better Robin sings with Kim if Kim sings, and better Robin sings without Kim if Kim does not sing. We also prefer all the live possibilities in (7) to the necessarily false proposition Ø. Thus, the relation R_1 that we get is given by the tuples in (8).

8. {⟨{ckrs, ckr, cks, ck, crs, cr, cs, c}, Ø⟩,
    ⟨{ckrs, ckr, cks, ck}, Ø⟩,
    ⟨{crs, cr, cs, c}, Ø⟩,
    ⟨{ckr, crs, cr}, Ø⟩,
    ⟨{cks, ck, cs, c}, Ø⟩,
    ⟨{ckrs, ckr}, Ø⟩,
    ⟨{cks, ck}, Ø⟩,
    ⟨{crs, cr}, Ø⟩,
    ⟨{cs, c}, Ø⟩,
    ⟨{ckrs, ckr, crs, cr}, {cks, ck, cs, c}⟩,
    ⟨{ckrs, ckr}, {cks, ck}⟩,
    ⟨{crs, cr}, {cs, c}⟩}}

This example might seem slightly involved, but it will allow us to give worked examples that walk through the definitions of updates precisely.

Capturing Dynamics

To describe discourse content, Starr moves from a level of formulas to a level of updates that transform the relationships that represent discourse state. For example, an update that contributes propositional information requires us to incorporate that information into all the available alternatives. The information may answer an open question: in this case the information will also eliminate the alternatives that are incompatible with the information it provides. We formalize these effects using the definition in (9). The notation $\triangleright\rho$ denotes an update that contributes the propositional information specified by the formula ρ.

9. $R[\triangleright\rho] := \{\langle a[\rho], a'[\rho]\rangle |\ aRa' \text{ and } a[\rho] \neq \emptyset\}$

According to the definition in (9), we update a context R with $\triangleright\rho$ by taking each of the tuples aRa' and restricting the alternatives a and a' to reflect the information ρ—as long as this is consistent with a. Thus, suppose we update R_1 with the information that Sandy will sing. In this case, we will simply refine the possibilities—eliminating all the worlds where Sandy will not sing from consideration. The relation we get for $R_1[\triangleright\text{sing}(\text{Sandy})]$ is therefore:

10. $\{\langle\{\text{ckrs, cks, crs, cs}\}, \emptyset\rangle,$
       $\langle\{\text{ckrs, cks}\}, \emptyset\rangle,$
       $\langle\{\text{crs, cs}\}, \emptyset\rangle,$
       $\langle\{\text{ckrs, crs}\}, \emptyset\rangle,$
       $\langle\{\text{cks, cs}\}, \emptyset\rangle,$
       $\langle\{\text{ckrs}\}, \emptyset\rangle,$
       $\langle\{\text{cks}\}, \emptyset\rangle,$
       $\langle\{\text{crs}\}, \emptyset\rangle,$
       $\langle\{\text{cs}\}, \emptyset\rangle,$
       $\langle\{\text{ckrs, crs}\}, \{\text{cks, cs}\}\rangle,$
       $\langle\{\text{ckrs}\}, \{\text{cks}\}\rangle,$
       $\langle\{\text{crs}\}, \{\text{cs}\}\rangle\}$

On the other hand, suppose we learn that Kim will sing. The discourse is already structured to distinguish alternatives where Kim will sing from alternatives where Kim will not sing: those where Kim will not sing will now disappear. The relation we get for $R_1[\triangleright\text{sing}(\text{Kim})]$ is therefore simply:

11. $\{\langle\{\text{ckrs, ckr, cks, ck}\}, \emptyset\rangle,$
       $\langle\{\text{ckrs, ckr}\}, \emptyset\rangle,$
       $\langle\{\text{cks, ck}\}, \emptyset\rangle,$
       $\langle\{\text{ckrs, ckr}\}, \{\text{cks, ck}\}\rangle\}$

Now imagine starting with a basic relation R_0 corresponding to complete ignorance about our example universe. We can specify R_0 as in (12).

12. $\{\langle\{\text{ckrs, ckr, cks, ck, crs, cr, cs, c, krs, kr, ks, k, s, r, -}\}, \emptyset\rangle\}$

Then $R_0[\triangleright\text{sing}(\text{Chris})]$ is simply:

13. $\{\langle\{\text{ckrs, ckr, cks, ck, crs, cr, cs, c}\}, \emptyset\rangle\}$

174 ERNIE LEPORE AND MATTHEW STONE

What about interrogatives? Contributing a new question just anticipates the possibility of a 'yes' answer or a 'no' answer as additional alternatives for the discourse. We formalize this in (14), where $?\rho$ denotes an update that raises the question whether ρ is true.

14. $R[?\rho] := R \cup R[\triangleright\rho] \cup R[\triangleright\neg\rho]$

It's best to start with a simple illustration: $R_0[\triangleright\text{sing(Chris)}][?\text{sing(Kim)}]$. We combine the alternatives specified in (13) with the alternatives we get from the update that Kim will sing and the alternatives we get from the update that Kim will not sing. That gives three possibilities:

15. $\{\langle\{\text{ckrs, ckr, cks, ck, crs, cr, cs, c}\}, \emptyset\rangle,$
    $\langle\{\text{ckrs, ckr, cks, ck}\}, \emptyset\rangle,$
    $\langle\{\text{crs, cr, cs, c}\}, \emptyset\rangle\}$

For a more complex example, consider constructing the relation $R_1[?\text{sing(Sandy)}]$. According to (14), we start with the relation R_1, as given in (8). Then we add the tuples in the relation $R_1[\triangleright\text{sing(Sandy)}]$, as given in (10). Finally, we add a complementary set of tuples derived from $R_1[\triangleright\neg\text{sing(Sandy)}]$. So the discourse allows for all the possible answers it did so far, allows any of those answers to be combined with the information that Sandy will sing if that's consistent, and also allows any of those answers to be combined with the information that Sandy will not sing if that's consistent. The preferences among these alternatives are inherited from the preferences already established in the discourse. The representation that results is rather cumbersome to write down, since the number of possible compound answers grows exponentially in the number of questions introduced. But the idea, as formalized in (14), should be clear.

What about establishing a preference for a proposition ρ? To start, this has to raise the issue of whether ρ is true; we will need to distinguish the ρ outcomes from the $\neg\rho$ outcomes. But we also have to relate the alternatives we have in the right way. We may have new alternatives of the form $a[\rho]$ that now should be preferred to corresponding alternatives of the form $a[\neg\rho]$. But, we also want to use our existing preferences of the form aRa' transitively, to encode our derived preference for consistent alternatives $a[\rho]$ over corresponding alternatives $a'[\neg\rho]$. This leads to the definition in (16), where $!\rho$ denotes the imperative update that establishes a preference for ρ over $\neg\rho$.

16. $R[!\rho] := R[?\rho] \cup \{\langle a[\rho], a[\neg\rho]\rangle | a \in \text{dom}(R[?\rho]) \text{ and } a[\rho] \neq \emptyset\} \cup$
    $\{\langle a[\rho], a'[\neg\rho]\rangle | aR[\rho]a' \text{ and } a[\rho] \neq \emptyset\}$

We leave it to the reader to check using definition (16) and the key intermediate result in (15) that $R_0[\triangleright\text{sing(Chris)}][?\text{sing(Kim)}][!\text{sing(Robin)}]$ gives precisely the relation R_1 presented in (8). As it happens, in this case, the order of the updates does not matter: we derive the same relation R_1 from $R_0[!\text{sing(Robin)}][\triangleright\text{sing(Chris)}][?\text{sing(Kim)}]$, $R_0[?\text{sing(Kim)}][!\text{sing(Robin)}][\triangleright\text{sing(Chris)}]$, and so forth.

As a matter of notation, we can introduce an operation of sequencing as in (17).

17. $R[\varphi; \psi] := R[\varphi][\psi]$

This allows us to compose together meanings that convey complex constellations of content—for example, to describe R_1 as obtained directly from R_0 by an update with the content of an entire discourse: $R_0[\triangleright\text{sing(Chris)}; ?\text{sing(Kim)}; !\text{sing(Robin)}]$.

The last ingredient of the formalism is the conditional. The definition has two parts: a *test* describing the import of conditional information, and an *update* describing the import of conditional questions and preferences.

18. $R[\text{if }(\varphi)\,(\psi)] := R \cup R[\varphi; \psi]$ if $\cup \text{dom}(R[\varphi]) = \cup \text{dom}(R[\varphi; \psi])$
Ø otherwise.

The test makes sure that the information $\cup\text{dom}(R[\varphi; \psi])$ given by the antecedent and consequent together does not go beyond the information $\cup\text{dom}(R[\varphi])$ obtained simply from considering the antecedent itself. In other words, we pass the test if the consequent is informationally redundant given the content we get by taking on the antecedent.[2] If the test fails, the conditional is inconsistent with our present information, so the output state of the conditional is trivial. Of course, raising questions and expressing preferences don't give any new information; they have other effects. So conditional questions and conditional preferences will always pass this test.

If the conditional generalization is already implicit in the information that we have, the rule will construct a new output state in a certain way, designed with questions and preferences in mind. The output makes reference to an updated state $R[\varphi; \psi]$—this captures the contributions made by φ and ψ. Normally φ contributes information, so this involves taking on the information given by φ, and then incorporating the contributions of ψ (adding information, raising questions or expressing preferences) that apply just to those worlds where φ is true. This state is then *combined* with the initial state R by *set union*. In other words, the update of the conditional preserves all the open questions and preferences we started with, but adds some new ones: we're interested in the answer if φ is true, as well as a range of further questions and preferences that will come into play if the answer is 'yes'.

For our purposes in this paper, the key thing about definition (18) is in the way it handles conditional imperatives. Let's return to R_0 and consider $R_0[\text{if }(\triangleright\text{sing(Chris)})$ $(!\text{sing(Robin)})]$. According to (18), we first compute $R_0[\triangleright\text{sing(Chris)}]$: recall that that's the relation given in (13). Then we compute $R_0[\triangleright\text{sing(Chris)}; !\text{sing(Robin)}]$. The reader can check that this is the relation given in (19).

19. {⟨{ckrs, ckr, cks, ck, crs, cr, cs, c}, Ø,
⟨{ckrs, ckr, crs, cr}, Ø⟩,
⟨{cks, ck, cs, c}, Ø⟩,
⟨{ckrs, ckr, crs, cr}, {cks, ck, cs, c}⟩}

It's easy to see that the these relations satisfy the conditional side condition $\cup\text{dom}(R_0[\triangleright\text{sing(Chris)}]) = \cup\text{dom}(R_0[\triangleright\text{sing(Chris)}; !\text{sing(Robin)}])$. In both cases, the relevant propositional information is just the information that Chris will sing. That means that $R_0[\text{if }(\triangleright\text{sing(Chris)})\,(!\text{sing(Robin)})]$ is the relation given in (20).

---

[2] We think it would be good to develop a version of Starr's system that gives conditionals content of their own. Such a system might be based on the work of Stojnic (2016), who provides a dynamic semantics for modal discourse that gives 'if' statements the truth conditions of strict conditionals, but it would need to be extended to handle questions and imperatives. Such an extension remains a project for future work. For now, we note that the substance of our paper—explicit indirection—does not depend on the content of conditional assertions; Starr's formalism is therefore enough to demonstrate the consistency of our ideas and give a precise system that substantiates our intuitive predictions.

20. $\{\langle\{\text{ckrs, ckr, cks, ck, crs, cr, cs, c, krs, kr, ks, k, s, r, --}\}, \emptyset\rangle,$
       $\langle\{\text{ckrs, ckr, cks, ck, crs, cr, cs, c}\}, \emptyset\rangle,$
       $\langle\{\text{ckrs, ckr, crs, cr}\}, \emptyset\rangle,$
       $\langle\{\text{cks, ck, cs, c}\}, \emptyset\rangle,$
       $\langle\{\text{ckrs, ckr, crs, cr}\}, \{\text{cks, ck, cs, c}\}\rangle\}$

Call this relation R_2. The key element of this relation is the final preference: better Chris and Robin both sing than Chris sings and Robin doesn't. This preference is part of the overall output state, but it's conditional. Our information doesn't say that Chris sings; Chris might or might not. If Chris doesn't sing, all bets are off. But if Chris does sing, Robin should sing too.

Interaction potential

Now we get the payoff. We can use this combination of raising questions, introducing preferences, conditionals, and sequencing to capture the indirection of utterances such as (1).

Let's give the insight by contrasting two further updates based on our most recent example R_2: $R_2[\triangleright\text{sing(Chris)}]$ and $R_2[\triangleright\neg\text{sing(Chris)}]$.

$R_2[\triangleright\text{sing(Chris)}]$ imposes the constraint, which most of the alternatives of R_2 already satisfy, that Chris will sing. That simply returns us to the relation given by (19). This illustrates the general fact about the system that if $R[\text{if }(\varphi)\ (\psi)]$ is nonempty then $R[\text{if }(\varphi)\ (\psi); \varphi]$ is exactly the same relation as $R[\varphi; \psi]$. The expected generalization of modus ponens holds. But in this case, it means that if we get the information specified by the antecedent, a conditional preference is not conditional any more. The preference holds generally.

$R_2[\triangleright\neg\text{sing(Chris)}]$, meanwhile, imposes the constraint that Chris will not sing. This is compatible with the overall information in the discourse, but it's inconsistent with all of the other alternatives; they all involve Chris singing. That means that these alternatives, and the preferences over them, get eliminated. The final result is just (21). In other words, if we get information ruling out the antecedent, then a conditional preference is again not conditional any more: The preference simply disappears.

21. $\{\langle\{\text{krs, kr, ks, k, s, r,--}\}, \emptyset\rangle\}$

Now, finally, consider the qualitative behavior of a relation specified as in (22).

22. $R[?\Diamond\text{sing(Chris)}; \text{if }(\triangleright\Diamond\text{sing(Chris)})\ (!\text{sing(Chris)})]$

This updates R in two ways. First it raises the question of whether it's possible for Chris to sing. The potential answers—that Chris can sing, that Chris can't—remain open issues in the discourse until at some point one or the other answer arrives. Then, it establishes a conditional preference: The worlds where it's possible for Chris to sing and Chris does sing are preferred to the worlds where it's possible for Chris to sing but Chris does not sing. Just as in the case we just considered, this preference comes into effect if we learn that Chris can sing. There's then nothing conditional about it any more. By contrast, if we learn that Chris cannot sing, the preference disappears. It's as though it was never there.

So where does (22) leave us, when we consider the results of the update as a whole? Well, it's still open whether Chris can sing or not. Nothing about the conditional changes that. So we would expect the discourse to continue with an answer, 'yes' or 'no'. If the answer is 'yes', the discourse now involves an unrestricted preference for Chris singing. Thus, if the answer is 'yes' (and the relevant background is in place), we'd expect the interlocutors to work to bring it about that Chris sings. Again, however, if the answer is 'no', there's no such preference, and no such implications about the interlocutors' actions.

In general, then, we claim that an update of the form '$?\Diamond p$; if ($\triangleright\Diamond p$) (!p)' captures the *indirect meaning* found in the key reading of (1). This update captures both the intuitive content of this kind of indirect utterance and the intuitive follow-ups that those utterances have in conversation.[3] But it's a meaning: indirection, on our analysis, describes the way the move is packaged together and bracketed so that it results in interactive effects that are different both from those of plain interrogatives and from those of unconditional expressions of preference. In particular, this move puts the preference forward only conditionally, and simultaneously raises an issue that the addressee can respond to in such a way as to silently neutralize that potentially problematic contribution. Thus, the move is indirect because its status (in some sense, even its very existence) depends on the addressee's answer. It should now be clear why we think indirection need not be a matter of pragmatic calculation. Our view is that indirect meanings such as '$?\Diamond p$; if ($\triangleright\Diamond p$) (!p)' are explicitly delivered by the grammar, whenever an utterance type is conventionally used to accomplish this indirection.

Discussion

In this section, we expand on the implications of the view that we have just articulated and formalized.

Politeness

Indirect requests, such as (1), are more polite than corresponding direct imperatives, such as (23).

23.   Pass the salt.

---

[3] Given our formal theory, we note that there will be a range of possible ways to develop similar ideas. For one thing, we need not take '$?\Diamond p$; if ($\triangleright\Diamond p$) (!p)' as an *analysis* of indirect meaning. It's enough that whatever the meaning is of indirect utterances such as (1), that meaning has the entailments that we show that '$?\Diamond p$; if ($\triangleright\Diamond p$) (!p)' has. Thus, philosophers who insist that lexical meanings must be semantic primitives (e.g., Fodor 1970) can still accept the idea of primitive indirect meanings. Moreover, philosophers who contest Brown and Levinson's (1987) account of politeness might deny that the preference expressed by utterances such as (1) is in any sense conditional. They are free to base an account of indirection on something like '$?\Diamond p$; !p'. The formalism shows that it is possible to specify indirect meaning in these terms as well. However these choices are resolved, it won't challenge our key claim: that indirect meanings can be specified by the ordinary semantic conventions of grammar. Finally, of course, it remains to derive indirect meanings for utterances compositionally from their parts and the way they are put together. To pursue this would require enriching Starr's formalism with the resources of the λ-calculus, so that we could factor meanings of the form '$?\Diamond p$; if ($\triangleright\Diamond p$) (!p)' into suitable lexical elements and the contributions of rules of combination. For example, one strategy might be to describe a new interrogative meaning for 'can', parameterized by individual x and property P, as in '$\lambda x \lambda P$: $?\Diamond Px$; if ($\triangleright\Diamond Px$) (!Px)', and allow meaning to compose with a particular subject and predicate via function application. We might go further and represent this meaning as the output of a lexical rule, an option that Asher and Lascarides (2001) recommend.

Brown and Levinson (1987) offer an explanation. They see politeness as a reflection of a range of ideals that we aim to foster in our dealings with one another, including showing our good feelings for others and respecting their independence and autonomy. Politeness, for them, is a strategy that helps to defuse potential conflicts between these ideals and certain kinds of utterances. For example, to make a request is to threaten your interlocutor's autonomy: you are telling them what to do. Politeness demands that you make it easy for your interlocutor to opt out of the request. Explicit indirection offers a way to do this. It lets the addressee who's so inclined fib, saying that the request would be impossible to fulfill. Then it's as if the request was never made, and the addressee's autonomy, never challenged. Our formalism transparently implements this explanation.

You might think that Brown and Levinson's explanation of the politeness of indirect requests would be compatible with a wide range of views about the meanings of utterances and the contributions they make. We disagree. We think that making Brown and Levinson's proposal precise *depends* on our view that utterances merely update the conversational record, an abstract construct that is removed from speakers' actual beliefs and intentions. For example, you cannot give this kind of explanation, we think, if you assume that declarative utterances are conventionally used in attempts to produce beliefs on the part of the addressee. If speakers who make excuses are obligated to convince hearers that they are true, or if hearers must believe excuses to accept them, then making requests through indirection won't make declining them any smoother. It merely pushes the problems down the road. However, we think English speakers understand that excuses in these contexts are *pro forma,* and should neither be believed nor challenged. That's why indirection makes it easy to offer excuses. In short, if Brown and Levinson are right about the politeness of indirection, "putting information on the record" is the attitude that most happily reconciles the public commitments utterances are used for with interlocutors' private interests and perspectives.

Intention Recognition

Issues of autonomy and politeness also loom large when we consider the role of intention recognition in indirection. Let's start with an example. We're at a yoga studio, and the speaker is late to reserve a spot at a future class that often fills up. She might use either (24) or (25) to open a discussion with the staff at the registration desk about getting herself added to it.

24.   Can I still get a spot in tomorrow's 6:30 class?
25.   Is it still possible to reserve a spot in tomorrow's 6:30 class?

On our view, (24) appeals to conventional indirection to establish a conditional preference, but (25) does not. However, when we consider the implications of the utterances for the speaker's intentions, the difference between them seems very small indeed. In both cases, the speaker doesn't know if there is a free spot, but the speaker would like one if there is one. In both cases, the speaker expects her interlocutor to take this into account—for example, by checking availability through a reservation system that will allow her to be quickly added to the class if the opportunity arises. And of course, in both cases, it is the utterance that signals to the audience that this is what the speaker has in mind. A cooperative interlocutor will think the same thing about the speaker's plans no matter which utterance the speaker uses.

But a polite interlocutor may well respond differently to the two utterances, with (26) for (24) but with (27) for (25).

26. Sure. You're in.
27. It is. Would you like one?

In Brown and Levinson's framework, there's no problem with complying with explicitly encoded requests. However, autonomy demands that polite interlocutors ask before acting towards a speaker's inferred goals on her behalf.

Because we are skeptical that meaning can be reduced to a speaker's intentions for getting information across to her addressee, we think it's no surprise that there's a difference between encoding one's preferences and making those preferences obvious. And, we have argued, conventionalized indirection is a case of encoding.

Ambiguity

Our discussion so far has focused on the ability of our account to capture intuitive judgments about indirection. But the dissatisfaction that linguists and philosophers have with the idea of conventionalized indirection often depends on its relationships to broader issues. One of these is ambiguity.

Indirection is ambiguous. For example, sometimes 'can' questions just raise questions about ability. Sometimes they convey a richer meaning involving indirection. Lepore and Stone (2015) use (28, their 89) to make these different readings palpable.

28. Can you play Chopin's E minor prelude?

With (1), it's normally obvious that the addressee can pass the salt, so it's hard to make sense of the utterance as a mere question. By contrast, (28) raises a substantive issue. (28) makes sense as a question about how good a pianist the addressee is; it also makes sense as a case of indirection, which also expresses a (conditional) preference for the addressee to play the piece now. As expected, we can formalize the two readings as in (29) and (30).

29. $?\Diamond p$
30. $?\Diamond p$; if $(\triangleright \Diamond p)$ $(!p)$

Our view, of course, is that the (29) interpretation and the (30) interpretation are alternatives that are both made available by the grammar, just as in the case of any other ambiguity. The formalism makes it clear that we predict the possibility of including a direct answer in response to the indirect meaning observed by Bach and Harnish (1979) and Clark (1979). Both (29) and (30) raise the issue of whether playing the E minor prelude is possible and so both afford an answer as a response.

Readers unused to thinking about lexical semantics may be surprised to find grammatically specified alternative meanings with such close affinities between them as (29) and (30) exhibit. In fact, this state of affairs is so common that it has its own name: "autohyponymy" (Horn 1984). We think 'can' is one of many verbs that have these kinds of overlapping senses. For an analogous example, consider 'climb', discussed extensively by Jackendoff (1990) and Hanks (2013). The action of climbing sometimes involves upward motion, sometimes involves hand-over-hand clambering, and prototypically involves both. The availability of these different interpretations depends in complex ways not only on what does the climbing, but also on which other arguments are present and how they are realized syntactically. Thus, the different interpretations are clearly a matter of English grammar. But now imagine the conversation in (31) and (32), uttered by interlocutors on the middle deck of a New York City fire escape.

31.   A: How did you get here?
32.   B: I climbed.

B's response in (32) probably suggests that she climbed up from the ground. But it's also true, on the weaker but related sense of 'climb', if she climbed down from the roof. The different interpretations of 'climb' at play in (32) stand in exactly the same semantic relationships to one another as do the different interpretations (29) and (30) that our account of conventionalized indirection posits for (28).

Explanation in Semantics

Ambiguity, then, is a possible view, but many linguists and philosophers think it is an unattractive one. If we showed how to derive the indirect interpretation from the literal one by general principles, wouldn't we strike the indirect interpretation from the roster of grammatical meanings and so reduce the complexity of speakers' knowledge of language? Grice argued that we would: this general argument in favor of pragmatic accounts, his "modified Ockham's razor" (1975), has come to be known as Grice's razor.

In the case of conventionalized indirection, we think the question is moot. There are no general interpretive principles that can derive indirect meanings from literal ones exactly where they occur within and across languages. Languages vary in how they accomplish indirection; you have to learn how each one does it. You have to learn, for example, that (33) in Hungarian is an apology or that (34) in Japanese is a request.

33.   Ne haragudjon.
      (Don't be angry.)
34.   Kikasete itadakemasen ka?
      (Can't you do us the favor of having us listen?)

Lepore and Stone (2015) discuss these examples—(33) is their (99), taken from Suszczyńska (1999); (34) is their (101), taken from Horvat (2000)—and make the case for conventionality in detail. Despite frequent claims otherwise in the literature, going back to Searle (1975) and Morgan (1978), Lepore and Stone argue that the conventions involved are semantic in the most straightforward sense. English speakers use the formulation "I'm sorry" and not "Don't be angry" to express an apology indirectly. In so doing, they are coordinating on the update the utterance makes to the conversational record, and using only their learned mutual expectations to do so. In short, this is a conventional meaning, in Lewis's (1969) sense of convention.

Nevertheless, the persistence of pragmatic accounts of indirection shows how convincing researchers find Grice's razor. We find the principle much less compelling, however. We think that researchers would often be led to better empirical theories, and a deeper and more nuanced understanding of linguistic meaning, if they approached the principle more skeptically.

Conventional meaning grows out of improvised meaning through a mixture of insight, luck, precedent, and repetition. That's a key feature of Lewis's (1969) account of convention—one that later approaches, such as Millikan (2005) or Ludlow (2014) have only sought to strengthen and extend. The dynamic evolution of language through improvisation and conventionalization readily transmutes word meanings from their established senses into new related but distinct ones. Polysemy is thus ubiquitous in language. To attempt to explain it away synchronically through pragmatic principles is to miss the historical contingencies that really are at work in shaping speakers' linguistic knowledge, as evidenced in examples such as (33) and (34).

Conclusion

Indirection is a kind of meaning: meaning that combines multiple contributions— a first, explicit contribution that can be addressed unproblematically, and a second, more difficult contribution whose potential embarrassment can be neutralized by certain of the coherent responses that the first makes available. Indirection is not diagnostic of implicature or other kinds of pragmatic reasoning in interpretation. The indirect contribution is not in any sense derived from the literal one; both are specified by grammar. Speakers' linguistic judgments and their conversational interactions make sense only if indirection is explicitly encoded. Some ambiguities inevitably result, but they are attested, comparable to other semantic ambiguities, and to be expected given the nature of meaning in language.

We have presented a formal account that makes these claims precise, for the specific case of English 'can' questions as indirect expressions of preferences, based on the work of Starr (2010, to appear). We have grounded our philosophical interpretation of the formalism in the perspective of Lepore and Stone (2015). This shows that our account of explicit indirection is consistent, and is consonant with the general approach to semantics that we favor.

We noted, however, that Starr's formalism can be interpreted in different ways. Moreover, we expect that a category of conventional indirect meaning can be formalized on similar lines using speech act approaches to meaning (Charlow 2011, Harris 2014) or truth-conditional reductions of imperative and interrogative meaning (as in Han 1998 or Kaufmann 2012). Thus, substantial opportunities remain for future explorations of conventional indirect meaning. Those investigations will certainly have to address the full range of polite indirection, not only in English but across languages.

Nevertheless, we think our discussion has revealed some subtle philosophical and linguistic challenges that must be met to describe indirection as conventional. In retrospect, Lepore and Stone (2015) are too cavalier in making the claims about conventionalized indirection that they do, without specifying the formal and philosophical details. In explicating and formalizing the view, we hope to illustrate the kind of detailed development that remains to be done to get clear on the rules of language and their role in guiding people's communicative interactions with one another.

Acknowledgments

This paper is informed by an author meets critics session on our book *Imagination and Convention* at the Eastern APA in Philadelphia, December 2014 (with Ann Bezuidenhout and Zoltan Szabo), a symposium on the semantics-pragmatics interface at the Pacific APA in Vancouver, April 2015 (with Kent Bach and Jeff Pelletier) and particularly the Workshop on the Philosophy of Language and Linguistics in Dubrovnik in September 2015, where we presented a preliminary version of this paper. Thanks to the other speakers and the audiences at these meetings for helpful discussion, and to Daniel Harris for feedback on our initial draft. Preparation of this paper was supported in part by NSF grant IIS 1526723 and a sabbatical leave from Rutgers to Stone.

References

Asher, Nicholas, and Alex Lascarides. 2001. "Indirect speech acts." *Synthese* 128(1–2): 183–228.

Austin, J. L. 1962. *How to Do Things With Words*. Oxford: Oxford University Press.

Bach, Kent, and Robert M. Harnish. 1979. *Linguistic Communication and Speech Acts*. Cambridge, MA: MIT Press.

Bezuidenhout, Ann. 2016. "What properly belongs to grammar? A response to Lepore and Stone." *Inquiry* 56(2): 175–94.

Bezuidenhout, Ann. To appear. "The conversational record." In G. Preyer (ed.), *Semantics, Pragmatics and Interpretation*.

Boër, Steven E., and William G. Lycan. 1980. "A performadox in truth-conditional semantics." *Linguistics and Philosophy* 4: 1–46.

Brown, Penelope, and Stephen C. Levinson. 1987. *Politeness: Some Universals in Language Usage*. Cambridge: Cambridge University Press.

Burge, Tyler. 1979. "Individualism and the Mental." In P. A. French, T. E. Uehling, and H. K. Wettstein (eds.), *Midwest Studies in Philosophy*, IV, 73–121. Minneapolis: University of Minnesota Press.

Charlow, Nathan A. 2011. Practical Language: Its Meaning and Use. PhD Dissertation, University of Michigan.

Chomsky, Noam. 2005. "Three factors in language design." *Linguistic Inquiry* 36(1): 1–22.

Ciardelli, Ivano, Jeroen Groenendijk, and Floris Roelofsen. 2015. "On the semantics and logic of declaratives and interrogatives." *Synthese* 192(6): 1689–728.

Clark, Herbert H. 1979. "Responding to indirect speech acts." *Cognitive Psychology* 11: 430–77.

Cresswell, Max J. (1973). *Logics and Languages*. London: Methuen.

Fodor, J. A. (1970). 'Three reasons for not deriving "kill" from "cause to die".' *Linguistic Inquiry* 1(4): 429–38.

Ginzburg, Jonathan. 2012. *The Interactive Stance*. Oxford: Oxford University Press.

Grice, H. Paul. 1975. "Logic and conversation." In P. Cole and J. Morgan (eds.), *Syntax and Semantics III: Speech Acts*, 41–58. New York: Academic Press.

Han, Chung-Hye. 1998. The Structure and Interpretation of Imperatives: Mood and Force in Universal Grammar. PhD Dissertation, University of Pennsylvania.

Hamblin, C. L. 1958. "Questions." *Australasian Journal of Philosophy* 36: 159–68.

Hanks, Patrick. 2013. *Lexical Analysis: Norms and Expectations*. Cambridge, MA: MIT Press.

Harris, Daniel. 2014. Speech Act Theoretic Semantics. PhD Dissertation, City University of New York.

Horn, Laurence R. 1984. "Toward a new taxonomy for pragmatic inference: Q-based and R-based implicature." In Deborah Schiffrin (ed.), *Meaning, Form, and Use in Context: Linguistic Applications*, 11–42. Washington, DC: Georgetown University Press.

Horn, Laurence R. 1989. *A Natural History of Negation*. Chicago: University of Chicago Press.

Horvat, Andrew. 2000. *Japanese beyond Words: How to Walk and Talk like a Native Speaker*. Berkeley, CA: Stone Bridge Press.

Jackendoff, Ray. 1990. *Semantic Structures*. Cambridge, MA: MIT Press.

Kaufmann, Magdalena. 2012. *Interpreting Imperatives*. Heidelberg: Springer.

Kripke, Saul. 1972. "Naming and necessity." In Gilbert Harman and Donald Davidson (eds.), *Semantics of Natural Language*, 253–355. Dordrecht: Reidel.

Lakoff, George. 1973. "Some thoughts on transderivational constraints." In B. B. Kachru (ed.), *Issues in Linguistics*, 442–52. Champaign, IL: University of Illinois Press.

Lepore, Ernie and Matthew Stone. 2015. *Imagination and Convention: Distinguishing Grammar from Inference in Language*. Oxford: Oxford University Press.

Lewis, David K. 1969. *Convention: A Philosophical Study*. Cambridge, MA: Harvard University Press.

Lewis, David K. 1970. "General semantics." *Synthese* 22(1/2): 18–67.

Lewis, David. 1979. "Scorekeeping in a language game." *Journal of Philosophical Logic* 8(3): 339–59.

Ludlow, Peter. 2014. *Living Words: Meaning Underdetermination and the Dynamic Lexicon*. Oxford: Oxford University Press.

McCawley, James D. 1985. *What Price the Performative Analysis? University of Chicago Working Papers in Linguistics*, Vol. 1, 43–64. Chicago: Department of Linguistics, University of Chicago.

Millikan, Ruth G. 1998. "Language conventions made simple." *Journal of Philosophy* 95(4): 161–80.

Millikan, Ruth G. 2005. "Semantics/pragmatics: (Purposes and cross-purposes)." In *Language: A Biological Model*, 187–220. Oxford: Oxford University Press.

Morgan, J. L. 1978. "Two types of convention in indirect speech acts." In Peter Cole (ed.), Syntax and Semantics, IX. Pragmatics, 261–80. New York: Academic Press.

Portner, Paul. 2005. "The semantics of imperatives within a theory of clause types." In Kazuha Watanabe and Robert B. Young (eds.), *Proceedings of Semantics and Linguistic Theory* 14, 235–52. Ithaca, NY: CLC Publications.

Putnam, Hilary. 1975. "The meaning of 'meaning'." In *Mind, Language and Reality*, 215–71. Cambridge: Cambridge University Press.

Roberts, Craige. 2012. "Information structure: Towards an integrated formal theory of pragmatics." *Semantics and Pragmatics* 5(6): 1–69.

Ross, John Robert. 1970. "On declarative sentences." In R. Jacobs and P. S. Rosenbaum (eds.), *Readings in English Transformational Grammar*, 222–72. Waltham, MA: Ginn.

Sadock, Jerrold. 1974. *Towards a Linguistic Theory of Speech Acts*. New York: Academic Press.

Sadock, Jerrold. 2004. "Speech acts." In Laurence R. Horn and Gregory Ward (eds.), *The Handbook of Pragmatics*, 53–73. Oxford: Blackwell.

Searle, John R. 1969. *Speech Acts*. Cambridge: Cambridge University Press.

Searle, John R. 1975. "Indirect speech acts." In P. Cole and J. Morgan (eds.), *Syntax and Semantics III. Speech Acts*, 59–82. New York: Academic Press.

Stalnaker, Robert. 1978. "Assertion." In Peter Cole (ed.), *Syntax and Semantics, IX. Pragmatics*, 315–32. New York: Academic Press.

Stalnaker, Robert. 2002. "Common ground." *Linguistics and Philosophy* 25(5–6): 701–21.

Starr, William B. 2010. Conditionals, Meaning and Mood. PhD Dissertation, Rutgers University.

Starr, William B. To appear. A preference semantics for imperatives. *Semantics and Pragmatics*.

Stojnic, Una. 2016. "One's modus ponens: Modality, coherence and logic." *Philosophy and Phenomenological Research* 95: 167–214.

Suszczyńska, Małgorzata. 1999. "Apologizing in English, Polish and Hungarian: Different languages, different strategies." *Journal of Pragmatics* 31(8): 1053–65.

Thomason, Richmond H. 1990. "Accommodation, meaning and implicature." In Philip R. Cohen, Jerry Morgan, and Martha E. Pollack (eds.), *Intentions in Communication*, 325–63. Cambridge, MA: MIT Press.

Wierzbicka, Anna. 1985. "Different cultures, different languages, different speech acts: Polish vs. English." *Journal of Pragmatics* 9(2–3): 145–78.

8

On Covert Exercitives
Speech and the Social World

Mary Kate McGowan

8.1 Introduction

It is familiar from speech act theory how saying so can make it so. When the C.E.O. declares that no more overtime will be approved, the C.E.O. thereby changes company policy. Her words effect an immediate change to the norms and policies operative in that company. Her saying so makes it so. Similarly, when a parent declares a new bedtime for her child, she thereby changes the rules of the household. She exercises her authority over her child and verbally enacts a new bedtime. Her saying so makes it so.

Clearly, speech can make things so. It can enact facts about what is permissible. The familiar way to do this via speech is illustrated by the examples above. In this paper, though, I argue for a different way that speech does this. Starting in the kinematics (i.e. the mechanics) of conversation, I first argue that conversational contributions routinely alter norms for the very conversation to which they contribute. I then argue that this phenomenon generalizes and I then briefly explore important potential consequences of this alternative model of norm-altering speech.

How might being thorough during a tax preparation interview add to racist social structures? How might complimenting a girl's outfit undermine her performance on a math exam? How might an offhand sexist comment made by someone with relatively little social power actually manage to oppress? I shall argue—briefly and schematically—at the end of this paper that the phenomenon identified here (of covert exercitives) sheds light on these and related questions thereby opening up new possibilities for the crucial role of speech in enacting and perpetuating unjust social hierarchies.

8.2 Preliminaries: Permissibility Facts and the Constitution of Harm

Before beginning my argument, some preliminaries are warranted. Since I am primarily interested in speech that alters norms or as I shall say enacts permissibility facts, it is prudent to say a bit more about the nature of permissibility facts, the nature of enacting and why focusing on the enacting of such facts is important.

8.2.1 Permissibility Facts

Permissibility facts are facts about what is permissible or appropriate in some realm. The rules of baseball are permissibility facts in that game and norms about how much physical space to give a conversational partner are culturally specific permissibility facts. This notion of permission does not require that some agent grant the permission. What is permissible is just what is appropriate in the practice. Permissibility facts also include prohibitions (and thus what is impermissible) as well as what is required (that is, what it is impermissible to refrain from doing). Permissibility is also a matter of degree and may function along more than one axis.

8.2.2 On Enacting

Some forms of enacting are really easy to do. In fact, we do it all the time. Simply by being and doing things, we thereby routinely affect what's true of the world and thereby enact these truths about it. Very roughly, enacting is a fairly direct way to make something true. When I skip to work, for example, I change what is true about the world; I make it the case that I skipped to work. That I skipped to work is enacted by my skipping. Although enacting involves an immediate way of making truths true and it is thus "truth-making" in this minimal sense, I am here entirely agnostic about the underlying metaphysics.[1]

Some forms of enacting depend on institutional structures. When Leo dies, for example, his death enacts the fact that his wife Sue is a widow. That this widowhood fact is enacted by this death event depends, among other things, on the institution of marriage.

Finally, a single utterance can enact several different facts and do so via different sorts of enactment mechanisms. Suppose, for example, that I verbally set a new bedtime for my children. When I do so, I thereby enact various facts. I enact the fact that I spoke; I also enact a new bedtime and these different facts are enacted in different ways. One of the differences concerns the role of intention. I can enact the fact that I spoke without intending to enact that fact but it seems that I must intend to enact a bedtime in order to successfully do so. There are, of course, other important differences. My main point now is merely that enacting comes in many forms and through various mechanisms.

8.2.3 On the Constitution of Harm

I am primarily interested in *speech* that enacts permissibility facts. One reason to focus on permissibility facts is that such facts can be harmful and one reason to focus on the *enacting* of such facts concerns the important difference between (merely) causing *harm* and constituting it. This distinction arises in the legal literature but has been precisified in the philosophical literature.[2]

---

[1] What truth-makers are ontologically (states of affairs, tropes, . . .), which sorts of things bear truth-value (sentences, propositions, . . .), which relation obtains between truth-makers and truth-bearers (necessitation, entailment, grounding, . . .) and even which truths, if any, require their own truth-maker are here left entirely open.

[2] Catharine MacKinnon is one legal theorist who relies heavily on this distinction. See, for example, her *Feminism Unmodified: Discourses on Life and Law* (Cambridge, MA: Harvard University Press, 1987).

To say that speech causes harm is to say that it causes harm but it does not also constitute it. In such a case, I shall say that the speech in question *merely* causes harm. To say that speech constitutes harm, by contrast, is to say that it brings the harm in question about *via* the enacting of a permissibility fact (or norm) that prescribes the harm in question.[3]

An example will help to illustrate this difference. Suppose that I convince my friends that redheaded people are genetically inferior, disposed to evil, and a threat to all things decent and, as a result of coming to believe these things, my friends discriminate against redheaded persons. In this case, my utterance causes discrimination against those redheaded persons. My words cause my friends' beliefs (attitudes and dispositions) to change and these changes in turn cause my friends' harmful discriminatory conduct. The connection between the speech and the harm in this case is (by hypothesis merely) causal.

Contrast that with a different case. Suppose instead that I am an employer and I implement a company hiring policy when I say, "From now on, we no longer hire anyone with red hair." This utterance will no doubt cause discriminatory conduct on the part of my employees. Despite this, since that discriminatory conduct is brought about by my employees' adherence to a policy that I put into place with my utterance, my utterance enacts the policy (or permissibility fact) that prescribes the harmful discriminatory practice in question. As a result, my utterance constitutes (and does not merely cause) the harm of discrimination.

This difference between causing and constituting harm matters to the law. In general, speech that (merely) causes discrimination is protected by a free speech principle but speech that constitutes discrimination is not. Furthermore, being clear about the relationships between speech and its associated harms will aid attempts to remedy those harms. By identifying an alternative model for permissibility-fact-enacting speech, we thereby identify an alternative model for speech constituting (as opposed to merely causing) harm.

8.3 Speech Acts and Exercitives

Illocution is one way for speech to enact norms and thus it is one way for speech to enact harmful norms. Since exercitive speech acts are the sort of speech act that enact

It has been picked up and precisified in the analytic feminism literature. See, for example, Rae Langton 1993, "Speech Acts and Unspeakable Acts," *Philosophy and Public Affairs* 22 (4): 293–30, and I. Maitra and M. K. McGowan, "Introduction and Overview," in Maitra and McGowan (eds.), *Speech and Harm: Controversies over Free Speech* (Oxford: Oxford University Press, 2012): 1–23.

[3] Ontological questions about the precise metaphysical nature of norms are also here left open. I am primarily interested in social norms and such norms are at least apparently prescriptive. Consider, for example, current norms of femininity. I am aware of these norms and whether I embrace them or not, my actions and choices are nevertheless responsive to them. Moreover, since others judge me with respect to these norms, they have at least apparent prescriptive force. After all, as a person socially positioned as a woman, there is a socially strong sense in which I am supposed to be feminine. That said, such norms might nevertheless fail to be genuinely prescriptive if, ultimately, I ought to reject them and thus should not abide by them. In what follows, I am interested in norms that are at least apparently prescriptive in this way. For an excellent recent discussion of the complex nature of gender norms, see C. Witt, *The Metaphysics of Gender* (Oxford: Oxford University Press, 2011).

norms, I now focus on them. The term 'exercitive' comes from Austin but Austin's taxonomy of speech acts has been criticized.[4] Although Austin's terminology is still used in some literatures, the term 'exercitive' is not used in the mainstream philosophy of language, linguistics or pragmatics literatures. Despite this, I use the term and I have two reasons for doing so. First, my work has arisen out of a separate literature that does use the term.[5] Second, and more important, I find the category of exercitive to be both illuminating and fruitful, as I hope this paper will demonstrate.

For our purposes, *exercitive* speech acts enact facts about what is permissible in a certain realm. In Austin's own words, an exercitive speech act is the "exercising of powers, rights or influence."[6] Suppose, for example, that while enacting college policies, the President of Wellesley College declares: "Smoking is no longer permitted in any college building." This utterance is an exercitive because it takes away certain (in this case, smoking) privileges and thereby changes what is permissible on the Wellesley College campus.

There are several things worth noting about exercitive speech acts. First, exercitives *enact* permissibility facts; they do not merely cause such facts to obtain. When the president declared that smoking is no longer permissible in any college building, her saying so made it so. Second, Austin's exercitive speech acts (I will argue for a different sort later) are *authoritative* speech acts since the speaker must have the requisite authority over the appropriate domain.[7] The case of the college president enacting a new smoking policy is an example of what I call a standard *exercitive*.[8] Standard exercitives enact permissibility facts *via an exercise of speaker authority*. They also enact the permissibility fact via illocution and they typically express the content of the permissibility fact being enacted. I shall now argue that there is another— quite different—way that our utterances enact permissibility facts.[9] Our investigation begins in the kinematics of conversation.

8.4 Conversational Score

Conversational score is a specification of a conversational context.[10] It tracks that which is relevant for the proper development and assessment of that conversation.

---

[4] Austin, J. L. *How to Do Things With Words* (Cambridge, MA: Harvard University Press, 1973): 151–2. For John Searle's classic criticism of Austin's taxonomy, see his "A Taxonomy of Illocutionary Acts," in *Expression and Meaning* (Cambridge: Cambridge University Press, 1979): 1–29. Several contributions to this volume weigh in on this set of taxonomic issues: Roberts, this volume; Murray and Starr, this volume; and Hanks, this volume.

[5] This literature is sometimes called the speech act approach to free speech; it is also sometimes called (feminist) applied philosophy of language. It has its roots in Langton, "Speech Acts and Unspeakable Acts," 293–330.

[6] Austin, *How to Do Things With Words*, 151.

[7] I shall later argue that this is true of only one sort of exercitive speech act. As we shall see, there are non-authoritative exercitives.

[8] Elsewhere, I called them Austinian exercitives. See my (2003) "Conversational Exercitives and the Force of Pornography," *Philosophy and Public Affairs* 31 (2): 155–89 and my (2004) "Conversational Exercitives: Something Else We Do With Our Words," *Linguistics and Philosophy* 27 (1): 93–111.

[9] As we shall see, speech that enacts permissibility facts is virtually ubiquitous; on my view, most if not all utterances do so. Exercitive speech is thus too widespread to be a type. Furthermore, I am not exclusively interested in illocution.

[10] I am working with a Lewisian conception of conversational score. It tracks everything relevant. See D. Lewis, "Scorekeeping in a Language Game," *Philosophical Papers Volume I* (Oxford: Oxford University Press, 1983): 240–3.

This includes, among other things, the presuppositions, the appropriate standards of accuracy, and the relevant topics. (It is thus not about who "wins" the conversation!) Since the various components of conversational score affect such a wide variety of linguistic phenomena (which may not be familiar to some readers), it is worthwhile to consider some examples.

Definite descriptions are one such linguistic phenomenon; they are descriptions that purport to uniquely refer.[11] In other words, definite descriptions seem to refer to exactly one thing. Examples include 'the tallest student in my 207 class', 'Helen McGowan Gardner's oldest son' and 'my favorite color.' Each of these descriptive expressions is routinely used on particular occasions to uniquely refer; on each occasion, it seems that these expressions refer to one and only one thing. As is well known, many definite descriptions appear to succeed in uniquely referring even though these descriptions fail to uniquely describe their referent. The expression 'the desk,' for example, may pick out a particular desk even though there are many desks in the universe and there may even be several desks in the room in question. Salience appears to account for this.[12] On this account, a definite description refers to the most salient satisfier of the description.[13] Suppose, for example, that Bobby mentions that his dog has just been to the vet and I ask if the dog is healthy. Bobby's dog is certainly not the only dog in the universe and his dog may not even be the only dog present, but I have nevertheless managed to refer to his dog with this use of the expression 'the dog.' This is because Bobby's dog is the most salient dog in the context of this particular conversation. Salience is a component of the conversational score and this salience component of the conversational score helps to settle the appropriate use of definite descriptions in the conversation at hand by fixing the unique referent of such descriptions.[14]

Consider now another linguistic phenomenon that draws our attention to a different component of the conversational score, the scope of quantifiers. When we use words like 'all', 'some', 'every' or 'any', we are making claims about groups of things. We might be saying that *all* of the things in the group have some property or that *some* of

---

[11] I leave it open whether this uniqueness condition is required for reference. I also leave it open whether this uniqueness condition is a semantic or pragmatic one. See Russell, Bertrand (2005), "On Denoting," *Mind* 14 (56): 479–93; Szabo, Zoltan Gendler, "Descriptions and Uniqueness," *Philosophical Studies* 101: 29–57; and Roberts, Craige, "Information Structure: Towards an Integrated Formal Theory of Pragmatics," in Yoon, Jae-Hak and Andreas Kathol (eds.), *Ohio State University Working Papers in Linguistics No. 49*, Papers in Pragmatics. Available at: https://linguistics.osu.edu/sites/linguistics. osu.edu/files/workingpa-pers/osu_ wpl_49.pdf

[12] There are other ways to try to account for this. Perhaps 'the desk' is shorthand for a longer description that satisfies the uniqueness condition. Russell himself used this ellipsis strategy by taking proper names to be shorthand for definite descriptions. See Russell, Bertrand (1918/1956), "The Philosophy of Logical Atomism," in R. Marsh (ed.), *Logic and Knowledge* (London: Allen and Unwin, 1956): 29. Alternatively, one might argue that the objects under consideration are restricted in such a way that this uniqueness condition is met. For an especially accessible discussion of this uniqueness problem, see Lycan, William, *Philosophy of Language: A Contemporary Introduction* (London and New York: Routledge, 2000): 24–5. For further details see, for example, Neale, Stephen, *Descriptions* (Cambridge, MA: MIT Press, 1990) and Stanley and Szabo (2000), "On Quantifier Domain Restriction," *Mind and Language* 15 (2 and 3): 219–61.

[13] Many theorists appeal to salience. Lewis does. See his "Scorekeeping in a Language Game," 240–3. So does Herbert Clark although his account is a bit more detailed. See Clark, H., *Using Language* (Cambridge: Cambridge University Press, 1996): 62–70.

[14] There will be many salience components of conversational score, each tracking salience facts about the different sorts of things under discussion.

them do. The *scope* of these quantificational terms is a technical way of specifying the group of objects in question. To see that the scope of such terms is a component of conversational score, consider the following. Suppose that Whitney, while talking to her husband Steve about her shopping list, asks him if there is any sour cherry juice. In this conversational context, the group of objects in question is the collection of things in their possession right now. Whitney is not asking whether there is any sour cherry juice anywhere in the universe and she is not asking whether there is any sour cherry juice at the store in Fairhaven (where she normally buys it). She is asking, of the things in their possession right now, is any of it sour cherry juice. As one can see then, the scope of quantificational terms is a component of conversational score.

Other components of conversational score include standards of accuracy, presupposition, and relevance. This list is not meant to be exhaustive. In fact, this notion of score is highly inclusive and includes, by definition, *whatever* is relevant to the assessment and proper development of the conversation. Thus, if some factor Y is shown to be relevant to the assessment and proper development of a conversation then (so long as Y is distinct from the other components of the score) Y is a component of the score.[15] Nothing else needs to be shown. The score just is the combination of that which matters for the purposes of that conversation.

I am operating with an especially inclusive notion of score. There are of course many ways to specify the score—in terms of what it does and does not track, in terms of how it works, and in terms of what it is ontologically—and not all ways of specifying the conversational score are as inclusive as mine.[16] Camp, for example, (this volume) defines the score as tracking obligations and thus as tracking only the on-record contributions to the conversation.[17]

This inclusive conception of score also tracks various meta-linguistic facts. The fact that a conversation is taking place and that all participants speak the same language are meta-linguistic facts that are also components of score. There are also other sorts of meta-linguistic facts tracked. Suppose, for example, that Greg asserts something that is then rejected by his interlocutor. Although the *content* of Greg's assertion is blocked from being accepted by both participants, the meta-linguistic fact that he asserted it is a component of the conversational score.[18] Furthermore, score change (sometimes called 'updating') is an ongoing and temporally complex process.[19] To see

---

[15] Technically, the distinctness qualification is unnecessary. A score with redundant components is perfectly adequate. Although I hope to avoid unnecessary (and ultimately irrelevant) complications regarding the distinctness of components, I am nevertheless inclined to exclude obviously equivalent components.

[16] Further examples of narrower conceptions of score include Lepore, Ernest and Matthew Stone, *Imagination and Convention: Distinguishing Grammar and Inference in Language* (Oxford: Oxford University Press, 2015), and Thomason, Rich, "Accommodation, Meaning, and Implicature," in, P. Cohen, J. Morgan, and M. Pollack (eds.) *Intentions in Communication* (Cambridge, MA: MIT Press, 1990): 325–63.

[17] Doing so marks a different difference between score and common ground and enables Camp (this volume) to analyze insinuation in terms of that difference.

[18] Langton (this volume) argues that blocking can retroactively render the blocked speech act a misfire. Elsewhere, I treat blocked moves differently (3 §6.2 of *Just Words: Speech and the Constitution of Harm*, forthcoming).

[19] These sorts of successive score (or common ground) changes are discussed in Stalnaker, Robert, (1998), "On the Representation of Context," *Journal of Logic, Language and Information* 7 (1): 3–19 and Kai von Fintel's (2008) "What is Presupposition Accommodation Again?" *Philosophical Perspectives* 22: 137–70.

this, consider what happens with an accepted assertion. Suppose, for example, that Albert says, "I love Rolling Road" and his interlocutor gladly accepts his assertion. Even in this simple case, though, an ongoing series of score changes are enacted; the score must be updated multiple times and in multiple respects. Since the score tracks what is relevant for the proper development of the conversation, it essentially captures all contextual information required for the proper interpretation of Albert's conversational contribution. Since Albert uses the word 'I' (and the referent of 'I' depends on who is speaking), the score must already include the fact that Albert is speaking. Of course, the score could not reflect that fact *before* Albert started speaking. Moreover, Albert's accepted assertion adds the content of his assertion to the score and that can happen only *after* his assertion. As one can see, a single conversational contribution will involve several successive score changes.

8.5 Common Ground

Common ground is an alternative (but complementary) framework for tracking conversational context;[20] it is the set of propositions that the participants in a conversation take for granted for the purposes of that conversation.[21] These propositions need not be believed; they may merely be accepted for the purposes of the conversation.[22] The common ground, like the score, changes as the conversation develops. (It is usually understood to be a set of possible worlds; those worlds in which the accepted propositions are true.) In short, as a specification of the conversational context, common ground functions in much the same way as the conversational score.

That said, there are important differences between these two frameworks. One such difference concerns their respective content. The common ground is tracking (only) facts about the psychology of participants; it tracks participants' belief-like psychological states of acceptance. The content of the score, by contrast, is not limited to the psychology of participants. Since not everything relevant to a conversation will be recognized by all participants, the score tracks more than the common ground. Another difference is that the common ground tracks only that which is *shared* (mutually recognized and recognized as mutually recognized) by participants. Although the various components of score are often shared by the participants in the conversation, they need not be. Facts relevant to the conversation but unshared are tracked by the score but they are not of the common ground.

Although both frameworks are useful and important, the scorekeeping framework is preferable for my purposes. (I argue for this in more detail elsewhere.)[23] Since I am primarily interested in identifying further ways in which speech can enact (harmful)

---

[20] Langton first treats them as complementary in her "Beyond Belief: Pragmatics in Hate Speech and Pornography," 72–93 and Langton (this volume).

[21] Some components of the common ground will be broad cultural beliefs (e.g., Donald Trump is the President of the Unites States) and others will be more specific to the conversation at a time (e.g., Uncle Charlie is speaking now).

[22] For a discussion of this, see Stalnaker, Robert, "Pragmatic Presupposition," in M. Munitz and P. Unger (eds.) *Semantics and Philosophy* (New York: New York University Press, 1974): 202; Stalnaker (1998), "On the Representation of Context,"; and Stalnaker, Robert, *Context* (Oxford: Oxford University Press, 2014).

[23] *Just Words: Speech and the Constitution of Harm*, forthcoming.

norms and thus constitute (as opposed to merely cause) harm, I am especially interested in identifying further ways in which speech can enact norms. (I will later argue that enacting score changes is tantamount to enacting norms.) Simply put, the score framework is preferable because it tracks the relevant enactments more directly than common ground does.

8.6 Conversational Exercitives

Speech constitutes harm by enacting norms that prescribe that harm. I now explore the kinematics of conversation in order to argue that conversational contributions routinely enact norms and they do so in a previously overlooked manner. Later I shall argue that this conversational mechanism generalizes in a way that affords an alternative model for how speech can constitute harm.

Since conversational contributions enact changes about what is true about that conversation and since the score tracks that which is relevant to the proper development of a conversation, conversational contributions enact changes to the conversational score. Since what counts as fair play depends on the score, changing the score thereby changes the bounds of conversational permissibility. Thus, any conversational contribution enacts changes to what is subsequently permissible in that conversation. For this reason, such contributions are *conversational exercitives*. They are *exercitives* since they enact facts about what is permissible in some realm and they are *conversational* exercitives since the realm in question is a particular conversation.

Since the phenomenon of conversational exercitives is so subtle and since my argument thus far is both general and abstract, some examples may help to illuminate the phenomenon. Consider first changes regarding which possibilities are relevant to a conversation. Suppose, for example, that my adulterous friend Maureen and I are discussing what she should do about her husband's suspicions and we have been considering only those courses of action that would keep her adulterous activities secret. There are plenty of things she *could* do (e.g., kill or hypnotize her husband) that are, in this context, simply beside the point. They are not within the class of possibilities under conversational consideration. Suppose, however, that I were to then say something that required the scope of relevant possibilities to broaden. Suppose I said, "Why don't you just come clean and tell the truth for once!"[24] In such a case, my utterance requires that a previously irrelevant possibility (that Maureen tell the truth) be relevant. The score automatically adjusts, though, through a rule of accommodation, so that the possibility I mention is conversationally relevant. My utterance effectively broadens the scope of relevant possibilities. Moreover, by enacting a change to the score, my utterance enacts changes to what is subsequently permissible in the conversation. Unless things change again, Maureen is no longer conversationally permitted to ignore these options.[25] Since my utterance enacts changes to the bounds of conversational permissibility, my utterance is a conversational exercitive.

---

[24] This example is similar to one in Lewis, his "Scorekeeping in a Language Game," 247.

[25] Of course, participants are free to try to block one another's moves. For an interesting discussion of blocking, see Langton (this volume). Maureen might ignore what I said and there may be contexts where her doing so counts as a conversational move and even one that changes the score right back to

Here is another example illustrating the phenomenon of conversational exercitives. Conversational contributions that introduce presuppositions also enact facts about what is subsequently appropriate in the conversation at hand. Suppose that I have just finished jogging (without my dog) and I meet a friendly stranger who is walking her dog along the trails. While we are chatting about the weather, her dog starts chewing on my shoes and I say, "My dog Fido also loves chewing on shoes!" Notice that this utterance introduces a presupposition. At the time of my utterance, my being a dog owner is not already a component of the conversational score but my utterance requires for its conversational appropriateness that my being a dog owner is a component of the score. Suppose that my new friend does not question this presupposition (that I have a dog) and we go on to have a lengthy and informed discussion about the best vets in the area. In such a case, the proposition that I own a dog has become a part of the score; it would be conversationally inappropriate for my new dog-walking friend to then ask me if I have any pets. This query is conversationally weird because my being a dog owner has become a shared part of the conversation. To later question that presupposition is conversationally inappropriate. Since my utterance enacts a change to the score (through a rule of accommodation, namely that for presupposition introduction), this conversational contribution thereby changes facts about what subsequently constitutes fair play in this conversation.[26] Thus, although it may not be obvious, my utterance enacts changes to what is conversationally permissible and is therefore an exercitive speech act; it is a conversational exercitive.

In this case, my interlocutor did not verbally question my presupposition but that does not mean that she actually believed it. In fact, she could have thought that I was faking being a dog owner all along. Even if this is the case, however, my being a dog owner is nevertheless a component of the conversational score. By treating my presupposition-introducing contribution as apt and by continuing the conversation as if I am a dog owner, my interlocutor treats my being a dog owner as a background fact for the purposes of this conversation. As such, it is a component of the conversational score. Were she to question that presupposition after our lengthy and detailed discussion of area vets by saying, "I've been wondering, do you own any pets?" her contribution would be conversationally out of bounds; it would violate the conversational norms operative and this is true even though she does not believe that I am a dog owner.

Of course, conversational contributions are open to ongoing challenge. This means that it is possible to conversationally question presuppositions. After all, my dog-walking interlocutor might have immediately questioned my presupposition-introducing conversational contribution by responding, "Wait! What? You have a

---

what it was. That said, conversationally broadening what is conversationally relevant seems easier than narrowing. In other words, for reasons that are not entirely understood, it is more difficult to say something that makes previously relevant options irrelevant than it is to make previously irrelevant options relevant. This asymmetric pliability of conversation is noted or discussed in Lewis, "Scorekeeping in a Language Game," 240–3; McGowan, Mary Kate (2007), "Oppressive Speech," *Australasian Journal of Philosophy* 87 (3): 389–407; Simpson, Robert M., "Unringing the Bell: McGowan on Oppressive Speech and the Asymmetric Pliability of Conversation," *Australasian Journal of Philosophy* 90 (3): 555–75; and Langton, this volume.

[26] There are complexities about the *timing* of score change, but this issue will not be explored here.

dog? But I've seen you at this park, running or walking, every day for two years and I've never seen you with a dog!" Were she to say this, she would prevent (or at least postpone) the presupposition that I am dog owner from being an ongoing component of the conversational score.[27]

So open to ongoing challenge are conversational contributions that it is even permissible to question a presupposition long after it has been introduced and even after it has been relied on repeatedly. To see this, suppose that, after having a lengthy and informed discussion of area vets, my dog-walking interlocutor says, "I know we've been talking about dogs all this time but it's really been bothering me and I didn't know how to bring it up but my friend Sean knows someone who doesn't have a dog but who likes to pretend to have one just to see if anyone says anything and . . . well . . . are you doing that right now?" Even conversationally entrenched presuppositions can be conversationally questioned in (highly unlikely but) conversationally appropriate ways.

But, as we just saw above, there are conversationally inappropriate ways to conversationally question entrenched presuppositions. It would not be conversationally apt for the my interlocutor to simply ask me if I have any pets after we have been discussing my dog's experiences with area vets for the last twenty minutes. That the presupposition that I am a dog owner is a component of the conversational score affects what is conversationally permissible. Since my presupposition-introducing utterance enacts that score change, it therefore also enacts the conversational permissibility facts enacted by that score change. Thus, despite the ongoing challengability of conversational contributions, my utterance is nevertheless a conversational exercitive.

8.7 How This Generalizes: Covert Exercitives

This phenomenon generalizes. After all, many activities—not just conversations—are such that contributions to them thereby change what is subsequently appropriate in them. In fact, any move in a norm-governed activity thereby enacts permissibility facts for that token instance of that activity. Moreover, when the action in question is speech, it is exercitive and is thus what I am calling a *covert* exercitive. (Note that I am using the term 'covert' in a way that departs from its technical use in pragmatics.)[28]

In order to argue for this general claim (i.e. that any move in a norm-governed activity thereby enacts permissibility facts in that particular activity), it is first necessary to say more about what is required for an activity to be norm-governed.

---

[27] I say 'ongoing' since she either prevents my utterance from introducing the presupposition or she changes the score back (by removing it). For ease of presentation, I sometimes speak as if the hearer blocks the score change when really the hearer's rejection of the contribution changes the score back in the relevant respect. I argue for this in *Just Words: Speech and the Constitution of Harm*, forthcoming. On Langton's account (this volume), her rejection makes it the case that my contribution misfires as a presupposition introduction.

[28] According to its use in pragmatics, an intention to perform an action is covert if the success of that action depends on the failure of the recognition of that intention. My intention to deceive is covert, for example, because my deception depends on that intention not being recognized. See, for example, Bach, Kent and Robert M. Harnish, *Linguistic Communication and Speech Acts* (Cambridge, MA: MIT Press, 1979).

8.7.1 On Being Norm-Governed

An activity counts as norm-governed just in case some actions count as inappropriate with respect to that activity. This is sufficient to show that the activity in question is governed by norms. This condition is easily and widely met. All practices, for example, are norm-governed activities.

Note that the norms in question need not be explicit, formal, exception-less or even consciously recognized.[29] If at least some actions would count as out of bounds or otherwise inappropriate with respect to that activity then that activity is norm-governed in the relevant sense. Conversations, dancing with a partner, informal social interactions, playing improvisational jazz, chess, checkers, and baseball are all norm-governed in this sense.

Some of the norms operative in norm-governed activities will not be peculiar to that norm-governed activity.[30] After all, the norms in question may very well be more general than that. Consider for example the norms of cooperation; these norms will guide a wide variety of practices. In so far as all of these activities are subject to the norms of cooperation, they are norm-governed in the relevant sense. Thus, to be norm-governed does not require that all of the norms guiding the activity are specific to that activity.

Note that the prescriptive force of norms can be quite complex and such norms can interact in nuanced ways with one another. Consider, for example, social norms pertaining to gender.[31] In what sense really do the norms of femininity apply to me? After all, as a feminist, I reject those norms. As a woman in American society, however, I am nevertheless judged in terms of these norms and I am sometimes socially sanctioned for my failure to abide by them. Thus, these norms have at least apparent prescriptive force even though I do and should reject them. Moreover, that I should reject these norms does not mean that they do not have some sort of prescriptive force; it means only that that force is overridden by other normative considerations.

8.7.2 Moves Enact Permissibility Facts

We are now in a position to see that any move in a norm-governed activity thereby enacts permissibility facts for that activity. To see this, notice first that moves enact score changes. Since a move is an action governed by the norms of the activity in question, moves are relevant to the proper development and assessment of that activity. Since the score, by definition, tracks all such relevant factors, the score tracks all moves. Consequently, any move enacts a change to the score. Furthermore, since what is permissible at any point in a norm-governed activity depends on what has happened so far in that activity (along with the norms governing it) and since what has happened so far is captured by the score, enacting a change to the score thereby

---

[29] I am agnostic about the ontology of these norms. I leave it to others to determine how best to account for them metaphysically and I am also open to them being explained away ontologically. What matters for my purposes is only that their apparent prescriptive force be retained.

[30] I thank Mark Richard for raising this issue.

[31] Murray and Starr (this volume) argue that social norms play a crucial role in communication. See also Bicchieri, Cristina, *The Grammar of Society: The Nature and Dynamics of Social Norms* (Cambridge: Cambridge University Press, 2005).

enacts permissibility facts for the activity in question. In this way, we see that a move in a norm-governed activity enacts permissibility facts for that activity.

Examples abound. When my opponent moves her checker, for example, her doing so made it permissible for me to subsequently move mine. As soon as Pat mentions a certain in-joke, he thereby makes it permissible for others to mimic Charles being drunk at last year's picnic. When an Irish session player starts a tune at a certain pace, it thereby makes it impermissible for other players to play at a different pace; it also makes it impermissible for other players to play other tunes and it makes it permissible for the other players to play that tune at that pace.[32] As one can see, our actions are often contributions to norm-governed activities and when they are they enact changes to what is subsequently permissible in those activities.

Although all moves enact score changes, not everything that enacts a score change is a move. Suppose, for example, that while I am talking to Bob about his sailboat, we both witness our friend Mike falling off his boat. In this case, Mike falling off his boat enacts a change to the conversational score (and, since we both notice it and are aware of each doing so, it also causes changes to our psychological states that then enact changes to the common ground). Moreover, this score change has permissibility consequences: now that Mike's boat is the most salient boat in the context of this conversation, it is now conversationally permissible for me to refer to Mike's boat with the expression 'the boat' whereas it would have been conversationally inappropriate to do so before that score change. Although Mike's fall enacts a score change, it is not a move in the conversation. Mike's fall is not governed by the norms of our conversation; it is not a contribution to that conversation; it is merely an event that is relevant to the conversation. Being relevant to a norm-governed activity falls short of being a contribution to it and moves are contributions.

8.7.3 Covert Exercitives

Thus far, we have focused on the permissibility-fact-enacting property of moves in norm-governed activities but we have not focused specifically on cases where the move in question is speech. Clearly, speech is sometimes a move in a norm-governed activity other than conversation. When it is, it enacts permissibility facts for the activity and is thus exercitive. Since the exercitive feature of the utterance in question is somewhat hidden, I call these utterances *covert exercitives*.[33] Covert exercitives enact norms in the norm-governed activity in which they are a move.

As one can now see, conversational exercitives are but a special case of covert exercitives. Since conversations are norm-governed activities and since conversational contributions are moves in that activity, conversational contributions are covert exercitives; they enact permissibility facts for the very conversation in which they are a move.

Now notice that speech can constitute a move in norm-governed activities other than (although typically in addition to) conversation. To see this, consider the following. Suppose that while discussing high school memories with my friend Greg

---

[32] The norms are quite different in other musical traditions (e.g., improvisational jazz).
[33] Again my use of 'covert' departs from its technical use in pragmatics. See fn. 28.

I say, "Grace was ironically named. She recently fell off her platform shoes and landed on top of the casket during the funeral for her boss. I must admit, I enjoyed hearing this; I still hate her. Don't Germans have a word for this?" My utterance is a move in the conversation; it thereby enacts permissibility facts for the conversation and is thus a conversational exercitive. In addition to this, however, my utterance is also a move in the norm-governed activity of social interaction. Suppose further that my expressed contempt for, and mockery of, Grace is accepted by Greg with relish. (Suppose, that is, that he is as petty and nasty as I am.) In such a case, my utterance (and his reaction to it) has permissibility consequences for our further social interaction. Depending on the broader g-norms operative (and these would need to be determined empirically) it might make it permissible between the two of us for Greg to mock Grace; it might make it permissible for him to roll his eyes at me were she to walk into the room and, in so far as it marks her as out of our little in-group, it might make it permissible for him to exclude her from our future gatherings. As one can see, conversational contributions can be moves in norm-governed activities in addition to conversation and thus such utterances can enact permissibility facts in these other norm-governed activities too. In addition to being a covert exercitive because it is a conversational exercitive, my utterance is also covertly exercitive in virtue of enacting permissibility facts in the additional norm-governed activity of social interaction.

8.8 Different Sorts of Norms

As one can see, it doesn't take much for an activity to be norm-governed. So long as some actions would count as somehow inappropriate with respect to a certain activity then that activity is norm-governed in the relevant sense. That some actions are (or would be) inappropriate shows that there are norms guiding the activity and this is all that is required for it to be norm-governed.

That said, there are different sorts of norms governing these activities and they ought to be distinguished. There is an important difference between norms that govern all instances of the (sort of) activity in question and those norms that govern only a particular instance of that (sort of) activity. Consider first the general or global norms. I call them *g-norms*.[34] G-norms govern all instances of the norm-governed activity in question and the performing of any particular such activity does not enact them. Consider, for example, conversations. The g-norms governing conversations include the (relatively rigid) rules of grammar and (the accommodating norm of) Grice's cooperative principle.[35] Note that these conversational g-norms apply to all conversations and they are not enacted by any particular conversation.[36]

Some of these g-norms are very general and others are more localized. The norms of cooperation that Grice stresses, for example, are very general norms of conversation. One ought to speak in a manner that enables one's interlocutor to understand what

---

[34] See my "Oppressive Speech," 389–407.

[35] Grice, H.P., "Logic and Conversation" in *Studies in the Way of Words* (Cambridge, MA: Harvard University Press, 1989): 26–31.

[36] To say that these norms are conversational does not require that they be peculiar to conversation. These "conversational" norms may just be more general norms of cooperation.

you mean by what you say. This is a very general norm of conversation. Of course, the appropriate to way to do this can vary from one context to another. In other words, there are more localized g-norms of manner operative in specific contexts. Using technical philosophical language while conversing with a supermarket teller is likely to violate local g-norms of manner of expression while failing to use that technical language would likely violate those local g-norms at an APA session on indexicals. G-norms can be more or less localized.

Other norms, by contrast, are quite specific and they are enacted by the performing of the very token-instance of the norm-governed activity over which they preside. I call such (token-activity-specific) norms *s-norms*.[37] Consider another example from a conversation. Suppose that my Uncle Jack and I are talking about his house when I say, "Oh yeah, well, when we bought our house, we thought about how difficult it would be to maintain it but we decided that we loved the house so much that we just had to buy it!" When I said this, I changed the salience facts for the conversation (making my house the most salient house) and this in turn changes what is subsequently permissible in that conversation. My utterance constitutes a move in the conversation that makes it conversationally impermissible (for the time being) to try to refer to any other house with the expression 'the house.' My utterance enacts a new s-norm for the conversation.

Several things are worth noticing about these s-norms. First, they are of limited duration. The s-norm I enact, for example, will be altered as soon as another house is made more conversationally salient. Second, s-norms are of limited scope. Unlike the rules of grammar (which are g-norms), this norm applies only to this particular conversation. Third, s-norms are enacted by the performing of the particular token instance of the norm-governed activity in which such norms preside. When I made a move in the conversation, I thereby enacted a new s-norm *for that particular conversation*. In fact, the performing of *any* norm-governed activity (not just conversations) will involve the perpetual creating and altering of s-norms, the constant creating and destroying of fleeting activity-specific permissibility facts. Fourth, the permissibility facts enacted by covert exercitives just are s-norms. When one makes a move in a norm-governed activity, one enacts new permissibility facts or s-norms for that activity. As one can see then, the more or less local g-norms governing norm-governed activities ought to be distinguished from the s-norms enacted by particular moves made in such activities.

8.9 Extremely Brief Exploration of Potential Applications

Utterances that enact score changes in a norm-governed activity thereby enact permissibility facts (or s-norms) for that (token instance of that) norm-governed activity. How might this mechanism shed light on the perplexing but powerful effects of speech

---

[37] See my "Oppressive Speech," 389–407. The distinction between g-norms and s-norms may not be a sharp one and there is likely to be a complex feedback system between the two sorts of norms. (G-norms clearly affect which s-norms are enacted by any particular move. Moreover, s-norms may (collectively) affect the g-norms.) Although interesting, such details are not pursued here.

in the social world? I shall now argue—all too briefly and in only the broadest of strokes—how the mechanism of covert exercitives can help to explain the social power of microaggressions, the verbal triggers for heightening stereotype threat, and the often unintended normative force of offhand sexist remarks.

Consider first microaggressions. "Microaggressions are subtle verbal and non-verbal insults directed toward non-Whites, often done automatically and unconsciously. They are layered insults based on one's race, gender, class, sexuality, language, immigration status, phenotype, or surname."[38] Here is an example:

> H&R Block employee when my best friend (who's black) and I went to get our taxes done together: "Employed?"
> Me: "Yes."
> H&R: "Any children?"
> Me: "No."
> H&R, turns to my friend: "Okay, and you. Employed?"
> Him: "Yes."
> H&R: "Any children?"
> Him: "No."
> H&R: "Are you sure?"
> Him: "Um . . ."
> H&R: "Just checking."
> Him: "Yes, I'm sure."[39]

I am assuming that the black best friend is male. Let us also assume that the H&R employee did not consciously intend to insult; the employee was merely conscious of trying to do the job well by being thorough and careful. Now, one might think that microaggressions such as this one are merely symptoms of the underlying problem of racism. One might think, that is, that such microaggressions merely signal or reflect antecedent and unjust facts about negative stereotypes and compromised social standing. The phenomenon of covert exercitives, however, shows that such microaggressions can do considerably more than this.

Notice first that the H&R employee's question is also a (non-conversational) covert exercitive. That is, in addition to being a conversational exercitive that enacts s-norms for the conversation, this question is also a move in the norm-governed activity of social interaction. As such, it enacts a score change in this token instance of that activity and thus it enacts s-norms in this token instance of that activity. The precise content of the enacted s-norm will depend on the g-norms operative, the move, and the score at the time of the move, and these are empirical matters that are not settled here. That said, we know that social interactions in our society are currently governed by g-norms that systematically disadvantage non-white persons relative to white

---

[38] Daniel Solorzano, Walter R. Allen, and Grace Carroll. "Keeping Race in Place: Racial Microaggressions and Campus Racial Climate at the University of California, Berkeley" 23 *Chicago-Latino Law Review* 15, 17 (2002). Quoted in Wells, Catherine "Micoraggressions in the Context of Academic Communities," unpublished manuscript. See also Brennan, Samantha, "The Moral Status of Micro-inequities: in Favour of Institutional Solutions," unpublished manuscript, available at http://philpapers.org/rec/BRETMS-4.

[39] From http://www.microaggressions.com/. Posted January 20, 2013.

persons and so there is ample reason to believe that the s-norm enacted in this case is problematic along a racial dimension.[40] If this is correct, then the microaggression actually enacts racist norms; it enacts racist parts of the racist social structure. It does not merely reflect antecedent racism, it (partially) constitutes it.

Were we to focus exclusively on the conversational exchange and thus on the participants' conscious intentions (as theorists normally do with speech), we would miss this crucially important aspect of the case. Once we recognize, however, that our utterances routinely constitute moves, and thus score-enacting actions, in broader social activities, such hitherto overlooked possibilities emerge. Whether intentional or not and whether the H&R employee was aware of doing so or not, the H&R employee's question is a covert exercitive; it enacts racially problematic s-norms. Thus, although this may seem like an isolated example of just one insensitive H&R employee, the phenomenon of covert exercitives shows how such utterances interact with (and also constitute mini-norms in) broader social structures.

Although I have here been stressing the constitutive aspect of covert exercitives, it is worth emphasizing that important causal processes are also illuminated by this phenomenon. Consider, for example, verbal triggers for stereotype threat. Stereotype threat, the "real-time threat of being judged and treated poorly in settings where a negative stereotype about one's group applies,"[41] is a well-documented psychological phenomenon. Persons made aware of their membership in negatively stereotyped social groups underperform on some cognitive tasks. The data suggest that one's awareness of the relevance of one's social group membership both taxes working memory and triggers psychological defense strategies, each of which undermines performance.

When I was in high school and about to take a challenging math test, my teacher complimented my outfit. In addition to being a conversational exercitive (that enacts s-norms for the conversation), the teacher's compliment is also a (non-conversational) covert exercitive that enacts score changes (and thus s-norms) to the social setting. In short, it made my gender relevant and it made my gender relevant to me; it triggered stereotype threat. The teacher's compliment enacted relevance facts that had the unintended but well-documented causal effect of undermining my performance.

Elsewhere I have argued that offhand sexist remarks can constitute acts of gender oppression.[42] Even when such remarks are made by someone with relatively little social power, the utterance nevertheless enacts oppressive s-norms because it enacts a score change in a norm-governed activity with gender unjust g-norms and because it enacts these s-norms in a social setting where women are systematically disadvantaged relative to men. As one can see, the "power" of the utterance resides more in the

---

[40] I have shown that s-norms are enacted, I have not proven which particular s-norms are enacted (but I have suggested that we have reason to believe they are racially problematic).

[41] C. M. Steele, S. J. Spencer, & J. Aronson, "Contending with a Group Image: The Psychology of Stereotype and Social identity Threat." In M. P. Zanna (ed.), *Advances in Social Experimental Psychology*, Vol. 34 (San Diego, CA: Elsevier, 2002): 385. Quoted in Fine, Cordelia, *Delusions of Gender* (New York: Norton, 2010): 30.

[42] McGowan, "Oppressive Speech,": 389–407. For an interesting discussion and partial development, see R. M. Simpson, "Unringing the Bell: McGowan on Oppressive Speech . . .": 555–75.

social context than in the speaker and the covertly exercitive force of such utterances brings this to light.

Finally, there is reason to believe that covert exercitives can help to explain plenty of other phenomena. They might, for example, help to explain the meaning and social force of pornography, the sneaky functioning of political dog whistles or the pernicious workings of racist jokes.[43] Thus, although our investigation started in the technical arena of conversational kinematics, we have nevertheless uncovered a socially important speech-mechanism of norm-enactment. We have identified a crucial role that we and our words unwittingly play in enacting the harmful social structures surrounding us.

[43] Saul (this volume), argues that my framework cannot account for dog whistles but she overlooks the fact that being explicit changes the move and thus alters which particular score changes are enacted by the move and this in turn alters which s-norms are enacted by the move. (In short, the g-norms could be such that making it explicit diminishes the effect.) Although I do not have an account of dog whistles on offer, an adequate account appears compatible with the framework. Moreover, if the causal effects of interest are brought about via adherence to norms enacted, then my framework would be especially helpful in accounting for how dog whistles work.

9

Force and Conversational States

Sarah E. Murray and William B. Starr

9.1 Overview

Classical speech act theory (Austin 1962; Searle 1969; Searle & Vanderveken 1985) drew attention to a phenomenon neglected by previous philosophers of language: our everyday utterances have a variety of forces, that is, they are used to make commands, promises, assertions, and so on.[†] These theorists took force to arise from social conventions or constitutive rules governing the use of particular linguistic forms: uttering *Dance!* counts as a command in virtue of its linguistic form and a rule which dictates when utterances of that form count as commands. As surveyed in §9.2.1, this work did not explain force in convincing empirical or conceptual detail. Principally, it does not capture the indirect relationship between linguistic form and utterance force, but it also leaves force unanalyzed in certain important respects. Neo-Gricean approaches to force, like Bach & Harnish (1979: §2.5) and Cohen & Perrault (1979), make this relationship more indirect and focus on the speaker's communicative intention.[1] This allows one to distinguish, as we will, between **utterance force** and **sentential force** (Chierchia & McConnell-Ginet 2000). The former is the total force of an utterance, while the latter is the way a sentence's semantics constrains utterance force. As we will argue, this feature is crucial to a sophisticated linguistic model of speech acts. But neither of the above accounts have figured prominently in recent efforts to formulate such a model.

Much of the recent work on speech acts in linguistics, philosophy, and artificial intelligence develops ideas from the discourse dynamics tradition, where speech acts are modeled in terms of how they change the context or 'score' of the conversation (Hamblin 1971; Stalnaker 1978; Lewis 1979; Gazdar 1981). These developments associate distinct sentence types (imperative, declarative, interrogative) with characteristic effects on what the agents in a discourse are mutually assuming for

[†] We would like to thank the participants in our Cornell seminar and ESSLLI course on speech acts, as well as audiences at the 2nd Cornell Workshop in Linguistics and Philosophy, the 1st conference on Philosophical Linguistics and Linguistic Philosophy (PhLiP), the *New Work on Speech Acts* conference and the Philosophy Desert Workshop for feedback on various stages of this project. Josh Armstrong provided crucial feedback on animal communication at several stages. We would like to thank Adam Bjorndahl for his comments and collaboration on a parallel joint project. We would also like to express special gratitude for the feedback and encouragement of Daniel Fogal, Daniel Harris, and Matt Moss.
[1] See also Cohen & Levesque (1985, 1990).

that exchange (Roberts 1996; Poesio & Traum 1997; Portner 2004; Farkas & Bruce 2010; Murray 2010b; Starr 2010; Murray & Starr 2012). Crucially, these particular effects are only taken to be *part* of an utterance's force (Stalnaker 1978: 86–7; Portner 2004: 237–8). This also allows one to distinguish sentential force and utterance force: the former is the characteristic way that a sentence type changes the context, while the latter consists of other unspecified changes. This clearly leaves open what a general theory of utterance force will look like and how one fills the gap between utterance force and sentential force. In this paper we extend models of communicative dynamics to explore these two open questions.

One might expect that there is not much exploration to be done: it seems simple enough to unify existing discourse dynamic approaches with the Neo-Gricean approach (Sbisá 2002). We consider such a unification here, but argue for a quite different approach. Unlike Speech Act Theorists or Neo-Griceans, we will *not* use the concept of utterance force to systematize our intuitive classifications of utterances, e.g. as assertions, commands, etc. Instead, we will use it to capture the communicative function(s) of an utterance (Millikan 1984, 2005): how the utterance can serve to coordinate us in our joint activities (see also Clark 1996). Speech Act Theory and Neo-Gricean analyses not only regard this as a perlocutionary effect external to the speech act itself, but offer theories of perlocution that are poorly suited to this process.[2] We propose that this shift in focus yields a more useful and explanatory conception of utterance force in three domains.

First, our account better integrates with the understanding of communication emerging in the biological and social sciences (e.g. Maynard Smith & Harper 2003; Scott-Phillips 2008; Scott-Phillips & Kirby 2013). That work has three key features, discussed at length in §9.3.1. It highlights the intrinsic conflict of interest in communication, it seeks to explain how communication can nonetheless emerge as a stable state of nature and focuses on the important role coordination plays in this process. We argue that a Neo-Gricean approach appeals to the wrong tools and is built on the wrong conception of communication to fit into a general account with these features. By contrast, our account is built around them and recent insights on sentential force in linguistics. In particular, we show that social norms have a crucial role to play in explaining how communication can succeed despite conflicts of interest. Our more unified and naturalistic picture of speech acts is at least an interesting alternative to the complex *a priori* accounts found in the classic literature (e.g. Bach & Harnish 1979; Searle & Vanderveken 1985).

Second, our concept of utterance force offers a better account of various empirical phenomena. It will offer a better account of particular ways in which sentential and utterance force diverge. In particular, it will allow complex sentences like *I love you*

---

[2] See Marcu (2000) for an extensive discussion of just this point. The gist is that the key division assumed by Neo-Gricean and Speech Act Theoretic accounts conflicts in various ways with all of the experimental studies that focus on how conversations influence people's private commitments. These accounts assume that hearers form private commitments in two distinguishable steps. First, they recognize what effect the speaker intended to achieve with their utterance. Next, hearers decide whether to form corresponding private commitments. This picture suggests that the two effects should be at least somewhat distinguishable, but empirical studies suggest the opposite.

and don't you forget it to have multiple utterance forces, each of which can diverge from its sentential force. We integrate this account with an independently motivated dynamic semantics for imperative, declarative and interrogative moods. The meaning of these moods can be straightforwardly specified in terms of how they update the conversational score, without assuming that this update wholly constitutes or determines the force of an utterance. That additional work is not done by interpreting intentions, as the Neo-Griceans propose. It is done by the social norms that are independently motivated by our more general discussion of communication in §9.3.

Finally, our concept of force is better-suited to the needs of recent work in social philosophy which highlights the ways language can be a tool of subordination, oppression, and violence (e.g. Maitra & McGowan 2012). Often, subordination is effected by the way hearers construe an utterance without regard to the speaker's intention (Fricker 2007), and an audience can amplify a speaker's message in un-envisioned and catastrophic ways (Tirrell 2012). Further, it is insulting at best, and quite obviously false, to view oppressed people as opting in to a language game whose rules systematically abuse and further oppress them. On our account, oppressive norms give certain agents limited control over their utterances and actions, and other agents enhanced control and reach with theirs. This approach predicts the oppressed have limited ability to opt out without opting out of society itself, and that the oppressors have a unique capacity to inflict verbal harm.

Our account of utterance force is comprised of two central proposals, one about the *nature* of utterance force and one about the *mechanisms* that generate it. We propose that the force of an utterance should be identified with the communicative function that utterance serves. We argue below that the communicative function of an utterance reaches beyond what it makes mutually assumed in a conversation. It concerns the actual private commitments that can result from changing these mutual assumptions.[3] Agents cannot actually accomplish things in the world by mutually attending to the conversational score. That score has to have some force, or bearing, on their private commitments to provide reasons to act. Thus, the force of an utterance is not simply one of the components registered on what Lewis (1979) called the *conversational scoreboard*. We agree that each speech act includes a particular contribution to those mutual assumptions or scoreboard. But, we will argue, the force of that speech act goes further: it consists in how that mutual contribution bears on the agents' private commitments (§9.4), something which is not generally itself part of those mutual assumptions.[4] While the mutual assumptions and scoreboard are transparent to the conversationalists, the agents' private commitments need not be. On this approach, force consists in the various ways a population of agents is using their mutual commitments or scoreboard to influence each other's private commitments. With this in mind, we introduce the concept of a **conversational state** which models both the mutual, transparent, commitments and the private individual commitments at play in a conversation.

How does one fill the gap between the conventional meaning of a sentence and the force an utterance of it has? The conventional meaning makes an attitude mutual,

---

[3] See Yalcin (2007: 1008) for the kindred idea of *conversational tone* which we discuss in §9.2.2.

[4] Cohen & Levesque (1990) seem to operate with a similar notion of force, but they do not speak directly to this issue.

and this act manages to influence the private commitments of the agents involved. We propose that social norms are the central *mechanism* governing this process, but grant that social conventions or rules are sometimes involved. More specifically, we take these norms to govern the relationship between public commitments and private commitments, and how they interact with important features of our social lives like reputation, power, relationship and activity type. It is thus crucial to have the basic distinction between social norms and conventions clear from the beginning. Indeed it is only recent work on these phenomena that makes it possible to see issues that are passed over in the founding texts of speech act theory.

Social conventions, like driving on one side of the road, are arbitrary ways of coordinating our interests, and can succeed only when our interests coincide (Lewis 1969; Bicchieri 2005). This has two crucial consequences. Social conventions must be explicitly formulated and taught to new members of the community, and in a population where self-interests are divergent in a given domain, conventions cannot emerge, e.g. people perversely desiring to cause wrecks would conspire against our driving conventions. Recall we are assuming, with economists and biologists, that there is a general conflict of interest between speaker and hearer, and that this conspires against communication. Social conventions are of little use here. What is needed is a tool for transforming a situation where interests conflict to one where they coincide. This is precisely what **social norms** do according to Bicchieri (2005).[5] They are self-fulfilling expectations about what particular kinds of agents are to do in particular kinds of situations, and these expectations are often reinforced with social penalties for non-conformity. Consider the practice in soccer of one team kicking the ball out of play when the opposing team appears to have a seriously injured player, and the opposing team returning possession after the player has received treatment. This is not a formal rule with formal sanctions for violation, but this practice is viable because there are costs associated with being called unsporting by other teams and spectators.

Human society is suffused with social norms that have evolved to make coordination possible in the face of conflicting interests (Bicchieri 2005), and our linguistic interactions are no exception. It is crucial, however, to highlight that while social norms are an essential tool for social existence, the actual norms at work in a society are usually suboptimal and oppressive, e.g. female footbinding in China (Bicchieri 2005: 41). We believe this point is essential for capturing how language can be used as a tool of subordination, oppression, and violence. It also provides useful insight into how norms work. They are not rationally calculated or democratically adopted, and may not even be rules we would accept if explicitly prompted. They dynamically emerge in response to existing contingencies in agents' psychological, social, and physical environments. For example, they exploit unconscious psychological processes sensitive to basic social cues like reputation, relationship type (Fiske 1992) and schema/activity type (Schank & Abelson 1977; Levinson 1979),

---

[5] While forms of life (Wittgenstein 1953) and social norms play large roles in work on language by Habermas (1998, 2000) our reliance on social norms is more specific. Viewing social norms as ways of making coordination possible where it otherwise wouldn't be is unique to Bicchieri (2005), and carves out the unique role we use them to play in our own theory of force.

which frequently lie beyond humans, conscious reach. This allows agents to fluidly adapt their actions to their social environment without interpreting the intentions behind each other's actions or learning to act in accord with formal rules. In assuming that these are the mechanisms driving utterance force, we are proposing to treat utterance force as a kind of distributed *social significance*: it consists in individual commitments that form a broader social pattern—one which may or may not be laudable, and may or may not manifest the intentions of any one individual.[6] This facilitates an integration with recent attempts to fit our linguistic behavior into a larger picture of social dynamics.[7]

9.2 Speech Acts and Utterance Force

Utterances have a somewhat mysterious and quite varied force over us. For example, some command us, some advise us, others inform us and yet others subordinate or elevate us. What exactly is this force and how does it arise from the linguistic and pragmatic features of an utterance? We will begin in §9.2.1 with the first attempts of the modern era to address this phenomenon, namely speech act theory and Neo-Gricean pragmatics. The chief advantage of the latter is that it allows for an indirect relationship between the form of a sentence and the force of its utterance. It does this by focusing on what the speaker intends to communicate with an utterance, while allowing that the semantics of sentences can constrain this. However, we will explain that this account does not allow one to characterize the communicative function of an utterance. That requires appealing to the private commitments that actually result from communication, while Neo-Gricean accounts focus exclusively on a process quite distant from the hearer's actual commitments: the state of mind a speaker intends to express and the hearer's recognition of this intention. In §9.2.2 we observe that the same is true of existing work in the discourse dynamics tradition. §9.3 will then argue that this limitation is problematic because our best accounts of communication require attending to the actual commitments that prompt and result from an utterance.

9.2.1 From Speech Act Theory to Neo-Gricean Analyses

In the seminal study of speech act theory, Austin (1962) alleged that previous work had focused only on the **locutionary act**: the act of saying something, e.g. uttering sounds that count as words in an order that counts as a sentence which counts as having a particular meaning. He proposed that speech acts also involve performing an **illocutionary act**: what one does *in* saying something, e.g. apologizing, betting,

---

[6] This approach is inspired by the similar analysis of figurative and evocative language in Lepore & Stone (2014), where the interpretive effects of, say metaphor, are neither part of the conventional meaning of the words uttered nor part of what a speaker means by their utterance. It also bears some resemblance to Geis' (1995: 33) *transactional significance*, which is embedded in a dynamic theory of speech acts.

[7] E.g. Brown & Levinson (1987); Langton (1993); Clark (1996); van Rooy (2004); Pinker *et al.* (2008); Skyrms (2010); Clark (2012); Maitra (2012); Tirrell (2012); Scott-Phillips *et al.* (2012); Asher & Lascarides (2013).

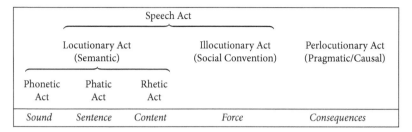

Figure 9.1 Austin (1962) Analysis of Speech Acts.

asserting. Only the illocutionary act has 'force' and it has force in virtue of social conventions:

[W]e also perform illocutionary acts such as informing, ordering, warning, undertaking, etc., i.e. utterances which have a certain (conventional) force.   (Austin 1962: 108)

We must notice that the illocutionary act is a conventional act: an act done as conforming to a convention.   (Austin 1962: 105)

On Austin's (1962) approach, an utterance's force consists of the effects it has in virtue of the social convention governing that type of utterance, e.g. the commitments a speaker produces by making a promise. Austin (1962) contrasts these effects with further by-products of a speech act. That is what he traced to the **perlocutionary act**: what one does *by* saying something, e.g. convincing, offending, alarming. The general analysis is depicted in Figure 9.1, though the key feature for us is the idea that force consists in the effects of social conventions that govern our utterances. On this theory, the nature of, and mechanism driving, utterance force is as follows:

Austin (1962) Theory (see Figure 9.1)
1. *Mechanism*: social conventions
2. *Utterance Force*: individual commitments brought about by utterances and social conventions

There are three major, interrelated issues for the Austinian analysis. Austin (1962) offers no theory of social conventions, and in the absence of this it is difficult to assess or apply the theory in much detail. For example, the Austinian says little about how a particular utterance and its context invokes any particular social convention. This also makes it extremely difficult to distinguish the conventional effects that constitute force from the perlocutionary effects that do not. This is evident when Austin (1962: 115–18) struggles to articulate the exact distinction. This issue is further compounded by the fact that it is difficult to find the requisite social conventions for most utterances occurring outside the rigid confines of marriages, card games, and the like (Strawson 1964). While it is easy to point to social conventions for promising, it is hard to find parallel conventions for, e.g., asserting, warning, suggesting, or inform-ing. Whatever social mechanism regulates the latter utterances, it is disanalogous to the explicitly taught and enforced rules that regulate marriages and card games.

Searle (1969) and Searle & Vanderveken (1985) propose a view well-positioned to address these issues. They propose that force arises via constitutive rules (Rawls 1955),

Speech Act					
Illocution (Semantic, Constitutive Rules)				Illocutionary Intent (Pragmatic)	Perlocutionary Act (Pragmatic/Causal)
Phonetic Act	Phatic Act	Propositional Act	Illocutionary Point		
Sound	*Sentence*	*Content*	*Force*	*Speaker Meaning*	*Consequences*

Figure 9.2 Searle (1968, 1969) Analysis of Speech Acts.

on the analogy with the rules of chess and baseball. These rules not only regulate the games they govern, they constitute those games: if you allow the knight to move in straight lines as well, you are playing a different game. Just as certain rules govern the use of a chess piece and the consequences of doing so, there are rules that govern the use of certain linguistic forms and the consequences of doing so. For example, Searle (1968) proposes that uttering, 'I promise ...', with the appropriate intentions, triggers such a rule which dictates that the speaker has made certain commitments. This requires Searle (1968) to reject the claim that force resides purely at the level of utterances: it arises at the level of particular linguistic forms and is part of the semantics of a language. In other words, Searle rejects Austin's distinction between illocutionary and locutionary acts. On this theory, the nature of, and mechanism driving, utterance force is as follows:

Searle (1969) Theory (see Figure 9.2)
1. *Mechanism*: constitutive rules, e.g. chess
2. *Utterance Force*: understood, intended commitments brought about by utterance and constitutive rules

One concern about this account is that most of the rules proposed for utterance force (Searle & Vanderveken 1985: §§3.2, 5.1) still contain primitive terms, like *illocutionary point*, which are dangerously close to the concept of utterance force itself (Siebel 2002). One is not told what an illocutionary point is, just that there are five of them and they roughly follow the metaphor of 'direction of fit'. Philosophically, this leaves room for a more revealing approach and empirically it makes the theory difficult to apply to particular linguistic data, especially outside the friendly confines of English. Related approaches like Stenius (1967) and Lewis (1975: 172) do without these primitives, but all make a problematic assumption, which Levinson (1983: 263) dubs the Literal Force Hypothesis: a sentence's form determines the force an utterance of it has. Levinson (1983: §5.5) takes indirect speech acts to sink the Literal Force Hypothesis. But even setting these aside, it does not stand up to a cursory look at human language use.

One sentence can have quite varied utterance forces (Davidson 1979; Bach & Harnish 1979: 130–1): *Run!* can serve to advise, command, suggest, or even rally. Maintaining that each such difference is traceable to a distinct *linguistic form* is simply not plausible. There are far more utterance forces than potential linguistic indicators of force. Further, simply treating force variation as widespread ambiguity misses clear generalizations connecting sentence types and contextual features to utterance forces. For example, it would fail to capture the fact that in particular exchanges *Is it raining?* and *I wonder if it's raining* can both have the force of an inquiry, but that their forces could diverge if uttered in a different context.[8] These generalizations are what our theory aims to predict.

Ironically, exactly the same empirical limitations result from denying that conventional meaning in any way constrains utterance force. For example, Davidson (1979) and Levinson (1983, 1979: 30) assume that any sentence can have any utterance force, because conventional meaning does not at all constrain utterance force. The middle ground occupied by Neo-Gricean approaches like Bach & Harnish (1979) and Cohen & Levesque (1985) is appealing precisely for this reason. They see utterance force as part of what a speaker means by an utterance, rather than part of a sentence's meaning. A sentence's meaning constrains, but does not determine, what a speaker can mean by its utterance. This flexibility is perhaps the most desirable property a theory of utterance force can have. The Neo-Gricean approach spells out what a speaker means and communicates in terms of Gricean (1957) communicative intentions:

Communicative Intention   Using a signal σ, X intends to bring about some particular effect in Y's state of mind by means of Y recognizing X's intention to do so.

Communication is construed as the mutual recognition of this intention, not the achievement of intended effects. Neo-Griceans maintain that hearers *infer* the speaker's communicative intention, and so the key task in a theory of speech acts is to spell out how this inference goes. Bach & Harnish (1979: §2.5) hold that a given sentence mood is primitively constrained to producing only certain kinds of effects.[9] This stipulation provides a mutual constraint that the hearer can exploit when inferring an interpretation. This account allows room for conventional utterances like *Hello* by simply saying that the speaker may intend to invoke a social convention. Perlocutionary effects like convincing the hearer are treated as intended consequences of the speech act itself, as Figure 9.3 illustrates.

On this approach, the force of an utterance consists merely in understanding the hearer's communicative intention.

Neo-Gricean Theory (see Figure 9.3)
1. *Mechanisms*: communicative intentions, inference; social conventions
2. *Utterance Force*: understanding intended commitments brought about by utterance and intention recognition

---

[8] A loophole: Searle & Vanderveken (1985) might attempt to treat force underdetermination as context-dependence, on the model of *I* and *here*. Starr (2014) argues that this loophole is closed: there is no function from contextual features to utterance forces that identifies a standing contribution of force indicators that is parallel to the function from contexts to speakers in that context that serves as the character of *I*. This is because each component of force can vary, and on the Searle & Vanderveken (1985) analysis force just is the cluster of contextual features that 'determine' force. This makes it impossible to specify a function which *predicts* the force of an utterance from relevant contextual features.

[9] See the rather brief remarks on 'locutionary-compatibility' or 'L-compatibility' in Bach & Harnish (1979: 11,34,36,173).

Speech Act						
Locutionary Act (Semantic)				Illocutionary Act (Pragmatic)		Perlocutionary Act (Pragmatic)
Phonetic Act	Phatic Act	Propositional Act	Sentence Type	Communicative Intention	Social Convention	
Sound	*Sentence*	*Content*	*Force Potential*	*Communicated Force and Content*		*Intended Consequences*

Figure 9.3 Neo-Gricean Analysis (Bach & Harnish 1979; Cohen & Perrault 1979).

Many objections have been raised to the Neo-Gricean analysis, but we will focus here on three criticisms that have not been highlighted in previous literature. First, the account of how sentence meaning constrains utterance force is not entirely satisfying. It does not explain why declaratives are constrained to expressing beliefs, it merely stipulates that they are. This would be fine if it was an account of the conventional meaning of declarative mood, but it is not. The Neo-Gricean analysis assumes a simple truth-conditional semantics where the only way of encoding this connection is to build it in to the truth-conditions of the sentence itself. But this is obviously incorrect, as the truth of *Mars is red* says nothing about the speaker's beliefs. Our analysis in §9.4 and Murray & Starr (2012) addresses this by allowing meanings to be the dynamic procedures by which sentences affect mutual attitudes, rather than just the state of the world they depict.

The second concern bears on mixed mood sentences, discussed extensively in Murray & Starr (2012). A sentence like *I'm making tortillas but don't expect to eat them all* simultaneously conveys information and a directive, but the inference of utterance force detailed by Bach & Harnish (1979) is limited in practice and principle to sentences of a single mood. Their actual theory only applies to sentences of a single mood that express a unified attitude. Further, their pragmatic inference would have to operate sub-sententially to capture this phenomenon. The latter would blur perhaps the only clear boundary between semantics and pragmatics: that which is part of recursive composition and that which is not. Our third objection is more general: the notion of communication embodied by this approach is far too weak and incomplete to actually capture what we want to explain when we theorize about communication. Developing this point will require more care.

Our first contention will be that mutual recognition of the speaker's communicative intention is not enough to actually coordinate two agents. We will later (§9.3) argue that the coordination of agents is the key phenomenon to be explained in a naturalistic theory of communication. Towards the first contention, consider a scenario where Janis wants to get together with Jimi to play music and says *Meet me at Hotel Chelsea around 11*. Now suppose Jimi recognizes that Janis intends him to choose his actions accordingly, and this is clear to Janis. This is not enough to actually coordinate Janis and Jimi's actions. Merely recognizing that Janis intends him to choose his actions accordingly does not yet provide Jimi with a reason to actually choose his actions accordingly. But that is precisely what needs to happen to coordinate Janis and Jimi. Neo-Griceans don't say false things about this process, they say *nothing* about it. They dismiss it as a perlocutionary effect. We think this perfectly illustrates a rather general issue for Neo-Gricean analyses. Their theory of communicative intentions is tailored to systematizing our intuitions about how to classify certain speech acts, but entirely ignores the central explanatory goal in a theory of communication: the explanation of how agents use signals to coordinate. We think that this methodology gives the wrong priority to our intuitive classifications. There is good reason to think that we should begin with a general, naturalistic investigation of communication, and once its capacity to coordinate agents has been explained we can return to the question of how that bears on our ordinary ways of describing utterances.

Now, we realize that it might sound tendentious to claim that using signals to coordinate is the central fact to be explained by a theory of communication. However, as mentioned in §9.1, it is the central assumption of naturalistic theories communication in the sciences, and deservedly so. We will present the evidence in favor of this idea, as well as addressing two very basic objections to it in §9.3. For now, we will turn to discussing work in the discourse dynamics tradition where we will make essentially the same point: the work in this tradition does not address the question of how language could actually coordinate two agents in a joint activity, and so is at most a partial theory of communication and utterance force.

9.2.2 Force and Discourse Dynamics

Ideas from classical speech act theory have been noticeably absent in more recent work by linguists and philosophers. Instead, that work has focused on discourse dynamics (Hamblin 1971; Stalnaker 1978; Lewis 1979). This approach offers detailed models of the mutual assumptions at play in conversation, and how utterances change those assumptions. In particular, each distinct sentence type is associated with a characteristic effect on what the agents in a discourse are mutually assuming for the purposes of that exchange (Roberts 1996; Portner 2004; Farkas & Bruce 2010; Murray 2010b; Starr 2010; Murray & Starr 2012). For example, declaratives provide information, interrogatives introduce issues, and imperatives promote alternatives (Starr 2010; Murray & Starr 2012). Such an approach better reflects linguistic typology and so provides a better starting point for an empirically adequate approach to utterance force. This has large empirical payoffs when considering phenomena on which speech act theory provides little insight.

Roberts (2003, 2005, 2012) reveals surprising and powerful connections between the questions under discussion in a discourse, discourse goals and the interpretation of 'incomplete' definites like *the guy*. Portner (2007) is able to explain several interesting interactions between deontic modals and imperatives, without assimilating one to the other. Murray (2011, 2010a,b, 2014) captures the distinctive contribution of evidentials as a distinctive kind of update with a broader application to other phenomena—not-at-issue assertion—where speech act theorists were compelled to posit a new primitive speech act 'present' (Faller 2002). More recently, Roelofsen & Farkas (2015) have used discourse dynamics to model the function of polarity particles like *Yes* and *No*. This sophisticated model can handle the complexities that arise from different polarity systems across languages and the variety of interrogatives and declaratives that license them, including the interaction of interrogatives with negation, disjunction and intonation. The fruits of this research program, with little comparative success in speech act theory, has seen interest in speech act theory among linguists decline.

Some working in this tradition are explicit that the characteristic effect of a sentence type is only *part* of an utterance's force (Stalnaker 1978: 86–7; Portner 2004: 237–8). But what more is there to utterance force and what phenomena does such a theory explain? Some, like Gazdar (1981), assume that there is an answer to this question within the basic models offered and that it will allow us to systematize our ordinary categorizations of speech acts. There is virtually no work on this issue, but one idea is to integrate elements of the Neo-Gricean approach. In addition to having a constant effect on the mutual assumptions, the utterance of a sentence will also trigger a pragmatic inference that depends on particular details of the utterance. For example, a speaker S's utterance of *Janis was a singer* to H counts as an assertion not only when it updates the mutual information with the proposition that Janis was a singer, but also when when (1) is true (Bach & Harnish 1979: 42):[10]

(1) S intends H to recognize that:
    a. S believes that Janis was a singer and
    b. S intends H to form this same belief

On this model, the assertion will make the proposition that Janis was a singer mutually assumed, and prompt a pragmatic inference to arrive at something like (1) also being mutually assumed for the purposes of the exchange.

This way of supplementing the discourse dynamics model inherits most of the problems highlighted for the Neo-Gricean account in §9.2.1.[11] Most importantly, it offers no account of why this utterance would lead H to conform to S's intention (1b) and actually form the belief that Janis was a singer. It also does not explain why this utterance would commit S to being sincere and actually believing that Janis was a singer. But this is precisely what one wants to explain if the force of an utterance is supposed to reflect the way it serves to coordinate speaker and hearer. Of course, one may not want to explain that—we return to this issue in §9.3.

The discussion above relies on a crucial fact that is sometimes ignored in work on discourse dynamics, e.g. Farkas & Bruce (2010). Discourse dynamics says nothing about the individual commitments, or even the mutual beliefs, that result from an utterance. These approaches only track what the agents are mutually and *provisionally assuming* for the purposes of the exchange.[12] This understanding of the view is essential to make it sufficiently general and useful. In order for it to model the parallel discourse kinematics involved in speculation, pretense, sarcasm, cooperative suspension of disagreement, and much else, it is essential to characterize utterances

---

[10] Additional qualifications ensure that the utterance is literal, communicative, and that the intention in (1) is appropriately transparent and recognized in the right way (Bach & Harnish 1979: §1.6).

[11] There's more room here for saying why, given the semantics of declaratives, belief or knowledge is associated with declarative mood. Declarative mood updates an informational acceptance-like attitude. However, problems lie in wait for speech acts like inquiries where the Neo-Griceans attempt to analyze utterance force in terms of the speaker wanting information. Yet interrogatives update inquisitive attitudes like wondering, not conative attitudes like wanting (Hamblin 1973; Heim 1992; Lahiri 2002).

[12] There are many definitions of these mutual assumptions, or common ground (Clark 1996: Ch.4). We prefer defining them as assumptions that are rationally transparent to all the agents involved: not only is each agent assuming p, they are justified in assuming that everyone is assuming p, in assuming that everyone is assuming that everyone is assuming p and so on (Lewis 1969). Note that this characterization does not assume that agents are aware of their justification or have reasoned through it themselves.

as changing mutual assumptions rather than the more committal attitudes of mutual belief, knowledge or desire (Stalnaker 2002). It is possible to converse with someone that has entirely different beliefs on a given subject matter, even if the two parties disagree entirely what the take-home message of the conversation is. However, it is precisely this justified assumption which prevents discourse dynamic models from capturing the communicative function of an utterance.

We think it is instructive here to consider the notion of conversational tone discussed by Yalcin (2007: 1008):

Conversational Tone   An attitude is the conversational tone of a group of interlocutors just in case it is common knowledge in the group that everyone is to strike this attitude towards the propositions which are common ground.

It is rather natural to consider applying this idea to the analysis of utterance force. While an actor's utterance and a policeman's utterance of /You're under arrest/ update the mutual assumptions in exactly the same way, they involve different conversational tones. Utterance force, then, is a discourse-level phenomenon whereby *all* of the mutual assumptions are mutually known to bear some relation to the private commitments of the conversationalists. Fictional discourse could be captured by mutual knowledge that neither the speaker nor hearer are committed to the mutual assumptions. By contrast, scientific discourse might be captured by mutual knowledge that both speaker and hearer are indeed committed to the mutual assumptions. It is worth noting that this account may not vindicate the intricate variety tracked by our ordinary categorizations of utterances into, e.g., suggestions, hints, and warnings. But we agree that should not be the empirical focus in the study of speech acts.

A more serious concern arises when considering the mechanisms by which this common knowledge is supposed to arise. The common knowledge cannot itself be communicated by speech acts, i.e. explicitly taught, to someone that does not yet possess it. By hypothesis, such hearers would not know what attitude to strike to the propositions made common ground by such instruction. Further, when one thinks about the wide variety of conversational tones that correlate with very nuanced social circumstances, e.g. close friends vs. new acquaintances vs. authority figures, it becomes difficult to even think of conversational tone as managed by 'common knowledge'. Common knowledge is information that the agents may not be actively entertaining, but would agree to if prompted. The large literature in behavioral economics suggests that the principles guiding our social behaviors do not have this feature, indeed most subjects reject the principles when prompted with them (Cialdini *et al.* 1991; Bicchieri 2005: Ch.2). Further, in a single discourse, this principle seems to apply differentially to different parts of an utterance. A complex imperative like, *Take off your shoes and try the tacos!* could be used as a sign at the entrance to a party to direct speakers to take off their shoes, but merely suggest trying the tacos. Similarly, it is extremely well-established that the social identity of an individual within a discourse radically shapes the uptake of their (attempted) contributions to the common ground (Labov 1972; Brown & Levinson 1987; Clark 1996; Hulstijn 2003; Hulstijn & Maudet 2006; Fricker 2007). While the idea of conversational tone has much in common with the approach we will develop, it differs on all of these crucial points.

9.3 Norms and the Communicative Function of Speech Acts

In §9.4 we will propose that the force of an utterance should be identified with its communicative function, which is in turn understood partly in terms of coordination. This section will articulate and defend this link between coordination and communication, as well as saying how the communicative function of an utterance emerges from understanding this link. The first step will be to present Lewis' (1969: Ch.4) simple account of communication as coordination, and contrast it with the Neo-Gricean model. The chief explanatory advantage of the Lewisian model here is that it explains how communication can be a self-sustaining method of coordinating our actions. We then explain how this feature of communication is the central property that biologists have sought to explain in their work on communication. But this work in biology also highlights ways in which Lewis' approach is far too simple.

The best way of moving past this simple model appeals to the communicative function of signals. We will argue that this allows one to address a number of problems for the Lewisian view, including deception, without defining communication immediately in terms of intentions. While this appeal to function does explain how deception can cohere with viewing communication as coordination, it does not explain how communication can persist in interactions which are not *prima facie* coordination games. The importance of this fact is illustrated powerfully in recent work on subordinating and altruistic speech. In these interactions, there is enough conflict of interest to make coordination of immediate self-interests impossible. It is here that we will draw on and articulate more carefully the idea of a social norm, which transforms what would be a game of conflict into a game of coordination. §9.4 will apply the idea of communicative function developed in this section to the study of utterance force.

9.3.1 Coordination and Communicative Function

The idea that communication involves coordination was central to Lewis' (1969: Ch.4) analysis of communication, signaling games, and convention. There, Lewis considers the Sexton of Old North Church hanging one lantern in the belfry to communicate that Redcoats are coming by land to Paul Revere. Communication occurs only when Paul Revere actually responds to that lantern signal by appropriately warning the countryside (Lewis 1969: 124). It is only when Revere interprets the lantern in this way, assuming it is truthfully issued by the Sexton, that their joint actions will bring about a mutually preferred state of affairs: an appropriately defended countryside. In other words, communication only occurs when the production and response to the signal coordinates the agents' actions.[13]

Lewisian Communication   (Lewis 1969: 124)
X communicated with Y using signal σ if and only if:
  1. Y's responded to σ by doing R,

---

[13] Lewis (1975) later allowed communication to also coordinate beliefs. One can imagine extending this approach to other mental states.

2. X produced σ by doing C and
3. C and R solved a coordination problem for X and Y.

Solving a coordination problem is a technical notion from game theory:

Solving a Coordination Problem   (Lewis 1969: 14)
C and R solve a coordination problem for X and Y, if and only if:
1. X could not have become better off by doing something other than C or from Y doing something other than R,
2. Y could not have become better off by doing something other than R or from X doing something other than C.

In the example above, C is the Sexton producing one lantern in the belfry after observing the Redcoats preparing a land invasion and R is Revere appropriately warning the countryside. No way of changing just the action executed by the Sexton or Revere would make the Sexton better off, and no way of changing just the action executed by Revere or the Sexton would make Revere better off. This game-theoretic understanding of coordination is one useful way to sharpen the intuitive notion of coordination, and will be assumed from here on. This is not, however, the definition of communication we will ultimately endorse. Yet it is instructive to see how it differs from the Neo-Gricean approach.

The Lewisian account maintains that communication itself provides the hearer with a reason for action: if communication has occurred, Revere must plan to appropriately inform the countryside. But the Neo-Gricean model does not provide such a reason: if communication has occurred, Revere would simply need to *understand* which action the Sexton intended Revere to perform, and Revere need not actually plan to perform that action. The Lewisian objects that the Neo-Gricean model of communication is useless for explaining how agents use signals to get things done, and useless for explaining the surprising stability of this capacity: why does communicating in a given way persist once it has been established? For that purpose, the Neo-Gricean would have to focus on the cases where the speaker and hearer actually satisfy the relevant intentions and explain why—but that is precisely what Neo-Griceans do not offer a theory of. In reply, the Neo-Gricean might suggest that Lewis' model construes hearers as automatons controlled by the speaker's signals. This objection is not quite right, but foreshadows a real issue.

Lewis' model allows that the hearer's response is rationally mediated and may not be a direct causal product of the speaker's signal. Indeed, the hearer may sometimes fail to respond in the way needed for coordination to result. Those instances do not count as communication, but they may be a common occurrence in the signaling system. Lewis' model does treat such instances as undeserving of systematic explanation. Lies and deception may be the cases where this matters. If one does want a systematic explanation of these cases, coordination seems only indirectly relevant and the speaker's intention seems more important. This concern is an important one, but we wish to set it aside until §9.3.1.1. Instead, we want to amplify the merits of Lewis' approach by looking at work on animal communication. This work shows that the property Lewis focused on was indeed the crucial one for understanding the natural phenomenon of communication. However, this work will also illustrate that the Lewisian picture is far too simple.

As Gillam (2011) and Maynard Smith & Harper (2003) survey, animals crucially rely on communication to achieve the most basic functions of habitation, nutrition, and reproduction. Male túngara frogs attract female conspecifics with a mating call that consists of low-pitched chucks and high-pitched wails (Ryan 1985). In doing so, the male exposes himself to predation: his calls not only attract females, but the predatory fringe-lipped bat. In fact, the female túngara and bat use the signal in *the same way*: they both respond to more low-pitched chucks and they use their general echolocation skills to find the signal's source—an irony not lost on ethologists. The male is communicating with the female frog, but is not communicating with the bat. This is not an intuition about how to apply the ordinary word *communication*. These two processes have different properties and different explanations. The male frog's call does not persist in the species because of its effects on bats, but because of the effects it has on other frogs (Maynard Smith & Harper 2003). So, the fact that these signals occur in the species is explained by their effects on frogs and *not* their effects on bats. This account of communication can be more precisely characterized as follows:

Adaptationist Communication   (Maynard Smith & Harper 2003: 3)
X communicated with Y using signal σ if and only if:
1. σ affected the behavior of Y,
2. The production of σ by X evolved because of that effect on Y,
3. σ is effective because Y's response to it also evolved.

Now note two key commonalities between this approach and Lewis'. Both accounts aim to explain why a pattern of interactive behavior *persists* in a given population, and they propose to explain it in terms of the signal's actual cause and consequences, i.e. the actual way the signal is produced and its actual effects on the receiver's actions or intentions. This commonality is telling, as it articulates a clear explanatory goal for a theory of communication and specifies the natural properties that are to be involved in such explanations. And yet the definitions seem rather different in two other respects: the Adaptationist model applies only to genetically controlled communication that influences behavior, and it does directly mention coordination. Exploring this difference will be revealing.

The Adaptationist perspective can be generalized by replacing evolutionary selection with the teleological notion of a *function* (Millikan 1984) and appealing to the more general idea of a signal causing 'a reaction'.

Functional Communication   (Scott-Phillips & Kirby 2013: 430–1)
X communicated with Y using signal σ if and only if:
1. σ caused a reaction in Y,
2. The function of producing σ is to cause that effect,
3. The function of Y's reaction is to be caused by σ.

This definition eliminates superficial differences between Lewis' account and the Adaptationist one, and in doing so highlights the key one. The Lewisian account and the Functional account explain the persistence of communication in very different ways. Lewis (1969: 42) explains persistence in terms of individual rationality: coordination persists because the agents expect it to make them better off. As soon as this expectation is disrupted, so too will communication be. But this is clearly implausible for the túngara frog: a single male could chuck and whine his whole life without a response, and yet his signal could persist in the species. As long as females respond often enough to enough of the calls of enough of the males, then this form of interaction will persist. While this call persists because it achieves coordination often enough, it is possible, depending on the population statistics and dynamics, that this coordination is in the statistical minority among uses of the signal. In such a scenario, Lewis (1969) predicts that communication will cease. Where Lewis (1969) requires frequent coordination to persist, the functional approach requires only enough coordination for the signal to keep its function or purpose. Millikan (1984) characterizes the function of a signal in a way that makes perfect sense of this:[14]

Function of a Signal   (Millikan 1984, 2005)
The function of σ in a population P is what σ does for the agents in P which explains why they reproduce it.

Millikan (2005) grants that coordination is the typical communicative function of signals, even though signals or behaviors may be used in other domains for other ends that confer them with a different function.

9.3.1.1 DEFEATING DECEPTION

With these details in place, it becomes clear why Lewis' theory of communication is too simple. The Neo-Gricean was right to be concerned with lying, but their concern was misplaced. One does not really need to invoke intentions to explain deception, only agents acting out of narrow self-interest. Lying might be deception that involves reasoning about other minds, but it's still a simple form of self-interested behavior whose persistence does not demand explanation. But the fact that lying occurs frequently in any population that communicates cannot be explained by Lewis' account. The existence of liars should make communication grind to a halt, and yet we know from our everyday experience that human society is surprisingly resilient in this respect. While our general interactions cannot be described as coordination games, some of them can be and the mere existence of successful coordination in these cases provides sufficient insulation from deception. How could this be?

The difference between Lewis and the biologists is not surprising, since game-theoretic analyses of biology are not executed in the rationalist tradition embodied by Lewis and Grice. Maynard Smith & Price (1973) introduced the idea of an *evolutionarily stable strategy*: a strategy such that, if all the members of a population adopt it, then no mutant strategy could invade the population under the influence of natural selection. This explains persistence of a behavior or trait without requiring rationality to maintain it. Recently, work on human communication has taken note of the promise here and begun its own turn from rationalist pragmatics. van Rooy (2004), drawing on Parikh (1991, 2000), is a special landmark here, where classic

---

[14] It is important to note that Millikan (1984, 2005) offers a sophisticated theory of reproduction whereby the original does not completely determine the reproduction. This is crucial for language where *A and B* could be a reproduction of *A, B* and *C and D*, and inherit its function from *and, A* and *B*.

manner implicatures are explained using the tools of evolutionary game theory rather than the classical rationalist game theory that Lewis employed. The key question to ask when applying these models to human language use is how social interaction and culture can operate in ways reminiscent of reproduction and genes, and how individual psychology conditions those interactions. As we will propose in the next section, social norms can be understood as an evolved cultural tool for making coordination possible in the face of conflicting interests. These norms govern our interactions in ways that make successful coordination possible while insulating us from deception, but they do so unconsciously and sub-personally. Many of the norms that govern our interactions are not principles we would endorse if asked about. They are heuristics of social cognition that we absorb from our social environment without being explicitly formulated or taught (Cialdini *et al.* 1991). The coordination that these norms make possible endows our utterances with a communicative function, which will be the focus of §9.4.

9.3.2 Social Norms and Coordination

Bicchieri (2005: x) succinctly contrasts social norms, as she analyzes them, from other familiar and related concepts:

Descriptive norms such as fashions and fads, for example, arise in contexts in which people desire to coordinate with (or imitate) others and prefer to do what others do on the condition that they expect a sufficient number of people to act in a certain way. A 'sufficient number' may be just one person, as in the case of a celebrity we want to imitate, or the number may vary from person to person, depending on how cautious one is in assessing the threshold at which to take action. Conventions are descriptive norms that have endured the test of time. If one's main objective is to coordinate with others, and the right mutual expectations are present, people will follow whatever convention is in place. Social norms, on the contrary, are not there to solve a coordination problem. The kinds of situations to which social norms most often apply are those in which there is a tension between individual and collective gains. Pro-social norms of fairness, reciprocity, cooperation, and the like exist precisely because it might not be in the individuals immediate self-interest to behave in a socially beneficial way.

Recall the soccer norm mentioned in §9.1. This is not a formal rule with formal sanctions for violation. This practice is not a coordinating convention followed due to precedent (Lewis 1969): there is no alternative pair of actions that would produce an equally good outcome for both parties. Furthermore, unlike a convention, e.g. driving on one side of the road, either team could defect from it and become better off, at least in the short-term (on occasion, some do). So it is not immediate coincidence of self-interest which sustains this practice—there is a conflict of immediate self-interest. This practice is sustained, like other social norms, because each agent A prefers to conform to the practice given that conditions (i) and (ii) obtain, and those conditions do obtain (Bicchieri 2005: 11):[15]

---

[15] Slightly more precisely: a behavioral rule R is a social norm just in case almost everybody knows that R exists and prefers to conform to R on the condition that (a) almost everybody believes that almost everybody conforms to R and either (b) almost everybody believes that almost everybody

(i) *A* expects others to conform and

(ii) *A* either believes that others expect *A* to conform or that others prefer *A* to conform and will informally sanction non-conformity (shame, disgust, etc.).

It is crucial to clarify, as Bicchieri (2005: 3) does, that this is a rational reconstruction of what a social norm is, but is consistent with a psychological implementation that is sub-personal, unconscious and economically approximates the concept defined by the rational reconstruction.

In general, our communicative exchanges cannot be described as simple coordination games. Our interests are too mixed: the speaker may want to show how much they know while the hearer may need some information to complete an urgent task, the speaker may want the hearer to believe some information which will cause them to act in a way that is beneficial to the hearer, and so on. It is here that social norms play a key and inadequately appreciated role in communication. While Austin focused on social conventions and Searle focused on constitutive rules, these social tools are of no use in mixed-motive games. If we can't coordinate, then we can't establish social conventions and could not agree on constitutive rules because our practical ends are at odds. Likewise, good Griceans could understand what each other meant, but would have no reason to express their states of mind to each other. However, a body of social norms—self-fulfilling expectations about what agents like us to in particular circumstances—operating in the shadows of our unconscious minds do just the trick. The Maxims of Quantity and Manner (Grice 1975) are likely examples of such norms, since they allow coordination in the fact of conflicting interests (van Rooy 2003). But, contra Grice (1975), we do not follow them because we are rational. Instead, we follow them because they are part of our cultural inheritance that has been shaped by our practical needs as social animals.

Many socio-biologists believe human interaction in general is governed by large-scale norms that are particular to the relation-types of the agents involved (Fiske 1992). For example, some interactions naturally evoke an understanding that one agent is a subordinate of the other, and is thereby expected to weight their self-interests less than the dominant's. Yet others are understood to be communal, in which case it is crucial not to make efforts to equalize costs since that is indicative of mistrust. Since norms are also sensitive to the circumstances of the interaction, they are not only sensitive to who is interacting, but what kind of task they are engaging in. Work in social psychology on scripts, schema, and activity types (Schank & Abelson 1977; Levinson 1979; Bicchieri 2005: Ch.2) illustrate that classifying some interaction as being of some familiar type automatically triggers self-fulfilling expectations about how that interaction will unfold. Just think of your elliptical utterances and interactions when ordering food, or saying 'here' to a teammate while playing basketball (Levinson 1979). Just as research in artificial intelligence (Schank & Abelson 1977) struggled and failed to articulate these practices in terms of precise rules, the true utility of these norms are that we can follow them and coordinate without explicitly

expects almost everybody to conform to *R* or (b') almost everybody believes that almost everybody expects almost everybody to conform to *R*, prefers them to conform to *R* and may sanction those that don't (Bicchieri 2005: 11).

representing or teaching precise rules of interaction. The question, then, is whether there are distinctive norms that pertain to our communicative interactions.

While Williamson (1996), Sellars (1956), Brandom (1994), and Kukla & Lance (2009) have emphasized the importance of characterizing language use in normative terms, they do not construe the role of normative ideas as we have here. Williamson (1996) proposes that knowledge is the norm of assertion, but to even assess this we have to do a bit of groundwork. For us, assertion, if it plays any role in a theory of communication, is the communicative function some class of utterances serve. One function utterances sometimes serve is to convey information from speaker to receiver. To speak of the norm of assertion is therefore to speak of how some self-fulfilling expectations transform the mixed-motive game of information transmission into a coordination game. This invites the question of what conflict such a norm solves and how the unconscious heuristics of social cognition support that solution.

The conflict of information sharing is clear enough: speakers may prefer to misinform certain hearers and hearers may prefer to ignore certain information. How do humans solve this problem? The emerging consensus is that our social memory and systems of reputation and authority are the crucial mechanism here (Scott-Phillips 2011, 2015). As long as these projections of authority and reputation somewhat reliably track a speaker's trustworthiness and competence, trusting their contributions and expecting them to be sincere will keep deception at bay, and allow information to flow. This speaker norm can only operate with a parallel hearer norm: reputable authorities can only sustainably share information when there are proportionately vigilant, receptive, and curious hearers. From this perspective, knowledge is not the actual norm of assertion, but the ideal norm that we would follow if we were not using the heuristics of social cognition to communicate. To study the actual norms of human communication is to understand what social problem they are solving and how established mechanisms of social cognition can solve it.

Talk of authority and assertion immediately brings to mind an issue which might initially seem like a problem for thinking about communication in terms of coordination: subordinating speech and uptake of speech. How can slurring or verbally oppressing someone be viewed as coordination? In response to this question, it is crucial to clarify that while some social norms produce a joint good—a more fair game in the soccer example above—from a scenario where acting out of immediate self-interest would not, this is not true for all social norms, e.g. footbinding in China (Bicchieri 2005: 41). Social norms work by discounting the self-interests of an agent or group of agents in order to promote the interests of a collective or some other individuals. While this can lead to self-sacrifice for a social good, it can also lead straight to oppression where one group of individuals systematically benefits from the sacrifices of another. Norms of this more malevolent kind are behind the uptake of utterances of 'Whites only' in the 1960s segregated South, and the Jim Crow laws that enforced them. They illustrate just how drastically social norms can warp our social reality and what counts as coordination (McGowan 2012, this volume). In a society where norms of oppression are operative, the oppressed respond in a way that is not in their narrow self-interest, but is in the end in their self-interest given the sanctions that will be exacted upon them for non-conformity. The phenomenon of *illocutionary disablement* or *silencing* in feminist work on speech acts reflects the norms at play on the production side of communication (Langton 1993: 315; MacKinnon 1993; Langton & West 1999; Fricker 2007). There, a speaker is unable to achieve a particular communicative end because hearers *mistakenly* deprive that speaker of the requisite authority. For example, a widespread belief among males that womens' utterances of *no* in response to sexual advances are not to be trusted, along with authority concentrated among male speakers, will deprive women of the authority needed to successfully reject their advances by uttering *no*.

One point emphasized in this work is that speech which invokes a norm, thereby supports or sometimes creates that norm (McGowan 2012, this volume; Maitra 2012). Often this happens despite the norm being outside the conscious reach of the speaker and largely because of the way hearers construe the utterance. This kind of phenomena is yet another example where a Neo-Gricean perspective, focused exclusively on speaker's intentions, provides little insight. To see this, consider an example of subordinating speech where the speaker was oblivious of the means by which they achieved their end. In the 2015 Republican primary, Donald Trump said, in an interview with *Rolling Stone*, the following about Carly Fiorina: *Look at that face! Would anyone vote for that? Can you imagine that, the face of our next president?* This comment appropriately drew criticism, since it appears to assume that for a woman candidate, appearance is relevant to one's qualification for a job (Trump did not make similar comments about male candidates). This utterance subordinates women by relying on, and thereby sustaining, the expectation that a woman's appearance is the salient dimension along which to assess her value—the frequency with which he praises his wife's and daughter's beauty compared to the infrequency with which he praises any of their other traits supports this explanation.[16] Is it a consolation that Trump did not intend this act of subordination? This much was clear from his exchange with Fiorina in a primary debate. Fiorina said *I think women all over this country heard very clearly what Mr. Trump said*, and Trump replied *I think she's got a beautiful face and she's a beautiful woman*. If Trump was just a devious and conscious misogynist, he would not have replied this way. He would have actually said something that spoke to Fiorina's subtle but clear rejoinder.

There are two distinctive linguistic features of this example. First, the relevant social mechanisms for achieving subordination were not within reach of the speaker's intentions. Second, the utterance's reliance on a gender norm not only produced subordination but strengthened others' capacity to subordinate by bringing the norm to salience (McGowan 2012, this volume; Maitra 2012). It is clear that one could explain these features in terms of norms and low-level social cognition, but far from clear that a Neo-Gricean perspective can say anything interesting about such cases. While the Neo-Gricean slant of contemporary philosophy of language might therefore lead some to ignore cases like this—Hornsby (2000) and Tirrell (2012) make this

---

[16] Starr is indebted to conversations with Lucia Munguia about this example.

case—we hope to have shown in §9.3.1 that the stronger naturalistic commitments of philosophy of language pull in the other direction.[17]

While it is initially difficult to see how subordinating speech can fit into a picture where communication is thought of in terms of coordination, Bicchieri's (2005) revolutionary analysis of social norms shows how this model can actually implement many of the foundational insights emerging from that literature. Indeed, it provides a different way of making precise the reliance on social conventions in Austinian approaches, constitutive rules in Searlean or scorekeeping approaches or constitutive inferences in inferential role approaches. As suggested above, none of these mechanisms are quite at home in the domain where social norms operate. Further, this approach is better equipped to implement the insights of this work than the Neo-Gricean framework that focuses on communicative intentions and their recognition. We now turn to spelling out in more detail how this picture of social norms and the communicative function of speech acts can speak to the distinction between sentential and utterance force that figured so prominently in §9.2.

9.4 Modeling Utterance Force: conversational states and norms

The key idea from §9.3 is that different utterances have different communicative functions, and these different functions should be thought of in terms of how they coordinate agents' private commitments. In this section we use this idea to return another thread from §9.2: what is utterance force and how is it constrained by the semantics of sentential mood? We will propose that part of the communicative function of every utterance is to affect the mutual assumptions of the conversationalists. This is the semantic contribution of mood, i.e. sentential force. The communicative functions of various utterances diverge in how this mutual contribution is supposed to bear on the agent's private commitments. This is the force of an utterance. To formally model this element of discourse dynamics, we introduce conversational states. Like previous models, conversational states capture the kinematics of mutual assumptions. But unlike previous accounts, it also tracks the individual commitments of the conversationalists. In doing so, we can precisely specify not just sentential force, but utterance force. This allows us to capture how social norms mediate the relationship between the two. We will begin (§9.4.1) with our model of how sentence mood updates the mutual assumptions of a conversation. In §9.4.2 we introduce conversational states and use them to analyze utterance force, highlighting the fact that this analysis, unlike the Neo-Gricean one, can allow for one complex utterance to have multiple forces.

9.4.1 Mutual Assumptions and Dynamic Meaning

Recent work on discourse dynamics and speech acts begins with the idea that each major sentence type has a characteristic effect on what's mutually assumed in a

---

[17] Lepore & Stone (2014) argue similarly against Neo-Gricean approaches to metaphor, irony, and sarcasm.

conversation (Roberts 1996; Portner 2004; Farkas & Bruce 2010; Murray 2010b; Starr 2010; Murray & Starr 2012). Following Sadock & Zwicky (1985) and König & Siemund (2007), we assume there are three major sentence types/moods in natural language:

(2) a. Dale ate pie. (*Declarative*)
     b. ▷D

(3) a. Did Dale eat pie? (*Interrogative*)
     b. ?D

(4) a. Dale, eat pie! (*Imperative*)
     b. !D

This work assumes that declaratives change the mutual information assumed in the conversation—the *common ground*—and interrogatives change the mutual questions guiding the conversation—the *questions under discussion*. Portner (2004) adds that imperatives change the 'To Do List', a record of which properties each conversationalist is committed to making true for the purposes of the conversation. On these accounts, it would be natural to model the mutual assumptions in a conversation A_C as a triple consisting of the mutually assumed information I_C (a set of possible worlds; Stalnaker 1978), the mutually adopted questions Q_C (a set of sets of possible worlds; Hamblin 1973) and the mutual To Do List T_C (a function from individuals to sets of properties; Portner 2004).[18] One can then model the characteristic effect of each sentence type with a particular change to the corresponding element of $\langle I_C, Q_C, T_C \rangle$ (Portner 2004, this volume). We follow roughly this approach, with some crucial differences.[19] One crucial difference is that we will assume that these effects are built in to the semantics of sentence mood, a view we argue for at length in Murray & Starr (2012). Other accounts attempt to pragmatically infer them (Portner 2004) or treat them as non-compositional 'discourse rules' reminiscent of Stenius (1967).

The basic idea of our model is that declaratives update information (eliminate worlds), interrogatives introduce issues (alternative propositions), and imperatives introduce preferences for one alternative proposition over its negation. Figure 9.4 depicts these three basic operations.[20] This idea is formally implemented by modeling the **mutual assumptions in a conversation** $A_C := \{r_0, \ldots, r_n\}$ as a **preference state**: a set of preference relations r over propositions ($p \subseteq W$). Each r can simultaneously model (a) assuming the information that p (dom $r \cup$ ran $r \subseteq p$); (b) questioning whether p ($\langle p, \emptyset \rangle, \langle \bar{p}, \emptyset \rangle \in r$); and (c) a preference for p over not-p ($\langle p, \bar{p} \rangle \in r$) (Starr 2013; Murray & Starr 2012). In simple cases, only a single preference relation will be in play: $A_C = \{r\}$. The capacity to put alternative competing preference relations into play

---

[18] A 'property' is the standard meaning of a predicate: a function from individuals to functions from worlds to truth-values.

[19] These differences are discussed in more detail in Starr (2013); Murray & Starr (2012). Some are aesthetic and some are substantive, but we will not belabor these issues here.

[20] In the diagram (Figure 9.4), the points are worlds and the letters indicate which atomics are true at that world, with a capital letter indicating truth and a lower case indicating falsity. The gray boxes indicate alternatives, and preferring one alternative to another is indicated by boxing the preferred alternative in a lighter shade of gray. When multiple preferences are depicted, the size of the boxes indicate which alternatives are compared to which—as in the bottom left of Figure 9.5.

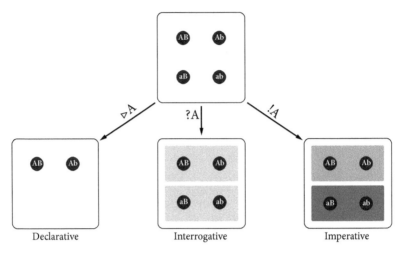

Figure 9.4 How moods update mutual assumptions.

is used in the analysis of disjunction, imperatives, and modals (Murray & Starr 2012; Starr 2013; Starr 2016)—it is also useful for characterizing an agent who is merely considering ϕ rather than accepting it. The basic idea is a twist on alternative semantics for disjunction (e.g. Simons 2005), namely that they can introduce alternative competing informational and perspectives of what the conversational information, preferences and issues are. Below, this will be useful for modeling the idea that some speech acts merely involve the hearer *taking into consideration* information, issues or preferences proffered by the speaker. But, setting aside these complications, a simple declarative $\triangleright$A will provide information by eliminating ¬A-worlds from the propositions in r, a simple interrogative ?A will introduce alternatives (propositions) by ranking both the A-worlds and the ¬A-worlds over the empty set, and a simple imperative !A will introduce a preference by ranking the A-worlds over the ¬A-worlds. While this specifies the core semantic contribution of sentential mood, one more resource is necessary for fully capturing the meaning of mood.

In our previous work (Murray 2010b; Murray & Starr 2012), we also motivated keeping track of the propositions that are at-issue, or under discussion, in the conversation. This allows us to model scenarios in which the conversationalists are mutually considering a certain proposition without mutually assuming that it is true. This is a key component of Murray's (2010b) analysis of evidentials and not-at-issue assertion. Further, we take the felicity of propositional anaphors such as *That, Yes* and *No* to be evidence that the retrieved proposition is in D. But, for now, we will simply say that these **propositions under discussion** D form an ordered list of propositions $\langle A_0, \ldots, A_n \rangle$.[21] While this element of the model is crucial for a number of semantic

---

[21] D is reminiscent of Farkas & Bruce's (2010: 86) *Table* of a conversation, but there are important differences. Farkas & Bruce (2010: 86) use the Table as a sort of 'buffer zone' to model the contributions of all matrix clauses, which can then be shifted to the common ground or rejected. Our D is limited to

and pragmatic phenomena, it will not feature essentially in what follows. The general idea here is what's important: conversationalists track the mutual information, issues and preferences encoded in A_C, as well as the propositions to which the agents are attending D.[22]

Work on discourse dynamics has been divided about the nature of linguistic meaning. Advocates of **dynamic semantics** have maintained that the update effect of a sentence on A_C is its compositional meaning (Heim 1982; Groenendijk & Stokhof 1991; Groenendijk *et al.* 1996). Advocates of a static semantics instead maintain that the update effect of a sentence on A_C is either a pragmatic effect (Stalnaker 1978; Portner 2004), or a clause-level convention that is distinct from a sentence's compositional meaning (Portner 2012; Roberts 2012). Our previous work (Murray 2010b, 2014; Starr 2010, 2013; Murray & Starr 2012) offers arguments in favor of the dynamic approach, and so we will assume it here. We will, however, take some care in later sections to consider whether one has to embrace the dynamic semantics in order to accept our analysis of utterance force. In the present setting, assuming that sentence meanings are dynamic comes to this: they specify how, given an arbitrary starting A_C and D, a given sentence ϕ will change A_C and D.

Formally, a sentence meaning $[\phi]$ is a function from one $\langle A_C, D \rangle$ to another. Using the notation of update semantics (Groenendijk *et al.* 1996; Veltman 1996), we will write $\langle A_C, D \rangle [\phi]$ to indicate the result of updating $\langle A_C, D \rangle$ with ϕ. The applications and system described here will be limited to a simplified logical language. A sentence is built by taking an atomic propositional phrase $A, B, C, A_0, \ldots$ and marking it for mood: $\triangleright A$ (declarative), $!A$ (imperative), and $?A$ (interrogative). We specify the exact meanings of these sentences in Murray & Starr (2012); Starr (2010), but the pictures will suffice for our purposes here. To say that the meaning of ϕ is an update function on the mutual assumptions is to say that all communicative utterances of that sentence have the communicative function of updating the mutual assumptions in that way. This is our semantic account of sentential mood. Our pragmatic account of utterance force requires saying how an utterance may serve the function of making certain private individual commitments. As discussed in §9.2.1, this division of semantic and pragmatic labor is essential to explain how sentence mood constrains, but does not determine the force of an utterance. But as discussed in §9.2.2 existing discourse dynamic models are not able to capture utterance force because they are, by their nature, constrained to modeling the mutual assumptions at play in discourse. Our notion of a conversational state will relax this constraint, while preserving the insights of previous work.

---

propositions, and we allow non-matrix clauses, for example the complements of propositional attitude verbs and the scope of evidential operators, to add propositions to D. Furthermore, we do not assume that the goal of adding a proposition to D is to eventually add it to the common ground, and we do not assume that a proposition can only get in to the common ground via that table, crucially for Murray (2010b). The Table of Farkas & Bruce (2010: 86) therefore plays a rather different theoretical role, and future work is needed to see how to integrate these two frameworks and the complementary data they cover.

[22] In a more comprehensive formulation we would actually allow for one D for each $r \in A_C$. This would allow disjunctions to introduce two competing lists of at-issue propositions. Since we treat *Yes* and *No* as propositional anaphors that pick up on propositions in D, this makes importantly different predictions for the answers licensed by $?A \vee ?B$ and $?(A \vee B)$.

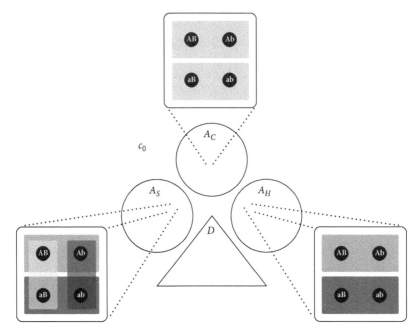

Figure 9.5 A conversational state c.

9.4.2 Conversational States: a model of utterance force

While a sentence updates the mutual assumptions $\langle A_C, D \rangle$, this does not capture the communicative function of an utterance. Following §9.3.1, we assume that one can capture utterance force by specifying how the utterance aims to bear on the agents' private commitments. To track this dimension our formal model of a conversation needs to be expanded beyond $\langle A_C, D \rangle$ to capture the dynamics of private commitments. Towards this, we proposed the concept of a **conversational state** $c = \langle A_S, \langle A_C, D \rangle, A_H \rangle$, depicted in Figure 9.5. Formally, A_S and A_H have the same structure as A_C: they are all 'preference states' in the sense defined in §9.4.1. However, they have a crucially different application. A_S models the speaker's private commitments, i.e. the information, questions and preferences to which they are genuinely committed. So unlike Hamblin (1971)'s *commitment slates*, A_S and A_H track each participant's *private* commitments. This difference is essential to distinguish the semantic effects an utterance has on the mutual commitments from the pragmatic effects it aims to have on private commitments.

In our model, a speech act has two essential components: **sentential force**, a semantically determined update effect on $\langle A_C, D \rangle$ and **utterance force**, a non-semantically determined effect on A_S and/or A_H. Figure 9.6 depicts this schematically. This formalism allows one to systematically investigate the relationship between these two processes. The semantic effect of a simple declarative sentence $\triangleright p$ is depicted in Figure 9.7: it adds the proposition that p to A_C and also draws attention to that proposition, thus adding it to D. The communicative function of such an update can

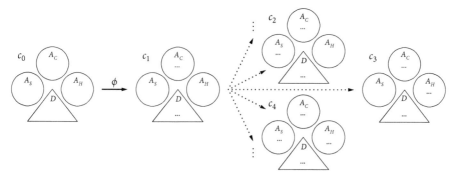

Figure 9.6 Semantic contribution and possible forces.

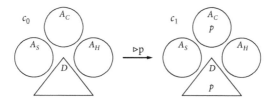

Figure 9.7 Semantics for a declarative sentence.

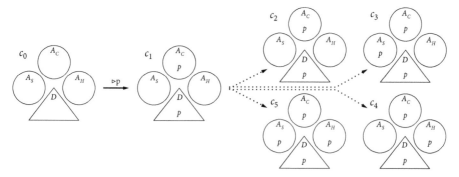

Figure 9.8 Possible forces of an utterance of a declarative.

vary widely and may theoretically involve arriving at any of the states after c_1 depicted in Figure 9.8. These states differ from c_1 only by the speaker or hearer accepting or rejecting the change induced by the sentence in the mutual assumptions.[23] On our approach, different forces correspond to the stable, i.e. coordinating, ways agents can use public commitments to express and influence their private commitments. For a given utterance of a sentence ϕ, this can be done by considering all conversational

---

[23] There may be yet further conversational states where the speaker or hearer merely considers rather than rejects or accepts the change induced in the mutual assumptions. This can be modeled in our formalism by taking the preference state modeling the agent's private commitments $A_X = \{r\}$ and forming the union of that with the result of updating with $\triangleright p$: $\{r\} \cup \{r\}[\triangleright p]$. Intuitively this captures the idea that the information that p is competing to be among X's beliefs.

states where ϕ has had its semantic effect, and that effect has also been accepted in A_S and A_H. One must then ask whether these configurations are stable states, i.e. repeatable coordinations. Consider, for example, states c_2–c_5. State c_2 represents an utterance where neither speaker nor hearer come to be committed to the information carried by the declarative. Are there circumstances where this outcome would be of sufficient value to the agents that they would attempt to replicate successful utterances in the past that brought about c_2? This is a big question, but we can only speculate that some dimensions of saving face, humor, sarcasm, and pretense fit this mold.[24] The state c_4 represents an utterance where the speaker has not committed to the information, but the hearer has. This utterance is a lie. While states like c_4 can come to exist, they will never serve a communicative function and will never therefore count as an 'utterance force'—lies are not the kinds of things which both speaker and hearer collaboratively reproduce because they worked in the past. Other theories like Searle (1969) and Bach & Harnish (1979) don't classify lies as a possible utterance force, but they do not say exactly why. Our story about utterance force as communicative function captures this elegantly.

State c_3 could be used to capture an utterance where a speaker sincerely makes certain information mutual, not with the aim to influence a clearly incredulous hearer, but to enter it into the 'social memory' that they have put this information out there. Due to the role of reputation in human communication, it seems likely that such a conversational move could achieve coordination of a sort and thereby acquire a communicative function. By contrast c_5 takes little imagination. It captures something like what we call assertion, and its communicative function is the transmission of information in a way that is sensitive to social power.

This brief illustration shows how our model allows one to distinguish the possible forces of different utterances by articulating different conversational states, and investigating the coordination function those states might serve. To show that a particular utterance has given utterance force requires much more than we've done here. It not only involves showing how an utterance could coordinate the agents, it requires showing that utterances with that function are reproduced in the population of language users. This is a rather expansive project which will have to draw on techniques from social psychology and behavioral economics. It will also involve specifying in detail the social norms that are responsible for bringing about these conversational states. We cannot even begin to carry out this project here. But we can illustrate it further by working a couple of examples and contrasting it with Neo-Gricean analyses.

9.4.3 Application: declarative and imperative utterances

Consider an utterance of *Cooper likes jelly donuts* by Norma, the waitress and owner of the Double R Diner where Cooper frequently dines. She utters this declarative sentence to Shelly who has just taken a maple donut to Cooper.

---

[24] It is worth highlighting that our model only captures the content, and not the affective or phenomenological impact of an utterance. We regard it as an interesting open question whether these are the kinds of effects that count as solutions to coordination problems.

(5)   a. *Norma*: Cooper likes jelly donuts.
     b. *Shelly*: Oh, I see.

This utterance has assertive force since it aims to coordinate the actions and beliefs of two agents by having their beliefs match. This is a persistent and common process, and can be straightforwardly explained in terms of social norms activated by Shelly and Norma's relationship type (employee-boss), joint activity (serving customers), and common ground (Shelly just gave Cooper a maple donut). These norms will involve self-fulfilling expectations the conversationalists form about how they should respond to this utterance in these circumstances.

(6)   *Genesis of Assertive Force*
    a. *Semantics*: S made the information that Cooper likes jelly donuts mutually assumed.
    b. *Speaker Expectation*: It's expected that S is privately committed to the information S has made mutual.
    c. *Hearer Expectation*: It's expected that H privately commits to information that is made mutual before them by an authority.

(7)   *Goal of Assertive Act*
    a. S is privately committed to the information that S made mutual.
    b. H is privately committed to the information that S made mutual.

An assertion would still have been performed if Shelly responded *No, Cooper's gotten sick of those*. In this case, the assertion simply fails to achieve part of its purpose: Shelly would not be privately committed to the content of Norma's assertion. Indeed, depending on the exact nature of their social relationship, Norma, with acknowledge-ment, might also give up her commitment to it. In either case there is a similar story to tell: utterances and social context conspire to generate particular expectations, and the agents act so as to conform to these expectations. There is much work left to be done here to fully specify the content of the operative norms, and to understand their psychological underpinnings. But as a sketch, this provides a direction for such further enquiry to pursue.

An imperative utterance by Norma to Shelly in the same circumstances of *Get a jelly donut!* would have a communicative function that one might call a *command*. It is expected that Shelly will privately adopt the preference this sentence makes mutual, and it is expected that this preference reflects Norma's own practical ends. This would coordinate Norma and Shelley's interests in achieving their joint activity. Wherever there are practical authorities, there will be communicative exchanges like these. But as authority is relaxed, interactions like these become more nuanced. The fact that doing something for someone often incurs a cost to one's perceived autonomy/authority can incentivize the inclusion of politeness particles in the signal to balance this cost. These mechanisms of face-maintenance are well-studied and nicely amenable to the style of analysis sketched here (Goffman 1959; Brown & Levinson 1987; Clark 2012).

Note that on this approach a hybrid utterance like *I got Cooper some fresh cherry pie, but don't tell him it's coming* and *Take off your shoes and try a taco!* can be smoothly analyzed. Norms specify whether an agent is committed to a particular change to the mutual assumptions. These speech acts involve two such changes. In the first case this means that one can have a single norm apply to both changes despite the fact that they induce different kinds of changes. In the second case, this means that the two changes can be subjected to different norms, one which calls for uptake by the hearer and another that merely aims to activate their deliberation about a given action. This flexibility is a crucial advantage of the account articulated here over the Neo-Gricean and Conversational Tone analyses.

Not all communicative exchanges rely on authority. Consider the same imperative sentence *Get a jelly donut!* inscribed on a little sign placed on the bar where patrons eat. These utterances do not impose a preference from a place of authority. It works by merely activating the hearer's imagination of getting a jelly donut, which may activate their own latent desires for a jelly donut. If they did not succeed in doing so often enough, they would not be such a persistent form of advertisement: they would be replaced by utterances that worked better. This example highlights not only that social norms are not essential for generating utterance force, but that the generation of utterance force relies on rather low-level psychological facts about how humans work. The fact that imagining X may activate actual beliefs or desires about X, and the fact that one is more likely to act on desires that are immediately activated are central to understanding this utterance. This highlights how many exciting advances in psychology have immediate bearing on the study of language use. Indeed, it suggests that the experimental methods used to make those advances will be indispensable in the study of utterance force as well.

9.5 Conclusion: a new analysis of speech acts

On our view, the conventional meaning of a sentence constrains the force of an utterance by encoding a procedure for updating the mutual assumptions. But the particular force of an utterance concerns how that utterance fits into the agent's social lives. To give an analysis of utterance force, one must how an utterance changes private commitments or psychological states, and how those changes count as coordination. Further, to be of interest, one must show that this is a stable and reproduced way of coordinating. While the semantics only determines what the words do to our mutual assumptions, this update crucially constrains which private commitments can result from the utterance. In these explanations of utterance force, we have downplayed the role of social conventions, constitutive rules and communicative intentions. But we do not mean to say that these mechanisms are not crucial tools for understanding language use. In interactions like marriages and promises, it is likely social conventions that coordinate us rather than social norms—and in many cases it may be a surprisingly vast array of norms and conventions. Further, we agree that there is good evidence for thinking that communicative intentions are involved in establishing novel ways of manipulating our mutual attitudes (Scott-Phillips *et al.* 2012) and thus expanding the range of our semantic conventions. However, we aim to have cast light on the most elusive but perhaps this most efficacious mechanism of coordination relevant to language use: social norms. It is only with recent contributions like

Bicchieri (2005) to our understanding of norms, conventions, and the like, that we are able to see which tools are best-suited to a theory of speech acts.

In conclusion it may be helpful to explicitly set our view against those that we began with. We are able to join Austin (1962) and Searle (1969) in saying that the force of an utterance is tied to the kind of social act it constitutes. We also are able to join Searle (1968) in holding that conventional meaning is not force-neutral. But our new way of capturing these insights allowed us to reconcile them with the contemporary methodology of semantics and pragmatics, as well as the focus on conflict and stability in the social sciences. Like Neo-Griceans, we have adopted a theory where the semantics of a sentence constrains, but does not determine the force of a speech act. However, we have grounded that theory in a radically different theory of communication. This theory of communication focuses on how language enables coordination that allows us to do things together in the real world that we would otherwise be unable to do. By contrast, the Neo-Gricean theory focuses only on mutually entertaining certain contents—leaving it entirely open *why* agents would do that and how they do it in the face of conflicting interests. Where they focus on understanding each other's communicative intentions, we focus on the coordination-driven stability of certain utterance types. The Neo-Gricean theory ably systematizes the daunting complexity of our ordinary thought and talk about speech acts, but our theory has left that project to the side. In this paper, we sought to explain how certain patterns of verbal interaction are valuable, and how they persist in seemingly hostile conditions. Perhaps our approach will vindicate common sense thought and talk about speech acts, but doing so is not the central task in the study of speech acts.

References

ASHER, N. & LASCARIDES, A. (2013). 'Strategic Conversation.' *Semantics and Pragmatics*, **6(2)**: 1–62.
AUSTIN, J. L. (1962). *How to Do Things With Words*. Oxford: Oxford University Press.
BACH, K. & HARNISH, R. M. (1979). *Linguistic Communication and Speech Acts*. Cambridge, MA: MIT Press.
BICCHIERI, C. (2005). *The Grammar of Society: The Nature and Dynamics of Social Norms*. Cambridge: Cambridge University Press.
BRANDOM, R. B. (1994). *Making It Explicit: Reasoning, Representing, and Discursive Commitment*. Cambridge, MA: Harvard University Press.
BROWN, P. & LEVINSON, S. (1987). *Politeness: Some Universals in Language Use*. Cambridge, UK: Cambridge University Press.
CHIERCHIA, G. & MCCONNELL-GINET, S. (2000). *Meaning and Grammar: An Introduction to Semantics*. 2nd edn. Cambridge, MA: MIT Press.
CIALDINI, R. B., KALLGREN, C. A. & RENO, R. R. (1991). 'A Focus Theory of Normative Conduct: A Theoretical Refinement and Reevaluation of the Role of Norms in Human Behavior.' vol. 24 of *Advances in Experimental Social Psychology*, 201–34. Academic Press. http://dx.doi.org/10.1016/S0065-2601(08)60330-5.
CLARK, H. H. (1996). *Using Language*. New York: Cambridge University Press.
CLARK, R. (2012). *Meaningful Games*. Cambridge, MA: MIT Press.

COHEN, P. R. & LEVESQUE, H. J. (1985). 'Speech Acts and Rationality.' In W. MANN (ed.), *Proceedings of the Twenty-Third Meeting of the Association for Computational Linguistics*, 49–59. Morristown, NJ: Association for Computational Linguistics.

COHEN, P. R. & LEVESQUE, H. J. (1990). 'Rational Interaction as the Basis for Communication.' In P. COHEN, J. MORGAN & M. POLLACK (eds.), *Intentions in Communication*, 221–55. Cambridge, MA: MIT Press.

COHEN, P. R. & PERRAULT, C. R. (1979). 'Elements of a Plan-Based Theory of Speech Acts.' *Cognitive Science*, **3**: 177–212.

DAVIDSON, D. (1979). 'Moods and Performances.' In A. MARGALIT (ed.), *Meaning and Use: Papers Presented at the Second Jerusalem Philosophy Encounter*, 9–20. Dordrecht: D. Reidel Publishing Co. Page references to reprint Davidson (1984: Ch.8).

DAVIDSON, D. (1984). *Inquiries into Truth and Interpretation*. Oxford: Oxford University Press.

FALLER, M. (2002). *Semantics and Pragmatics of Evidentials in Cuzco Quechua*. Ph.D. thesis, Stanford University, Palo Alto, CA. http://personalpages.manchester.ac.uk/staff/martina.t.faller/documents/Thesis.pdf.

FARKAS, D. F. & BRUCE, K. B. (2010). 'On Reacting to Assertions and Polar Questions.' *Journal of Semantics*, 27(1): 81–118. http://jos.oxfordjournals.org/content/27/1/81.full.pdf+html, http://jos.oxfordjournals.org/content/27/1/81.abstract.

FISKE, A. P. (1992). 'The Four Elementary Forms of Sociality: Framework for a Unified Theory of Social Relations.' *Psychological Review*, **99**(4): 689–723. http://search.ebscohost.com.proxy.library.cornell.edu/login.aspx?direct=true&db=pdh&AN=1993-05502-001&site=ehost-live.

FRICKER, M. (2007). *Epistemic Injustice: Power and the Ethics of Knowing*. New York: Oxford University Press.

GAZDAR, G. (1981). 'Speech Act Assignment.' In A. K. JOSHI, I. A. SAG & B. WEBBER (eds.), *Elements of Discourse Understanding*, 64–83. New York: Cambridge University Press.

GEIS, M. L. (1995). *Speech Acts and Conversational Interaction*. Cambridge, UK: Cambridge University Press.

GILLAM, E. (2011). 'An Introduction to Animal Communication.' *Nature Education Knowledge*, **2**(11): 10. http://www.nature.com/scitable/knowledge/library/an-introduction-to-animal-communication-23648715.

GOFFMAN, E. (1959). *Presentation of Self in Everyday Life*. New York: Anchor Books.

GRICE, H. P. (1957). 'Meaning.' *Philosophical Review*, **66**(3): 377–88. http://www.jstor.org/stable/2182440.

GRICE, H. P. (1975). 'Logic and Conversation.' In D. DAVIDSON & G. H. HARMAN (eds.), *The Logic of Grammar*, 64–75. Encino, CA: Dickenson Publishing Co.

GROENENDIJK, J. & STOKHOF, M. (1991). 'Dynamic Predicate Logic.' *Linguistics and Philosophy*, **14**(1): 39–100.

GROENENDIJK, J., STOKHOF, M. & VELTMAN, F. (1996). 'Coreference and Modality.' In S. LAPPIN (ed.), *The Handbook of Contemporary Semantic Theory*, 179–213. Oxford: Blackwell Publishers.

HABERMAS, J. (1998). *On the Pragmatics of Communication*. Cambridge, MA: MIT Press. Edited by Maeve Cook.

HABERMAS, J. (2000). *On the Pragmatics of Social Interaction*. Cambridge, MA: MIT Press.

HAMBLIN, C. L. (1971). 'Mathematical Models of Dialogue.' *Theoria*, **37**: 130–55.

HAMBLIN, C. L. (1973). 'Questions in Montague English.' *Foundations of Language*, **10**(1): 41–53.

HEIM, I. R. (1982). *The Semantics of Definite and Indefinite Noun Phrases*. Ph.D. thesis, Linguistics Department, University of Massachusetts, Amherst, MA.

HEIM, I. (1992). 'Presupposition Projection and the Semantics of Attitude Verbs.' *Journal of Semantics*, **9**(3): 183–221.

HORNSBY, J. (2000). 'Feminism in Philosophy of Language: Communicative Speech Acts.' In M. FRICKER & J. HORNSBY (eds.), *Cambridge Companion to Feminism in Philosophy*, 87–106. Cambridge: Cambridge University Press.

HULSTIJN, J. (2003). 'Roles in Dialogue.' In I. KRUIJFF-KORBAYOVÁ & C. KOSNY (eds.), *Diabruck 2003: Proceedings of the 7th Workshop on the Semantics and Pragmatics of Dialogue*, 43–50. Saarbrücken: Universität des Saarlandes.

HULSTIJN, J. & MAUDET, N. (2006). 'Uptake and Joint Action.' *Cognitive Systems Research*, **7(2–3)**: 175–91. Introduction to special issue on Cognition, Joint Action and Collective Intentionality, http://dx.doi.org/10.1016/j.cogsys.2005.11.002.

KÖNIG, E. & SIEMUND, P. (2007). 'Speech Act Distinctions in Grammar.' In T. SHOPEN (ed.), *Language Typology and Syntactic Description: Clause Structure*, vol. 1, 2nd edn., 276–324. Cambridge: Cambridge University Press. http://dx.doi.org/10.1017/CBO9780511619427.

KUKLA, R. & LANCE, M. (2009). *'Yo!' and 'Lo!': The Pragmatic Topography of the Space of Reasons*. Cambridge, MA: Harvard University Press.

LABOV, W. (1972). *Sociolinguistic Patterns*. Philadelphia, PA: University of Pennsylvania Press.

LAHIRI, U. (2002). *Questions and Answers in Embedded Contexts*. New York: Oxford University Press.

LANGTON, R. (1993). 'Speech Acts and Unspeakable Acts.' *Philosophy & Public Affairs*, **22(4)**: 293–330. http://www.jstor.org/stable/2265469.

LANGTON, R. & WEST, C. (1999). 'Scorekeeping in a Pornographic Language Game.' *Australasian Journal of Philosophy*, **77(3)**: 303–19. http://dx.doi.org/10.1080/00048409912349061.

LEPORE, E. & STONE, M. (2014). *Imagination and Convention: Distinguishing Grammar and Inference in Language*. New York: Oxford University Press.

LEVINSON, S. C. (1979). 'Activity Types and Language.' *Linguistics*, **17(5–6)**: 365–400.

LEVINSON, S. C. (1983). *Pragmatics*. Cambridge, UK: Cambridge University Press.

LEWIS, D. K. (1969). *Convention: A Philosophical Study*. Cambridge, MA: Harvard University Press.

LEWIS, D. K. (1975). 'Languages and Language.' In K. GUNDERSON (ed.), *Language, Mind, and Knowledge*. Minnesota Studies in the Philosophy of Science, Vol. 7, 3–35. Minneapolis: University of Minnesota Press. Page references to reprint Lewis (1983).

LEWIS, D. K. (1979). 'Scorekeeping in a Language Game.' *Journal of Philosophical Logic*, **8(1)**: 339–59. http://www.jstor.org/stable/30227173.

LEWIS, D. K. (1983). 'Languages and Language.' In *Philosophical Papers*, vol. 1, chap. 11, 163–88. Minneapolis: Oxford University Press.

MACKINNON, C. (1993). *Only Words*. Cambridge, MA: Harvard University Press.

MAITRA, I. (2012). 'Subordinating Speech.' In I. MAITRA & M. K. MCGOWAN (eds.), *Speech and Harm: Controversies Over Free Speech*, 94–120. New York: Oxford University Press.

MAITRA, I. & MCGOWAN, M. K. (eds.) (2012). *Speech and Harm: Controversies Over Free Speech*. New York: Oxford University Press.

MARCU, D. (2000). 'Perlocutions: The Achilles' Heel of Speech Act Theory.' *Journal of Pragmatics*, **32(12)**: 1719–41. http://www.sciencedirect.com/science/article/pii/S03782166990-01216.

MAYNARD SMITH, J. & PRICE, G. (1973). 'The Logic of Animal Conflict.' *Nature*, **246**: 15–18.

MAYNARD SMITH, J. & HARPER, D. (2003). *Animal Signals*. New York: Oxford University Press.

MCGOWAN, M. K. (2012). 'On 'Whites Only' Signs and Racist Hate Speech: Verbal Acts of Racial Descrimination.' In I. MAITRA & M. K. MCGOWAN (eds.), *Speech and Harm: Controversies Over Free Speech*, 121–47. New York: Oxford University Press.

MILLIKAN, R. G. (1984). *Language, Thought and Other Biological Categories*. Cambridge, MA: MIT Press.

MILLIKAN, R. G. (2005). *Language: A Biological Model*. New York: Oxford University Press.

MURRAY, S. E. (2010a). 'Evidentiality and Questions in Cheyenne.' In S. LIMA (ed.), *Proceedings of SULA 5: Semantics of Under-Represented Languages in the Americas*. Amherst, MA: GLSA Publications. http://www.semanticsarchive.net/Archive/DRiZTUyN/.

MURRAY, S. E. (2010b). *Evidentiality and the Structure of Speech Acts*. Ph.D. thesis, Rutgers University, New Brunswick, NJ. http://hdl.rutgers.edu/1782.1/rucore10001600001. ETD.000056638.

MURRAY, S. E. (2011). 'A Hamblin Semantics for Evidentials.' In E. CORMANY, S. ITO & D. LUTZ (eds.), *Proceedings from Semantics and Linguistic Theory (SALT) 19*, 324–41. Ithaca, New York: eLanguage. http://elanguage.net/journals/salt/article/view/19.19/1878.

MURRAY, S. E. (2014). 'Varieties of Update.' *Semantics and Pragmatics*, **7(2)**: 1–53. http://dx.doi.org/10.3765/sp.7.2.

MURRAY, S. E. & STARR, W. B. (to appear). 'The Structure of Communicative Acts.' *Linguistics & Philosophy*.

PARIKH, P. (1991). 'Communication and Strategic Inference.' *Linguistics and Philosophy*, **14(5)**: 473–514.

PARIKH, P. (2000). 'Communication, Meaning, and Interpretation.' *Linguistics and Philosophy*, **23(2)**: 185–212. http://dx.doi.org/10.1023/A%3A1005513919392.

PINKER, S., NOWAK, M. A. & LEE, J. J. (2008). 'The Logic of Indirect Speech.' *Proceedings of the National Academy of Sciences*, **105(3)**: 833–8. http://www.pnas.org/content/105/3/833.full. pdf+html, http://www.pnas.org/content/ 105/3/833.abstract.

POESIO, M. & TRAUM, D. R. (1997). 'Conversational Actions and Discourse Situations.' *Computational Intelligence*, **13(3)**: 309–47. http://citeseer.ist.psu.edu/cache/papers/cs/ 103/http:zSzzSzwww.cogsci.ed.ac.ukzSzpoesiozSzpublicationszSzCI_journal.pdf/poesio97 conversational.pdf.

PORTNER, P. (2004). 'The Semantics of Imperatives within a Theory of Clause Types.' In R. B YOUNG (ed.), *Proceedings from Semantics and Linguistic Theory 14*, 235–52. Ithaca, NY: CLC Publications. http://semanticsarchive.net/Archive/mJlZGQ4N/PortnerSALT04.pdf.

PORTNER, P. (2007). 'Imperatives and Modals.' *Natural Language Semantics*, **15(4)**: 351–83. http://dx.doi.org/10.1007/s11050-007-9022-y.

PORTNER, P. (2012). 'Permission and Choice.' In G. GREWENDORF & T. E. ZIMMER-MANN (eds.), *Discourse and Grammar: From Sentence Types to Lexical Categories*, Studies in Generative Grammar. Berlin: Mouton de Gruyter. http://semanticsarchive.net/ Archive/jI1YjMyY/Permission_Choice_Portner.pdf.

RAWLS, J. (1955). 'Two Concepts of Rules.' *The Philosophical Review*, **64(1)**: 3–32. http://www. jstor.org/stable/2182230.

ROBERTS, C. (1996). 'Information Structure in Discourse: Towards an Integrated Formal Theory of Pragmatics.' In J. H. YOON & A. KATHOL (eds.), *OSU Working Papers in Linguistics*, vol. 49. Columbus, OH: Ohio State University Press. References to Roberts (2012).

ROBERTS, C. (2003). 'Uniqueness in Definite Noun Phrases.' *Linguistics and Philosophy*, **26(3)**: 287–350.

ROBERTS, C. (2005). 'Pronouns as Definites.' In M. REIMER & A. BEZUIDENHOUT (eds.), *Descriptions and Beyond*, 503–43. New York: Oxford University Press.

ROBERTS, C. (2012). 'Information Structure in Discourse: Towards an Integrated Formal Theory of Pragmatics.' *Semantics and Pragmatics*, **5(6)**: 1–69. http://dx.doi.org/10.3765/sp.5.6.

ROELOFSEN, F. & FARKAS, D. F. (2015). 'Polarity Particle Responses as a Window onto the Interpretation of Questions and Assertions.' *Language*, **91(2)**: 359–414. https://muse.jhu.edu/ journals/language/v091/91.2.roelofsen.html.

VAN ROOY, R. (2003). 'Quality and Quantity of Information Exchanges.' *Journal of Logic, Language, and Information*, **12(4)**: 423–51.

VAN ROOY, R. (2004). 'Signalling Games Select Horn Strategies.' *Linguistics and Philosophy*, **27**(4): 493–527. http://dx.doi.org/10.1023/B%3ALING.0000024403.88733.3f.

RYAN, M. J. (1985). *The Túngara Frog: A Study in Sexual Selection and Communication*. Chicago, IL: University of Chicago Press.

SADOCK, J. M. & ZWICKY, A. M. (1985). 'Speech Act Distinctions in Syntax.' In T. SHOPEN (ed.), *Language Typology and Syntactic Description*, vol. 1, 155–96. Cambridge University Press.

SBISÁ, M. (2002). 'Speech Acts in Context.' *Language & Communication*, **22**(4): 421–36. http://dx.doi.org/10.1016/S0271-5309(02)00018-6.

SCHANK, R. C. & ABELSON, R. (1977). *Scripts, Plans, Goals, and Understanding*. Hillsdale, NJ: Lawrence Erlbaum Associates.

SCOTT-PHILLIPS, T. (2015). *Speaking Our Minds: Why Human Communication is Different, and How Language Evolved to Make it Special*. New York: Palgrave Macmillan.

SCOTT-PHILLIPS, T. & KIRBY, S. (2013). 'Information, Influence and Inference in Language Evolution.' In U. STEGMANN (ed.), *Animal Communication Theory: Information and Influence*, 421–42. Cambridge: Cambridge University Press.

SCOTT-PHILLIPS, T. C. (2008). 'Defining Biological Communication.' *Journal of Evolutionary Biology*, **21**(2): 387–95. http://search.ebscohost.com.proxy.library.cornell.edu/login.aspx?direct=true&db=a2h&AN=28807716&site=ehost-live.

SCOTT-PHILLIPS, T. C. (2011). 'Evolutionarily Stable Communication and Pragmatics.' In A. BENZ, C. EBERT, G. JÄGER & R. VAN ROOIJ (eds.), *Language, Games, and Evolution*, vol. 6207 of *Lecture Notes in Computer Science*, 117–33. Springer Berlin Heidelberg. http://dx.doi.org/10.1007/978-3-642-18006-4_6.

SCOTT-PHILLIPS, T. C., BLYTHE, R. A., GARDNER, A. & WEST, S. A. (2012). 'How do Communication Systems Emerge?' *Proceedings of the Royal Society B: Biological Sciences*, **279**(1735): 1943–9. http://rspb.royalsocietypublishing.org/content/279/1735/1943.abstract.

SEARLE, J. R. (1968). 'Austin on Locutionary and Illocutionary Acts.' *Philosophical Review*, **77**: 405–24. http://www.jstor.org/stable/2183008.

SEARLE, J. R. (1969). *Speech Acts*. Cambridge, UK: Cambridge University Press.

SEARLE, J. R. & VANDERVEKEN, D. (1985). *Foundations of Illocutionary Logic*. Cambridge, UK: Cambridge University Press.

SELLARS, W. (1956). 'Empiricism and the Philosophy of Mind.' In H. FEIGL & M. SCRIVEN (eds.), *Minnesota Studies in the Philosophy of Science*, vol. 1, 1st edn. Minneapolis, MN: University of Minnesota Press.

SIEBEL, M. (2002). 'What Is an Illocutionary Point?' In G. GREWENDORF & G. MEGGLE (eds.), *Speech Acts, Mind, and Social Reality*, vol. 79 of *Studies in Linguistics and Philosophy*, 125–39. Springer Netherlands. http://dx.doi.org/10.1007/978-94-010-0589-0_9.

SIMONS, M. (2005). 'Dividing Things Up: The Semantics of Or and the Modal/or Interaction.' *Natural Language Semantics*, **13**(3): 271–316. http://dx.doi.org/10.1007/s11050-004-2900-7.

SKYRMS, B. (2010). *Signals: Evolution, Learning, and Information*. New York: Oxford University Press.

STALNAKER, R. C. (1978). 'Assertion.' In P. COLE (ed.), *Syntax and Semantics 9: Pragmatics*, 315–332. New York: Academic Press. References to Stalnaker 1999.

STALNAKER, R. C. (1999). *Context and Content: Essays on Intentionality in Speech and Thought*. Oxford: Oxford University Press.

STALNAKER, R. C. (2002). 'Common Ground.' *Linguistics and Philosophy*, **25**(5–6): 701–21.

STARR, W. B. (2010). *Conditionals, Meaning and Mood*. Ph.D. thesis, Rutgers University, New Brunswick, NJ. http://hdl.rutgers.edu/1782.1/rucore10001600001.ETD.000056780.

STARR, W. B. (2013). 'A Preference Semantics for Imperatives.' Ms. Cornell University, http://williamstarr.net/research/a_preference_semantics_for_imperatives.pdf.

STARR, W. B. (2014). 'Mood, Force and Truth.' *ProtoSociology*, **31**: 160–81. http:// williamstarr. net/research/mood_force_and_truth.pdf.

STARR, W. B. (2016). 'Dynamic Expressivism about Deontic Modality.' In N. CHARLOW & M. CHRISMAN (eds.), *Deontic Modality*, 355–394. New York: Oxford University Press.

STENIUS, E. (1967). 'Mood and Language-Game.' *Synthése*, **17**(3): 254–74. http://www.jstor.org/stable/20114558.

STRAWSON, P. F. (1964). 'Intention and Convention in Speech Acts.' *The Philosophical Review*, **73**(4): 439–60. http://www.jstor.org/stable/2183301.

TIRRELL, L. (2012). 'Genocidal Language Games.' In I. MAITRA & M. K. McGOWAN (eds.), *Speech and Harm: Controversies Over Free Speech*, 174–221. New York: Oxford University Press.

VELTMAN, F. (1996). 'Defaults in Update Semantics.' *Journal of Philosophical Logic*, **25**(3): 221–61. http://dx.doi.org/10.1007/BF00248150.

WILLIAMSON, T. (1996). 'Knowing and Asserting.' *The Philosophical Review*, **105**(4): 489–523. http://www.jstor.org/stable/2998423.

WITTGENSTEIN, L. (1953). *Philosophical Investigations*. Oxford: Basil Blackwell.

YALCIN, S. (2007). 'Epistemic Modals.' *Mind*, **116**(464): 983–1026. http://mind.oxfordjournals.org/content/116/464/983.

10

The Social Life of Slurs

Geoff Nunberg

Chaque mot a son histoire.

—Jules Gilliéron

The Emergence of Slurs

We wear two hats when we talk about slurs, as engaged citizens and as scholars of language. The words had very little theoretical interest for philosophy or linguistic semantics before they took on a symbolic role in the culture wars that broke out in and around the academy in the 1980s.[1] But once scholars' attention was drawn to the topic, they began to discern connections to familiar problems in meta-ethics, semantics, and the philosophy of language. The apparent dual nature of the words—they seem both to describe and to evaluate or express—seemed to make them an excellent test bed for investigations of non-truth-conditional aspects of meaning, of certain types of moral language, of Fregean "coloring," and of hybrid or "thick" terms, among other things. There are some writers who take slurs purely as a topical jumping-off point for addressing those issues and don't make any explicit effort to bring their discussions back to the social questions that drew scholars' attention to the words in the first place. But most seem to feel that their research ought to have some significance beyond the confines of the common room.

That double perspective can leave us a little wall-eyed, as we try to track slurs as both a social and linguistic phenomenon. The distinction between the two perspectives isn't always obvious. To listen to the way people talk about slurs and to judge from the number of papers, conference sessions, and special journal numbers with "slur" in their title, people often assume that slurs are an essentially linguistic rather than rhetorical category—that *slur* is a term more like "proper name" or "factive verb" than

---

[1] Such words have long been grist for philologists and dialectologists (a well-known example is H. L. Mencken's "Designations for Colored Folk," which appeared in 1944 in *American Speech* (Mencken 1944)). Slurs have also figured in work on racist and homophobic discourse by linguists, sociologists, and social psychologists. But until recently, the subject has played little role in semantic theory. Derogatives first made their way into the philosophical literature in 1973, when Dummett (1993) used them to exemplify the difference between the grounds for applying a concept and the consequences of its application, without considering slurs as a social phenomenon.

it is like "euphemism" or "jargon." So it's worth bearing in mind that the slur as such is a fairly recent addition to both our common metalanguage and our moral inventory. Of course languages like English have a long history of words that disparage people on the basis of their membership of a certain group (though as the sociologist Irving Allen (1983) noted, the proliferation of ethnic derogations is chiefly a modern urban development). But before the mid-twentieth century there was no one English term that gathered such words as a class. One could describe them only with elastic labels like "derogatory," "abusive," or "pejorative," whose various equivalents (e.g., *dépréciatif*, *abschätzig, spregiativo*) are still the only terms available in most other languages for words like these. It was only in the 1960s that the noun *slur* itself became generally accepted as a term for a particular kind of derogative word, rather than simply as "an insulting or disparaging remark or innuendo," as in "the accusation of theft was a slur on my honor"—still the only definition that Merriam-Webster gives for the relevant sense of the noun.[2]

The new use of *slur* was part of the new vocabulary of race and social diversity that entered public discourse in the 1950s and 1960s: notions like "colorblind," "hate speech," "racial sensitivity," and "racism" itself, all of them connected to a sweeping revision of the framework of civic virtue.[3] The new framework implied a doctrine of linguistic self-determination, which entails that every group should have the right to determine what it should—and, more important, should not—be called, with *slur* the name we now give to certain infractions of that doctrine. That isn't to say that slurs and related concepts required new words to express them. The appearance of a new moral vocabulary was a sign of their emergence, not a precondition for it. There have been parallel cultural developments in many other Western nations, some marked by the introduction of new words, some by the repurposing or redefinition of old ones.[4] But the emergence of *slur* in Anglophone cultures puts the conceptual revisions in relief.

---

[2] The linguistic sense of *slur* (as in "a four-letter slur") shows up earlier in the African-American press of the 1940s and 1950s, but it wasn't mainstreamed until the 1960s. The phrase "racial slur" appeared just 17 times before 1960 in Proquest's newspaper and magazine corpus, which includes the records of the *New York Times*, the *Washington Post*, and other major publications, and the majority of those instances referred to slights or disparagements, rather than to specific words—a judge's observation that a white male defendant who had lived with a colored woman was beyond rehabilitation, a baseball remark about watermelons in connection with Jackie Robinson. The phrase appeared 126 times in the 1960s, 400 times in the 1970s, and 2015 times in the 1980s, almost always in reference to a derogatory word or expression.

[3] Some of these words originated well before this period but were rarely used in the language of public life. Others, like *slur*, acquired new senses; *bias*, for example, was no longer restricted to a mental disposition, but could refer to active discrimination, as in "housing bias." *Racism* itself underwent a similar shift. The 1989 OED definition read, "The theory that distinctive human characteristics and abilities are determined by race"; the 2008 revision added, "prejudice, discrimination, or antagonism directed against people of other racial or ethnic groups." (On the evolution of this term, see, e.g. (Miles 2004), (Garcia 1996)).

[4] Making allowances, we find similar attitudes toward certain derogative words in other Western language communities, whether or not they have a specific word that corresponds to *slur*. Italian philosophers and linguists have published papers with titles such as "La Semantica Multi-Atto Degli Slur" (Tenchini and Frigerio 2014) and "Slurs: Un'introduzione" (Bianchi 2013).We can read in those titles not just an acknowledgment that *slur* has no precise translation in Italian, where such items are usually described with the more general *spregiativi*, but also that *slur* has an application in that language even so. One indirect sign of the diffusion of these concepts is the wide cross-linguistic use of the phrase "politically correct," either under its English name or others like "rectitude politique," which signals a similar reaction to the perceived excesses that a reflexive avoidance of words that might be construed as slurs can lead to. Perhaps more basic

Like those other terms, *slur* is one of those culturally saturated keywords—words that are "strong, difficult, and persuasive," as Raymond Williams (1976) described them—that cry out for thick description. The word is both more specific and more value-laden than a term like *derogative*, in three connected ways. For one thing, a derogative word qualifies as a slur only when it disparages people on the basis of properties such as race, religion, ethnic or geographical origin, gender, sexual orientation, or sometimes political ideology—the deep fatalities that have historically been the focus of discrimination or social antagonisms that we see as rents in the fabric of civil society. Sailing enthusiasts deprecate the owners of motor craft as "stinkpotters," but we probably wouldn't call the word a slur—though the right-wingers' derogation of environmentalists as "tree-huggers" might qualify, since that antipathy has a partisan cast.

Second, unlike *derogative*, *slur* is a hybrid word (Bernard Williams' "thick term") that mixes categorization and attitude, like *bigot*, *boor*, or *toady*. We might speak of a word for the members of a group as derogative even if we personally think they merit derogation, such as the label *clamheads* for Scientologists or the French *facho* for fascists. But most of us would demur from calling either word a slur, since we feel the groups have it coming. When someone writes "neocon is a slur for Conservatives," we don't have to read further to surmise that she considers the label unfair.

The third distinctive feature of slurs is connected to the first two. Because we see slurs as the expressions of antipathies that are considered matters for civic concern, they count as a distinct kind of social transgression. To describe a word as a slur isn't just to say that it's offensive, but to assign a particular moral or political tenor both to the offense it gives and the offense one commits in uttering it. Using a slur isn't simply a breach of personal manners or a sign of coarseness, which is the grounds on which white critics condemned the use of *nigger* in the nineteenth century. For us, a slur is a kind of verbalized thought-crime: it perpetuates social inequities, infects even innocent minds, and undermines the conduct of public discourse. And as such, slurring—the verb, too, acquired a new sense around this time—becomes a speech act in which institutions and the law may take an official interest.[5]

In that sense, the slur as such is a new addition to the moral or at least civic life. To say that *nigger* was a racial slur in Mark Twain's time or that *Sassenach* was a slur for an Englishman in the age of Walter Scott is not just a linguistic anachronism but a cultural one. It would be like describing Lovelace's violation of Clarissa as date rape or taxing Lear's daughters with ageism—or to take Lionel Trilling's example, like accusing Achilles of being insincere in his boasts. Not that those actions wouldn't merit reproach, but the contemporary words diagnose them in terms of an inapposite moral frame.

---

are the parallel meaning changes that the term *racism* and its cognates have undergone in just about all of these languages.

[5] As the Washington Supreme Court put it in 1977, "racial epithets which were once part of common usage may not now be looked upon as 'mere insulting language.'" 88 Wash. 2d 735, 565 P.2d 1173 (1977) (en banc).

The Risks of Reduction

For all their cultural particularities, slurs clearly rely on some more general linguistic ploy or device—it's not as if the possibility of using words to disparage people in virtue of the groups they belong to didn't arise until modern English developed an app for them. That's the mechanism that semanticists want to explain, abstracted from the specific features that lead people to classify certain of its applications as slurs. As a purely linguistic process, it certainly isn't going to be restricted to words that derogate only certain kinds of social groups, much less to the words that do so unreasonably, or to the kinds of words whose use strikes us as a matter for civic concern. But our specific conception of slurs has become so much a part of the cultural wallpaper that many writers fail to see how local and ideologically charged it is. That often leads them to essentialize the features that lead us to classify certain derogative words as slurs, so that slurs-as-we-think-of-them comes to seem a linguistic natural kind. When you see someone using "slur" to describe a general linguistic phenomenon, the problem isn't usually that the word is being used polysemously, but that it isn't—people don't notice that there's a distinction to be made here. That can create a deceptive impression of explanatory harmony between semantics and cultural criticism, as if we could read the moral implications of using the words straight off their lexical surface.

It would probably help to clarify things if we reserved *slur* for the sorts of words that count as slurs in English, along with the analogous words that people in other modern societies classify in a similar category. Then we might use *derogative* for the general linguistic type of which slurs are a particular instance. That's what I'll do here, when it's appropriate, though I'll suggest later that the mechanism at work here isn't restricted to words that convey a negative evaluation of their referents. But the confusion here isn't simply terminological. Whether semanticists describe the object of their inquiry as slurs or as derogatives, pejoratives or epithets, they almost always identify that object with the particular set of words that *slur* picks out. When it comes to exemplifying the phenomenon, for example, they most often fasten on one or two culturally prototypical derogations based on race, ethnicity or sexual orientation, or the circumspect meta-slur S*, which stands in for some "odious racial slur" (Richard 2008). The assumption is that the characteristic features of *nigger* or *faggot*, say, are going to be representative of the important features of derogatives in general. In their practice, most writers seem to agree with McCready that "pejoratives behave more or less alike in terms of their basic meanings, differing only in the degree of approbation assigned to the individual or group under discussion" (McCready 2010).

This approach reflects a *déformation professionelle* that manifests itself in a kind of methodological incuriosity, where aspects of the phenomena that seem inessential are either marginalized or neglected. There has been very little discussion of other kinds of derogative words, for example, though those seem to undermine some of the claims that people make on the basis of observations about prototypical ethnic slurs and the like.[6] Someone says "That building is full of flacks [publicists]" or "Mes voisins sont tous fachos" or complains that the neighborhood is filling up with techies

---

[6] An exception is Bach (2014), who elaborates a vocabulary of different types of evaluative words but without distinguishing, e.g. between slurs other hybrid terms.

(in present-day San Francisco, a derogative for the overpaid tech workers who are driving up rents). I don't think many people would want to argue that those utterances aren't truth-evaluable, or that they're purely expressive, or that they're useless to us, all claims that people have made about words like *nigger*. Not that the claims about the use of that word are wrong—that's another question—but they seem to apply only to words that convey unfounded or indefensible contempt for the members of a racial or ethnic group, which make for a poor candidate for a universal linguistic type.

That isn't the only kind of variation that has been slighted in the literature. As McCready's remark suggests, writers realize that the slurs for different groups may vary in intensity according to the degree of abuse or discrimination each has endured, so that slurs for blacks are generally more offensive than those for Frenchmen, say. But no one has had much to say about the differences among slurs for a single group, other than to suggest they may differ in intensity. There's nothing in anyone's account of *nigger* that might provide a point of comparison for other slurs for blacks, such as *coon, spade* or *jungle bunny*, though these are different from one another in more than just their relative intensity. Nor is there anything in those accounts that might explain how whites' slurs for blacks are *functionally* different from blacks' slurs for whites, as some empirical research seems to suggest (Embrick and Henricks 2013). Even the very notion of *whites'* slurs for blacks isn't often expressed—nor, what's more striking, is the idea that such slurs might be expressions of the notion of whiteness itself. Writers focus almost entirely on what slurs convey about their targets and the insult or offense they give, not on what they have to say about the groups that coin and use them, though those group-identifying or group-affiliating uses are more prevalent, more universal, and arguably prior to their uses as terms of direct abuse. The motivations of the people who use slurs are pretty much discharged by describing the prototypical speaker as "the racist."

I don't mean to suggest that writers are unaware of all these points. Many touch on one or more of them in passing. But there's a widespread assumption that we can abstract away from these matters and reduce slurs to their semantic kernel, leaving it to pragmatics and sociolinguistics to fill in their broader cultural and social implications and background. That assumption enables semanticists to come at the phenomenon with familiar methods, building their arguments by appeals to intuitions about the meaning or acceptability of the sorts of constructed sentences that live out their entire lives on scholars' blackboards. The idea is that we can intuitively assess what is meant by sentences like *Germans are boches* or *There are Ss* in that building* in the same way we can with sentences about farmers beating their donkeys, by burrowing down into our own idiolects. And with the range of relevant data so constricted, it's not always clear what would count as an empirical disconfirmation of one or another theory of these words, beyond appeals to intuitions about other constructed examples.

One obvious difficulty here is that, as a rule, most of these words are mercifully alien to most of the philosophers and linguists who write about slurs: they don't use them or frequent the sorts of people who do.[7] It's only at the risk of presumption that we academics can assume we can intuitively assess what someone who describes his

---

[7] I'm talking about the strong ethnic and racial slurs, not derogatives like *techie* or *flack*.

neighborhood as filling up with spics has precisely in mind, or why he's putting things that way. And while intuitions are useful shortcuts for getting at semantic properties such as scope, they can play us false even there. The judgments about decontextualized examples like, "If I were racist, I probably wouldn't like niggers" and, "I used to think kikes were bad" may lead us to conclude that slurs invariably scope out or are invariably speaker-oriented. But it isn't at all hard to find lots of counterexamples in the field: "Everybody loves to hate a homo," the gay playwright Harvey Fierstein said on MSNBC. One might claim that such a sentence is atypical, but on what grounds? It's well-known that speakers are not terribly good at making judgments about such things as typicality; that's a statistical claim that depends on how we determine the baseline and expected frequency, which isn't all obvious here.

Actually, though, the problem isn't so much that slurs don't belong to most scholars' idiolects; it's that where slurs are concerned, there really are no idiolects. You can't secure a judgment about slurs against criticism by confining it to "what the word means for me." What we are reporting when we offer judgments about sentences containing slurs are just unacknowledged ethnolinguistic hypotheses, very often drawn from second-hand accounts and colored by ideology and cultural preconceptions. If we don't immediately notice this, it's partly because we're none of us immune to those preconceptions and partly because the data we consider are so reduced and circumscribed that they rarely force us to confront complications or disconfirming phenomena.

These methodological limitations come at a cost. We can come away from much of this literature having learned not much more about slurs, or about racism, than we thought we already knew going in—we're rarely surprised by it. So while I'm not averse to appealing to these methods where appropriate, I want to augment them here with a different line of approach. In fact I don't think that slurring is a semantic phenomenon in the first place. What makes the phenomenon interesting, over and above its independent sociopolitical importance, is that it opens a window on aspects of language use and of the sociolinguistic organization of languages that have seemed marginal to the questions at the heart of semantics and pragmatics.

This paper is going to be philologically thick, so to speak. One of my objects here is to widen the range of explicanda, in the hope that our theorizing about slurs will benefit from a more challenging selectional environment. That includes not just the phenomena I mentioned above that writers tend to pass over, but others that no one seems to have noticed. What should we say about words which we count as slurs but which none of their users regard as negative or derogatory? How does it happen that there are groups and social categories that are often regarded with antipathy or disrespect but for whom there are no common Standard English slurs—that is, words that express a negative attitude toward the entire class? (Muslims are one such group, and we'll see, surprisingly, that women are another.) To this end, I'm going to spread the net more widely and dip into the history and social background of particular words in more anecdotal detail than these discussions typically do. Most of these words are particular to American English, and I'll sometimes appeal to some fairly subtle connotations and distinctions, for which I'll have to ask for the indulgence of nonnatives. I'm not offering an account of contemporary American slurs as such; you can't build sociolinguistics in one country. But it's difficult to say anything definitive about slurs in general without saying a good deal about particular slurs in their cultural settings.

Semanticizing Slurs

Slurring meanings

Virtually all accounts of slurs try to answer several questions. First, what do the words convey, over and above identifying their referents as members of the relevant group? Do they impute certain stereotypical properties to the members of a group, or do they describe or express the speaker's attitude toward members of the group, or do they do something else? Call this the question of import. And whichever it is, how do certain strong slurs come by their power to inflict injury on their targets or to evoke anger of such intensity that courts have sometimes assigned them to a legally distinct category of "fighting words"? Call this the question of impact.

Then there's the related question of mechanism: how do the words convey their import? In almost all accounts of slurs, the mechanism is made part of the words' conventional linguistic meanings, whether as additional descriptive content, as a conventional implicature or as a presupposition, which serves to distinguish a slur semantically from a nonslurring descriptive equivalent. (There are few exceptions, such as Anderson and Lepore's (2013) "prohibition" theory and Bolinger's Contrastive Choice Account (Bolinger 2017), which I'll discuss later.) This semanticist hypothesis, or if you prefer, this family of semanticist hypotheses, has largely circumscribed the discussions of these words. People debate whether this or that mechanism is best suited to produce the effects associated with the words and to predict their apparent idiosyncrasies, but without stepping outside the basic assumption that the conventional meaning of the word itself is what makes it the bearer of the attitude that speakers use it to convey.[8]

On the face of things, the semanticist view seems not only plausible but inevitable. If (*American*) *Indian* and *redskin* denote the same group of people but consistently convey different attitudes toward them or beliefs about them, how could that be anything but a consequence of a difference in their conventional meanings? And having accepted that conclusion, it seems natural to go on to assimilate slurs and words like them to other words whose conventional meanings convey evaluations or connotations, or alternatively to expressives, words and constructions that conventionally indicate heightened emotional states. But semanticism is an empirical claim about the use and interpretation of these words, and I'll be arguing here that it's wrong, on several grounds. Broadly speaking, semanticist accounts introduce formal mechanisms which have no functional motivation and which don't account either for

---

[8] To speak of semanticist theories isn't to say that the import of a slur couldn't also depend on additional pragmatic inferences. One could reserve the term "semantic theories" for those which hold that the derogatory content of a slur affects the truth-conditions of the sentences in which it appears, as Sennet and Copp (2014) do, or equivalently, that it constitutes part of what Potts (2005) calls the "at issue" content of a sentence. In that case, though, to say that an account of slurs is nonsemantic is to leave open whether the derogation follows from a linguistic convention or arises from a conversational inference, which is precisely the question I want to raise here.

the way the words are actually used or for their effects on their targets or on other members of the communities they belong to.

Sketch of an Alternative

Without getting too far ahead of myself, let me say a word about the alternative account of slurs I'll be offering here. From a semantic point of view, I'm proposing as minimal a story as one could tell. Slurs and words like them are just plain vanilla descriptions like *cowboy* and *coat hanger*, no different in any semantic respect from their nonslurring equivalents. There's nothing in their linguistic meanings that conveys any disparagement of their referents, whether as content, conventional implicature, presupposition, "coloring" or mode of presentation. As plain descriptions, they have nothing in common with hybrid words that mix categorization and attitude, such as *bigot*, *boor*, or *toady*, or as I noted, the label *slur* itself. Nor is there anything in the meanings of slurs that makes them the direct expressions of strong emotion. That is, they don't share any *semantic* properties with items like vulgarities and interjections—they may sometimes engender analogous kinds of discomfort in listeners, but for independent reasons. As plain descriptions, moreover, they figure in the truth-conditions of the sentences that they appear in exactly as their nonslurring equivalents do: the sentence *The krauts won the cup* says neither more nor less about the world than *The Germans won the cup*. And just to round out the picture, although a few of these words have become phonetically toxic, their effects and behavior owe virtually nothing to any blanket proscriptions on their use.

I'll be arguing, rather, that the effects of words like *redskin* and *kraut* are the results of a routinized conversational implicature, an exploitation of Grice's Maxim of Manner or some analogous conversational principle. In particular, the implicature plays off a submaxim of the form, "Use appropriate language." That would cover not just the requirement of using English among Anglophones and French among Francophones, which is usually just the limiting case of avoiding obscurity, but the need to use an appropriate register—for example, to avoid describing someone's behavior as egregious in an informal context, or as crummy in a formal one. Beyond that, it implies an obligation to make appropriate choices among the welter of conventions that might govern the choice of words in a given speech situation, depending on the social norms that are contextually pertinent. Opting out of these maxims can set up various conversational implicatures. I'll argue that *redskin* is distinguished from *Indian* not by any additional evaluative or expressive features of its meaning, but merely in being the description of Indians prescribed by the conventions of a group whose members have disparaging attitudes about American Indians. Then the implications of pointedly choosing to use *redskin* arise not from the meaning of the word but from its association with the discourse of a certain group of speakers. That's what sets this account apart from semanticist theories that try to pack the effects of these words into their conventional meanings. In a nutshell: racists don't use slurs because they're derogative; slurs are derogative because they're the words that racists use.

I'll be focusing here on slurs and analogous derogative terms. But once we accept that slurs are just descriptions that have no distinctive semantic properties, we aren't going to see them as a natural linguistic category nor can they be lumped with expressives, hybrid terms or other categories that convey an evaluation or an attitude via their conventional meanings. Rather, the recognition of slurs as a distinct class has to be made on sociopragmatic grounds, grouping slurs with other words whose extra-denotative import results from an exploitation of the same conversational maneuver that gives slurs their effect. This category of expressions I'll describe as prejudicials, a class of words that turns out to be quite broad.[9] It includes not just most racial and ethnic slurs, but derogatives that disparage people for their occupations, like *flack* and *shyster*; for their avocations, like the French *tou-tou* for tourists and the sailor's *stinkpotter* for motor boat owners; for their geographical origin, like *Canuck* for Canadians or the Italian *terrone* for southerners; for their social status, like *bougie* and *pleb*; or for their political orientation, like *commie, lib-lab*, French *facho* for fascists, *Trots* for Trotskyists, and what Republicans like to style as "the Democrat Party." There are prejudicial proper names, such as La La Land for Los Angeles, Dubya for George W. Bush, Drumpf for Donald Trump, and a whole phonebook of soubriquets for Barack Obama, including Obumma, Ohlowme, Obozo, Bammy and just BHO. There are political prejudicials, both negative and positive, such as *socialistic, death tax* for the estate tax, and *free enterprise* for market capitalism. There are hypocoristics that convey affection, such as the Chicago Cubbies, dysphemisms like *retard*, and euphemisms like *senior citizen*.[10] As we'll see, all of these items pattern with slurs in ways that make them distinct from words that convey an evaluation via their linguistic meanings. I don't claim that prejudicials as such constitute a universal category; that would entail the universality of both the conversational maneuver that creates them and the conception of societally divided opinion that it exploits. But the phenomenon is very general in the languages of socially complex speech-communities.

Critique of Semanticist Accounts

Import as Content

The questions of import and mechanism are by no means the only ones one should be asking about words like these, as we'll see later on. But because it's on these issues that most accounts have concentrated their attention, they're the obvious points of departure for a critique of semantic theories that will set up the pragmatic theory I'm going to develop. And while most writers blend their accounts of mechanism and import, it will be convenient here to deal with each of these issues separately.

Some semanticist accounts of slurs hold that their import arises from representing their targets in some ways, either by imputing a stereotype to them or depicting them as despicable. The most straightforward way of incorporating this material, and perhaps the one that accords most easily with naïve intuition, is simply to add the descriptive content to what one asserts in using the term. This is the approach

---

[9] See the note on terminology at the end of this paper.

[10] One could argue that in some of these cases the evaluation follows entirely from the descriptive content of the term: what could *Obozo* or *stinkpotter* be but derogatives? But the line is fuzzy, and most of these descriptions underdetermine the precise evaluation they convey. There's nothing in the compositional meaning of the phrase *free enterprise* that tells us it's associated with the political right. *Cubbies* expresses affection for the Chicago Cubs, but *Yalie* is traditionally a derisive term for Yale students and alumni (Lassila 2009). BHO is disparaging, unlike FDR and JFK.

developed by Hom (2008), who packs the meaning of the term with both a stereotype and its social consequences, so that:

... the epithet 'chink' expresses a complex, socially constructed property like: ought to be subject to higher college admissions standards, and ought to be subject to exclusion from advancement to managerial positions, and ..., because of being slanty-eyed, and devious, and good-at-laundering, and ... all because of being Chinese.

This leads Hom to the morally satisfying conclusion that to describe someone as a chink is necessarily to make a false assertion, because there are no chinks; the word has an empty extension. In a sparer version of this approach, Hom and May (2013, 2014) assign to the sentence, "X is a chink" a meaning like, "X ought to be the object of negative moral evaluation just because X is Chinese." The disparaging sense of *chink* remains part of the content of the assertion, however, so that, "X is a chink" and, "X is Chinese" have different truth-conditions.

The Hom-May position is subject to several kinds of objections. First, and to my mind most telling, it doesn't capture the way these words are actually used. By and large, a speaker who uses a slur isn't asserting anything about the group the word refers to, other than in the prototypical but rare cases where someone is actually venting his hostility toward one of its members. A man who tells his wife, "I'll pick up some dinner from the chinks on Church Street" isn't trying to communicate anything about what Chinese people are like or what he thinks about them—what would that have to do with the point of the utterance? You may be able to infer something about what he thinks about the Chinese, or perhaps more likely, about what passes for common wisdom about the Chinese in his social circle. But none of that is part of the content of what he said, whether at-issue or not.

A second group of objections to these approaches is more purely mechanical, and involves the interaction of slurs with various operators (see among others Jeshion 2013b; DiFranco 2014; Sennet and Copp 2014; and Rappaport MS). The Hom-May thesis fails to explain why slurs are offensive even when their content is not asserted, as in conditionals such as, "If a chink applies for the job, tell him it's filled" or in negated sentences like, "There are no chinks in the class."[11] It leads to awkward conclusions about the truth-conditions of negated sentences. If *kike* has a null extension, then as Rappaport observes, the Nazi concentration camp commandant who tells a war crimes tribunal, "I never killed any kikes" can't be accused of perjury. And as Sennet and Copp note, this position entails that, "All kikes are Mormons" is necessarily true.

Moreover, this view leaves us wondering why one can't directly contest the description of someone as a chink or a kraut by denying the aptness of the stereotype that the word putatively conveys. Under normal circumstances, "Oskar isn't a kraut" can

---

[11] Hom and May argue that the offensiveness of sentences like this can be explained via a conversational implicature: in saying, "If a chink applies for the job ..." or, "There are no chinks in my class," the speaker implicates that there are Chinese who deserve to be the target of negative moral evaluation because of being Chinese, since to use a predicate is to imply that it has a non-null extension. That assumption is dubious; as Rappaport points out, it would entail that the parent who tells a child, "There are no monsters in the closet" believes in the existence of monsters. And even if the assumption were plausible, it would entail, implausibly, that the offensive effects of the sentences, "There are kikes in the building" and, "There are no kikes in the building" have different sources, one semantic and one pragmatic. (See Jeshion 2013b)

only mean that Oskar isn't German, not that he's not cruel.[12] Potts (2005) describes this phenomenon by saying that the content of such words is "scopeless"; I prefer to say that it simply isn't there. When we hear somebody described with a prejudicial, that is, we don't interpret the speaker as having predicated anything about either him or the class he belongs to over and above his membership in it.

Slurs as Conventional Implicatures

One way to avoid some of these consequences is to bury the stereotype associated with a derogative in a conventional implicature, as a number of people have proposed.[13] One can understand the motivation here. Conventional implicature is a mechanism designed to accommodate cases where a term has two dimensions to its meaning, so that its application can be right in one way and wrong in another: "Anna is wealthy but a Republican" might make a true statement about Anna's wealth and political allegiance yet also convey the dubious implication that there is something unexpected about the connection between the two. In that regard, there's an apparent parallel to "Jules is a redskin," if you take that sentence to assert truthfully that Jules is an American Indian but imply wrongly that he is savage or contemptible. This approach has other advantages. It seems to explain why such stereotypes are impervious to negation. The negative implications of using *boche* survive when one says "Oskar is

---

[12] I say "under normal circumstances" because a slur can sometimes acquire a transferred meaning in which it denotes only those members of the group who share the negative properties stereotypically assigned to the group—what Rappaport (Rappaport MS) calls the "stereotype essentializing" uses of the terms. That's what makes possible such utterances as "He's a gentile but not a goy," headlines such as "DC's PR Luminaries Explain Why 'I'm Not a Flack'," and Chris Rock's riff on the difference between blacks and niggers. In these cases, however, the word is no longer functioning as a slur for the group as a whole, but rather as a hybrid term for certain of its members, so that the stereotypical properties implied by its use as a slur become part of its lexical meaning. Thus one could say, "Oskar isn't one of those krauts— he's actually easygoing and kind," where *kraut* is functioning as a hybrid term for those Germans who are cruel or brutal. (Note that this essentialization is a general characteristic of the extended uses of words: the pragmatic connotations attached to *tiger* as the name of a feline become part of its semantics when it is used to denote a person who is fierce and determined.)

The failure to recognize this distinction has led to a lot of confusion. In defense of their theory that *Jew* and *kike* have distinct lexical meanings, Hom and May (2013) point to the nonequivalence of "Kikes are supposed to be Jews that are bad" and "Jews are supposed to be Jews that are bad." That example does indeed show that *kike* and *Jew* have different lexical meanings in this context, but if *kike* means "Jews that are bad," it denotes a subset of Jews, not the entire kind. *Kike* has the same hybrid meaning in a sentence like, "Jews are all kikes," which a more judicious anti-Semite might counter by saying, "No, some are generous and honest."

In actual usage, sentences asserting the identity of bare plurals, such as "Jews are kikes" or "The Chinese are chinks" are invariably used to make metalinguistic assertions, e.g.: γ "Japanese are nippers, Vietnamese are gooks, Filipinos are flips, Chinese are chinks or chinamen. Get your slurs straight." (In this paper I follow Horn (2013) in using "γ" to indicate a Googled example.) There is no evidence that anyone has ever used a sentence such as, "Jews are kikes" in the wild to assert the identity of two kinds, e.g., as in, "Cougars are pumas."

[13] Among those who have advocated or entertained this view are Boisvert (2008); Williamson (2009); Copp (2001); Hay (2011); McCready (2010); and Whiting (2013). Potts (2007, 2012) has developed an explicit framework for representing conventional implicatures of this type, but what is conveyed, on his view, is the expressive content of the term rather than a descriptive stereotype. (It should also be noted that Potts himself has less to say about slurs than others who have cited his work in this connection.)

not a boche," in the same way the contrary-to-expectations implication established by *but* is preserved when we say "It's not true that Mary is wealthy but a Republican."

I see two kinds of problems with this approach. One is conceptual: why would ethnic and racial stereotypes work their way into the semantics of these terms in just this form? What could it be about the word *boche* that makes it semantically more like *but* than like *German*—not just in having a different lexical meaning, but a different kind of meaning?[14] Are there other kinds of descriptions that have this feature? If not, why not—what do these quirks of meaning and use have to do with derogative words and the practices that surround them? That doesn't mean by itself that the view is wrong, but only that it's incomplete.

The other objections are mechanical, and apply to not just to CI accounts but to all representationalist accounts, whether the stereotype or descriptive import is made part of the at-issue content or a conventional implicature. Proponents of both of those approaches have observed that the stereotype associated with a slur need not necessarily apply to everyone in the target category. An individual might be exempted: "He's a chink, yeah, but he's terrible at math, he's a careful driver and his collars are always dirty." In advocating the CI view, Williamson (2009) suggests that *boche* implies only a tendency for Germans to be cruel: "A xenophobe may easily say 'He's a Boche, but he's not cruel—he's one of the few decent ones.'" (Camp (2013) and Tirrell (1999) make the same observation.) But on these analyses, it's not clear *why* this should be so. After all, the conventional implicature associated with *but* doesn't indicate that the relation signaled by "A but B" is *typically* contrary to expectations. What's more, even the generic condition is too restrictive; as Camp (2013) notes, many slurs appear to permit the denial of any negative feeling. Someone could say, "You know, these boches get a bum rap. They're actually a kind and clement people, if a bit impetuous and disorganized." Granted, that would be unexpected thing for someone who refers to Germans as boches to say. But the statement isn't semantically contradictory, the way it would be if the speaker said, "The boches come from Italy." We wouldn't say the speaker is misusing *boche* or is confused about its meaning. The most one can say, then, is that *boche* is typically used to convey that Germans are typically cruel. But that sounds a lot more like a cultural association than a lexical meaning. The fact is that the sentence "Oskar is a boche" doesn't say anything categorical about the properties of either Oskar in particular or Germans in general.

The second mechanical point that counts against the CI approach is connected to the previous one. Since words like *boche* and *chink* don't necessarily impute any specific properties to the group they refer to, such properties can be informatively

---

[14] Some have assumed that this is the sort of analysis required by Frege's examples of "coloring," in order to explain the difference between using *dog* and *cur* in, "The dog/cur howled all night." But as Picardi (2006) points out, there's no reason to suppose that *dog* and *cur* (or *Hund* and *Köter*) are in fact synonymous. One can deny that one's dog is a cur without denying that it is a dog, whereas one can't ordinarily deny that one's neighbor is a boche without also denying that he is German. By way of analogy, suppose my neighbor parks his new Mercedes in front of my driveway and I say to him, "Would you mind moving your jalopy so I can get my car out of the garage?" You wouldn't conclude that *jalopy* was a negatively colored synonym for *automobile*, rather than a name for a battered old car; I'm just indulging in a little neighborly meiosis. Richard makes this same point using the example of someone who refers to his horse as a nag in a jocular way (Richard 2008).

predicated of the terms. If cruelty were actually inherent in the linguistic meaning of *boche*, whether as content or a conversational implicature, then an assertion of "The boches are cruel" (or "inhuman" or "brutal," etc.) would strike us as conversationally tautological, but it doesn't.[15] And similarly for "Commies are devious"—or "godless," or "fanatical," or "ruthless," or whatever you take the stereotypically invidious traits of communists to be—which a militant anti-communist wouldn't find so redundant as to go without saying. Someone who speaks of free enterprise presumably holds that market capitalism is the fairest and most productive economic system, but we don't sense a tautology when someone asserts that claim outright. Some of those properties may be hovering in the background when you use a prejudicial, but they aren't part of the semantics of the word, which is why they can be explicitly reinforced, like other conversational implicatures. As Sadock (1978) notes: "Since conversational implicatures are not part of the conventional import of utterances, it should be possible to make them explicit without being guilty of redundancy." In this regard prejudicials contrast with the hybrid words with which they're often lumped, where the evaluation is genuinely part of the word's meaning and hence can't be nonredundantly predicated of it.[16] Utterances like "Toadies are obsequious," "Fleecing someone is unfair," and "Shrill sounds are unpleasant" are likely to elicit the reaction, "So what else is new?"[17]

These two features—the possibility of denying the putative stereotypes and the possibility of explicitly reinforcing them—provide a useful diagnostic for distinguishing slurs and other prejudicials from hybrid words that convey their evaluations semantically. That boundary is easy to lose sight of, particularly when it comes to pejorative terms. There are a number of pejorative hybrid words that are linked to categories like race, gender or ethnicity, such as *Uncle Tom* for a black person who behaves obsequiously toward whites, *slut*, JAP (*Jewish-American princess*) for a spoiled Jewish woman, and *wetback* for an illegal Mexican migrant. These words are often described as slurs, and they unquestionably draw on the same kinds of social attitudes that words like *coon*, *yid*, and *beaner* do.[18] But they can't convey a merely generic

---

[15] As Jeshion (2013a) crisply observes, "'Chinks should be subject to higher admissions standards' is not an analytic truth."

[16] One could say, of course, "You obsequious toady!" but the adjective serves only to intensify, not to inform or to restrict the reference of the noun.

[17] Many of the arguments I've offered here apply as well to accounts that treat the import of slurs as semantic presuppositions, such as by Schlenker (2007) and Cepollaro (2015). For example, if *commie* presupposed the deviousness of communists, then "Commies are devious" should sound redundant, in the same way that "John stopped beating his wife, and he has" does. People have mounted semantic arguments against this view, but I won't go into these here, since I'll be arguing that neither the stereotype nor the attitude associated with a slur can be identified with its conventional meaning in any form. But other arguments against the presuppositional view are less persuasive. Richard (2011) argues that slurs don't push their content into the conversational background, but rather function to insult the addressee. On the contrary, we'll see that insulting the addressee is not the main purpose of slurs, but only an occasional and relatively rare effect of their use. In fact pushing their implications into the conversational background is exactly what slurs are for, which is what makes them such effective instruments for socializing the members of a group into its communal values, though this isn't a matter of the semantic presuppositions of the words.

[18] People very often use *slur* to cover pejorative hybrid words like these, as well as for other terms that reduce people to their ethnicities or play on ethnic stereotypes—given names like Sambo, Ikey, and Hiawatha or expressions like *Indian giver* and *Chinaman's chance* and the verb *Jew down*. It makes perfect

reading: it would be odd to say, for example, "He's an Uncle Tom, but he's one of the proud and assertive ones," denying the stereotype that the word evokes, in the same way that it would be odd to say, "He's a toady, but not a fawning or deferential one," suggesting that servility is only a typical feature of toadies. And there's a sense of redundancy when one explicitly predicates of the term the evaluation or stereotypical content it semantically conveys, as in "JAPs are spoiled" or "Uncle Toms are servile." Note that most of the disparaging words for women that are loosely described as slurs also fall into this group: *bitch* and *slut* are hybrid pejorative words like *idiot* or *asshole*, not prejudicials like *commie* or *nigger*.[19]

The Priority of Attitude

One can understand the temptation to say that slurs semantically convey negative stereotypes of their targets. As Dummett (1993) says of the word *boche*, both German nationality and cruelty are "involved in the very meaning of the word; neither could be severed without altering its meaning." This is an intuitively plausible picture, which is very common in the psychological and sociological literature on slurs. The psychologist Leon Rappoport (2005) describes it thus:

Ethnic slurs serve as a kind of shorthand way of referring to the negative qualities associated with any particular group. They are quite specific. Hispanics might be called "spics" and Jews "kikes"; each term would stand for a specific cluster of traits assumed to be typical of Hispanics and Jews . . .

Stereotypes, negative and positive, are among the cognitive shortcuts we rely on to make sense of the world and to guide our responses to it. The utterance of a slur very often evokes or foregrounds a negative stereotype of its target, which is one reason why people use these words: "What do you expect from a ____?" Those stereotypes in turn can serve to legitimate various responses to the group, sometimes by dehumanizing

---

sense to extend *slur* in this way, so long as we bear in mind that the different types involve different semantic processes. (Allen (1983) uses "slurring nicknames" to distinguish the prototypical derogatives like *nigger*, a term that nicely emphasizes that they are pointed alternatives to other words.)

[19] One reason why it's easy to lose sight of the distinction between hybrid terms and prejudicials is that words sometimes migrate from one class to the other. *Bitch* has long been a hybrid pejorative for a woman with certain unpleasant characteristics, but in a part of hip hop culture it is also used as a dismissive term for women in general. When Abner says, "I went out with a lot of bitches," his utterance is ambiguous: he might mean either that he dated a lot of nasty or unpleasant women, or just that he dated a lot of women, with the implication that he doesn't hold women in high regard. In the first instance you can contest his utterance by rejecting either component; you can say either "That's not true; you've never been out on a date" or "No, your dates were always considerate and good-natured." But if he's using *bitch* simply as a derogative for women in general you can only make the first objection; you can't say "Well, it's true you went out with a lot of women but they were all very nice." The maliciousness that's evoked by the hybrid term *bitch* may still be resonating in the background when it's used as prejudicial (i.e. a slur, in the strict sense I'm using the word here). But it isn't part of what one asserts with the word. In the same way, when *bitch* is used as a prejudicial the speaker doesn't necessarily convey a negative attitude about the particular person it refers to, any more than "My neighbor is a chink" does. The derogation may fall only on the category to which the referent belongs. In the hip hop sense of the word, there's no contradiction in saying "That bitch is kind and sweet" though that utterance sounds contradictory if *bitch* is being used as a routine hybrid pejorative. I'll have more to say about below about why this sort of change hasn't happened in Standard English.

or marginalizing its members, and other times merely allowing us to discount them (when we call a publicist a flack it's by way of questioning her journalistic integrity, not her basic humanity).

But as I've shown, those stereotypes can't themselves be part of the conventional semantic content of the term. *Redskin* and (*American*) *Indian* both contain only as much semantic information as is required to pick out their common referent. And however the stereotype is evoked, the relation between slur and stereotype is not as straightforward as Rappoport's remarks suggest. It's misleading to say that "each term [stands] for a specific cluster of traits assumed to be typical" of the targeted group. For one thing, it isn't easy to identify the "negative qualities" from among the various traits that are stereotypically associated with the group. Racial and ethnic stereotypes are rarely categorically negative—they're typically compounded of contrasting or inconsistent traits. As the sociologist Ali Rattansi (2007) observes:

Stereotypes . . . reveal contradiction and ambivalence rather than completely invariable hostility or admiration toward other groups . . . Attitudes toward Asians in Europe and the US, for instance, reveal admiration for supposed community unity, thrift, ambition, hard work, respect for education, and "family values," but also hostility for insularity, suspicion regarding their loyalties to the Western nation-states in which they have come to live, and a sense of superiority toward their more "backward" cultures . . .

The antithetical features of these stereotypes aren't independent of one other. The positive traits are usually the more genial manifestations of the conflicted racial attitudes that also shape the negative ones. But *chink* doesn't convey any ambivalence about the Chinese; as Jeshion (2013b) notes, the word is "unequivocally and exclusively contemptuous." One might argue that the slur semantically selects only the negative features of the stereotype. But just about any feature of a stereotype can be seen as positive or negative on a given occasion. On Monday it's "You have to give it to the chinks; they work hard"; on Tuesday it's "No wonder those damn chinks all get As— they don't do anything but study until two in the morning." The same traits that suggest the clannishness of Jews can be cited to testify to their strong sense of family. Whatever ethnic traits a given utterance of the word *chink* or *kike* brings to mind, if any, are usually just those that can be interpreted as contextually consistent with an antecedent attitude of condescension or contempt—though as we saw, one can convey disparagement even while asserting the virtues of the target group. The speaker who says, "Whatever you may have heard, the krauts are really a kind and clement people" isn't repudiating the attitude that's implicit in the slur, just contesting the stereotype that other people invoke to justify it.[20]

---

[20] Blackburn (1992) misses this point when he writes that while *kraut* is a term of abuse used by some Englishmen for Germans,

> . . . it is very easy to think of contexts in which it is not that: faced with some marvel of engineering in my new BMW you might shake your head in wonder: 'typical of the krauts to think of that' you say in awe, and all the term does is emphasize a sense of difference, that in turn reinforces the admiration. A few such cases, and the derogatoriness starts to slide into history, while the appreciation of the difference as a positive thing may come to be the default.

The attitude comes first. To suggest that invidious stereotypes are the source of bigotry is credit the bigot with a weirdly misplaced rationality, as if his antipathies were sound logical conclusions drawn from what happen to be false premises. But racism, anti-Semitism, homophobia, and xenophobia are generally rooted in the basic fact of alterity rather than the stereotypes that people cite to justify or rationalize the attitude—of contempt, loathing, fear, or condescension, as the case may be.

That's how it is that stereotypes can vary from one person to another or change over time without dramatically shifting the significance of a slur. At one time or another *kike* has conjured up images of Jews as Christ-killers, as money-grubbing trades-men, as clannish and superior, as conspiratorial international bankers, as depraved deviants, as wild-eyed radicals, as Stalin's "rootless cosmopolitans," as Zionist oppres-sors, and even, in the 1930s, as possessing a duplicitous genius for basketball (a game which "appeals to the Hebrew with his Oriental background," Paul Gallico wrote in 1938, because it "places a premium on an alert scheming mind, flashy trickiness, artful dodging and general smart-aleckness" (Sclar 2008)). But it isn't as if the word has had seven or nine different meanings over the years, or as if there's any semantic misunderstanding between the speaker who denounces kikes with Emma Goldman in mind and the listener who agrees with him while thinking of Goldman Sachs. The animus transcends the specific pretexts we give for it.[21]

True, certain derogatives tend to bring specific stereotypes to mind. Sometimes the stereotype is suggested by the name itself, particularly when it's transparently derived from a description—*fairy* for homosexuals, *beaner* for Mexicans. Or sometimes the stereotype is shaped by the particular historical context in which the term emerged. The connection of *boche* to cruelty, for those who still retain any feel for the word, reflects its origin in the slang of World War I Tommies, who got it from the French *poilus*. The terms that soldiers apply to the enemy naturally evoke his savagery and inhumanity, rather, say, than his bombastic music or turgid scholarship; that's the theme historically evoked by soldier slang like *Hun*, *jerry*, *Jap*, and *gook*. Even then, though, the point of the stereotype is to legitimate a certain attitude: as used by a Tommy, *boche* didn't imply simply that the Germans were cruel, but that their cruelty made them so contemptible as to deserve killing.

What Slurs Are For

The general concern with the injuriousness of slurs had led writers to focus almost exclusively on the effects they can have on their targets, whether by legitimating their

---

But the speaker's admiration for German engineering doesn't suspend the disparagement that is still implicit in *kraut*, though it's no longer colored by fierce belligerence. Compare the adjective *Gallic*, which is airily condescending even when it's being used to praise the French for their charm, their flair or their savoir-faire.

[21]   As Jeshion (2013b) puts this point:

There are many reasons why bigots take their attitudes to be warranted. . . . The roots of rationales for anti-Semitism are notoriously multi-faceted but, to be sure, some people hate and hold contempt for Jews, and regard it as warranted, because they are not Christian or because members of more religious branches are insular, and look, act, and dress different.

Hornsby (2001) makes a related point when she notes that "if speakers' involvement with the ideology went as deep as it would need to in order to be implicit in their very use of words, then common understandings would be difficult to preserve."

exclusion or brutalization or by inducing feelings of helplessness or rage. That's what's implied when slurs are described as "terms of abuse" and what Jeshion is getting at when she typologizes the uses of slurs as "weapon" and "non-weapon," uses, the former derogative uses and the latter reclaimed uses by the groups the words target.[22] As she puts it, it is a fundamental property of slurs that they "function to derogate or dehumanize, by which I mean, that they function to signal that their targets are unworthy of equal standing or full respect as persons, that they are inferior as persons." Jeshion (2013a), Bolinger (2017), Richard (2008), and Croom (2013) are among others who focus primarily on the use of slurs to offend a targeted addressee. But while it's reasonable to distinguish reclaimed and non-reclaimed uses of slurs, it's misleading to characterize all of the latter in terms of their use as "weapons" or for that matter to say that they're in their nature tools for insulting or offending others. Those are unquestionably among the most troubling effects of the uses of certain slurs, and I'll return to them at the end of this paper. But the focus on the offensiveness of slurs tends to obscure what is usually their primary *raison d'être*.

We should bear in mind that vast majority of the uses of these words occur among the members of the group they belong to, out of earshot of any of the people they target.[23] Indeed, a community may have a slur for a group of people that its members have no expectation of ever encountering. It's safe to assume that there are a lot of languages with slurs for Jews which no Jew has ever heard or is likely to hear, and most of the people who use *redskin* have never to their knowledge met a Native American face-to-face. And to the primary users of a slur—which is to say, those who "own" the word—it's often a matter of indifference how it would actually land in the ear of its target. The person who uses *commie* to refer to communists or loosely to leftists doesn't care whether actual leftists are going to be offended by it. These days, in fact, leftists are more likely to be amused or flattered by the label—there's a brisk trade on the web in t-shirts saying, "You say 'commie' like it's a bad thing." (One might point to an obvious exception here in the frequent use of pejoratives for women in direct address with the intent to offend or injure, but these words don't function like prejudicials either semantically or socially, as we'll see below.)

If we want to know what a slur is *for*, we'll need to ask first what it conveys about the members of the group that it belongs to—its speakers, rather than those that it targets. Those people may use a slur in direct address to put someone it targets in their place, it's true, but the words are far more often used for other reasons: to create solidarity in a common sense of resentment or superiority; to enjoy the complicit schoolyard-variety naughtiness in using forbidden words, particularly in the form of racial or homophobic humor; or to underscore the normative values of the group. Those implications usually arise via the suggestion that the members of the targeted group are unworthy of respect, of course, though the targets may also fill a symbolic role that's largely removed from their actual social presence. Adolescent boys who

---

[22] Jeshion's distinction is echoed by Camp (2013) and Popa (2016), among others.
[23] In a case study of discourse about race among employees at a large Southwestern baked good company, Embrick and Henricks (2013) note that whites almost never used *nigger* in racially mixed company, confining it to casual conversation with other whites in what Picca and Feagin (2007) call backstage settings.

throw the word *fag* around loosely aren't focused on disparaging homosexual men as such so much as communing with each other over their own macho heterosexuality.[24] Or sometimes, as Jane Hill notes, the use of the words signal a "a tough, hyper-masculine register of American English, where [slurs] are emblematic of straight talk and the right to unconstrained and 'irreverent' expression" (Hill 2009; see also Eliasoph 1999).

The point is easiest to see when we focus on slurs that belong to a non-hegemonic subgroup, such the Hawaiian *haole*, black *honky*, Hispanic *gringo*, or *shiksa* as used by American (or Anglophone) Jews. No one would say that the import of *shiksa* was exhausted by saying that it denotes a non-Jewish woman and enumerating the properties that such women are held to possess. One can't understand the import of the word without understanding something about how Jews see themselves in relation to gentile culture: to its owners, the word says as much about "us" as it does about "them," and a gentile who uses it will be taken as consciously affiliating him- or herself with a Jewish point of view or identity. But while the use of slurs to mark group identity is obvious enough when the words belong to groups defined in opposition to hegemonic culture, it's harder to discern when the slur belongs to the hegemonic culture itself. No one would try to describe the import of *honky* without referencing black identity. But when people describe the import of *nigger*, they almost always limit themselves to what it conveys about the speaker's beliefs or feelings about its target, not about himself. *Nigger* is treated as *the* paramount slur for blacks, rather than as whites' (or nonblacks') paramount slur for blacks. Reading through the philosophical and linguistic literature on slurs, you rarely encounter any mention of whiteness or of the other hegemonic categories in terms of which alterities are defined (a notable exception is Hill (2009)). That isn't surprising—whiteness is in its nature invisible, unmarked; as Richard Dyer (1997) has written, whiteness is the "framing position." But as the sociologists Joe Feagin, Hernan Vera, and Pinar Batur (2000) have observed, "racialized attitudes and actions require not only a representation of the stereotyped other but also a representation of oneself." The very existence of a stereotype for an out-group entails the existence of a corresponding ideal of identity among the people who own it. When you stereotype the members of a group as indolent or greedy, you evoke conceptions of your own group as industrious or generous, each in a rather specific way.

Multiple Slurs for a Single Target

The significance of the self-affiliating or self-identifying functions of slurs can be easily lost sight of when it comes to arch-slurs such as *nigger*, which seems to be defined simply in terms of a white (or non-black) identity. But specific subgroups and subcultures of whites (or straights or Christians) can also use other slurs to carve out and reinforce narrower social allegiances and more specific identities, which in turn

---

[24] Croom (2013) cites a monologue by the comedian Louis C.K.:

> faggot didn't mean gay when I was a kid, you called someone a faggot for being a faggot, you know? . . . I would never call a gay guy a faggot, unless he was being a faggot. But not because he's gay, you understand.

leads to the existence of multiple slurs for the same target group. That phenomenon has been almost entirely unexplored. Writers sometimes talk about what Hom calls "derogative variation," but by that they mean that slurs for different groups vary in intensity according to the extent of the discrimination and enmity that the group has faced (see Hornsby (2001); Tirrell (1999); Hom (2008)). This is generally true as far as it goes—in American English, slurs for blacks or Hispanics are going to be stronger than those for Englishmen or white Protestants. But that principle doesn't explain the differences in tone, affect and intensity among the various disparagements for the same group, such as *nigger, coon, spade, jigaboo, spook*, and *jungle bunny* for blacks and *fag(got), queer, pansy, poof, fairy, fruit*, and *homo* for gays.[25] These words may or may not evoke different stereotypes of their targets. Someone who simply wants to impute laziness to blacks or tightfistedness to Jews can choose pretty much any slur for the group—on the web, *kike, jewboy*, and *yid* have almost exactly the same probability of being modified by *greedy*.

But different subgroups may evaluate the very same stereotypes in different ways, each implying a distinct sense of group identity. *Spade*, for example, was the term of choice for blacks among by mid-twentieth-century bopsters and hipsters and later among the hippies (it originated as underworld slang a bit earlier). In a flier by that was circulated in San Francisco's Haight in 1967, the Beat writer and editor Chester Anderson said: "The spades . . . are our spiritual fathers . . . . They gave us jazz & grass & rock & roll . . . if it weren't for the spades we would all have short hair, neat suits, glazed eyes, steady jobs, and gastric ulcers" (Peck 1985). Like other prejudicials for blacks, *spade* evoked the familiar stereotypes of indolence, insouciance, and drug-use, but in a tone of sentimentalized admiration rather than out-and-out contempt, an expression of the hipster self-image that Norman Mailer described in the title of his famous essay "The White Negro," which celebrated the attachment to jazz, mari-juana, and "cool."

Within a broad hegemonic culture, multiple slurs for a single group are often distinguished by the specific social identity that they encode. That's one reason why there's so much turnover in the slurs for a particular group (think of the passé *nance, nellie*, and *pansy* for homosexuals or *ikey, mockie* and *sheenie* for Jews). Like slang, slurs are usually coined by younger speakers to differentiate themselves linguistically from the attitudes of their elders, for which purposes a new proprietary word for blacks or gays can be as useful as one for sex or beer.[26] And it's why slurs often

[25] Langton, Anderson, and Haslanger are among those who mention multiple slurs in passing, but only to remark that "there can be variation among slurs for the same group; 'nigger' is more offensive than 'darkie' or 'coon,' " as if the difference in offensiveness exhausted the distinctions among the words. (Langton, Anderson, and Haslanger 2013).

[26] As Allen (1983) notes modern slurs are usually slang words. Slang is a category that's notoriously hard to pin down, but standard slang dictionaries such as Jonathan E. Lighter's *Historical Dictionary of American Slang* and Jonathon Green's *Dictionary of Slang* list most common slurs, and the words seem to satisfy Otto Jespersen's definition of slang as "something that is willfully substituted for the first word that will present itself" (Jespersen 1922). Still, some slurs, such as *jungle bunny*, are clearly slangier than others, such as *nigger*. Indeed, it's reasonable to assume that *jungle bunny* is more often a substitution for *nigger* than for a nonslurring term like *Negro* or *black*. The slanginess of slurs (as of other words) reflects, among other things, the degree to which they are associated with a specific local subcommunity.

Wescott (1971) observes that labio-velar (i.e., noncoronal) obstruents are overwhelmingly predominant in the onsets and codas of derogative words (cf. *nigger, spook, dago, chink, mick, spic, redneck, gook*,

manifest what Irving Allen calls a "low comedy" that enhances their usefulness as tokens of common sensibility—*jungle bunny* and *spearchucker* for blacks, *mackerel-snapper* for Catholics, greaseball for Italians, Buddhahead for (Hawaiian) Japanese, Jew canoe for a Cadillac, and so forth (on the uses of ethnic humor, see Howitt and Kwame Owusu-Bempah (2005) and Rappoport (2005)). It's a reminder that the main reason why people coin slurs is to provide pleasure and gratification for their friends rather than to visit humiliation upon their targets.

In fact a great proportion of the active slurs in modern society are relatively short-lived and mutable, along with the social identities they index. They tend to be replaced as the perceptions of their targets change, entailing a change in the group self-conception defined in opposition to the target. *Chink*, for example, has been increasingly set aside as the crude "no tickee no washee" anti-Chinese racism that was dominant in earlier periods yielded to the more decorous anti-Asian racial aversions of modern academic and corporate life. (*Chink* is still heard, but it is far less common in books and newspapers than it was in the 1920s.)[27] More recent terms such as *ching-chong* and the pan-Asian *slant* are more expressive of resentment of Asian overachievers and the anxiety they induce than the virulent racialist Orientalism of earlier eras. Even those few words that have persisted as active slurs since the nineteenth century have changed their import from period to period as speakers reinterpret the words' histories: the modern use of *nigger* reflects a modern conception of whiteness (or really several such conceptions), though as filtered through a historical lens.[28]

The Nonconventionality of Affect

A full description of the import of any of these words belongs to folklore or ethnography, not to semantics or pragmatics. Thirty years ago, Irving Allen deplored the sociological neglect of the folkloric aspects of this vocabulary:

This vocabulary is too often read only as malice and too seldom as folklore with all the inventiveness, ideological utility, and inadvertent confession of other folklores. I hear in these words more than the din of Billingsgate. They are the echoes and re-echoes of historical situations, of issues wrangled over, and of the very incidents of contention.   (Allen 1983)

It's clear that one can't decontextualize the import of a word such as *spade*, or for that matter *nigger*, and reduce it to some descriptive content that can be incorporated in the conventional meaning of the term, in whatever form. But what of the affect that

---

cracker, kraut, kike, coon, dink, redskin, greaser, Ikey, honky with velars; also wop, hebe, Jap, flip, beaner with labials and polack, frog, jig-a-boo, wog, peckerwood, fag with both). He argues, more speculatively, that this tendency is evident in pejorative and vulgar words in general (cf. punk, prick, crook, boob, creep, etc.) and that it is cross-linguistically associated with derogation and aggression

[27] For more on the complex history of this word, see Mieder (1996); Roy (2011); and Wu (1972). Saka (2007) notes in passing that *chinaman* is less offensive than *chink*, a difference he lays to the circumstances that have sustained the existence of the each term.

[28] Most of the still-potent slurs of modern American life (such as *kike*, *spic*, *wop*, *faggot*, and *chink*) were twentieth-century inventions. The nineteenth-century slurs that are still remembered and occasionally heard, such as *mick*, *kraut*, and *frog*, generally denote groups toward whom there is now so little real antipathy that there's no incentive to coin new derogatives for them. *Nigger* and *white trash* are the important exceptions (*redskin* has been a slur since the nineteenth century but is a special case).

the word signals? Could we say, for example, that *spade* is a word denoting blacks that conveys either the speaker's contempt for them or his belief that they warrant it? There are different ways to formulate this approach, which I'll come back to later. But they all come down to claiming that we can associate the use of the word with a particular affect, and for now I'll describe these positions, loosely, as "affectivist."[29]

One problem here is that many of the same arguments that make a semantic treatment problematic for the descriptive view create problems for affectivist views, as well. Like the stereotypes that the use of a slur can evoke, the affect it conveys can be explicitly reinforced without creating a sense of tautology, which would be puzzling if it were inherent in the term's conventional meaning. An utterance like "Wops are despicable" strikes us as potentially informative, and when someone says, "Ugh, commies—I despise them" we aren't tempted to respond, "Well, duh! Why else would you call them commies?"

But the problems go deeper than that. The feeling-tones that these words convey— the affect they express toward their targets and the sense of common identity that they reinforce—are generally much too nuanced and socially embedded to be rendered in meaning-schemas like "contemptible because Italian" or "Jewish and I despise them for it," which reflect the simplistic picture of the words' effect that's implicit in the term *slur* itself. Could we then get away with saying that *chink* in the mouth of a white Los Angeles policeman in the 1920s expresses the same affect toward the Chinese as *ching-chong* in the mouth of a white female USC student in 2015? Perhaps the conventions for using these words don't have to mention all their social implications; perhaps the conventional meanings provide only summary evaluations like "despicable" or "used to express contempt," or maybe just a bald "negative," while the more nuanced social attitudes are part of what the words pragmatically convey.[30] In this way, the lexical entries for these words might look something like the entries provided by standard dictionaries, which are simply tagged with metadata labels such as "derog." for the benefit of users who are unfamiliar with the term. This is basically the same idea that writers seem to be getting at when they say that the meanings of slurs are equivalent to the meanings of their "neutral" counterparts as modified by *fucking*, or as accompanied by a raised middle finger or a sneering tone of voice, all of which imply that at its core, all derogation is the result of a single operator.

These claims are more speculative than empirical, even as they regard arch-slurs like *nigger*, and in any case they don't generalize. The affect conveyed by a slur can't

[29] I'll reserve "expressivist" for the view that the utterer of a slur expresses contempt for its target, perhaps together with a second identifying component (the "hybrid expressivism" of Jeshion) and follow Bach (2014) in using "loaded descriptivism" to describe the position that a slur for N's means something like "N and therefore despicable." What these views have in common is the idea that a slur is conventionally associated with a particular affect, which is the claim I'm taking up in this section. For varieties of these views, see e.g. McCready (2010), Saka (2007), Blackburn (1984), Richard (2008), and Jeshion (2013b) among others. I'll have more to say about some of these proposals below, when I can contrast them with my own approach.

[30] For example, Bach suggests that "the negative attitude [conventionally associated with the term] should be unspecific enough to be compatible with the property of being any of the following (insofar as these are all distinct from one another): abominable, despicable, detestable, disgusting, inferior, loathsome, offensive, repugnant, subhuman, or vile" and uses "contemptible" only as a stand-in for the terms in that range.

always be reduced even to minimal polarities like "negative" and "positive." There are often discrepancies between the evaluation of the referent that users of the word believe they're conveying and the evaluation perceived by the word's targets. What polarity would we assign to the attitude expressed by the hipsters and hippies of the 1950s and 1960s who described blacks as spades, for example? The word certainly wasn't intended contemptuously—Ken Kesey was no doubt speaking for most of his fellow beats and hippies when he described it as a "term of endearment." (As the cultural historian John Beckman notes, "It was hip for hippies to *appreciate* 'spades' " (Beckman 2014).) If one were going to incorporate that attitude into the convention for using the word, accordingly, one might frame it as something like, "Use *spade* to convey a warm and positive evaluation of blacks." But many blacks regarded the word as condescending and obtuse; as one black critic paraphrased it, "those fay cats . . . don't want us to be Uncle Toms, but they still want us to be spooks. They don't really dig us as a people; they just dig us for our music and our pot" (Forman 1998).

Most of us would agree now with those critics—contemporary dictionaries all label this use of *spade* as offensive or disparaging. But how would we translate what the word's critics were saying into a statement about of the content of the convention for using it? They weren't charging that the hipsters had gotten their own convention wrong or were using the word inappropriately—that whatever the speakers who used the word might think, the relevant convention really prescribed using *spade* to unwittingly condescend to blacks. (How could a convention prescribe unwitting behavior?) But they also weren't claiming that the hipsters were conveying honest respect when they used the word, as they believed they were. Yet there's no uncertainty about what was actually going on here; the confusion comes of trying to work the evaluation into an account via linguistic convention. The hipsters used *spade* to articulate a construction of urban blackness that was central to their own self-conception as outsiders. The disagreement is over whether that construction of blackness was accurate or reductive. But nobody was actually in doubt about what the word conveyed.

Spade isn't as current as it once was, but this sort of situation isn't that unusual. Most Americans are familiar with the very public campaign to persuade the Washington Redskins football team to change what many regard as an offensive name. The team's owners and many of its supporters maintain that the term is meant as a tribute to the toughness, bravery, and perseverance that are part of the "the proud legacy and traditions of Native Americans," as the team's president puts it. Opponents of the name reply that fight songs that begin with an apostrophe to "braves on the warpath," accompanied by marching bands in war bonnets and cheerleaders in Indian regalia, are no less dehumanizing and demeaning than the evocations of more derisive or hostile stereotypes. That's the evaluation of the word provided by standard dictionaries, which label it as derogatory or offensive, as well as by the US federal courts.[31]

---

[31] In June of 2014, Trademark Trial and Appeals Board of the US Patent and Trademark Office canceled the team's mark on the grounds that trademark law doesn't permit the registration of marks that "may disparage persons or bring them into contempt or disrepute," noting that the word was offensive to a "substantial composite" of American Indians. In August of 2015, the TTAB's decision was upheld by a US

But here again, we get ourselves into a muddle if we try to frame the dispute in terms of the content of the linguistic convention for using the word. Are the team's defenders mistaken about the word's meaning when they use the term in what they, along with what polls say is a majority of Americans, take to be a positive and respectful way? (This is not an atypical view, like that of the speaker who uses *spic* or *kraut* without holding any personal animus toward its targets.) Or are they are conforming to a convention that prescribes using the word respectfully, and in that case why shouldn't dictionaries and the TTAB acknowledge the fact? Does *redskin* become a slur only when a substantial proportion of those who use it come to realize that it expresses contempt or disrespect for present-day Native Americans? That's one of the arguments the team offers in its defense, claiming that the word was not disparaging when the team was first named in 1933 since no one considered it such. And in fact it would seem as if an affectivist might have to go along with that view, and claim that a word can't be derogative if none of its users find it so; at the most, it could be expressive of an attitude that others consider contemptuous.

Yet, again, the facts are not in dispute. The attitude that the team's defenders regard as respectful is a reading of the attitudes that *redskin* expresses in the word's historical provenance, as largely embodied, in this case, in the mythologized discourse of Western literature and movie and TV Westerns. According to the conservative columnist Pat Buchanan, defending the team's use of the name, that discourse demonstrates that "these were people who stood, fought and died and did not whimper" (Buchanan 2013).[32] Others watch the same movies that Buchanan did and conclude that conception of Native Americans that the word expressed in those sources was condescending and racist. But again, this isn't an argument about the meaning of the word; neither side has an interest in claiming that *redskin* is ambiguous.

These cases may seem exceptional, but such discrepancies between intention and reception are quite common. Think of various usages of *lady*, *gal*, and *girl* (as in "I'll have my gal set up a meeting") or of démodé terms like *colored*, *half-breed*, *mulatto*, *Oriental*, and in certain regions, *Spanish* for Latinos, all of them considered neutral or respectful by the diminishing number of speakers who still use them and disrespectful or clueless by many of the rest of us. Or think of the various terms associated with physical and mental disabilities. Does an older speaker who refers to someone as "a poor cripple" manifest his contempt for her? Not by his own lights, certainly; he means it as an expression of genuine compassion and solicitude. It's others who see the usage as troubling in the light of contemporary attitudes about disability; they hear *cripple*

District Court, and subsequently by a Court of Appeals. I served as the linguistic expert on behalf of the Native Americans who petitioned the USPTO to cancel the mark. On June 19, 2017 the Supreme Court ruled that the law's prohibition of the registration of disparaging marks was an unconstitutional restriction on free speech, so that the team could continue to use the mark, whatever its connotations. See Shapira and Marimow (2017).

[32] A curious feature of *redskin* is that the stereotypes it brings to mind are associated with the prototypical Plains Indian or Southwest Indian of the late nineteenth century, though the group actually denoted by the term is not historically circumscribed in the way, say, that *Viking* refers just to ninth-through eleventh-century Scandinavians and not to their modern descendants. That is, *redskin* imputes historical stereotypes of bloodthirstiness and savagery to contemporary Indians as well. But its users are not frequently aware of that implication, which is what leads them to deny the word is a slur.

as conveying not just excessive pity, but suppressed revulsion—and as having always conveyed those things, even when all its users thought it was polite. Even when terms are unequivocally negative, as with many prototypical slurs, there are considerable ranges of affective variation that would have to be filled in by pragmatic inferences. But if such inferences are capable of sorting out the nuanced distinctions among *spade*, *coon*, and *nigger*, why would they be unable to tell us that the words are all negative, so that a convention becomes necessary to do the work? If you're steeped in the period and know that *spade* was the word the hipsters used for blacks, what more would you need to figure out what affect it conveyed? What could a convention contribute that you didn't know already?

Like all popular language, slurs arise from the ground up and reflect the textures of the immediate experience of a group—Allen's "historical situations . . . issues wrangled over, and . . . the very incidents of contention." Those are the contexts and encounters that invest each slur with its singular color and attitude and that generate the inevitable misunderstandings that can make the words land differently for the speaker and hearer. There's no grounds for assuming that we could reduce all of these attitudes to a uniform affective element that figures in the meaning of each of these words. Even if we could, it wouldn't advance our understanding of how they work. What we want to understand, rather, is how people use the words to express the particular identities and attitudes that they evoke. That turns out to be part of a larger story that takes the phenomenon in a different direction.

A Note on "Perspectives"

A good deal of what I've argued here is consistent with Camp's suggestion (Camp 2013) that slurs signal "allegiance to a perspective: an integrated, intuitive way of cognizing members of the targeted group." In her sense of the term, a perspective doesn't necessarily commit one to certain characterizations of the target; rather it's a "disposition to structure one's thoughts" about them in certain ways. It need not entail either acceptance of particular propositions about the referents. Nor does it require a certain affective response to them, such as contempt, though that will often follow from a more amorphous derogating attitude that the perspective implies. This view isn't susceptible to many of the critiques I've offered here of views that identify the import of a slur with either a stereotype or the expression of a certain affect. It seems to accommodate cases where the users of slurs don't see themselves as expressing contempt for the targeted group, such as in the examples of *redskin* and *spade* that I mentioned, and perhaps the impression that the import of slurs is ineffable and unparaphrasable.

There are several points of departure between this view and mine. First, Camp argues that the association of a slur and a perspective has to be part of the word's conventional meaning, in virtue of the defeasibility of the words' import. We'll see below that this doesn't follow—implicatures arising from floutings of the maxim of manner are typically nondefeasible—but by itself it doesn't undermine the thesis that the import of a slur is the perspective it signals. Second, "perspective" seems a rather vague notion when it comes to teasing apart the specific colorings of the slurs for a particular group. Whatever distinguishes *redskin* from *injun* or *nigger* from *coon*, it's more precise and richer than simply a disposition to think about the referents in certain ways. And if we want to get at the perspective implicit in the use of *redskin*, we'll need to talk not just about dispositions to think in certain ways about race, but of mode of reading a certain tradition of American historical representations and their significance in national life. What many slurs really bring to mind is neither a stereotype nor an affect but a set of narratives. Not that "perspective" is the wrong notion to use here, but it needs to be situated and filled in to be of real explanatory use.

The third point of difference is related to the second: to speak of signaling an allegiance to a perspective seems to make the latter a full-fledged citizen of cultural life, something that's independently abroad in society. That may not be a misleading way to think of things like political orientations, which Camp cites as a paradigmatic instance of a perspective: when we signal an allegiance to liberalism, say, we're not necessarily allying ourselves with some particular group of liberals. But as we've seen, most slurs signal the speaker's self-affiliation with a particular group or community. To take an obvious case, when you call a woman a shiksa you're not just allying yourself with a disposition to think about gentile women in certain ways, but with the people who have that disposition. That group affiliation is primary and prior to the perspective it evokes: you can use *shiksa* appropriately without having any specific views of gentile women at all, but not without identifying with Jews.[33] I'll be arguing below that self-affiliation is central both to the sense of complicity slurs can occasion in their nontargeted listeners and the explosive impact they can have on their targets.

Slurs as Conversational Implicatures

The Counterpart Condition

Having argued at some length that the import of slurs—what they convey about the speaker and the referent—couldn't be part of their conventional linguistic meanings, I want to offer a positive account of how import arises as a pragmatic inference. In a way, that assumption has always been implicit in most semanticist approaches to slurs. On these views, slurs acquire their derogatory powers from their conventional meanings. Yet when it comes to defining or characterizing slurs, many writers feel the need to add an additional clause that implicitly suggests a role for conversational inferences. Take Richard's (2008) definition of slurs. He first reprises the semanticist hypothesis:

A word is a slur when it is a conventional means to express strong negative attitudes towards members of a group, attitudes in some sense grounded in nothing more than membership in the group.

But Richard adds another stipulation:

Every slur so far as I can tell, has or could have a "neutral counterpart" which co-classifies but is free of the slur's evaluative dimension.

---

[33] Camp does note at one point that the use of a slur signals an in-group allegiance but doesn't otherwise explore the connection between perspectives and the groups that hold them.

This "counterpart" condition is cited by a number of philosophers who otherwise offer varying accounts of the semantics of slurs, some making it a part of the definition of a slur and others a characteristic feature; see e.g. Bach (2014), Bianchi (2014), Camp (2013), Croom (2013), DiFranco (2014), Hedger (2012), Hom (2008), Hornsby (2001), Jeshion (2013b), Whiting (2013) and Williamson (2009), among others.[34]

On consideration, the conjunction of the two prongs of the standard characterization of slurs raises some puzzles for semanticist accounts. The idea, to put it more generally, is that the effect of slurs depends upon the existence of a coreferential word that doesn't convey the same evaluation of its referent—a word, not just a coreferential descriptive phrase.[35] (The condition that its counterpart be "neutral" is a separate criterion, which isn't justified either, as we will see.) That is, *boche* can convey what it does about Germans because there is another word, *German*, that doesn't. But then what if *German* should suddenly disappear from the language—such things have been known to occur, often for extraneous phonetic reasons—so that speakers who want to refer to Germans can do only by improvising descriptive phrases like "Schiller's compatriots" or "the inhabitants of the nation that keeps France from bumping into Poland"? Would the meaning of *boche* then change so it ceased to be a slur? It's hard to see how such a thing could happen; it seems to call for a kind of semantic action at a distance.

This poses a difficulty for defenders of semantic accounts of slurs. To introduce the counterpart condition is to implicitly acknowledge that the effect of a slur depends at least in part upon the recognition that the speaker has pointedly chosen to refer to something with one word rather than with another. That suggests that some sort of conversational implicature is a work, particularly since the condition seems to accord with the well-documented generalization that marked or periphrastic expressions induce conversational implicatures only when they contrast with a lexicalized synonym. As McCawley (1978) observed, for example, the periphrastic causative "cause X to die" is usually interpreted as implying indirect cause, whereas "cause X to laugh" is not. Yet why should we need to appeal to an implicature, if the slur is already doing the work of disparagement all by itself? And indeed, how could the disparagement not be part of the meaning of the word; how else would we know that *boche* is disparaging rather than a flattering term?

One could argue that there is no genuine inconsistency here, that the fact that speaker has pointedly chosen to use the slur S rather than the alternative term A initiates an implicature that reinforces the derogative force of S or the speaker's commitment to it. As Camp puts it:

---

[34] Interestingly, the counterpart condition isn't usually mentioned by those linguists who have dealt with slurs from a semantic point of view, such as Potts (2007), McCready (2010), and Gutzmann (2013). That may be because "having a neutral synonym" doesn't seem to be a natural lexical feature; there's no slot in a formal semantic description for a stipulation on the order of "w denotes A and conveys that the speaker feels X about A, on condition that the language contains another word w' that denotes A and does not convey that the speaker has any particular feeling about A."

[35] I will assume here Arnold Zwicky's (2006) definition of a word as "an ordinary-language fixed expression of some currency," by which standard the category includes noncompositional collocations such as *Jewish American princess* and *Uncle Tom*.

... a slur's very optionality is part of what makes it so expressively powerful—slurs are arguably constituted as slurs in part through their contrast with (comparatively) neutral counterparts. That is, a [group]-referring expression S becomes increasingly perspectively marked to the extent that a co-referring expression becomes increasingly salient as an alternative.

(Camp 2013)

Croom makes a similar argument in suggesting that a speaker chooses to use a slur rather than a neutral term such as African American "in order to most aptly communicate to others, through their lexical choice, the corresponding attitude that they are intending to express towards their target." And on Bolinger's Contrastive Choice Account (Bolinger 2017), in choosing to address someone with a word associated with a negative attitude toward its referent rather than one with no such associations, the speaker "signals that he endorses or holds ... an attitude of disrespect" toward the addressee and thereby allows the hearer to feel warranted offense.[36]

These discussions assume that a slur is an independently marked alternative to a "neutral" term. This doesn't explain the markedness, but does get at an important point about slurs. The effect of a slur will ordinarily depend on our recognition that the speaker has made a point of using that particular word, whether as a term of abuse or to reinforce or emphasize group solidarity. But then most lexical choices are going to be interpreted in terms of Gricean principles. A speaker will have presumably have had some reason for describing a member of the school board as obdurate in her opposition to the building plan rather than as adamant or steadfast. But there are plenty of hybrid words that express strong evaluations of their referents which have no synonyms that don't express the same evaluation. The force of calling somebody an asshole isn't attenuated by the absence of a word denoting someone who is not obtusely self-considering. Similarly for hybrid words such as *toady*, *slut* or *goon* ("a bully or thug, especially one hired to terrorize or do away with opposition"). There are no nonevaluative synonyms for derogations such as *Uncle Tom* and *Jewish American princess*, but their use is offensive all the same. In fact not all of the words we clearly think of as slurs have synonyms with alternate evaluations. Some notable examples are umbrella derogatives for what on the consensus view are collections of distinct groups that ought not to be conflated, such as *slope* for East Asians and *wog* for what Merriam-Webster defines as "a dark-skinned foreigner; especially one from the Middle East

---

[36] Bolinger offers what she describes as a pragmatic theory of slurs, in which semantics has no role to play: the connotations of their use follow from the awareness that they are dysphemisms associated with the derogation of their targets, which speakers infer on the basis of their correlation with the expression of certain attitudes toward the members of a group. This is consistent with what I'll be arguing here (Bolinger draws on an unpublished version of this paper), but the mechanism it invokes is too general by itself to distinguish slurs from hybrid terms whose evaluation is incorporated in their conventional meaning. It's on the basis of observations about correlations, after all, that language learners conclude that words such as *bitch* and *toady* are used to disparage the people they're applied to, and in fact Bolinger cites examples like these in making her point. There's more to be said about the particular kinds of correlations that figure in the use of slurs and their implications for the identity of the speaker herself, as we will see.

or Far East."[37] (So too were words like *fairy* and *nancy* for homosexuals until recent times, a point I'll come back to below.)[38]

So the effect of a slur can't arise simply because the speaker has chosen to use a negative or disparaging term where a neutral one was available. If slurs are marked, it's because their use is a pointed conversational transgression—a departure from the norms that would ordinarily govern referential practice in that situation. That explains why slurs are different from pejorative hybrid terms such as *goon*, and why the relevant alternative, if there is one, has to be another lexical item, rather than a compact descriptive phrase that denotes the same category but doesn't express the same evaluation. That follows only when we bear in mind that slurs and their alternatives are socially anchored in communities of speakers who have developed specific conventions for referring to particular categories; that is, who "have a name for it." This point—that slurs are interpreted relative to the conventions of the communities who own them—is going to be crucial to the account I'll be developing from here on in.

Meaning and Metadata

Let me try to spell this point out in terms of the notion of lexical metadata. Clearly the fact that *redskin* is derogatory is an arbitrary fact about that word that speakers have to know in order to use or understand it. Somebody who is ignorant of that fact is deficient in her knowledge of English, not in her knowledge of racism, American Indians or the rules of conversational interaction. But there are a lot of things we know about words which affect the way we use them but which are all the same not themselves part of its meaning. Consider the metadata labels that dictionaries use to define *redskin*:

> **redskin**   *usually offensive* American Indian (Merriam-Webster)
> **redskin**   *dated, offensive*. An American Indian. (Oxford American)
> **redskin**   *Slang (often disparaging and offensive)* A North American Indian. (Random House)

---

[37] *Squaw* is another example of a slur with no default lexicalized equivalent (one can of course speak of a Native American woman). As Hill (2009) observes, the paradigm *buck-squaw-papoose* is a way of "animalizing" lesser breeds such as blacks and Indians, on the model of *buck-doe-fawn* and *stallion-mare-colt*. It parallels the paradigm *Jew-Jewess-Jewling* (that last term is attested in nineteenth- and twentieth-century use).

[38] DiFranco (2015) notes that a certain class of idiomatic expressions, such as *slanty-eyed, curry muncher* and *Jewish American Princess*, don't have neutral equivalents, but should be considered slurs all the same. These fall, I think, into several classes. DiFranco identifies *slanty-eyed*, correctly, I think, as an "idiomatically combining expression" (per Nunberg, Sag and Wasow 1994), but the absence of a default synonym is likely due to the fact that, like *wog* and *gook*, it denotes what most consider an illegitimate social category—i.e. those who "look Oriental"—and hence lacks a coreferential default equivalent. As I noted, individual-denoting terms such as *Jewish-American princess* and *Uncle Tom*, while also described as slurs, really behave like hybrids rather than prejudicials, so the absence of default synonyms isn't surprising. DiFranco also lists *redskin* here, but that is simply a slur with the default equivalent (*American) Indian*; the fact that it references a putative physical feature of the group doesn't mean it works as a compositional idiom (cf other terms like *darkie, blackie, burrhead* for blacks etc.)

These entries make no mention of any properties that *redskin* imputes to its referents; they don't say anything about redskins being savage, stupid, inarticulate or alcoholic. They simply attach a label like "disparaging" or "offensive" to the entry as a kind of metadata. Metadata labels like these can indicate a word's geographical or social provenance (*Southern, nonstandard*), its currency (*rare, archaic*), the genre or discourse type it's associated with (*formal, colloq., poet.*), the field it's used in (*bot., ling.*) or its typical effect or reception (*disparaging, humorous*), among other things.

Such metadata features don't belong to the conventional meaning of a word. The linguistic conventions that govern the meanings of *anon* and *alas* don't specify that they're archaic, and the conventional meaning of *asshole* doesn't specify that it's vulgar. It is not a matter of semantic convention that *ain't* is associated with the English of uneducated or working-class speakers (it is conventional among certain groups of speakers, many of whom are uneducated or working-class, to use the word, but that's not the same thing).[39] But these features can give rise to conversational implicatures. Tom Wasow once pointed me to an article in the *Chronicle of Higher Education* that quoted a dean at an Eastern university: "Any junior scholar who stresses teaching at the expense of research *ain't* gonna get tenure." In the dean's mouth, the use of the demotic *ain't* rather than *isn't* implied that his conclusion wasn't based on expert knowledge or a research survey; it was as if to say, "You don't need an advanced degree to see that; it's obvious to anyone with an ounce of sense." That's what makes *ain't* appropriate to the expression of nitty-gritty verities like "If it *ain't* broke don't fix it." And while "Alas, the Warriors lost" conveys an arch or ironic tone that isn't present with "Damn! The Warriors lost," the difference doesn't follow from the meanings of the words—it's implied by the use of an archaic literary word rather than a vulgar colloquialism to express one's disappointment.

These are familiar conversational moves, and there's a temptation to think of their effects as having been folded into the semantics of the expressions. One might conclude, for example, that *alas* has become a conventional signifier of ironized lamentation. But it is more accurate to say that the word is regarded as an archaism, like *anon* and *perchance*, and that such words provide a convenient way of coloring the expression of an attitude with literary distance. That is, *alas* can only convey what it does because it's what we think people *used* to say in the elastic literary past of Walter Scott and Shakespeare.[40] If *alas* no longer had an archaic character—if it were merely a formal word of modern English like *regrettably*—it couldn't evoke the same

---

[39] People may say things like "*redskin* has a disparaging meaning" in the same way they might say "*asshole* has a vulgar meaning" and "*bloviate* has a jocular meaning," using "meaning" to refer simply to what one expects a dictionary to say about the word or what one has to know about the word in order to use it appropriately. And one might ask whether it isn't simply hair-splitting to ask whether such features count as metadata or semantic content. But as we'll see, conventionality in the narrow sense is precisely the property we want to focus on when it comes to explaining the social grounding that slurs and other terms exploit to achieve their effects.

[40] I say "what we think people used to say" because the label "archaic" describes the contemporary view of a word, unlike "obsolete," which refers to its actual history. Indeed, words like these can retain their archaic flavor for centuries without becoming obsolete. *Behest* and *anon* have been regarded as archaisms since the eighteenth century; *alas* since Victorian times.

sensibilities.[41] And if its status as an archaism is sufficient to evoke those sensibilities all by itself, there's nothing arbitrary about that effect that would require further conventionalization. In short, these effects defy semanticization, a point I'm going to keep coming back to.

Ventriloquistic Implicatures

The maneuvers involved here belong to a family of conversational implicatures that arise out of Grice's Maxim of Manner. Horn (1984) and Levinson (2000) have reformulated that maxim and its consequences in somewhat different ways, though both in terms of markedness, and have laid out the implicatures that arise from flouting them. Here is Levinson, explicating the effects of his M-Principle:

> Where S has said "p" containing marked expression M, and there is an unmarked alternate expression U with the same denotation D which the speaker might have employed in the sentence-frame instead, then where U would have I-implicated the stereotypical or more specific subset d of D, the marked expression M will implicate the complement of the denotation, namely $\bar{d}$ of D.

Or as Levinson puts it more succinctly, "What's said in an abnormal way, isn't normal." This is a powerful principle. It can be evoked to explain the interpretive differences between pairs like *can/be able to, tired/fatigued, happy/not unhappy, stop the car/cause the car to stop, pink/pale red,* and *very rich/very very rich,* among many other types.

Markedness is a capacious notion, but for most writers it comes down to a difference in frequency, prolixity, processing difficulty, or morphological or syntactic complexity, in various combinations, which in turn gives rise to interpretations that are more atypical, more specialized, or less predictable. But the cases we're concerned with here differ from the standard examples both in what makes them marked or abnormal and in the kind of inferences that their markedness gives rise to.

Take the dean's remark that "junior faculty who don't concentrate on research ain't gonna get tenure." *Ain't* is no more prolix, infrequent, or difficult to process than *isn't* is. Nor is the difference the same as one of register, such as between saying, "Her house is on the corner" and, "Her residence is on the corner," each of which would be considered an appropriate form to use depending on the communicative setting, independent of the speaker's social background. *Ain't* is "marked" here because it isn't the variant prescribed by the conventions of the group whose norms should govern the behavior of these participants in this context. And in interpreting this use of *ain't,* we don't look for a nonstereotypical meaning or range of application, which is what we do when we interpret *pale red* as denoting a color between pink and red or take *Sue made the car move* to mean something other than that she drove it. The dean's sentence has exactly the same truth-conditions whether he uses *isn't going to* or *ain't gonna.* What's different, rather, is that in using the nonstandard form, the speaker evokes or impersonates a member of the community among whom *ain't* is the conventional

---

[41] One probably wouldn't say, for example, "Alas, I was unable to get my child to the hospital in time to save him," where the ironic distancing would be inappropriate—the context calls for *sadly* or *regrettably.* François Recanati tells me a Frenchman might use *hélas* in a similar context. But *hélas* is not an archaism in French; Google ngrams shows that, unlike *alas,* it is about as frequent now as it was a century ago.

third-person negative form of *be*, as if he were just a regular Joe schmoozing with other regular Joes. The implication is that the evaluation of the assertion requires no more intelligence or expertise than such people are stereotypically held to possess. That is, in using the "marked" form the speaker associates himself with the attitudes of a group whose norms wouldn't ordinarily govern linguistic choices in the speech-situation. One could say that the example suggests a variant interpretation of Levinson's heuristic "What's said in an abnormal way, isn't normal," in that "normal" literally suggests a connection to social norms. But with that proviso, Levinson and Horn's general schemas apply in these cases as well.

I'll describe this conversational maneuver as ventriloquism. In a particular context, a speaker pointedly disregards the lexical convention of the group whose norms prescribe the default way of referring to A and refers to A instead via the distinct convention of another group that is known to have distinct and heterodox attitudes about A, so as to signal his affiliation with the group and its point of view. Ventriloquistic implicatures are often triggered by the use of words from a dialect or language other than the one that would normally be used in the conversation. The week after the Monica Lewinsky story broke, the *New York Times* Week in Review section ran its story about it under a picture of the White House at night that was headed *Scandale*. When I asked an editor at the section why they felt the need to put that final *e* on the word, he said, "Oh, that's so readers will know it's about sex and not money." Now most Americans would assume, correctly, that French *scandale* and English *scandal* are synonyms: when Frenchmen say *Quel scandale!* they express pretty much the same thought that we would express with "What a scandal!" The added implications of using the French word in an English context arise from a familiar cultural stereotype of the French. The effect is ventriloquistic: when the speaker (or here, the headline writer) uses a French word in place of its English synonym, he's impersonating a Frenchman, or more accurately, a cliché Frenchman, so as to convey the impression that he regards the affair with an attitude of Gallic worldliness.

Features of Ventriloquistic Implicatures

These implicatures have several properties that are relevant to the behavior of slurs, some of which they share with other implicatures arising from the Maxim of Manner. First, they're very difficult to cancel, bearing in mind that the inferences one is trying to revoke usually involve the speaker's attitudes rather than the truth-conditions of the utterance. Someone who says, "Alas, the Warriors lost" could finish the remark, "and I'm deeply despondent about it," but in that case we'd be more likely to interpret the second clause ironically than to assume that the speaker's "Alas!" was actually an expression of genuine distress. If he was really upset, why would he have put it that way? Analogously, the dean who predicts that "junior faculty who concentrate exclusively on teaching ain't gonna get tenure" might go on to cite quantitative studies to reinforce his point, but we'd still read him as having implied that the conclusion is obvious on its face. (Hence the conversational oddness of saying, "Our initial clinical trials seem to show that the drug ain't gonna significantly reduce cardiac arrest in older patients.")

Second, the attitudes evoked by these implicatures tend to be speaker-oriented, even in embedded contexts. When a supervisor says, "The *billet-doux* that Bill sent out complaining about the new work schedule was way out of line," the use of *billet-doux* rather than *message* or *email* conveys a sarcastic attitude about the communication. If I report her utterance as, "The boss said she was angry about the *billet-doux* Bill sent out about the new work schedule," I would be taken as conveying my own sarcastic attitude about Bill's message, even if the boss had used *billet-doux* herself, since I was under no obligation to repeat that her term in indirect speech, unless I wanted to make a point about her pretentiousness. Similarly, a middle-class assistant professor who has heard the dean's remark might say to a colleague, "The dean said that if we don't concentrate on research we ain't gonna get tenure." In that case she too implicates both that the truth of the conditional is obvious to anyone. If what matters to her and her colleague is only the importance of doing research, then she'll convert his *ain't* to *isn't*, lest she trigger an inference that isn't conversationally relevant.

The third feature of these implicatures is a special case of a general principle that I mentioned earlier, which affects a number of types of manner implicatures, such as those arising from the periphrastic constructions like "cause to die." With a few exceptions, these implicatures are triggered only when the word used by the speaker replaces one prescribed by the convention that would be the contextual default. In other words, there has to be a normal conventional (i.e., a lexicalized) means of saying what the speaker is saying abnormally. The use of a foreign word can trigger this kind of implicature only when English has "a perfectly good word" for the very same thing, as with the *Times' scandale* or the boss's *billet doux*. It isn't sufficient that one should be able to render the sense of the foreign word with a more-or-less synonymous English phrase, as one can for French terms like *cinéma vérité* or *crème brulée*, since the English calques aren't themselves conventional, so those terms engender no implicatures of this type. It's only when a group has a conventional way of referring to such-and-such a thing (that is, a word for it, in our sense) that we can assume that its members perceive a common interest in being able to individuate and discuss it, so that the use of an alternate term implies a rejection of the group's received attitudes about it. This is the principle that has led English-speakers in the past to plunder the French lexicon for items like *affair(e)* and *dalliance* to suggest a more urbane tolerance than our Anglo-Saxon attitudes stereotypically countenance. (We sometimes invest the words with more explicitly sexual meanings than the French themselves do—in French, to say something is *risqué* doesn't necessarily mean it's naughty, and a *ménage à trois* isn't really a threesome. But then this isn't about the French as they actually are but as we fancy them to be.)

If slurs involve a ventriloquistic implicature, as I'm claiming here, then it isn't surprising that they should exhibit the same features that other implicatures of this type do. We've already seen that slurs are possible only when there is a nonslurring lexicalized default, a point I'll come back to below. In addition, slurs are often speaker-oriented or "nondisplaceable" wherever they appear in linguistic structure. This is sometimes framed as a categorical constraint that affects not just slurs but all types of expressives. But this generalization is actually quite leaky, as several writers have noted. (See, among others, Guerts (2007), Anand (2007), and Gutzmann (2103) as well as Potts (2005) for discussion of the more general principle.) It's not hard to find unexceptionable, naturally occurring sentences in which the attitudes implicit in a slur are not attributed to the speaker. I already mentioned the example produced by the playwright Harvey Fierstein, "Everybody loves to hate a homo," where clearly the import of *homo* was being ascribed to the haters rather than assumed by Fierstein himself. Here are a few others:

γ We lived, in that time, in a world of enemies . . . but beyond enemies there were the Micks, and the spics, and the wops, and the fuzzy-wuzzies. A whole world of people not us.

γ So white people were given their own bathrooms, their own water fountains. You didn't have to ride on public conveyances with niggers anymore. These uncivilized jungle bunnies, darkies. . . . You had your own cemetery.

γ At the Saturday movies, "Time Marches On" told us how bad-unfair-stupid the enemy was . . . The guys were determined to kill a German or a Jap for freedom, democracy, Betty Grable, and the American Way.

γ [Marcus Bachmann] also called for more funding of cancer and Alzheimer's research, probably cuz all those homos get all the money now for all that AIDS research.

There may still be a tendency to be explained here, depending on how we determine what the expected frequency of examples like these should be.[42] But if slurs often do scope out, there's a straightforward pragmatic explanation for it. If you are reporting the speech of someone who has replaced an unmarked term with its marked synonym in order to implicate a particular attitude toward the referent or the proposition expressed—irony, disdain, obviousness, amusement or whatever—you're under no informational obligation to repeat the speaker's word unless the implicated attitude is conversationally relevant; otherwise, you are unnecessarily asking the listener to rehearse the inferences that the word triggers. Say your apparently pacific and sweet-tempered neighbor is a World War II veteran who tells you one day to your surprise that he was awarded a medal for killing five Japs on Tarawa. When you report the story to your wife—"You'll never guess what I heard from that nice Mr. Owens next door"—you'll most likely say he killed five Japanese. If you made a point of repeating his use of the marked alternative *Jap*, you'd be apt to imply that his contempt for the Japanese he killed was a significant element of the story—say that it was what motivated his action. That kind of inference is sometimes justified; what Fierstein was saying is that everybody loves to hate a homosexual in virtue of the homophobia that expresses itself in words like *homo*. But if there's no reason to suppose that the speaker's choice of words was pertinent to the point at issue, as is most likely the case in reporting your neighbor's story, then your pointed decision to use *Japs* will be taken as an indication of your own racial attitude. In other words, slurs tend to be speaker-oriented because they are marked alternatives to a conversational default, so the speaker always has an ulterior reason for using them, over and above the proposition he asserts.[43]

---

[42] Actually, the great majority of occurrences of strong slurs in nonfiction books that do not appear in quotations have narrow scope, like the first three of the ones cited here. But then most authors wouldn't use the words in contexts where they might be read as speaker-oriented. Things are no doubt different in other settings.

[43] Unlike slurs, vulgarities such as *asshole* and *fucking* are virtually always speaker-oriented, which is one of a number of reasons for not conflating them under a single semantic category.

The same principle explains why these implicatures are hard or even impossible to cancel. When you make a point of using a word that's an alternative to the contextual default, whether it's *alas*, *ain't*, or *Jap*, you evoke the attitude or a point of view that is implicit in the word, which once out there can't be walked back. What you can do, rather, is disclaim your own commitment to the attitude by displacing it, often by embedding the slur in reported speech or thought, as in the examples above. Note that the import of a slur isn't suspended even when the word is used ironically or defiantly by its targets—indeed, it's because the attitudes it evokes are still present that the irony has its bite, a point I'll come back to. In short, there's no need to introduce any formal mechanism or distinction to explain the basic features of slurs or prejudicials. Those follow naturally from conversational principles taken together with the notion of a default convention, which is what I want to turn to now.

Lexical Conventions and Their Provenances

Slurs work as foreign words like *scandale* do: they derive their significance and force from the attitudes we associate with the people who use them. By itself, that's not a novel insight. Hornsby (2001) says, "About derogatory words . . . one finds oneself saying that negative or hostile attitudes of *their users* have rubbed off onto them"; Blackburn (1984) says of *boche* that the word "*belongs* to people who accept a certain attitude—that being a German is enough to make someone a fit object of derision" (my italics). But what exactly does it mean to say that a derogative "belongs to" certain people? One assumes it means pretty much the same thing as to say that the word *scandale* belongs to the French; that is, that it is the conventional descriptive term for A's among the members of certain group—in this case, one whose members are thought to have distinctive attitudes about A's. And it implies that the word does not belong to those who don't identify with those attitudes: *boche* is not the property of people who don't belong to that particular group, even if they happen to share some of those attitudes. Not everybody who uses a slur can claim ownership of the word, no more than everybody who uses a French word can.

The lexicon has a sociolinguistic structure, as well as a semantic and morphological one: the words we use are drawn from the lexical conventions of various intersecting communities, roles, and discourses, only some of which are actually in some sense "ours." At a first pass, we can think of a lexical convention as a rule for using a word that a certain group of people conforms to because they collectively believe it answers to their common communicative interests. Then we can describe the provenance of a convention simply as the social projection of that interest, the group of people who recognize a distinct common stake in having a word for such-and-such a thing.[44]

---

[44] I'm interested here only in lexical conventions. I assume, roughly following Lewis (1969) that a convention is an understanding among the members of a group that they will try to coordinate their practices around a certain regularity in a particular situation because they believe it is in their common interest to do so. But the arguments I'm giving here don't rest crucially on accepting that conception of a convention rather than some other, and one could as easily reformulate these arguments in terms of Gilbert's notion of plural subjects (1989), which might actually be more congenial to my purposes.

The crucial point of departure is that in Lewis's idealized conception, the content of a linguistic convention is the practice of using an entire language, so that whether we're talking about baseball or cricket,

Sometimes that's because the word denotes a category the members of the group have a proprietary interest in individuating—*ergativity* for linguists, *triple net* in commercial real estate. Or sometimes it's just because the members of a group want to suggest they have an interest in defining a particular category for themselves, whether or not it's functionally necessary. Adolescents coin their own words for friends or intimates, not because efficient reference demands it, but because it implies a distinct conception of those relationships and hence signals a distinct social identity. In either case, we want to distinguish between the people who perceive themselves as sharing those common interests, that is, the parties to the conventions, and the people who merely conform to the convention deferentially on some occasions. I can speak of emotivism, but only in deference to the way philosophers use the word. I can tell my daughter I've been chillin' with my mains, but who am I kidding? Another way of saying this is that there's nothing the nonparties to a convention can say or do that will alter its form, in the same way that my use or misuse of the French subjunctive isn't going to have any effect on the way French people use it. Though over time, of course, a convention can be extended to a broader community, sometimes in virtue of a more widespread acceptance of the interest it answers to, often accompanied by a reinterpretation of that interest—in which case the meaning of the word may change, as well.

I'm using "group" and "community" in a very general way. The social provenance of a convention may be an independently constituted "robust" social type—New Yorkers, philosophers, Jewish Americans, inner-city adolescents, real-estate brokers, sailing enthusiasts. Those are the sorts of linguistic practices we typically describe with terms like "dialect," "jargon," and "slang." But conventions can also be defined relative to a register, medium, or style. There are conventions that apply only among those engaged in formal address, in meetings, and on the telephone. Or the provenance of a lexical convention can correspond simply to the self-conscious social extension of a certain set of beliefs or attitudes, which themselves can sometimes be inferred from the existence of the word itself. That is, you could say that the provenance of the convention for using *w* to denote A is just whatever group is such that its members recognize a common interest in having a common word for A. That definition isn't necessarily circular or uninformative. It's enough to say that the provenance of the convention for using *free enterprise* is the group of people who perceive a common interest in having a distinct approbative name for market capitalism, which by itself actually tells us quite a bit about them. That interest corresponds to a collection of other attitudes that define

we're conforming to a single convention that prescribes the use of English. (Lewis (1975) touches sketchily on internal linguistic heterogeneity, but not so as to affect the general point.) The implicit assumption is that all or most of the speakers of a language want to be able to talk to each other about everything and anything. Whereas when we talk about individual lexical conventions it's in order to acknowledge that things are messier than that. A language, in reality, is "a sprawling mass of crisscrossing, overlapping conventions," as Millikan (2005) puts it in another context. Americans and Englishmen perceive no overriding common interest being able to talk to each other about knitted garments or vegetables, which is why the former speak of sweaters and rutabagas while the latter speak of jumpers and swedes. But English-speakers as a whole do seem to wind up trying to coordinate their use of words like *vanity* or *dissolution*—words for which the usage of the writers of one nation can establish valid precedents for writers from the others. In a sense, those alone are the words that belong to the English language as a whole.

a political identity and give rise to other conventions, such as prescribe referring to the wealthy as job creators or using the adjective *socialistic*. But in cases like that we might better think of the provenance of the convention as the participants in a certain discourse, rather than as a speech-community. If you did the demographics you might discover that those people tend to be Republicans, *Wall Street Journal* subscribers, or Hummer owners. But it's the discourse that's matters, because however you describe its participants, they don't use the terms on all occasions.[45] (Think of the discourse of modern corporate life, in which employees may be expected to refer to their goals as missions and their team leaders as champions. But not even human resources managers use that language when they're talking about their plans for themselves and their families.)

With this in mind, we can think of the individual speaker's sociolinguistic conception of the lexicon as resembling the dictionary entries I mentioned earlier, with words tagged with a pointer to the provenance whose conventions prescribe their use. True, actual dictionaries tag only those metadata features of words that depart from the norms of formal written English that govern the language of the dictionary itself. They label words as substandard but not standard, as regional but not national, as archaic but not current, and so on. That corresponds to the way we tend to think about these things: we assign a marked status only to words that seem to be alternatives to an implicit default. But the defaults aren't semantically or socially "neutral," any more than Standard English is something distinct in kind from other English dialects.

Default Conventions

Relative to a particular speech situation, we can talk about the default convention for referring to A as the one that participants would ordinarily expect one another to use. It may be a convention to which one or both of the participants in the exchange are themselves parties, or which belongs to the practices of some other group, say if the participants belong to no group that has a word for A. On occasion, though, we make a point of flouting or opting out of the default convention for referring to A in favor of some other convention. One reason for doing that is to claim or simulate membership

---

[45] One reason for preferring "provenance" to Lewis's "population" for the social domain of a convention is that a provenance can be a group of people in their capacity as participants in a certain discourse or discourse genre. But neither of those words gets directly at the sense of common social identity that a convention requires. "Speech-community" is used in a lot of different ways and usually implies a well-defined and more-or-less stable geographic or social grouping. But as Dwight Bolinger (1975) defined the term, it comes close to what I mean here by a provenance:

> There is no limit to the ways in which human beings league themselves together for self-identification, security, gain, amusement, worship, or any of the other purposes that are held in common; consequently there is no limit to the number and variety of speech communities that are to be found in a society.

In this sense the speech-community needn't exactly correspond to an objective population like "Berkeley students" or "Brooklynites." Often it's better thought of as the set of (perhaps fuzzy) properties that define a social group in the mind of an individual speaker or group of speakers. As Hudson (1996) observes of speech-communities, " . . . their reality is only subjective, not objective—and may be only loosely based on objective reality…No self-respecting dialectologist would recognise a dialect area called 'Northern' (or 'Southern') [British] English, but some lay people certainly think in such terms…" In this sense the idealized speech-communities with which the conventions for words like slurs are identified are not exceptional.

in another group whose members have an alternative or heterodox attitude toward A, which is what I've been describing as ventriloquism. We can think of this as a case of an "affiliatory" speech act (I owe the term to Daniel Harris), whereby a speaker pointedly claims an affiliation with a particular group. People have various reasons for doing this. Sometimes the object is to suggest an affinity with a group one doesn't belong to, as when white teenagers adopt hip hop slang in order to intimate that they are down with the bros. (Emulation is the chief engine of lexical diffusion.) Sometimes it's to signal solidarity with the fellow members of a group or to distance oneself from the group whose norms would ordinarily establish the conventions that should govern the speech situation—for example when an African American academic injects inner-city slang into a formal discourse when the default convention would prescribe a Standard English term. And sometimes it's to insult or offend someone by referring to him with a term associated with a group by whom he is thought to be held in contempt. In an appropriate context, an Anglophone anti-Semite can suggest hostility to Jews simply by using the German word for Jew, without actually presenting herself as being a German.

Slurs and prejudicials involve a particular kind of affiliatory speech acts, which arise with words that denote a socially disputed category. By that I mean that people are generally aware that there is a significant difference of opinion or attitude about the category which corresponds to an independent social division between groups that have distinct linguistic conventions for referring to it. By that criterion, not all widespread disagreements will qualify. There are a lot of people who hate dogs, for example (cynophobes? misocynists?), but the attitude doesn't correspond to a basic seam in the social fabric: dog haters don't constitute the kind of self-conscious collectivity whose members are going to come up with their own distinctive name for dogs, which is why there is no derogative for dogs as such, Frege's example of *cur* notwithstanding.

The default term corresponds to what's usually called the "neutral counterpart" of a slur; that is, a word which as Richard puts it, "co-classifies but is free of the slur's evaluative dimension." This notion of neutrality is an artifact of the semanticist approach, which makes the slur's "evaluative dimension" a component of its conventional linguistic meaning in addition to its purely identifying function. From that point of view, a term that merely identifies a group will be "neutral" in the sense that it doesn't *semantically* evaluate its referent. But as I've argued here, the evaluative force of a slur isn't part of its conventional meaning but arises from the attitudes of the group that uses the slur towards the word's target. And when it comes to categories defined along racial, ethnic, political grounds and the like, the vocabulary of every group is colored by further connotations or evaluations. Terms such as *white* and *black* are "neutral" only in the sense that they encode the unreflecting body of opinion—the taken-for-granted—that Bourdieu calls the doxa.

That point is crucial to understanding how changing social attitudes can alter the status of words, as new defaults appear and old ones are either abandoned or themselves become prejudicials. Thus *Negro* yielded to *black* and *African American*, and *Oriental* to *Asian*. Note that if those original defaults had been genuinely neutral, there would have been no call for replacing them. It's only when an existing default term is challenged by a new contender that most people come to acknowledge its implicit connotations, whether they're critiquing or defending it ("*Lady* demonstrates respect for the fair sex"). The usurpers are apt to be denounced as euphemistic or deceptive, and perhaps as a perversion of language ("a lifestyle that is anything but gay"). As the new term gains currency its connotations are absorbed into an altered doxa and it becomes an alternative default in certain subdiscourses. At the point where the new word becomes widely accepted, an insistence on sticking with the old one triggers the implicature of pointed nonconformity, and it may even come to be regarded as a slur.

The notion of "neutrality" that's relevant here is cultural or journalistic, and can't be reduced to a simplistic semantic opposition. To see how defaults arise and shift in response to changing attitudes, we might consider the twentieth-century history of words for homosexuals. As I noted earlier, ordinary Americans of 1925 who wanted to describe someone as a homosexual had at their disposal only slang words such as *nance*, *fairy*, and, loosely, the informal *sissy*. Terms such as *homosexual, invert, pederast* and, in relevant senses, *Sapphic* and *lesbian* were largely restricted to clinical or learned use until they gradually became part of general educated use in the 1940s and 1950s.[46] In one sense, then, one could say that *fairy* became a slur only a few decades ago. But the fact that the word was considered slang is an indication that people didn't consider homosexuality a matter to which one could refer directly in polite discourse, other than by means of euphemisms or circumlocutions. Even when *homosexual* did enter wider use, it would initially have been heard as a marked choice for the average speaker, a rejection of the assumptions implicit in slang or euphemistic reference, though often colored by negative stereotypes and assumptions. By the late 1970s *homosexual* was being supplanted as a default term by *gay*, before then a term used among a relatively small in-group. Now the words' positions are in a way reversed, with *homosexual* as a tendentious alternative to *gay*, particularly as applied to cultural categories like marriage and lifestyle. Yet one wouldn't want to argue that *gay* is free of connotations, either; the word is saturated with contemporary attitudes about sexual orientation. Rather, *gay* has come to occupy what the political scientist Daniel Hallin (1986) calls the "sphere of consensus" in journalism, a domain in which the requirements of balanced reporting are suspended and "journalists do not feel compelled to present an opposing view point or to remain disinterested observers." (Hallin opposes the sphere of consensus to "the sphere of legitimate controversy.") In American public discourse, that is, you can speak of "gays in the military" without any strong implication that you are personally signing on to its implications, whereas to speak of the "homosexuals in the military" commits you personally to the retrograde connotations that the older term evokes. That is, the default term is not necessarily one without evaluative connotations, but rather the one for whose

---

[46] The number of articles in the Proquest historical newspapers corpus containing the word *homosexual* went from 9 in the 1920s to 118 in the 1940s to 3529 in the 1960s to 18,139 in the 1980s (by which time *gay* was making inroads). The slang truncation *homo* didn't appear till 1929 and was rarely used before the 1940s; *faggot* and *queer* weren't widely used in this sense outside of the gay community until around the same time.

connotations the speaker can assume the least personal responsibility, beyond tacitly acknowledging them as a basis for conversation.[47]

The difference in detachability here—the fact that the speaker can disavow the associations of a default term but not of its alternative—follows from the logic of the implicature itself. There's a nice example of the principle in the history of the antiquated *Sassenach*, the Gaelic name for the English. Given the history of Anglo-Caledonian and Anglo-Hibernian relations up to the nineteenth century, we can assume that the word had accumulated a rich set of unflattering connotations—that if you gave a Gaelic-speaking Highlander or Irishman from the age of George II a word-association test and offered *Sassenach*, he'd come back with the Gaelic words that translate as "arrogant," "sybaritic," "cruel," "snooty," and so on, which was how pretty much everybody in those communities regarded the English. But in the unlikely event that he wanted to say something flattering about the English, *Sassenach* was the only name he had to hand. *Sassenach* became a derogative only when it was adopted by English-speaking Scots and Irish who had the alternative term *Englishman* at their disposal. At that point, a speaker could use *Sassenach* to symbolically affiliate himself with the Gaelic-speaking Celts in order to evoke their attitudes about the English, either in earnest or in jest, as Buck Mulligan does in the Telemachus chapter of *Ulysses* when he applies it to the English houseguest Haines. But in that context the word can't be used with the neutral implications it could potentially have in Irish. If Mulligan should say in English, "The Sassenach have always treated us decently," the remark would almost certainly be interpreted ironically, though he could make the same utterance in Irish and perhaps be counted sincere. Yet the narrowing of the word's implications follows from a purely pragmatic inference, not because it had acquired a conventional derogative meaning in its English use. If Mulligan had intended to say something positive about Englishmen while speaking English, after all, why would he make a point of using a word that signaled his affiliation with a group whose members stereotypically detest them?

At no point, then, do the associations of these words work their way into their semantics. There's nothing in the meaning of the phrase *free enterprise* that's explicitly approving of capitalism (there's no such implication when we speak of the "free market system"). It's not a hybrid term like *nanny state*, which semantically disparages its referent. Rather it's just the default descriptive name for free-market capitalism in the ideological discourse of people who hold that the capitalist system is a bully idea. That's why the evaluation associated with the phrase isn't accessible to contestation or negation. In response to somebody's claim that the regime encourages free enterprise, you wouldn't ordinarily say, "That's not true; they encourage dog-eat-dog capitalism." And it's why someone can assert that free enterprise is the fairest and most productive

---

[47] Note though that when views about a category are highly polarized, there is often no single default convention that answers to the interests of everyone in the larger discourse of public life. Journalists can't describe the parties to the debate over abortion as being either "pro-life" or "pro-choice" without seeming to compromise their claims to objectivity, so they are obliged to resort to paraphrases like "pro-abortion rights," which almost never appear outside of news stories or formal policy discussions. Neither "illegal alien" nor "undocumented immigrant" is a "neutral" term; to use either one is to identify oneself with the views of a particular discourse. (The *New York Times* goes with "illegal immigrant," but that's not really neutral, just a way of Solomonically splitting the difference.)

economic system without suggesting redundancy: she's simply repeating what counts as the received wisdom about free-market capitalism among people who have their own special name for it. By way of analogy, think of a Catholic priest telling his parishioners that the Holy Mother Church is the one true religion. They don't take him as having asserted a tautology, even though anyone who describes Catholicism in earnest as the Holy Mother Church is very likely to believe in the unique truth of the faith. Nor would even the most dogmatic anti-Catholic say that the sentence "The Holy Mother Church is addressing the problem" has no truth-value, just because the phrase seems to imply the truth of the Catholic religion. It's simply the phrase used by devout Catholics to denote an institution about which others hold different beliefs.

Note that these points seem to obviate the position that Bach (2014) describes as loaded descriptivism, which takes the conventional meaning of a term like kike to be something like "Jewish and contemptible on that account," with the second clause interpreted as a kind of supplement that isn't accessible to negation. Once we recognize slurs as a kind of ventriloquism, that stipulation is no longer necessary. Suppose that S is a member of a culture in which it is considered normal and healthy for adults to take a sexual interest in young children, so that the word that translates as "pedophile" in the language of that culture has no particular negative connotations. S, however, believing that such people are pathological and abhorrent, decides to take advantage of widespread familiarity with English and English-speakers and refer to such adults using the English word pedophile, so as to evoke the well-known Anglophone abhorrence for the disposition. One wouldn't say that in saying X is a pedophile, using the English word, S has said that X takes a sexual interest in children and is contemptible on that account. He has merely expressed himself in the manner of those who are known to hold such a view. Substitute racists for Anglophones and some racial slur for *pedophile*, and the story is the same.

From Description to Derogation

The example of *Sassenach* foregrounds the importance of stereotypes in fixing the implications of a prejudicial term—not of its targets, but of the people who use them. When you pointedly substitute an exogenous term for the default name for a group, it will be colored by the attitudes toward that group that are *stereotypically* held to prevail in the term's native provenance as a descriptive term. The imputed attitudes may be genuinely prevalent in that setting, as they were with the Gaelic uses of *Sassenach*, but they can also be folkloric or fictive, as they are when we use a French word like *scandale*.[48]

---

[48]   At one point Williamson (2009) entertains an account of slurs very like the one I'm developing here:

> ... there can be non-semantic sociological differences between terms with the same reference. For instance, the expressions E and E* both refer to X, but E predominates in the dialect of a social group G whose members tend to view X positively, while E* predominates in the dialect of a social group G* whose members tend to view X negatively. But it does not follow that a member of G who uses E thereby conversationally implies (perhaps by manner) something positive about X, or that a member of G* who uses E* thereby conversationally implies (perhaps by manner) something negative about X. For E may simply be the default, neutral term for X in G, smoothly available even to the few members of G who view X

Things work in the same way when the appropriation is intra-linguistic, though the starting point is different. There was an actual speech community whose members used *Sassenach* as the default descriptive term for the English and who were stereotypically held to despise them. But there's no actual community or region in contemporary America in which *nigger* is the default descriptive word for blacks in all contexts, as it arguably was among laboring class whites in the ante-bellum South, whose use of *nigger* was typically unreflecting and routine rather than tendentious. Even among the most virulent modern racists, saying *nigger* is a pointed choice. With what community, then, is the person who uses the word affiliating himself? Who are the actual parties to the relevant convention?

One way to answer, which is in one form or the other the standard view, is to say that *nigger* is the English-language word that's conventionally used to refer to blacks when one wants to convey a contemptuous attitude towards them—in effect, that the desire to disparage blacks is just a condition on the felicitous utterance of the word. May (2005) says that *kike* means "Jewish and used to refer to Jews with hatred or hostility." Blackburn (1984) proposes that it is a convention to use *kraut* to refer to Germans when one has a contemptuous attitude toward them. And Saka (2007) explicates the meaning of *kraut* as "For any member S of the Anglophone community, S thinks "X was a kraut" ≡ (a) S thinks that X is a German and (b) S disdains Germans as a class." Whatever their differences, these and similar proposals have in common the idea that slurs are governed by a convention of the (entire) language that restricts their utterance (outwardly or inwardly as the case may be) to those who have a negative attitude toward the group they refer to. In Kaplan's (2005) terms, it suffices that the speaker have a derogatory attitude toward the reference for the utterance to be "expressively correct."

I'm suggesting something else: the convention governing the use *nigger* belongs to the participants in a discourse in which blacks are viewed with contempt. The obvious difference is one of scope. On the utterance-condition view, it's conventional among English-speakers to use *nigger* to refer to blacks in order to express racist attitudes (leaving aside reclaimed and metaphorical uses of the word). On my view, roughly, it's a convention among certain English-speakers who have racist attitudes to use *nigger* to refer to blacks. Now the first version can't be right. To say that a word is conventional among the members of a group is to say, among other things, that they

negatively, while E* is the default, neutral term for X in G*, smoothly available even to the few members of G* who view X positively.

But Williamson (hastily, to my mind) rejects this analysis:

> Those who used 'Boche' were not presenting themselves as members of a social group in which anti-German feeling was commonly known to predominate; they were insulting Germans much more directly. The failure of cancellability for 'Boche' confirms this difference. One does not cancel the implicature by saying 'Lessing was a Boche, but I'm not one of those German-hating people who use "Boche."'

Those conclusions don't follow: someone who makes a point of presenting himself as belonging to a group whose members despise blacks has quite directly signaled an insulting attitude toward them—and as we'll see, with more intensity than if he were merely reporting his own feelings about the target. As for the failure of cancellability, we've seen that implicatures that arise from certain floutings of the Maxim of Manner can't be walked back.

discern a common interest to which it answers. But English-speakers in general don't recognize a common interest in having a disparaging word for blacks. One can argue that most people are susceptible to one or another strain of the endemic racism of modern society, but that doesn't entail that they all want to have an explicit vocabulary to express it. A great many of them genuinely abhor the attitudes that slurs are used to express; others are less troubled by those attitudes than by the vulgarity of expressing them in such a coarse manner, or don't want to engage in any practice that might brand them as "racists," which has become a universal execration. One way or the other, none would consider themselves parties to any convention for using the word.

That doesn't mean, though, that we can describe the social provenance of the convention for using *nigger* simply as "racists" or "people with a contemptuous attitude toward blacks." As we've seen, the provenance of a convention can correspond to the social extension of a certain set of attitudes only if the group of people who hold those attitudes are self-consciously aware of their common interests and associate the attitudes with a distinctive social identity. It follows that prejudicials of this type are possible only when a socially distinctive subgroup or subdiscourse holds a self-consciously heterodox view of the denotation of a word.[49] The provenance of *nigger*, then, is the discourse of a group of people (or in this case, of several groups of people) who see their common attitudes about blacks as in some way shaping or reinforcing a social identity, attitudes that warrant having their own distinct name for blacks, a word that they alone can own. That doesn't mean that such people invariably use that word to refer to blacks, no more than American teenagers invariably use *mad* to mean "very." They use it in settings in which that social identity is foregrounded or when attitudes toward blacks are at-issue, typically in conversation with others who share their views.[50]

To be sure, *nigger* is a special case, an arch-slur with a long history and a socially and geographically extended provenance. Looking at the word over the *longue durée*, one could describe it as a pure expression of racism, which is to say that it implies no relation between its speaker and its referent beyond the historical fact of black-white alterity. In that way it's unlike slurs such as *spade* and *coon*, which by themselves evoke more specific settings and tonalities, and hence more specific self-conceptions.

---

[49] Blakemore (2015) argues that the derogative force of slurs is derived not from their meaning but rather from the metalinguistic knowledge that the word is used offensively by people who are "generally prone to hold specific beliefs about the members of the group which the slur denotes–beliefs which are the result of negative social stereotyping and prejudice." I think this is close to what I am arguing here. What is missing is the association of a slur with a provenance and social identity with which the speaker affiliates himself, and which is what shapes its specific affective force.

[50] Virtually all Americans are familiar with *nigger*, and in that sense it counts as a word of American English, even if many Americans would never utter it. It recalls Grice's (1968) example of his prim Aunt Matilda, who is familiar with the expression "he is a runt" to mean "he is an undersized person," but who has no "degree of readiness to utter the expression in any circumstances whatsoever." What one wants to say, Grice suggests, is that his aunt is "equipped to use the expression." But that leaves open the question of whether she is a party to the convention that prescribes it, since she is presumably equipped to understand any number of expressions to which she neither can nor would claim ownership. It's hard to know how Grice understood her distaste for the expression. Was it because she considered the word vulgar slang, which it originally was? In that case she wasn't a party to the convention for using it. Or was it because she considered the observation itself a vulgar one, in which case she may have been?

Heard in isolation, an utterance of "He's a spade" tells us more about how the speaker thinks of both blacks and himself than "He's a nigger" does. But it's misleading to ask what an utterance of *nigger* signifies in isolation. Whiteness can be constructed in various specific ways, which generally emerge "in encounters or challenges from black Americans," as Feagin, Vera, and Batur (2000) observe, the only occasions which are likely to move whites to reflect on their identity. In that way, *nigger* can be the vehicle for expressing a variety of social identities—in America, not just of virulent skinhead racists, but also of sectors of the threatened urban working-class, and of the good ol' boys whose pickup trucks sport Confederate flags and bumper stickers that read, "If I knew they were going to cause this much trouble, I would have picked the damn cotton myself."

Absent Slurs

If one passes over the role of the communities to which slurs belong, it can seem natural to see their meanings and functions as directly shaped by abstract societal forces—to speak of them as enforcers of a racist system or as the product of the racist institutions that support them. But without discounting the causal role of societal racism, it's important to recognize that the import of these words is always mediated by the interests and self-conception of the specific communities that coin and own them. Without such mediation, even a strong and widespread antipathy toward a group may have no lexical expression. Since 9/11, many Americans have felt intense hostility towards Arabs and Muslims (to xenophobes, the distinction between the groups isn't always clear). But there is no commonly used slur for either group—none, that is, whose usage is remotely as extensive as the emotions they evoke.[51] Americans are content to vent their rage with chants of "death to Muslims" and "Arabs suck." The absence of such a slur suggests that the alterity of Muslims/Arabs isn't constitutive of the sense of social or national identity of Americans or American Christians—that it doesn't define a social category that's analogous to whiteness, heteronormativity or Anglo or gentile identity. That might be because Muslims and Arabs have been historically and geographically remote from the everyday experience of most Americans. But whatever the reason, the absence of such a slur would be puzzling if slurs were simply the expression of general societal attitudes about race and religion.

Even more curious is the absence of Standard English slurs for women. There's a long historical register of words that denote women who are afflicted with various of the flaws and vices women are held to be specifically liable to—*bitch, slut, whore, shrew, slag, cunt, ditz,* and so on (for a historical survey, see Hughes 1998). But these are all hybrid pejorative words that apply to individual women (as shown by the fact that their evaluative content can be contested, but not reiterated without a sense of

---

[51] It's not that no such slurs have been coined. The online Racial Slur Database lists a few slurs for Muslims along with a number of them for Arabs, such as *raghead* and *hadj*, which were used by soldiers in Iraq. But while most Americans have probably heard one or two of these, none of them has caught on widely in the way *Japs* did in World War II or that *boche* did among the British in the First World War. It's not as if such a slur couldn't easily be diffused, say by the vehicle of right-wing talk radio. It just hasn't happened so far.

redundancy).[52] In Standard American English, there are few if any disparaging words for women that work as prejudicial slurs such as *nigger* and *kike* do; i.e., that derogate women as a class.

Consider the frame "What else could you expect from a _____?" as used to account for someone's faults or misbehavior. When a black employee fails to show up on time for an appointment, one racist co-worker might say to another, "What else could you expect from a black person?" or "What else could you expect from a nigger?" Both utterances imply that the employee's lateness can be attributed to the fact of his race rather than his individual character, but the second foregrounds the stereotype of irresponsibility and indolence. Analogously, a man might say to a male friend whose wife has been cruel or unfaithful, "What else could you expect from a woman?" so as to attribute her behavior to the simple fact of her sex. But there is no Standard English word that one could substitute here to explicitly evoke the stereotypes of female malice or inconstancy. One could only say, "What else could you expect from a bitch?" (or "cunt" or "slut" etc.) but those lay the blame on the wife's personal failings. Of course the man could inject a tone of disrespect for women in general by using a vernacular word for women, such as *broad* or *dame*. But while those words can evoke a stereotypically crude working-class sexism, they can also be admiring (recall Rogers and Hammerstein's "There is Nothing like a Dame!"). That is, they're not essentially misogynistic in the way *nigger* is essentially racist.[53]

Why should that be? It's not as if men in their misogynistic moments wouldn't have a use for a whole battery of terms to fill out the sentence, "Frailty thy name is__ ." And linguistically speaking, it would be easy enough to derive such a word, simply by projecting one of those hybrid pejoratives to a prejudicial, in the process that gave rise to slurs such as *cracker* for Southern whites and *sheeny* for Jews. As I noted earlier, that's how things have gone in the strain of hip hop culture in which *bitch*—and *ho*— are used as prejudicials for women in general. But like the homophobia that usually accompanies it, that "cartoonish misogyny" (George 1999) is meant to be read as a sign of the artists' gangsta authenticity. That is, it's their means of expressing a particular social identity, not by casting themselves in opposition to women but in opposition to those who are "fake," "soft" or failing to "keep it real" (see McLeod 1999). *Chick* played a similar role as a marker of social identity in its progress from the slang of jazzmen to its use by the hipsters, then the hippies, then youth slang in general (Lighter 2014). In the broader culture, by contrast, misogyny may be pervasive but it isn't localized: it doesn't define the kind of self-conscious group or community that could constitute itself as the provenance of a linguistic convention—nor, needless to say,

[52] As I noted earlier, one can call a woman a nasty bitch or a silly ditz, where the adjective intensifies the force of the noun but doesn't further restrict its reference. (With "Ditzes are silly," by contrast, the adjective feels purely otiose.)

[53] Two people have suggested to me *cunt* could be used in a way parallel to *nigger*. I don't have that intuition (and frankly don't have a lot of faith in theirs, either). I haven't been able to find any unambiguous example of such a usage among several hundred instances of the word on the web or in the BYU corpora—that is, sentences such as, "Now they're going to make management pay cunts the same as men" or "I don't know any cunts who want to serve in combat." If this usage is out there, it's not very common.

does misandry.[54] That point calls out for elaboration, I realize, But for the immediate purposes it's enough to note that while some people might find such a word useful, in the same way dog-haters might welcome a prejudicial for dogs, circumstances aren't congenial to its emergence.

Community and Complicity

The self-affiliating function of slurs is also behind the sense of reluctant involvement that the use of a slur can induce in its audience. Camp is one of a number of writers who have observed that the use of slurs can "produce a sense of *complicity* in their hearers in a way that other taboo expressions do not" (Camp 2013). Croom says that the "the racial slur *nigger* is explosively derogatory, enough so that just hearing it mentioned can leave one feeling as if they have been made complicit in a morally atrocious act" (Croom 2011). These observations have to be qualified. Obviously, the hearer who feels a sense of complicity in the speaker's attitude is not going to be a person that the word targets, who is more likely to feel a victim of the act than a party to it. Moreover, the sense of complicity will only be evoked when the speaker seems to be assuming that the hearer belongs to the group whose identity the word signals, who shares his attitudes about the target group. That is, the word is presumably not being used to shock or provoke the hearer, as it can be when speakers use slurs in order to affirm the social identity that's encoded in the label "politically incorrect."

The sense of complicity that slurs can evoke among the members of the group is crucial to socializing them into its communal attitudes. It can also serve a ritual function, when it works to connect the participants in a shared naughtiness. Reporting on her ethnographic research among working whites in an American suburb, Eliasoph notes that in group contexts, participants, particularly men, often used racist slurs and jokes in the same way they made bathroom jokes and sex jokes, in order to bond around a common defiance of polite norms (Eliasoph 1999). In that sense, she notes, "the group was often more racist than the sum of its parts."[55] (Eliasoph also points out how difficult it is for participants in such a context to object to the use of the words—it would have required "getting on a high horse," she notes, which would in turn have made the objector the butt of another round of jokes.)

But when the speaker wrongly attributes his own social identity to his hearer (who is presumably personally unfamiliar to him), that same behavior can induce a sense of insult, all the more because these words typically have strong working-class associations. Historically, genteel whites have often taken offense at the use of *nigger* in

---

[54] Robin Jeshion has suggested to me that men might be reluctant to embrace a slur that applied to all women, wives, sisters, and mothers included, the idea being, I think, that misogyny is more selective than racism.

[55] It strikes me that these two functions of the use of slurs are connected: they induce a sense of solidarity because their users can envision the reaction they would evoke among the elitist hypocrites who self-righteously condemn any language that might offend some group. The willingness to use a slur thus becomes a demonstration of one's candor and authenticity. As the Irish critic Fintan O'Toole (2004) observes, "We have now reached the point where every goon with a grievance, every bitter bigot, merely has to place the prefix, 'I know this is not politically correct, but …' in front of the usual string of insults in order to be not just safe from criticism, but actually a card, a lad, even a hero." The solidarity invoked by the use of slurs isn't always a collateral effect of the contempt they express for their explicit targets—they can be directed up as well as down.

their presence, chiefly for the speaker's effrontery of assuming that his addressees were of the same social cut as he. A speaker who used the word before respectable whites, an English traveler to America wrote in 1835, spoke "in defiance of decency and in scorn of those rules which every man who respects himself, and is unwilling to be classed with the lowest of the vulgar, observes" (Abdy 1835). Members of nontargeted groups may still react to slurs in this way, when the words are uttered in the apparent belief that the listener shares the identity they signal. I might bristle at being told by a man standing next to me, "There are a lot niggers living in that building." But my indignation probably arises not because the remark obliges me to think of blacks as the speaker does, but because he seems to assume that I already do.[56]

How Slurs Offend

Cases like these demonstrate the connection between the social identities that slurs signal and the offense they can offer to those who don't share those identities. But of course when people talk about offensiveness of slurs, they're thinking not of their effects on nontargeted listeners, but their use as terms of abuse, as instruments aimed at injuring, intimidating, or provoking their targets. Those uses of the words may not be very common or fundamental to the nature of the category: as I noted, people can have slurs for a group whose members they could never encounter. But even so, these are the uses of the words that evoke the most social concern, the ones that the label *slur* itself brings to mind. So any account of slurs has to enable us to explain why their utterance can have the explosive effect I'm describing as their impact. In this section, I want to show that here too, the sense of injury that the words create follows from their self-affiliating function.

For semanticists, explaining the impact of a slur requires explaining how it arises from what the word itself conveys about its targets or about the speaker's attitude towards them. If you think that a slur semantically imputes a negative stereotype to its target, then the impact is a response to that predication. As Hom (2008) puts it:

To predicate a slur of someone is to say that they ought to be treated in such-and-such a way for having such-and-such properties, all because of being a member of a particular group. Depending on the practices and the properties, such a claim can be highly derogatory, and even threatening.

Or if you think of slurs as semantically expressive, you'll locate that the source of their impact in the affect they demonstrate. Jeshion (2013a) explains the offensiveness of the "weapon" uses of slurs via the contempt they convey:

---

[56] The class associations of strong slurs are not attenuated when middle-class speakers use the word in something like the way they use *ain't*, in a gesture of transgressive insolence. That's arguably what's going on when a group of middle-class college fraternity members use the word among themselves, knowing it would not be appropriate at the family dinner table. The same principle may also cover some public versions of this maneuver: in 1853 Thomas Carlyle provocatively retitled his pro-slavery 1850 essay "Occasional discourse on the negro question," substituting *nigger* for *negro*, at a time when the former word was generally regarded in Britain as a vulgar Americanism, particularly after the 1852 publication of *Uncle Tom's Cabin*. (See Campbell 2003).

As a matter of their semantics, slurs function to express the speaker's contempt for his target in virtue of the target's group-membership and that his target ought to be treated with contempt in virtue of that group-membership, because what the target *is, as a person*, is something lesser, something unworthy of equal or full respect or consideration.

Now I've already argued that a slur doesn't conventionally convey either a stereotype of its targets or the speaker's contempt for them. But by way of setting up an alternative account of the words' impact consistent with the story I've developed here, I want to show why those semanticist accounts couldn't explain the phenomenon even if they were correct in other respects.

There are several difficulties here, some of them more familiar than others. First, it has been noted that the impact of a slurring utterance can be independent of the speaker's attitudes or beliefs about the target. A slurring utterance can be offensive even when the speaker makes it clear he doesn't harbor any animus against its target or hold any negative opinions about them—recall the Germanophile who says, "You know, the krauts have gotten a bum rap," and goes on to proclaim his affection for them and attribute to them virtues that run counter to all the invidious stereotypes about Germans.

To account for this disparity, Hom introduces a principle of "derogative autonomy": "The derogatory force for any epithet is independent of the attitudes of any of its particular speakers." For him, this entails that the content of the utterance has to be augmented externally, so as to invest it with the invidious stereotypes that will kindle the feeling of threat or injury. To this end, he appeals to what he calls "combinatorial externalism," modeled on Putnam's framework:

According to CE, because the predicative material is causally determined externally from the speakers' psychology . . . The explosive, derogatory force of an epithet is directly proportional to the content of the property it expresses, which is in turn directly proportional to the turpitude and scope of the supporting racist institution that causally supports the epithet.

The idea is that people can use *chink* in the way they use *arthritis* or *annuity*: the word denotes what authorities say it denotes—or here, perhaps, connotes what authorities say it connotes—whatever the speaker and listener may think it means. If "racist institutions" impute highly negative properties to the Chinese, then that's what any utterance of *chink* predicates of them, which in turn is what gives the utterance its "explosive force." But the analogy to Putnam's externalism doesn't work here. There's a reason why we describe the nonexpert uses of words like *arthritis* and *annuity* as "deferential": in the normal case, the speaker and hearer are willing to defer the determination of the meanings of their utterances to expert judgment. But would we want to say that the speaker who uses *chink* but who has benign and positive opinions of the Chinese is willing to defer to the judgment of racist institutions to determine the actual meaning of her utterance? Suppose that those institutions hold, unbeknownst to her or her listener, that the Chinese are devious, despicable and unfit for management positions. Then on Hom's view, those are the properties that her utterance ascribes to them: she may have thought she was saying the Chinese are candid but she really said they're shifty. But if neither she nor her listener knows that, how could that stereotype possibly invest the utterance with "explosive force" in the immediate context? And how could you hold the speaker morally responsible for predicating those features of the Chinese, if she's unaware of the stereotype and herself attributes only positive traits to them? If the utterance does offend, and if the speaker can be taxed for making it, it's in virtue of something other than what she actually asserted.

From these observations three points follow. First, the impact of a slurring utterance doesn't depend on what the speaker actually predicates (or conventionally implicates) about its target. Second, the impact has to be a consequence of some act for which the speaker can be held culpable. Third, the impact of a slurring utterance is also dependent on some external considerations; there has to be something out there that makes the speaker's *chink*-utterance a slur.

Expressivists wouldn't seem to have the same difficulties here as the representationalists do. If the use of a slur conventionally signals the speaker's contempt for members of the target group in virtue of their race, ethnicity, etc., then a slurring use of the word conveys that they are unworthy of respect and so on. (It conveys that even if the speaker is misrepresenting his actual attitude for some ulterior motive.) On that analysis, it would seem as if the slurring utterance doesn't require any Putnam-type apparatus to augment its content. But things aren't that simple. As we've seen, the users of a slur don't always see it as the expression of negative feelings, yet it can evoke an angry reaction from its targets even so. The majority of people who use *redskin* think that they're conveying their respect for American Indians, but the Indians themselves hear it as the expression of racial animus. (Similarly *squaw*, *cripple*, *mulatto*, and many others.) That's why one can't say that the attitude conveyed by an utterance of a slur is prescribed by the linguistic convention governing its use. And it means that here, too, the impact of the utterance must be determined in part by what the speaker intends and in part by external considerations.

We can demonstrate the need for externalism without having to consider the semantic variation and divisions of linguistic labor that typically figure in these discussions. Even when a speaker obviously despises the targets of a slur and holds invidious beliefs about them, it's not clear why his utterance of the word should invariably be "explosive" or even particularly disturbing. The impact of a slur more often than not exceeds any insult that an individual could inflict simply by manifesting his attitudes about the target, however malignant they are. Why should I care about the attitudes of some pseudonymous bozo who rails about "the kikes" in a Twitter post—why should it matter to me or to anyone what *he* thinks or feels about Jews? Not that his remark isn't annoying in and of itself, if only in the way it's annoying when another driver raises a middle finger to indicate that he thinks I didn't make my left turn with sufficient alacrity. But considered just as an individual, the tweeter has no standing that should drive me to rage. And yet neither his insignificance nor my indifference is sufficient to palliate the offensiveness of the usage.

Thus the offensiveness of a slur follows from the utterance of the word itself, independent of anything the speaker is saying with it. One way of explaining this is via the deflationary account proposed by Anderson and Lepore (2013), who argue that a slur is phonetically toxic in the way an obscenity is, so that merely to pronounce it, whether in indirect or direct discourse, is to violate a taboo. But that story is another example of the presentism that dogs these discussions, where very recent and local features of these words are unwittingly made the basis for general explanations of their use. As a matter of historical fact, only a handful of strong slurs such as *nigger* are genuinely toxic, and even these have been treated as such only since the last part of the twentieth century, as a deliberate response to the perception that they were already highly offensive. (If one were to accept Anderson and Lepore's hypothesis, one would conclude that words such as *redskin* and *faggot* didn't become slurs until objections were raised to them in the 1970s.) Moreover, the mere mention of a slurring word, while often unsettling, is nowhere near as offensive as when it is applied to someone. In fact the interdiction is much stronger in speech than print. You'll virtually never hear someone's use of *nigger* repeated on broadcast news, but the *New York Times* has few qualms about quoting someone's use the word without the need for trigger warnings to protect the sensibilities of readers.[57]

Some have suggested that the mere existence of a slurring word evokes its social backing. As Camp (2013) puts this view, "The very fact of the slur's existence demonstrates that the speaker's perspective is not hers alone, but sufficiently culturally established for a conventional signal of it to maintain widespread use." Saka (2007) develops a similar point; to use a pejorative for someone, he says,

. . . one must belong to a linguistic community in which pejoratives exist. Since the conventionalization of contempt relies, like all convention, on societally recognized norms, every pejorative utterance is proof not only of the speaker's contempt, but proof that such contempt prevails in society at large. This is why pejoratives make powerful insults, why repeated exposures to pejoratives can create feelings of alienation, inferiority, and self-hatred . . .

But as we've seen, the conventions for using words like these aren't defined over society as a whole but only over certain subgroups, some more prominent or extensive than others. There are slurs or derogatives for just about every racial, ethnic and religious group, but that doesn't entail that the attitudes that each of them expresses "prevail in society at large." Online databases list hundreds or thousands of derogative words and phrases, the vast majority of them obscure. The effect of a slur depends on the speaker's prior recognition of its currency, rather than testifying to it. And if disparaging attitudes toward a group actually are pervasive, the hearer presumably doesn't require the evidence of a slur to be reminded of that, nor does society as a whole necessarily need to coin one; as I noted, anti-Muslim feeling has flourished without the help of lexical derogatives.

I've argued here that slurs function by evoking the attitudes about the target that are associated with the group who have constituted the word's historical provenance, which doesn't sound that different from what Camp and Saka say. Similarly, Jeshion points out that slurs can derogate by activating stereotypes and by "raising to salience

---

[57] According to Nexis, in 2013 the word *nigger* was spoken only three times on US broadcast and cable TV news networks, in each instance by blacks recalling the insults they endured in their childhoods. People are more tolerant of its use in print; in that same year, the word appeared 42 times in the *New York Times* alone. The journalism blogger Jim Romenesko (2013) reports that when a TV news reporter in Bloomsburg, Pennsylvania tried to get people in the street to say that the local newspaper had "crossed the line" in repeating the word *nigger* in a story about a school board member who had resigned after using it, he found no takers: "An older white woman said: 'They're just quoting what the man said, so that's not a fault of the newspaper.'"

histories of group oppression." But none of that alone is sufficient to give a slurring utterance its full impact. That follows as well from the speaker's act of self-affiliation with that group. In that sense the force of a slur isn't independent of the speaker's intentions. But what matters is his affiliatory intention, his declaration of solidarity with the speakers who own the word, rather than his own opinions—even, as with the Twitter anti-Semite, when he happens to personally share the views typical of the native provenance of the word. By affiliating himself with the historical owners of the word, the speaker doesn't simply evoke the word's background but materially obtrudes it into the context. Langston Hughes made that point eloquently in his 1940 memoir *The Big Sea*:

The word *nigger* sums up for us who are colored all the bitter years of insult and struggle in America: the slave-beatings of yesterday, the lynchings of today, the Jim Crow cars . . . the restaurants where you may not eat, the jobs you may not have, the unions you cannot join. The word *nigger* in the mouths of little white boys at school, the word *nigger* in the mouth of the foreman at the job, the word *nigger* across the whole face of America! *Nigger! Nigger!*

(Hughes 1993)

As Hughes tells it, that is, the force of *nigger* goes beyond anything the speaker believes or feels about blacks, or for that matter, beyond anything that others who have used the words have thought or felt about blacks. It also evokes the things such people have *done* to blacks—with the speaker pointedly affiliating himself with the perpetrators. The word can turn a bigot from a hapless, inconsequential "I" into an intimidating, menacing "we." That's all there is or could be to the "explosive force" of a slur like *kike* or *nigger*. There is no need to charge the word with an independent expressive component or a similar mechanism. The effect is less like accompanying the word with a threatening gesture or tone of voice that expresses an individual attitude than donning Nazi armband, a Ku Klux Klan hood or some other affiliatory symbol. As Judith Butler puts it, "The speaker who utters the racial slur is…making linguistic community with a history of speakers" (Butler 2013).[58]

That explains how the impact of a slur can be more explosive and threatening than any expression that merely gives voice to the speaker's point of view, however charged it is or how emphatically it is uttered. "You fucking Jew!" can be terribly offensive, but "You kike!" is more intimidating and more ominous. (So is "you dirty Jew," a collocation with a "harsh and hateful . . . cultural pedigree" (Lambert 2009).) It explains, as well, why we don't discern any derogation when a slur is used by someone who is ignorant of its marked status or who can't plausibly pretend to affiliate with its provenance. That can happen because the speaker is a child, or perhaps a nonnative speaker misled by a connotational faux ami, like the Italian who assumes that *redskin* is the equivalent of the neutral *pellerossa*, or the Anglophone who translates *Negro* into French as *négre*, not realizing that the latter term is a slur. Or it might be because

[58] Butler treats slurs as performatives, which succeed "not because an intention successfully governs the action of speech, but only because the action echoes prior actions, and accumulates the force of authority through the repetition or citation of a prior and authoritative set of practices." This is a position widely accepted by Critical Race Theorists, and I think it's consistent with what I've been arguing here, though I'd put the point differently.

the term is regional or obscure, such as *coonass* for Cajuns; or because the speaker is unaware that word is no longer an acceptable designation, such as *Oriental* for Asians or *midget* for those who prefer to be called little people. There's no assumption in such cases that the speaker has pointedly chosen to use this word rather than the default term—as far as he's concerned, it *is* the default term. Those situations can be awkward, particularly if the slur is one of the handful, such as *nigger*, that have become phonetically toxic. But so long as there's a plausible explanation for the speaker's ignorance, we're disposed to let him off the moral hook and offer a polite correction: "By the by, Helmut, we don't say 'Orientals' anymore—it's 'Asians' now."[59]

But speakers do bear moral responsibility when they manifest an intention to affiliate with the provenance of a slur in the knowledge that it is not the default term for a group, even when they disclaim any derogatory intent and insist that the word itself is not a derogation at all. A contemporary American who refers to an Indian as a redskin or who defends the use of the term by others, as we saw, may believe in all sincerity the word is being used in a respectful way. But we're apt to hold her morally accountable even so if she is connecting the word to its appropriate provenance—affiliating herself with those who used it in old Western movies and TV shows, for example. In the judgment of critics and of many Native Americans, to hear those usages and the attitudes they signal as respectful is not just ignorant but culpably obtuse. To be familiar with those contexts and not discern the racism the word expresses is to be the victim of "sincere fictions"; that is, "personal ideological constructions that reproduce societal mythologies at the individual level" (Feagin, Vera, and Batur 2000). But those fictions aren't exculpatory. Here again, it's the affiliatory intention that is morally decisive.

Thus the explosive impact of strong slurs such as *kike* and *nigger* follows from the affiliatory gesture that a speaker performs with a slurring speech act, which is why I say that it's the self-affiliating function of slurs that gives them their power to injure and intimidate. With this in mind we can turn to a third challenge for semanticist accounts of these effects, which is to account for the fact that different slurs for the same group can land with very disparate impact. That point was illustrated in a famous sketch in the opening season of Saturday Night Live (Henry and Henry 2014). Chevy Chase is a job interviewer who asks a job applicant, Mr. Wilson, played by Richard Pryor, to take a word association test. Chase begins with standard pairs—"tree" evokes "dog" and so forth—and then begins to offer a series of increasingly offensive racial terms for blacks. Pryor responds to each with a term for whites of roughly equivalent strength—"Negro" evokes "whitey," "tar baby" evokes "ofay," "colored" evokes "redneck," and so on, until the exchange ends:

INTERVIEWER: Spearchucker!Mr. Wilson: White trash!
INTERVIEWER: Jungle Bunny! Mr. Wilson: Honky!
INTERVIEWER: Spade!Mr. Wilson: Honky honky!
INTERVIEWER: Nigger! Mr. Wilson: *Dead* honky!

---

[59] I say that the speaker's ignorance has to be plausible because there are clearly limits. An adult white native speaker of English who uses *nigger* in apparent ignorance of its associations can be taxed for hanging out with the wrong crowd.

Why do the words that each race uses for the other land with such disparate impact? Nobody has had much to say about that question, or as I noted, about the general phenomenon of variant slurs for a single group. But if these variants correspond to distinct provenances, as I've been arguing, then the utterance of one or another of them suggests an affiliation with a distinct social identity, with its own history, attitudes and practices. If a mid-twentieth century utterance of *nigger* evoked the vitriolic contempt of a diehard segregationist like Strom Thurmond or George Wallace, Norman Mailer's use of *spade* evoked a condescending claim to spiritual kinship with urban black culture—both of them racial sensibilities that were characteristic of the age, but in very different settings and different consequences for the people they were directed at. That's why *spade* didn't have the same malefic effects that *nigger* did, at least in its historical context (a black detective in a 1971 Ed McBain novel speaks disparagingly of the "white phonies who consider it hip to call blacks 'spades,'" which is far from the way that character would have described whites who called blacks niggers (Dove 1985)).

Appropriation, Reclamation, and Meaning Change

It's no wonder that an arch-slur such as *nigger* can be perceived as hurtful or threatening when directed at its target, particularly when the speaker's affiliatory claim isn't implausible. But the effect of the maneuver depends on how we read the speaker's intentions, particularly if he himself is a member of the targeted group speaking to other members. Not always, it's true; the self-directed use of a slur can signal introjected racism, as *nigger* does in the mouth of the servile house slave played by Samuel Jackson in Quentin Tarantino's *Django Unchained*. But when it's contextually implausible that the targeted speaker sincerely endorses the attitudes associated with the native provenance of the word and when her listeners can be expected to perceive the humor or irony of her impersonating those who use it in earnest, the use can create the shared sense of defiance or repudiation that can be the first step toward the reclamation of the word.

It's important to realize, however, that at this stage the word doesn't lose any of its derogatory import—if it did, the effect would be lost. When gays took to using *faggot* in arch self-reference, it was to evoke and ridicule the homophobes who used it in earnest—an instance of what Croom (2013) describes, citing Goffman, as "mock impoliteness."[60] But the appropriated use may also be directed outwards, in a tone of defiance or challenge. Native American high schools that took the name Redskins for their football teams in the 1950s and 60s were playing on the savage connotations of the word, for example as it was used in the ads for Western movies of the period: "Redskin hordes on the vengeance warpath." Their use of the name accomplished two speech-acts, depending on its presumptive addressee: the one ironic, for the benefit of other members of the group, the other defiant, aimed at the white high schools they played—as if to say, "Okay, we'll show you some savage redskin hordes . . . " This

---

[60] For an analogy, think of the way marijuana smokers in the 1960s took to referring to the drug as dope, not with the idea of purging the word of its old-fashioned *Reefer Madness* associations but to emphasize them, in a comic riff on the clueless denunciations of those who lumped the drug with heroin and other narcotics.

dual function is characteristic of many appropriated uses of these words, particularly when they're used in a public way, such by the Dykes on Bikes motorcycle club, whose members traditionally lead off the San Francisco Pride parade, or by the Asian American rock group the Slants.[61]

Since the derogatory import of a slur is unchanged in first-stage (ironic or defiant) appropriation, there's no need to assume that it has become polysemous, as required by theories that incorporate the expression of contempt into the word's conventional meaning.[62] In fact the inferences that give rise to the word's derogatory import are unchanged, except that we don't take the speaker's affiliatory claim in earnest. It's only at the second and third stages of appropriation, which the majority of slurs never reach, that the word really ceases to be a slur and becomes instead the content of a new convention, no longer parasitic on its derogatory use. Gays who use *queer* nowadays are no longer satirizing the homophobes who coined the term, and once that positive sense became a default term in certain contexts, even among straights, a description like Queer Studies has no disparaging implications. (See, e.g., Brotsema 2004, Zwicky 1997.)

Coda: Racism Without "The Racist"

It's a telling peculiarity of the philosophical and linguistic literature on slurs that when writers speak of the "in-group" uses of the words, they're invariably referring to the reclaimed uses by the members of the groups they target.[63] That obviously reflects their focus on the effects of the words on the people they disparage. But when

---

[61] I should make it clear that I'm not endorsing the position that slurs conventionally accomplish two speech acts, one representational or identificational, the other expressive (see Camp 2014, Popa 2016, Tenchini and Frigerio 2016). On the analysis I'm offering, someone who asserts "There are two redskins in my class" performs only one illocutionary act in virtue of the conventional meaning of her words, and in virtue of its manner achieves the perlocutionary effect of signaling a certain social connection to the addressee. But an act of naming potentiates an indefinite number of perlocutionary effects, depending on the context of interpretation and the presumptive addressees. The same name can be calculated to induce solidarity among one group of addressees and to intimidate another, the two effects corresponding to distinct speech acts.

[62] Those who favor treating reclaimed slurs as polysemous include Jeshion (2013b), and Richard (2008), who says, "It is not at all clear that 'queer' preserved its meaning on appropriation by the gay community." In a thoughtful discussion of reclamation, Tirrell (1999) also concludes that the meanings of slurring and reclaimed uses of the words "overlap but are not the same." The problem here, as in many of these discussions, may lie in the failure to distinguish among the successive stages of appropriation and reclamation. On my account, we can assume polysemy only when an originally derogative term can be used by outsiders without its original negative force. By that standard, appropriated terms such as *redneck* and *slut* remain monosemous, whereas *queer* and *Obamacare* are polysemous, though one should bear in mind that to speak of polysemy on this account is to say only that the word is prescribed by the conventions of two or more distinct speech-communities with different attitudes toward its reference. But reclaimed terms often acquire new extensions: *queer* now denotes a range of nonconforming gender identities. This third-stage polysemy is inherently unstable: once the reclaimed use of a slur has been normalized, its original derogative use is likely to be abandoned, as has happened with formerly derogative terms such as state nicknames (e.g., North Carolina tarheels, Indiana hoosiers) and political designations such as Tory and Whig.

[63] See, e.g. Jeshion (2013b), Hom (2008), Saka (2007), Anderson and Lepore (2013), Tirrell (1999), Croom (2013), and Bianchi (2014) among others. The sociologist Irving Allen (1983), by contrast, more appropriately refers to the targets of the words as the out-group.

sociologists or social psychologists speak of the in-group uses of language, they mean its use among the members of the group that owns it. (Think of a phrase like "in-group jargon.") This would be merely a quibble, except that it reflects the pervasive neglect of what I take to be the primary and prior role of these words as the means of expressing the social identity and reinforcing the self-esteem of their users. That point is suppressed when the prototypical speaker is simply "the racist"—not wrong, exactly, but not of much explanatory value, either.

From a sociolinguistic or sociological point of view, that insight is crucial to understanding the role these words play in the formation and reproduction of group attitudes, mirroring a point that has been amply demonstrated in the literature on phonological and syntactic variation (Eckert 2008). With few exceptions, the words are anchored in the everyday experience of the members of the groups that use them—as Allen puts it, they're "the echoes and re-echoes of historical situations, of issues wrangled over, and of the very incidents of contention." What's more immediately relevant here, it's largely the self-identifying function of these words that determines what they convey about their speakers and about their targets—even when, as with reclaimed uses, the pretense of affiliation is patently specious. That perspective allows us to explain some of their familiar properties without having to introduce slur-specific mechanisms—why their import seems impervious to negation, why they tend to be speaker-oriented, why they're usually marked alternatives to a default way of picking out their referents. It also explains a number of the social features of slurs that have played little or no role in this literature: why there should be multiple slurs for a single group; how it can happen that almost all the users of a word can be deluded about its significance: why the utterance of a slur can provoke a stronger reaction in its targets than the attitudes of the speakers would warrant; why slurs evoke a feeling of complicity in certain listeners (and why they often don't); why there are no slurs for certain groups that are the objects of widespread social antipathies.

At the most basic level, it leads us to reframe the question of why there are slurs. From the point of view I'm advocating here, slurring is just a special case of the way speakers exploit sociolinguistic variation to create self-presentations and invest their utterances with attitude. Slurring is no different in method, if not in its effects, from using slang to connect with the members of one's immediate social group or using recondite or foreign words to make an impression. The temptation is always to pack those effects into the meanings of the words themselves—historically, a way of thinking that dictionaries have done a lot to foster. But if slurring were at root a semantic phenomenon, it wouldn't be worth the time we give it.

A Note on Terminology

In the literature on these phenomena, terms like *derogative*, *pejorative*, and *slur* are used in loose and often interchageable ways. In this paper, I've given each of them a distinct and more precise meaning and introduced some new terms such as *prejudicial*. The following sets out the taxonomy of evaluative language I've adopted here.

Semantic mechanism: hybrid words ("thick terms")

Evaluative content can be negated ("John's not a toady; he speaks his mind to his boss") but not asserted without redundancy (¿"Toadies are obsequious"). Often have no nonevaluative descriptive equivalent.

> **Laudatives:**   *steed, paragon, angel* (fig.), *plucky, valiant*
> **Pejoratives:**   *slur, toady, goon, deadbeat, sashay* (v.), *floozie, wierdo*

Pragmatic mechanism: prejudicials

Evaluation conveyed can't be negated (¿"She's not a commie; she's a dedicated socialist revolutionary") and can be independently asserted without redundancy ("Commies are devious"; "Free enterprise is fair"). Typically have a socially unmarked ("neutral") equivalent.

> **Approbatives:**   *jurist, free enterprise, warfighter* (combat soldier)
> **Euphemisms:**   *senior* (n.), *pass away, collateral damage* (civilian casualties)
> **Derogatives:**   *stinkpotter* (motor craft), La La Land, Drumpf (Trump), Obumma, Yalie, *facho* (Fr. "fascist"), *clamhead* (Scientologist).
> → **Slurs:**   derogatives that convey unwarranted contempt for the members of certain socially sensitive categories (typically race, ethnicity, class, nationality, sexual orientation, or religion).[64] E.g. *kraut, pleb, redskin, redneck, hadj* (US military slang for Arabs), *terrone* (It. "Southerner").

Acknowledgments

Earlier versions of this paper were circulated under the title "Slurs Aren't Special." I've presented this material at the CNRS conference on Context and Interpretation at Cérisy-la-Salle, France in June of 2012 and a session on slurs at the American Philosophical Association Pacific Division meetings in March, 2013, as well as at colloquia and seminars at the University of Chicago, Cambridge University, the University of California at Berkeley, and the Institut Jean Nicod, at all of which I received useful feedback. For discussion and comments, I'm grateful to Paul Duguid, Joseph Hedges, Robert Newsom, Geoff Pullum, Jesse Rappaport, Tom Wasow, Seth Yalcin, and François Recanati, and in particular for the extensive notes and suggestions I received from Adam Simon, Robin Jeshion, Daniel Harris, and two sets of reviewers for the *Philosophical Review*.

References

Abdy, E. S. 1835. *Journal of a Residence and Tour in the United States of North America: From April, 1833, to October, 1834*: London: John Murray.
Allen, I. L. 1983. *The Language of Ethnic Conflict: Social Organization and Lexical Culture*: New York, Columbia University Press.
Anand, Pranav. 2007. "Re-expressing Judgment." *Theoretical Linguistics* 33(2): 199.

---

[64] As I noted, *slur* is sometimes used for terms that apply only to certain members of a sensitive category, such as *Uncle Tom* and *bitch*. These are better analyzed as pejorative hybrid terms, since their derogative force is part of their conventional meaning.

Anderson, Luvell, and Ernie Lepore. 2013. "Slurring Words." *Noûs* 47(1): 25–48.

Bach, Kent. 2014. "Mean and Nasty Talk: On the Semantics and Pragmatics of Slurs." Pacific APA, San Diego, April 19, 2014.

Beckman, J. 2014. *American Fun: Four Centuries of Joyous Revolt*: New York: Vintage Books.

Bianchi, Claudia. 2013. "Slurs: un'introduzione," in *Senso e Sensibile: Prospettive tra Estetica e Filosofia del Linguaggio*, vol. 17, edited by Paolo Leonardi and Claudio Paolucci, 41–6. Rome: Edizioni Nuova Cultura.

Bianchi, Claudia. 2014. "Slurs and Appropriation: An Echoic Account." *Journal of Pragmatics* 66(5): 1–62.

Blackburn, Simon. 1984. *Spreading the Word: Groundings in the Philosophy of Language*: Oxford: Oxford University Press.

Blackburn, Simon. 1992. "Morality and Thick Concepts." *Proceedings of the Aristotelian Society* 66: 285–99.

Blakemore, Diane. 2015. "Slurs and Expletives: A Case Against a General Account of Expressive Meaning." *Language Sciences* 52: 22–35.

Boisvert, Daniel R. 2008. "Expressive-Assertivism." *Pacific Philosophical Quarterly* 89(2): 169–203.

Bolinger, Dwight. 1975. *Aspects of Language*. New York: Harcourt Brace Jovanovich.

Bolinger, Renée Jorgensen. 2017. "The Pragmatics of Slurs." *Noûs* 51(3): 439–63.

Brotsema, Robin. 2004. "A Queer Revolution: Reconceptualizing the Debate over Linguistic Reclamation." *Colorado Research in Linguistics* 17: 1–17.

Buchanan, Patrick. 2013. "Hail to the Redskins!" *The American Conservative*, October 22. Accessed: http://buchanan.org/blog/hail-redskins-5953

Butler, Judith. 2013. *Excitable Speech: A Politics of the Performative*: London and New York: Taylor & Francis.

Camp, Elisabeth. 2013. "Slurring Perspectives." *Analytic Philosophy* 54(3): 330–49.

Camp, Elisabeth. 2014. The Semantics of Slurs: A Dual Speech-Act Analysis. MS.

Campbell, D. A. 2003. *English Public Opinion and the American Civil War*: Suffolk: Royal Historical Society/Boydell Press.

Cepollaro, Bianca. 2015. "In Defence Of A Presuppositional Account Of Slurs." *Language Sciences* 52: 36–45.

Copp, David. 2001. "Realist-Expressivism: A Neglected Option for Moral Realism." *Social Philosophy and Policy* 18(02): 1–43.

Croom, Adam. 2011. "Slurs." *Language Sciences* 33: 343–58.

Croom, Adam. 2013. "How To Do Things With Slurs: Studies in The Way of Derogatory Words." *Language & Communication* 33(3): 177–204.

DiFranco, Ralph. 2014. "Pejorative Language." In *Internet Encyclopedia of Philosophy*. Accessed: http://www.iep.utm.edu/pejorati/

DiFranco, Ralph. 2015. "Do Racists Speak Truly? On the Truth-Conditional Content of Slurs." *Thought: A Journal of Philosophy* 4(1): 28–37.

Dove, G. N. 1985. *The Boys from Grover Avenue: Ed McBain's 87th Precinct Novels*: Bowling Green, OH: Bowling Green State University Popular Press.

Dummett, Michael. 1993. *Frege: Philosophy of Language*. Cambridge: Harvard University Press.

Dyer, R. 1997. *White*: London and New York: Routledge.

Eckert, Penelope. 2008. "Variation and the Indexical Field." *Journal of Sociolinguistics* 12(4): 453–76.

Eliasoph, Nina. 1999. "'Everyday Racism' in a Culture of Political Avoidance: Civil Society, Speech, and Taboo." *Social Problems* 46(4): 479–99.

Embrick, David G., and Kasey Henricks. 2013. "Discursive Colorlines at Work: How Epithets and Stereotypes are Racially Unequal." *Symbolic Interaction* 36(2): 197–215.

Feagin, Joe R., Hernan Vera, and Pinar Batur. 2000. *White Racism*. London: Routledge.

Forman, S. 1998. *Blacks in the Jewish Mind: A Crisis of Liberalism*: New York: New York University Press.

Garcia, J. L. A. 1996. "The Heart Of Racism." *Journal of Social Philosophy* 27(1): 5–46.

George, N. 1999. *Hip Hop America*: New York: Penguin Books.

Gilbert, Margaret. 1989. *On Social Facts*: New York: Routledge.

Green, Jonathon. 2010. *Green's Dictionary of Slang*: London: Oxford University Press.

Grice, H. P. 1968. "Utterer's Meaning, Sentence-Meaning, and Word-Meaning." *Foundations of Language* 4(3): 225–42.

Guerts, Bart. 2007 "Really Fucking Brilliant." *Theoretical Linguistics* 33: 209–14.

Gutzmann, Daniel. 2103. "Expressives And Beyond: An Introduction to Varieties of Conventional Non-Truth-Conditional Meaning." In *Beyond Expressives. Explorations In Use-Conditional Meaning*, edited by D. Gutzmann & H.-M. Gärtner. Leiden: Brill.

Hallin, Daniel C. 1986. *The Uncensored War: The Media and Vietnam*. New York: Oxford University Press.

Hay, Ryan. 2011. "Hybrid Expressivism and the Analogy between Pejoratives and Moral Language." *European Journal of Philosophy* 21(3): 450–74.

Hedger, Joseph. 2012. "The Semantics of Racial Slurs." *Linguistic and Philosophical Investigations* 11: 74–84.

Henderson, Anita. 2003. "What's in a Slur?" *American Speech* 78(1): 52–75.

Henry, David, and Joe Henry. 2014. "Saturday Night Live and Richard Pryor: The Untold Story Behind SNL's Edgiest Sketch Ever." *Salon*, Nov. 3.

Hill, J.H. 2009. *The Everyday Language of White Racism*: Oxford: Wiley.

Hom, Christopher. 2008. "The Semantics of Racial Epithets." *Journal of Philosophy* 105: 416–40.

Hom, Christopher, and Robert May. 2013. "Moral and Semantic Innocence." *Analytic Philosophy* 54(3): 293–313.

Hom, Christopher, and Robert May. 2014. "The Inconsistency of the Identity Thesis." *Protosociology* 31: 113–20.

Horn, Laurence R. 1984. "Toward a New Taxonomy for Pragmatic Inference: Q-Based and R-Based Implicature." In *Meaning, Form, And Use In Context: Linguistic Applications*, edited by Deborah Schiffrin, 11–42. Washington: Georgetown University Press.

Horn, Laurence R. 2013. "I Love Me Some Datives: Expressive Meaning, Free Datives, and F-Implicature." In *Expressives And Beyond: An Introduction To Varieties Of Conventional Non-Truth-Conditional Meaning*, edited By D. Gutzmann and H.-M. Gärtner. Leiden: Brill.

Hornsby, Jennifer. 2001. "Meaning and Uselessness: How to Think about Derogatory Words." *Midwest Studies In Philosophy* 25(1): 128–41.

Howitt, Dennis and Kwame Owusu-Bempah. 2005. "Race and Ethnicity in Popular Humour." In *Beyond a Joke: The Limits of Humour*, edited by Sharon Lockyer and Michael Pickering, 45–62. New York: Palgrave Macmillan.

Hudson, R. A. 1996. *Sociolinguistics*: Cambridge University Press.

Hughes, Geoffrey. 1998. *Swearing: A Social History of Foul Language, Oaths and Profanity in English*: London: Penguin Books Limited.

Hughes, Langston. 1993. *The Big Sea: An Autobiography*: New York: Farrar, Straus and Giroux.

Jeshion, Robin. 2013a. "Slurs and Stereotypes." *Analytic Philosophy* 54(3): 314–29.

Jeshion, Robin. 2013b. "Expressivism and the Offensiveness Of Slurs." *Philosophical Perspectives* 27(1): 231–59.

Jespersen, Otto. 1922. *Language; Its Nature, Development And Origin*: New York: Henry Holt.

Kaplan, David. 2005. The Meaning of 'Ouch' and 'Oops': Explorations in the Theory of Meaning as Use, MS.

Lambert, Josh. 2009. "A Literary History of the Dirty Jew." *Jbooks.com*. Accessed: http://jbooks. com/interviews/index/IP_Lambert_DJ.htm

Langton, Rae, Luvell Anderson, and Sally Haslanger. 2013. "Language and Race." In *Routledge Companion to the Philosophy of Language*, edited by Gillian Russell and Delia Graff Fara, 763-7. New York: Routledge.

Lassila, Kathryn. 2009. "What's a Yalie?" *Yale Alumni Magazine*, Jan-Feb.

Levinson, S. C. 2000. *Presumptive Meanings: The Theory of Generalized Conversational Implicature*: Cambridge: MIT Press.

Lewis, David. 1975. "Languages and Language." In *Minnesota Studies in the Philosophy of Science*, edited by Keith Gunderson, 3-35. University of Minnesota Press.

Lewis, David K. 1969. *Convention: A Philosophical Study*. Cambridge, MA: Harvard University Press.

Lighter, J. E. 2014. *Historical Dictionary of American Slang*: Oxford University Press.

May, Robert. 2005. "Bad Words: Remarks On Mark Richard's 'Epithets And Attitudes.' " USC Workshop in the Linguistics/Philosophy Interface, Los Angeles, CA, April 18.

McCawley, James. 1978. "Conversational Implicature in the Lexicon." In *Pragmatics*, edited by P. Cole. New York: Academic Press.

McCready, Eric. 2010. "Varieties of Conventional Implicature." *Semantics & Pragmatics* 3: 1-57.

McLeod, Kembrew. 1999. "Authenticity Within Hip-Hop and Other Cultures Threatened With Assimilation." *Journal of Communication* 49(4): 134-50.

Mencken, H. L. 1944. "Designations for Colored Folk." *American Speech* 19(3): 161-74.

Mieder, Wolfgang. 1996. " 'No Tickee, No Washee': Subtleties of a Proverbial Slur." *Western Folklore* 55 (1): 1-40.

Miles, R. 2004. *Racism*: London: Taylor & Francis.

Millikan, R. G. 2005. *Language: A Biological Model*: Oxford: Oxford University Press.

Nunberg, Geoffrey, Ivan Sag, and Thomas Wasow. 1994. "Idioms." *Language* 70(3): 491-538.

O'Toole, Fintan. 2004. "The Words We Use." *The Irish Times*, May 5.

Peck, A. 1985. *Uncovering the Sixties: The Life and Times of the Underground Press*: New York: Pantheon Books.

Picardi, Eva. 2006. "Colouring, Multiple Propositions, and Assertoric Content." *Grazer Philosophische Studien* 72(1): 49-71.

Picca, L. H., and J. R. Feagin. 2007. *Two-faced Racism: Whites in the Backstage and Frontstage*: New York: Routledge.

Popa, Michaela. 2016. "Role Assignment: Explaining The Variable Offense Of Slurs." American Philosophical Association, Pacific Meeting, San Francisco.

Potts, Christopher. 2005. *The Logic of Conventional Implicatures*: Oxford: Oxford University Press.

Potts, Christopher. 2007. "The Expressive Dimension." *Theoretical Linguistics* 33(2): 165-97.

Potts, Christopher. 2012. "Conventional Implicature And Expressive Content." In *Semantics: An International Handbook of Natural Language Meaning*, edited by Klaus von Heusinger Claudia Maienborn, and Paul Portner, 2516-36. Berlin: Mouton de Gruyter.

Rappaport, Jesse. Communicating with Slurs. MS.

Rappoport, L. 2005. *Punchlines: The Case for Racial, Ethnic, and Gender Humor*: Westport, CT: Praeger Publishers.

Rattansi, Ali. 2007. *Racism: A Short Introduction*: Oxford: Oxford University Press.

Richard, Mark. 2008. *When Truth Gives Out*: Oxford: Oxford University Press.

Richard, Mark. 2011. "Reply to Lynch, Miščević, and Stojanović " *Croatian Journal of Philosophy* 32: 197-208.

Romenesko, Jim. 2013. TV Station Tries to Get People to Criticize Paper for Printing School Board Member's N-Word Quote. *JimRomensko.com* (March 15).

Roy, P. E. 2011. *The Oriental Question: Consolidating a White Man's Province, 1914–41*: Vancouver: UBC Press.

Sadock, J. M. 1978. "On Testing for Conversational Implicature." In *Syntax and Semantics: Pragmatics, 9*, edited by P. Cole, 281–98. New York: Academic Press.

Saka, Paul. 2007. *How to Think About Meaning*. Vol. 109, Philosophical Studies. Dordrecht: Springer.

Schlenker, Philippe. 2007. "Expressive Presuppositions." *Theoretical Linguistics* 33(2): 237–45.

Sclar, A. 2008. *"A Sport at which Jews Excel": Jewish Basketball in American Society, 1900–1951*: State University of New York at Stony Brook.

Sennet, Adam, and David Copp. 2014. "What Kind Of A Mistake Is It To Use A Slur?" *Philosophical Studies* 172(4): 1–26.

Tenchini, Maria Paola, and Aldo Frigerio. 2014. "La Semantica Multi-Atto Degli Slur." *Rassegna Italiana di Linguistica Applicata* 46(1): 261–75.

Tenchini, Maria Paola, and Aldo Frigerio. 2016. "A Multi-Act Perspective on Slurs." In *Pejoration*, edited by Rita Finkbeiner, Jörg Meibauer and Heike Wiese. Amsterdam: John Benjamins.

Tirrell, Lynne. 1999. "Derogatory Terms: Racism, Sexism, and the Inferential Role Theory of Meaning." In *Language and Liberation: Feminism, Philosophy, and Language*, edited by Christina Hendricks and Kelly Oliver. Albany NY: SUNY Press.

Wescott, Roger W. 1971. "Labio-Velarity and Derogation in English: A Study in Phonosemic Correlation." *American Speech* 46(1/2): 123–37.

Whiting, Daniel. 2013. "It's Not What You Said, It's the Way You Said It: Slurs and Conventional Implicatures." *Analytic Philosophy* 54(3): 364–77.

Williams, Raymond. 1976. *Keywords: A Vocabulary Of Culture And Society*. New York: Oxford University Press.

Williamson, Timothy. 2009. "Reference, Inference, and the Semantics of Pejoratives." In *The Philosophy of David Kaplan*, edited by Joseph Almog and Paolo Leonardi, 137–58. Oxford: Oxford University Press.

Wu, C. T. 1972. *"Chink!": A Documentary History of Anti-Chinese Prejudice in America*: New York: World Pub.

Zwicky, Arnold. 1997. "Two Lavender Issues for Linguists." In *Queerly Phrased: Language, Gender, and Sexuality*, edited by Anna Livia and Kira Hall. Oxford: Oxford University Press.

Zwicky, Arnold. 2006. Does Anybody Have a Word for This? Probably Not. In *Language Log*. Accessed: http://itre.cis.upenn.edu/ myl/languagelog/archives/003846.html

11

Commitment to Priorities

Paul Portner

11.1 Strong and weak imperatives

We have a clear sense that some imperatives are "stronger" than others:

(1) a. Soldiers, march! (Strong)
     b. Have a cookie! (Moderate or Weak)

What are we judging when we describe one imperative as stronger than another? Several different factors seem to be involved. First, with some examples, the imperative is imposed upon the addressee; with others, the addressee's choice determines whether it takes effect:

(2) a. Sit down, and don't get up until I tell you to!
     b. Have a seat. You'll be more comfortable.

Second, in some cases, the imperative "makes true" the corresponding modal statement (in an intuitive sense which we need to understand further); in others, the modal statement seems to be already true at the point when the imperative is used, and expresses the justification for the use of the imperative:

(3) a. Friends, begin your meditation now!
     b. They should begin to meditate now.

(4) a. Do not park in the dry cleaner's lot!
     b. They should not park in the dry cleaner's lot.

At the point when (3a) is uttered, it is not the case that the students should begin to meditate, but after their teacher says so, they should. The imperative makes it the case that they should begin to meditate. In contrast, when (4a) is uttered, it's already the case that they should not park in the lot (because they will get a ticket). The imperative serves to remind the addressee of this fact or to urge the addressee to make the right choice.

A third type of difference involves the relation between imperatives and different levels of necessity. In some cases, an imperative allows an inference to a strong necessity statement, for example one involving *must* or *have to*; in other instances, the imperative does not imply the truth of a strong necessity statement, but we can infer a weak necessity (*should* or *ought to*) or a possibility statement:

(5)   a. Soldiers, march! → They must march.
      b. Have a cookie! → He #must/should have a cookie.

Intonation affects the intuitive strength of imperatives in a way parallel to its effect on declaratives. In (6)–(7), the arrows represent forms of rising and falling intonation.

(6)   a. It's cold out.[↓]
      b. It's cold out?[↑]

(7)   a. Have a seat⇊
      b. Have a seat⇑

The notation ↓ represents the falling intonation which goes along the sentence being uttered "as an assertion", while ↑ represents the rising intonation when it is used "as a question". See Gunlogson (2001) for this use of ↓ and ↑. Similarly, ⇊ represents the intonation associated with the imperative being uttered "as a command", while ⇑ represents that associated with its use "as a request or permission".[1]

In this paper I will suggest that the last observation is important for understanding all of the others. Specifically, I will explore the idea that the contribution of an imperative to discourse should be explained using (i) a pragmatic model which tracks the commitments of individual participants in a conversation, as well as the joint commitments, and (ii) a theory of the grammar-meaning interface in which intonational patterns help indicate the ways that sentences affect these commitments. Models of the type in (i) have been used to represent the "fact-seeking" side of discourse since at least Hamblin's (1971) early formal work on dialogue, and they have been used recently to analyze the discourse meanings of declaratives, interrogatives, and polar particles (Gunlogson 2001; Farkas and Bruce 2010; Roelofsen and Farkas 2015). Gunlogson (2001) proposes that rising and falling declaratives differ in whether they primarily express speaker or addressee commitment. I will argue that similar models and a similar connection to intonation are applicable to the deontic or "prioritizing" side as well.

11.2 Dynamic pragmatics

My analysis will be presented in terms of the framework of DYNAMIC PRAGMATICS. Dynamic pragmatics is a theory of discourse meaning which makes use of the following fundamental ideas:[2]

(8)   **Dynamic pragmatics**:
    1. Sentences have standard static semantic values.

---

[1] The patterns ↑ and ⇑ are not identical. *Have a seat* ↑ is an echo question. Bolinger (1989) generally confirms the intuition that steadily falling intonation is associated with commands and a rise with permission and invitation; see his work for additional discussion.

[2] "Dynamic pragmatics" is a new term, to my knowledge, though the approach has been developing for more than forty years. See Portner (2018) for more detailed discussion. Lauer (2013) uses the term "dynamic pragmatics" for a rather different set of ideas. Schlenker (2010) uses it to describe Stalnaker's work, in much the same sense as used here, and Stalnaker (2014, this volume) continues to develop the the approach.

2. The communicative effect of utterances in discourse is modeled as the effect they have on the discourse context.
3. The effect of an utterance of a particular sentence is determined by pragmatic principles on the basis of syntactic or semantic features.

There is important work on both imperatives and the meaning associated with into-nation within dynamic pragmatics, and since our interest here is in the intersection of these two topics, it it perhaps the most appropriate approach on which to build. Later in this section, I will make some remarks on the relation between dynamic pragmatics and other, closely related frameworks (dynamic semantics and speech act theory).

11.2.1 The development of dynamic pragmatics and the structured discourse context

Dynamic pragmatics is a framework, not a theory, and there are many versions around. In this section, I'll trace the lineage of some key ideas within dynamic pragmatics. Figure 11.1 provides a visually-oriented summary. (Darker lines indicate what I take to be the most important contribution of each scholar to the state of the art.)

Hamblin and the structured discourse context Hamblin (1971) can be understood as giving a series of generative grammars for dialogue. His various systems explore different ideas about the structure of dialogue and the contributions of utterances to dialogue. For our purposes, the most important system is his System 7. Here's my formulation of that system:

1. **Dialogue**
   (a) There are five types of LOCUTIONS: assertions, retractions, inquiries, retraction-demands, and *I don't know.*
      In symbols: The set L consists of five non-overlapping subsets $\lambda, \mu, \xi, \eta, L_0$.
   (b) A DIALOGUE is a sequence of locutions $\langle l_0, l_1, \ldots, l_i \rangle$.
2. **Commitment slates**
   (a) A COMMITMENT SLATE is a set of assertions.

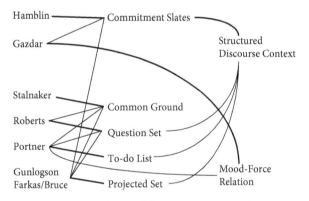

Figure 11.1 Evolution of dynamic pragmatics theories

(b) The relation between locutions and commitment slates: For each locution in a dialogue $D = \langle l_0, l_1, \ldots, l_i \rangle$, $CS_j(p)$ is a commitment slate representing participant p's commitments in D after locution j.

Note that Hamblin's system associates a commitment slate with each participant in the dialogue (see Figure 11.1).

Rules define the set of well-formed dialogues. Some of the relevant rules are paraphrased below:

(9) a. Following an assertion, everyone's commitment slate includes that assertion.

   b. Following a retraction by participant p, p's commitment slate does not include what was retracted, but every other participant's commitment slate remains unaltered.

   c. An inquiry (i.e., question) is not allowed if its answer is in anyone's commitment slate.

   d. Following an inquiry, the next locution must be an assertion by someone other than the speaker of the inquiry and must answer it.

Because Hamblin's ideas are formulated as a grammar of dialogue, its relation to more familiar dynamic theories is somewhat obscured, but we can easily reformulate Hamblin's ideas in a more familiar context-and-update format. In order to re-express Hamblin's approach, we begin by defining a "context" as follows:

(10) **Contexts.** A HAMBLIN CONTEXT is a locution and an associated assignment of commitment slates to individuals.

Specifically, the context for locution l_j is:

$C_{j-1} = \langle l_{j-1}, CS_{j-1} \rangle$, where CS_{j-1} assigns a set of propositions to every participant p in the discourse.

Here we have an important early exemplar of the STRUCTURED DISCOURSE CONTEXT. The discourse context is modeled as a set-theoretic object with components doing the job of representing different aspects of the discourse. In this case, the context has p+1 parts (where p is the number of participants) which serve to represent (i) the most recent locution and (ii) each of the participants' commitments. By building the model this way, Hamblin hypothesizes that such information is all that is needed to explain the meaning of the dialogue and to predict the contribution of the next utterance.

Given the definition of a context, (11) is a formalization of Hamblin's first rule (9a).

(11) For any context $C = \langle l, CS \rangle$: If l' is an assertion (i.e., $l' \in \lambda$), $C + l' = \langle l', CS' \rangle$, where for every participant p, $CS'(p) = CS(p) \cup \{l'\}$.

We can readily formalize the other rules in (9b–d) in a similar way, but it is not worthwhile to do so here. See Portner (2018) for more discussion of Hamblin's ideas in relation to modern discourse semantics.

Gazdar and sentential force Gazdar (1981) sketches an approach to sentential force which builds on Hamblin's version of the structured discourse context. The key ideas of Gazdar's model can be summarized as follows:

1. **The content of a speech act.** The semantic value of any sentence can be the propositional content of a speech act. These contents have various semantic types:
   (a) The meaning of a declarative sentence is a proposition.
   (b) The meaning of an interrogative sentence is a set of propositions.
2. **Illocutionary force.** An illocutionary force is a function from contents to update potentials.
3. **Update potential.** An update potential is a function from contexts to contexts.
4. **Contexts.** Though Gazdar doesn't commit to understanding contexts this way, he suggests Hamblin's (1971) commitment slates as a good basis for providing a definition of contexts.
5. **Speech act assignment.** A speech act assignment is a pair $\langle f, c \rangle$ consisting of a force f and a content c.
6. **Speech acts.** A speech act is $f(c)$, for any speech act assignment $\langle f, c \rangle$.

These ideas of Gazdar's are important because they make explicit a possible way of linking grammatical categories to functions with the dynamic pragmatics model. It will be helpful to make explicit some terminology (Portner, 2018):

(12)   SENTENCE MOOD is an aspect of linguistic form conventionally linked to the fundamental conversational functions within semantic/pragmatic theory.

(13)   These fundamental functions can be called SENTENTIAL FORCES.

It is often assumed that sentence moods correspond closely to syntactically defined clause types like declarative, interrogative and imperative. Given this, we can see that Gazdar proposes an important role for sentence mood within the system. In combination with the provisionally-assumed model of context from Hamblin, his analysis implies that declaratives are normally associated with speech act assignments $\langle f, c \rangle$ where $f(c)$ updates one or more individuals' commitment slates, while interrogatives are normally associated with speech act assignments where $f(c)$ creates a context in which an answer must come next.

It is easy to read the part of Gazdar's paper in which the above framework is sketched out as implying an analysis of sentential force. It would be natural to build on his ideas to say that declaratives are conventionally associated with a force f_{assert} which updates every commitment slate by adding c, and that interrogatives are associated with f_{ask} which adds c as the most recent locution without affecting any commitment slates.[3] But Gazdar in fact raises such an approach (as a form of the LITERAL FORCE HYPOTHESIS, the claim that every sentence has a literal force with which it is associated in every context of use), and explicitly denounces it. For example, he specifically argues that the classic example, *Can you pass the salt?* is only associated with the force of requesting, and not with the force of asking at all.

For Gazdar, because there is no literal or basic force associated with the various sentence moods, sentential forces are identical to illocutionary forces. As we will see, later work in the dynamic tradition has departed from Gazdar on this point, but

---

[3] Perhaps it would add to the speaker's commitment slate "speaker wants to know whether c", or something similar.

it is worth noting that, because Gazdar's use of Hamblin's model has been largely overlooked in the subsequent literature, the scholars in this tradition have never dealt explicitly with his arguments against the literal force hypothesis.

Stalnaker and the common ground Stalnaker's (1974; 1978) COMMON GROUND is the set of propositions mutually assumed by the participants in a conversation. The common ground differs from the Hamblin context in that there is only one set of propositions representing *mutual commitments*,[4] rather than a record of commitments for each participant. As is well known, Stalnaker uses the common ground (and its reduction to the **context set**) to analyze acts of assertion and pragmatic presupposition.

Lewis and the sphere of permissibility Lewis (1979a,b) gives an analysis of imperatives which treats them as having the semantics of modal sentences but with a discourse effect which can be seen as extending the dynamic pragmatics approach. In the context of describing a language-game involving a master and a slave, Lewis proposes a truth-conditional semantics for imperatives involving two accessibility functions (functions from world-time pairs to sets of worlds or world-time pairs):

1. The SPHERE OF PERMISSIBILITY $f_{sp}(\langle w, t \rangle)$ is the set of worlds representing the requirements governing the slave's actions at w and t.
2. The SPHERE OF ACCESSIBILITY $f_{sa}(\langle w, t \rangle)$ is the set of worlds compatible with the actual history of w up to time t.

The sphere of permissibility represents the requirements governing the slave's actions at w and t, and the sphere of accessibility identifies the set of worlds compatible with the actual history of w up to time t. An order-type imperative is interpreted as a strong necessity statement with respect to the intersection of these two relations. That is, $!\phi$ is true with respect to $\langle w, t \rangle$ iff ϕ is true at every world both permissible and accessible from w and t (i.e., iff $f_{sp}(\langle w, t \rangle) \cap f_{sa}(\langle w, t \rangle) \subseteq [\![\, \phi \,]\!]$).

Lewis made a number of important contributions to dynamic pragmatics, including a well-known evaluation of the prospects for a dynamic analysis of permission. I'd like to focus on the directive force which is sometimes associated with sentences with the logical form $!\phi$. Lewis proposes that, if the master uses an imperative $!\phi$ when it is not true with respect to f_{sp} and f_{sa}, a rule of accommodation applies which adjusts f_{sp} (if possible) so as to make the imperative true. In general, $f_{sp}(\langle w, t \rangle)$ adjusts to $f_{sp}(\langle w, t \rangle) \cap [\![\, \phi \,]\!]$.

(14)   **Rule of accommodation for imperatives.** When $!\phi$ is spoken by the master to the slave but $!\phi$ is not true with respect to f_{sp} and f_{sa}, $f_{sp}(\langle w, t \rangle)$ adjusts to $f_{sp}(\langle w, t \rangle) \cap [\![\, \phi \,]\!]$ if this makes $!\phi$ true.

This intersective effect of an imperative on the sphere of permissibility is analogous to assertion on Stalnaker's analysis. However, Lewis's use of a rule of accommodation is an important difference from other dynamic pragmatics theories, including Stalnaker's. According to Lewis, the dynamic pragmatic effect of an imperative is not a

---

[4] The mutual commitments can be called *shared* or *joint commitments*. It is not clear whether any difference in status is implied by these different terms (or others one may find).

basic matter of the updating of the sphere of permissibility by the imperative's content, but rather derived indirectly from three factors: its modal necessity semantics, the principle of accommodation, and an unstated rule which requires that accommodation apply in just this way to imperative sentences.[5]

Roberts and the question set Roberts (2012, a revised version of Roberts 1996) builds a theory of discourse "moves" (divided into **assertions** and **questions**) using a dialogue-grammar similar to Hamblin's. Translated into a context-and-update format, Roberts' theory has the following crucial features:

(15) **Contexts.** A ROBERTS CONTEXT is a common ground and a question set.
- The most recent member of the question set is the QUESTION UNDER DISCUSSION.

(16) **Relevance.** A move m is RELEVANT to the question under discussion Q if and only if:
a. m is an assertion, and it provides at least a partial answer to Q, or
b. m is a question and a complete answer to m entails at least a partial answer answer to Q.

(17) **Context change potential.** An assertion-move, if accepted, updates the common ground. A question-move, if accepted, updates the question set.

Roberts' ideas are similar to Hamblin's but her notion of the question set is an improvement upon Hamblin's analysis of inquiries, because it allows questions to have an effect on the evolution of the discourse beyond the immediately subsequent move. Moreover, in her use of Relevance, she gives a deeper explanation of this effect. (Around the same time, Ginzburg 1996 and Hulstijn 1997 present similar ideas in frameworks more closely related to speech act theory and dynamic semantics.) Though it is suggestive that she employs the terms "assertion" and "question" for different types of moves, in Roberts' usage assertions and questions are act-types, not clause types; for this reason, we cannot confidently attribute to Roberts a theory of sentence mood and sentential force.

Portner and the To-do List Portner (2004), building on Hausser (1980, 1983), presents a dynamic pragmatics model of the sentential forces of the three basic clause types. His version of the structured discourse context contains a common ground, question set, and function which assigns a TO-DO LIST to each participant in the conversation:

(18) **Contexts.** A PORTNER CONTEXT is a common ground, a question set, and a to-do list function.
1. Common ground: a set of propositions
2. Question set: a set of questions

---

[5] By limiting his attention to the master-slave scenario, Lewis is able to state that the sphere of permissibility adjusts, if it can, to make whatever the master says about permissibility true. But such a formulation does not allow an explanation of the difference in actual function between imperatives and explicit modal necessity sentences. In other words, Lewis does not explain why imperatives, according to his theory, always (or virtually always) trigger accommodation when not true, while sentences with overt modals only do so sometimes.

3. To-do list function: a function from participants in the conversation to to-do lists.
   - The to-do list of an individual a is a set of properties restricted to a.

Portner assigns sentential force on the basis of the compositional meaning of a sentence.

(19) **Semantic values.**
   a. The semantic value of a declarative sentence is a proposition.
   b. The semantic value of an interrogative sentence is a set of propositions.
   c. The semantic value of an imperative sentence is a property restricted to one individual (the addressee).

(20) **Force assignment.** The force of a root sentence S is a function updating the discourse context by adding $[\![\,S\,]\!]$ to the component of the context which is a set of objects from the same semantic domain as $[\![\,S\,]\!]$.

The to-do list is understood to represent the mutual assumptions in the conversation about which actions are preferred. (Technically, the to-do list defines a pre-order over the context set and an action is deemed rational and cooperative if it tends to make it the case that the actual world is maximally highly ranked.)

In Portner's work, we see a further development of Hamblin's, Gazdar's and Roberts' ideas. While the most obvious new claim is that the discourse context contains a component specifically designed to handle imperatives, Portner also takes the step of associating each sentence mood with a single sentential force. He says that the Force assignment principle must be used whenever it can be; for example, unless there is some reason why a particular declarative cannot be assigned the force of assertion (=update the common ground), it will be assigned that force. In combination with his assumptions about semantic values, this means that declarative type as a whole has a direct, conventional connection to the force of assertion (and similarly for interrogatives and imperatives). Portner does not discuss the exact parameters which would lead to a particular sentence's not receiving the force normally associated with its type, so it is not clear how he would respond to Gazdar's arguments against the literal force hypothesis. In particular, it's not clear whether he would say that *Can you pass the salt?* has the literal force of asking, or whether the contextual inappropriateness of the literal question in context would be enough to block the assignment of this force. Either way, however, it is clear that Portner sees clause type as the most important factor in force assignment, with contextual factors playing a secondary filtering role.

The Santa Cruz school and the utility of commitment slates Both Roberts and Portner assume that assertion is to be modeled with reference to the common ground rather than individual commitment slates for each participant. In this, they represent the majority of formal work in discourse semantics over the past thirty years; it has become a standard assumption that the common ground (or a similar construct) is the right tool for the job of modeling assertion. However, individual commitment slates have not been entirely lost to the literature. With the project of analyzing rising declaratives like (6a), Gunlogson (2001) presents a dynamic pragmatics model which, like Hamblin's, keeps track of the individual commitments of the speaker and addressee. Her key idea is the following:

1. Falling declaratives commit the speaker towards the proposition expressed.
2. Rising declaratives commit the addressee towards the proposition expressed.

Gunlogson's theory is somewhat inexplicit on some important points which play a role in her informal discussion. For example, it doesn't really make sense to say that rising declaratives commit the addressee in the same way that falling declaratives commit the speaker. The speaker can hardly commit the addressee in this way. Rather, rising declaratives seek confirmation that the addressee really is committed towards the proposition expressed. In addition, the theory does not incorporate an analysis of assertion, understood as the type of speech act which aims to create joint commitment towards a proposition. A falling declarative only commits the speaker, and if the speaker intends for the addressee to share the commitment, this is must be inferred indirectly. In this respect, Gunlogson does not account for the intuition that falling declaratives normally aim for joint commitment.

It is also noteworthy that Gunglogson contradicts standard assumptions concerning clause type and sentence mood; specifically, she classifies rising declaratives as questions and her theory does not have a clear concept of sentential force. These properties might be seen as problematical or refreshing, depending on one's perspective.

Farkas and Bruce (2010) develop Gunlogson's framework in a way which clarifies some of the issues on which her discussion was inexplicit or incomplete. Their notion of the structured discourse context incorporates the question set (called the "table") and adds a new component, the PROJECTED SET, which indicates anticipated future developments of the conversation.

(21) **Contexts.** A FARKAS/BRUCE CONTEXT is a tuple $\langle CS, cg, qs, ps\rangle$, where:
   a. CS is a function from discourse participants p to p's discourse commitments.
   b. cg is a common ground.
   c. qs is a stack of issues to be resolved. [treated as a set below]
   d. ps is a set of projected extensions of cg.

With ps, the system is able to represent the effect of a falling declarative as not only indicating the speaker's commitment, but also proposing its addition to the stock of shared commitments.

(22) **Context change of a falling declarative.** The conventional effect of a falling declarative $S\downarrow$ in context C is: $C + S = C'$, where:
   1. $CS'(speaker) = CS(speaker)\cup\{[\![\,S\,]\!]\}$
   2. $cg' = cg$
   3. $qs' = qs\cup\{[\![\,S\,]\!]\}$
   4. $ps' = \{c \cup cg\cup\{[\![\,S\,]\!]\}|c \in ps\}$

The presence of $[\![\,S\,]\!]$ in each element of ps indicates that the sentence's content will enter the common ground, unless a participant raises an objection. In other words, this theory makes the assumption that, though speakers do not normally have the right to make a proposition into a joint commitment simply by asserting it, they do normally have the right to create a bias in favor of its becoming a joint commitment. Farkas and Bruce do not discuss rising declaratives, but it would capture Gunlogson's idea to say that $S{\uparrow}$ affects $CS(addressee)$ rather than $CS(speaker)$, but affects qs and ps in the same way.[6]

Looking ahead I am going to argue that a dynamic pragmatics model which incorporates distinct representations of the speaker's and addressee's committed priorities allows us to address in an insightful way the variation in strength among imperative clauses. Building on the works discussed above, in particular Portner (2004) and Farkas and Bruce (2010), I propose a structured model of the context which separates individual commitments, mutual commitments, and projected commitments towards both factual information and priorities:

(23)   A CONTEXT is a tuple $\langle MC, IC, PC \rangle$, where:
   1. $MC = \langle cg, tdl \rangle$
   2. For each participant p, $IC(p) = \langle cs_p, tdl_p \rangle$
   3. $PC = \langle pc_{cg}, pc_{tdl} \rangle$

Intuitively, the members of MC are the **mutual commitments** (the common ground and function tdl, which assigns a to-do list to each participant in the conversation), the members of $IC(p)$ are the **individual commitments** of p (towards information and priorities), and PC represents the **projected extensions** of MC.

11.2.2 Other approaches

Dynamic pragmatics is closely related to two other important approaches to the relation between semantics and discourse meaning. The first of these is DYNAMIC SEMANTICS (e.g. Groenendijk and Stokhof 1990, 1991; Heim 1992; Groenendijk et al. 1996; Aloni and van Rooy 2002; Starr 2013). The key difference between dynamic pragmatics and dynamic semantics concerns the assumptions about sentence meaning, and indeed we can define dynamic semantics by its adherence to the following tenet.

(24)   **Dynamic semantics**: Sentence meanings are update potentials.

Dynamic semantics and dynamic pragmatics have been intertwined throughout their development. For example, we see in Heim's work (Heim 1982, 1983a,b, 1992) a change from a dynamic pragmatics perspective grounded in Stalnaker's system to an endorsement of full dynamic semantics: "the meaning of a sentence is its context change potential (CCP)....A CCP is a function from contexts to contexts" (Heim 1992, 185). Portner (2018) compares dynamic pragmatics and dynamic semantics at length, and Stalnaker (this volume) explicitly argues in favor of the former. It is

---

[6] This approach would also let us assign a reasonable sentential force to all declaratives, namely the addition of the sentence's content to ps. But despite this apparent traditionalism in their understanding of sentence mood, later work in the same tradition (such as Roelofsen and Farkas 2015, similarly to Groenendijk and Roelofsen 2009) even more radically breaks down the difference between declaratives and interrogatives.

useful to have a term for what's shared by the two, and I will say they are both varieties of the DYNAMIC APPROACH.

Some influential work in the tradition of classical speech act theory builds on ideas originating with the dynamic approach. Specifically, we find scholars who assume the DYNAMIC FORCE HYPOTHESIS (Gazdar 1981; Krifka 2001; Charlow 2011; Kaufmann 2012):

> (25) **Dynamic force hypothesis**: Classical speech act theory combined with the idea that illocutionary force should be modeled using the tools of the dynamic approach.

It is difficult to say whether Gazdar's ideas should be classified as falling within dynamic pragmatics or speech act theory (under the dynamic force hypothesis). He was thinking through how to improve upon the assumptions of classical speech act theory, and as he did this, he seems to present a prescient version of a dynamic pragmatics model. However, other (more well-recalled) parts of his paper are widely seen as having helped to refute a key tenet of classical speech act theory, the literal force hypothesis, and for many interested scholars, this leads to his work being seen as puncuating the end of a line of research, rather than forming the beginning of one (see Levinson 1981).

The more recent analyses given by Charlow (2011) and Kaufmann (2012) very clearly accept the dynamic force hypothesis. Both situate their theories within the tradition of speech act theory. Charlow then argues that root sentences which perform basic speech acts update one of the parameters of a structured discourse model; imperatives, in particular, update the "body of preferences" of a discourse model. Kaufmann understands the illocutionary force of both declarative and imperative utterances to involve updating the common ground.

It seems to me that, because dynamic pragmatics uses pragmatic principles to associate a given sentence's content with an update potential, it is particularly well-suited to making use of intonational factors in the assignment of force. Intonation can be one factor among several which plays a role in this assignment. In contrast, and while I believe that the fundamental ideas about imperative force and intonation developed below could be incorporated into either dynamic semantics or speech act theory, these approaches seem less well-suited to the task. To give a flavor for why this is the case, note that many scholars who follow these theories make the traditional assumption that a root sentence is divided into a force-indicator and a sentence radical which gives its propositional content; on such assumptions, the ideas we are developing here would then imply that intonation contributes in a systematic way to the force indicator. I do not know of any precedent for analyzing force compositionally within dynamic semantics; within speech act theory, Searle and Vanderveken (1985) and Vanderveken (1990, 1991) do derive force in a compositional way, but their work does not follow the dynamic force hypothesis.

11.3 Individual and mutual commitment to priorities

In this section, I develop an analysis of imperatives which builds in crucial respects on the line of research respresented by Gunlogson (2001) and Farkas and Bruce

(2010). Then I will argue that it can explain the differences between strong and weak imperatives on all of the different ways of understanding what "strong" and "weak" amount to. Finally, I will discuss some problematic cases.

11.3.1 The basic idea

If the commitment slate approach, with its separation of the commitments of speaker and addressee, is relevant to imperatives, the first place to look might be intonational patterns. Can we analyze intonational differences in imperatives in a way similar to rising and falling declaratives? To test out the basic idea, let's examine how a translation of Gunlogson's ideas to imperatives would work. For this project, let's call (7a: *Have a seat*⇑) a "rising imperative" and (7b: *Have a seat*⇓) a "falling imperative".

Rising imperatives propose the addressee's commitment to treating the imperative's content as a priority, while falling imperatives propose the speaker's commitment. We can express this using the context model of (23) as follows:[7]

(26) The conventional effect of a falling imperative $S{\Downarrow}$ in context C is:
$C + S {\Downarrow} = C'$, where:
1. $tdl'_{speaker}(addressee) = tdl_{speaker}(addressee) \cup \{[\![\,S\,]\!]\}$
2. $pc'_{tdl}(addressee) = \{c \cup tdl(addressee) \cup \{[\![\,S\,]\!]\} \mid c \in pc_{tdl}(addressee)\}$

(27) The conventional effect of a rising imperative $S{\Uparrow}$ in context C is:
$C + S{\Uparrow} = C'$, where:
1. $tdl'_{addressee}(addressee) = tdl_{addressee}(addressee) \cup \{[\![\,S\,]\!]\}$
2. $pc'_{tdl}(addressee) = \{c \cup tdl(addressee) \cup \{[\![\,S\,]\!]\} \mid c \in pc_{tdl}(addressee)\}$

According to these definitions, both rising and falling imperatives add an expectation in pc_{tdl} that the imperative's content will be added to tdl, i.e. an expectation that the interlocutors will come to a mutual commitment about how to judge the addressee's actions. But falling imperatives in addition add the imperative's content to $tdl_{speaker}(addressee)$, while rising imperatives add it to $tdl_{addressee}(addressee)$.

The basic analysis captures some basic intuitions about rising and falling imperatives.

1. (a) *Have a seat*⇓ would naturally be used in a context in which the speaker has directed the addressee to sit down, and doesn't care whether the addressee wants to.
    (b) The analysis correctly implies that the speaker rates futures in which the addressee sits down higher than those in which he does not, and creates an expectation that this judgment will become mutual.
2. (a) *Have a seat*⇑ would naturally be used in a context in which it is assumed that the addressee will be more comfortable if he sits down, and is being invited or given permission to do so.

---

[7] In general, apart from the differences stated, C' will be very similar to C. I do not say it is identical because there may be other parts of S, such as presupposition triggers and expressive elements, which independently affect C.

(b) The analysis correctly implies that the addressee rates futures in which the addressee sits down higher than those in which he does not, and creates an expectation that this judgment will become mutual.

Only one point is perhaps less than obvious: that *Have a seat*⇑ creates an expectation that 'you sit down' will be on the mutual to-do list. But I think this is correct. The sentence implies that the speaker wants the addressee to be comfortable, and is seeking confirmation that his sitting down should be preferred on those grounds.

Update or presupposition? I am not sure whether the relation between the imperative's content and $tdl_{speaker}$ or $tdl_{addressee}$ should be modeled as an update or a presupposition. I suspect it should be a backgrounded update. We don't have a standard dynamic model of this kind of relation, but it seems to me that the proposed updates to *IC* are, in effect, backgrounded, in the sense that they are never put "on the table" (see Horn 2002, Herburger 2011, Murray 2014 for relevant recent discussion).

11.3.2 Strong and weak imperatives

The model continues to be useful as we go back to the earlier inventory of ways in which some imperatives are strong and others weak.

A. With some examples, the imperative is imposed upon the addressee; with others, the addressee's choice determines whether it takes effect:

(28) a. Sit down, and don't get up until I tell you to!
      b. Have a seat. You'll be more comfortable.

This distinction is related to the basic difference between rising and falling imperatives. Example (28b) would be uttered with rising intonation; it is just (7a) with some more context.

Example (28a) would naturally be uttered with falling intonation, and adds 'sit down' to $tdl_{speaker}(addressee)$ and $pc_{tdl}(addressee)$; this indicates that it's the speaker's preference which serves as the basis for the expectation that 'sit down' will be added to the addressee's mutually assumed to-do list.

In some contexts, like that assumed for (1a) and maybe that of (28a) as well, the speaker has a type of **authority** which really leaves the addressee with no role to play in determining whether the imperative takes effect. We can model this by saying that such imperatives go directly onto the to-do list, without a stage at which they are projected (in $pc_{tdl}(addressee)$) but not yet shared (in $tdl(addressee)$).

B. In some cases, an imperative makes true the corresponding modal statement; in others, it is justified by it:

(29) a. Friends, begin your meditation now! ⇒ They should begin to meditate now.
      b. Do not park in the dry cleaner's lot! ⇐ They should not park in the dry cleaner's lot.

When (29a) is used, the proposition that the students begin to meditate goes onto $tdl_{speaker}(addressee)$ and $pc_{tdl}(addressee)$, indicating that the meditation teacher has as a priority that the students begin to meditate and that he projects this as a mutual commitment. At this point, the teacher's preferences can serve as the basis for the modal statement. (Technically speaking, we say that $tdl_{speaker}(addressee)$ can serve as an ordering source for *should*, cf. Portner 2007.) The teacher has authority similar to that of the officer who orders his soldiers to march in (1a), but the spirit of the meditation class does not involve imposing his will directly on the students; we can say that a meditation teacher employs a gentle form of authority. Thus, the priority does not immediately become a mutual commitment, but it is expected that the teacher's mere projection of mutual commitment is enough to motivate its subsequently becoming a mutual commitment.

Turning now to (29b), its initial effect is to add 'do not park' to $pc_{tdl}(addressee)$ and $tdl_{addressee}(addressee)$. This indicates that the speaker thinks the addressee prefers not parking in the dry cleaner's lot and that she expects that this preference will be promoted to the mutually committed status. But why would it be so promoted? This utterance is not based on authority in any sense, not even the gentle authority of the meditation teacher, and so the speaker must have a reason in mind why the addressee would want to accept the priority of not parking in the cleaner's lot. This reason—namely, that parking there will be worse for the addressee because his car would be towed—makes true the modal statement even prior to the imperative being uttered. This is why (29b) is understood to urge the addressee to make a choice which is already justified by modal fact.

An alternative way of thinking about the imperative in (29b) might be that it just means 'you should not park in the dry cleaner's lot'. That is, we might identify the meaning of the imperative here with that of the *should* sentence, rather than saying it has a separate directive meaning.[8] However, the following contrast seems to show that such an approach to (29b) would not work:

(30)   You should not park in the dry cleaner's lot, because you'll get a ticket if you do. So, . . .
  a. do not park in the dry cleaner's lot!
  b. ??you should not park in the dry cleaner's lot!

The imperative *Do not park in the dry cleaner's lot!* has a function here, namely urging the addressee to do something for her own good, which the modal declarative cannot have in this context.

C. Some imperatives license an inference to a strong necessity statement; others license an inference to a weak necessity statement.

(31)   a. Soldiers, march! → They must march.
  b. Have a cookie! → He #must/should have a cookie.

To understand this contrast, we must begin with an idea about the difference between *must* and *should*. I would like to build on recent work which argues that *must* claims

---

[8] In very rough outline, this is the modal theory of Kaufmann (2012). In fact, (30) appears to be a counterexample to Kaufmann's proposal that imperatives are synonymous with *should* sentences, except for the fact that they are restricted to contexts in which the latter are understood performatively. The felicity of the imperative in (30a) shows that this would have to be a context in which a *should* sentence would have a performative meaning, and yet the infelicity of the *should* sentence in (30b) cannot be used in that way.

are based only on assumptions to which all parties to the conversation are committed in the context, while *should* claims may involve some assumptions which are not so contextually committed (Rubinstein 2012; Portner and Rubinstein 2016).[9] The intuition behind this work can be illustrated with the following, based on examples in Rubinstein 2012 and Portner and Rubinstein 2016:

(32)   a. We must make sure all our citizens have proper health insurance.
       b. We should make sure all our citizens have proper health insurance.

In the case of (32a), the speaker is saying that ensuring universal coverage follows from assumptions which are not up for debate. (Of course the addressee might actually debate them, but the speaker doesn't grant that they are under debate.) It is a bid to cut off further discussion. With (32b), the speaker says that ensuring universal coverage follows from a contextually relevant set of assumptions, but does not assume that none of those assumptions are up for debate. For this reason, (32b) seems to invite further discussion.

Given this way of looking at *must* and *should*, (31) makes sense. Because of the authority behind it, (31a) adds 'march' directly to the addressee's to-do list, where it has a mutually assumed status. As such, it can be used as a premise for a *must*-statement. In contrast, (31b) projects 'have a cookie' as a future shared assumption about the addressee's priorities, but does not automatically give it this status. Since it is not yet represented as being mutually assumed, it cannot serve as the basis for a strong, *must*-type necessity statement. However, as a projected mutual commitment, it is a perfect candidate to serve as a premise for a *should*-type modal statement.

11.3.3 Imperatives which are not fully directive

Several kinds of imperatives have posed problems for previous dynamic analyses because they are not used with the intention to create a mutual commitment to judge some action positively. In other words, their directive force seems somehow incomplete or deficient. In terms of the current theory, they do not seek to update the addressee's to-do list. I would like to discuss briefly how they fit into the picture being developed here.

Instructions, directions, disinterested advice Charlow (2011) discusses the instruction (33), asked to a stranger on the street:

(33)   a. How does one get to Union Square from here?
       b. Take Broadway to 14th (for example).

(See also Kaufmann 2012 and Condoravdi and Lauer 2012.) We can describe the pragmatics of instruction imperatives in this model as adding the imperative's content to the addressee's individual plans (i.e., to $tdl_{addressee}(addressee)$) but not to the projected mutual commitments (i.e., not to $pc_{tdl}(addressee)$). This makes sense because the person giving the instruction is not going to judge the stranger positively for taking Broadway, or negatively for not doing so. He simply doesn't care. More generally, he does not expect to form any mutual commitments with the person who asked for directions, since their conversation is going to end after (33b) with a "Thanks."

---

[9] Rubinstein's work builds directly on that of von Fintel and Iatridou (2008).

COMMITMENT TO PRIORITIES 311

Absent wishes Kaufmann (2012) discusses the wish (34):

(34)   Please, be rich! [On one's way to a blind date] (absent wish)

(See also Charlow 2011 and Condoravdi and Lauer 2012.)[10] In terms of the model, absent wishes are the opposite of instructions. They can be described as adding the imperative's content to the speaker's preferences $tdl_{speaker}(addressee)$ while not treating it as a projected commitment. The speaker is representing himself as committed to preferring that the addressee be rich, but not expecting a mutual commitment toward this preference.

Example (34) shows another property noted by Mastop (2011): the individual being treated as addressee is not really an addressee. She is not even truly in the context of utterance, and so some sort of context-shifting is involved in such examples.[11] The fact that the "addressee" is absent may be part of the reason why 'be rich' is not added to $pc_{tdl}(addressee)$—there can be no expectation of a mutual commitment with someone who is not really present.

Counterfactual imperatives Mastop (2011) discusses example (35), considering it a type of imperative:

(35)   Was toch lekker thuisgebleven.
        Was prt   prt   at.home.stay-pp
        'You should just have stayed at home.'

I do not think this type can be accounted for just with the separation of speaker's and addressee's commitments. The reason is that 'you stayed at home' will not establish a non-trivial ordering relation among worlds compatible with the common ground, since there are no worlds in which the addressee stayed home in that set. Nor will turning attention to the speaker's commitment slate help, since the speaker is also assumed to know that the addressee did not stay home.

As Mastop argues, such examples (if they are to be treated as imperatives on the dynamic pragmatics approach) require that the range of alternatives under consideration be expanded. This expansion of the set of relevant alternatives would be quite similar to what happens with factive and anti-factive predicates like *be glad* and *wish* in the analyses of Heim (1992) and Villalta (2008).

(36)   a. I want to order the steak.
        b. I wish I had ordered the steak.

On the assumption that desire predicates have a comparative modal semantics, (36a) can analyzed as saying that in the most desirable worlds compatible with the speaker's

---

[10] It might be thought that the stativity of (34) is the reason for its wish-type interpretation. However, the following shows this is not the case:

(i)   Please, don't ask what I do for a living! [On one's way to a blind date]

(The speaker doesn't want to have to explain what a linguist does.) Rather, not expecting mutual commitment towards a member of $tdl_{speaker}$ is a basic property in itself.

[11] In fact, (34) does not mean that the speaker prefers that the particular person who will actually show up for the date be rich, but rather than the speaker prefers that a rich person be the addressee. If his date turns out to be poor Jill, he would not complain that Jill is not rich, but rather that he was not set up with a different, richer person.

beliefs, she orders the steak. However, in (36b) it is presupposed that the speaker did not order the steak, and so the desirability ordering of the speaker's belief worlds would not distinguish worlds in which she has steak from worlds in which she does not. In order for the comparative semantics to work, the set of relevant worlds must be expanded from just the belief worlds, to include other worlds in which the speaker ordered steak. These are the ones ranked as more desirable.

In terms of the theory of imperatives being developed here, we would expand the set of relevant alternatives by removing propositions from the common ground (or speaker's commitment slate) or by replacing some propositions with weaker ones. Then the counterfactual imperative would lead to a to-do list which non-trivially ranks worlds compatible with this adjusted context. What's not clear at this point is what we want to do with the weakened common ground. Should it be a fundamental component of the structured discourse context itself, or is it somehow encoded implicitly?[12]

11.4 Summary and further issues

In this paper, I hope to have accomplished two things: First, I aimed to review the dynamic pragmatics approach in a way which both distinguishes it clearly from dynamic semantics and speech act theory and highlights its insights and contributions. And second, I proposed an analysis of imperatives which makes use of both individual and shared commitments to explain certain aspects of the variation in function among imperatives.

The ideas developed in this paper raise a number of important issues, and I would like to call attention to the following in particular:

A. The semantics of intonation. How reliably does intonation indicate the function of imperatives in the ways relevant to semantic/pragmatic theory?

Note that an addressee-benefit imperative like (29b) can be uttered with falling intonation (esp. with focus on *not*: *Do NOT park in the cleaners!*). And Bolinger states that (37) can be uttered with rising intonation "if I wish to threaten imminent retribution" (Bolinger 1989, 152).

(37) Put it down!

(Here the intonation may indicate an implicit conditional interpretation ... *or I'll shoot!*) These points may only indicate that we do not understand in enough detail which intonational features are relevant to sentential force. Matters are also more complex than they've been portrayed with declaratives; note, for example, that an assertion-type declarative can be uttered with rising intonation (and a wince) when the speaker is in fear of immediate retribution:

---

[12] The distinction between expanded and original context set is closely related to that between the CONTEXT OF JUSTIFICATION and the CONTEXT OF DELIBERATION in deontic logic (Thomason 1981a,b). van der Torre and Tan (1998) and Portner (2009) describe a dynamic logic which keeps track of both, and Portner (2018) discusses its usefulness for analyzing sentence mood.

(38) I crashed the car.

At our current stage of understanding it's reasonable to limit our attention to the few intonational patterns about which we have some understanding.

B. Compositionality. Do intonational features contribute to sentential force in a compositional way? More generally, do those features have meaning independent of the clause type they are associated with?

A starting point would be Gunlogson's hypothesis that the overall sentential force of a declarative is compositionally derived from a declarative "proto-force" and an intonational specification of whether this force targets the speaker's or addressee's commitment slate. An alternative view would hold that sentence mood and intonation specify two separate dimensions of discourse function, with the ultimate force of the utterance being a combination of the two.

C. The nature of sentence mood. The traditional view distinguishes sentence moods syntactically, for the most part identifying each with the root occurrences of one clause type. However, Gunlogson, Farkas, and Bruce, and the authors of inquisitive semantics have implicitly challenged the status of declaratives and interrogatives as separate sentence moods (although they are analyzed as separate clause types).

Our discussion of imperatives suggests that a standard association of clause type and sentence mood is correct (at least when it comes to imperatives and declaratives). The imperative clause type is associated with the sentential force of updating the addressee's to-do list, although it often does so indirectly through IC and PC, and occasionally not at all. This qualifies it as a sentence mood. Non-directive imperatives like instructions and idle wishes would also have imperative sentence mood, although they do not have the associated sentential force, because they have grammatical properties which lead to that force in more canonical contexts.

These issues are obviously of both great difficulty and fundamental importance to semantics and pragmatics. The goal of this paper has merely been to motivate a better dynamic pragmatics model in which they can be studied.

Acknowledgements

I would like to thank audiences at the University of British Columbia, Yale University, MIT, and the Hebrew University of Jerusalem for very helpful feedback on the material presented here. Daniel Fogal, as editor of this volume, gave comments which led to significant improvements. This research has been supported by NSF award BCS-1053038 'The Semantics of Gradable Modal Expressions' to Graham Katz, Elena Herburger, and Paul Portner.

References

Aloni, Maria, and Robert van Rooy. 2002. The dynamics of questions and focus. In *Proceedings of semantics and linguistic theory 12*, ed. Brendan Jackson, 20–39. Ithaca, NY: CLC Publications.

Bolinger, Dwight L. 1989. *Intonation and its uses: Melody in grammar and discourse*. Stanford, CA: Stanford University Press.

Charlow, Nathan. 2011. Practical language: Its meaning and use. Doctoral Dissertation, University of Michigan.

Condoravdi, Cleo, and Sven Lauer. 2012. Imperatives: Meaning and illocutionary force. In *Empirical issues in syntax and semantics 9*, ed. Christopher Piñón, 37–58. Paris: Colloque de Syntaxe et Sémantique à Paris. http://www.cssp.cnrs.fr/eiss9/.

Farkas, Donka, and Kim B. Bruce. 2010. On reacting to assertions and polar questions. *Journal of Semantics* 27: 81–118.

von Fintel, Kai, and Sabine Iatridou. 2008. How to say *ought* in foreign: The composition of weak necessity modals. In *Time and modality*, eds. Jacqueline Guéron and Jacqueline Lecarme, 115–41. Berlin: Springer. http://web.mit.edu/fintel/fintel-iatridou-2008-ought.pdf.

Gazdar, Gerald. 1981. Speech act assignment. In *Elements of discourse understanding*, eds. A. Joshi, Bruce H. Weber, and Ivan A. Sag, 64–83. Cambridge: Cambridge University Press.

Ginzburg, Jonathan. 1996. Dynamics and the semantics of dialogue. In *Language, logic and computation, volume 1*, ed. J. Seligman, CSLI Lecture Notes. Stanford: CSLI, 221–37.

Groenendijk, Jeroen, and Floris Roelofsen. 2009. Inquisitive semantics and pragmatics. Presented at the Stanford workshop on Language, Communication and Rational Agency.

Groenendijk, Jeroen, and Martin Stokhof. 1990. Dynamic Montague grammar. In *Papers from the symposium on logic and language*, eds. L. Kálman and L. Pólos, 3–48. Budapest: Adakémiai Kiadó.

Groenendijk, Jeroen, and Martin Stokhof. 1991. Dynamic predicate logic. *Linguistics and Philosophy* 14: 39–100.

Groenendijk, Jeroen, Martin Stokhof, and Frank Veltman. 1996. Coreference and modality. In *The handbook of contemporary semantic theory*, ed. Shalom Lappin, 179–213. Oxford: Blackwell Publishers. https://staff.fnwi.uva.nl/f.j.m.m.veltman/papers/FVeltman-cm.pdf.

Gunlogson, Christine. 2001. *True to form: Rising and falling declaratives as questions in English*. New York: Routledge.

Hamblin, Charles L. 1971. Mathematical models of dialogue. *Theoria* 37: 130–55.

Hausser, Roland. 1980. Surface compositionality and the semantics of mood. In *Speech act theory and pragmatics*, eds. J. Searle, F. Kiefer, and M. Bierwisch, 71–95. Dordrecht and Boston: Reidel.

Hausser, Roland. 1983. The syntax and semantics of English mood. In *Questions and answers*, ed. F. Kiefer. Dordrecht: Reidel, 97–158.

Heim, Irene. 1982. The semantics of definite and indefinite noun phrases. Doctoral Dissertation, University of Massachusetts, Amherst.

Heim, Irene. 1983a. File change semantics and the familiarity theory of definiteness. In *Meaning, use, and interpretation of language*, eds. R. Bauerle, C. Schwarze, and A. von Stechow, 164–89. Berlin: Mouton de Gruyter. Reprinted in Paul Portner and Barbara H. Partee (eds.) (2002). *Formal Semantics: The Essential Readings*. Oxford: Blackwell Publishers, 223–48.

Heim, Irene. 1983b. On the projection problem for presuppositions. In *Proceedings of WCCFL 2*, ed. M. Barlow, D. Flickinger, and N. Wiegand, 114–25. Stanford: Stanford University. Reprinted in Paul Portner and Barbara H. Partee (eds.) (2002). *Formal Semantics: The Essential Readings*. Oxford: Blackwell Publishers, 249–60.

Heim, Irene. 1992. Presupposition projection and the semantics of attitude verbs. *Journal of Semantics* 9: 183–221.

Herburger, Elena. 2011. Negation. In *Semantics: An international handbook of natural language meaning*, eds. Klaus von Heusinger, Claudia Maienborn, and Paul Portner, volume 2, 1641–60. Berlin: de Gruyter.

Horn, Laurence R. 2002. Assertoric inertia and NPI licensing. In *CLS 38: The panels*, eds. Mary Andronis, Erin Debenport, Anne Pycha, and Keiko Yoshimura, 55–82. Chicago: Chicago Linguistics Society.

Hulstijn, J. 1997. Structured information states. raising and resolving issues. In *Proceedings of MunDial97*, eds. A. Benz and G. Jager, 99–117. Munich: University of Munich.

Kaufmann, Magdalena. 2012. *Interpreting imperatives*. Dordrecht: Springer.

Krifka, Manfred. 2001. Quantifying into question acts. *Natural Language Semantics* 9: 1–40.

Lauer, Sven. 2013. Towards a dynamic pragmatics. Doctoral Dissertation, Stanford University.

Levinson, Stephen C. 1981. The essential inadequacies of speech act models of dialogue. In *Possibilities and limitations of pragmatics: Proceedings of the conference on pragmatics, Urbino, July 8–14, 1979*, eds. H. Parret, M. Sbisà, and J. Verschueren, 473–492. Amsterdam: John Benjamins.

Lewis, David K. 1979a. A problem about permission. In *Essays in honour of Jaakko Hintikka*, eds. E. Saarinen, R. Hilpinen, I. Niiniluoto, and M. Provence Hintikka, 163–75. Dordrecht: Reidel.

Lewis, David K. 1979b. Scorekeeping in a language game. *Journal of Philosophical Logic* 8: 339–59.

Mastop, Rosja. 2011. Imperatives as semantic primitives. *Linguistics and Philosophy* 34: 305–40. http://dx.doi.org/10.1007/s10988-011-9101-x.

Murray, Sarah E. 2014. Varieties of update. *Semantics and Pragmatics* 7: 1–53.

Portner, Paul. 2004. The semantics of imperatives within a theory of clause types. In *Proceedings of semantics and linguistic theory 14*, eds. Kazuha Watanabe and Robert B. Young, 235–52. Cornell University Linguistics Department: CLC Publications. https://staff.fnwi.uva.nl/f.j.m.m.veltman/papers/FVeltman-cm.pdf.

Portner, Paul. 2007. Imperatives and modals. *Natural Language Semantics* 15: 351–83.

Portner, Paul. 2009. *Modality*. Oxford: Oxford University Press.

Portner, Paul. 2018. *Mood*. Oxford: Oxford University Press.

Portner, Paul, and Aynat Rubinstein. 2016. Extreme and non-extreme deontic modals. In *Deontic modals*, eds. Nate Charlow and Matthew Chrisman, 256–82. Oxford: Oxford University Press.

Roberts, Craige. 1996. Information structure in discourse: Towards an integrated formal theory of pragmatics. In *Papers in semantics*, eds. Jae-Hak Toon and Andreas Kathol, OSU Working Papers in Linguistics, Vol 49, 91–136. Columbus: Department of Linguistics, Ohio State University.

Roberts, Craige. 2012. Information structure in discourse: Towards an integrated formal theory of pragmatics. *Semantics and Pragmatics* 5: 1–69.

Roelofsen, Floris, and Donka Farkas. 2015. Polarity particle responses as a window onto the interpretation of questions and assertions. *Language* 91(2): 359–414.

Rubinstein, Aynat. 2012. Roots of modality. Doctoral Dissertation, University of Massachusetts, Amherst.

Schlenker, Philippe. 2010. Presuppositions and local contexts. *Mind* 119: 377–91.

Searle, John R., and Daniel Vanderveken. 1985. *Foundations of illocutionary logic*. Cambridge: Cambridge University Press.

Stalnaker, Robert. 1974. Pragmatic presuppositions. In *Semantics and philosophy*, eds. M. Munitz and P. Unger, 197–213. New York: New York University Press.

Stalnaker, Robert. 1978. Assertion. In *Syntax and semantics 9: Pragmatics*, ed. P. Cole, 315–32. New York: Academic Press.

Stalnaker, Robert. 2014. *Context*. Oxford and New York: Oxford University Press.

Starr, William B. 2013. A preference semantics for imperatives. MS., Cornell University.

Thomason, Richmond H. 1981a. Deontic logic and the role of freedom in moral deliberation. In *New studies in deontic logic*, ed. Risto Hilpinen, 177–86. Dordrecht: D. Reidel Publishing Co.

Thomason, Richmond H. 1981b. Deontic logic as founded on tense logic. In *New studies in deontic logic*, ed. R. Hilpinen, 165–76. D. Reidel Publishing Co.

van der Torre, Leon W. N., and Yao-Hua Tan. 1998. An update semantics for deontic reasoning. In *Proceedings of DEON'98*, 409–26.

Vanderveken, Daniel. 1990. *Meaning and speech acts*, Volume 1: Principles of language use. Cambridge: Cambridge University Press.

Vanderveken, Daniel. 1991. *Meaning and speech acts*, Volume 2: Formal semantics of success and satisfaction. Cambridge: Cambridge University Press.

Villalta, Elisabeth. 2008. Mood and gradability: an investigation of the subjunctive mood in Spanish. *Linguistics and Philosophy* 31: 467–522.

12

Speech Acts in Discourse Context

Craige Roberts

12.1 Introduction: Speech acts in a QUD model of discourse

If one is committed to the development of a scientific account of human language, aiming to explain how linguistic form is related to meaning in context, then an adequate theory of speech acts would need to satisfy the following desiderata:

Linguistic desiderata for speech act theory:
A theory of speech acts should be linguistically motivated—grounded in the conventional content of the utterances used to make them—and explanatory, offering testable predictions about both (a) the kinds of speech acts attested across languages, and (b) in particular utterances, the kind of speech act we would take a speaker to proffer, given the conventional content of what she says and the context of utterance.

Then what is a speech act, and how do we differentiate different types? The Austinian tradition best exemplified by the work of Searle aims to classify the kinds of speech acts we perform. For example, here's the taxonomy from Searle (1969, 1975):

Assertives:
Commit the speaker to the truth of a proposition: suggesting, putting forward, swearing, boasting, concluding. *No one makes a better cake than me.*

Directives:
Atttempt to make the addressee perform an action: asking, ordering, requesting, inviting, advising, begging. *Could you close the window?*

Commissives:
Commit the speaker to some future course of action: promising, planning, vowing, betting, opposing. *I'm going to Paris tomorrow.*

Expressives:
Express how the speaker feels about a state of affairs: thanking, apologizing, welcoming, deploring. *I am sorry that I lied to you.*

Declarations:
Change the state of the world to bring it into conformity with the propositional content: *You are fired, I swear, I beg you, I hereby pronounce you man and wife.*

This taxonomy may be of interest from the point of view of the theory of action or social theory. But it isn't clear that it would satisfy the linguistic desiderata above. I will offer an alternative, simpler taxonomy that's better motivated linguistically and, I will argue, under the proper understanding of the character and role of the goals and intentions of interlocutors in a discourse interaction, permits one to predict, for a given utterance in a particular context, which type of Searlean function that utterance might serve.

Searle offers several parameters which distinguish his speech acts. But the most important is *direction of fit*, of which there are two values: Speech acts display **word to world** fit just in case they portray the world as being so-described. Speech acts display **world to word** fit in case they propose that interlocutors behave in such a fashion that the world comes to fit the description. Searle (1975:158) notes "Direction of fit is always a consequence of illocutionary point. It would be very elegant if we could build our taxonomy entirely around this distinction in direction of fit, but though it will figure largely in our taxonomy, I am unable to make it the entire basis of the distinctions."

I'm going to argue that we can, and in fact should, do this. We can profitably distinguish speech acts in terms of this two-way distinction, with one natural elaboration:

- **assertion**: an act of proposing an addition to the interlocutors' C(ommon) G(round) (Stalnaker 1979). If adopted, this addition would commit the interlocutors to accepting that (and behaving as if) the *world fits the words*. Note that this is a weaker commitment than belief, in keeping with Stalnaker's (1979) characterization of the interlocutors' Common Ground.
- **suggestion**: an act of proposing that interlocutors adopt intentions to act in specific ways. There are two types of speech act proposals reflecting an essential distinction in the types of goals interlocutors may propose in discourse:
  - **direction**: an act in which a speaker proposes to her addressee that he adopt a particular intention to act in the world. This is the sort of speech act typically performed with an imperative. It is a proposal to *make the world fit the words*.
  - **interrogation** or **question**: an act of proposing that the interlocutors collectively commit to collaborative inquiry, thus an act which would establish a direction for the discourse itself. It is a proposal that the interlocutors endeavor to *discover the proper fit between world and words*, thereby resolving the question.

In other words, on this view all speech acts propose to one's interlocutor that they make some type of commitment, and the central distinction between them lies in whether the proposal involves a commitment to the world being truthfully portrayed by the content of the utterance (assertion), a commitment to adopt intentions to make the world change so as to conform to the way it is portrayed by the utterance (direction), or a proposal to find the correct fit between world and word among those alternatives associated with a question (interrogation). The distinction among the two types of suggestions is about whether the proposed intentions should be adopted by one of the interlocutors (typically the addressee) as a spur to action, or whether inquisitive intentions should be jointly adopted with a view to the direction of discourse.

This taxonomy cross-cuts Searle's at several junctures. Some of his Directives would be interrogations on this view (for example *asking*); while others would be directions (*ordering, inviting, advising, …*); and some might be classed here as assertions (*I hereby request that you close the window*). Speech acts which fall under my category of assertions may be found in all five of his types. Besides the Directive just noted and the Assertives, these would include most Commissives (*vowing*, as in the example *I'm going to Paris tomorrow*), Expressives (*I am sorry that I lied to you*) and Declarations (including performatives like *I hereby pronounce you man and wife*, to be discussed in §12.4.3). So it is clear that the present account approaches the question of what a speech act is, and how we might distinguish different types of speech acts, from a different angle.

If we are to develop a linguistically satisfying account of speech acts, and speech act types, we need to provide empirical evidence for the types of speech acts proposed and a theoretically interesting explanation of how they are differentiated and recognized by interlocutors. While most of the classical work on speech acts tended to focus on verb types, especially performative verbs, the linguistic evidence suggests that the foundation of such an account should instead be a theory of the semantics and pragmatics of clause types. In this connection, there are two observations about grammatical mood, which I take to reflect language universals. Here is the first:

Mood (grammatical universal):   All known languages display three basic clause types, characterized as a distinction in grammatical mood:
Declarative
Interrogative
Imperative

As Sadock and Zwicky (1985:160) put it, one might find it "a surprising fact that most languages are similar in presenting three basic **sentence** types with similar functions and often strikingly similar forms. These are the declarative, interrogative, and imperative."[1] These moods may be realized quite differently from language to language or even in one and the same language. For example, interrogative mood may be reflected morphologically in some languages (e.g. Japanese verbal morphology), syntactically in others (English word order and extraction), or even prosodically (English utterance final phrase accent and boundary tone). But it is generally agreed that mood arises as a function of the compositional morpho-lexical and structural semantics of the clause. Moreover, as Sadock and Zwicky observe, there are a number of notable syntactic similarities in the imperative across languages, including both the fact that even in ergative languages the addressee is almost always the subject in imperative sentences, whether transitive or intransitive, and a strong tendency for subjects and subject-verb agreement to be suppressed in imperatives, even in

---

[1] See Portner (2018; this volume) for an excellent discussion and overview of the literature on the relationship between clause types, sentence types, and sentence force, and how (and why) we need to differentiate these notions. I assume that *grammatical mood* is what distinguishes the three types of clauses of interest here, a distinction which may be syntactically and morphologically complex, as Portner discusses in detail.

languages which otherwise display an obligatory subject agreement feature on the main verb.

The grammatical mood universal is reflected cross-linguistically in a second universal, a robust generalization about the pragmatics of mood:

Mood (pragmatic universal):   There is a strong correlation between choice of grammatical mood and intended type of move in a language game:
Declarative mood is typically used to make an **assertion**
Interrogative mood is typically used to pose a **question**
Imperative mood is typically used to issue a **direction**

We should be careful not to confuse this correlation with the *semantic content* of grammatical mood itself. One important reason is that each of these moods may be used in embedded clauses, which carry no illocutionary force themselves. Moreover, even in main clauses, one mood may be used to perform different types of acts, e.g. a declarative used to pose a question (looking at someone quizzically, I say *you're not hungry*, even without final prosodic rise) or issue an order (*you* WILL *clean your plate!*). Most formal semantic work on declarative and interrogative mood has taken them to conventionally indicate the semantic type of the resulting interpretation: a declarative denotes a proposition: type $<s,t>$, whereas an interrogative denotes a set of propositions: type $<<s,t>, t>$ (intuitively, the set of alternative possible answers to the question). Recent work on the semantics of imperatives by Portner, Zanuttini and their colleagues (Portner 2007, 2018; Pak, Portner & Zanuttini 2008, 2015; Zanuttini, Pak & Portner 2012) has taken a similar tack, treating them as denoting a particular type of property: type $<s,< e,t>>$ (indexed to the addressee via an abstract agreement feature). If this were correct, then we could conclude that mood determines semantic type, the type then correlated by default with type of move, as summarized in Table 12.1:[2]

Table 12.1. Semantics and pragmatics of mood

Mood	Type	Move
Grammatical	**Semantic**	**Default**
Declarative	$<s,t>$	Assertion
Interrogative	$<<s,t>,t>$	Question
Imperative	$<s,<e,t>>$	Direction

[2] The idea that there is a semantic type assigned to each clause and pragmatically correlated with a basic illocutionary force is not new. See Hausser (1980), Huntley (1984), Pendlebury (1986), Wilson & Sperber (1988), and Portner (2004) for other ways of developing it; and Portner (2018, this volume, §3.1.3) for an excellent critical discussion of this literature. Of these, only Hausser and Portner take imperatives to denote properties, as here; and Hausser fails to offer an explanation for why this correlation should obtain, or how it works in discourse. Pendlebury and Wilson & Sperber are vague about the semantics of the different clause types. Only Portner offers an account of why the correlation obtains, in a version of the framework in this volume, in §12.2.

A declarative clause may denote a proposition, but its use does not, of course, inevitably amount to an assertion. As noted above, such clauses may occur embedded, as in *John believed that his breakfast was ready*, where the complement clause is not asserted. In parallel fashion, though a semantic question is a set of propositions, it is important not to confuse that object with a pragmatic question, as we also see in embedded uses: *John wondered whether his breakfast was ready* reports on John's consideration of a set of alternatives; it doesn't pose the corresponding question for discussion in the discourse in which the utterance occurs. Though it is less common, it is now generally recognized that imperative clauses may occur embedded as well in several languages (Pak, Portner & Zanuttini 2008, 2015; Charlow 2010; Kaufmann & Poschmann 2013; Kaufmann 2014a; Stegovec & Kaufmann 2015). In such uses, as with the other mood-types, the imperative clause is not used to propose a direction to the addressee, but instead to report such an event of proposing.

Moves—assertions, questions, suggestions—are types of utterances; and utterances (Bar-Hillel 1971) are uses of a constituent in a context of utterance. Given the proposed conventional contents of the clause-types, we can see that their default use for the corresponding types of moves is functionally natural. This should be fairly obvious for the declaratives: Their semantic type is that of a proposition and what one asserts is a proposition. Similarly, interrogatives denote a set of propositions, and asking a question poses such a set of alternatives—the possible answers to the question—for consideration. We'll say more about imperatives in §12.3. As a first pass, take the meaning of an imperative clause to be its realization conditions: it specifies what the world would be like if the targeted agent (typically the addressee) were to realize the property denoted. Then if the imperative is issued as a direction, it is a proposal that the addressee realize that property. If, as below, we take these three types of moves to be constitutive of the language game, then this suggests an explanation for the grammatical mood universal. Each language has some way of distinguishing the three basic semantic types because these are designed to serve those basic roles of an utterance in discourse. Of course, as Wittgenstein famously pointed out, just because a tool was designed for a particular use, that doesn't mean that it cannot be used in other ways. Just so, these natural correlations between mood and speech act type are defeasible. I will argue that this defeasibility, too, is natural and readily understood, as a function of the intentional structure of the discourse in which a move takes place.

This natural correlation contrasts with the lack of regular correlation between the conventional content of utterances and the classical speech act types of Austin or Searle. Thus, it seems, those classical speech act theories have no account of the two universals pertaining to mood.

The proposal here relies heavily on preceding literature: I assume the account of assertions of Stalnaker (1979) and of questions of Roberts (1996/2012a). I draw on Portner (2004, 2007, 2018), Schwager (2006)/Kaufmann (2012, 2014b), and Charlow (2011) for understanding important features of the semantics of imperative mood; the latter authors and Starr (2013) for an account of the relationship between the imperative and deontic modality; on Condoravdi and Lauer (2011) for their basic approach to performatives; and on Allen, Cohen, Perrault, et al. (as cited in the acknowledgements at the end of this paper) for basic ideas about the relationship between plans and speech act determination. I only provide enough detail about those accounts to flesh out and support the basic theory I am proposing here. What I offer is: (i) support for the mood-type correlation in Table 12.1, crucially resolving the tension between those accounts of the semantics of the imperative which treat it as property denoting and those which treat it as denoting a modal proposition; and (ii) the use of an independently motivated theory of formal pragmatics to reveal how the observations from the previous literature fit together to provide an empirically motivated, elegant account of what a speech act is, how it's canonically reflected in the conventional content of the constituent uttered, the default nature of the content-speech act correlation, and how we infer the *intended* speech act type for a given utterance as a function of its grammatical mood and the context of utterance.

In what follows, in §12.2 I offer a brief overview of an approach to discourse in which the evident goals and intentions of the interlocutors, as partly reflected in the Question Under Discussion (QUD) and the interlocutors' evident domain goals, play a central role in structuring interlocutors' interaction in discourse and, especially, in facilitating and constraining interpretation. Then in §12.3, I turn to the semantics of grammatical mood. The standard assumptions about declarative clauses (denoting propositions) and interrogative clauses (denoting sets of propositions) are quite generally accepted, with only minor variations between theories. So there I'll focus on sketching a particular semantics of imperative mood, one which is well-supported empirically and is consistent with the proposed view of speech acts. Given these underpinnings, in §12.4, I discuss how they make possible a simple, non-stipulatory account of speech acts, explaining the universals about grammatical mood, while predicting that the observed correlations between mood (and semantic type) and move type can be overridden in context as a function of other pragmatic principles. In §12.4.3 we'll discuss the theoretical pay-off of this view for the classic issue of how to account for performative speech acts. In §12.5, I present some conclusions.

12.2 Discourse Structure and Context of Utterance

The proposed view of speech acts has its place in a general theory of the nature of human linguistic interaction, i.e. of discourse, proposed independently in Carlson (1982), van Kuppevelt (1996), Ginzburg (1996, 2012) and Roberts (1996/2012a); in these theories, a question or topic under discussion both drives and constrains the interpretation of individual utterances. In Roberts' version, adopted here, discourse is a game in which the interlocutors conduct a collaborative inquiry about the way things are, on the basis of their common fund of information about that world, the Common Ground (CG). Following Stalnaker (1979), we don't know which world we're in, but the CG is the set of propositions which we all purportedly take to truthfully characterize it (though some may be false, whether we know it or not). A proposition is represented by the set of worlds in which it's true. Hence, the intersection of the CG at a given point in discourse is the Context Set (CS), the set of candidate worlds for reality according to these interlocutors at that time.

Here are the basic assumptions of this view of discourse and of the context of utterance:

1. Language is **a game of collaborative inquiry structured by the recognized intentions of the interlocutors.**
   A **discourse** is one round of this game.
2. Intentions involve commitments to goals. In the language game, players attend to two principal kinds of goals:
   - **Domain goals** and the associated **plans** to achieve them are the things the interlocutors are publicly committed to achieving in the world and the strategies they adopt to do so. These are relevant in the language game insofar as they may indirectly motivate and constrain the interlocutors' linguistic interaction.
   - **Discourse goals** are a distinguished type of domain goal, those the interlocutors are jointly committed to achieving in the discourse itself. These are represented by questions, often implicitly posed, which guide the interlocutors' inquiry. You can think of these as issues or topics under discussion. These, too, are organized, to reflect an underlying plan for achieving these goals, into **strategies of inquiry** (see point 7).

   One's goals are generally partially ordered, both hierarchically, some feeding others (as in a complex plan), and by priority, some more important than others (especially among goals at the same level in the hierarchy, which might otherwise conflict). Hence the structure over goals may be quite complex.
3. The main goal in any round of the game is to share information about the way things are, adding to the interlocutors' **Common Ground**.
4. There are three kinds of moves in a language game:
   a) **Interrogations** pose questions; they are **set-up moves** in the language game: If accepted by the interlocutors, a question establishes a discourse goal to which the interlocutors are cooperatively committed: resolving the accepted Question Under Discussion (QUD).
   b) **Assertions** offer partial answers to the QUD at the time of utterance; if accepted, they are **payoff moves**, in which the interlocutors come closer to achieving their immediate discourse goal of addressing the QUD.
   c) **Directions** propose domain goals to the addressee, and hence are set-up moves as well. If accepted, they are added to the addressee's individual domain goals, with a consequent modification of her associated plans.
5. If discourse is to be maximally effective, it must be orderly. What serves to organize any game is the players' immediate goals and intentions in playing the game. Typically, interlocutors in a discourse are already committed to certain domain goals. If a group of collaborating agents are rational, then in keeping with general constraints on rational agency (Bratman 1987):
   - the goals they adopt, and the plans they form to achieve them, are consistent, and in particular,
   - discourse goals (QUD) should subserve pre-existing or over-arching domain goals.

   Hence, addition of information to the CG is not random and unconstrained, but is guided by the mutually agreed upon topics for discussion, these in turn constrained by recognized domain goals. Interlocutors choose a topic for discussion and stick with it, even complaining if others inappropriately change the subject: *What's that got to do with the price of eggs?* As we might expect in a theory of linguistic pragmatics—of how context comes to bear on interpretation—the orderliness which characterizes felicitous discourse is surely in the interest (a) of more efficient information retrieval and storage, and (b) of the practical reasoning involved in intention recognition, and hence in meaning recognition:

The intentional structure of discourse:
The structure of a discourse interaction is designed to help retrieve the speaker's intended meaning for a given utterance, in view of the goals of the interaction. This is what makes it reasonable to intend that one's audience will recognize that one intends them to grasp a particular meaning (Grice 1957), even when it is underdetermined by the conventional content of what one says.

A rational agent's intentions are ideally intrinsically bound up with her plans for action (Bratman 1987). Hence we have:

Rational Cooperation in a Discourse D: Make your utterance one which promotes your current intentions in D. (cf. Grice's Cooperative Principle 1967, and its counterpart in Thomason 1990)

6. This orderliness is reflected in the crucial role of the QUD in interpretation. Thus, we can derive Grice's (1967) maxim of Relation from the nature of the game and standard assumptions about rational agency:

RELEVANCE: Since the QUD reflects the interlocutors' goals at any point in a discourse, in order for an utterance to be rationally cooperative it must address the QUD.

An utterance m **addresses a question** q iff m either contextually entails a partial answer to q (m is an assertion) or is part of a strategy to answer q (m is a question) or suggests an action to the addressee which, if carried out, might help to resolve q (m is a suggestion).

7. Just as we develop plans to achieve our domain goals, to address complex questions, interlocutors usually develop **strategies of inquiry**, involving a series of related questions. These are sequences of moves designed to (at least partially) satisfy the aims established in a particular round of the game while obeying the game's general constraints. To be a strategy of inquiry, such a sequence must display a hierarchical structure based on a set of questions partially ordered by entailment. The constitutive moves and the overall strategy are constrained by Relevance and what it is to be a rational cooperative agent. Rhetorical relations between utterances (Mann & Thompson 1987, Asher & Lascarides 1994, 2003) pertain to features of such strategies (Roberts 2004).

8. The context of utterance in a language game can profitably be characterized as a **scoreboard** (Lewis 1979) tracking the distinguished bodies of information relevant for interpretation as these evolve under the rules of the game. A non-defective context is one in which the interlocutors share the same content in their individual representations of what's on the scoreboard. Here is a somewhat simplified version of the scoreboard for a language game (see Roberts 1996, 2012b for more details), characterized as a tuple of bodies of information:

The **scoreboard for a language game** is a tuple, $<I, G, M, <, CG, QUD>$, where:

I is the set of interlocutors at t

M is the set of moves made by interlocutors up to t, with distinguished sub-sets:

$A \subseteq M$, the set of assertions
$Q \subseteq M$, the set of questions
$S \subseteq M$, the set of suggestions
$Acc \subseteq M$, the set of accepted moves

$<$ is a total order on M, the order of utterance

CG, the common ground, is the set of propositions treated as if true by all $i \in I$ at t

$QUD \subseteq Q \cap Acc$ is the ordered set of questions under discussion at t, such that for all $m \in M$ at t:

   a. for all $q \in Q \cap Acc$, $q \in QUD(m)$ iff CG fails to entail an answer to q and q has not been determined to be practically unanswerable.
   b. QUD is (totally) ordered by $<$.
   c. for all $q, q' \in QUD$, if $q < q'$, then the complete answer to q' contextually entails a partial answer to q.

and in addition:

   d. for all $Q \in QUD$ there is a $g \in G_{com}$ (see just below) such that g is the goal of answering Q, and
   e. for all $Q \in QUD$, it is not the case that CG entails an answer to Q.

G is a set of sets of goals and priorities in effect at t, such that

for all $i \in I$, there is a (possibly empty) G_i which is the set of i's publically evident prioritized desiderata, including those goals which i is publicly committed at t to trying to achieve; and
$G = \{G_i \mid i \in I\}$.

Moreover:

for all $i \in I$, for all $g \in G_i$, g is a conditional goal, representing the intention to achieve the target goal should certain conditions be realized in the actual world.

and we can define:

$G_{com} = \{g \mid \forall i \in I: g \in G_i\}$, the set of the interlocutors' common desiderata at t.

$G_Q = \{g \in G_{com} \mid$ there is some $Q \in QUD$ and g is the goal of answering Q$\}$.

For all $i \in I$, if i is a sincere, competent and cooperative interlocutor in D, we can use G_Q to characterize two kinds of publicly evident desiderata and goals held by i (at time t):

Discourse Goals of i = G_Q
Domain Goals of i = $G_i \backslash G_Q$
$G_{com} \backslash G_Q$: the set of common Domain Goals of all the interlocutors

There are three main types of moves tracked on the scoreboard, A, Q, and S, corresponding with the three main types of speech acts from §12.1, the latter characterized below in terms of their contribution to the score. We track all moves, even those that are not accepted, because interlocutors do respond to and discuss moves, even when rejected (e.g. see Ginzburg 2012 for extensive illustration), and can characterize them in terms of their order (*what you just said...*). Similarly, there are three main bodies of information on the scoreboard, CG, QUD, and G, and these are the loci of the main changes to the scoreboard when moves in A, Q, and S are accepted. CG is the standard Stalnakerian Common Ground (a set of sets of possible worlds). The QUD is as defined in Roberts (1996/2012a), a push-down store where each question on the stack must be a (contextual) sub-question of the one below it, so that a complete answer to the new question will contextually entail a partial answer to the question(s) below it. G includes a set of goals and priorities for each interlocutor. Each goal is conditional, to be realized by the agent in question only in case certain conditions obtain; one might model this as an ordered pair <c,t>, c the set of circumstances in which the realization is called for (the applicable circumstances), t the target property to be realized by the agent in those circumstances. Alternatively, one could model such a goal as Kratzerian conditional necessity, necessity making explicit the commitment of the agent whose goal this is, the applicable conditions serving to restrict its domain, and the realization by the agent of the target property as prejacent. I take it that like other elements of the scoreboard, G is not a set of linguistic expressions, but a body of information; so it isn't crucial here to determine the exact form of such conditional goals. The idea is that we only aim to achieve a given goal (intending to realize a corresponding property) under certain conditions, not come what may; this plays an important role in the semantics of imperatives in Roberts (2015), sketched in §12.3 below.

Since the CG includes all that the interlocutors take to be true, it includes information about the discourse scoreboard as well. The point of the more articulated scoreboard is not to *replace* the CG so much as to clarify the different types of information that interlocutors crucially track in discourse and the different roles these types of information play in the evolution of felicitous discourse.

Clause (d) of the definition of the QUD ensures that each of the questions under discussion, as agreed upon by the interlocutors, corresponds to a shared goal, that of answering that question, so that all of the questions in QUD are reflected in G_Q. Hence, any rational, cooperative interlocutor should address the QUD (unless more important goals, as reflected in priorities over G, interfere). Then we formally define RELEVANCE:

Given QUD q, a move m is **RELEVANT** iff m addresses q.

The role of a given utterance in the speaker's plans can be inferred using the assumption of relevance to the QUD at the time of utterance, and in this way, the intended interpretation can be inferred, especially if we understand that the QUD subserves the larger domain goals of the interlocutors. As we know from Grice (1957), meaning recognition depends on intention recognition.[3]

Part of the information available in the interlocutors' scoreboard is an indication, for each interlocutor i, of the set G_i of i's evident goals. But in a rational agent, goals do not exist in a vacuum. Rather, they are the targets which drive and constrain behavior; and that behavior is strategic—organized so as to maximize the realization of the agent's goals. Further, because we typically have many goals, some of them difficult to reconcile, they must be prioritized. So the strategies we adopt to achieve them must take into account those priorities, as well as the circumstances in which the agent finds herself at potential realization times. Finally, goals themselves may be conditional, in the sense that we may adopt a goal which is to be realized just in case certain conditions obtain in the circumstances in which we find ourselves. This is all reflected in the features of G_i for interlocutor i, via the conditional nature of goals and other relations over G, such as subservience and prioritization. Since both the circumstances and even our goals may change (be realized, abandoned, etc.) and one may change one's priorities, the character and organization of one's plans are complex and non-monotonic. Thus G_i is merely the tip of a complex, dynamic planning structure, always mediated by the agent's awareness of circumstances and the determination of priorities, as evident to all interlocutors (see Charlow 2011 for excellent discussion).

The three principal kinds of moves in a discourse game, for which the above is the scoreboard, can now be characterized formally as follows, where for constituent κ $|\kappa|^D$ is the interpretation of κ in discourse context D, and the diacritics ., ?, and ! stand for declarative, interrogative, and imperative mood, respectively.

Assertion: (following Stalnaker 1979)
If an assertion of $.\alpha$ is accepted by the interlocutors in a discourse D, $|.\alpha|^D$ is added to CG.

Interrogation: (Roberts 1996)
If a question posed by $?\alpha$ is accepted by the interlocutors in a discourse D, then $|?\alpha|^D$, a set of propositions, is added to the QUD.

A question is removed from QUD iff either its answer is entailed by CG or it is determined to be unanswerable.

Direction:[4](cf. related proposals in Roberts 2004, Portner 2007)

If a proposed direction $!_iP$ is accepted by the addressee i in a discourse D, then G_i and i's associated evident plans are revised to include the realization, under the applicable circumstances, of $!_iP$.

G_i is revised to remove the realization of $!_iP$ once it *or the larger goals it subserves* are no longer potentially applicable (e.g. it has been realized, or else it is determined that it cannot be practically realized).

---

[3] See Roberts (2012b) for discussion of the realization of this insight via G in the QUD framework.

[4] This characterization of Direction is incomplete, since it does not cover what Kaufmann (2012) calls Expressive uses of imperatives, like *Be well!* See Roberts (2015) for modification of this pragmatics to cover those uses.

The conceptual foundations of this approach to pragmatics are Gricean. And the implications for pragmatic theory are wide-ranging. One reason for this is that the way the three kinds of moves are modeled in the QUD framework is designed to dovetail with the independently motivated compositional content, realized in a formal semantics, of utterances with declarative, interrogative, and imperative mood, as I'll illustrate with the imperative in the next section. Thus, there is a natural formal **congruence between conventional content and the default pragmatic function given by the rules above**. In the matter of speech acts, the semantic types of the three types of clause are the right sorts of objects to play the roles of the constitutive moves in the language game as characterized above. Thus, the formal pragmatic framework not only coordinates smoothly with compositional semantics, but is compatible with the formal logics commonly used to model inference in discourse, including erotetic logics like the inquisitive semantics of Groenendijk and his associates (for introductions, see Groenendijk & Roelofsen 2009, Ciardelli et al. 2013, and Cross & Roelofsen 2015).

There are some additional consequences of this view of pragmatics for speech act theory. Making a given type of speech act entails that the speaker incurs certain commitments. For example:

- **All moves carry a commitment to RELEVANCE.** This goes well beyond information sharing *simpliciter*, and so marks a difference from Stalnaker's (1979) account of assertion. But unlike Sperber & Wilson's (1986) notion of Relevance, this one is inherently relational, a function of goals and intentions, and hence arguably closer to Grice's original notion.[5]
- **Assertions have a doxastic flavor**: making an assertion involves a commitment to believing (purporting to believe) that the proposition asserted is true and based on adequate evidence.
- **Directions pertain to priorities**, as reflected in the interlocutors' goals: These are often **deontic** (pertaining to permission and obligation), or under certain circumstances **buletic** (pertaining to wishes). If suggested to an addressee, they propose the adoption of desiderata and/or goals, with a consequent adjustment of the addressee's plans. These goals are conditional, intentions to realize some property or other *should the relevant conditions obtain*. If accepted by an addressee, then she is (conditionally) committed to those goals—she *ought* or she *should* or she *must* do what's necessary to accomplish them, under the appropriate conditions, and under standard semantic accounts of the meanings of those modals.

These commitments, which follow from the nature of the game, amount to what Searle called **sincerity conditions on the performance of these acts, arising from the function of their canonical roles in the language game**. For speakers, assertions are associated with a commitment to truth, questions with a sincere commitment to

---

[5] Sperber & Wilson's (1986 and subsequent work) Relevance is purely quantitative—defined in terms of maximum inferential pay-off for minimum cognitive effort. This notion is not relativized to goals or other contextual desiderata, unlike the notion defined above. Grice (1967), on the other hand, repeatedly talks about "the purposes of the conversation", which I take to correlate to the goals and plans in G in the present theory.

inquiry, directions with a sincere belief that the realization of the proposed act by an addressee would further certain aims. Of course, this doesn't entail that speakers actually *have* the relevant intentions. But making a speech act does incur commitments: it puts the speaker and/or addressee under obligation, and as we shall see:

(a) This has consequences for our understanding of the way that imperatives interact with deontic modality, and hence for what the class that Searle called *Directives* has in common with my class of Directions.
(b) It provides the foundation of an explanatory account of performatives—Searle's Declaratives—and of performativity.

Moreover, the three basic speech act types, and the associated commitments to sincerity, relevance and other reflexes of Gricean cooperation are together **essentially constitutive of what it is to play the language game**. These acts are basic to the nature of the game. To display competence in the game is to be able to understand and use these three types of moves under the associated constraints on cooperativity and rationality. To grasp the use of these moves and their conditions and effects is to understand the language game. Thus, to the extent that understanding the structure of discourse in this way proves useful in explaining how we interpret the things speakers say, this argues that the proposed three-way distinction reveals a great deal about the way in which we share meaning in the Gricean sense. If so, then this is an illuminating taxonomy: It helps to explain the mechanisms by which we grasp a speaker's intended non-natural meaning.

Of course, in many languages grammatical mood is realized morphologically, e.g. with verbal affixes or particles. Once we have a paradigm, nothing prevents language users from extending it in various language-particular ways, to include other morphologically realized moods. So, for example, in English and many other languages we also have exclamatives: *What a lovely day it is!*, *How odd that was!*. But so far as I know this clause-type is not universally realized across languages.

12.3 Clausal mood and the semantics and pragmatics of the imperative

As noted above, the correlation between declarative and interrogative mood, on the one hand, and the semantic type of proposition or question, on the other, is well accepted, as is the default correlation between clauses in these moods (with their associated types) and what it is to be an assertion or a question in discourse. But the formal work on the imperative is more recent and as yet controversial, so that will be my illustrative focus here. I will offer a brief sketch of a new semantics and pragmatics for the imperative, with only a few illustrations to show how it works for the core cases. A full justification and comparison of this account with others in the literature can be found in Roberts (2015), along with detailed applications to a broader range of uses of the imperative, and to the more general mood that Zanuttini et al. (2012) call the *jussive*.[6]

---

[6] This term is used slightly differently by different authors. In Zanuttini et al. (2012) and that group's related work, it is used to refer to the mood in a class of Korean clauses that include the imperatives,

A **clause** is any sentential constituent with mood, even though clauses with different moods have different semantic types and differ in important syntactic features. Hence, a clause is not necessarily a constituent that denotes a proposition (e.g. an interrogative clause denotes a *set* of propositions), though it may denote a "complete thought" in the old-fashioned sense (e.g. there's nothing intuitively elliptical about a question). Nor need all clauses have overt subject constituents in the syntax. One can take imperative clauses to lack a syntactic subject, but they do typically carry subject-agreement features, and always have a semantico-pragmatic subject, the entity (usually the addressee) which serves as target for the directed property denoted by the clause. So they are not simple VPs, but sentential.

There are two main types of proposals for the semantics of the imperative in the recent literature: The first type, exemplified by Wilson and Sperber (1988), Han (2000), Schwager (2006)/Kaufmann (2012), and Condoravdi and Lauer (2012), takes an imperative clause to denote a proposition with a built-in modal component. This is closely related to the proposal in Charlow (2014), who takes an imperative to denote a property of a plan, always carrying the force of necessity. The most subtle and detailed formal realization of this general approach is that of Kaufmann (2012), who **focuses on the modal** component of the meaning of an imperative clause. Here, modality is modeled on the approach due to Kratzer (1977, 1981, etc.), relativized to contextually-given parameters, the modal base and ordering source. These functions together yield a modal accessibility relation which determines the set of worlds over which the modal is to range in order to determine the truth conditions for the proposition in which it occurs; if the modal's force is that of necessity, it will have to be true in all the accessible worlds, if possibility, true in at least some of them. For Kaufmann, the modal base and ordering source capture the "relevant criteria" for the directive, characterizing the types of worlds in which the proposed action is to be implemented. Because of this flexible parameterization, the account can capture attested features of a wide range of uses of imperatives, both matrix and embedded; directive and desiderative, and including "weaker" uses of the imperative, such as suggestions and depictives, as well as "stronger" commands. The deontic character of the modal base and ordering source for an imperative explains the attested relationship between directives and deontic assertions. For example, the following are synonymous on this account, though they have different presuppositions for felicitous use:

(1)   Go to school!
(2)   You should go to school!

---

promissives, and exhortatives. When the subject of such a clause is 2nd person, it receives an imperative interpretation; with 1st person it is understood to be promissive—to commit to speaker to realizing the property denoted; with 1st person plural subjects, it has an exhortative interpretation, urging the group to make this commitment. Wheelock (LaFleur 2011) uses the term *jussive* to refer to a mood in Latin which occurs in subjunctive main clauses to express a command or exhortation, e.g. 'let us study this lesson carefully' (Chapter 28) or in subordinate clauses which denote indirect reports of "what someone has ordered, commanded, urged, persuaded, begged, etc." (Chapter 36). The Summer Institute of Linguistics Glossary of Linguistic Terms (http://www01.sil.org/linguistics/GlossaryOf linguisticTerms/WhatIsJussiveMood.htm) defines jussive mood as "a directive mood that signals a speaker's command, permission, or agreement that the proposition expressed by his or her utterance be brought about". The general idea seems to be that jussive in such languages may have an imperative sense if the understood subject is 2nd person, but unlike imperative mood may also take 1st person subjects to yield a promissive or exhortative interpretation, as in Zanuttini et al.'s (2012) use.

Kaufmann's Kratzerian account naturally explains the common occurrence of conditional imperatives and gives them an intuitively plausible semantics. Kratzer treats conditionals as modal statements (which may have a merely implicit necessity modal in the main clause) with the *if*-clause serving as part of the restriction on the modal operator; technically, the proposition denoted by the *if*-clause is added to the propositions contextually retrieved by the modal base, and their intersection, further constrained by the ordering source, serves as the set of worlds over which the modal operator ranges. We see this in (3) and the corresponding modal conditional (4):

(3)   If you have trouble updating your software, delete the current copy and re-install.

(4)   If you have trouble updating your software, you must delete the current copy and re-install.

The instructions in (3) include criteria for their application: in case of trouble with one's software. The deletion and reinstallation are only suggested if the addressee has trouble updating.

Kaufmann's account also readily extends to embedded imperatives. Some languages, such as Slovenian (Stegovec & Kaufmann 2015) have a wide range of uses of embedded imperatives. But even English has embedded imperatives, though their occurrence is more limited; e.g. in this language the understood target of the embedded imperative must be the actual addressee: *John said eat his share of the chicken. He won't get home til late.* This is an important argument against including the illocutionary force of the imperative in its semantics, *pace* Han (2000), since such clauses do not display illocutionary force.

But there are problems with the modal proposition approach. One is that it fails to satisfactorily explain the lack of truth conditions associated with imperatives or why they cannot be used to make assertions. If someone tells me to wash my car, I can neither judge that true nor false. Since one can certainly make such a judgment about *You should wash your car*, this argues that the imperative and the deontic modal assertion are not synonymous. Kaufmann appeals to various pragmatic aspects of their meaning in order to explain this difference; for example, she argues that they cannot be used to make assertions because they are performative, and (supposedly) performatives cannot be used to make assertions. But ultimately it is a rather unsatisfactory feature of this type of account. Questions don't have truth conditions, and their semantic type explains why. We feel that the type of imperatives should offer the same kind of explanation.

Another problem, observed by Gärtner (2015), is that imperatives do not take sentential adverbials that are acceptable with declaratives. We cannot felicitously say (5), though its modal counterpart (6) is felicitous.[7] And performatives can have sentential adverbials of this sort, as we see in (7):

(5)   #Unfortunately, marry him!

(6)   Unfortunately, you must marry him.

(7)   Unfortunately, I now pronounce you man and wife.

---

[7] Matt Moss (p.c.) notes the acceptability of the following:

(i)   [to a friend who's considering not taking his meds:] Obviously, take them!

Finally, this account by itself doesn't offer an adequate pragmatics of the canonical use of imperatives to issue directions; I refer the reader to Roberts (2015) for a critique in that vein.

The second prominent contemporary approach to imperative mood,[8] exemplified by Portner (2004, 2007), Roberts (2004), and Starr (2013), takes an imperative clause to denote a property indexed (typically) to the addressee; these accounts typically focus on the pragmatics of direction. For example, in Portner (2007) if an imperative is proffered as a direction and accepted, the indexed property it denotes is added to the addressee's To-Do list. He then offers a pragmatic explanation of the evident relationship between imperatives and deontic assertions, so that while on this account (1) above is not synonymous with (2), its use and acceptance entail it. Roughly, as noted in the previous section, all content on the scoreboard is reflected in the CG, so that (a) any publicly evident goals and intentions of the addressee count as commitments to act (if possible) to realize them, and (b) such commitments are reflected in the CG, in this case as deontic propositions. Portner (2007) works this idea out in formal detail; see also Portner (this volume).

But there are problems with this approach, as well. Briefly, because there is no modality in the semantics of the imperative clause itself, unlike in Kaufmann's imperative propositions, there is no way to relativize interpretation to the flexible Kratzerian modal parameters, the modal base and ordering source, and so it is difficult to explain the full range of imperative flavors. Portner is aware of this issue, and addresses it by introducing multiple To-Do lists, with slightly different flavors, but this doesn't seem entirely satisfactory. Given the broad variety of ways in which different modal bases and ordering sources can come to bear, how many To-Do lists would we need for a given interlocutor, and how should those be related? Furthermore, without a modal base there is no way to naturally capture the semantics of conditional imperatives like (3).

In Roberts (2015) I propose an alternative which attempts to reconcile these two general approaches and preserve the best in each, without building illocutionary force into the semantics of the imperative mood, by making an imperative clause denote an indexically targeted property (in English, always anchored to the addressee) which carries conditional presuppositions retrieved by a modal base and ordering source. Like Portner's account, the denotation of an imperative is a property. But this account does not use a To-Do list. Instead, when such a property is proffered as a move in the language game—used to make a speech act—that use proposes a modification of the indexically targeted agent x_i's goals, plans and priorities G_i.

I agree with his judgment. Ernst (2000) classifies *obviously* as an evidential (epistemic modal) speaker-oriented adverb, whereas *unfortunately* in (5)–(7) is an evaluative speaker-oriented adverb. I find his other evidential adverbs to be acceptable with imperatives, as well: *clearly, plainly* can acceptably replace *obviously* in (i). Other evaluatives (*luckily, oddly, significantly, unbelievably*) and Ernst's discourse-oriented adverbs (*frankly, honestly*) are, for me, as unacceptable as *unfortunately*. Hence, Gärtner's generalization seems a bit too broad. Nevertheless, all the evaluatives and discourse-oriented adverbs are acceptable with deontic modal statements (the counterparts of (6)), leaving a distinction between imperatives and modal declaratives which cannot be explained on the modal proposition approach to clauses in the imperative mood.

[8] See also Bolinger (1977), a precursor.

Recall that G_i consists of a set of x_i's evident goals and priorities. A goal in this set is represented by a property that x_i is conditionally committed to realizing; and these goals are organized by relations over goals indicating subservience, organization into plans, and priorities. We can keep the advantages of Kaufmann's modal account by using Kratzer's modal parameters, the modal base and ordering source, to relativize the denotation of the indexically targeted property-denotation. Those parameters effectively make the goal conditional: the modal base and ordering source determine the applicable circumstances for the conditional goal—those in which the agent is to attempt to realize the targeted property. Adding a new goal, corresponding to the targeted property denoted by an imperative indexed to addressee x_i, involves not only adding that to the set G_i, but in some cases relating that goal via subservience, etc., to others in G_i. Recall also that the CG tracks all changes to shared information on the scoreboard. So if the imperative is accepted and G_i updated as proposed, then, as in Portner's proposal, this addition is automatically reflected in a deontic proposition in the CG—that x_i is committed (and so 'ought to') realize that goal, under the applicable circumstances, thereby explaining the correlation between imperatives and deontic modal statements.

Something slightly more abstract works for all the remaining imperative (and jussive) systems I'm familiar with, but with different constraints on resolution of the contextual parameters (e.g. for anchoring the indexical) from language to language.[9]

Formally,[10] take $!_{f,g}[_S VP_i]$ to be the logical form of an English imperative clause, and take it to be uttered in context K (the scoreboard, including information about the interlocutors, their CG, QUD, evident plans and goals, etc.), indexed to the addressee x_i, and relativized to modal base f and ordering source g. As in Kratzer, f takes a world w and time t (the circumstances of issuance) as argument to yield a set of propositions, each a set of worlds; their intersection $\cap f(<w,t>)$, the set of worlds in which all those propositions are true, is then further constrained by g. Technically, $g(<w,t>)$ also yields a set of propositions—reflecting some relevant ideals (e.g. the wishes of either the speaker or addressee)—and $g(<w,t>)$ orders the worlds in $\cap f(<w,t>)$ according to how close they come to realizing all those ideal propositions. Then the worlds of interest are those in $\cap f(<w,t>)$ that are most ideal under g. Hence, these parameters work here exactly as they do in Kaufmann's modal theory.

We define the applicable circumstances for a directed property, relative to f, g, and the world and time of issuance $<w,t>$ as a set of circumstances (world/time pairs):

$$\mathbf{Applic}_{f,g}(<w,t>) = \{<w',t'> \mid w' = w \,\&\, t \leq t' \,\&\, <w',t'> \in \cap f(<w,t>) \,\&\, \forall <w',t''> \in \cap f(<w,t>): <w',t> \leq_{g(<w,t>)} <w'',t''> \}$$

Paraphrasing, the applicable circumstances relative to f, g at a given circumstance $<w,t>$ are those circumstances in the actual world w which are non-past with respect

---

[9] As noted before, for simplicity here I ignore Kaufmann's Expressive imperatives, but address them in Roberts (2015) with a slight modification of the pragmatics for imperatives.

[10] All formal definitions below are paraphrased, so if you trust those you can ignore the formal definitions.

to the issuance time and are most g(<w,t>)-ideal among those where all the propositions in f(<w,t>) are true.[11]

Then given felicity (satisfaction of its presuppositions), an imperative's proffered
content is its **realization conditions**, what would have to be the case for the proposed
goal to be realized:

> CONVENTIONAL CONTENT of English $!_{f,g}[_s\underline{VP_i}]$:
> Given context K and circumstance of evaluation <w,t>:
> **Presupposed content:**
> $x_i =$ addressee(K),
> f is a circumstantial modal base
> g is an ordering source reflecting x_i's goals, plans and priorities in <w,t>
>
> **Proffered content:** (type <s,<e,t>>)
> $\lambda <w',t'> \lambda x \in \{x_i\}$. $\text{Applic}_{f,g}(<w',t'>) \subseteq ([x \in VP]^{\mathfrak{c}})$[12]

The use of the imperative presupposes a targeted addressee, modal base and ordering
source. The circumstance of evaluation < w, t > will be the circumstance of issuance;
in matrix clauses, this will be the speech time/world < w*, t* >, and in embedded
clauses, it will be the eventuality reported in the matrix. The presupposed modal base
f and ordering source g determine the applicable conditions in the actual non-past in
which the prejacent is to be realized.

An imperative is **conditional** under the proposed semantics in that the applicable
conditions for which the property is defined are determined by the contextually given
parameters f and g for a modal base and ordering source. f and g are the usual
Kratzerian parameters used for modal operators, the modal base here presupposed
to be circumstantial and g to reflect the target's goals, plans, and priorities. As in
Kratzer, a modifying *if*-clause adds its proposition to the modal base determined
by f.[13] Then as in Kaufmann (2012), the identities and relationship of the issuer and
the addressee x_i, and the character of f and g all play a central role in determining the
ultimate flavor of any direction issued with this clause—command, suggestion, etc.
On this semantics, this comes about in the determination of the non-past applicable
circumstances, Applic(<w,>), those in which, should the imperative clause be used
to issue a direction, the direction is intended to be realized. One might say that the
semantics is modal, not only because of the use of f and g, but also because the proffered content involves a relation between sets of circumstances, effectively necessity.
But unlike in Kaufmann's account, there is no (modal) proposition expressed by an
imperative clause; its proffered content is a property.

In some contexts there may be but one set of applicable circumstances; e.g. if
someone whose plane has been cancelled asks, 'What do I do now?', one might answer

---

[11] Given the pragmatic role of a Direction, to add to the target's goals, and the fact that goals are of their
nature future-oriented, this stipulation may be unnecessary. But it remains to be seen how this plays out
in embedded imperatives across languages, so I add this condition here for clarity. Similarly, it may be that
the applicable circumstances are those in which the addressee 'soon after' realizes the prejacent. I ignore
that here.

[12] $[x \in VP]^{\mathfrak{c}}$ is the sense of $[x \in VP]$, the set of worlds where x has the property denoted by VP.

[13] I ignore here the so-called biscuit conditionals of Austin (1970).

'Rent a car', and in that case the current situation is the single applicable circumstance and it does obtain. Or, as in a recipe or directions, this may be a general instruction, intended whenever circumstances conform to the described scenario.

Recall from the previous section that the default use of a matrix imperative clause, the natural use in view of its directed semantics, is to issue a direction to the target agent:

Direction:

If a proposed direction $!_iP$ is accepted by the addressee i in a discourse D, then revise G_i, and i's associated evident plans to include the realization, in the applicable circumstances, of $!_iP$.

G_i is revised to remove the realization of $!_iP$ once it or the larger goals it subserves are no longer potentially applicable (e.g. it has been realized, or else it is determined that it cannot be practically realized).

So the semantics of mood merely determines the semantic type of the clause in which it occurs, and it is the pragmatics of sincere use that makes it an update. Addressee x_i's acceptance of a direction leads to integrating the targeted property into G_i, which means that x_i's plans are revised to prioritize realizing VP should the relevant conditions of applicability obtain. Then, should x_i find herself in one of the circumstances in Applic($<w,t>$), she (ideally) implements a plan to realize VP. But anytime one adopts a goal, whether as a consequence of a Directive or in the course of elaborating a group plan, etc., the resulting update of G_a for a given agent a may itself be quite complex. First, addition of a new goal to which the agent is committed also typically includes elaboration of a plan to achieve that goal, which plan itself may be complex and interact with other goals and with preconditions on achieving the plan. And just like belief revision in the CG, revision of a set of goals, plans and intentions G_a requires that a consider any pre-existing commitments that would conflict with the addition of the new goal (and the plans to achieve it), determine the relative priority of conflicting goals, and revise and re-order accordingly, which may require dropping some pre-existing goals or at least giving them lower priority. All of these revisions take into account a's relationship to the speaker who proffered the Directive, a's goals and commitments with respect to that speaker, etc. For example, relativizing the realization conditions to the target agent's other goals, plans, and priorities via g, gives us a way of capturing the differences between, e.g., a command and a suggestion. The latter are typically intended by the issuer to suggest to the target how to proceed in the applicable circumstances *if* the proposed action is consistent with the target's other priorities. A command, on the other hand, assumes that obeying the issuing authority is high priority, even obligatory, and that this would be reflected in the agent's G_a. But, again like belief revision in the CG, this is a practical matter, not part of what it is *per se* to proffer or accept a directive.

Then we might say that the proffered directive is 'given your current goals and plans, then if and when the applicable circumstances obtain and the proposed action is consistent with those goals and plans, you should realize the prejacent property'. As this makes clear, then, the pragmatics of issuing a Directive amount to making a proposal to update the ordering source g; since g reflects (at least in part) the target a's G_a, proffering the imperative amounts to proposal for update of G_a. Charlow (2011, 2014) would make the *semantics* of the imperative clause itself be an update function on G (not his term, but the substance of his proposal). I note that Charlow's semantics for an indicative clause makes it denote an update function on (his counterpart of) the CG, while an interrogative clause is an update on the QUD, so that his update semantics for the imperative is consistent with a general view of how the illocutionary force associated with grammatical mood is encoded semantically. But that is not the view reflected here, where illocutionary force is not semantic. So while related, these accounts propose quite different semantics.

As we saw in the scoreboard above, goals and the plans they motivate are themselves conditional, contingent on conditions of applicability; and a given agent's goals are complexly organized. Accordingly, the goals of an interlocutor are not a simple To-Do list. A change in one's goals is reflected in a change in one's plans and priorities, and constitutes a commitment reflected in the CG. We have many conditional goals— intentions to realize some property or other *should the relevant conditions obtain*. We see this in instructions like (3) above. This does not imply that it's ideal to delete and re-install one's software. But **in case** one has trouble—under the applicable conditions—these instructions tell us that that *is* the best way to proceed. Similarly, with a recipe or directions, some are designed to be realized *at some appropriate time in the future*, when other conditions are right:

(8)   When the egg whites are stiff from beating, fold in the sugar.
(9)   When you see the red firehouse on the left, turn right at the next corner.

When the goal proposed by an imperative is added to G_i, the applicable conditions given by f and g restrict the set of applicable circumstances, and the resulting interpretation is effectively conditional in Kratzer's sense. But in the present account, we can say more. I take the use of f and g with an imperative to represent, respectively, information available in the interlocutors' CG and the goals, plans, and priorities of one or more interlocutor x_i (the issuer of a command, the target of a helpful suggestion, etc.), G_i. That is to say, the interpretation of an imperative both draws on and leads to changes in these parameters of the context of utterance.

We see this in how the account of imperatives as proposals to adopt a conditional goal not only yields a natural account of overtly conditional imperatives like (3), but explains yet further facts about how context affects the interpretation of imperatives, as illustrated in (10):

(10)   A and B are strategizing about how their gang is going to rob a bank:
   i. A: Suppose the police arrive while we're cleaning out the vault.
   ii. B: We'll elude them by escaping over the roof.
   iii. A: What if our short-circuiting software fails and the alarm goes off?
   iv. B: Grab the cash in the drawers and run!
   v. A: Suppose the guard gets untied.
   vi.   Should I shoot him?

In (10) the interlocutors are negotiating a plan. Besides directly planning how to achieve their goals, they consider various possible obstacles and contingencies and speculate about alternative ways of proceeding if/when they arise. So there are branching possibilities. In each branch, they consider 'what to do' *as if* acting out the plan. Earlier B might have said *then tie up the guard*, etc., just *as-if* they were in an actual situation in which that action was appropriate, modulo the anaphoric *then*. In this extended irrealis context, all proffered content is relativized to the hypothetical scenario being entertained, and as in modal subordination generally (Roberts 1989), the relativization has implications for the resolution of anaphora and other presuppositions. In (10i) A proposes consideration of one possible contingency; since this is a planning discourse, this raises the practical question of what to do in that circumstance. In (ii), B offers a plan to address that contingency; notably, the Reference Time for (ii) is clearly the immediate aftermath of the event described in (i), and *them* is resolved to the police. In (iii) A directly poses a question about how to plan for yet another possible contingency, and in (iv) B suggests what to do in that hypothetical circumstance, with the same relativization of Reference Time, and also domain restriction of *the cash* and *the drawers* to those in the bank. In (v), A proposes consideration of yet another contingency, and then in (vi) asks whether she should adopt a particular provisional plan in that case, shooting the arbitrary guard under discussion, thereby resolving *him* and, once again, the Reference Time— she's asking whether she should shoot the guard *at that point in time*. Note that the imperative in (iv) is a conditional suggestion: 'if the alarm goes off, grab the cash and run'. The modal *should* in (vi) takes the background scenario in the bank plus (v) as part of its modal base, and as its ordering source the understood goals and priorities both immediate (get the money) and longer-term (get away, avoid the worst potential legal consequences, stay alive), yielding a conditional interpretation of the question, 'should I shoot the guard if he gets untied'. And just so, the imperative in (iv) takes (iii) as one of the premises for its modal base, and the same general priorities for the ordering source. In all these cases, relevance to the question under discussion (as part of the practical strategy being developed) and the interlocutors' understood joint and individual goals in G play a direct role in restricting the applicable circumstances to yield the natural interpretation.

Deontic modality generally is a reflex of such complex planning structures, and the goals, circumstances, and priorities which drive and constrain them. The proposed goal (for the subject) associated with a deontic proposition Modal-p is the realization of the prejacent p—making the world fit the word; and the circumstances in which the realization of the goal is applicable are those given by a combination of a modal base f and ordering source g, the latter reflecting some agent's relevant priorities (e.g. speaker's or addressee's, God's rules or the law, and/or the relevant permissions and obligations of the issuer or the target x_i). And not all an agent's ideals and goals are straightforwardly modified as a consequence of acceptance of a deontic modal proposition targeted to that agent, so that, e.g. the adoption of a goal corresponding to a bouletic permission modal may be conditional on whether the permitted action pleases the target.

Imperatives, as characterized in the semantics above, are deontic in just this way. Via f and g, with the same range of factors bearing on their selection as in the deontic modal statements, we derive the observed wide range of flavors of the imperative. And just as the requirement that a modal proposition be Relevant to the QUD at the time of utterance helps to resolve the intended f and g, as we saw in (10v–vi) a competent cooperative speaker will intend that her Directives be Relevant to the QUD at the time of utterance, and expect her addressee to expect that as well, as in (10iii) and (iv), as well as in the over-arching set of decision problems ('what to do') being explored strategically in (10). Hence, Relevance to the QUD and other contextual factors is crucial for the recognition of the particular intended speech act intended by the speaker—here, differentiating among the different types of Directive in Searle's taxonomy: asking, ordering, requesting, inviting, advising, begging, and more besides.

Thus, like the theory of Kaufmann (2012), the account of the imperative here has the flexibility to account for a far wider range of uses than that of Portner (2007), but without predicting that the resulting interpretation is propositional.

Note, finally, that $!_{f,g}[_S\underline{VP_i}]$ is **indexical** in that it is targeted to one of the interlocutors—typically, as we have seen in English, the addressee. In Korean (see Pak et al. 2008, 2015) the target might instead be the speaker (for a promissive), or the joint interlocutors (for a desiderative), so that we replace the first presupposition, $x_i =$ addressee(K), with: $x_i \in \{$addressee(K), speaker(K)$\}$. Just as we find shifting indexicals in some languages when embedded under certain attitude predicates, in Korean the target of an embedded imperative under a verb of telling may be the third person addressee in a reported issuance event, as we see in:

(11)   ku salam-i   inho-eykey   [swuni-lul towacwu-la]-ko
       that person-NOM   inho-DAT   [swuni-ACC help-IMP]-COMP
       malhayss-ta.
       said-DC
       'He told Inho to help Swuni.'   (Pak et al. 2008:170)

Here the third person addressee Swuni is the target of the embedded imperative clause headed by *towacwu*. An imperative is **directed** in that its extension is only defined for the targeted agent x_i in the applicable circumstances. So, as argued in Roberts (2015), the semantics proposed for English imperatives above can readily be generalized to address the variety of imperatives found across languages.

Summarizing, the semantic denotation of an imperative clause is not a proposition, but a property. But it is a very special property, one which gives the **realization conditions** for the clause, indexically targeted to the addressee. These semantics involve no illocutionary force operators, and hence are suitable for embedded uses. It is only in the *use* of an imperative to make a speech act that it comes to propose a goal to the target, through the pragmatics of directions.

Assuming this analysis, then given the correlation standardly assumed between the other clausal moods and semantic types, we get the three-way distinction noted above:

Declarative: proposition, type $<s,t>$
Interrogative: question, type $<<s,t>,t>$
Imperative: property, type $<s,< e,t>>$

12.4 Speech acts as moves in the language game

Against the background of the pragmatic framework in §12.2 and the characterization of the semantics of the three universal types of sentential mood filled out with the discussion of the imperative in §12.3, in §12.4.1 I argue that the Searlean speech act performed by a given utterance can be predicted as a function of (a) the semantics of the constituent uttered, (b) the specific context of utterance, and (c) general principles for discourse evolution and for plan recognition. Though space precludes an exhaustive survey of all the types of classical speech acts, the examples considered, building on insights from earlier work on planning theory and speech acts, are designed to show how the resources offered should generally suffice. In §12.4.2 I briefly consider again the default correlation between sentential mood and speech act type, and use the discussion up to that point to support the contention, reflected in the Force Linking Principle of Portner (2004) and Zanuttini et al. (2012), that this correlation, though quite robust, is merely pragmatic, not part of the conventional content of the sentences uttered. And in §12.4.3 I briefly consider a view of performatives due to Condoravdi and Lauer (2011), defending it from criticisms by Searle, in light of the general framework proposed here.

12.4.1 Speech Act recovery as intention-recognition

How do we recognize a particular type of speech act when we encounter it? We have just considered how the different types of Directives expressed by an imperative may be contextually differentiated. Here we consider a broader variety.

Consider utterance U by speaker S to hearer H, pertaining to act A. This utterance can be characterized as a Request or a Promise only if it satisfies these criteria, drawn from Searle (1975):

Directive (Request):

Preparatory Condition:	H is able to perform A.
Sincerity Condition:	S wants H to do A.
Propositional Content Condition:	S predicates a future act A of H.
Essential Condition:	U counts as an attempt by S to get H to do A.

Commissive (Promise):

Preparatory Conditions:	S is able to perform A.
Sincerity Condition:	S intends to do A.
Propositional Content Condition:	S predicates a future act A of S.
Essential Condition:	U counts as the undertaking by S of an obligation to do A.

In the work of Austin and Searle, the development of such inventories tends to be lexically driven, the speech act typologies reflecting the acts we canonically perform in uttering an indicative with a verb like *request* or *promise*. But as definitions of act types, these conditions stand alone.

Now consider:

(12)   Joan: a) I want you to get a checkup.

b) Please get a check-up!

c) Will you please get a check up?

Bart: OK. I'll make an appointment with Dr. Josephson for my annual physical.

Would any of these possible utterances by Joan constitute making a request of Bart? (12a) clearly does. Use of *want* instead of counterfactual *wish* (Heim 1992) implicates that so far as Joan knows Bart is able to get a check up, satisfying the Preparatory Condition of a Request. The Sincerity Condition is explicitly satisfied—*I want*. And the infinitival pertains to a future action on the part of the object, here the addressee, satisfying the Propositional Content Condition. Does (12a) count as an attempt by Joan to get Bart to get a check up? That depends on their relationship. If she is his wife, mother, sweetheart or close friend, one might assume that what she wants matters to Bart, who wants to please her; if she is his boss, he is *required* to please her by doing what she wants insofar as is reasonable. In any such case, Bart is motivated to adopt any reasonable obligation Joan suggests, and they both know this. Thus telling him what she wants him to do constitutes an attempt by Joan to get Bart to get a check up. Satisfying all these criteria, Joan's (12a) is a request. Of course, here only the Sincerity Condition and the Propositional Content Condition are explicitly satisfied by Joan's utterance itself, the Preparatory Condition and Essential Condition being contextually inferable, i.e. pragmatically implicated. So the classical theory would say that Joan's (a) is only an indirect request. But it is quite clear in the context of utterance that this *is* the speech act performed. If it is also an assertion about Joan's desires, so be it.

(12b) is a direct request: By virtue of the fact that the imperative is directed to Bart, Joan proposes that he add the future realization of this property to his goals, thereby satisfying the Propositional Content Condition and the Essential Condition. Proposing that an addressee add a goal to their plans is only reasonable (and thus cooperative) if the speaker believes that the addressee is capable of realizing that goal, so in directing Bart to get a check-up, we can assume that the Preparatory Condition of a Request is satisfied so far as Joan knows. As for Sincerity, I think that proposing that someone do something, absent evidence that this is something the target himself wants, can typically be counted as direct evidence that one wants him to do it (under the applicable conditions); but here *please* makes that explicit. So we only have to figure out whether we think Joan means what she says in order to determine whether the Sincerity Condition is satisfied. But presumably that's the case more often than not with speech acts—one always has to gauge the sincerity of one's interlocutors (as opposed to, say, a sarcastic delivery). In the absence of evidence to the contrary, we take it that she does.

Asking if the addressee will do something as in (12c) implies that so far as the inquirer knows he is capable of doing so (Preparatory Condition)—otherwise, why ask?—and the future *will* satisfies the Propositional Content Condition. *Please* plays the same role in this question as in the imperative, satisfying the Sincerity condition. But even more, it marks the question as an indirect request, since just like *want* it conveys that the speaker hopes for a positive commitment to this action; then as in (12a) and (12b), the Essential Condition is satisfied by virtue of this evident desire on the part of Joan plus the same kind of contextual knowledge about Joan and Bart's relationship that played a role in the other examples. So, as in (a), (c) is an indirect Request, but its status in that regard is perfectly clear from the context. Further, though *please* helped to make the Sincerity Condition clear in these examples, if Bart knows Joan well the request would be clear without it.

Then immediately following one of these utterances by Joan, I would argue that Bart's full response counts as a Promise to endeavor to see Dr. Josephson, fulfilling the conditions on that speech act type *in this context of utterance*. *OK* is a reply indicating agreement on the part of the speaker, Bart, with what the addressee, Joan, proposes, here understood by both to be a direct or indirect Request. The Preparatory Conditions and Propositional Content Condition on Promises are satisfied by Bart's reply in virtue of its being a positive, agreeable response to what counted as a felicitous (direct or indirect) Request: since those conditions were satisfied for Joan's utterance, they're entailed by the Common Ground at the time of Bart's. If Bart is understood to be making a sincere response and follow-up assertion, this satisfies both the Sincerity Condition and the Essential Condition: First, agreeing with a Request by saying *OK* in itself commits Bart to agreeing to accept Joan's proposal. Then in order to be relevant, his immediate follow up will be understood to indicate how he intends to fill that request. Sincerely asserting that one will do something, as an indication of a plan to fulfill an accepted goal, publicly commits one to intending to do it. Bart's failing to make the appointment would clearly disappoint Joan (given the satisfied Sincerity Condition of her request), and thus due to his motivation to please her, his *OK* plus this assertion about how he will do what she requests constitutes his undertaking an obligation towards Joan. So even though if it were uttered out of the blue *I'll make an appointment with Dr. Josephson for my annual physical* might not be understood as a promise (it could be just a strange kind of prediction, uttered in a trance by a medium foretelling his own future behavior), all of Searle's conditions are satisfied in this context of utterance, the Sincerity Condition directly.

Of course, one might say that in Bart's reply *will* is ambiguous, with one reading wherein it is simple future (the medium's trance), the other indicating an inclination on the part of the subject Bart (the promise). But given a general Kratzerian account of how modal auxiliaries are understood in context, the question is how we know which modal base and ordering source for *will* the speaker intends, and in the absence of an *if*-clause this is purely a matter of context. The same kind of abductive inference is required to resolve the intended domain restriction for the modal as we use in determining whether the Searlean conditions are satisfied generally.

This conception of the speech acts performed in (12) might not conform to standard Speech Act theory analyses. But I want to underline how what matters on the analysis I've given is not the words uttered, but the meaning of an utterance and its *implications in context*. Searle's characterizations of the speech acts of Requesting and Promising and the more general description of the various features of a speech act developed by Searle and Vanderveken (1985), make these out to just be things one does in saying something or other. The conditions jointly define what it is to do that sort of thing. Though Searle and various others have attempted to root illocutionary force in particular conventional features of what is said, there has never been a consensus that this is successful.[14] Searle, Austin before him, and speech act theorists generally have tended to focus on acts associated with the use and meanings

[14] On Searle & Vanderveken (1985), see the nice summary in Green (2015:19–20) and the overview of some of the relevant literature in Green (2015, §4).

of particular verbs which, when used in an indicative sentence, might constitute an act of the relevant sort. But if you just take their characterizations seriously, without assuming any necessary correlation between the conventional content of what is said (e.g. the use of particular verbs) and the presuppositions and implications of what is said *in context*, we find that there are many ways of committing a certain type of speech act, not all involving utterance of the canonically correlated verbs. If all the conditions on a particular speech act type are apparently satisfied, then the utterance counts as an instance of that type of speech act. That is to say, on the present approach there's nothing deep about the distinction between direct and indirect speech acts.[15]

Generally, Searle takes it that a speaker performs an illocutionary act only if he intends that the hearer recognize his intention to perform that act. As Perrault and Allen (1980) point out, this is a Gricean condition. The sketch I have given here is intended to show how the realization of Gricean Relevance in the intentionally structured theory from §12.2, given transparent assumptions about the relationships between the interlocutors as reflected in the CG, make it reasonable for the speaker to intend and the addressee to recognize what they say *in context* as particular illocutionary acts, without necessarily using the performatives or other verbs that inspired these speech act characterizations to begin with.

This general approach to speech act recognition derives from the work on speech acts in Planning Theory, work that was formally implemented by a number of researchers working in computational linguistics in the 1980s and 1990s.[16] All emphasize the role of practical reasoning: how we construct and implement joint plans and *recognize* the plans underlying the speech acts of our interlocutors. The basic thesis was that speech act type could be derived from conventional content plus the perceived goals and intentions of the interlocutors. For example, Cohen and Levesque (1990) offer a theory of speech acts based on:

- an account of propositional attitudes like belief, knowledge, intention
- a theory of action and its relation to the attitudes, describing those conditions necessary to engage in action and those resulting from it
- a description of the effects of locutionary acts on the mental state of the participants
- definitions of the performance of illocutionary acts as "the performance of any action…under appropriate circumstances, by a speaker holding certain intentions."

The particular realization of the Planning Theory approach proposed here, in the framework for pragmatic analysis utilizing the notion of context sketched in §12.2, has another important payoff, already mentioned above. It affords the same kind of account as that pioneered by Portner (2004, 2007) of the attested entailment

---

[15] See Charlow (2011) for extended discussion of the topic of indirect speech acts, generally compatible with the view promoted here.

[16] I have given only an informal discussion here for reasons of space. See especially Cohen & Perrault (1979), Allen & Perrault (1980), Perrault & Allen (1980), Cohen & Levesque (1990), Perrault (1990), Thomason (1990), and the more recent developments in Asher & Lascarides (2001), Thomason, Stone & DeVault (2006) and Charlow (2011), all of which influenced the present proposal.

relationships between imperatives and declaratives with deontic modality, without imputing modal propositional content to the imperative *per se*.

Though, on the account in §12.3, directions contain no modal operator *per se*, any directions issued using imperatives lead, **indirectly but regularly**, to modifications of the CG in the context of utterance, as Portner and others have proposed. But here this needn't be stipulated, and instead follows directly from the nature of the language game and its scoreboard (§12.2) and the essentially deontic (though non-propositional) semantics of the imperative (§12.3). The adoption of the goal associated with a direction is not an isolated matter, but requires revision of the target agent's complex structure of plans, with the understood f and g in the interpretation of the imperative reflecting relevant contingencies and priorities *in those plans*. Since the state of G on the scoreboard is always reflected in CG *as deontic propositions about the relevant agent(s) goals, etc.*, the primary pragmatic effect of acceptance of a direction—update of G_i for the target x_i—regularly leads to the update of CG with corresponding deontic propositions.

Consider some of Portner's examples, illustrating a range of deontic flavors for paired imperatives and modal propositions:

(13) a. Sit down right now! (order)
      b. Noah should sit down right now (given that he's been ordered to do so).

(14) a. Have a piece of fruit! (invitation)
      b. Noah should have a piece of fruit (given that he's hungry).

(15) a. Talk to your advisor more often! (suggestion)
      b. Noah should talk to his advisor more often (given that he wants to finish).

Because of the commitments involved in adopting a goal (see, e.g., Bratman 1987), when an imperative is accepted (as it must be in the case of an order issued by a legitimate authority), this publicly commits the addressee to intend to achieve that goal. Since all information on the scoreboard is reflected in the CG, knowledge of such commitments is encoded in propositions in CG to the effect that the addressee has those goals.

A proposition about goals is a modal proposition. Consider the proposition that agent x intends to bring it about that ϕ is true. This is a complex type of propositional attitude, a teleological attitude towards ϕ on the part of x. In terms of a Hintikka-style (1969) treatment of the attitudes, if the proposition that x bears this attitude toward ϕ is true in world w at time t, it means that all worlds x-teleologically accessible from w at t are worlds in which ϕ is true at some time t' s.t. $t \leq t'$. Hence, an agent's goals are reflected in teleological modal accessibility relations.

Typically a direction whose acceptance is appropriately reflected in the CG (and corresponding Context Set CS) may have an additional deontic flavor. For instance, if a Directive is issued (via utterance of an imperative) by a speaker who has authority over the addressee, this amounts to an order or demand, as in (13a). In that case, the addressee may have no choice but to accept the goal so proposed, and in addition, the corresponding proposition in the CG will not only be teleological, but also a very high priority—something the agent *must* do, according to the authoritative speaker. If Noah accepts the invitation of a friend in (14a), thus intending to eat a piece of fruit, the deontic in (14b) may be understood to range over worlds in which Noah is hungry (and presumably wants something healthy to eat), characterizing as ideal those in which he eats a piece of fruit. Without any authority of the speaker of (14a) over Noah, this will be a much less binding obligation than that in (13a), and accordingly (14b) may be true without Noah necessarily striving to realize his goal. We might say that for social reasons, the realization of (13a) has to be a higher priority for Noah than the realization of (14a). Thus, a variety of social circumstances (pecking order, etc.) and relations between the interlocutors will color the accessibility relations imposed on the CS as a consequence of acceptance of a Directive.

In the framework in §12.2, such propositions about goals for agent x restrict the worlds in the Context Set (CS, the worlds compatible with the CG) to those such that the x-teleological modal accessibility relation maps them to worlds in which x has achieved that goal at some future time. So all x's goals as reflected in G_x on the scoreboard will be reflected in various kinds of teleological propositions in the CG. But this same type of teleological relationship between x and x's ideal intentions is entailed by statements involving deontic modals like *should* in (13b), (14b) and (15b), on the standard Kratzerian account: In these examples, the speaker asserts a proposition which entails that the real world is one in which Noah ideally has certain goals—sitting down, eating fruit, talking with his advisor—and, if accepted, this assertion restricts the worlds in the CS to those which the *Noah*-teleological modal accessibility relation maps to worlds in all of which *Noah* has achieved the relevant goals at some future time. Accordingly, the resulting CG after (13a), (14a) or (15a) has been addressed to, and accepted by Noah, will entail the truth of their (b) counterparts. No stipulation is required.

On the other hand, it is a pragmatic consequence of (i) the meaning of the modal and (ii) the authenticity of the deontic authority appealed to, that the subject of (13b) is under obligation to perform the action in question. Thus *You should sit down right now!*, spoken to Noah by his father, when accepted by Noah has the same effect on the discourse scoreboard, and in particular on the publicly evident goals for Noah, as if his father had issued a direct command to perform the act. Accordingly, corresponding to such modal propositions in the CG, there arise appropriately conditioned goals in G_{Noah}.[17]

Moreover, the relationship just sketched follows naturally on the present account, where goals and plans are taken to be a central factor in the organization and direction of discourse. In contrast:

I do not see any way to account for this close connection between imperatives and modals within a classical speech act theory, since the effect of a directive act is not given a linguistically relevant representation. [Portner 2018, p. 26]

Finally, in the QUD framework in §12.2, a Directive response to a QUD may have a particular deontic flavor as a consequence of the meaning of the question itself.

---

[17] See Mastop (2005), Charlow (2010, 2011) and Portner (2018) for detailed technical expositions of the general approach to the relationship between imperatives and deontic modality (and other "priority" modalities—Portner 2018) just sketched here.

To see this, first consider the following three contexts for the use of the direction, *Take a taxi*.

(16) [Joan is tired and has a lot of bags to carry home after a long day shopping. Her usual way home would be via the subway, but her girlfriend says sympathetically:] Take a taxi.

(17) [The boss is angry and irritated with an employee Joan who has been late to work several times lately because her car keeps breaking down. She claims he can't afford to get a new car, but the boss gives her a withering look and says:] Take a taxi.

(18) [Joan had to work late and her husband is worried about her traveling home late at night on the subway alone. Talking to her on the phone before she leaves the office, she insists she'll be just fine, but he says:] Take a taxi!

The speakers in (16)–(18) are all proposing to the addressee Joan that she adopt the goal of taking a taxi to the relevant location. But they have different power relationships to Joan in these three scenarios, the speakers themselves have different motives for proposing this goal, and in each case Joan herself would be understood to have different motives for possibly adopting it. As a consequence, we understand these speech acts in different ways. In (16), presumably the friend's goal is to help Joan, but she may have no particular desire for Joan to adopt this plan, and Joan's motives to adopt the proffered advice may be relatively weak, so this constitutes a suggestion or advice. In (17), the boss's goal is to force the employee to get to work on time, and Joan, subject to his authority, wants to keep her job, so this constitutes an order. In (18), we might take the husband's goal to be to protect Joan, and Joan herself might be afraid. Depending on the husband's tone of voice and the general relationship between them, we might take this to either be a plea (begging), a request (there's something in it for the husband too), or even an order.

But now consider cases where the Directive is issued in response to a question by Joan:

(17′) Seeing the boss's anger, Joan asks: What must I do?

(18′) In response to her husband's concern about her safety on the subway, Joan says: Honey, I have to get home. What can I do?

In these cases, the force of the interlocutors' reply is understood partly as a function of the nature of the modal in the question. Deontic *must* implicitly recognizes the boss's authority over Joan. But *can* in (18) is circumstantial: This is a question of what Joan's practical options are, and no authority is implied.

In all these cases, the evident goals and intentions of the interlocutors, as well as their common knowledge, including knowledge of their power relationships, play a role in the calculation of the intended effect of the speech act. But when there is a QUD, it plays an over-riding role: Even though the situations are the same, if Joan asked her husband the question, *What must I do?*, she'd be acknowledging her husband's Biblical authority over her, and his answer would be understood as an order. Following such a question, the only way to avoid taking (18) as an order is if the husband explicitly denied that authority, as with presupposition rejection generally—*Honey, you can do whatever you want, but I suggest that you take a taxi.*

This illustrates the special force of the QUD in interpretation, in this case in speech act determination.

In sum, as in the Planning-based accounts, speech act recovery is intention-recognition, involving abductive inference to the best explanation, in view of the score and the nature of the game. And in the framework in §12.2, the nature of the context of utterance puts strong constraints on the type of speech act which it would be felicitous to make with a given utterance.

Note that, as reflected in the theory of Cohen and Levesque (1990) sketched above (p. 342, the classical Planning-based approach wasn't entirely satisfactory. This is partly because it failed to note any regular relationship between conventional form and speech act type. Morgan (1990:189ff) remarks on this problem: What is the bridge between the conventional truth-conditional content of an utterance and the kinds of beliefs, desires, and intentions which Perrault and his colleagues take to be basic features of how speech acts arise? And, extending this observation, why should we expect to find the universally attested three types of clausal mood and their correlation to specific speech act types? The missing component in these accounts is the canonical relationship between grammatical mood and illocutionary force, via semantic type. This is remedied in the present account by making the default force of an utterance—assertion, direction, or question—to be given by its grammatical mood, as discussed in the following section, and by the standard pragmatics of these three kinds of speech acts, as spelled out formally in §12.2.

12.4.2 The default correlation between mood and speech act type

Recall from §12.2 above, the default correlation between sentence form and speech act type:

Mood	Speech Act
declarative	assertion
interrogative	interrogation/question
jussive/imperative	direction

One central issue has been evident in speech act theory from the outset, as reflected in Searle's (1975) taxonomy, from §12.1 above. Portner (2018) calls this the **conventionalization** question. Generally, how do particular utterances of questions come to be associated with the force they are attested to have? Here is how he poses the question for imperatives:

The conventionalization question: How do imperative sentences come to be associated with directive sentential force? In particular, what are the linguistic principles that associate certain grammatical representations, namely those which we identify as imperatives, with directive force, rather than with some other force, or no force at all? (Portner 2018)

Zanuttini et al. (2012), Kaufmann and Poschmann (2013), and Portner (2018) offer several reasons to take the correlation to be pragmatic rather than semantic. Among them, as Portner notes:

- There are distinct means of formally marking clausal mood even within a single language: "The syntactic diversity of imperative sentences within languages like Greek and Italian shows that there is no simple correlation between grammatical form and the imperative speech act type. This fact poses a problem for speech act theory's approach to the conventionalization question. As pointed out by Zanuttini and Portner (2003), it seems that it is not possible to identify any discrete piece of the morphosyntactic representation with the force marker."
- The same morphological form may be used in different moods: "Kaufmann and Poschmann (2013) present evidence that colloquial German allows wh-interrogatives with imperative morphology and the associated directive meaning. They point out that this combination of the interrogative and imperative meaning is difficult to account for on the view that sentences are typed through the presence of an operator which assigns them their illocutionary force."

In addition to these complex many-one correlations between mood and speech act type, in both directions, there are other reasons to take the correlation to be merely pragmatic—a function of the rules of the game, and not grammatical—determined by the semantics of the moods. One, noted above, is that embedded uses are not speech acts, have no independent illocutionary force; insofar as the semantics proposed above gives the correct contribution to truth conditions in these embedded uses, then it seems preferable to leave illocutionary force out of the compositional semantics.

But what counts as a move in a discourse game of the sort sketched here? This is a question posed clearly in Murray and Starr (to appear), and I can only briefly address it here. I argued above that what potentially carries illocutionary force is an utterance, not a sentence alone. Recall that following Bar-Hillel (1971), an utterance is the ordered pair of a constituent (under an analysis, hence with its compositional semantics) and a context of utterance; call the first element of such a pair the uttered constituent. But what constraints are there on what kinds of utterance may serve as speech acts, as moves in the sense explored here? At first blush, it seems that only utterances whose uttered constituent is a main clause potentially carry illocutionary force. But this would ignore non-sentential utterances—cases where the utterance of a non-clausal constituent counts as, e.g., the answer to a question. And are subordinate clauses ever treated as moves in themselves, as speech acts? There is a tradition, recently represented by the work of Krifka (2014), in which they may be. If not, why not?

I think this is not a syntactic matter, *per se*, and hence not a matter for simple compositional semantics, but a question about what potentially constitutes a complete speech act. I would argue that the answer lies in the constraints imposed by compositionality, as well as its limits:

A **complete speech act** is one such that the proffered content of the uttered constituent is coherent and compositionally maximal, and has the type of denotation (either on its own or with contextually implicit modification) which can serve as one of the standard types of discourse move.

What someone says is semantically **coherent** if all of the functions denoted in what's said are saturated with appropriate argument(s). An uttered constituent is **compositionally maximal** if it doesn't serve as part of a larger semantically composed constituent.

If you have two clausal contents side-by-side, with no connectives, there's nothing to make them cohere; neither is a functor taking the other as argument. In that case, we can say that each is compositionally maximal, and (given that each is the right type to be asserted) hence potentially serves as a speech act in itself, so long as the speaker's delivery suggests that that is what she intends. If a fragment cannot be understood to implicitly (in the context of utterance) have the content of a standard move (for which, see Ginzburg 2012, *inter alia*), then its utterance doesn't count as a complete speech act. Not all complete speech acts have explicit content denoting propositions or questions or directed properties (again, see Ginzburg); but any of the latter denotata, *if maximal (e.g. not argument to a higher functor), so that the entire utterance is altogether coherent* (all its functors saturated) may constitute a complete speech act.

This characterization fails to admit of embedded speech acts because by themselves embedded constituents are not compositionally maximal (since they serve as arguments to the main clause verb, conjunction, etc.). Also, since there are no clear examples where a single constituent plays a role in two distinct speech acts simultaneously, if an embedded constituent by itself constitutes a speech act, then the whole utterance in which it occurs could not be understood as a speech act, since without the embedded constituent it is incoherent (the argument of one of its functors unsaturated).

Further, the proposed definition of what it is to be a complete speech act is not semantic, since nothing about the utterance-internal semantics tells us, "This is a complete speech act". A proposition-denoting declarative clause can serve as argument to a modifier or embedding predicate, a question-denoting interrogative ditto; a directed property-denoting imperative can serve as main clause in a conditional. Nothing semantic ever says, "This is it!". The only purported exceptions that I know of from the literature are (a) so-called "speaker-oriented adverbials" and (b) evidentials. Ultimately, careful consideration of those two purported exceptions are crucial to my case. Potts (2005) has argued that the speaker-oriented adverbials are Conventional Implicatures, and so do not bear directly on the proffered content of the utterance. Evidentials are a more complex case, and still quite controversial; see Murray and Starr (to appear) for extended discussion and additional references. This issue goes well beyond the purview of the current paper, but it should be noted that it has a direct bearing on the proposed account of speech acts.

Finally, the fact that features of speech acts can be derived from features of the language game, as illustrated in the previous section, and so needn't be stipulated in the semantics of the moods themselves, argues that the principled separation of semantics from illocutionary force, the latter a function of pragmatics, results in a more explanatory account of speech acts.

Portner (2004) and Zanuttini et al. (2012) argue in detail for a picture along similar lines, where root sentences have non-illocutionary, compositionally derived semantic objects as their semantic values, and the linkage between sentence type and force is determined by basic theses of pragmatic theory. Semantic type explains the correlation with force, inspiring the present proposal. They assume that declaratives denote propositions and that imperatives denote properties formed by abstracting over the subject; they take a To-Do list to be a set of properties, in contrast to the common ground, which is a set of propositions. Given this, a basic principle answers the conventionalization question:

Force Linking Principle (Portner 2004, Zanuttini et al. 2012)
a. Given a root sentence S whose denotation [[S]] is a proposition, add [[S]] to the common ground.
b. Given a root sentence S whose denotation [[S]] is a property, add [[S]] to the addressee's To-Do list.

We might add a third clause:

c. Given a root sentence S whose denotation [[S]] is a set of propositions, add [[S]] to the QUD stack.

The Force Linking Principle is realized in the present framework by the default correlations between mood and speech act type in §12.2. Though the mood-force correlation is not part of the conventional grammar on this account, it is canonical in the following sense: The correlation noted in the Force Linking Principle is natural. The semantic types of the root sentences lend themselves naturally to the tasks they canonically serve. The *canonical part*, the rule government, lies in the rules of the game, and in the requirement that the moves in question have the right content to contribute to the scoreboard as such a move should.

Mandy Simons (p.c.) suggests that we think of the Force Linking Principles as *conventions of use* in the sense of Morgan (1978): norms associated with particular forms, for reasons based in general pragmatic considerations. Because the norm is associated with a particular form, it need not be "calculated" on each occasion of use. But because a norm has this pragmatic foundation, it can also be overridden when other general pragmatic considerations or other linguistic conventions indicate a different intended interpretation. In any case, a convention of use isn't a *grammatical rule*.

12.4.3 Performatives

A central motivation for speech act theory was Austin's observations about performatives, a special class of speech acts which are self-verifying, in the sense that their very performance accomplishes a conventionally associated perlocutionary act:

I now pronounce you man and wife.
You're fired!
I promise that I'll fix dinner next Sunday.
You're hereby ordered to report to jury duty.

These are all included in Searle's (1989) Declarations.

There have been many attempts over the years to provide accounts of the performatives which reduce them to some form of assertion (Lemmon 1962, Hedonius 1963, Bach & Harnish 1979, Ginet 1979, Bierwisch 1980, Leech 1983, *inter alia*). These are accounts in which, as Searle (1989) puts it "it is just a semantic fact about certain verbs that they have performative occurrences". In other words, their conventional semantic contents guarantee that when a speaker makes a felicitous assertion using one of these verbs as head in a first-person present tense root declarative sentence, the result is automatically true. Most of these accounts, including the Planning Theory views discussed in §12.4.1, have not been entirely satisfactory in the terms established by Austinian Speech Act theory as developed by Searle.

Searle (1989:539) takes the following to be among the central features of performatives, and hence as establishing desiderata for an adequate theory of explicit performative speech acts:[18]

(1) Performative utterances are performances of the act named by the main verb (or other performative expression) in the sentence.
(2) Performative utterances are self-guaranteeing in the sense that the speaker cannot be lying, insincere, or mistaken about the type of act being performed.
(3) Performative utterances achieve features (1) and (2) in virtue of the literal meaning of the sentence uttered.

We might take (2) to mean that explicit performatives' content gets added to the CG automatically (Jary 2007), unlike assertions, which are conditioned on the acceptance of the addressee. (3) argues that there should be a uniform lexical meaning of the main verb across performative and reportative uses.

Searle takes performatives to involve in their essential meaning a speaker's intention corresponding to their sincerity condition. E.g. in the case of a promise (1989: 545):

in what does [a statement's] being a promise consist? Given that the preparatory and other conditions are satisfied, its being a promise consists in its being intended as a promise.

Hence, to satisfy (2), an adequate account of performatives has to guarantee that this aspect of the meaning of a performative is automatically added to the CG. Searle then argues that assertoric accounts of performatives are inadequate because they cannot guarantee that the speaker has the requisite intention (1989: 546):

Such an assertion [as proposed in those accounts] does indeed commit the speaker to the existence of the intention, but the commitment to having the intention doesn't guarantee the actual presence of the intention.

Further, Condoravdi & Lauer (2011: 2) point out that if we take the speaker's having the relevant intention to be required for the utterance to constitute a promise, then

It should be immediately clear that inference-based accounts cannot meet [(1)–(3)]. If the occurrence of the performative effect depends on the hearer drawing an inference, then such sentences could not be self-verifying, for the hearer may well fail to draw the inference.

But Condoravdi & Lauer's (2011) assertoric theory of performatives seems to me to successfully address these issues. They give detailed formal semantic analyses of three performatives, *claim*, *promise*, and *order*. For each, in keeping with desideratum

[18] There are others (see Searle 1989: 539–40), but they are more easily addressed. These are the most problematic for the assertoric accounts.

(c), they begin by giving the lexical semantics for the predicate *based on its meaning in non-performative uses*, with third person subjects and non-present tense. On the basis of this analysis, they then explain how its use with first person subject and present tense satisfies desideratum (b), whereby in making the assertion the speaker makes the assertion true, leading to its automatic addition to the Common Ground. With respect to criterion (a), they agree that this should obtain, but argue that Searle has misunderstood what it is to be a promise or a claim or an order. For example, a promise does *not* require that the speaker intends to keep his promise, but only that he is *committed* to doing so. Thus, they call into question Searle's Sincerity Condition on promises, discussed in §12.4.1 above.

Here is how one might understand their rebuttal (though this is not how they present it): Consider Jason Stanley's (2013) complaint about Fox News' misrepresentation of their commitment to presenting a Fair and Balanced view of public affairs: Trust is crucial to the maintenance of the social compact underlying the language game. Fair enough. It's trust that leads us to assume that a speaker is observing Gricean Quality, hence to be inclined to add the propositions they assert to the CG. Without this trust, we cannot achieve the goals of the game, to make progress in joint understanding. Similarly, it's trust that leads us to *expect* that someone who has made an explicit promise intends to keep it. But though *dis*trust can generally lead us to refuse to add an assertion to the CG, it doesn't prevent us from adding a promise when it's explicitly made, even if we think the speaker does not intend to keep his promise. This is because **the act of asserting that one promises just *is what a promise is*:** It's about incurring an explicit commitment to act, and it is that commitment which is all that is required for it to *be* a promise. Thus, in this case the assertion is self-verifying, so is added to the CG despite one's lack of confidence in the speaker's intentions to meet her commitments. And there will be consequences if she fails to do so.

This account is consistent with the non-performative use of *promise*. Consider:

(19) He promised to come, but none of us believed he really meant it.

This sounds true and non-contradictory. If the fellow didn't come, we can say he broke his promise, though nobody expected he'd come.

Hence Condoravdi and Lauer "circumvent [Searle's first problem for assertoric accounts] by requiring only that the speaker be committed to having a belief or an intention (in our terms, an effective preference). On our view, **what matters for speech acts, or at least the truth conditions of performative verbs, is public facts**" [CR's emphasis]. I concur.

About the automatic update of the Common Ground, they argue that no hearer inferences are required to derive the self-verifying nature of performatives. In the language game sketched in §12.2, the fact that an assertion happened always automatically enters the CG, even if that assertion is not accepted. But with the performatives, by virtue of the meanings of the predicates in question and certain social facts, **the utterance is a witness for its own truth**, i.e. "the content of the assertion is entailed by the fact that the assertion happened, and so this content will become part of the common ground automatically." In my terms, the meaning of the performative predicate plus the way the game works together guarantee an update that entails the truth of the performative utterance.

More generally, successful, felicitous speech acts don't guarantee speaker *intentions*, only speaker *public commitments*.

Consider the related issue for the common ground: As Stalnaker (1979) argued, the common ground isn't really a joint doxastic state—the set of propositions that the interlocutors believe and reflexively believe that each other believe—but instead is the set of propositions that they jointly *purport to believe*. Thereby they incur certain commitments, and these have consequences in the language game, and beyond. But we all know that it is likely that the common ground CG is nonveridical in certain respects; someone may have lied, and certainly some of our beliefs are false. Similarly, for any interlocutor *i*, the representation of their goals on the scoreboard in G_i isn't the set of goals that that agent *intends to (attempt to) achieve*, but instead those that it is publicly apparent that she is committed to achieving. The same can be said for the QUD: These represent the discourse goals that the interlocutors are committed to addressing. And here again, there are consequences in the language game for such commitments: One can be called to task for not sticking to the subject, and whatever one *does* say will be taken to be relevant to the QUD unless it is explicitly noted that it is an aside (i.e. irrelevant from the point of view of that question). But that's all that's required for the game to work as it does. To require sincere intentions is more than is needed or is attested by our colloquial understanding of verbs like *assert* or *ask* or *order*, as in the example (19) above.

Condoravdi and Lauer give a similar account of the other performatives they consider, and I think it generalizes quite nicely. Also, they note that their account, unlike the speech act story, can explain the interaction of performative predicates with the progressive, which cannot be used performatively even in the present tense. If performatives are accomplishments, then the progressive form doesn't commit the speaker to the existence of an accomplishment (progressive doesn't entail the culmination of the described event); but only the accomplishment entails the commitment.

One more point: Searle claims that Performatives have both directions of fit, word-to-world and world-to-word. The performatives considered in this section have word-to-world fit, on the present account, by virtue of the fact that they are assertions. But as we saw in §12.4.1, a performative Promise also has world-to-word fit, in the same way that a deontic assertion, *you must do P* can put the addressee under an obligation to act if the interlocutors are in an appropriate power relationship. In the case of the Promise, this world-to-word fit is a pragmatic consequence of (a) the meaning of the predicate in question, (b) the nature of the act denoted by that predicate, and (c) the commitments incurred in making an assertion, since the utterance itself is witness to the truth of the proposition expressed. In virtue of the fact that the meaning of the assertion is clear, and that the goals on the scoreboard are introduced whenever they are publicly evident, then this goal is automatically added to those of the speaker. Similar explanations can be given for other performatives that have deontic consequences. Hence, the only uptake required for such speech acts is that they be understood. Any other uptake—a belief in their justice or truth, commitments to achieving goals—is not necessary for the agent to incur the relevant commitments.

12.5 Conclusion

A central focus of classical speech act theory is on the kinds of speech acts made with particular verbal predicates, with special attention to those typically used to make performative speech acts with first-person subjects. Instead, on the present view, the core conventional distinction that bears on speech act type is clausal mood—declarative, interrogative, imperative, each determining the semantic type of the clause in which it occurs: a proposition, set of propositions, or property, respectively. In turn, these semantic types are canonically correlated with particular speech act types—assertion, question, direction—though unlike the semantic type, the correlation between mood and illocutionary force is pragmatic and hence can be contextually over-ridden. I.e., on the account of speech acts proposed above, though sentences are conventionally marked with clausal mood, what carries illocutionary force is not a sentence, but an utterance.

The resulting account is simple and non-stipulative. The formal characterization of the notion of context of utterance as the scoreboard in a language game is independently motivated, and has been shown over the past twenty years to support illuminating accounts of a wide variety of pragmatic phenomena.[19] Against this theoretical backdrop, the three basic illocutionary forces constitute the three basic types of moves in a language game, resulting in three basic types of update of the scoreboard. Making a move using one of these basic types is a speech act. All other speech act types discussed in the literature, including those in Searle's taxonomy in §12.1, are more specific instances of those three types, their differences pragmatically implicated in particular contexts of use. The bridge between conventional content and illocutionary force is a pragmatic, default correlation, Portner's (2004) Force Linking Principle, between the grammatical mood of the utterance and illocutionary force.

The proposed semantics of grammatical mood, determining the semantic type of the utterance in which it occurs, is empirically well-founded, arguably yielding the correct semantic types for embedded as well as matrix clauses. This is illustrated in §12.3 with a natural, elegant account of the semantics of imperative clauses which has these empirically superior features:

- An imperative clause is not propositional, so we avoid Kaufmann's incorrect predictions in this regard. Its semantic type is that of a property.
- Imperative mood presupposes a Kratzerian modal base f and ordering source g, which permit us to capture the deontic, conditional character of imperatives but without modal operators *per se*. This permits us to retain what's best in Kaufmann, including the wide variety of flavors found in directions issued with imperative clauses.
- The imperative interacts pragmatically, both in the essential effect of its default use as a move in the game (as a direction) and in the way that f, g are selected, with the independently motivated, complexly structured record of the interlocutors'

---

[19] See the evolving bibliography at http://www.ling.ohio-state.edu/~croberts/QUDbib/ for a sample of this work.

evident goals G, in a fashion that's natural given the nature of the language game and discourse scoreboard. Thereby:

- The account avoids Portner's problems with the too-simple To-Do list(s).
- It affords a natural implementation of Portner's (2007) characterization of imperative-deontic relations. This turns out to be a specific instance of the way that indirect speech acts are generated, through regular pragmatic effects rooted in plan recognition and update in a context structured by intentions. So again, no stipulation is required.

A similar account of the illocutionary force of interrogatives as questions is given in Roberts (1996/2012a), and all this is consistent with Stalnaker's (1979) account of declaratives as Assertions.

This account is not only empirically superior, it is explanatory, offering a functionally motivated explanation for the linguistic universals noted in §12.1: These three basic speech act types are universal because they serve as the three main types of moves in a language game. Each directly contributes to one of the three central repositories of information on the discourse scoreboard: assertions to the common ground (CG), imperatives to the interlocutors' evidence goals and plans (G), and questions to the distinguished set of goals that drive and constrain felicitous utterances and their interpretations (QUD). Since we assume that the nature of the game, as reflected in this model of the context of utterance, is not language-specific but reflects what it is to engage in discourse, it is not surprising that (a) the three clause types occur across languages, universally correlated with the semantic types argued for here, and (b) the pragmatic correlation between semantic type and illocutionary force obtains across languages as well.

Moreover, this view of illocutionary force affords an account of how contextual factors evident to the interlocutors (as reflected in the scoreboard, and in particular in CG, G, and QUD) regularly determine both,

- what counts as a felicitous speech act in a given context, thereby constraining the speaker's production in that context, and
- how the particular illocutionary force of an utterance is to be understood, thereby guiding interpretation.

It does this by implementing insights into speech act determination and indirect speech acts from the earlier work in Planning Theory and Charlow (2011). We can derive the kinds of speech acts which the Austin/Searle theory takes to be basic, without stipulation or the implication that there is some finite list of speech act types. Not only do speech acts contribute to the scoreboard, but we understand what someone means by an utterance—what speech act they intend to make—as a function of the interlocutors' evident information (CG), goals and plans (G), and the question under discussion (QUD). In an imperative or modal assertion or a question, CG contributes directly to the determination of the modal base f, while G contributes to the ordering source g; and in any case the resulting interpretation must be relevant to the resolution of the QUD. Speech acts needn't be direct or fully explicit, so long as the context makes clear only one contribution that would satisfy all the constraints contextually imposed. But this particular implementation of the pragmatic derivation of illocutionary force addresses Morgan's (1990) problem for the earlier work, by offering a bridge between the conventional truth conditional content of an utterance and the kinds of illocutionary force an utterance can be taken to have—the default Force Linking Principle of Portner (2004).

Finally, the proposed theory is consistent with a natural account of performatives as self-verifying assertions, meeting Searle's (1989) objections to such accounts.

I don't mean to suggest that Searle's speech act types are without interest. He isn't taxonomizing verb types, of course, but types of act (which can be performed with these verbs). Thus, the resulting taxonomy may be of interest in its own right in a theory of action, and especially in a theory of status functions and their role in social institutions (as he discussed in Searle 2013). However, it arguably isn't motivated by linguistic pragmatics *per se*. With an adequate theory of the latter, I have argued, we can explain how particular "performative" verbs, in their basic meaning, give rise to acts of the relevant sorts when used with a first person subject and present tense. More generally, we can derive Searle's speech act types from the simpler taxonomy I propose, in combination with the conventional content of the utterances involved, the nature of the acts in question, and contextual information in the discourses in which they are used.

Most of the present account of speech acts, as acknowledged above, derives from prior work on the linguistic semantics of clause types, and on the role of plans and intention recognition in the determination of the speech act intended by an utterance in a given context. The contribution here is to use the discourse framework in §12.2 and a particular account of the semantics of imperatives in §12.3 to make clear how multiple factors simultaneously come to bear on speech act recognition: conventional content, including clausal mood and the corresponding semantic type, background information and presuppositions (CG), the interlocutors' evident goals and plans (G), and the question under discussion (QUD). On this model, interpretation is like solving a simultaneous equation with multiple variables. The scoreboard tracks the contextual factors that enter in, and in turn its update *in all those dimensions* is the target of speech acts. All these factors are independently motivated by other pragmatic phenomena, but they play exactly the role we need for speech act retrieval.

Acknowledgment

This paper developed out of a talk at the NY Philosophy of Language Workshop, conference *New Work on Speech Acts*, at Columbia on September 29, 2013. My thanks to the organizers, Daniel Fogal, Daniel Harris and Matt Moss, for an excellent conference, and to the participants for a lively conversation. Thanks as well to the OSU Pragmatics working group, the MASZAT group at the Research Institute for Linguistics of the Hungarian Academy of Sciences, and the OSU Synners working group, for comments on earlier versions, and to B. Chandrasekaran, Hans-Martin Gärtner, and Mandy Simons for helpful conversations as the work evolved. Hans-Martin's challenges and suggestions were especially important in driving me to consider more carefully the semantics of the imperative.

But whatever merit there may be in this work depends in large measure on the excellent earlier work acknowledged throughout, and most especially that of John Searle; James Allen, Phil Cohen, Ray Perrault, and Rich Thomason; Magdalena (Schwager) Kaufmann, Paul Portner, and Nate Charlow, as well as Cleo Condoravdi and Sven Lauer, and Sarah Murray and Will Starr. I hope I have managed to adequately convey my debt to all these scholars.

This work was largely completed while I was a Senior Fellow in 2014–15 at the Institute for Advanced Studies at Central European University, Budapest, Hungary, sponsored by Budapesti Közép-Európai Egyetem Alaptvány, The theses promoted herein are the author's own, and do not necessarily reflect the opinion of the CEU IAS. I am deeply grateful for their support, as well as to The Ohio State University, which also helped to make possible that fellowship year.

References

Allen, James & C. Raymond Perrault (1980) Analyzing intention in utterances. *Artificial Intelligence* 15: 143–78.

Asher, Nicholas & Alex Lascarides (1994) Intentions and information in discourse. In *Proceedings of the 32nd Annual Meeting of the Association of Computational Linguistics (ACL94)*, Las Cruces, New Mexico, 34–41.

Asher, Nicholas & Alex Lascarides (2001) Indirect speech acts. *Synthese* 128(1–2): 183–228.

Asher, Nicholas & Alex Lascarides (2003) *Logics of Conversation*. Cambridge University Press.

Austin, J. L. (1970) Ifs and cans. In Austin, *Philosophical Papers*, 2nd edition. Oxford: Oxford University Press, 205–32.

Bach, K. & R. M. Harnish (1979) *Linguistic Communication and Speech Acts*. Cambridge, MA: MIT Press.

Bar-Hillel, Yehoshua (1971) *Pragmatics of Natural Language*. Dordrecht: Reidel.

Bierwisch, Manfred (1980) Semantic structure and illocutionary force. In John R. Searle, Ferenc Kiefer & Manfred Bierwisch (eds.) *Speech Act Theory and Pragmatics*. Dordrecht: Reidel, 1–35.

Bolinger, Dwight (1977) *Meaning and Form*. London: Longman.

Bratman, Michael E. (1987) *Intentions, Plans, and Practical Reason*. Cambridge, MA: Harvard University Press.

Carlson, Lauri (1982) *Dialogue Games:An approach to discourse analysis* (Synthese Language Library 17). Dordrecht: D. Reidel.

Charlow, Nathan (2010) Restricting and embedding imperatives. In Maria Aloni, Harald Bastiaanse, Tikitu de Jager & Katrin Schulz (eds.) *Logic, Language and Meaning*, volume 6042 of Lecture Notes in Computer Science, Berlin/Heidelberg: Springer, 223–33.

Charlow, Nathan (2011) *Practical language: Its meaning and use*. Ph.D. Dissertation, University of Michigan.

Charlow, Nate (2014) Logic and semantics for imperatives. *Journal of Philosophical Logic* 43: 617–64.

Ciardelli, Ivano, Jeroen Groenendijk, & Floris Roelofsen (2013) Inquisitive semantics: A new notion of meaning. *Language and Linguistics Compass* 7(9): 459–76. DOI: 10.111/lnc3.12037.

Cohen, P. R. & H. J. Levesque (1990) Rational interaction as the basis for communication. In P. Cohen, J. Morgan, and M. Pollack (eds.) *Intentions in Communication*. Cambridge, MA: MIT Press, 221–55.

Cohen, Philip R. & C. Raymond Perrault (1979) Elements of a plan-based theory of speech acts. *Cognitive Science* 3(3): 177–212. Available at DOI:10.1207/s15516709cog0303_1.

Condoravdi, Cleo & Sven Lauer (2011) Performative verbs and performative acts. In Reich et al. (eds.) *Proceedings of Sinn & Bedeutung* 15. Saarbrücken, Germany: Universaar–Saarland University Press, 1–15.

Condoravdi, Cleo & Sven Lauer (2012) Imperatives: Meaning and illocutionary force. In Christopher Piñon (ed.) *Empirical Issues in Syntax and Semantics* 9: 37–58.

Cross, Charles & Floris Roelofsen (2015) Questions. In Edward N. Zalta (ed.) *Stanford Encyclopedia of Philosophy*. Accessed at https://plato.stanford.edu/entries/questions/.

Ernst, Tom (2000) Semantic features and the distribution of adverbs. *ZAS Papers in Linguistics* 17: 79–97. Available at http://www.zas.gwzberlin.de/fileadmin/material/ZASPiL_Volltexte/zp17/zaspil17-ernst.pdf.

Gärtner, Hans-Martin (2015) Root infinitivals and modal particles. An interim report. MS, HAS-RIL, Budapest.

Ginet, Carl (1979) Performativity. *Linguistics and Philosophy* 3(2): 245–65.

Ginzburg, Jonathan (1996) Dynamics and the semantics of dialogue. In Jerry Seligman & Dag Westerståhl (eds.), *Logic, Language and Computation*, vol. 1 (CSLI Lecture Notes 58), Stanford, CA: Center for the Study of Language and Information (CSLI), Stanford University, chap.15, 221–37.

Ginzburg, Jonathan (2012) *The Interactive Stance*. Oxford University Press.

Green, Mitchel (2015) Speech acts. In Edward N. Zalta (ed.) *Stanford Encyclopedia of Philosophy*. Accessed at http://plato.stanford.edu/archives/sum2015/entries/speech-acts/.

Grice, H. P. (1957) Meaning, *The Philosophical Review* 66: 41–58. Reprinted in Grice (1989).

Grice, H. P. (1967) Logic and conversation, William James Lectures, Harvard. In Donald Davidson & Gilbert Harman (eds.), 1975, *The Logic of Grammar*, 64–75. Encino: Dickenson Press. Reprinted in Grice (1989).

Grice, H. P. (1989) *Studies in the Way of Words*, Cambridge, MA: Harvard University Press.

Groenendijk, Jeroen & Floris Roelofsen (2009) Inquisitive semantics and pragmatics. Stanford workshop on Language, Communication and Rational Agency, Mary 30–1, 2009. Available at www.illc.uva.nl/inquisitivesemantics/papers/publications.

Han, Chung-hye (2000) *The Structure and Interpretation of Imperatives, Mood and Force in Universal Grammar*. New York: Garland.

Hausser, Roland R. (1980) Surface compositionality and the semantics of mood. In J. R. Searle, F. Kiefer & M. Bierwisch (eds.) *Speech Act Theory and Pragmatics*, Dordrecht: Reidel, 71–95.

Hedonius, I. (1963) Performatives. *Theoria* 29: 115–36.

Heim, Irene (1992) Presupposition projection and the semantics of attitude verbs. *Journal of Semantics* 9: 183–221.

Hintikka, Jaako (1969) *Models for Modalities*. Dordrecht: Reidel.

Huntley, M. (1984) The semantics of English imperatives. *Linguistics and Philosophy* 7: 103–34.

Jary, Mark (2007) Are explicit performatives assertions? *Linguistics and Philosophy* 30(2): 207–34.

Kaufmann, Magdalena (2012) *Interpreting Imperatives*. Studies in Linguistics and Philosophy 88. Berlin: Springer. Revised version of Schwager 2006, below.

Kaufmann, Magdalena (2014a) Embedded Imperatives Across Languages: Too rare to expect, too frequent to ban. Handout from a talk, Department of Linguistics, SUNY Stony Brook.

Kaufmann, Magnalena (2014b) Fine-tuning Natural Language Imperatives: Between logic and linguistics. Slides of a talk at DEON, Ghent, July 2014.

Kaufmann, Magdalena & Claudia Poschmann (2013) Embedded imperatives and echo-questions. *Language* 89(3): 619–37.

Kratzer, Antelika (1977) What 'must' and 'can' must and can mean. *Linguistics and Philosophy* 1: 337–55.

Kratzer, Angelika (1981) The notional category of modality. In H. J. Eikmeyer & H. Rieser (eds.), *Words, Worlds and Contexts*. Berlin: de Gruyter, 38–74.

Krifka, Manfred (2014) Embedding illocutionary acts. In Tom Roeper & Margaret Speas (eds.), *Recursion, Complexity in Cognition* (Studies in Theoretical Psycholinguistics 43). Berlin: Springer, 125–55.

LaFleur, Richard A. (2011) *Wheelock's Latin 7th Edition*, New York: HarperCollins.

Leech, Geoffrey N. (1983) *Principles of Pragmatics*, vol. 30 of the Longman linguistics library. London and New York: Longman.

Lemmon, J. E. (1962) Sentences variable by their use. *Analysis* 12: 86–9.

Lewis, David (1979) Scorekeeping in a language game. In R. Baüerle, U. Egli, and A. von Stechow (eds.) *Semantics from a Different Point of View*. Berlin: Springer, 172–87.

Mann, W. C. & S. A. Thompson (1987) Rhetorical Structure Theory: Description and construction of text structures. In G. Kempen (ed.) *Natural Language Generation: New Results in Artificial Intelligence, Psychology and Linguistics*. Dordrecht: Martinus Nijhoff, 279–300.

Mastop, Rosja (2005) *What can you do: Imperative mood in semantic theory*. Ph.D. dissertation, University of Amsterdam.

Morgan, J. L. (1978) Two types of convention in indirect speech acts. In Peter Cole (ed.), *Syntax and Semantics Volume 9: Pragmatics*. New York: Academic Press, 261–80.

Morgan, Jerry (1990) Comments on Jones and on Perrault. In P. Cohen, J. Morgan, and M. Pollack (eds.) *Intentions in Communication*. Cambridge, MA: MIT Press, 187–94.

Murray, Sarah & Will Starr (to appear) The structure of communicative acts. *Linguistics and Philosophy*.

Pak, Miok, Paul Portner & Raffaella Zanuttini (2008) Agreement in promissive, imperative, and exhortative clauses. *Korean Linguistics* 14: 157–75.

Pak, Miok, Paul Portner & Raffaella Zanuttini (2015) Embedded imperatives in English and Korean. Class notes, LSA Summer Institute, University of Chicago, July 2015.

Pendlebury, M. (1986) Against the power of force: Reflections on the meaning of mood. *Mind*, 95(379): 361–72.

Perrault, C. Raymond (1990) An application of default logic to speech act theory. In P. Cohen, J. Morgan, and M. Pollack (eds.) *Intentions in Communication*. Cambridge, MA: MIT Press, 161–85.

Perrault, C. Raymond & James Allen (1980) A plan-based analysis of indirect speech acts. *American Journal of Computational Linguistics* 6(3–4): 167–82.

Portner, Paul (2004) The semantics of imperatives within a theory of clause types. In K. Watanabe & R. Young (eds.) *Proceedings of SALT 14*. Cornell University Linguistics Department: CLC Publications. Available at http://semanticsarchive.net/Archive/mJlZGQ4N/.

Portner, Paul (2007) Imperatives and modals. *Natural Language Semantics* 15: 351–83.

Portner, Paul (2018) Imperatives. In Maria Aloni & Robert van Rooij (eds.) *Cambridge Handbook of Formal Semantics*. Cambridge University Press.

Portner, Paul (2018) Mood. In Oxford Surveys in Semantics and Pragmatics. Oxford: Oxford University Press. Chapter 3: Sentence Mood.

Potts, Chris (2005) *The Logic of Conventional Implicatures*. New York: Oxford University Press.

Roberts, Craige (1989) Modal Subordination and Pronominal Anaphora in Discourse. *Linguistics and Philosophy* 12(6): 683–721. Reprinted in Javier Gutierrez-Rexach (ed.) *Semantics: Critical concepts in linguistics*, Volume 4: *Discourse and dynamics* 197–233, London: Routledge, 2003.

Roberts, Craige (1996/2012a) Information Structure: Toward an integrated theory of formal pragmatics. In Jae Hak Yoon and Andreas Kathol (eds.) *OSUWPL Volume 49: Papers in Semantics*, 1996. The Ohio State University Department of Linguistics. Published, with a new afterword, in *Semantics and Pragmatics* 5(7): 1–19. Also available at http://semprag.org/article/view/sp.5.6.

Roberts, Craige (2012b) Information Structure: Afterword, with bibliography of related work. *Semantics and Pragmatics* 5(7): 1–19. Also available at http://semprag.org/article/view/sp.5.7.

Roberts, Craige (2004) Discourse context in dynamic interpretation. In Laurence Horn and Gregory Ward (eds.) *Handbook of Contemporary Pragmatic Theory*, Oxford: Blackwell 197–220.

Roberts, Craige (2015) Plans and imperatives: A semantics and pragmatics for imperative mood. MS, The Ohio State University and the Institute for Advanced Studies of Central European University, Budapest. Revised 2017.

Sadock, Jerrold M. & Arnold M. Zwicky (1985) Speech act distinctions in syntax. In Timothy Shopin (ed.) *Language Typology and Syntactic Description I: Clause Structure*. Cambridge University Press, 155–96.

Schwager, Magdalena (2006) *Interpreting imperatives*. Ph.D. Dissertation, University of Frankfurt. See her subsequent work under the name *Kaufmann*, above.

Searle, John R. (1969) *Speech Acts: An essay in the philosophy of language*. Cambridge University Press.

Searle, John R. (1975) A taxonomy of illocutionary acts. In K. Gunderson (ed.) *Language, Mind, and Knowledge*. Minneapolis: University of Minnesota Press, 344–69.

Searle, John R. (1989) How performatives work. *Linguistics and Philosophy* 12(5): 535–58.

Searle, John R. (2013) Speech act theory after fifty years. Talk at the New York Philosophy of Language Workshop, Columbia University, September, 2013.

Searle, John R. & Daniel Vanderveken (1985) *Foundations of Illocutionary Logic*. Cambridge: Cambridge University Press.

Sperber, Dan & Deirdre Wilson (1986) *Relevance: Communication and cognition*. Cambridge, MA: Harvard University Press.

Stalnaker, Robert (1979) Assertion. In Peter Cole (ed.) *Syntax and Semantics* 9: 315–32.

Stanley, Jason (2013) Counterbalancing and communication in politics and the media. Talk at the New York Philosophy of Language Workshop, Columbia University, September, 2013.

Starr, William B. (2013) A Preference Semantics for Imperatives. MS, Cornell University. Available at http://williamstarr.net/research/a_preference_ semantics_for_imperatives.pdf.

Stegovec, Adrian & Magdalena Kaufmann (2015) Slovenian Imperatives: You can't always embed what you want! In Csipak & Zeijlstra (eds.), *Proceedings of Sinn und Bedeutung* 19: 620–37. Göttingen.

Thomason, Richmond (1990) Accommodation, meaning, and implicature: Interdisciplinary foundations for pragmatics. In P. Cohen, J. Morgan, and M. Pollack (eds.) *Intentions in Communication*. Cambridge, MA: MIT Press, 325–64.

Thomason, Richmond H., Matthew Stone & David DeVault (2006) Enlightened Update: A computational architecture for presupposition and other pragmatic phenomena. MS, University of Michigan, Rutgers University, University of Edinburgh. Talk at the NSF-sponsored Workshop on Accommodation, OSU.

van Kuppevelt, Jan (1996) Inferring from topics: Implicatures as topic-dependent inferences. *Linguistics and Philosophy* 19(4): 393–443. Available at http://dx.doi.org/10.1007/BF00630897.

Wilson, Deirdre & Dan Sperber (1988) Mood and the analysis of non-declarative sentences. In J. Dancy, J. Moravcsik & C. Taylor (eds.) *Human agency: Language, duty and value*. Stanford University Press, 77–101. Reprinted in A. Kasher (ed.) (1998) *Pragmatics: Critical concepts*, Volume 2. London: Routledge, 262–89.

Zanuttini, Raffaella & Paul Portner (2003) Exclamative Clauses at the Syntax-Semantics Interface. *Language* 79(1): 39–81.

Zanuttini, Rafaella, Miok Pak & Paul Portner (2012) A syntactic analysis of interpretive restrictions on imperative, promissive and exhortative subjects. *Natural Language and Linguistic Theory* 30(4): 1231–74.

13

Dogwhistles, Political Manipulation, and Philosophy of Language

Jennifer Saul

You start out in 1954 by saying, "N*****, n*****, n*****." By 1968, you can't say "n*****"—that hurts you. Backfires. So you say stuff like forced busing, states' rights and all that stuff. You're getting so abstract now [that] you're talking about cutting taxes, and all these things you're talking about are totally economic things and a byproduct of them is [that] blacks get hurt worse than whites. And subconsciously maybe that is part of it. I'm not saying that. But I'm saying that if it is getting that abstract, and that coded, that we are doing away with the racial problem one way or the other. You follow me—because obviously sitting around saying, "We want to cut this," is much more abstract than even the busing thing, and a hell of a lot more abstract than "N*****, n*****."

Lee Atwater, quoted in Lamis (1990)

In recent years, two very welcome changes have come to philosophy of language. The philosophy of language that I was "raised" in was that of the 1980s and 1990s in the US. Our focus was almost exclusively on semantic content, reference and truth conditions. I say "almost exclusively" because Grice's notion of conversational implicature was a notable exception to this—this notion was a topic of some interest, because it allowed semantic theorists to explain away intuitions that seemed to conflict with their preferred theory as "merely pragmatic".

Recently, philosophy of language has broadened in two significant ways. The most important shift, to my mind, is a move to consider the ethical and political dimensions of language. These were never forgotten by philosophers more broadly, but until recently they were left almost exclusively to ethicists and political philosophers. Now, however, philosophers of language are working to understand hate speech, political manipulation, propaganda and lies. These issues—vital in the real world—have not yet become central to philosophy of language. But they are at least a part of the conversation, in a way that they weren't twenty years ago. With this shift (though not wholly as a result of it), has come an increasing philosophical interest in matters other than semantic content and reference. Implicature, accommodation, and speech acts are the central notions in these new debates, rather than semantic content.[1]

And yet, I will be arguing, these new discussions have not yet moved far enough away from the focus on content. Fully making sense of politically manipulative speech will require a detailed engagement with certain forms of speech that function in a less conscious manner—with something other than semantically expressed *or* pragmatically conveyed content; and with effects of utterances that are their very point and that nonetheless vanish as soon as they are made explicit. None of the machinery developed in detail so far is equipped for this task.

This task, however, is an absolutely vital one. Dogwhistles, we will see, are a disturbingly important tool of covert political manipulation. They are in fact one of the most powerful forms of political speech, allowing for people to be manipulated in ways that they would resist if the manipulation was carried out more openly— often drawing on racist attitudes that are consciously rejected. If philosophers focus only on more overt speech, which does its work via content expressed or otherwise consciously conveyed, they will miss much of what is most powerful and pernicious in the speech of our political culture. This paper is a call to start paying attention to these more covert speech acts, and a first attempt at beginning to theorize them.

13.1 Dogwhistles

My focus in this paper is on dogwhistles. 'Dogwhistle' is a relatively new term in politics, arising out of US political journalism in the 1980s. The first recorded use of the term seems to have been by Richard Morin of the *Washington Post*, discussing a curious phenomenon that had been noticed in opinion polling:

Subtle changes in question-wording sometimes produce remarkably different results . . . researchers call this the 'Dog Whistle Effect': Respondents hear something in the question that researchers do not.   (Morin 1988, quoted in Safire 2008: 190)

The idea of a political dogwhistle shifted somewhat over the next decades to focus mainly on a kind of deliberate manipulation, usually by politicians (or their handlers), designed to be unnoticed by most of the public. (We will refine this definition over the course of this paper.) We will see, though, that this sort of manipulation comes in importantly different varieties, which we will tease apart and examine over the course of this paper. Dogwhistles may be overt or covert, and within each of these categories they may be intentional or unintentional.

13.2 Intentional Dogwhistles

13.2.1 Overt Intentional Dogwhistles

Kimberly Witten (forthcoming) is one of very few linguists who has worked on dogwhistles. Her focus is exclusively on the sort of dogwhistle that I call an overt

---

[1] This isn't meant to suggest that speech act theory is new, just that it had fallen out of fashion at least in the circles I moved in.

intentional dogwhistle, and her definition (of 'dogwhistle') is an excellent one for an overt intentional dogwhistle.

A[n overt intentional] dogwhistle is a speech act designed, with intent, to allow two plausible interpretations, with one interpretation being a private, coded message targeted for a subset of the general audience, and concealed in such a way that this general audience is unaware of the existence of the second, coded interpretation.   (Witten forthcoming: 2)

Although the main interest of dogwhistles lies in their political use, Witten rightly argues that the concept applies more broadly. As a parent, I was shocked to revisit some of my favourite childhood entertainments and see much that I had missed as a child. Watching Bugs Bunny with my small son, I was surprised to see references to old movies that children couldn't be expected to know, and even more surprised to see that one of these was *Last Tango in Paris*. Finding these references of course made the endless re-viewings less tedious. And, of course, this was the intent of their makers. Witten suggests that this should be considered a dogwhistle—a concealed message for a subset of the cartoons' general audience.[2]

The most important sort of intentional overt dogwhistle, however, is that used by politicians. Dogwhistle utterances allow a candidate to send a message to one portion of the electorate that other portions might find alienating. These will be my main focus here. We'll start with some examples.

13.2.1.1 "WONDER-WORKING POWER"

George W. Bush faced a tricky situation with respect to his faith throughout his candidacies. He desperately needed the votes of fundamentalist Christians, and yet it was also clear that many others—whose votes he also needed for the general elections— were made nervous by fundamentalist Christianity. The solution his speech-writers used was to dogwhistle to the fundamentalists. A nice example of this is Bush's utterance in his 2003 State of the Union speech:

Yet there's power, wonder-working power, in the goodness and idealism and faith of the American people.   (Noah 2004)

To a non-fundamentalist this is an ordinary piece of fluffy political boilerplate, which passes without notice. But a fundamentalist Christian will hear the dogwhistle. Amongst fundamentalists, "wonder-working power" is a favoured phrase that refers specifically to the power of Christ. There are two messages a fundamentalist might take from this. The first is a kind of translation into their idiolect, to yield an explicitly Christian message that would alienate many:

Yet there's power, the power of Christ, in the goodness and idealism and faith of the American people.[3]

---

[2] Witten discusses different examples, but the idea of dogwhistles for parents in children's entertainment is hers.

[3] Presenting this paper to audiences in the US, I've found that this interpretation is controversial. Some Christians think it's exactly right, while others think it would be wrong to read it this way, and that doing so would yield a heretical utterance. For the latter group, obviously the second interpretation in the text will make more sense.

The second is simply the fact that Bush does speak their idiolect—indicating that he is one of them.[4]

The first message is very clearly an overt intentional dogwhistle: it is a coded, concealed message, intended for just a subgroup of the general audience. In fact, it functions rather like the exploitation of a little-known ambiguity. The second is a little messier. It is somewhat like speaking in a regional accent that gives a feeling of kinship to a particular audience. But it's crucially different because, unlike an accent, it can't be heard by everyone. Arguably, then (assuming that it is done intentionally), this is still an overt intentional dogwhistle—it is a coded message for a subgroup, concealed by an apparently straightforward message.

13.2.1.2 "DRED SCOTT"

George W. Bush also, like many conservatives, makes a point of declaring his opposition to the *Dred Scott* decision, which in 1857 held that no black person, free or slave, could be a US citizen. This is somewhat baffling to those it's not directed to, who take it for granted that even a right-wing Republican opposes slavery, and who think this opposition should go without saying. But most viewers were not who Bush was addressing with this dogwhistle. Bush was addressing the anti-abortion right, and he was dogwhistling about his opposition to abortion.

This dogwhistle functions somewhat differently: it works because it is very common for right-wing commentators to discuss the Dred Scott decision when discussing abortion rights, but in a variety of ways. Sometimes it is as an example of a bad Supreme Court decision in need of overturning (like *Roe v. Wade*). Sometimes it is a part of an analogy between the unrecognized personhood of slaves and (purported) unrecognized personhood of fetuses. But it is so common to discuss it when discussing abortion—and, crucially, so baffling to discuss it otherwise—that it can serve to signal Bush's opposition to abortion, and his desire to see *Roe* overturned.

The exact details of how this one works are a little bit murky. It may work like the old movie references in children's cartoons: designed to trigger allusions for those in the know. Those who know the prominent role of Dred Scott in anti-abortion discussions will know that Bush is deliberately reminding them of these, and take from this the message that he too is anti-abortion, and thinks *Roe* should be overturned. Alternatively, it may even be that "I oppose Dred Scott" and similar utterances have come to serve as generalized conversational implicatures indicating opposition to abortion. One can certainly tell a story of how they'd be calculated: *He's stating his opposition to Dred Scott. But everyone opposes Dred Scott, and that's not relevant to the question he was being asked. He must be trying to convey something else—that he is opposed to abortion, like those other people who talk about Dred Scott.*

Either way, this is an overt intentional dogwhistle: it is a conveying of a coded, concealed message to a subset of the general audience.

---

[4] This idea of signaling group membership by word choice finds a nice parallel in Nunberg's account of slurs (this volume).

13.2.2 Covert intentional dogwhistles

Covert intentional dogwhistles are far more complicated to make sense of. They play a special role in American race discourse, due to the presence of what Tali Mendelberg in her (2001) calls the Norm of Racial Equality. (Mendelberg does not use the term 'dogwhistle' for these, though later writers such as Ian Haney Lopez 2014 do. She simply refers to 'implicit political communication'.) Prior to the 1930s, Mendelberg argues that it was acceptable to explicitly express racist attitudes in American political discourse. More specifically, she notes that it was acceptable to use obviously pejorative terminology; to assert that black people are innately inferior to white people; and to express support for legal discrimination, such as legally enforced segregation or refusal to hire black people. Not everyone did so, of course—but doing so did not render one beyond the bounds of acceptable political engagement. Those courting racist voters could do so by simply proclaiming their racist views. From the 1930s to the 1960s, according to Mendelberg, the prevailing norm of racial inequality "began to erode" (Mendelberg 2001: 67). After the 1960s, however, overt racism became increasingly unacceptable. Most voters now no longer wanted to think of themselves as racist.

However, this aversion to overt racism conceals a more complicated picture. Most white voters are highly unlikely to endorse claims of innate black inferiority, or legally enforced segregation. However, a belief system that psychologists have called 'racial resentment'[5] remains widespread. Racial resentment includes four main claims: "(1) blacks no longer face much discrimination, (2) their disadvantage mainly reflects their poor work ethic, (3) they are demanding too much too fast, (4) they have gotten more than they deserve" (Tesler and Sears 2010: 18). Psychologists standardly test for racial resentment by asking for degree of agreement or disagreement with the following statements (Tesler and Sears 2010: 19):

- Irish, Italian, Jewish and many other minorities overcame prejudice and worked their way up. Blacks should do the same without any special favours.
- Generations of slavery and discrimination have created conditions that make it difficult for blacks to work their way out of the lower class.
- Over the past few years, blacks have gotten less than they deserve.
- It's really a matter of some people not trying hard enough; if blacks would only try harder they could be just as well off as whites.

The various possible responses are assigned scores ranging from most racially liberal to most racially conservative. White Americans are, overall, on the racially conservative end of the spectrum, and Republicans significantly more so than Democrats.

Mendelberg describes this situation as one in which a "norm of racial equality" is in place, despite the persistence of racial resentment. Her phrasing may be somewhat misleading, however. It seems to me certainly not the case that the majority of white Americans assent to any very strong notion of racial equality, if they give the answers that count as racially resentful on the above items. Moreover, it is clearly still quite

---

[5] Tesler and Sears, who I quote below, use the term 'symbolic racism', but they note that they use it interchangeably with Mendelberg's preferred term, 'racial resentment'.

socially acceptable to make reference to the ills of black *culture,* blaming black poverty and even police killings of unarmed black people on this cause. What Mendelberg calls the "norm of racial equality" clearly doesn't preclude these sorts of utterances. Indeed, she herself notes a tendency to conform to the norm "in the most minimal, symbolic way possible" (Mendelberg 2001: 92). One plausible way of understanding this is that white Americans feel the need to pay lip service to something that could be called "racial equality". Exactly what this comes to may vary somewhat, but it seems to preclude the use of obvious pejoratives, assertions of *genetic* (though not cultural) inferiority, and support for obviously discriminatory behavior (legally enforced seg- regation, rules against hiring black people, etc.). The only kind of racial equality this commits one to is an extremely thin sort of formal equality. But Mendelberg is clearly right that the bounds of permissible racial discourse have shifted somewhat, even if they do not yet require support for any substantive sort of equality—e.g. one which rejects structural racism, acknowledges the existence of implicit bias, inquires into equality of outcomes, and so on.[6] Despite these reservations about terminology we will follow Mendelberg and refer to the current situation as one in which the Norm of Racial Equality is in force.

Politicians who might in a different era have explicitly expressed obviously racist views in order to reach proudly racist voters now need to find a subtler way to signal a kind of psychological kinship with these "racially resentful" voters.[7] An explicit racist dogwhistle might not work—while it would improve on an unambiguously racist utterance, it would very likely still be recognized as racist by its intended audience.[8] And most of this audience would reject something that was explicitly and unambiguously racist—doing otherwise would call into question their now-cherished commitment to egalitarianism. Certainly, it would be a risky move to use a dogwhistle of this sort. (Importantly, of course, not everyone would reject explicit racism. But our focus here is on the large segment of the population that would.)

This is where what Mendelberg calls "implicit political communication" comes into its own. A dogwhistle that people fail to consciously recognize turns out to be a very powerful thing. I will call this a 'covert dogwhistle'. Such an utterance would appear on its face to be innocuous and unrelated to race—lending deniability if confronted with racism accusations. And, if the dogwhistled content could do its work outside the dogwhistle-audience's awareness, it would not be rejected in the way that an explicitly racist dogwhistle would be.

---

[6] It is also worth noting, and exploring at a different time, that many white Americans have come to think of *themselves* as victims of racial discrimination, and to openly assert this (Lopez 2014: 71, citing the work of political strategist Stanley Greenberg). This may be another way that racial resentment can be expressed without violating the Norm of Racial Equality: those who express this view would claim that they support *equality,* but that they (not black Americans) are the ones being treated less well.

[7] Which utterances are obviously racist is obviously a matter on which disagreement arises. It seems to me that assertions of black cultural inferiority are obviously racist, but it is clear that for many white people these are not obviously racist. But as noted, these have survived the presence of the "norm of racial equality".

[8] I'm genuinely uncertain how well it would work. Of course its efficicacy would vary from voter to voter, but the deniability it would bring might well allow for a substantial degree of success. When I initially drafted this paper, I thought an explicit racial dogwhistle would fail, but I'm now (post-Trump) not at all convinced. Many thanks to Daniel Harris for raising this point.

But how could a dogwhistle work in this way? How can a racist message be communicated effectively enough to influence an audience's voting decisions, without the audience being aware of it? Working through examples will help us to see this.

13.2.2.1 WILLIE HORTON

The most famous example of a covert intentional dogwhistle is the immensely successful Willie Horton advertisement, used in George H. W. Bush's campaign against Michael Dukakis. (I take my discussion of this from Mendelberg 2001, chs. 5–8.) This ad criticized the prison furlough program that was in place during Dukakis's time as governor by telling the tale of a furloughed convict, Willie Horton. Horton assaulted a couple in their home, raping the woman and stabbing the man. Race is not mentioned at any point in the ad. However, the illustration for the ad is a photo of Willie Horton, and Horton is black. The Bush campaign made Horton a key issue, and this led to the ad receiving enormous airplay on the news.

Prior to the Willie Horton ad, Dukakis was substantially ahead in the opinion polls. As the ad aired and was discussed, he immediately began to plummet. During most of this time, the ad was not discussed in connection with race. It was discussed as a part of stories on the role of crime in the campaign, or negative campaigning. However, quite late, Jesse Jackson called the Willie Horton ad "racist". This charge was at the time viewed with great skepticism (though it's extremely widely accepted now), and viewed as an illicit attempt by Democrats to "play the race card". But it was widely discussed. As soon as the possibility of racism was raised, the ad ceased to function wholly on an implicit level. Viewers began to consider the possibility that something racial might be going on. And at this point, Dukakis started to rise in the polls again—some indication that the ad had ceased to be effective once race was explicitly under discussion.

But of course, none of this really shows that the ad was responsible for these effects, or that race had anything to do with it (though the effect of the Jackson intervention is suggestive.) Far more informative is the data gathered during the campaign about the effects on voters. These data show that while levels of racial resentment were unaffected by viewing the ad, *the relationship between racial resentment and voting intentions* was strongly influenced by it. Specifically, increasing exposure to the ad increased the likelihood of racially resentful voters favouring Bush. And, crucially, as soon as Jackson criticized the ad as racist, this correlation began to decline.

Mendelberg argues that the dogwhistle acts upon pre-existing racial attitudes, unconsciously bringing them to bear where they might previously not have been drawn upon—in this case on voting preferences. But she also notes something else that is vital: once race starts to be consciously reflected on, the dogwhistle ceases to be fully implicit. This drastically diminishes its effectiveness, presumably due to the widespread conscious acceptance of the norm of racial equality. As Mendelberg writes, "As soon as a person is alerted to the need to pay conscious attention to her response, accessibility is no longer sufficient to make her rely upon racial predispositions" (Mendelberg 2001: 210). Mendelberg's experimental data back this up, showing a sizable relationship between racial resentment and policy preferences after viewing an implicitly racial ad, but no relationship after viewing an explicitly racial ad (ch. 7).

13.2.2.2 'INNER CITY'

In the United States, 'inner city' has come to function as a dogwhistle for *black*. Thus, politicians who would be rebuked if they called for harsher measures against black criminals can safely call for cracking down on inner city crime. Psychologists have studied the effects of the phrase "inner city", and it seems to function very similarly to the Willie Horton ad. Horwitz and Peffley (2005) randomly assigned subjects to two groups, with one group being asked question A below, and one group being asked question B (difference underlined by me, from pp. 102–3):

A. Some people want to increase spending for new prisons to lock up <u>violent criminals</u>. Other people would rather spend this money for antipoverty programs to prevent crime. What about you? If you had to choose, would you rather see this money spent on building new prisons, or on antipoverty programs?

B. Some people want to increase spending for new prisons to lock up <u>violent inner city criminals</u>. Other people would rather spend this money for antipoverty programs to prevent crime. What about you? If you had to choose, would you rather see this money spent on building new prisons, or on antipoverty programs?

This small change—the addition of 'inner city'—turned out to have a significant effect on the answer that subjects gave, but the nature of this effect was strongly influenced by subjects' pre-existing racial attitudes. Prior to being asked A or B above, subjects were questioned about their acceptance of racial stereotypes and their beliefs regarding the racial fairness of the justice system. "Racial conservatives" tended to hold negative stereotypes of black people and to believe the system to be racially fair. "Racial liberals" were the opposite.

When 'inner city' was added to the question (as in B) subjects' attitudes toward spending were strongly influenced by their pre-existing racial attitudes—with racial conservatives more likely to favour prison spending and racial liberals more likely to oppose it. But when 'inner city' was not present (as in A) there was *no relationship* between racial attitudes and answers to the question. This shows that 'inner city' serves to raise subjects' pre-existing racial attitudes to salience and bring them to bear on a question, where they would not otherwise be brought to bear—just as the Willie Horton ad does.[9]

13.3 Unintentional Dogwhistles

Thus far, our focus has been on intentional dogwhistles. However, a crucial fact about the way that dogwhistles do their work in the world is the way in which they can be unintentionally passed on, with identical effects to the original dogwhistle. This is wholly predictable, from the fact that audiences will very often be unaware of a dogwhistle's presence—they may, and do, repeat the dogwhistle unwittingly. I will call

---

[9] It is not clear what the cause was of racial liberals' response. It is possible that racial liberals reflected consciously on the use of 'inner city' as a euphemism for 'black', rather than simply having their racial attitudes raised to non-conscious salience. In general, racial liberals have not been the focus of studies on racial priming and dogwhistles. Many thanks to Rosie Worsdale for raising this question.

these utterances unintentional dogwhistles, and in this section of the paper we will work through a few examples. My working definition of 'unintentional dogwhistle' will be as follows:

> Unwitting use of words and/or images that, used intentionally, constitute an intentional dogwhistle, where this use has the same effect as an intentional dogwhistle.

To see that this is possible, just reflect briefly on the Dred Scott dogwhistle that we've already discussed. Now imagine a debate, in which the left-wing candidate is puzzled by the right-wing candidate expressing their opposition to Dred Scott: they had not taken slavery to be a live issue, and they are unaware of the dogwhistle. Confused, they become worried that they might be taken to support slavery if they do not also start expressing their opposition to Dred Scott—so they, too, start waxing eloquent on the wrongness of this decision. But since discussing Dred Scott dogwhistles opposition to abortion they unintentionally (and falsely) dogwhistle their opposition to abortion.

Very importantly, though, we don't need to rely on fanciful cases like this. Unintentional dogwhistles are real, and they are in fact often a part of the primary dogwhistlers' plan.

13.3.1 Willie Horton and the Reporters

There is by now ample evidence that the Bush campaign was deliberately dogwhistling about race with the Willie Horton ad. However, there is no reason to believe that the reporters and TV producers of the time were doing this. Certainly some may have been, but many were not. Yet nonetheless they replayed the ad over and over, and discussed Horton and his crimes over and over in the context of the election. This, in fact, was what allowed the effects Mendelberg discusses to be so widespread and so powerful: the original advertisement was only shown briefly in a small area, but it was re-shown again and again as a part of news reports ostensibly about "negative campaigning" or "crime". I take these re-showings to be unintentional dogwhistles. This shows just how important such unintentional dogwhistles can be in accomplishing an intentional dogwhistle's goals. Indeed, such is their importance that they deserve a term of their own. I will call these 'amplifier dogwhistles', since they greatly increase the reach of the original dogwhistle. And, just as an amplifier is not responsible for the original sound that it amplifies, those who carry out acts of amplifier dogwhistling are not responsible for the original dogwhistle whose reach they are enhancing.

13.3.2 Racialization of 'government spending'

Throughout the 1980s, a concerted effort was made by the Republican Party in the US to associate government spending with racial minorities. (Ronald Reagan was especially important to this campaign.) This effort was enormously successful: Media coverage of government assistance, for example, came to focus disproportionately on black recipients of assistance, despite the fact that they are the minority of those on such assistance (Valentino et al. 2002: 75). And, we will see, these efforts have brought it about that even terms like 'government spending' now serve as racial dogwhistles. Utterances containing such terms are, as a result, sometimes intentional dogwhistles—when the utterances are made with the intention of making racial attitudes salient. But these terms are widely used, as what the country should spend money on is an issue that simply has to be discussed. And so they will extremely often function as unintentional covert dogwhistles. Indeed, they will often serve as amplifier dogwhistles.

We'll begin by examining the evidence that utterances of these words can function as covert racial dogwhistles. We can see very clearly that this is the case from Valentino et al.'s study of racial priming and political advertising. Their study involves showing participants one of several versions of a carefully constructed advertisement. In every version, the words of the ad, ostensibly for George W. Bush, criticizes Democrats for "wasteful spending" and says (to take one example from a complex ad) that Bush will "reform an unfair system that only provides healthcare for some, while others go without" (Valentino et al. 2002: 79). What varies across versions is the visuals. One version, Neutral, uses wholly neutral visuals, like medical files and the Statue of Liberty. The second, Race Comparison, uses images of e.g. a black family being helped while the words "healthcare for some" are uttered; and images of a white mother and child while the words "others go without" are uttered. The third, Undeserving Blacks, does not contain images comparing treatment of whites and blacks, but does show images designed trigger associations of race and government spending. So, it shows the black family being helped just as in Race Comparison; but it shows medical files while "others go without" are uttered. A control group viewed a totally non-political advertisement. After viewing the advertisements, subjects completed a test to assess the accessibility of racial attitudes. They then completed a questionnaire regarding their assessment of presidential candidates, the importance of various issues, and their racial and political attitudes. Below see Table 13.1 (Valentino et al. 2002: 79) showing the workings of the various versions of the advertisement.

Valentino et al. found that racial resentment had little effect on preference between candidates unless subjects had viewed one of the political advertisements. But if they had viewed one of the political advertisements, the impact of racial resentment on candidate preference was increased—even in the neutral condition in which the advertisement contained no racialized imagery, just words about government spending. Indeed, the effect in the Neutral condition was just as strong as in the Race Comparison condition (though less strong than in the Undeserving Blacks condition). This shows very clearly that "government spending" has become an covert dogwhistle, which functions like the Willie Horton ad or "inner city". And this fact should be enormously disconcerting, as it indicates just how very widespread such priming is. The widespread nature of such priming makes it extremely difficult to discuss issues absolutely central to democracy—such as what a government should spend its money on—without opinions being influenced by racial attitudes.[10]

Importantly, Valentino et al. also tested the impact of *counter-stereotypical images*. In these versions of the advertisement, the images of black families appear as the ad discusses "hard-working families", and so on. These ads are designed to jar with the racist stereotypes that viewers have likely absorbed through cultural exposure. The effects were dramatic.

---

[10] This sort of concern is very important to Stanley (2015).

Table 13.1. Transcripts of implicit race cue advertising manipulation

Narrative	Neutral Visuals	Race Comparison	Undeserving Blacks
George W. Bush, dedicated to building an America with strong values.	George Bush in crowd shaking hands	George Bush in crowd shaking hands	George Bush in crowd shaking hands
Democrats want to spend your tax dollars on wasteful government programs, but George W. Bush will cut taxes because you know best how to spend the money you earn.	Image of Statue of Liberty, Treasury Building. Bush sitting on couch, residential street (no people)	**Black person counting money, black mother and child in office.** Bush sitting on couch, **white person writing check, white person counting money, white teacher**	**Black person counting money, black mother and child in office.** Bush sitting on couch, residential street (no people)
Governor Bush cares about families.	Laboratory workers (race unclear) looking into microscopes	**White parents walking with child**	Residential street (shot continued as above)
He'll reform an unfair system that only provides health care for some, while others go without proper treatment because their employer can't afford it.	Medical files	**White nurse assisting black mother, child. White mother holding child**	**White nurse assisting black mother, child.** Medical files
When he's president, every hard-working American will have affordable, high-quality health care.	X-rays against lit background	**Bush talking to white family, talking to white child, Bush kissing white girl**	X-rays against lit background
George W. Bush, a fresh start for America	Bush, arm around wife. Screen reads "George W. Bush" and "A Fresh Start"	Bush, arm around wife. Screen reads "George W. Bush" and "A Fresh Start"	Bush, arm around wife. Screen reads "George W. Bush" and "A Fresh Start"

When the black racial cues are stereotype-inconsistent, however, the relationship between racial attitudes and the vote disappears . . . Violating racial stereotypes with positive images of blacks dramatically undermines racial priming. The presence of black images alone, therefore, does not prime negative racial attitudes. The effect emerges only when the pairing of the visuals with the narrative subtly reinforces negative stereotypes in the mind of the viewer. (Valentino et al. 2002: 86)

This is a crucial point, as it raises another possible way of combatting the influence of covert dogwhistles. It shows that it *is* possible to discuss government spending without priming racial attitudes. But avoiding racial imagery is *not* the way to do this— instead, one must make a concerted effort to include the right racial imagery. The right racial imagery will be counter-stereotypical imagery that can serve to undermine the dogwhistles (primary or unintentional) that would otherwise be present (whatever one's intentions). This requires awareness and effort on the part of the speaker, who might otherwise think that they have avoided triggering racial attitudes by avoiding overtly racial imagery or words. (See Table 13.2 below, from Valentino et al. 2002: 80)

13.4 What Existing Accounts Cannot Fully Capture

13.4.1 What existing accounts <u>can</u> capture

Existing accounts do fairly well with an overt intentional dogwhistle. As noted in the discussion above, it is quite plausible to suppose that 'Dred Scott' utterances carry conversational implicatures about opposition to abortion.

Elisabeth Camp (this volume) goes a step further and introduces the notion of *insinuation*. A speaker *insinuates* some proposition P just in case she communicates P without entering P into the conversational record. The speaker intends her intention to be recognized, but without a willingness or responsibility to own up to it.[11] This is an important notion.

Camp treats Bush's Dred Scott dogwhistle as a paradigm case of insinuation, and this seems plausible. Bush intends to have his anti-abortion message recognized, and recognized as intended. At the same time, though, use of a code phrase gives allows him to avoid placing his contribution on the record—thus achieving deniability.

13.4.2 More difficult cases

Covert intentional dogwhistles are substantially more challenging to capture. There are two key reasons for this. First, what is dogwhistled is not a particular proposition. Instead, certain pre-existing attitudes are brought to salience, without the audience being aware of it. This means that any theory relying on the communication (via semantics or pragmatics) of a particular proposition (or even a range of propositions) will fail. Second, this occurs *outside* of consciousness. Crucially, when an audience becomes conscious of the dogwhistle, it fails to achieve its intended effect. Success of a covert intentional dogwhistle, then—unlike most communicative acts—depends

---

[11] Camp describes this as 'implicit' communication. This is clearly a different usage from Mendelberg's, as Camp is interested in cases in which at least part of the audience recognizes the speaker's intention, and is expected to do so.

Table 13.2. Transcripts of counter-stereotypic advertising manipulation

Narrative	Deserving Blacks	Deserving Whites	Undeserving Whites
George W. Bush, dedicated to building an America with strong values.	George Bush in crowd shaking hands, black woman with American flag in background, black veteran smiling	George Bush in crowd shaking hands	George Bush in crowd shaking hands
Democrats want to spend your tax dollars on wasteful government programs, but George W. Bush will cut taxes because you know best how to spend the money you earn.	Treasury building Bush sitting on couch, **black person laying money on a counter**	Bush sitting on couch, **white person writing a check, white person counting money**	**White person counting money, white mother and child in office** Bush sitting on couch, residential street (no people)
Governor Bush cares about families.	**Black family using a computer, black family eating at a restaurant**	**White teacher, white parents walking with child**	Residential street (shot continued as above)
He'll reform an unfair system that only provides health care for some, while others go without proper treatment because their employer can't afford it.	Laboratory workers (race unclear) looking into microscopes **Black woman holding baby**	Laboratory workers (race unclear) looking into microscopes **White mother holding child**	**White mother holding newborn receiving medical care in hospital** Medical files
When he's president, every hard-working American will have affordable, high-quality health care.	**Bush shaking hands with black children, black kids sitting in school yard, Bush sitting in classroom reading with black kids**	**Bush talking to white family, Bush talking to white child, Bush kissing white girl**	X-rays against lit background
George W. Bush, a fresh start for America	Bush, arm around wife. Screen reads "George W. Bush" and "A Fresh Start"	Bush, arm around wife. Screen reads "George W. Bush" and "A Fresh Start"	Bush, arm around wife. Screen reads "George W. Bush" and "A Fresh Start"

on the audience *not recognizing* the speaker's intention.[12] Any theory which includes the idea that recognition of the speaker's intention is required for success will fail entirely as a way of accommodating covert dogwhistles. Covert intentional dogwhistles only succeed where this is absent; uptake prevents such dogwhistles from being effective.[13]

Two sorts of theories, however, hold out some promise for capturing them: Langton and McGowan's work on conversational accommodation, especially McGowan's notion of conversational exercitives; and Jason Stanley's recent work on propaganda and not-at-issue content. We will see, however, that neither of these is fully able to capture the complexity of these cases.

13.4.2.1 STANLEY

Jason Stanley is the only philosopher to have discussed what I call 'covert dogwhistles' (both intentional and unintentional), which he takes to be a particularly insidious form of propaganda. On Stanley's view, these function by introducing into conversation some pernicious "not-at-issue" effects. Not-at-issue content is material that becomes part of the conversation's common ground without being explicitly put up for consideration in the way that asserted content is. This makes it more difficult to notice that this content is being added to the common ground, and also more difficult to object to. It also cannot be canceled: the associated meaning will always be conveyed, as not-at-issue content, and a speaker cannot block this from happening (Stanley 2015: 139). Stanley argues that certain words come to carry not-at-issue content of a highly problematic sort:

> When the news media connects images of urban Blacks repeatesdly with mentions of the term "welfare," the term "welfare" comes to have not-at-issue content that Blacks are lazy. At some point, the repeated associations are part of the meaning, the not-at-issue content.
>
> (Stanley 2015: 138)

Stanley also suggests that the not-at-issue effect of a term can take the form of a preference ordering, taking the form of a ranking of groups in terms of worthiness of respect. So, a term may cause those who encounter it to rank groups differently, in a way that erodes respect for some groups. One might even come to rank groups as worthy of more or less empathy, which for Stanley is an especially important sort of not-at-issue effect.

Stanley's approach is able to accommodate the way that audiences may be unaware of what is really going on in a covert dogwhistle utterance. Not-at-issue content is (sometimes) entered into the common ground without an audience's explicit awareness that this is taking place: this is a key part of what makes it so insidious.

---

[12] One might suggest that the audience is unconsciously recognizing the speaker's intention. But I see no reason to attribute such unconscious recognition of intention. It is far more straightforward to accept the cases at face value—as ones in which intention is not recognized.

[13] Dogwhistles are not alone in having this latter feature. Most acts of deception are also like this: if the audience recognizes the speaker's intention to deceive the deception fails. For more on covert speech acts, see Bach and Harnish (1979).

Nonetheless, Stanley's approach does not accommodate all that psychologists have taught us about how these utterances work. Stanley suggests that words like 'welfare' erode respect for black people either by carrying a not-at-issue content *that black people are lazy* or causing people to implement a preference ranking according to which black people are less deserving of empathy than white people are. Moreover, he suggests that this cannot be canceled, and that it will be present in every use of a term like 'welfare'.[14] But this fails to fit with the data in certain key ways.

The first problem is that the use of covert dogwhistle terms like 'welfare' or even the viewing of advertisements like the Willie Horton ads do not (in general) cause *changes* in racial attitudes.[15] Instead, they make accessible pre-existing attitudes, and bring them to bear on issues where they might not otherwise have played a role in decision-making. This is quite different from Stanley's picture, on which the terms either cause new claims to be added to the common ground, or cause changes in people's preference rankings.[16]

The second problem is related to this one. It is that the effects of covert dogwhistle terms are not quite so monolithically negative as Stanley takes them to be. We can see this either intuitively or by looking at the empirical evidence. Intuitively, we can imagine a black speaker addressing a left-wing black audience and saying, "My mother was on welfare while she did the engineering degree that lifted our family out of poverty." This use of 'welfare' seems extremely unlikely to carry any suggestion that black people are lazy, nor will it erode respect for black people. If we prefer to look back on the empirical data, we can return to the findings discussed earlier. Adding 'inner city' to the question about prison funding caused those low in racial resentment to be *less* likely to agree that more prisons should be built. Pre-existing racial attitudes—*whatever they are*—are activated by covert racial dogwhistle terms. If the attitudes are racially resentful, then there is likely to be an outcome that indeed fits with a lack of respect for black people. But if the attitudes are not racially resentful, the outcome is likely to be entirely different.

Finally, challenging a dogwhistle successfully may not be as difficult as Stanley suggests. The priming of racial resentment only works if it remains covert. If a dogwhistle term like 'welfare' is used but race is made explicit, the effect vanishes. Recall also that as soon as Jesse Jackson raised the issue of race, the Willie Horton ad ceased to be effective. This shows that at least some challenges can succeed rather easily.

[14] He does allow for the possibility of change over time, but only when there is "sufficient control of the media and other instruments of power" (Stanley 2015: 162) by those advocating a change. He does not allow for conversation-by-conversation variation.

[15] It is worth emphasizing that the worry I am raising here is specific to the claim that racial dogwhistles cause changes in racial attitudes, based on specific study of these utterances. I am not at all skeptical about the general idea of linguistic utterances causing changes in attitudes—indeed I think this is widespread. Nor am I even skeptical about the idea that racial dogwhistles cause *some* changes in attitudes: After all, viewing the Willie Horton ad caused many voters to change their voting intentions and their beliefs about who was the best candidate.

[16] Some of Stanley's claims are also at odds with the idea that dogwhistles alter attitudes. For example, he writes, "As Tali Mendelberg shows, stereotypes of black Americans have remained constant throughout the history of the Republic." (2015: 135)

13.4.2.2 LANGTON AND McGOWAN

Langton (2012) discusses many ways that hate speech might function. For our purposes here the most promising is one based on Lewis and Stalnaker's work on conversational score.

[Utterances of hate speech] may implicitly *presuppose* certain facts and norms, rather than explicitly enacting them; but these implicit presuppositions may nonetheless work in ways that are comparable to classic Austinian illocutions. Consumers then change their factual and normative beliefs by taking on board the 'common ground' (in Robert Stalnaker's phrase) or the 'conversational score' (in David Lewis's phrase) that is presupposed in the ... 'conversation'.   (Langton 2012: 83)

Langton further suggests that emotions like desire and hate may be introduced into the common ground through roughly the same procedure—or, in Lewis's terms, their appropriateness may become part of the conversational score. Langton tentatively suggests that the two accounts may be related as follows: Lewis's account captures the immediate way that what counts as acceptable may change, and this then leads to changes in the attitudes and emotions that are part of the taken-for-granted common ground of the conversation.

It is useful to understand this in terms of Mary Kate McGowan's model (2004, 2012). McGowan suggests that these alterations in the conversational score should be understood as due to covert exercitives. These are speech acts which do not require any special authority on the part of the speaker (unlike more standard exercitives such as ruling a play in football as a foul). Crucially, they may or may not be intended by the speaker or recognized by the audience. McGowan suggests that these acts will be very widespread in any norm-governed activity (and that a huge variety of activities are norm-governed). What is permissible in such activities depends both on the rules (implicit or explicit) of those activities, and on what has happened before. In a conversation, what is permissible adapts quickly and seamlessly in response to what people say. Suppose Jeff makes an utterance that carries a presupposition, such as (1):

(1)   Yes, my wife and I like to do that.

If nobody protests, then it becomes permissible (in this context) to make other utterances in this conversation that assume that Jeff has a wife. Similarly, McGowan suggests that if Jeff makes a racist utterance and nobody protests, it becomes permissible (in this context) to make further racist utterances.[17] Depending on the context and the nature of the utterance, it may also enact further racist permissibility facts (McGowan 2012: 137–9).

---

[17] In fact, I think that a changing of norms in this manner will be a very rare occurrence. In a context where the Norm of Racial Equality is in force an openly racist utterance will generally not be seamlessly accommodated. Even if people don't outwardly object, they will be very uncomfortable and will psychologically distance themselves from the utterance, rather than adding what's needed to the common ground. In a context where the Norm is not in force, there will not be a *change*. I discuss this further, and explore a mechanism that enables the changes of norms, in my "Racial Figleaves, the Shifting Boundaries of the Permissible, and the Rise of Donald Trump" (2017).

The most appealing elements of this picture for dealing with covert dogwhistles are that (a) significant changes to common ground or to score may occur without explicit acknowledgment of their occurrence; and (b) it is not just focused on *propositions* believed or taken for granted, but also on norms and emotions. The suggestion would be, then, that e.g. the Willie Horton ad implicitly alters the facts about what it is appropriate to take into account in making voting decisions. The normative score—regarding what one's voting decisions should be based on—is subtly altered by the Willie Horton ad, outside of the awareness of those who view it. This leads viewers to take race into account in their voting decisions. And since McGowan allows that this may occur unintentionally, we can accommodate both intentional and unintentional covert dogwhistles.

At first, this seems like a very good fit. However, there is a crucial problem: if dogwhistles were *actually* changing permissibility facts, discussing what has been implicitly added would not destroy their effects in the way that it does. When Jesse Jackson raised the possibility that the Willie Horton ads were related to race, viewers stopped allowing their vote to be influenced by their racial attitudes. If the ad actually *had* made it permissible to base their voting decision on racial attitudes, this would not have happened. When we reflect on something that we genuinely take to be permissible, we don't reject it—even if it's something we haven't reflected on. Imagine, for example, that I am immersed in a country with different conventions about personal space, and I take on those conventions without realizing it. If someone in this country remarks on the fact, I don't reject it: instead, I realize that the permissibility facts have changed for me, at least for the duration of my time in this country. When one calls attention to a racial dogwhistle, what happens is very different: what happens looks, for all the world, like a discovery that one was doing something *impermissible*.[18] This shows that the Langton/McGowan story cannot capture these cases.[19]

13.4.2.3 COVERT INTENTIONAL DOGWHISTLES AS COVERT PERLOCUTIONARY SPEECH ACTS

My view is that covert intentional dogwhistles must be understood as a species of perlocutionary speech acts. (I am taking perlocutionary speech acts to be the acts of making utterances with certain effects.)[20] Perlocutionary speech acts are not much discussed by philosophers of language, and with good reason. They are quite a motley and unsystematic collection of acts, difficult to theorize. (Contrast the simple illocutionary act of getting married with the intended perlocutionary acts of being

---

[18] Another move Langton and McGowan might make is to distinguish between the linguistically and morally permissible. But it seems to me crucial to their argument that linguistic moves are affecting *not just* what's linguistically permissible but also what's seen as morally permissible. That, after all, is why hate speech and pornography are meant to be so dangerous.

[19] It might, however, be possible for them to argue that the sort of permissibility facts they are concerned with are ones that can change in this way: something previously permissible can become impermissible once it is reflected upon consciously. However, this would diminish the force of their argument concerning the dangers of hate speech. If the permissibility facts they are concerned with can be so fleeting then hate speech does not look quite so clearly dangerous. Still, this response merits further consideration.

[20] Austin describes these as the "consequential effects upon the feelings, thoughts, or actions of the speaker, or of other persons" (1962: 101).

happy, making one's ex jealous, getting to wear that lovely dress, acquiring citizenship, becoming financially secure; and the unintended perlocutionary acts of making one's parents cry, devastating a secret admirer, inspiring some friends to get married, and so on.) Austin does not provide much at all in the way of perlocutionary theory. However, individual kinds of perlocutionary acts can be extremely important. And the perlocutionary seems very much the right category for covert intentional dogwhistles upon brief reflection: covert intentional dogwhistles, after all, are very much a matter of intended *effects* on their audiences.

My suggestion is that covert intentional dogwhistles should be understood as what I will call *covert perlocutionary acts*. A covert perlocutionary act is one that does not succeed if the intended perlocutionary effect is recognized as intended.[21] Although this category has not been much discussed as a category, covert dogwhistles are not the only covert perlocutionary acts. Another important kind of covert perlocutionary act is deception. One who deceives can usually only succeed if their intention to deceive is *not recognized*. This is the defining feature of a covert perlocutionary act. A covert intentional dogwhistle cannot succeed if the intended effect is recognized as intended, so it is a covert perlocutionary act.

There are some clear advantages to this account. Since I understand covert intentional dogwhistles as perlocutionary acts, I need not understand them as about propositions. Nor need I claim that they are added to the common ground, or in any way consciously available to their audience. I can also very easily make sense of the sorts of variation we have seen: Not every utterance using a particular dogwhistle term will be intended to have the same effect, so we can give the right understanding of the black speaker describing his mother's use of welfare to earn an engineering degree. And not every perlocutionary effect will be intended—so we can accommodate the fact that *anti-racist* attitudes will be raised to salience for some voters, even when this effect is not intended. Finally, perlocutionary effects can be prevented, as Jesse Jackson's utterance eventually began to prevent the intended effects of the Willie Horton ad.

13.4.2.4 UNINTENTIONAL COVERT DOGWHISTLES

There is more than one way to fit unintentional covert dogwhistles into this picture.

Option 1: Unintentional covert dogwhistles are not themselves covert perlocutionary acts, since the intention of the speaker is not related to the dogwhistle, which the speaker is unaware of. So there can be no question of the act failing if the speaker's intention is recognized. Unintentional covert dogwhistles, on this story, are simply speech acts which have particularly pernicious unintended perlocutionary effects. Unintended perlocutionary effects are extremely common, so there's nothing particular special going on, except that these unintended effects are a part of someone else's (not the speaker's) plan. This option perhaps underplays the role of manipulation.

---

[21] This, then, is a perlocutionary act for which intention is a necessary condition. I do not take this to be true of all perlocutionary acts.

Option 2: The second option puts more of an emphasis on the way that unintentional covert dogwhistles fit in to the manipulation that is taking place. Those who create the initial covert dogwhistles are very good at attaching pernicious associations to words and images (and possibly other things as well) and sending them out into the world in the hope that they will be taken up and used by others, bringing with them these associations. One might, then, take the creators of the dogwhistles to be in some important sense the utterers of the unintentional covert dogwhistles. This would allow one to treat the unintentional dogwhistles as covert perlocutionary acts, fully recognizing the way that they fit into this sort of manipulation. The problem with this story, though, is that it underplays the agency of those who repeat the dogwhistles. These people really are the speakers, and they need to be thought of as such, and held accountable for the effects of their speech.

On balance, the best approach seems to me to be Option 1. But it is important in adopting this approach that one not lose sight of the way that the utterers of the unintentional covert dogwhistles have been manipulated—and important to remember that somebody *did* intend the pernicious effects of these utterances, even though their utterers did not. And, in fact, this helps us to see more about what is so insidious: as they unknowingly utter unintentional covert dogwhistles, people are made into mouthpieces for an ideology that they reject. The actual utterers are the speakers, and this is why they need to pay attention to the effects of what they say, and to the careful manipulation that has caused them to say these things.

A further advantage of this approach is that we can accommodate two distinct varieties of unintentional covert dogwhistle. The first is what I have called 'amplifier dogwhistles', which help to spread the effects of intentional covert dogwhistles. The second, which is not my focus here, is unintentional covert dogwhistles which *don't* originate in deliberate attempts to manipulate. It has been suggested to me that 'crafty' functions this way in sports commentary, dogwhistling whiteness but without any deliberate attempt to manipulate the salience of audience members' racial attitudes.[22]

13.5 Political Upshot

Of course, what makes this underexplored topic so important is that dogwhistles represent a vital part of strategies by which we are influenced—in fact, manipulated—in our thinking, and in our decisions. In particular, these have enormous and important political effects. The political implications of dogwhistles have not been much discussed by philosophers. Robert Goodin and Michael Saward (2005), however, have discussed the political implications of overt dogwhistles; and Jason Stanley has discussed the political implications of covert dogwhistles. All three of these theorists argue that dogwhistles pose serious problems for democracy, although the problems they identify differ. I certainly agree that dogwhistles can pose problems for democracy, but I don't fully agree with any of these philosophers on the nature and seriousness of the problems.

---

[22] I am grateful to Tyler Doggett and Randall Harp for this suggestion.

13.5.1 Dogwhistles and Democratic Mandates

Goodin and Saward argue that overt intentional dogwhistles (they don't discuss covert or unintentional dogwhistles, so in fact they just use the term 'dogwhistle') may undermine democratic mandates for particular policies, but that they do not pose difficulties with regard to a mandate to rule. Their focus is on cases in which a political party (or a politician) advocates a particular policy using a phrase that dogwhistles a message to one audience which another audience is unaware of. To take an artificial (though not totally artificial) example, imagine a party that trumpets its opposition to Dred Scott in many of its campaign commercials. The party gets the support of both anti-racism and anti-abortion voters. This party, when victorious, could not declare a mandate for banning abortion, because only some of the voters took this to be what they were voting for. Hence, Goodin and Saward argue, policy mandates are undermined when policy preferences are merely dogwhistled. However, Goodin and Saward hold that a mandate to rule is not undermined in this way, because everybody who votes for politician P knows exactly what they are voting for: that politician P should rule.

A conservative party dog-whistles an encouraging message to racists that its own traditional supporters would instantly repudiate. It wins the ensuing election. Half its voters voted for it purely because of its (coded) support for racist policies; half voted for it purely because of its traditionally decent policies on race. Clearly, the party won a majority; clearly, it has a mandate to rule. But under those circumstances, it equally clearly could not claim a policy mandate to pursue either of the two contradictory policies that won it its votes.

(Goodin and Saward 2005: 475)

Goodin and Saward argue, then that a party cannot claim a mandate for its policies unless it refrains from engaging in dogwhistle politics (and more than this may be needed as well):

It is worth firmly reminding political parties that when they engage in dog whistle politics in ordinary general elections, the same phenomenon that they are counting on to increase their share of votes also undercuts the authority that they might secure by winning the vote.   (Goodin and Saward 2005: 476)

It seems to me, however, that Goodin and Saward's arguments do not go quite far enough. If they are right about the policy mandate, then the mandate to rule may also often be undermined. This will happen, for example, in the case of single-issue voters, of which there are likely to be many. If a voting decision is based on abortion policy, and different messages are sent about this to different groups of voters, then surely the mandate to rule is also—in any meaningful sense—undermined.

Now let's turn to the case of covert dogwhistles, which Goodin and Saward don't discuss. Covert dogwhistles don't involve the same sort of deception. It's not the case that some viewers of the Willie Horton ad will think that Dukakis's prison policy is Q, while others will take it to be R. What will happen, however, is that the ad's target audience will vote for Bush on the basis of their racial attitudes, without realizing it. Human psychology being what it is, being unaware of one's reason for making a voting decision is surely widespread. People are unaware of the extent to which, for example, their decision of which socks to buy is based on the location of the socks on the table. It stands to reason that people would be unaware of the degree to which they are influenced by music in a commercial, subtleties of tone or body language, being reminded of a loved (or hated!) one, and so on. If such lack of awareness of influences were enough to undermine democratic authority, we would need to give up all hope of democracy.

However, more than this goes on with covert dogwhistles. In covert dogwhistle cases, people make decisions on the basis of reasons that they would reject if they became aware of them—as we know from what happens when they are raised to consciousness. Moreover, they do this as a result of being deliberately manipulated. This looks, on the face of it, much more like a threat to democratic mandates.

But if this is sufficient to undermine a mandate, then once more there may in fact be no mandates. What voter, after all, thinks that they *should* base their vote on music played during a campaign commercial, or on a candidate's physical appearance? And yet, all that we know about psychology suggests that factors like these are sure to impact voter choices. And all that we know about the running of campaigns (and about advertising more generally) tells us that things like this are bound to be used by campaign operatives to deliberately manipulate the voters. Being influenced by factors that we don't think should influence us is, it seems to me, an inevitable part of the human condition. And, since this is relatively widely known, using such factors to influence others will also be a standard feature of human life. If this is sufficient to undermine democratic mandates, then there are no democratic mandates.

13.5.2 Stanley

Stanley is particularly concerned about what I am calling 'dogwhistles', because of the function that they serve in undermining democracy. The terms that particularly concern him—like 'welfare'—have devastating properties:

1. Use of the relevant expression has the effect on the conversation of representing a certain group in the community as having a perspective not worthy of inclusion, that is, they are not worthy of respect.
2. The expression has a content that can serve simply to contribute legitimately to resolving the debate at issue in a reasonable way, which is separate from its function as a mechanism of exclusion.
3. Mere use of the expression is enough to have the effect of eroding reasonableness. So the effect on reasonableness occurs just by virtue of using the expression, in whatever linguistic context. (Stanley 2015: 130)

If every use of one of these terms has these effects, then every use erodes respect for black people, and every use erodes reasonable discussion by excluding their perspective. This is obviously enormously damaging for democracy, even though the official *content* of the term might be a perfectly reasonable contribution to discussion.

If Stanley is right, then dogwhistle terms would indeed be utterly devastating—we simply could not have a debate using terms like 'welfare' because all participants would unwittingly be introducing racist not-at-issue content with every utterance, no matter what the context, and no matter what the rest of their utterance contained. If this were right, then the standard liberal remedy for problematic speech—more speech—faces enormous barriers.

There is much that is right in this: It is indeed trickier to challenge dogwhistles than it is to challenge, for example, overtly racist claims. If a campaign commercial explicitly asserts that "black men are dangerous criminals and Dukakis is insufficiently racist," it is exceptionally easy to point out what is wrong with the ad. The racism is undeniable, and even the most timid of journalists will feel comfortable asserting that racism is present. Those who made the ad will have no recourse but to either apologize or confine their electoral prospects to the explicitly racist voter. But the Willie Horton commercial is very different. Many viewers will be unaware that they have watched an ad that makes their racial attitudes salient. The ad contains no overtly racist assertions that are easily pointed to. And politicians can, and did, easily deny that there was racism in the ad or in their intentions. Moreover, Jesse Jackson was vilified as "playing the race card" when he pointed to the racism of the ad, and the suggestion was said to be ludicrous by mainstream commentators.

But as we have already seen, the truth is not quite this bleak. The effects of terms like 'welfare' vary depending (at least) on the racial predispositions of one's audience, on whether race is explicitly under discussion, and upon the rest of what one says. Also, recall that as soon as Jackson raised the issue of race the ad *stopped working*. This shows that in an extremely important sense it could be challenged. And indeed challenged quite easily. Even those who thought Jackson was wrong to raise the issue of racism were no longer affected by it in the way that its makers intended. Although racism was now a part of the conversation, and so highly salient, it was *explicitly salient* rather than covertly. The ad could only cause them to use their racial attitudes in their voting decisions as long as race was *covertly* salient. A covert perlocutionary speech act is (in at least some cases) very easily challenged: all one needs to do is to make what has been covert into an explicit part of the conversation.

But to fully understand how to combat these speech acts, we must combine this fact with insights from Stanley: it will indeed be *conversationally* challenging to make what has been covert explicit. People will reject what challengers say, and deny that it is true. Sanity may be, and often is, called into question. Challengers will be accused of having a political agenda. The conversation will be derailed, and it will not flow smoothly. It *is* difficult, just as Stanley said, and as a result it is hard to make oneself do it, or to persist in the face of this resistance. There are, then, important lessons here for those seeking to fight pernicious covert perlocutionary acts. But if challengers are aware of how these speech acts work, then it becomes clear that despite this resistance it is well worth doing. As soon as the issue of race is raised—even if raising it is thought to be a mistake, and met with anger—the speech act we are trying to fight *stops working*. It is both very hard to fight and very easy to win. Those seeking to challenge these pernicious speech acts need to remind themselves of the ease of winning in order to gear themselves up for the difficulty of the fight. And importantly, they need to realize that winning will not *feel* like winning: those responsible for the speech acts will not back down, concede the truth about what they were doing, or apologize; the intended audience of the speech acts will probably insist that the analysis is wrong and deny the existence of the covert material. Yet nonetheless the battle will be won: the speech acts will be neutralized.

Importantly, of course, we will only win these battles if the norm of racial equality is actually in place. And whether it is or not may vary a great deal over time and place. We know from the sad and terrible history of genocide that a community where this norm is in place can change remarkably quickly into one in which it has disappeared (Smith 2011; Tirrell 2012). And we also know that what is unacceptable to say in one location may be considered perfectly normal just 30 miles away. For this reason, it is undoubtedly an oversimplification to claim that the norm of racial equality is in force. It is, broadly speaking, in force. But there will be times and places where it isn't. And at those times and places, raising the issue of race will not neutralize a racial dogwhistle. (For more complexities on this point, consider the difficulties raised earlier concerning the content of the norm.)[23]

Another limitation is also important to emphasize. What I have argued is that explicitly raising the issue of race can defuse a racial dogwhistle. This is a defensive maneuver against a very particular sort of political manipulation. It seems to be highly effective. But it does not alter *attitudes*: the racial resentment may not be brought to bear on the voting choice, but it remains. Nor does it alter concrete realities in the world. Centuries of violence, discrimination, and segregation are not changed via a rhetorical maneuver. The world we live in remains just as much structured by racism after a dogwhistle has been openly discussed as it was before. It is vital to openly discuss the dogwhistles, but this should not be mistaken for something more powerful than it is. I have presented this paper to so many wonderfully helpful audiences that I have sadly lost track, but I am grateful to all of them. It was written before the 2016 election, though a few footnotes have been added since.

References

Austin, J. L. 1962. *How to Do Things With Words*. Oxford: Oxford University Press.

Bach, Kent and Robert Harnish. 1979. *Linguistic Communication and Speech Acts*. Cambridge, MA: MIT Press.

Goodin, R. and M. Saward. 2005. "Dogwhistles and Democratic Mandates", *Political Quarterly* 76(4): 471–6.

Horwitz, J. and M. Peffley. 2005. "Playing the Race Card in the Post-Willie Horton Era: The Impact of Racialized Code Words on Support for Punitive Prison Policy", *The Public Opinion Quarterly* 69: 1, 99–112.

Lamis, Alexander P. 1990. *The Two Party South*. New York: Oxford University Press.

Langton, R. 2012. "Beyond Belief: Pragmatics in Hate Speech and Pornography", in I. Maitra and M. K. McGowan, eds. *Speech and Harm: Controversies Over Free Speech*, 72–93. Oxford: Oxford University Press.

Lopez, I. 2014. *Dog Whistle Politics: How Coded Racial Appeals Have Reinvented Racism and Wrecked the Middle Class*. New York: Oxford University Press.

McGowan, M. K. 2004. "Conversational Exercitives: Something Else We Do With Our Words", *Linguistics and Philosophy* 27(1): 93–111.

---

[23] Nor will it neutralize it for those individuals who simply disagree with the norm, for even when and where the norm is in place there are openly racist people who explicitly deny the norm. But, of course, those people don't need to be dogwhistled to in order to activate their racism: they are happy to deliberately vote for the racist candidate.

McGowan, M. K. 2012. "On 'Whites Only' Signs and Racist Hate Speech: Verbal Acts of Racist Discrimination", in I. Maitra and M. K. McGowan, eds. *Speech and Harm: Controversies Over Free Speech*, 121–47. Oxford: Oxford University Press.

Mendelberg, T. 2001. *The Race Card: Campaign Strategy, Implicit Messages, and the Norm of Equality*. Princeton, NJ: Princeton University Press.

Noah, T. 2004. "Why Bush Opposes Dred Scott", accessed at http://www.slate.com/articles/news_and_politics/chatterbox/2004/10/why_bush_opposes_dred_scott.2.html.

Saul, Jennifer. 2017. "Racial Figleaves, the Shifting Boundaries of the Permissible, and the Rise of Donald Trump", *Philosophical Topics* 45(2): 97–116.

Safire, W. 2008. *Safire's Political Dictionary*. New York: Oxford University Press.

Smith, D. L. 2011. *Less Than Human: Why We Demean, Enslave, and Exterminate Others*. New York: St. Martin's Press.

Stanley, J. 2015. *The Problem of Propaganda*. Princeton University Press.

Tesler, M. and D. O. Sears. 2010. *Obama's Race: The 2008 Election and the Dream of a Post-Racial America*. Chicago: University of Chicago Press.

Tirrell, L. 2012. "Genocidal Language Games", in I. Maitra and M. K. McGowan, eds. *Speech and Harm: Controversies Over Free Speech*, 174–221. New York: Oxford University Press.

Valentino, N., V. Hutchings, and I. White. 2002. "Cues That Matter: How Political Ads Prime Racial Attitudes During Campaigns", *American Political Science Review* 96(1): 75–90.

Witten, Kimberley, forthcoming. "Dogwhistle Politics: The New Pitch of an Old Narrative".

14

Dynamic Pragmatics, Static Semantics

Robert Stalnaker

14.1 Introduction

Semantic-pragmatic theorizing took a dynamic turn in the 1970s, motivated by the recognition of at least three problems, or problem areas: first the problem of presupposition projection, second, puzzles about conditionals, which later generalized to problems about epistemic and deontic modals; third, problems about anaphora, including cross-sentential anaphora. At first the strategy was to explain discourse dynamics in pragmatic terms, retaining a more or less traditional static conception of compositional semantics. Later, in the 1980s and 90s, several versions of dynamic semantic theories were developed that built the dynamic processes into the compositional semantics. My aim in this paper is to clarify the contrast between the two approaches and to consider the costs and benefits of each. The dynamic semantic theories are more elegant and parsimonious in some respects, but I will argue that the phenomena that motivate the dynamic turn are best explained at the pragmatic level. All agree that there is considerable interaction between compositional rules and the dynamics of discourse, but I think we get a clearer view of this interaction if we represent the structure of discourse in a way that is independent of the linguistic mechanisms by which the purposes of the practice of discourse are realized, and if we retain the traditional distinction between the content of a speech act and the force with which it is expressed.[1]

By a "more or less traditional static conception of semantics," I mean a conception that treats semantics as a theory of the truth-conditional content of sentences, and of the compositional rules that determine those contents as a function of the meanings of their constituents. The conception is only "more or less traditional" since it allows for a semantics for context-dependent expressions such as tenses, demonstratives and personal pronouns. So David Kaplan's logic and semantics for demonstratives, and the formal semantic theory that Richard Montague called "Pragmatics" are more or

---

[1] I develop and defend the general view in more detail in Stalnaker 2014. In this paper I will not discuss problems concerning anaphora, but I address some of them in Chapter 5 of Stalnaker 1999. On this issue, see also K. Lewis 2014, which argues for a pragmatic treatment.

less traditional in this sense. While these theories allow for context-sensitivity, they abstract away from any substantive account of context, representing it by a sequence of parameters that are somehow determined by the situation in which an utterance takes place, but saying nothing about the features of the situation that determine what values those parameters take.[2]

My plan is this: in section 14.2 I will sketch the outlines of the pragmatic story developed in the 1970s, at least my version of it. In section 14.3 I will sketch a contrasting framework that builds the dynamic process into the semantics. There are a number of different dynamic semantic theories (Discourse representation theory, dynamic predicate logic, update semantics, for example), but I will focus on Irene Heim's file change semantics,[3] highlighting the central contrasts between this approach and the more traditional one. In section 14.4, I will focus on the notion of propositional content—*what is said* in a speech act, arguing that the partial notion of content that is recoverable from the dynamic semantic theory leaves out something important. Then in section 14.5, I will consider the notion of speech act force, arguing that it is useful to retain a notion of force that is abstracted from content.

14.2 Dynamic pragmatics

A notion of *context* plays a central role in both the dynamic pragmatic and dynamic semantic stories. A context, in the sense that is relevant to both approaches, is an information state represented by a set of possibilities. The intuitive idea is that the possibilities in the *context set* are all and only those that are compatible with the presumed common background knowledge shared by the participants in a conversation. This body of information plays two roles: first, it provides a resource that speakers may exploit in determining how to say what they want to say; second, it identifies the possibilities between which the participants aim to distinguish in their speech, and so provides a resource for the explanation of speech acts in terms of the way the act is intended to change the context. To play these two roles, the information state will include two different kinds of information: first, information about the participants in the conversation—about what they know about each other and their common environment; second, information about the subject matter of their discourse. The relevant information state is generally assumed to have an iterative structure, following the pattern of the notion of common knowledge (what a and b

<hr>

[2] I will say more below about the distinction between content and speech act force, but at this point I should note that most developments of the traditional static conception of semantics, including the theories of Montague and Kaplan, restricted themselves to a semantics for declarative sentences, and did not have much to say about uses of language to do things other than say how things are. But a semantic theory might be "more or less traditional" in the sense I intend even if it provided for wider uses of language, for example to ask questions, to make requests or to issue commands, as well as to make statements. On one traditional view, imperatives have the same kind of *content* as declarative sentences; the difference between assertions and commands is explained in terms of the force with which the content is expressed. Questions must have a different kind of content, but they are taken, in a traditional semantics for questions, to have, as their content, sets of propositions (the possible answers to the question).

[3] Heim 1982.

both know, what they both know that they both know, what they both know that they both know . . . etc.)

The context set is constantly changing as the conversational parties interact, and as their environment changes. The dynamic theories, both pragmatic and semantics, are theories about systematic ways that contexts change in response to what happens as a discourse proceeds. One can distinguish two kinds of changes: (1) changes in response to manifest events in the environment (including facts about what is said), and (2) changes in response to the conventional rules of a language, constitutive rules that specify how a speech act is intended to change the context. The pragmatic story[4] explains the second kind of context change by giving a general illocutionary-force rule. The rule for the speech act of *assertion* (the only rule specified in this early work) says that a successful assertion changes the context by adding the information that is the content of the assertion to the common ground (the context set). Assertions may be rejected, but in the simple idealized "language game" of assertion, the presumption is that an assertion changes the context in this way unless it is rejected.

The pragmatic story retains the traditional distinction between content and force. The idea is that the semantics, with its compositional rules, delivers a proposition, and then a speech act force rule specifies, in general, for an arbitrary proposition, how that proposition alters the context.[5]

But the semantics may specify the propositional content as a function of context (the same context which the speech act aims to change). So the process gives rise to a two-way interaction between context and content: first the context constrains content (as determined by the indexical semantics); second, the content of an assertion in turn changes the context (as determined by the speech act force rule), and this changed context will constrain the content of subsequent speech acts. This interaction may give rise to systematic relations between the contents of successive speech acts, relations that are not explained (with a traditional static semantics) on the semantic level. In particular there might be an inference that seems to be valid, and valid in virtue of the abstract form of the premise and conclusion, but where the force of the inference derives from the context-content interaction. The example that I used to illustrate this pattern[6] was an inference involving indicative conditionals, the or-to-if inference,

---

[4] See the papers reprinted in the first section of Stalnaker 1999 for the way I understood and developed the pragmatic dynamic story in the 1970s.

[5] The traditional distinction between content and force is compatible with a wide range of different accounts of just what speech act force is, and how it is marked in a language. In my account of assertion, the idea was to explain speech act force in terms of the way that a speech act is intended by the speaker to change the context. On the simple and highly idealized model of assertion that I offered, the intention is to add the content to the context set—the set of possible worlds representing the shared information, and that is the effect of the assertion if it is not rejected by one of the other participants. 'Assertion' is probably too narrow a term for speech acts with this force, since it has a connotation of seriousness not shared by all declarative speech acts with this aim.

The grammatical differences between declarative, interrogative, and imperative sentences certainly play a role in determining the force of a speech act, but it is not obvious that they are definitive. The commanding officer statement, 'you must return to base by noon tomorrow' seems as much a command as the imperative, 'return to base by noon tomorrow', and, 'you will be back in town by the weekend?' (with the question mark indicating a rising intonation), seems as much a question as, 'will you be back in town by the weekend?'

[6] See chapter 3 of Stalnaker 1999, first published in 1975.

which is an argument of the following form: either φ or ψ, therefore, if not-φ, then ψ. (Either the butler or the gardener did it; therefore, if the butler didn't, the gardener did.) The or-to-if argument presents a prima facie puzzle, since on the one hand it seems intuitively to be a valid argument. But on the other hand, it is semantically valid (in a truth-conditional semantics) only if the material conditional analysis is correct. But that analysis seems to have intuitively unacceptable consequences. The solution was to argue that while the argument is not *semantically* valid, its force could be explained by the interaction of context and content in something like the following way: first, the premise of the argument is appropriate only in a context in which it is an open question whether the butler did it, and also whether the gardener did it. Second, the content of the premise rules out all other options, so the posterior context, after the premise is accepted, includes possibilities in which the butler did it, possibilities in which the gardener did it, but only possibilities of one of these two kinds. Third, it was assumed that the semantic rule for the conditional was this: "if φ, then ψ" is true (in a given possible world) if and only if ψ is true in a selected possible world in which φ is true, but which otherwise differs minimally, if at all, from the given world. The relevant notion of minimal difference is determined by context. Fourth, it was assumed that for the *indicative* (as contrasted with the so-called *subjunctive*) conditional, it is a constraint on the interpretation of this context-dependent parameter (the notion of minimal difference) that possibilities compatible with the context have priority over those that are not.[7] It follows from these four assumptions that the conclusion of the argument (interpreted in its context) will be true if and only if the premise of the argument was appropriate, and accepted. But it does not follow that the proposition expressed by the premise semantically entails the proposition expressed by the conclusion.

This proposed account of the indicative conditional was idealized and schematic, but the main point was just to illustrate the way in which context-content interaction might help to explain some apparently logical (and so apparently semantic) relations between sentences in a discourse sequence.

A second example of the strategy of giving a pragmatic explanation for an apparently semantic phenomenon was the pragmatic response to the problem of presupposition projection. This problem, much discussed in the early 1970s in the linguistics literature on presupposition, was the problem of explaining the relation between the presuppositions required by speech acts performed with complex sentences in terms of the presuppositions required by the speech acts performed with their component parts. The problem was originally seen as a problem of compositional semantics, and it was taken for granted that presupposition was itself a semantic property of sentences: a sentence *presupposes* a proposition if and only if the sentence has a truth-value, true or false, only if the proposition presupposed is true. So it seemed that what is required, for example, to generate the presuppositions of a sentence of the form (φ and ψ)

---

[7] The fourth assumption, which specifies a constraint on indicative, but not subjunctive conditionals, is motivated by the following independently motivated thesis: the distinctive grammatical features—tense, aspect, and mood—that characterize the subjunctive conditionals are interpreted as markers that presuppositions are being suspended for the interpretation of the conditional, and the presumption is that without these markers, the presuppositions are maintained under the supposition.

was to generalize the two-valued truth table for conjunction to a three-valued rule that specified the truth-value of the conjunctive sentence (true, false or neither) as a function of the semantic values of the conjuncts. But the data suggested that the rule would have to be quite complex. It seemed to be non-truth-functional (depending on the meanings, and not just the truth-values of the constituent sentences), and also non-symmetric, unlike the two-valued rule for conjunction. The pragmatic response to the problem was, first, to redescribe the phenomenon to be explained in pragmatic terms, and second, to explain the redescribed data in terms of conversational dynamics.[8] Presupposition was understood, not as a semantic property of a sentence, but as a feature of context: what the speaker presupposes is what she takes to be entailed by the background information taken for granted by participants in the conversation. For a *sentence* to presuppose that **P** is just for its use to be appropriate only in a context in which the speaker takes for granted that **P**. It was taken to be a datum, for example, that "France is a kingdom, and the king of France is bald" does *not* presuppose that France has a unique king, even though the second conjunct does presuppose it. We redescribe this datum in pragmatic terms as follows: a speaker does not need to take it as given that France has a unique king in order to speak appropriately in saying, "France is a kingdom, and the king of France is bald," but she would need to take this as given in order to speak appropriately in saying, "The king of France is bald." Now the explanation is obvious: the presupposition required by the second conjunct need not be taken for granted for the appropriateness of the conjunctive statement since it is introduced by the first conjunct.

Both of these examples of pragmatic explanation of facts about discourse dynamics are oversimplified, and they are old news. The point of reviewing them is first to bring out the pattern of interaction between context and content, and second to set up the contrast between this kind of explanation and the kind of theory that builds the pattern into the semantics.

14.3 Dynamic semantics

A dynamic *semantic* story proposes to streamline the process of context change. Instead of context affecting content, that in turn affects context, we have a theory that goes directly from context to context, eliminating the middleman. The semantic value of a sentence is not a proposition, determined as a function of context, but instead a context-change potential: a function from contexts to contexts. In the traditional theory, the compositional rules specify how the proposition expressed by the complex sentence is a function of the propositions and other semantic values expressed by the parts; in the dynamic semantics, the compositional rules will specify the context-change potential of the complex sentence as a function of the context-change potentials of the parts.

To account for presupposition, the file-change semantic theory assumed that sentences would be *admissible* only in certain contexts, and part of the specification of the context-change potential of a sentence was a specification of the class of contexts in

---

[8] See chapter 2 of Stalnaker 1999 (first published 1974) and Karttunen 1974.

which the sentence could be used. So for example it will be an admissibility condition for the sentence, "Hazel's husband is a good cook" that the prior context be one that entailed that Hazel is married. That is, it must be true in all the possible worlds in the prior context set that Hazel is married. Then the context change rule for the sentence would specify, for any prior context meeting this condition, the posterior context that would result from an assertive utterance of the sentence. A sentence φ presupposes a proposition **P** if and only if all of the admissible contexts for φ entail the proposition **P**.

The dynamic semantic move then can use the same pattern of explanation for presupposition projection phenomena that the pragmatic account gave, but incorporate the pattern into the compositional semantics. So, for example, the compositional rule for a sentence of the form 'φ and ψ' says roughly the following: an assertive utterance of (φ and ψ) changes the context by first applying the context-change rule for φ to the given prior context, and then applying the context-change rule for ψ to the posterior context that results from the first change. So even though "Hazel's husband is a good cook" presupposes that Hazel is married, the conjunctive sentence, "Hazel is married and Hazel's husband is a good cook" does not have this presupposition, since the intermediate context (the one that results from the application of the context-change rule for the first conjunct) will satisfy the admissibility conditions for the second conjunct, even if the prior context for the whole sentence does not.

The old story about presupposition projection (before the introduction of the notion of pragmatic presupposition) was that the problem was a problem for compositional semantics in a language that allowed for truth-value gaps. The dynamic pragmatic account argued that while truth-value gaps may play a role in explaining why certain pragmatic presuppositions are required, the phenomena to be explained should be described in terms of conversational dynamics, and not compositional semantics. The dynamic *semantic* story is a kind of synthesis that builds conversational dynamics into the compositional semantics.

14.4 Propositional content

It is an elegant theory, but the streamlining of the dynamic process loses some distinctions that are made by the pragmatic account. As noted above, the pragmatic story retains the traditional distinction between *content* and *speech act force*, while the dynamic semantic theory builds speech act force into the semantic values of the constituents of sentences, and into the compositional rules by which the constituents are combined. I will consider in section 14.5 some reasons for retaining a general notion of speech act force, abstracted from content, but first I want to look at what the dynamic semantic theory has to say about truth-conditional content. In the streamlined theory, sentences do not express propositions at all, instead specifying the way that an arbitrary information state that meets certain admissibility conditions would be altered by a use of the sentence. But one can, as Irene Heim has emphasized, recover a notion of truth-conditional content from the prior context and the context-change rule in the following way: for any possible world w that is a member of a context set c, if w is in the posterior context set that results from applying the context-change rule for a sentence S to context c, then we can say that sentence S (as used in that context) is true in world w. On the other hand, if w is one of the worlds *eliminated* by the context-change rule, then the sentence is false in *w* in that context. On the traditional picture, the assertive utterance of the sentence changes the context as it does *because* the semantic rules for the sentence give it certain truth-conditions. Heim's proposal is that the explanation should go in the opposite direction. The semantic rules for the sentence define its CCP (context-change potential), and we then can "give an—albeit partial—definition of truth of a sentence in terms of the CCP of that sentence."[9] The definition is only partial because it "says nothing about the truth of S when *c* [the context] is false." That is, it gives truth-conditions for S (when used in context *c*) only for possible worlds compatible with that context. This means that if *anything* false is being presupposed, or taken for granted by the speaker in a particular context in which S is used to say something, then S, as used in that context, receives no truth-value in the actual world. Heim expresses the opinion that this partial definition is good enough, but I want to look more closely at the distinctions that are lost by restricting the truth-conditions of sentences in this way.

On either the dynamic pragmatic or the dynamic semantic story, a context for a particular token utterance is a specific information state defined by what the speaker in that particular situation is presuming to be common background knowledge. If the speech act performed in the context is appropriate, then the context will be an *admissible* context for the sentence used, but what is presupposed by the speaker will always be more than what she is *required* to presuppose in order for the sentence used to meet the admissibility conditions—more than what is presupposed in *all* admissible contexts. Even in a perfectly well behaved discourse, speakers may be presupposing *some* things that are in fact false. Any such case will be one where the dynamic semantic truth-conditions dictate that what is said is neither true nor false in the *actual* world.

Consider an old example that Saul Kripke used to make a point about reference:

Two people see Smith in the distance and mistake him for Jones. They have a brief colloquy: "What is Jones doing?" "Raking the leaves."

In the context of this banal exchange, it is presupposed by both parties that the person they see, who is in fact Smith, is Jones. So in all the possible worlds compatible with the context—all the worlds in the prior context set—it is Jones who they see in the yard, and the second speaker's statement changes the context by eliminating the possibilities in which Jones is doing something other than raking leaves. That is indeed what happens in this talk exchange, but we may also be interested in the question, was what the second speaker said true or false? The speaker said that Jones was raking leaves, and (assuming that Jones was not at the time raking leaves somewhere else), it seems obvious that what he said was false. That is, while the statement was true in the non-actual possible worlds compatible with the posterior context, it was false in the actual world—the world in which the statement was made, which is a world that is outside of the context set. We might contrast Kripke's case where a proper name is used with a variation where the questioner uses a demonstrative pronoun: "What is he doing?" the first speaker asks, as they both are looking at Smith. "Raking leaves," the second

---

[9] Heim 1988, 400.

speaker answers. The speaker's prior presuppositions are the same as they are in the original case: they both mistakenly take for granted that the person they see is Jones. But in this case, the presupposition that it is Jones rather than Smith who they see, seems to be irrelevant to the determination of the referent, and to the determination of what is said. In this case, it seems that it was Smith rather than Jones who the second speaker said was raking leaves, since his answer to the question picks up the referent of the demonstrative pronoun.[10] The two contrasting exchanges change what is essentially the same context in exactly the same way, but there seems to be a contrast in what is said in the two cases—a contrast that is made only by considering the truth-value of what is said in possible situations outside of the context set. But by Heim's definition of truth-conditional content, what the second speaker said, in both the original example and the variant, is neither true nor false.

Now I think it is intuitively clear that there is a contrast between the truth-conditional content of what is said in the two cases, and more generally clear that we routinely make judgments about the truth-values of statements in possible situations that are not compatible what is presumed to be common knowledge in the particular context in which the statement is made. But does it matter? One might argue that the semantic theorist's job is to explain what goes on in a discourse—the way it evolves in accordance with the rules governing the language. What matters for this purpose is not what is actually true, but what is true and false in the possible situations that are compatible with what the participants presuppose in the discourse. But I will argue that this is a mistake. Semantic theory should be part of a functional theory that aims to explain language as a device that serves certain purposes, including the exchange of information, rational deliberation, and debate. Success or failure in serving some of the functions of language will depend on whether what is said in a discourse is actually true. More generally, truth-values of what is said in possible situations that are outside of the specific local context in which they are made make a difference to the broader situation in which statements are used and assessed. If I understand and accept what is said in a context, then normally I acquire a belief that I can detach from the particular context in which it is acquired, leaving behind all of the parochial presumptions about the particular situation that define that context, presumptions that may have played a role in determining what was said, but do not become part of the content of what was said. Even if I later learn that some of what we were taking for granted about the situation of our discourse was false, I may continue to believe in the truth of something said in that discourse. Furthermore, we often retrospectively assess a speech act performed in an earlier context. I may concede that you were right, even though I was skeptical at the time. Judging that a statement made in a different context was true or false requires judging that the same statement that changed the earlier context in a particular way affects the present context, constituted by different possible situations. And by "same statement" we don't mean "sentence with the same context-

---

[10] At least this seems to me to be the right account of what is said with the demonstrative, but intuitions about the case may differ. The referent of the demonstrative is the person intended by the speaker, but in this case the speaker had two intentions that he mistakenly presupposed to come to the same thing: (to refer to the person they were seeing, and to refer to Jones). My judgment is that it is the first of these intentions that determines the referent.

change potential," since sentences with the same context-change potential may say different things in different contexts, and the same thing might be said, on different occasions, with sentences with a different context-change potential.

The difference between the meaning of a sentence and the statement that the sentence is used to make is a familiar one in the more orthodox truth-conditional semantics for a language with tenses, demonstrative, and personal pronouns. David Kaplan's semantics for demonstratives, for example, distinguishes the *character* of a sentence from its *content*.[11] When you and I use the sentence, "I was born in New Jersey," to make a statement, we say different things, but we use the same sentence, with the same character, to say them. Context-change potential is like character: the context-change potential of "I was born in New Jersey," when said by me, is the same as the context-change potential of your statement made with the same sentence. But there is no object distinguished by the dynamic theory corresponding to the intuitive notion of *what is said*.

Suppose I say, "It has just started snowing," and you say the next day, in a context in which the earlier conversation is remembered and salient, "It had then just started snowing." Your 'then' is anaphoric to the time of utterance of my earlier statement; what you say echoes what I said; what I said is true if and only if what you said is true. Recognizing this relation between our two statements, which used different sentences with different context-change potentials to change different contexts, requires cross-context comparison—cross-context calibration of content. These broader relations between what is said in different context are important for theorizing about speech behavior broadly construed.

One obvious place where cross-context comparison of content is important for the interpretation of speech is the interpretation of sentences or clauses embedded in speech and attitude ascriptions. We may talk explicitly in one context about what was said in another, or about what attitudes are held by a person who is not necessarily a participant in the context in which the attitude is attributed. The interpretation of embedded sentences or clauses will involve derived, subordinate, or "local" contexts, with their own presuppositions about what the subject believed or was presupposing. One can see these derived contexts as devices for calibrating what is going on in different contexts, and getting clear about embedding requires getting clear about the background problem of connecting different specific speech contexts, and the cognitive situations, at different times, of the parties to them.

The straightforward extension of a dynamic semantics to such constructions will treat the semantic value of a that-clause occurring in an attitude ascription as a context change potential. Malte Willer makes this proposal explicit: "We may . . . understand attitude verbs as expressing relations between individuals and CCPs." He argues that this proposal is not very different from a traditional view: "To say 'S believes that ϕ' is to claim that S stands in the belief relation to the meaning of ϕ, that is, [on the traditional view] a proposition or—if one prefers the dynamic view—a CCP."[12] But the meaning of a sentence (on a static semantics for a language that allows for context-dependence) is not a proposition but something that determines a proposition as a

---

[11] Kaplan 1989.   [12] Willer 2013, 62–3.

function of context. On either a static or a dynamic semantics, it should not be the meaning of a sentence that is the object of an attitude, or of an act of saying; it should be what that sentence is used to say in the relevant context. As I have noted, one of the things that is lost in the dynamic semantic streamlining of the pragmatic process of context change is the distinction between meaning ("character", in David Kaplan's terminology) and content, a distinction based on the contrast between two different roles that the facts play in determining the truth-value of a sentence, in context: first the facts determine *what is said* by a given use of a sentence; second the facts determine whether what is said is true or not.[13]

So we have two interconnected problems: first, dynamic semantics delivers only a partial proposition—a proposition that is defined only for the possible situations that are compatible with the presuppositions of the specific context in which the speech act takes place. Second, dynamic semantics does not distinguish the two roles that information plays in determining the truth value of what is expressed in a speech act.

I have argued that the restriction of truth-conditions to the possible worlds compatible with the context is a problem since we are, in many cases, interested in the truth-value of what is said relative to a wider range of possible situations. But while in many cases we can detach a piece of information expressed in a context from the context in which it is expressed, there are also cases where the information communicated is more difficult to separate from the situation in which it is communicated, and the means used to do it, and cases of this kind fit well with the dynamic semantic approach. I have used an example of John Perry's to illustrate the point:[14] the context is one in which it is presupposed that John and his interlocutor are looking out at the bow of a ship, most of which is blocked by a large building, and at the stern of a ship visible behind the other end of the building. The prior context is compatible with the possibility that there are two different ships, and also compatible with the possibility that the bow and stern are parts of the same ship. When John says, "*That* ship [pointing at the bow] is the same as *that* one [pointing at the stern]," he changes the context by excluding the first of these possibilities. If we think of the *information* communicated as an increment of information—the change from the prior to the posterior information state—then it is clear enough what information is conveyed. But if we look for a detachable item of information—a proposition that is independent of the particular circumstances in which John's identity claim was made—it is not so clear what was said. Suppose later John's interlocutor sees this ship out on the open sea, and says, pointing twice at it, "John told me that *that* ship is the same as *that* one." This report does not seem to be an accurate account of what John told her. She needs to tell a longer story about what the context was, but that story will not identify (in the later context) the proposition that was expressed.

Indicative conditionals and epistemic modals may (in some cases) also provide examples of what I have called "essentially contextual" statements. There are just

---

[13] It must be conceded that Kaplan himself at one point suggested that the *cognitive value* of a statement (which is presumably the belief expressed by the speaker in making the statement) was the character of the sentence used to make the statement. (See Kaplan 1989, 530.) But I don't think this suggestion withstands scrutiny.

[14] The original example is in Perry 1977. I discuss in in Stalnaker 2008, chapter 4.

three possible suspects, the butler, the gardener, and the chauffeur. I have information that decisively excludes the chauffeur, so I say, "If the gardener didn't do it, the butler did." You have information that excludes the butler, so you say (in a different context), "If the gardener didn't do it, the chauffeur did." As later becomes clear to both of us, the gardener did it, but which of us was right about who did it if it wasn't the gardener? In this case, retrospective assessment seems inappropriate; the question "no longer arises" after we learn that the culprit was in fact the gardener. The dynamic semantic story, with the information identified with the increment, seems to get things right. But the dynamic *pragmatic* story, with its representation of propositional information as a function from possible worlds to truth-values, can accommodate partiality. The function with which a proposition expressed by a sentence in a given context is identified may be defined for wider or narrow domains of possibilities. It is a minimal condition for appropriate speech that one use a sentence that expresses a proposition that is defined *at least* for the possible situations compatible with the particular local context in which the sentence is used. In some cases, truth-values may be undefined beyond that, but in other cases it may be straightforward how to assess the truth-value of what is said relative to a much wider range of possible worlds. In a reasonable semantic framework, cross-context comparisons, retrospective assessment, and ascriptions of speech and thought should be possible, but not necessarily easy or automatic. The combination of static semantics and pragmatic dynamics allows for this flexibility.

14.5 Speech act force

I have so far been focusing on the role of a notion of propositional content in the explanation of semantic/pragmatic phenomena. I will conclude with a brief look at the content–force distinction from the other side: at the role of a general notion of speech act force, abstracted from content.

On the pragmatic story, it is assumed, in general, that speech act force is to be explained in terms of the way that the expression of a proposition with that force changes the context. The speech act rules are thus what drive the dynamic process, to the extent that it is governed by rules of the language. In the development of this approach, just one speech act rule was given: a rule for assertion. The rule was highly idealized—best thought of as a rule for an artificial assertion game that provides a simplified model for the way one kind of discourse evolves. And "assertion" is probably not the best name for the kind of speech act modeled, since the rule applies to a wider range of speech acts, including some that do not necessarily satisfy the norms that serious assertions are supposed to satisfy. But all assertions, in the broad sense intended, are speech acts that aim to cut the context set down, which is to say to add information to what is presumed to be the common knowledge of the participants in the conversation. It was never assumed that this was the only speech act, or that others can be reduced to assertion, in this broad sense. Some speech acts will raise questions, rather than answering them, and as has recently been emphasized in the discussion of epistemic modals, a speaker may aim to expand rather than contract the context set: to subtract from what is presumed to be common ground, rather than to add to it. The dynamic semantic strategy for representing the idea that *might* statements affect contexts in this way is to build a rule for the expansion of the context set into the context-change potential for the modal word. Willer puts the idea this way: "my suggestion is that *might*-statements . . . are designed to change possibilities that are merely compatible with the agent's evidence into 'live possibilities'—possibilities that are compatible with the agent's evidence, and that the agent takes seriously in inquiry."[15] His formal implementation of this suggestion represents a context, not as a single set of possible worlds, but as an overlapping set Σ of sets of possible worlds. If a possible world w is a subset of *some* member of Σ, then it is not excluded from the context, but it is a "live possibility", one taken seriously in the context, only if it is a member of *every* set in Σ. So the context-change rule will change the context not by eliminating possible worlds from a context set, but by eliminating sets of possible worlds from a set Σ that provides a richer representation of a context.[16]

This rule is not, on the face of it, a rule for expanding, rather than contracting a context set, but if we think of the context set as the intersection of all the sets in Σ (that is, as the set of serious possibilities in the prior context), then by eliminating sets from Σ, we expand the set that is the intersection of the revised set of sets (the set of serious possibilities in the posterior context).

An alternative more constrained way of implementing the context-change rule, using more familiar semantic resources, is to think of a context as a set of nested spheres of possible worlds, or equivalently as a set of worlds plus an ordering source. The inner sphere, or the highest ranking possible worlds, form the basic context set, and the others provide a procedure for expanding the set as a function of a proposition that is compatible with the whole set of worlds, but incompatible with the inner sphere, or the set of highest ranking worlds.[17]

It is good to ask, in seeking a semantic analysis of the epistemic *might*, how a *might* statement changes the context, but I think it is also possible and useful to isolate a distinctive *content* for the modal statement, and to explain why its use has the context-change potential that it has in terms of both a distinctive kind of force and a distinctive content. A simple model for the kind of explanation I have in mind (a model I have used as an analogy for an account of epistemic modals) is provided by a simple language game of commands and permissions designed by David Lewis. Let me sketch Lewis's game, and then make the analogy between the deontic modals in the game and epistemic *might* and *must*.[18]

Lewis's game has a master who has the authority to issue commands, and to give permission, to a slave who is obliged to do what the master says. There are two deontic

---

[15] Willer 2013, 50.

[16] Willer's intuitive gloss on the meaning of this set is that it is something like a vague context set, where vagueness is given a supervaluationist representation. A world w is compatible with the context if it is a member of every set in Σ, and incompatible with the context if excluded by every set in Σ. If w is a member of some members of Σ and not of others, then it is indeterminate whether it is compatible with the context. In this case, w is not ruled out, but also not a salient possibility that is taken seriously.

[17] So *might*-ϕ will expand the context set by adding the set of worlds determined by applying the context-change rule for the prejacent, ϕ to the "context" determined by the smallest subset compatible with ϕ.

[18] See D. Lewis 1975 for his account of the game. See Stalnaker 2014, chapter 6 for a development of the analogy with epistemic modals.

modal operators, '!' and '¡' (pronounce 'fiat' and 'taif'): '!φ' says that the slave is obliged to bring it about that φ, and '¡φ' says that the slave is permitted to bring it about that φ. These deontic sentences are straightforwardly true or false at any point in the game, with their truth-values depending on what the master has commanded or permitted up to that point. So they have a distinctive deontic *content*: someone other than the master can make ordinary assertions with these sentences. (The game has a third player, a kibitzer who may comment on the state of play, or remind the slave or the master what the slave is required or permitted to do.) But when the master utters a deontic sentence, it has a distinctive illocutionary *force* in virtue of her authority. It is a rule of the game that when the master issues a command, the "sphere of permissibility" that determines what is required and permitted adjusts in the minimal way required to make the statement true.

In this game, both deontic content and a distinctive kind of illocutionary force play a role in explaining the effect of the master's commands and permission statements, and the content is truth-conditional content. What distinguishes the force of a command from the force of an assertion is that the content of the command is *prospective*: the deontic sentence is interpreted relative to the *posterior* context, rather than the prior context. In the case of an assertion, the content is first determined, relative to the *prior* context, and then the assertion is understood as a proposal to change the context by adding this content to the information in the common ground. With a command, the proposal is to change the context (by adjusting the sphere of permissibility) so that the proposition expressed by the deontic sentence is true in the context as adjusted. The prospective force rule introduces a potential circularity, since the content that changes the context is determined relative to the context that results from the change. To put it in dynamic semantic terms, if f is the CCP for a command and c is the prior context, then $f(c)$ must be a fixed point: a c' such that $f(c') = c'$. To get the uniqueness that the rule requires, we need to say that the context change is the *minimal* change that achieves a fixed point. For commands, it is clear enough what the minimal change required is: when the master says '!φ', this eliminates from the sphere of permissibility all the worlds in which φ is false. It is less clear what possibilities should be *added* to the sphere of permissibility when the master issues a permission, for example saying '¡φ' in a prior context in which bringing it about that φ was forbidden. There is no obvious minimal change, given the simple structure provided by the deontic framework, that make it the case that the slave is permitted to bring it about that φ. (This is the "problem about permission" that Lewis raises for his game.) So some additional structure needs to be added in order to have the resources to state a determinate force rule for permissions. For example if the sphere of permissibility was the smallest sphere in a set of nested spheres of the kind alluded to above, that might provide what we need.

Epistemic *might* statements, according the analysis I have suggested,[19] are analogous to the permission statements in Lewis's game. The *content* of a statement of the form "it might be that φ" is as given in a standard modal semantics: the statement is true (in world x, in a given context c) if the prejacent, φ, is true in

---

[19] Stalnaker 2014, ch. 6.

some possible world in a set of worlds determined by the context. In simple cases, the relevant set of worlds will be, simply the context set itself. But the force rule for the epistemic modals proposes to interpret them relative to the *posterior* context. The *might* statement is, in effect, a proposal to adjust the context to ensure that the prejacent is true in some possible world in the posterior context set. This account, because of the "fixed-point" rule, faces a problem exactly analogous to Lewis's problem about permission, and the solution is similar: we need a structure to provide "back-up" contextual possibilities, the kind of structure suggested above in the context of dynamic semantics.

In Lewis's artificial game, one player has authority: only the master can issue commands and give permission, and there is no provision for the rejection of these speech acts. With epistemic modals (and also with a more realistic account of deontic discourse), no one has this kind of absolute authority. *Might* statements, like assertions, can be rejected, and can be a subject of negotiation. You say that the keys that we are looking for might be in the car (to use a simple and familiar example), but I reply that, no, I remember having them after coming into the house, so they can't be still in the car. You were proposing to add to the context, or to make salient, keys-in-the-car possibilities. I reject your proposal, suggesting instead that we are in a position to rule out those possibilities. I am not suggesting that we *were* in a position to exclude those possibilities in our prior joint epistemic situation, but that (based on my knowledge) we now should adjust the context to exclude them: to make the *might* statement false in the posterior context. Neither of us has authority here. We are negotiating about how the context set, which represents the possibilities that are the live options for us, given our joint epistemic situation, should evolve. In the example of the car keys, my rejection of your *might* statement will normally settle the matter, but in other cases, disagreement may persist. We are considering, early in the 2016 presidential campaign, whether Donald Trump might win the Republican nomination. "No way," I say (along with most reasonable people at the time). "We can exclude that possibility." But while you are not prepared to say, at that point, that he *will* get the nomination, you insist that he *might*. We are, you think, not yet in a position to rule that possibility out. But I am not moved to concede that this might happen, I continue to contend that we have sufficient reason to conclude that it won't. I give you my reasons for thinking this surely won't happen, and you reply with reasons why my considerations are not sufficient.

On the kind of account I am suggesting, the context-change potential of a *might*-statement (in the case where it is accepted by the addressees) is exactly as it is in a dynamic semantic account such as Willer's. But I think it is useful, particularly in understanding the disagreement cases, to separate content from force in the explanation for why the statement changes the context in this way. When we are negotiating about how our context should change, we are carrying out that negotiation in a context, and in the context of that negotiation, it is common ground neither that Trump might win the nomination, nor that it is not the case that he might. To properly represent the context of our disagreement, we need possible situations in which it is true that he might win, and contrasting possibilities in which this is false. These are possibilities that the *content* of the *might*-statement distinguishes between, in the context of our negotiation.

As things developed, it turned out that you were right: we would not have been correct to rule out that possibility. But suppose things had gone differently, with Trump fading after the early primaries, and in the end losing out to Jeb Bush. That of course would not show that you were wrong—you only said that he *might* win. But depending on how things went, it could become clear, in a retrospective context, that I was right—that we were in a position, at the earlier time, to rule out the possibility, and that your skepticism about my reasons was unwarranted. Or alternatively, it could become clear that *you* were right—that even though my claim was true, my reasons were not sufficient, at the time, to know that it was.

There is also a third way that the retrospective assessment could go. Epistemic modal statements are fragile, and the account that gives them propositional content is not committed to the claim that there is always a fact of the matter about whether they are actually true. The distinctions we make between the possibilities that define the common ground at a given point in a debate, deliberation, or exchange of information are the distinctions we need in order to account for what we agree and disagree about in that situation. Some disagreements are practical disagreements about how (given its purposes and our epistemic situations at that point) the context should evolve, and the distinctions between possibilities that represent such practical disagreements may be more fine-grained than the distinctions between the possibilities that are decided by the facts. But the distinction between more robust propositions, defined for a wide range of possible situations beyond those that are compatible with the immediate local context, and more fragile propositions, about which one may say later, the question of whether they are actually true or false does not arise, is a distinction that cannot be made in advance. A static truth-conditional semantics, combined with a systematic pragmatic account of the dynamics of context change can account for the phenomena that motivate dynamic semantics, and also give us the flexibility we need to account for the role of discourse in our cognitive lives.[20,21]

References

Heim, I. 1982. *The semantics for definite and indefinite noun phrases*. PhD dissertation, University of Massachusetts.

Heim, I. 1988. "On the projection problem for presuppositions," in M. Barlow et al. (eds.) *Proceedings of WCCFL 2*, Stanford: Stanford University, 114–25. Reprinted in S. Davis (ed.) *Pragmatics: A reader*, Oxford: Oxford University Press, 1990. Page number references are to the reprinted version.

Kaplan, D. 1989. "Demonstratives," in J. Almog, J. Perry, and H. Wettstein, *Themes from Kaplan*, New York and Oxford: Oxford University Press, 481–563.

Karttunen, L. 1974. "Presupposition and linguistic context," *Theoretical Linguistics* 1: 181–94.

Lewis, D. 1975. "A problem about permission," in E. Saarinen et al. (eds.) *Essays in Honour of Jaakko Hintikka*, Dordrecht: Reidel, 163–75.

[20] In chapter 8 of Stalnaker 2014 I discuss in more detail the idea that in representing agreement and disagreement, we may individuate possibilities more finely than can be justified by the facts that determine which of the possibilities is the actual one.
[21] Thanks to Daniel Fogal for very helpful comments on an earlier draft of this essay.

Lewis, K. 2014. "Do we need dynamic semantics?" in A. Burgess and B. Sherman (eds.) *Metasemantics: New Essays on the Foundations of Meaning*, Oxford: Oxford University Press, 231–58.

Perry, J. 1977. "Frege on demonstratives," *Philosophical Review* **86**: 474–97.

Stalnaker, R. 1999. *Context and Content: Essays on intentionality in speech and thought*. New York: Oxford University Press.

Stalnaker, R. 2008. *Our Knowledge of the Internal World*. Oxford: Oxford University Press.

Stalnaker, R. 2014. *Context*. New York: Oxford University Press.

Willer, M. 2013. "Dynamics of Epistemic Modality," *Philosophical Review* **122**: 45–92.

15

Expressivism by Force

Seth Yalcin

15.1 Introduction

Here is what happens in this paper.[†] I make a certain distinction. I use the distinction to frame two directions that an expressivist view of normative language might take. I then plump for one of these directions.

Here is what happens in a bit more detail. I make a distinction: there is on the one hand the traditional speech act-theoretic notion of illocutionary force, and there is on the other hand the kind of notion of force we have in mind when we are theorizing in formal pragmatics about conversational states and their characteristic modes of update. I say these notions are different, and occur at different levels of abstraction. They are not helpfully viewed as in competition. I then say that the expressivist idea that normative language is distinctive in force can be developed in two sorts of directions, depending on which of the two senses of 'force' just distinguished is emphasized. One familiar tradition tries to develop expressivism as the thesis that the meaning of normative language is somehow to be explained via its putative connections to non-assertoric illocutionary forces. But that path is prone to Frege-Geach-style worries. Expressivists do better to take the other path, and start with the idea that normative discourse is distinctive in respect of its dynamic effect on the state of the conversation (Yalcin 2012a,b; cf. Lewis 1979a,b; Veltman 1996; Ninan 2005; Stalnaker 2014; Pérez-Carballo and Santorio 2016; Starr ;2016; Willer forthcoming). This approach is not in principle subject to special worries about compositionality. It can be developed further using static semantic or dynamic semantic tools. It coheres with familiar lines of thinking about the metaphysics of content. It goes far, I suggest, in accommodating the core ideas expressivists have traditionally wanted to capture.

That summarizes the first seven sections of the paper. You might like to stop there. From section 15.8 forward, I go on a bit more about how one might develop an expressivism about normative language in this style, building on Gibbard (2003)'s notion of a plan-laden state of mind, and his technical notion of a 'hyperplan'. I find much that is attractive in Gibbard's formal model of normative states of mind, but as for the question how best to philosophically gloss that model, I take a different

[†] I am greatly indebted to Daniel Harris for illuminating comments on an earlier draft. Thanks also to Selim Berker and Edward Schwartz.

approach. I pursue a way for the expressivist to approach answering the question: "In virtue of what does a state of mind have the plan-laden content it has?" The sort of answer I recommend is broadly 'functionalist' and 'representationalist' in character. I suggest that the expressivist can approach this question in the same general way that, e.g. Lewis (1979c, 1994) approaches the analogous question as it arises for his modeling proposal about content. I deny that an expressivist in this vein has any special problem about explaining what it is for two normative states of mind to be inconsistent. Ultimately the sort of expressivism I envisage is perhaps distinctive in that it does not call for a radical rethinking of semantics, its foundations, or the theory of content; on the contrary, it presupposes and conservatively extends a broadly non-deflationary and representationalist conception of the mental, and can be made to mesh with compositional semantic theories of familiar varieties.

15.2 Separating illocutionary force and dynamic force

There are many things one could mean (and that have been meant) by 'force' in theorizing about linguistic communication. As advertised, I want to start by separating two broad ideas. The first idea I will call *illocutionary* force. The second idea I will call *dynamic* force.

Begin with illocutionary force. The terminology owes of course to Austin, but as I want to frame it, this general way of approaching force corresponds to a big tent, and goes back at least to Frege on assertion. There are two key ways that Frege gives us a handle on the notion of assertoric force. First, force is contrasted with an intuitive notion of content. Frege would say that the assertion that p and the query whether p both "contain the same thought" or have the same content, namely, that p. 'Force' is the name for the remainder, for the dimension that varies across these speech acts. This way of introducing the notion of force remains common in contemporary work.[1] Second, drawing on aspects of Kant's theory of judgment, Frege described assertion as the outward manifestation of the inner act of judgment, where an act of judgment is something like an event of coming to believe, an event of taking-to-be-true. On such a view, assertoric force has a constitutive tie to the mental state of believing or judging, and (thereby) to the normative requirements governing these states of mind. You shouldn't believe (judge) that p unless you have the appropriate epistemic relation to p (whatever that epistemic relation may be exactly—sufficient evidence, justification, knowledge, etc.). Since on this view assertion just is a way of manifesting a mental state of belief or judgment, it is naturally taken to be subject to normative requirements of a similar character.[2]

---

[1] An example from the first page of Searle and Vanderveken (1985): "In general an illocutionary act consists of an illocutionary force F and a propositional content P. For example, the two utterances, "You will leave the room" and "Leave the room!" have the same propositional content, namely that you will leave the room; but characteristically the first of these has the illocutionary force of a prediction and the second has the illocutionary force of an order." See also Green (2015).

[2] A related approach is that of Williamson (1996, 2000), who argues that assertion is distinguished by a certain constitutive norm, one which makes reference to the knowledge state of the speaker. (Assertion could be said to 'manifest' a state of knowledge on this approach partly in virtue of the fact that the speech act itself is partly constituted by the rule one asserts p only if one knows p.) Williamson's general

Austin (1961, 1962) followed Frege in conceiving of the force of a speech act as the sort of thing that (*inter alia*) situates the content expressed with respect to extra-conversational aspects of the speaker's state of mind, but his work placed a special emphasis on the broader rational objectives that animate speakers. The answer to the question of what the illocutionary force of a speech act is, is approached by asking what the agent is trying to do in speaking. Speech acts are individuated in part by appeal to the kinds of state of mind they are normally associated with, but also in part by appeal to the typical sorts of rational objectives associated with performing them. The illocutionary force of a speech act locates it at a level of description incorporating a broad sphere of human activity and social interaction. Searle (1969) is an extended development of Austin's approach. Some in this tradition, drawing on Grice (1957), place a special emphasis on a particular subclass of objectives, namely those having to do with getting the addressee to recognize the speaker's intentions (see, e.g., Strawson 1964; Bach and Harnish 1979). Within this broad approach to force, there is of course considerable room for debate about how exactly to divide the space of forces, and about how to analyze the force of any given speech act.

Since there is a seemingly boundless array of things speakers might do by using language, this way of thinking about force tends to lead to a rich diversity of forces. Searle and Vanderveken (1985), for instance, suggest that the following kinds of speech acts all correspond to characteristically different forces: assertions, predictions, reminders, objections, conjectures, complaints, orders, requests, declarations, promises, vows, pledges, apologies, admissions, boasts, laments, and bets. (That is a selection; their official list is longer.) To perform any of these acts is in part to manifest that one's beliefs, desires, intentions, and/or actions outside of the context of the discourse are subject to certain norms. (Perhaps, as with performatives, in virtue of the very performance of the speech act.)

A second, very different thing one could have in mind by the 'force' of an utterance is (something like) the characteristic kind of change to the state of the conversation the utterance is apt to produce. This sort of idea—what I want to call *dynamic* force—began to come into focus in the seventies, when theorists like Karttunen, Stalnaker, Lewis, Kamp, and Heim began to formalize pragmatics and explore various ways of making the whole conversation or discourse itself the object of systematic formal investigation (Karttunen 1969, 1974; Stalnaker 1974, 1978; Lewis 1979b; Kamp 1981; Heim 1982; see also Hamblin 1971; Gazdar 1979).[3] The account of assertion in Stalnaker (1978) provides a paradigm case of this way of thinking about force. On this view, the characteristic conversational effect of successful assertion is to change the conversational state by adding information to it. Stalnaker models the state of a conversation by a set of possible worlds, the possible worlds left open by what is jointly presupposed by the interlocutors in the discourse—what he calls a *context set*. To gain information is, in the possible worlds setting, for there to be fewer possibilities

---

approach suggests that speech acts forces are individuated by their "constitutive rules"—rules which (like the knowledge rule for assertion) are typically articulated via appeal to the intentional mental states of the interlocutors—their knowledge, beliefs, preferences, etc.

[3] While the present paper is greatly indebted to these works, the particular way of framing the notion of dynamic force that will emerge here may not exactly align with any of them.

compatible with your information, so the effect of assertion is modeled as an operation that eliminates possibilities from the context set. When one says, 'It's raining' and all goes well,[4] possibilities in the context set where it is not raining are eliminated. This reflects the fact that our shared conversational information now ceases to be compatible with the possibility that it isn't raining.

The array of possible dynamic forces depends on the variety of interesting dynamical changes that conversational states are capable of—a matter which of course interacts with the question what kind of structure conversational states are best modeled as having. Theorists working with a dynamic conception of force often use richer objects than context sets in their models of conversational states, recognizing additional structure as necessary to model whatever language fragment is of target concern.

To give an illustration of this approach beyond ordinary assertion, consider questions. Here it is obvious that without elaboration, the simple context set picture is inadequate: a question like 'Is it raining?' does not characteristically add information (eliminate possibilities) to the conversation; but neither does it remove information (add possibilities). Abstractly, a question seems to "frame an issue" in a way that serves to steer the discourse in a particular direction. As Hamblin suggested in classic work, "Pragmatically speaking a question sets up a choice situation between a set of propositions, namely those propositions that count as answers to it" (Hamblin 1973, 254). Since the work of Hamblin, and Karttunen (1977), it has been usual to understand the semantic value of an interrogative sentence as the kind of thing that determines a set of propositions, the propositions that could serve to answer the question. Where the complete possible answers to a question are mutually exclusive, we can think of a question as determining a partition of logical space (Hamblin 1958; Belnap and Steel 1976; Groenendijk and Stokhof 1984). Now we can bring this idea into our model of conversational states in various ways, in order to clarify and model the dynamic force of questions of this kind. One simple possibility would be as follows (cf. Roberts 1996, 2012; Hulstijn 1997; Yalcin 2011):[5] we suppose that a conversational state includes, in addition to a set of open possibilities (a context set), a set of ways of partitioning logical space. We use the latter element to model the question(s) that are in focus in the discourse. The characteristic dynamic effect of a question would be to eliminate partitions from this set. Take for example the question, 'Is it raining?' This will semantically determine a simple bipartite partition of logical space into

---

[4] By "All goes well" I mean that speaker was heard by the addressee, that both speak English, that each takes herself to be in conversation with the other, etc.

Stalnaker glosses the dynamic update effect of assertion as a "proposal" to change the context set: my assertion of 'It's raining' changes the context set in the way described only if my interlocutor does not object. I think it is best to take the "proposal" talk metaphorically, and not view assertion as literally explained as an illocutionary act of proposing. (That would just pass the buck to the question of what proposing is.) I myself would favor dropping the "proposal" talk entirely, holding instead that assertions simply always change the state of the conversation in their characteristic fashion. That is to say, the update does not "wait" for the addressee's permission, implicitly or explicitly. Rejections of assertions do not stop the relevant changes to the conversational state from happening; rather, they undo a change that has taken place.

[5] It should be noted that the idea that the context set is interestingly partitioned in a manner that is sensitive to the distinctions of interest to the interlocutors is an idea Stalnaker has raised in various places; see, e.g., Stalnaker (1981, 1986, 2014).

rain possibilities and no-rain possibilities. The dynamic effect of the question would be to remove from the conversational state those partitions of logical space that fail to incorporate at least this distinction. That is, it serves to rule out partitions that fail to cut logical space in a manner that is sensitive to the question of rain.[6] By eliminating the partitions that fail to include the question of rain, the question of rain becomes, as it were, 'visible' or 'in focus' in the discourse.

Imperatives make for another illustration. Perhaps the best known recent account in the dynamic force style is due to Portner (2004, 2007, 2017). He suggests that imperatives semantically express individual (address-relativized) properties. He proposes (roughly) that a conversational state includes, for each interlocutor, a "To-Do List" for that interlocutor—a sequence of properties that the agent is mutually understood in the conversation to be under some kind of requirement to realize. He then proposes that the dynamic force of an imperative is to update the To-Do List of the addressee, adding the property expressed by the imperative to the addressee's To-Do List.

For at least a half-dozen more ways of enriching conversational states in order to associate certain fragments of language with distinctive dynamic forces, see Lewis (1979b). He postulated a rich "conversational scoreboard" including a number of dimensions beyond the context set, among them: (i) a ranking of comparative salience of objects (for, e.g., tracking the way that the referent of a definite description may be sensitive to the preceding discourse); (ii) a parameter tracking the prevailing standards of precision (for modeling vagueness; see also Lewis 1980, King 2003); (iii) a component registering the admissible modal accessibility relations (for modeling the dynamic effect of unembedded modal utterances); (iv) a parameter mapping names to their bearers (for modeling the dynamic effect of performative speech acts of dubbing); (vi) a component representing the possible plans of the interlocutors (for modeling talk of what to do).

I take it that dynamic force is basically the notion in play in what has lately come to be called 'dynamic pragmatics' (see, e.g., Stalnaker (this volume) and Portner (this volume)). But while typical proponents of dynamic pragmatics frame that view as packaged with a rejection of dynamic semantics, the notion of dynamic force operative here is meant to be neutral on that issue. (The notion of dynamic force occurs at what Rothschild and Yalcin (2016, 2017) call the 'conversation systems' level of description.) Whether or not the compositional semantic value of a sentence is identical to its way of updating the conversational state (its *context change potential*, or CCP), the dynamic semanticist and the dynamic pragmaticist agree that (unembedded) sentences *have* CCPs. Both can therefore ask, for various fragments of language, what interesting distinctions there are to be made amongst the CCPs they

---

[6] More exactly: say a partition of logical space (question) Π_1 *includes* partition Π_2 just in case every element of Π_2 is equal to the union of some set of elements of Π_1. Then the dynamic effect of a question is to eliminate from the conversational state those partitions that do not include the question. This is basically the notion of inclusion defined by Groenendijk and Stokhof (1984) and by Lewis (1988a,b).

(I don't mean to defend this particular theory of the dynamic force of questions here against relevant competitors, the most obvious being perhaps Roberts (1996, 2012), who postulates *inter alia* a component of the conversational state that tracks a sequence of questions ordered by priority. I just want a simple example of a dynamic force picture of (partition-like) questions on the table.)

recognize. And as I am understanding it, that is just the question: what the interesting distinctions are between dynamic forces.

15.3 That illocutionary force and dynamic force do not line up nicely

With illocutionary force and dynamic force distinguished, the next thing to emphasize is that they need not line up in any particularly neat way. The things we are apt to call assertions in the illocutionary sense may be diverse in respect of their dynamic forces; and in the other direction, it may be that a single underlying dynamic force is what is in play across speech acts with diverse illocutionary forces. I do not take this to be a new point. Stalnaker (1978) already noted that his idea about dynamic force seemed appropriate to cases of what we would naturally call, in the illocutionary sense, 'assertion' and also to what we would naturally call in the illocutionary sense 'supposition', and that therefore the account was not helpfully understood as an analysis of the traditional (illocutionary) notion of assertion. Indeed, it is rather misleading to use the same words—'assertion' and 'force'—in both the illocutionary way and the dynamic way. That can suggest competing analyses of the same phenomenon. But there is no conflict here. These concepts apply at different levels of description.

It might be right to suppose that Stalnakerian assertoric dynamic force is put to an especially common and important purpose in normal linguistic interaction, namely the purpose of transmitting belief or knowledge. That is why it made some sense for Stalnaker to describe his dynamic model of conversational update as a model of what assertion typically does, taking 'assertion' in tradition illocutionary sense. But this use to which the kind of dynamic force described by Stalnaker can be put—the use of transmitting belief or knowledge—should not be wrapped into its identity, or its conditions for individuation. To do that would be to lose some of the power of this way of theorizing about conversation.

Stalnaker's dynamic force account captures an abstract idea—basically, the idea of adding some more information to a certain existing body of information (viz., the conversational state). As I want to recommend we understand it, the story prescinds from the question what exactly the conversational state is taken by the interlocutors to be characterizing, and from the question what the speaker might be aiming to do, extra-linguistically speaking, by adding certain information to that state. In this way, it prescinds from exactly the kind of facts that are thought to be essential for individuating speech acts on illocutionary conceptions of force. This level of abstraction for theorizing about conversation is high—or if you prefer, narrow— but it is a fruitful one for modeling core features of discourse and of our linguistic competence. It makes sense to distinguish the game of updating conversational states from the diverse uses to which this game could be put—even when certain uses seem particularly canonical or salient or important. In making a series of declarative statements, a person may be recounting events that transpired yesterday, or they may be telling a story everyone mutually recognizes to be a fiction. In both cases, we should like to say that they are exploiting the meaning of their sentences and certain conventions about the dynamics of conversational update in their language to add information to something like a store of information already mutually held in common. In both cases we might naturally model the impact of these speech acts on the conversational state in Stalnaker's way, in terms of the elimination of possibilities from a context set. The concept of dynamic force enables us to capture key similarities about the dynamics of discourse across diverse uses of language. Thus if we use 'assertion' in the dynamic force sense, we should not be taken to be assuming anything very substantive about what the illocutionary force of the speech act in question was.

There is a certain point that is apt to get lost in the preceding, so let me pause to draw it out and emphasize it. One should not assume that the information captured by the conversational state, in the target technical sense of 'conversational state', must reflect what is common belief among the interlocutors. The information incorporated into the conversational state needn't be common belief or common knowledge.[7] Sometimes more is conversationally common ground than what is common belief— as when we converse under (explicit or tacit) hypothetical suppositions, or when we make polite conversation, allowing presuppositions into the conversation that we don't plan to take home. Other times, the state of the conversation does not include propositions that are common belief, as when we reason under counterfactual suppositions, or tell stories. Moreover, what exactly one comes away from a conversation actually believing or knowing always depends on subtleties about trust and authority (real and perceived). Such factors may, but needn't, influence what one lets into the conversational state. Whether they will or not in any given case depends on the goals and interests of the interlocutors, and on the mutually understood point of the conversation. A model of the abstract dynamics of conversation, and of the general way in which the state of the conversation is changed by speech acts, can to a great degree abstract from these factors.[8] We can postulate a basic mental state—call it *presupposition*, or the *conversational state*—to play the desired role in theorizing about linguistic communication. It is this state, in the first instance, that we are coordinating on in conversation. (Thus we can say, for example, that ϕ is *common ground* in a conversation just in case it is common knowledge, or common belief, among the interlocutors that ϕ is being presupposed.) We need not show how to reduce this state of mind to other, more familiar states in advance of theorizing. If it helps us to explain things, it will earn its own keep.[9]

[7] In this paragraph I repeat some points made in Yalcin (2012a).

[8] Kölbel (2011) puts the gist of it well:

the exchange of information is only one among many ultimate purposes that linguistic exchanges can have. When we converse in pursuit of the aim of information exchange, we do so *by* pursuing the language-internal objective of changing the conversational score, an objective that can serve many other aims too. We will gain a better understanding both of conversation and of information exchange if we keep this in mind. (51)

The basic point carries over to dynamic forces which are not (or not merely) information-adding moves.

[9] To be clear, I am not denying in advance of inquiry that the target notion of a conversational state might somehow be reduced to other mental states. What I am rejecting is the presupposition that some such reduction must be carried out in order for theorizing to proceed. One needs to moor the technical notion in a sufficient body of explanatory theory before clear questions of reduction can be framed and profitably pursued.

So again, there is no tension between the illocutionary and dynamic approaches to force. They are not competing analyses of the same phenomena, but are rather concerned with different explananda. Readers who enjoy Austinian taxa should perhaps situate dynamic force as a feature of what he called the "locutionary act", inasmuch as fixing the dynamic force of a speech act still generally leaves it substantially underdetermined what the speaker was up to, or was trying to do, in performing a speech act with that dynamic force.

In separating illocutionary and dynamic notions of force, I am not trying to attack those theorists who hope to theorize about illocutionary force by appeal to a notion of dynamic force—who want to offer a theory of illocutionary forces which appeals partly to an independently understood notion of dynamic force. On the contrary, such theorists should welcome the distinction I press, since in making this separation, I am drawing out a sense in which they can claim to be explaining features of illocutionary acts using independently understood materials.[10]

One kind of theorist in this vein holds that dynamic forces can be used to group illocutionary forces. Stalnaker's abstract treatment of the dynamic effect of assertion, for instance, might be argued to group together what ordinary speakers call "assertion", but also other speech acts like supposing or hypothesizing. I myself am not especially interested in the prospects for constructing a botany of illocutionary acts, so I leave it to others to show that such an approach might yield some explanatory insight.[11] In any case, whether such a theory can be worked out is orthogonal to the point I'm making, which is just that there is an interesting notion of dynamic force which does not reduce to, and is not a species of, illocutionary force.

It could well be that the specific array of dynamic forces we in fact find in natural language is explained, or partly explained, by the fact that we have an interest in using such forces to perform various illocutionary acts. That idea is entirely compatible with everything said so far.

On the view I favor, knowing the dynamic forces associated with the sentences of a language is part of linguistic competence with the language. If we think of language as complex tool that we do things with, I am situating dynamic force as a component of

---

[10] Am I one of these theorists? I see no problem with informal elucidations of familiar sorts of illocutionary acts in part by appeal to their dynamic conversational effects; on the contrary, I employ such elucidations on occasion below, and have done so elsewhere (e.g. Yalcin 2007, Yalcin 2012a). What is less clear to me is whether instructive, theoretically fruitful general analyses of illocutionary acts/forces are possible. It does not appear that the literature licenses great optimism about the prospects for a science of illocutionary acts, where such a theory is understood as taking us beyond a relatively shallow botanization of human speech behaviors, the latter stated mostly in terms of common sense categories. Theories in this vein seem at risk of devolving into conceptual analyses of common sense speech act notions, with concomitant loss of grip on what was supposed to be getting explained. There is, relatedly, a general worry, emphasized by Chomsky (2000), about the (un)fitness of ordinary common sense notions for use in scientific inquiry (especially when what is to be explained is human language and behavior). Common sense notions rarely perform well when pressed into service as theoretical notions; they have their own lives. (I try to expand on this latter worry in Yalcin (forthcoming).)

[11] The question here is whether a speech act's having an illocutionary force of a certain kind implies it has a dynamic force of a certain kind. On the face of it, it seems not: it seems one can know that, for instance, a speech act had the illocutionary force of a command without knowing whether it had the dynamic force characteristic of an imperative, declarative, or interrogative—plausibly one can issue commands in the illocutionary sense via various kinds of context-change potential.

the tool, not as a component of actions of using the tool. Once we start talking about actions of using the tool—once we are talking about interlocutors qua rational agents, using language to achieve various objectives, communicative and otherwise—we are at the speech act level of description.

15.4 Normative language as distinctive in force

Having now separated two very different sorts of thing one could mean by 'assertion', let us consider the idea that normative sentences are not assertion-like. This is an idea that has permeated expressivist approaches to normative discourse since those views began to take shape in the first half of the twentieth century. Some representative early statements of this idea, beginning with W. H. F. Barnes:

Value judgements in their origin are not strictly judgements at all. They are exclamations expressive of approval. This is to be distinguished from the theory that the value judgement, "A is good," states that I approve A. The theory that I am now putting forward maintains that "A is good," is a form of words expressive of my approval. To take an illustration :— When I say "I have a pain," that sentence states the occurrence of a certain feeling in me: when I shout "Oh!" in a certain way that is expressive of the occurrence in me of a certain feeling. We must seek then for the origin of value judgements in the expressions of approval, delight, and affection, which children utter when confronted with certain experiences.   (Barnes 1934, 45)

Carnap:

The rule, "Do not kill," has grammatically the imperative form and will therefore not be regarded as an assertion. But the value statement, "Killing is evil," although, like the rule, it is merely an expression of a certain wish, has the grammatical form of assertive proposition. Most philosophers have been deceived by this form into thinking that a value statement is really an assertive proposition, and must either be true or false. . . . But actually a value statement is nothing else than a command in a misleading grammatical form.   (Carnap 1935, 24)

Russell:

If, now, a philosopher says "Beauty is good," I may interpret him as meaning either "Would that everybody loved the beautiful" . . . or "I wish that everybody loved the beautiful" . . . The first of these makes no assertion, but expresses a wish; since it affirms nothing, it is logically impossible that there should be evidence for or against it, or for it to possess either truth or falsehood. The second sentence, instead of being merely optative, does make a statement, but it is one about the philosopher's state of mind, and it could only be refuted by evidence that he does not have the wish that he says he has. This second sentence does not belong to ethics, but to psychology or biography. The first sentence, which does belong to ethics, expresses a desire for something, but asserts nothing.   (Russell 1935, 236–7)

Ayer:

…in every case in which one would commonly be said to be making an ethical judgment, the function of the ethical word is purely "emotive". It is used to express feeling about certain objects, but not to make any assertion about them.   (Ayer 1936, 108)

Stevenson (1937), building on Ogden and Richards (1923):

Doubtless there is always *some* element of description in ethical judgments, but this is by no means all. Their major use is not to indicate facts, but to *create an influence*.   (18)

When you tell a man that he oughtn't to steal, your object isn't merely to let him know that people disapprove of stealing. You are attempting, rather to get *him* to disapprove of it. Your ethical judgment has a quasi-imperative force . . .   (19)

These views were set against what Austin (1962) and others later framed as the *descriptive fallacy*:

It was for too long the assumption of philosophers that the business of a 'statement' can only be to 'describe' some state of affairs, or to 'state some fact', which it must do either truly or falsely.   (1)

It has come to be seen that many specially perplexing words embedded in apparently descriptive statements do not serve to indicate some specially odd additional feature in the reality reported, but to indicate (not to report) the circumstances in which the statement is made or reservations to which it is subject or the way in which it is to be taken and the like. To overlook these possibilities in the way once common is called the 'descriptive' fallacy . . .   (3)

Considering now the thesis that normative sentences do not have the force of assertions, two questions confront us:

(i) What sense of 'assertoric force' is at issue? Do we mean 'force' in some illocutionary sense? Some dynamic sense? Both?

(ii) What is the nature of the link between the meaning of normative vocabulary and the putatively non-assertoric force of normative sentences?

Since as noted, the dynamic notion of force appeared on the scene only in the seventies, early forays into the prospects for expressivist approaches to normative language worked with conceptions of force in the illocutionary vein. As for the nature of the link between the meaning of normative vocabulary and the putatively non-assertoric force of normative sentences, the details here were often less than completely clear.[12]

15.5 Frege-Geach

However, it was clear what the opponents of these approaches, notably Geach (1965) and Searle (1969), took the view to be saying, or trying to say. They took the idea to be that the connection between the meaning of normative vocabulary and the putatively non-assertoric, non-descriptive force of normative sentences is very tight. The meaning of normative vocabulary was to be explained by appeal to the distinctive sorts of non-assertoric, non-descriptive illocutionary acts they ostensibly participate in. The meanings of 'good' and 'bad', for instance, were to be explicated

---

[12] None of the above cited authors offered anything like a detailed account, for instance. Undoubtedly Hare (1952) was the most detailed mid-century attempt at working out the details.

by appeal to the observations that 'good' is used to perform the speech act of commending, and the word 'bad' is used to perform the speech act of condemning. The semantics of normative terms was somehow to be a matter of associating them with the distinctive speech acts they enable. The usual thought was that these distinctive speech acts corresponded to the expression of distinctive non-doxastic (or not entirely doxastic) states of mind—perhaps desire-like states of mind if Carnap and Russell were on the right track; perhaps something more emotional in character, if Barnes and Ayer were on the right track; perhaps some mix, if Stevenson was on the right track.

The fundamental difficulty with this way of developing the idea, as Geach (1965) and Searle (1969) famously stressed, is that meanings are compositional, whereas illocutionary forces seem not to be. Here we can separate two related points.

First and most obviously, the mere appearance of a particular word in a construction cannot make it the case that a speech act of a particular illocutionary type is being performed with that construction.[13] There are ever so many sentences in which 'good' (etc.) appears wherein there is no plausibility that the corresponding speech act need be a commendation. On the contrary, choose virtually any speech act force you please, and we will be able to produce an example of an illocutionary act with that force which involves tokening a sentence wherein 'good' (etc.) figures. This point is widely appreciated, so I'll skip examples.

The second point emphasizes the degree of disanalogy between meaning and illocutionary force in respect of compositionality. Whatever the meaning of a complex expression is, it had better be by and large fixed by the meanings of its constituent parts plus the syntax of the expression. The assumption of compositionality is part of what is required for natural language semantics to play its part in explaining the productive character of language understanding and use.[14] The illocutionary force associated with the utterance of a sentence, on the other hand, is not helpfully understood as something somehow fixed by the forces putatively associated with the individual primitive parts of the sentence and their combination. Generally speaking, it rarely if ever even makes sense to speak of the illocutionary force of subsentential constituents of a sentence uttered. The locus of illocutionary force is the whole utterance-in-context qua intentional act. What force an utterance has may certainly be constrained in interesting ways by the meaning of the sentence uttered, but the illocutionary force of a whole utterance is not somehow built up out of out the putative forces of the sub-utterances of the constituent words.[15]

The classic Frege-Geach critique encourages a certain understanding of what the expressivist thesis is, or was supposed to be. It suggests that expressivism is a view that

---

[13] There may be some limited exceptions. Perhaps one performs a speech act of derogation in virtue of using a slur, no matter how deeply embedded it appears.

[14] I offer a more detailed discussion of this point in Yalcin (2014).

[15] Sometimes even anti-expressivist theorists, e.g. Geach (1965), slip into a way of talking that suggests that subsentential clauses of sentences may have illocutionary forces. But theorists who slip into this kind of talk rarely defend it or render it conceptually clear. Sometimes what theorists have in mind by this kind of thing is clearly something more easily rendered via the idea of dynamic force, about which more shortly. (Geach's slips are mostly in connection with facts that would be described from a modern perspective as facts about presupposition projection—a famous impetus for the development of the notion of dynamic force.)

is supposed to take on the challenge of delivering a theory which derives the forces of utterances compositionally—a theory which teaches how the meaning of normative expressions can be given by explicating their connections to distinctive illocutionary forces, in such a way as to respect the compositionality of meaning. We could call this kind of approach to developing expressivism *compositional force expressivism*.

Compositional force expressivism has a close cousin. According to it, expressivism is the view that is supposed to take on the challenge of delivering a theory which associates, not forces, but attitudes—various mental state types—with sentences compositionally. We could call this version *compositional attitude expressivism*. The meaning of (e.g.) 'good' is not given by directly associating it with speech acts of commendation; rather, it is associated with some kind of 'pro-attitude', or state of preference, or something along those lines. Calling *x* good still amounts to performing a distinctive speech act of commendation; but what makes the speech act a commendation is in part that the meaning of 'good' is somehow, as a matter of its meaning, tied to the attitude of favoring *x*. This is roughly the sort of way that expressivism has been understood by many in more recent times. Thus for example Rosen (1998), discussing Blackburn (1993):

The centerpiece of any quasi-realist (expressivist) 'account' is what I shall call a psychologistic semantics for the region: a mapping from statements in the area to the mental states they 'express' when uttered sincerely. The procedure is broadly recursive. Begin with an account of the *basic states*: the attitudes expressed by the simplest statements involving the region's characteristic vocabulary. Then assign operations on attitudes to the various constructions for generating complex statements in such a way as to determine an 'expressive role' for each of the infinitely many statements in the area.   (387–8)

Similar characterizations of expressivism can be found in Blackburn (1998), Wedgwood (2007), Schroeder (2008c), Gibbard (2003), and Charlow (2015).

On the face of it, the prospects for working out compositional attitude expressivism are as bleak as the prospects for working out compositional force expressivism. From the point of view of the skeptic versed in modern natural language semantics and pragmatics, they both seem based on the same kind of category mistake, mislocating the locus of compositionality.

I leave it to others to sort out whether some version of compositional force expressivism or compositional attitude expressivism could be rendered viable. It seems to me that there is a more promising path for developing the kind of expressivist themes sounded by the authors cited above. It is basically the sort of path I have explored elsewhere in connection, not with normative talk, but with epistemically modal talk (Yalcin 2007, 2011, 2012a). This path does not involve any radical reconception of the notion of illocutionary force. Nor does it involve any attempt at a compositional mapping from sentences to mental states. Nor does it require a total rethinking of the foundations of semantics. But to get to this kind of view, we need to say some things about how best to conceive of the relations between compositional semantic value, content, and dynamic force.[16]

---

[16] I regret I lack the space in this paper to chart the ways that my take on the Frege-Geach problem differs from others in the literature. The recent literature is especially influenced by the framing of Unwin

15.6 The locus of compositionality

The locus of compositionality is not force, and neither is it attitude—so in a nutshell goes the Frege-Geach critique of textbook expressivist views. But Frege and Geach themselves could be critiqued for mislocating the locus of compositionality. Specifically, they could be chided for failing to observe the distinction between content and compositional semantic value, and for misconstruing the relationship between content and the demands of compositionality.

The semantic value–content distinction is stressed in various ways in Dummett (1973, 1993), Lewis (1980), and Stanley (1997a,b), and more recently in Yalcin (2007, 2012a, 2014), Ninan (2010), Rabern (2012a,b, 2013), and Yli-Vakkuri (2013).[17] These works differ in where they place the stress, and in the terminology used (in Dummett, the distinction appears as that between 'ingredient sense' and 'assertoric content'). My preferred take appears in Yalcin (2014) (it owes significantly to Lewis (1980), Rabern (2012b), and to conversations with Ninan). Without rehearsing the full story told there, the basic thought is that the requirements on a notion of content suitable for modeling the mental states we traditionally call 'propositional attitudes' are importantly different from the demands appropriate to the notion of linguistic meaning (semantic value), and in such a way that we shouldn't expect the realizers of the content role to line up in some particularly straightforward way with the realizers of the semantic value role. In particular, there is little reason to theorize under the assumption that the semantic values of sentences (in context) are identical with the objects we find useful to call, in the theory of mental content, 'contents' ('propositions', 'propositional content', etc.).

This isn't to say that we don't or can't assert propositions in something like the traditional sense using ordinary declarative sentences. One can of course still have that view compatible with respecting the distinction between semantic value and content. It's just that in such cases, it sows less confusion to see the matter like this: the compositional semantic value of the sentence *determines*, as a function of context, the item of content asserted (cf. Lewis 1980). That is all that is necessary to uphold the idea that we can assert propositions using declarative sentences—viz., that there be some bridge principle, understood as a feature of the pragmatics or 'post-semantics' of the language, connecting the target class of sentences to propositional contents via the semantic values and relevant features of context. Thus the suggestion isn't that semantic value and content are wholly disconnected. On the contrary, most will naturally want to take the theory of mental content and the theory of linguistic meaning to have deep and important interconnections. The point is merely that we should distinguish these theoretical concepts and their associated explananda.

Semantic values are the locus of compositionality in natural language. It is hardly a contestable thesis that they are compositional, since it is their job to do their part in explaining the productive character of language understanding and use, and this job

(2001): see in particular Gibbard (2003), Dreier (2006), Schroeder (2008a,b,c). See also Charlow (2014), Ridge (2014), Woods (2017).

[17] Burge (1979) argues that theorists have exaggerated the extent to which Frege pressed senses into work as linguistic meanings. In a sense, Burge could be read as arguing that Frege was alive to what I am here calling the semantic value–content distinction. This isn't the place to pursue the exegetical question, but I discuss the issue briefly in Yalcin (2015, 242).

appears undoable without compositionality. Content, on the other hand, may not be compositional in anything like that sense. The assignment of contents to mental states may be a more global, holistic matter—so in fact go the kind of pictures of mental content advanced by theorists like Stalnaker (1984), Dretske (1988), and Lewis (1994), for instance. (Even the theory of content implicit in Kaplan (1977/1989) is (despite intentions) noncompositional, as Rabern (2013) shows.) What view one prefers here depends on what one expects the notion of mental content to do—what explanatory work it is supposed to perform—and it seems rarely the case that theorists are working with just the same conception of that work. In any case, the claim is not that it is necessary to sign up for one of these particular views of content to proceed. It is enough to see that we can still intelligibly debate the question whether content is compositional in some sense, even after having agreed that linguistic meaning is compositional.

When we separate the notion of content and of semantic value, we clear conceptual space for the possibility that:

> The semantic values of declarative sentences are of a uniform type in a manner conducive to compositionality, even though the communicative role of some declarative sentences is such as not to determine truth-conditional propositional content of some traditional sort.

That is, we make room for the possibility that the role of some sentences—stereotypically 'descriptive' sentences—in communication may be to express ordinary, world-characterizing truth-conditional propositional contents as a function of their semantic values, along traditional lines, whereas the communicative role of other declarative sentences—normative sentences, perhaps—may not be.

And that idea in turn can be sharpened via the notion of dynamic force. Even if the semantic values of declarative sentences take a uniform shape, there may yet be semantically notable subtypes of declarative sentences, subtypes that correspond to distinctive dynamic forces. A coherent possibility is that sentences we intuitively describe as having normative import, while being of the same semantic type as non-normative sentences, nevertheless form a semantically natural and distinctive class; and moreover that this class is associated with a distinctive kind of conversational update in a way that vindicates the intuitive thought that normative sentences are different in some communicatively important way from straight factual assertion.

15.7 Static and dynamic expressivist paths

What does it mean to say that declarative sentences could be of a 'uniform semantic type' despite also dividing into 'semantically distinctive classes' in such a way as to allow them to correspond to distinctive dynamic forces? This can be—indeed, has been—made precise in a variety of ways. Let me mention two possible paths, without presuming there aren't others. My objective here is not to lay out very detailed semantic-pragmatic proposals about specific expressions; rather it is to clarify two shapes that detailed proposals could take.[18]

---

[18] The basic contours of the picture I present here appear in Yalcin (2007, 2011, 2012c). I discuss normative language in particular in Yalcin (2012a,b).

The first trail was in essence blazed by Gibbard (1986, 1990, 2003), though notably he did not employ the notion of dynamic force I am recommending. Let me describe a version of the idea. Assume a textbook intensional semantics of the usual sort—say, in the style of the appendix of Kaplan (1977/1989). But in addition to parameters for context, possible world, and variable assignment, take it that semantic values are relativized also to 'systems of norms' in the style of Gibbard (1990). (Or better, to 'hyperplans' in the style of Gibbard (2003), and about which more later.) Thus formally speaking, all expressions have as their semantic values functions from this kind of tuple of parameters to extensions. The semantic values of declarative sentences in particular are functions from such tuples to truth-values. In this sense, declarative sentences are of uniform semantic type.

Nevertheless, we can isolate the subclass of sentences whose truth-values are sensitive to the value of the hyperplan parameter. The modeling idea is that the normative sentences will correspond to this class. We can isolate this class just as we can, e.g., semantically isolate the class of open sentences in first-order logic. The situation is analogous. Semantically speaking, the open sentences are (to an adequate first approximation) the ones whose truth-values are sensitive to the variable assignment; the closed sentences are the ones whose truth-values do not vary with the choice of variable assignment.[19] The analogy here is worth underlining. There is no Frege-Geach problem about open sentences—no problem about how it could be that the open and closed sentences of first-order logic, despite their very real semantic differences, can nevertheless intelligibly appear in the same places in a compositional way. So it is, too, with norm-sensitive sentences on Gibbard's approach. The fact that these sentences are sensitive to value of the norm parameter makes this class 'semantically distinctive' in the relevant sense.

Once we acknowledge this semantically distinctive subclass of declarative sentences, we are free to hypothesize that the sentences of this class may have a distinctive dynamic role in conversation—that their dynamic force is not, say, simply to add truth-conditional information to the conversational state along textbook Stalnakerian lines. Their role may be to change a different aspect of the conversational score, or anyway, to change *more than* just the 'world-describing' component of the conversational state. To use Gibbard's way of talking, normative sentences—or anyway, those of a paradigm sort—would serve to update conversational states in respect, not (or not only) of how things are, but also in respect of what is to be done. That is a way of getting at the expressivist idea, voiced in the quotes above, that normative talk is different from ordinary 'descriptive' assertion. To spell out this thought in detail, we would want to postulate the relevant component of the conversational state tracking "to be doneness"—perhaps Portnerian To-Do Lists are what is needed; perhaps the plans of Lewis (1979b); perhaps the hyperplans of Gibbard (2003) (explored in Yalcin (2012a); see also Pérez-Carballo and Santorio (2016)); perhaps all of the above; perhaps something else—and articulate how sentences of the target class serve to change that feature of conversational states.

---

[19] 'First approximation' because an open sentence like $(Fx \lor \neg Fx)$ may nevertheless be technically insensitive to the value of the assignment function. A more sophisticated definition of 'sensitive to (assignments, norms, etc.)' could be given, but the exercise isn't necessary here.

To an account like this we could add, further, that the relevant kind of conversational state change is often exploited to perform illocutionary acts we could call something like "expressing norms", acts that correspond to the expression of states of mind that are not "prosaically factual". (Just as we could say that the sort of conversational state change Stalnaker described is often exploited to perform illocutionary acts we could call "expressing beliefs" or "expressing knowledge".) Altogether, this path would seem to lead a coherent package of views about normative discourse, a package that could reasonably be called 'expressivist'.

This obviously is not yet to establish that this kind of path is the right one to take for some particular subfragment of English; that is an empirical matter that needs to be fought out in the usual way. It is just to clarify a coherent possible form a semantics-pragmatics for some language could take, a form that is recognizably expressivist in spirit.

Call this kind of expressivist plan 'static', as the details of implementation involve the assumption of a static intensional semantics. A second, alternative implementation would use the resources of dynamic semantics. The meaning of a sentence on the dynamic semantic approach is given by the way it is apt to change the state of the conversation. Formally, the compositional semantic values of all sentences take the form of functions from conversational states into conversational states—context change potentials. The semantic values of declarative sentences on this approach would again be of uniform semantic type in the sense relevant to compositionality. Still, we could isolate interestingly different subclasses of sentences, grouping sentences into characteristically similar context change potentials. Again the basic thought would be that normative sentences invoke a characteristic sort of change to a component of the conversational state, one not merely adding more information to the state about what the world is like. That they induce this kind of change would be something reflected, on the dynamic approach, directly in the semantic values of sentences. And again, the thought would be that the relevant kind of conversational state change is often exploited to perform illocutionary acts we could call something like "expressing norms".[20]

(The main difference between the static and dynamic approach is that on the static approach, we need some 'bridge principle' mapping the normative sentences to their context change potentials, whereas no such principle is needed on the dynamic approach (as it equips sentences with context change potentials directly in the compositional semantics). For example, if we accept Gibbard's idea that normative sentences are semantically the sort that determine a nontrivial condition on (centered) world-hyperplan pairs, then we'd want a rule, akin to Stalnaker's assertion rule, telling us how this condition is supposed to serve to change the state of the conversation—a rule that maps the output of the semantics to a context change potential. The simplest version of such a rule would perhaps postulate that the conversational state just is represented by a set of (centered) world-hyperplan pairs, and that update is just intersection.

[20] See Charlow (2015), Starr (2016), Willer (2016, 2017) for developments of expressivist ideas about normative language using tools from dynamic semantics. Veltman's work on the dynamic evolution of expectation patterns in discourse, in connection with words like 'normally', is one important relevant precedent (Veltman 1996).

On that simple kind of picture, normative sentences will be conversationally distinctive, because they will serve to eliminate (centered) world-hyperplan pairs in part as a function of the hyperplan-component.)

Expressivism is often thought of as a special kind of semantic theory. The version of expressivism I am now suggesting is not well-described that way. I am suggesting that on the most plausible development, expressivism is not a kind of semantic theory as model-theoretic truth-conditional semantics is a kind of semantic theory, or as (say) Heim (1982)'s dynamic semantics is a kind of semantic theory. Expressivism is not an alternative to these frameworks; on the contrary, an expressivist view can be developed entirely within the context of such frameworks. The misconception that expressivism must be seen as a special kind of semantic theory stems in part from the tendency to conflate semantic value with content, together with the idea that items of content each determine a 'factualist' truth-condition, understood as fixing a 'way the world might be'. Expressivism will seem radical if one thinks orthodoxy in semantics requires making these assumptions. But to think that is to misunderstand truth-conditional semantics in the familiar model-theoretic style.

Since the basic expressivist idea can be realized in the context of quite different compositional semantic theories, it is not itself well-characterized as a thesis about the shape of a compositional semantic theory. In general, one cannot necessarily read an expressivist view directly off a compositional semantic theory. Better to think of expressivism as a view in pragmatics, or at the semantics-pragmatic interface. It is a kind of view that may be seen as imposing some high-level constraints on semantics. Expressivism about a fragment of language comes in (or doesn't) when we take a certain stand on the relation between the compositional semantic values of the fragment and their dynamic force, and in the relation between dynamic force and the sorts of states of mind they are apt to express in various contexts.

15.8 Normative states of mind in an expressivist setting

To make some of the preceding slightly more concrete, let me walk through one conception of the underlying normative states of mind that normative language is, according to the expressivist, in the business of expressing. The story is substantially inspired by Gibbard (2003), though certain aspects will depart from Gibbard's preferred development.

The story begins with a model of normative states of mind. Formally speaking, Gibbard's way of modeling attitudes begins with the abstract, idealized model of attitudes given by Lewis (1979c), in which a state of belief is represented as a set of centered worlds, intuitively the centered worlds compatible with the way the agent takes herself to be situated in the world. Gibbard adopts this much structure to model what it is to have a factual view, a view about how the world is (and about where one is within it). He then adds further structure to model what it is to have normative view, which he takes fundamentally to be a view concerning what to do. To have a view about what to do is to have a plan. To model normative, plan-like states of mind, Gibbard introduces a technical notion, the *hyperplan*. As a single centered world might be used to characterize a state of mind completely opinionated concerning every matter of fact, so a hyperplan can be used to characterize a state of mind completely opinionated about what is okay to do in any situation. Thus a hyperplan is a maximal contingency plan:

> [it] covers any occasion for choice one might conceivably be in, and for each alternative open on such an occasion, to adopt the plan involves either rejecting the alternative or rejecting rejecting it. In other worlds, the plan either forbids an alternative or permits it.
>
> (Gibbard 2003, 56)

A hyperplan can thus be construed as a mapping from a set of available options to some subset of those options—the options deemed by the hyperplan as permissible.[21]

Equipped with this notion of a hyperplan, Gibbard modifies Lewis's model of belief states. Instead of modeling them as sets of centered worlds, he proposes we model them as sets of centered world-hyperplan pairs. We can say these are models of *plan-laden* states of belief, states of mind that intertwine a view about how things are with a view about what is to be done. One's view about purely descriptive, worldly matters of fact is settled by the centered worlds that one's plan-laden belief state leaves open. But one's normative views—for instance, one's views about what ought to be the case— depend at least in part on the hyperplans that one's plan-laden belief state leaves open. Just as what one believes in the prosaically factual sense is reflected in what is true at every centered world compatible with what one believes, so what one believes about what to do is reflected in what is common to every hyperplan left open by one's state of belief. If I plan to pack, for instance, then every hyperplan left open by my state of belief calls for packing relative to the options I take myself to have.[22]

To believe I ought to pack more or less just is, for Gibbard, to plan to pack. The story is aimed *inter alia* at clarifying the tie between normative thought and motivation, at removing the mystery of why the belief that I ought to pack motivates packing.

Planning states are understood broadly: one can have plans, both about what one is to do in the situation one takes oneself to be in, and also plans about what to do in situations that one does not take oneself to be in. Even if one recognizes that one is not Obama, one can have a view about what to do if faced with Obama's options. This view is a planning attitude in the relevant sense.[23]

---

[21] Schroeder (2008a) writes that Gibbard "assumes that hyperplanners are always decided either to do A or to not do A, for any action A" (53). Not so: a hyperplan (and thus any hyperplanner whose state is modeled by the hyperplan) may deem both A and ¬ A permissible.

[22] Note that the options one takes oneself to have are fixed by what one believes in the prosaically factual sense. In this way, one's view about what ought to be the case is sensitive to what one takes the facts to be.

[23] More carefully: the relevant sense of 'plan' and 'planning' here is quasi-technical. To plan in the target sense is to have a take on what is permissible to do in some class of situations. We are understanding "thinking what to do" in the sense of "thinking what is to be done" or "thinking what should be done". One might have a plan in this sense for a situation (a take on what is permissible in it) and yet still be undecided about what one will in fact do in that situation. Resolving that latter form of indecision is something we could call (following Gibbard 2006) forming a *strategy*. I am inclined to agree with Scanlon (2006), that the connection between planning and normative judgment shouldn't be overstated (and needn't be for the expressivist's purposes). Specifically, there isn't a need to reduce normative thinking to planning if we are going expressivist. There is just a need to model normative thinking as something other than prosaically factual belief, and to be able to specify the characteristic functional role of this sort of state in non-normative terms.

We could describe Gibbard as offering a model of the contents of belief states, a model aimed at capturing what is distinctive about normative thought. As we have stressed in earlier pages, a model of content still leaves much open from the point of view of compositional semantics. There are many ways one might try to bring these abstract ideas to bear on the semantics and pragmatics of normative language. But I first want to consider some questions about Gibbard's model of content of a more foundational nature.

Some theorists may have the feeling that the appeal to hyperplans in modeling normative states of mind engenders only an illusion of explanation or understanding. 'Hyperplan' may seem to be a name for a mystery, or a merely formal widget that distracts from the real philosophy. One aspect of the concern may trace to the postulation of a new primitive element. Most theorists who use (centered) possible worlds to model belief content would have them in their ontology anyway—the concept of a possible world is very plausibly intelligible independently from their particular use in modeling content. (Indeed, many theorists, notably Stalnaker (1984) and Lewis (1986, 1994), hope to explain the intentionality of the mental in part by relying on a non-intentional conception of modality.) Hyperplans, on the other hand, seem to arrive on the scene as a new primitive without independent motivation; and it can seem we have no independent grip on what they are that is analogous to the independent grip we have on the notion of a possible world. Gibbard eases us into the notion by an appeal to the idea of a completely decided agent—a hyperplanner. But if hyperplans are explained entirely in terms of normative states of mind—if all that can be said by way of clarifying the notion of a hyperplan is that it approximates the state of mind of a completely decided agent—then we seem to be modeling normative states of mind and their interrelations with the help of...a primitive notion of normative states of mind. This circle is rather tight. It can be hard to see any path here for understanding normative states of mind and their properties as explicable in other terms, as grounded in more basic facts.

Confronted with this kind of request to say more about the idea of plan-laden belief, I am inclined to react as follows. There are two parts to the response.

The first part of the response stresses that we needn't take hyperplans as primitive elements of the model. These objects can be constructed from antecedently available resources (as Gibbard himself observes (2003, 100)): sets and possibilia. We said that a hyperplan is basically a mapping from options to a subset of those options. Let's now take this literally: hyperplans are functions on sets of options. The question then arises what options are. We can model an option as a centered worlds proposition (a set of centered worlds)—the conditions under which the option can be said to be realized. Thus a hyperplan is a function from a set of centered worlds propositions (understood as a set of available options for some possible agent) to some subset thereof. So we can construct hyperplans from independent resources, resources we have a grip on independently of their application in modeling normative states of mind.[24] This does something to demystify hyperplans.[25]

---

[24] Even simpler, we could take a hyperplan to be a function from the union of the set of options to a union of some subset of those options. (So I suggested in Yalcin 2012a.) But this leaner description may be inadequate for cases where a plan-laden state seems somehow sensitive to the way the options are distinguished.

[25] Let me add another point of clarification. I am taking it (following Gibbard) that the plans that one's state leaves open will generally interact with/be sensitive to what worlds one's belief state leaves open

The second part of the response concerns the issue of how philosophically to gloss the formal model. It begins by framing the question:

> In virtue of what is an agent's state of belief well-modeled by a given set of centered world-hyperplan pairs?

This we could call the foundational question about plan-laden content. Any formal model of attitude states faces a foundational question of this sort. It asks what it is about a situated agent that makes it the case that their state of mind is representable by some formal object in the model rather than some other formal object. It may be that some of the concern about the extent to which Gibbard's approach to normative states of mind is adequately explanatory stems from unclarity about what the shape of the answer to this question is supposed to be. If one has no grip at all on what it could be about an agent that makes it the case that their state of mind has one body of plan-laden content rather than another, the account is apt to seem mysterious.

Theorists who agree about the shape of a formal model of the attitudes may nevertheless disagree about the answer to the corresponding foundational question. So we can expect there to be various responses that expressivists who enjoy Gibbardian modeling tools might have. But to sketch one direction in order to give a sense of things, it is natural to consider the corresponding foundational question as it arises for Lewis (1979c), especially since as noted, Gibbard's formal model is an extension of Lewis's.

Again, Lewis (1979c) models a state of belief as a set of centered worlds. We intuitively describe this as the set of centered worlds compatible with where, for all the agent believes, she is. Lewis also puts it like this: to believe that P is to *self-ascribe* the property corresponding to the set of worlds P. But of course, these intuitive descriptions are not meant to supply deep explanations: they just show how the formal talk is meant to connect with informal belief talk. If, given an agent A in w modeled with centered worlds belief content P, we ask:

(alternatively, sensitive to how one apportions credence across logical space), and suggesting that it is easier to understand the way they interact if hyperplans are not taken as primitive but built out of (formalized with) possibilia. But I am thinking of the plan structure of an agent's state as additional structure—structure that we can, as theorists, usefully separate out from the set of worlds (or probability space) that corresponds to the agent's doxastic state. So from the point of view of the modeling theory, we are separating the planning structure from the doxastic structure—much as, e.g., the decision theorist wants to separate out a state corresponding to belief and another state corresponding to preference.

Now this might seem confusing when it comes to approaching the semantics of natural language, because I want to allow that certain belief ascriptions (e.g. 'John thinks he ought to pay his taxes') might sometimes place conditions on the plans the subject's state leaves open (in addition to the worlds their doxastic state leaves open). So there is not a straight line from what the theorist calls a "doxastic state", which is to do only with modeling what the world is like according to the agent, and object-language belief ascription, which can mix ascription of factual and plan-like content. But there is no problem here. You might compare this to the semantics of 'wants'. As theorists, we find it fruitful to model preference as some sort of ordering over possible states of the world. But when it comes to the semantics of 'wants', it may turn out that 'wants'-ascriptions also place conditions on the subject's state of belief (as e.g. Heim (1992) suggests, drawing *inter alia* on Stalnaker (1984)). So ordinary talk of what an agent wants admixes features of what they prefer and what they believe. Still, again as theorists, there's a sense in which the agent's preference ordering alone gets at a natural psychological joint, and models the agent's desires in a pure but abstract sense.

As for whether to call the additional planning structure 'cognitive', the answer is 'no' if by 'cognitive' we just mean *doxastic*. But if 'cognitive' means something like *intentional mental state*, then certainly planning states are cognitive (as are states of preference). (Thanks to Mahrad Almotahari for discussion.)

What is it about A in w that makes it the case that P is the content of A's belief state in w?

Lewis has an answer. The basic contours of his answer are given in Lewis (1984, 1986, 1994). Not really needing a full review (and lacking space for it anyway), I stick to a crude highlight reel. Like many theorists, Lewis takes it that the contents of mental states are supposed to be (at least) causal-explanatory properties of those states. Particular hypotheses about the belief and desire contents of an agent generate *ceteris paribus* predictions about how the agent will be disposed to act in various circumstances. Belief and desire states are, Lewis thinks, constitutively rational. These states are the occupants of certain functional roles, and it is just part of the functional roles associated with belief and desire that beliefs and desires tend to cause behavior that serves the subject's desires according to her beliefs. Roughly, belief, desire, and action are constitutively related at least as follows:

> If agent A is in a belief state with the centered content B and in a desire state with centered content D, then A is disposed to act in ways that would tend to bring it about that he is located within D, were it the case that he occupied a centered world within B.

Belief and desire are causally efficacious inner states whose content is constitutively rational in (at least) this way. Roughly, the full belief-desire state of an agent is the one most apt to produce the agent's dispositions to act compatible with the above, and which otherwise maximizes the extent to which the agent's belief content is *eligible*— that is, sensitive to reality's objective structure.[26]

That is Lewis's approach to grounding facts about contentful states of mind. This story is responsive to the foundational question raised by the centered worlds modeling framework. It does much to clarify the subject matter of that model—the phenomena being modeled by it. In a certain sense, it offers a way of interpreting the model.

I don't have the aim of arguing that Lewis's particular foundational picture is correct. Rather, what I want to suggest is that the sort of expressivism I have described can approach the foundational question framed above along the same pattern. If we can see this expressivist and the Lewisian as basically on par—as facing similar foundational questions, and as having similar styles of answers at their disposal—that will suggest that no qualitatively different foundational or 'metasemantic' challenges are faced by the expressivist *per se*; and it will help to further demystify the role of hyperplans in the expressivist's model.

So how can the expressivist who models with Gibbard's tools approach the foundational question framed above in the same basic way as the Lewisian? She can do this by articulating the constitutive functional interconnections between belief (or credence), desire (or preference), and her postulated planning states. Moving beyond

---

[26] The appeal to eligibility is motivated by the fact that without it, many intuitively incorrect assignments of belief-desire content would nevertheless preserve constitutive rationality and make the correct predictions about action. The basic contours of that worry go back to Putnam (1980). See Stalnaker (1984) for a different approach. See also Stalnaker (2004) for a critique of Lewis's particular way of appealing to eligibility.

the familiar belief-desire framework assumed by Lewis, she can suppose that rational action centrally involves also states of planning. We can expect the detailed functional interconnections between these three states to be elaborate, but it seems safe to hypothesize that the functional interconnections will include at least something like the following. Agents are disposed to act in ways which would conform with their plans, in centered worlds with respect to which their (purely factual) belief content is true. Where such plans leave several options open, agents tend to elect those options which would serve best to satisfy their preferences. And where agents find themselves in unplanned-for situations, we appeal only to belief and desire. That is, we say that such agents will be disposed to act in ways that would tend to satisfy their desires, in centered worlds where their beliefs are true—leaving intention out of it.

Of course, that's brief—we should try to say more. But then, so should the Lewisian. The point is that Gibbard's kind of model of content need not, if explained in this way, be regarded as more mysterious than the sort of (unmysterious) accounts favored by theorists in the possible worlds tradition upon which he is building, such as those of Lewis (1994) or Stalnaker (1984). Moreover, as I read it, it seems to me much of Gibbard (2003)—not to mention important earlier work by Bratman (1987)— is anyway concerned to draw out and explore the rich functional interconnections between belief, desire, and planning—so that this is hardly work left entirely undone.

Gibbard himself embraces a very different way of philosophically glossing his own model. Theorists in the orthodox tradition of possible worlds modeling, like Lewis or Stalnaker, would say that to believe that grass is green is to be in a state which rules out possible worlds wherein grass is not green, and they would hold that these possible worlds that the state rules in or out are explicable independently of intentional mental states. Gibbard, however, prefers to explain the "possibilities" that mental states rule out *as themselves mental states*. (He has this view quite apart from his proposal to model in terms of hyperplans—this is how he would want to think about an ordinary, hyperplan-free possible worlds model of belief.) Gibbard will agree that to think grass is green is to "rule out a possibility", but fundamentally he will explain this state as the state of ruling out another mental state, the state of rejecting grass is green—the mental state of *rejecting that grass is green* is the "possibility" ruled out. Similarly, he would describe the state of believing that grass is not green as "disagreeing with believing" that grass is green—as rejecting believing grass is green. The centered worlds of the model are interpreted by Gibbard as maximally opinionated states of (factual) belief—they are not, as Lewis or Stalnaker would have it, maximally specific ways things might have been, understanding the relevant modality as fundamentally non-mental. Likewise, he glosses the hyperplans of his model as maximal states of decision.

This is apt to look like a pretty tight circle: it is a model of mental states whose basic resources for modeling mental states include…mental states. Out is the idea of characterizing propositional attitudes as relations to contents, if the latter are understood in the traditional way as some sort of mind-independent abstracta—sets of possibilities, for instance, as Lewis and Stalnaker would have it. We don't arrive on this picture at a conception of mental content giving us a handle on it in other terms. This seems to leave it mysterious, for instance, what makes it the case, when it is the case, that one content is incompatible with another. For example: the state *believing grass is green* and the state *believing grass isn't green* "disagree" with each other; they are in logical tension. In virtue of what?—Not, says Gibbard, in virtue of their having incompatible contents, if content elucidated in orthodox fashion, via a non-intentional notion of possibility. What, then? Gibbard says he has no further explanation of such disagreement facts; he takes them as primitive.

Gibbard argues that this is not a disadvantage, however:

> Proceeding this way might seem to be philosophical theft. The scheme amounts just to helping ourselves to the notion of disagreeing with a piece of content, be it a plan or a belief. A negation, we say, is what one accepts when one disagrees—and this explains negation. Now I wish, of course, that I could offer a deeper explanation of disagreement and negation. Expressivists like me, though, are not alone in such a plight. Orthodoxy starts with substantial, unexplained truth, eschewing any minimalist explanation of truth. I start with agreeing and disagreeing with pieces of content, some of which are plans. It's a thieving world, and I'm no worse than the others.
>
> (Gibbard 2003, 74)

Here I want to depart seriously from Gibbard. It seems to me a mistake to suggest that orthodoxy starts with "substantial unexplained truth", if that is meant to imply that it involves brute appeals to intentional relations between mental states and their contents, with no sense of a pathway for reduction or further clarification. We can model states of belief as having plan-laden content. Items of plan-laden content stand in various familiar logical relations. Inconsistency between states of mind traces to their inconsistent content. States have content in virtue of their functional interconnections to each other and in virtue of subsidiary requirements on prosaically factual belief (such as that its content be suitably eligible along the lines of Lewis, as sketched above; or that it be a state that normally carries information, as suggested by, e.g. Dretske (1981), Stalnaker (1984); or perhaps some two-dimensional admixture of these; or perhaps something else—debates continue). There is an array of choice-points about the details, familiar from much of the philosophical work on intentionality in the 1980s and early 90s, but it is hard to deny that there are well-trodden paths of analysis in this vein. Expressivists like Gibbard—the ones who embrace, not just his abstract formal model of normative states, but also his distinctive metatheoretic gloss on the model—are, I think, relevantly alone in their plight, and are at an explanatory disadvantage compared to orthodox rivals, like the account of this paper.

Gibbard seems to suggest in places that the expressivism of his account chiefly resides in his preferred metatheoretical gloss on the model—so that to reject that gloss just is to reject expressivism. He seems to be identifying expressivism with something like what I earlier called 'compositional attitude expressivism', giving a version of it wedded to deflationary views about truth and meaning. But I think this is the wrong way of styling expressivism. Expressivists do "explain in terms of mental states", but we need not take this in the direction of Gibbard's style of metatheory.

What is distinctive of expressivism, I suggest, is the way it exploits the strategy of psychological ascent. To go expressivist about ϕ, you first reject the question, "What is the world like when ϕ is the case?" You replace it with the question, "What is the state of mind of accepting ϕ like?" You answer this question in such a way that the state of mind is understood as not tantamount to ordinary factual belief that something is the case. You then approach the target discourse from this perspective: you seek a way to elucidate the semantics and pragmatics of ϕ consistent with the idea that accepting ϕ is being in this not-fully-factual state of mind.

The story I have advanced so far is expressivist in this sense. Normative thought is styled as not fully factual in character. To believe that one ought to pack is not to be belief-related to some possible worlds truth-condition, to a way things might have been. It isn't merely to represent the world, or one's position in the world, as being a certain way rather than other. It is to have a view about what is to be done, in the sense formalized and functionally explicated above. What still remains is to connect this model of normative states of mind to language—to matters of meaning and communication. But on natural ways of forging those connections, it is not hard to see how to end up with a view vindicating the traditional expressivist thought that normative talk is not purely factual in character.

15.9 Normative language in an expressivist setting

In a big picture way, we have already said how that story can go. Let me restate. To have a model of the state of the conversation that can comport nicely with the plan-laden conception of belief, we can make conversational states themselves plan-laden. We can, for example, model conversational states as sets of centered world-hyperplan pairs.[27] We then hold that normative talk is in the business of eliminating such pairs—or more broadly, of changing the state—in ways that are sensitive to the plan component. This characteristic difference in the way that normative sentences would be apt to change the state of the conversation is a difference in dynamic force.

Where does talk of "expressing a normative state of mind" come in? Here again it pays to be mindful of the distinction between illocutionary and dynamic force. In changing the conversational state in respect of the plans it leaves open, one is often expressing one's normative beliefs—the latter understood expressivistically as above. When we change the conversational state in this kind of way, is it *always* to express the normative view one in fact endorses? No—no more than ordinary factual conversational update is always a matter of expressing one's true state of belief. We stressed earlier that the dynamic notion of force prescinds largely from one's distal objectives in communication. Often we do change the state of the conversation in something like the way Stalnaker taught, and often (not always) we do that with the mutually understood aim of transferring belief, knowledge, a view about how the world really is, and the like. When those subsidiary elements are in place—aspects that come into focus when we approach the performance as an illocutionary act, locating it in a particular kind of space of human interests and objectives—we might then sensibly identify the speech act move made as an "expression of belief". We need the same kind of subtlety when it comes to talk of "expressing one's normative view" on an expressivist approach.

---

[27] Or, as I prefer, a pair of a set of centered worlds and a set of hyperplans; see Yalcin (2012a). Some orthogonal subtleties arise here in connection with using centered worlds in a model of the conversational state; see, e.g., Egan (2007), Stalnaker (2008). It may be preferable to generalize, using multi-centered worlds in place of centered worlds. For further discussion of that approach, see Stalnaker (2008, 2014), Ninan (2012).

It could be right to say that "expressing one's normative view" is what is happening in most ordinary cases we'll want to model dynamically in terms of elimination of hyperplans. When it is one's normative state that is prompting one's utterance, when the condition on hyperplans determined by the speech act accords with the speaker's actual normative state, and when it is mutually recognized that the speaker is attempting to engender coordination in respect of normative states, then it will seem natural to call what is happening "expressing one's normative view". When all these background factors (and perhaps more) are in place, the expressivist might want to further claim that normative sentences so deployed characteristically involve a distinctive illocutionary force—"norm expression", say. I myself am not sure what value it would add to make this kind of declaration, since I am not sure there is much of an interesting general theory of illocutionary force to be given;[28] but we needn't get into that. The point is to separate the vaguely illocutionary idea of "norm expression" from the idea that some fragments of language interact especially with the planning aspect of the conversational state. These will often go together, according to the sort of expressivist described, but they are not the same thing.

We should, in particular, be alive to other ways we might find ourselves messing with plan-laden conversational states. For example, just as the worlds compatible with a context set might be taken, in context, to be characterizing a fictional universe rather than the actual world, so the plans a conversational state leaves open might, in context, be mutually recognized as characterizing what is so according to some particular plan that no party to the discourse in fact endorses (cf. Lewis 1979b). That is logically possible, anyway. If there are such cases, we would want to describe the states of mind expressed as descriptive or factual in character, despite their similarity in dynamic respects to cases which clearly do involve the expression of normative states. There is no problem here for the expressivist—just distinctions to avoid tripping upon in imposing the vague word "express" upon an otherwise clear theory.

It should be acknowledged that the point we have reached is far in important respects from some of the early expressivists cited above. Normative talk is not much like exclamation (pace Barnes 1934); nor does it serve to express preference (pace Carnap 1935 and Russell 1935) or feeling (pace Ayer 1936). But in accord with these authors, and in the spirit of the quote from Austin above, the view is that normative talk serves express states of mind that are not straightforwardly factual in character.

15.10 Empirical plausibility

If the preceding seems to leave the impression that expressivism about normative discourse faces only smooth sailing, it is time to bring the bad news. Metaethical expressivism is, *inter alia*, supposed to be a thesis about the meaning of some fragment of natural language. About this sort of thesis we can separate two issues:

---

[28] There is the worry that such a theory verges on a "theory of everything" of the sort derided by Chomsky (2000). See footnote 10.

(i) LOGICAL POSSIBILITY Is the thesis even in principle compatible with a compositional semantics for some elementary possible language? Can we even make sense of a communication system that works along expressivist lines?

(ii) EMPIRICAL PLAUSIBILITY Can the thesis be well-motivated for a fragment of some actual natural language?

I have largely been concerned with describing affirmative answers to the LOGICAL POSSIBILITY questions, seeing these questions as prior. I have not said anything very substantive about EMPIRICAL PLAUSIBILITY. But of course, our expressivist means to say that a fragment of natural language actually works in the way described—it interacts with the plan structure of the conversational state, and is apt for giving voice to plan-laden states of mind. This places some abstract constraints on the semantics of natural language—in particular, normative expressions need to be given semantic values which interact with hyperplans in the right ways, generating sentences whose context change potentials are adequate for the expression and transmission of plan-laden states of mind. (Normative predicates would seem to need plan-sensitive extensions; deontic modal operators would seem to need to involve quantification over hyperplans, etc.) It is perfectly possible for there to be such semantic values. But is there empirical motivation for the thesis that sentences of natural language have such semantic values?

It is interesting that Gibbard (2003) never attempts to put hyperplans to non-trivial compositional semantic work—for instance, by articulating the compositional semantics of deontic modals, or the attitude verbs 'decides' or 'believes', etc., by appeal to hyperplans in the semantic metalanguage. This is the sort of thing that would be required to motivate the added structure from semantics-internal considerations.[29] A natural place to start might be with sentences like these:

(1)   John thinks that he ought to pack.

The first move the expressivist makes is to psychologically ascend: her story begins with a model of some mental states. It is natural to start here because our expressivist offers special truth-conditions for this sentence: on her theory, its truth turns on the hyperplans that John's state rules in and out. But to give truth-conditions is not yet to give a compositional semantics. The task for the expressivist is to show how to determine these truth-conditions via the compositional semantics of the sentence using the advertised hyperplans, and in a way that meshes with what is already known about the semantics of the constituent expressions of the sentence. (See Yalcin (2012a) for one start at this task.) A similar task awaits the expressivist for normative predicates in general. Much work remains to be done here. The expressivist approach needs to prove itself in the details in natural language semantics and pragmatics. But recent work developing expressivist ideas using tools from formal pragmatics suggests some cause for optimism—or anyway, an open mind.[30]

Further, theorizing in semantics and pragmatics with plans may teach us more about what plans must be like, what constraints they are subject to. Assigning plans

---

[29] This perhaps only highlights how different the present conception of expressivism is from Gibbard's.

[30] Besides the many works already cited in this vein, see also Santorio (2016), MacFarlane (2016).

semantic and pragmatic work to do is a way of constraining a theory of them. Seeking reflective equilibrium between a theory of normative language and a theory of normative thinking, we can make progress on both.

References

Austin, John Langshaw. Performative utterances. In J. O. Urmson and G. J. Warnock, editors, *Philosophical Papers*, pages 220–39. Oxford University Press, Oxford, 1961.

Austin, John Langshaw. *How To Do Things With Words*. Harvard University Press, Cambridge, MA, 1962.

Ayer, Alfred J. *Language, Truth and Logic*. Dover, New York, NY, 1936. Second edition, 1946.

Bach, Kent and Robert Harnish. *Linguistic Communication and Speech Acts*. MIT Press, Cambridge, MA, 1979.

Barnes, W. H. F. A suggestion about value. *Analysis*, 1(3):45–6, 1934.

Belnap, Nuel and Thomas Steel. *The Logic of Questions and Answers*. Yale University Press, New Haven, 1976.

Blackburn, Simon. *Essays in Quasi-Realism*. Oxford: Oxford University Press, 1993.

Blackburn, Simon. *Ruling Passions*. Oxford: Oxford University Press, 1998.

Bratman, Michael. *Intention, Plans, and Practical Reason*. MIT Press, Cambridge, 1987.

Burge, Tyler. Sinning against Frege. *The Philosophical Review* 88(3): 398–432, 1979.

Carnap, Rudolf. *Philosophy and Logical Syntax*. Kegan Paul, London, 1935.

Charlow, Nate. The problem with the Frege-Geach problem. *Philosophical Studies* 167(3): 635–65, 2014.

Charlow, Nate. Prospects for an expressivist theory of meaning. *Philosophers' Imprint* 15(23): 1–43, 2015.

Chomsky, Noam. *New Horizons in the Study of Language and Mind*. Cambridge University Press, 2000.

Dreier, James. Negation for expressivists: A collection of problems with a suggestion for their solution. *Oxford Studies in Metaethics* 1: 217–33, 2006.

Dretske, Fred. *Knowledge and the Flow of Information*. MIT Press, Cambridge, MA, 1981.

Dretske, Fred. *Explaining Behavior: Reasons in a World of Causes*. MIT Press, Cambridge, MA, 1988.

Dummett, Michael. *Frege: Philosophy of Language*. Harvard University Press, Cambridge, MA, 2nd edition, 1973.

Dummett, Michael. *The Logical Basis of Metaphysics*. Harvard University Press, Cambridge, MA, 1993.

Egan, Andy. Epistemic modals, relativism and assertion. *Philosophical Studies* 133(1): 1–22, 2007.

Gazdar, Gerald. *Pragmatics: Implicature, Presupposition and Logical Form*. Academic Press, New York, 1979.

Geach, Peter. Assertion. *Philosophical Review* 74(4): 449–65, 1965.

Gibbard, Allan. An expressivistic theory of normative discourse. *Ethics* 96(3): 472–85, 1986.

Gibbard, Allan. *Wise Choices, Apt Feelings*. Harvard University Press, Cambridge, MA, 1990.

Gibbard, Allan. *Thinking How to Live*. Harvard University Press, Cambridge, MA, 2003.

Gibbard, Allan. Reply to critics. *Philosophy and Phenomenological Research* 72(3): 729–44, 2006.

Green, Mitchell. Speech acts. In Edward N. Zalta, editor, *The Stanford Encyclopedia of Philosophy*. Summer 2015 edition, 2015.

Grice, H. P. Meaning. *Philosophical Review* 66: 377–88, 1957.

Groenendijk, Jeroen and Martin Stokhof. *Studies on the Semantics of Questions and the Pragmatics of Answers*. PhD thesis, University of Amsterdam, 1984.

Hamblin, Charles L. Questions. *Australasian Journal of Philosophy* 36(3): 159–68, 1958.

Hamblin, Charles L. Mathematical models of dialogue. *Theoria* 37(2): 130–55, 1971. ISSN 1755-2567.

Hamblin, Charles L. Questions in Montague English. *Foundations of Language* 10(1): 41–53, 1973.

Hare, R. M. *The Language of Morals*. Oxford University Press, New York, 1952.

Heim, Irene. *The Semantics of Definite and Indefinite Noun Phrases*. PhD thesis, University of Massachusetts, 1982.

Heim, Irene. Presupposition projection and the semantics of attitude verbs. *Journal of Semantics* 9(3): 183–221, 1992.

Hulstijn, Joris. Structured information states: raising and resolving issues. In A. Benz and G. Jager, editors, *Proceedings of MunDial97*, University of Munich, 1997.

Kamp, Hans. A theory of truth and semantic representation. In Jeroen A. Groenendijk, Theo Janssen, and Martin Stokhof, editors, *Formal Methods in the Study of Language*, pages 277–322. Mathematisch Centrum, University of Amsterdam, Amsterdam, 1981.

Kaplan, David. Demonstratives. In Joseph Almog, John Perry, and Howard Wettstein, editors, *Themes from Kaplan*, pages 481–563. Oxford University Press, Oxford, 1977/1989.

Karttunen, Lauri. Discourse referents. In: *International Conference on Computational Linguistics (COLING)* 1969: Preprint no. 70, 1–38. Research Group for Quantitative Linguistics, Stockholm, 1969.

Karttunen, Lauri. Presupposition and linguistic context. *Theoretical Linguistics* 1(1–3): 181–94, 1974. ISSN 0301-4428.

Karttunen, Lauri. Syntax and semantics of questions. *Linguistics and Philosophy* 1: 607–53, 1977.

King, Jeffrey C. Tense, modality, and semantic values. *Philosophical Perspectives* 17: 195–245, 2003.

Kölbel, Max. Conversational score, assertion, and testimony. In Jessica Brown and Herman Cappelen, editors, *Assertion: New Philosophical Essays*, pages 49–78. Oxford University Press, Oxford, 2011.

Lewis, David K. A problem about permission. *In Essays in Honour of Jaakko Hintikka*, pages 163–75. Reidel, Dordrecht, 1979a.

Lewis, David K. Scorekeeping in a language game. *Journal of Philosophical Logic* 8(1): 339–59, 1979b.

Lewis, David K. Attitudes de dicto and de se. *Philosophical Review* 88(4): 513–43, 1979c.

Lewis, David K. Index, context, and content. In S. Kanger and S. Ohman, editors, *Philosophy and Grammar*, pages 79–100. Reidel, Dordrecht, 1980.

Lewis, David K. Putnam's paradox. *Australasian Journal of Philosophy* 62: 221–36, 1984.

Lewis, David K. *On The Plurality of Worlds*. Blackwell, Malden, MA, 1986.

Lewis, David K. Relevant implication. *Theoria* 54(3): 161–74, 1988a.

Lewis, David K. Statements partly about observation. *Philosophical Papers* 17(1): 1–31, 1988b.

Lewis, David K. Reduction of mind. In S. Guttenplan, editor, *A Companion to the Philosophy of Mind*, pages 412–31. Blackwell, Oxford, 1994.

MacFarlane, John. Vagueness as indecision. *Proceedings of the Aristotelian Society* 90: 255–83, 2016.

Ninan, Dilip. Two puzzles about deontic necessity. In Bernard Nickel, Seth Yalcin, Jon Gajewski, Valentine Hacquard, editors, *New Work on Modality*, volume 51, pages 149–78. MIT Working Papers in Linguistics, 2005.

Ninan, Dilip. Semantics and the objects of assertion. *Linguistics and Philosophy* 33(5): 355–80, 2010.

Ninan, Dilip. Counterfactual attitudes and multi-centered worlds. *Semantics and Pragmatics* 5(5): 1–57, 2012.

Ogden, Charles Kay and Ivor Armstrong Richards. *The Meaning of Meaning*. Kegan Paul London, 1923.

Pérez-Carballo, Alejandro and Paolo Santorio. Communication for expressivists. *Ethics* 126(3): 607–35, 2016.

Portner, Paul. The semantics of imperatives within a theory of clause types. In Robert B. Young, editor, *Proceedings of SALT XIV*, pages 235–52, Northwestern University, 2004. Linguistics Society of America.

Portner, Paul. Imperatives and modals. *Natural Language Semantics* 15(4): 351–83, 2007.

Putnam, Hilary. Models and reality. *The Journal of Symbolic Logic* 45(03): 464–82, 1980.

Rabern, Brian. Against the identification of assertoric content with compositional value. *Synthese* 189(1): 75–96, 2012a.

Rabern, Brian. *Monsters and Communication: The Semantics of Contextual Shifting and Sensitivity*. PhD thesis, Australia National University, Canberra, 2012b.

Rabern, Brian. Monsters in Kaplan's logic of demonstratives. *Philosophical Studies* 164(2): 393–404, 2013.

Ridge, Michael. *Impassioned Belief*. Oxford University Press, Oxford, 2014.

Roberts, Craige. Information structure in discourse: Towards an integrated formal theory of pragmatics. In Jae-Hak Yoon and Andreas Kathol, editors, *OSU Working Papers in Linguistics*, volume 49, pages 91–136. The Ohio State University, Department of Linguistics, 1996.

Roberts, Craige. Information structure in discourse: Towards an integrated formal theory of pragmatics. *Semantics and Pragmatics* 5(6): 1–69, 2012.

Rosen, Gideon. Blackburn's *Essays in Quasi-Realism*. *Noûs* 32(3): 386–405, 1998.

Rothschild, Daniel and Seth Yalcin. Three notions of dynamicness in language. *Linguistics & Philosophy*. 39(4): 333–355, 2016.

Rothschild, Daniel and Seth Yalcin. On the dynamics of conversation. *Noûs*, 51(1): 24–48, 2017.

Russell, Bertrand. *Religion and Science*. Oxford University Press, Oxford, 1935.

Santorio, Paolo. Nonfactual know-how and the boundaries of semantics. *Philosophical Review* 125(1): 35–82, 2016.

Scanlon, T. M. Reasons and decisions. *Philosophy and Phenomenological Research*, 72(3), May 2006.

Schroeder, Mark. *Being For: Evaluating the Semantic Program of Expressivism: Evaluating the Semantic Program of Expressivism*. Oxford University Press, Oxford, 2008a.

Schroeder, Mark. How expressivists can and should solve their problem with negation. *Noûs* 42(4): 573–99, 2008b.

Schroeder, Mark. What is the Frege-Geach problem? *Philosophy Compass* 3(4): 703–20, 2008c.

Searle, John R. *Speech Acts: An Essay in the Philosophy of Language*. Cambridge University Press, Cambridge, 1969.

Searle, John R. and Daniel Vanderveken. *Foundations of Illocutionary Logic*. Cambridge University Press, Cambridge, 1985.

Stalnaker, Robert. Pragmatic presuppositions. In Milton K. Munitz and Peter Unger, editors, *Semantics and Philosophy*, pages 197–213. New York University Press, 1974.

Stalnaker, Robert. Assertion. In Peter Cole, editor, *Syntax and Semantics 9: Pragmatics*, pages 315–32. Academic Press, New York, 1978.

Stalnaker, Robert. Indexical belief. *Synthese* 49(1): 129–51, 1981.

Stalnaker, Robert. *Inquiry*. MIT Press, Cambridge, MA, 1984.

Stalnaker, Robert. Possible worlds and situations. *Journal of Philosophical Logic* 15(1): 109–23, 1986.

Stalnaker, Robert. Lewis on intentionality. *Australasian Journal of Philosophy* 81(1): 119–212, 2004.

Stalnaker, Robert. *Our Knowledge of the Internal World*. Oxford University Press, Oxford, 2008.

Stalnaker, Robert. *Context*. Oxford University Press, Oxford, 2014.

Stanley, Jason. Rigidity and content. In Richard G. Heck Jr, editor, *Language, Thought, and Logic: Essays in honor of Michael Dummett*, pages 131–56. Oxford University Press, Oxford, 1997a.

Stanley, Jason. Names and rigid designation. In B. Hale and C. Wright, editors, *A Companion to the Philosophy of Language*, pages 555–85. Blackwell, Oxford, 1997b.

Starr, William. Dynamic expressivism about deontic modality. In Nate Charlow and Matthew Chrisman, editors, *Deontic Modality*, pages 355–94. Oxford University Press, 2016.

Stevenson, Charles Leslie. The emotive meaning of ethical terms. *Mind* 46(181): 14–31, 1937.

Strawson, Peter F. Intention and convention in speech acts. *The Philosophical Review* 73(4): 439–60, 1964.

Unwin, N. Norms and negation: A problem for Gibbard's logic. *The Philosophical Quarterly* 51(202): 60–75, 2001.

Veltman, Frank. Defaults in update semantics. *Journal of Philosophical Logic* 25(3): 221–61, 1996.

Wedgwood, Ralph. *The Nature of Normativity*. Oxford University Press, Oxford, 2007.

Willer, Malte. Dynamic foundations for deontic logic. In Nate Charlow and Matthew Chrisman, editors, *Deontic Modality*, pages 324–54. Oxford University Press, Oxford, 2016.

Willer, Malte. Advice for noncognitivists. *Pacific Philosophical Quarterly* 98: 174–207, 2017.

Williamson, Timothy. Knowing and asserting. *Philosophical Review* 105(4): 489–523, 1996.

Williamson, Timothy. *Knowledge and its Limits*. Oxford University Press, Oxford, 2000.

Woods, Jack. The Frege-Geach problem. In Tristram McPherson and David Plunkett, editors, *Routledge Handbook of Metaethics*, pages 226–42. Routledge, London, 2017.

Yalcin, Seth. Epistemic modals. *Mind* 116(464): 983–1026, 2007.

Yalcin, Seth. Nonfactualism about epistemic modality. In Andy Egan and Brian Weatherson, editors, *Epistemic Modality*, pages 295–332. Oxford University Press, Oxford, 2011.

Yalcin, Seth. Bayesian expressivism. *Proceedings of the Aristotelian Society*, 112(2): 123–60, 2012a.

Yalcin, Seth. Comments on Mark Schroeder, *Being For*. Delivered at American Philosophical Association Central Division Meeting, 2012b.

Yalcin, Seth. Context probabilism. In Maria Aloni, Vadim Kimmelman, Floris Roelofsen, Galit Weidman Sassoon, Katrin Schulz, and Matthijs Westera, editors, *Logic, Language and Meaning*, volume 7218 of *Lecture Notes in Computer Science*, pages 12–21. Springer, Berliln and Heidelberg, 2012c.

Yalcin, Seth. Semantics and metasemantics in the context of generative grammar. In Alexis Burgess and Brett Sherman, editors, *Metasemantics*, pages 17–54. Oxford University Press, Oxford, 2014.

Yalcin, Seth. Quantifying in from a Fregean perspective. *Philosophical Review* 124(2): 207–53, 2015.

Yalcin, Seth. Semantics as model-based science. In Derek Ball and Brian Rabern, editors, *The Science of Meaning*. Oxford University Press, forthcoming.

Yli-Vakkuri, Juhani. Propositions and compositionality. *Philosophical Perspectives* 27(1): 526–63, 2013.

Name Index

Adler, Jonathan 12n15, 27n49, 150n36
Aloni, Maria 77n18, 305
Anderson, Luvell 146n16, 160n78, 243, 255n25, 284–5, 289n63
Asher, Nicholas and Alex Lascarides 26n40, 42n4, 58, 60, 61, 69, 70n5, 90n42, 169, 170, 177n3, 206n7, 324, 342n16
Austin, J. L.
  and felicity conditions 2, 47–8, 151–2, 155–8, 334
  and illocutionary acts 1–5, 21–2, 60, 102, 104, 109, 120–3, 125, 127, 133, 146, 148–9, 151, 154–7, 159, 188, 206–8, 341, 354, 376, 401–2, 407, 409, 424
  and performatives 152, 321, 339, 349–50, 355, 402
  and perlocutionary acts 1, 4, 6, 149, 154, 155, 157, 207–8, 349, 376–7
  and speech act theory 207, 208, 219, 222, 235, 317
  –Searle speech act theory 3, 22, 27, 109, 123–5, 127, 133, 141, 188n4, 339, 341, 350, 354, 402
Ayer, A. J. 1n1, 21n29, 408, 410, 424

Bach, Kent 3–5, 12n15, 27, 40, 53, 55, 139n19, 165, 179, 182, 194n28, 202, 203, 208–10, 212, 228, 240n6, 257nn29, 30, 262, 276, 349, 373n13, 402
Barker, Chris 24n36
Barker, Stephen 104n7, 114–16
Barnes, W. H. F 408, 410, 424
Belnap, Neul D. 105n9, 403
Bezuidenhout, Ann 165, 168, 182
Bhatt, Rajesh 77
Bicchieri, Christina 195n31, 205, 213, 218–19, 220, 222, 231
Bierwisch, Manfred 349
Blume, Andreas and Oliver Board 8n9, 42
Bolinger, Dwight 272n45, 297n1, 312, 332n8
Bolinger, Renee 29n55, 243, 253, 263
Brandom, Robert 13, 15, 59, 220
Bratman, Michael E. 223–4, 343, 421
Brown, Penelope 42, 44, 167–8, 177n3, 178–9, 206n7, 213, 229
Bruce, Kim, B. 17–18n24, 24n37, 25n40, 203, 211–12, 223, 224–5n21, 297–8, 304–6, 313
Buchanan, Ray 4n4, 54
Burge, Tyler 167, 412n17
Butler, Judith 27, 146nn12, 16, 157, 286

Camp, Elisabeth 11, 15–16, 20, 22, 28–9, 40n2, 42, 47n8, 54, 60, 63, 146n16, 149n33, 154n56, 160n79, 190, 248, 253n22, 260–3, 281, 285, 289n61, 371
Cariani, Fabrizio 79n26, 87n38, 90n43
Carr, Jennifer 79n26, 90n43
Charlow, Nate 18, 19n26, 21n30, 25, 68, 69, 70n5, 76n17, 77n18, 78–9, 80n28, 81, 83n32, 85n34, 86nn35, 37, 87n38, 89n41, 90nn42, 43, 44, 91n45, 92n47, 127n4, 166–7, 168, 181, 306, 310, 311, 321, 327, 330, 335–6, 342n15, 344n17, 354, 356, 411, 411–12n16, 415n20
Chomsky, Noam 166, 407n10, 424n28
Ciardelli, Ivano, Jeroen Groenendijk, and Floris Roelofsen 171, 328
Clark, Herbert H. 40, 165, 179, 189n13, 203, 206n7, 212n12, 213
Cohen, Philip R. 17n24, 190n16, 202, 204n4, 209–10, 321, 342, 346
Condoravdi, Cleo 10, 18, 25n40, 70, 78, 86n35, 310–11, 321, 330, 339, 350–2
Culicover, Peter 82n30, 88n40

Davidson, Donald 3n2, 4n4, 23n34, 53, 109–10, 208, 209
Davis, Wayne 9, 10, 101
Dummett, Michael 11, 109, 237n1, 250, 412

Egan, Andy 11, 423n27

Farkas, Donka, F. 18n24, 24n37, 25n40, 203, 211–12, 223, 224n21, 297–8, 304–6, 313
von Fintel, Kai 18, 21n30, 24n36, 25n38, 71n8, 82n30, 88n40, 150n38, 157n64, 190n19, 311n9
Fiske, Alan P. 205, 219
Fodor, Jerry 10, 177n3
Frege, Gottlob
  on "coloring" 237, 248n14, 273
  on force and content 23, 24n36, 25n39, 71, 99–100, 104n7, 109, 125–39, 141, 400–2, 409–12
Fricker, Elizabeth 42n4, 48, 50, 59–60
Fricker, Miranda 204, 213, 221

Gazdar, Gerald 17n24, 20, 22n31, 24, 202, 212, 298–301, 303, 306, 402
Geach, P. T. 135, 400, 409, 410–11, 412
Gibbard, Allan 87n38, 400, 411, 412n16, 414–22

Ginzburg, Jonathan 18n24, 69n3, 167, 170, 302, 322, 326, 348
Green, Mitchell S. 9–11, 26, 27n45, 99n2, 100n3, 102–3, 106, 107n13, 109n18, 110, 111n20, 112n22, 114n24, 136n16, 138n18, 341n14, 401n1
Grice, H. P.
  and his Aunt Matilda 279n50
  and conversational implicature 26, 42, 49, 165, 244, 360
  and the conversational maxims 12, 70, 244, 263, 266, 324, 328, 351
  and the cooperative principle 12, 14, 40, 197–8, 324, 329
  and the force/content distinction 23n34
  and intentionalism 4–7, 14, 15
  and speaker meaning 1n1, 5, 21–2, 53–5, 61–2, 101–2, 108n16, 166–7, 180, 327, 342, 402
Groenendijk, Jeroen 19n27, 24n35, 127n4, 134n12, 171, 225, 305, 328, 403, 404n6
Gunlogson, Christine 18n24, 24n37, 25n40, 297–8, 303–7, 313

Habermas, Jürgen 27n50, 205n5
Hamblin, C. L. 17n24, 24n35, 171, 202, 211, 212n11, 223, 226, 297–304, 402–3
Han, Chung-hye 71, 77n18, 181, 330–1
Hanks, Peter 25–6, 100n3, 111, 112n21, 113–14, 116–20, 126n3, 128n6, 129n7, 130n9, 135n13, 137n15, 136n16, 137n17, 138n18, 188n4
Hare, R. M. 1n1, 21, 23n34, 109, 124n2, 409n12
Harnish, Robert M. 3–5, 27, 53, 55, 139n19, 165, 179, 194n28, 202–3, 208–10, 212, 228, 349, 373n13, 402
Harris, Daniel W. 3n2, 4n4, 18, 21n28, 22, 25n41, 53, 86n35, 167–9, 181, 273
Hart, H. L. A. 27n46
Haslanger, Sally 146n16, 148, 225n25
Hausser, Roland 24n36, 105n10, 302, 320n2
Hawthorne, John 12n15, 48, 56
Heim, Irene 3n3, 14n20, 17n24, 19, 58, 87, 111n20, 212n11, 225, 305, 311, 340, 385, 389–91, 402, 416, 419n25
Hintikka, Jaakko 124n2, 343
Hom, Christopher 27n44, 29n54, 116n25, 137n17, 246, 247n12, 255, 262, 282–3, 289n63
Horn, Laurence R. 166, 179, 247n12, 251n21, 266–7, 308
Hornsby, Jennifer 28, 146n12, 151n44, 221, 252n21, 255, 262, 270
Hulstijn, Joris 213, 302, 403

Iatridou, Sabine 24n36, 71n8, 82n30, 88n40, 310n9

Jackendoff, Ray 82n30, 88n40, 179

Kamp, Hans 17n24, 19n27, 402
Kaplan, David 3n3, 277, 299, 384, 385n3, 392–3, 413–14
Karttunen, Lauri 24n35, 68n2, 388n9, 402–3
Kaufmann, Magdalena 19, 67–9, 71n8, 74, 77n19, 81–6, 88, 94, 105n10, 181, 306, 309n8, 310–11, 321, 327n4, 330–4, 338, 346–7, 353
King, Jeffery C. 3n3, 48, 56, 404
Kolodny, Niko and John MacFarlane 79n26, 90n43
Kukla, Rebecca 13, 146n12, 151, 157n65, 220
Kratzer, Angelika 77–8, 85n34, 88, 90n42, 111n20, 326, 330–4, 336, 341, 344, 353
Krifka, Manfred 13n18, 25nn38–40, 306, 347
Kripke, Saul 167, 390

Lackey, Jennifer 12n15, 59
Lakoff, George 148n26, 166
Lance, Mark 13, 220
Langton, Rae 28–9, 59n15, 103n5, 144n5, 145n7, 146nn12, 16, 147n18, 148nn25, 28, 149n32, 150n33, 37 151n44, 152nn45–8, 153nn52–3, 154nn54, 56, 157nn64, 66, 68, 159nn72–4, 160n75, 161nn81, 83, 187n2, 188n5, 190n18, 191n20, 192n25, 193n25, 194n27, 206n7, 221, 255n25, 373, 375–6
Lauer, Sven 10, 18, 25n40, 70, 78, 86n35, 297n2, 310, 311, 321, 330, 339, 350–2
Lee, James 42n4, 43, 44n6, 48, 50, 58, 60–1
Lepore, Ernie 3–4, 16–17, 25, 53–4, 70n5, 166–9, 179–82, 190n16, 206n6, 222n17, 243, 284–5, 289n63
Levesque, Hector J. 202n1, 204n4, 209, 342, 346
Levinson, Stephen C. 22n31, 42, 44, 167–8, 177n3, 178–9, 205, 208–9, 213, 219, 229, 266–7, 306
Lewis, David
  and accommodation 145, 148, 150–5
  and content 27n45, 72, 401, 412, 418–22
  and conversational score 14, 16, 17n24, 20, 53, 58–9, 62, 153–4, 159, 167, 188n10, 189n13, 192n24, 193n25, 202, 204, 211, 324, 375, 402, 404, 414, 424
  and coordination 212n12, 214–18
  and force 19n26, 23n34, 83, 124n2, 152–3, 169, 208, 301, 302n5, 395, 397
  and linguistic convention 16, 40–1, 53, 167, 180–1, 205, 270n44, 272n45
  and retroactivity 156–60
Lewis, Karen 17, 384n2
Lycan, William G. 169, 189n12

MacFarlane, John 12n15, 13, 59, 425n30
   joint work with Niko Kolodny 79n26, 90n43
MacKinnon, Catherine 28, 103n5, 186n2, 221
McGowan, Mary Kate 13, 15, 28–9, 146,
   153n53, 154n56, 159n74, 160, 187n2,
   193n25, 200n42, 204, 220–1, 373, 375–6
McKinney, Rachel 29
Maitra, Ishani 12n15, 28nn51, 53, 146n12, 152,
   187n2, 204, 206n7, 217, 221
Maynard Smith, John 203, 216–17
Mendelberg, Tali 364–6, 368, 371n11, 374n16
Michaelson, Eliot 3n3, 27n49
Millikan, Ruth G. 7–9, 11, 12n16, 13n17, 19,
   166, 181, 203, 216, 271n44
Montague, Richard 71, 384, 385n3
Murray, Sarah E. 8n9, 18n24, 19–20, 22, 25,
   28n51, 153n53, 188n4, 195n31, 203,
   210–11, 223–5, 308, 347–8

Neale, Stephen 3n3, 6n7, 7, 27n48, 53, 198n12
Ninan, Dilip 21n30, 72, 400, 412, 423n27

Pagin, Peter 9, 12n15
Pak, Miok 320–1, 338
Peirce, Charles S. 59
Pendlebury, Michael 104, 320n2
Pérez–Carballo, Alejandro 21n30, 400
Perrault, C. Raymond 17n24, 202, 210, 321,
   342, 346
Perry, John 393
Pinker, Steven 20, 42n4, 43, 44n5, 48, 50–1, 58,
   60–1, 146n14, 206n7
Portner, Paul 15, 17–19, 24, 67–9, 71n8, 72,
   74–81, 83–5, 90, 92, 94, 105n10, 127n4,
   167, 203, 211–12, 223, 225, 297n2,
   298–300, 302–3, 305, 309–10, 312n12,
   319n1, 320–1, 327, 332–3, 338–9, 342–4,
   346–9, 353, 355, 404, 414
Potts, Christopher 20, 110n19, 243n8, 247,
   262n34, 268, 348
Putnam, Hilary 167, 283–4, 420n26

Recanati, François 104n8, 127n5, 266n41
Reiland, Indrek 26n44, 116–17n25, 137n17
Roberts, Craige 14n20, 15, 17, 17–18n24, 19,
   20, 22n31, 24, 40, 58, 71n9, 72, 76, 86n35,
   152n48, 167, 188n4, 189n11, 203, 211, 223,
   225, 298, 302–3, 321, 322, 324, 326–7, 332,
   333n9, 337, 338, 354, 403, 404n6
Roelofsen, Floris 171, 211, 297, 305n6, 328
Rothschild, Daniel 82n30, 85n34, 88n40,
   93n48, 404
Russell, Bertrand 125–6, 128–9, 189nn11, 12,
   408, 410, 424

Sadock, Jerrold M. 23n34, 69, 166, 167, 169,
   223, 249, 319

Santorio, Paolo 21n30, 400, 414, 425n30
Saul, Jennifer 11, 27n49, 29, 41n3, 43,
   55, 60, 146nn12, 16, 159n74,
   201n43
Sbisà, Marina 103, 146nn11, 16, 147, 148–9,
   151n43, 154nn56, 57, 156, 158n74,
   159n74, 160n75, 203
Scanlon, Thomas 14, 417n23
Schiffer, Stephen 3n3, 5, 7, 18, 27n45, 55,
   124n2
Schroeder, Mark 21n29, 81n29, 411,
   411–12n16, 417n21
Schwartz, Jeremy 116n25, 137n17
Schwartzman, Lisa 146n12, 156, 157n68
Scott–Phillips, Thom 5n5, 9n11, 27n45, 203,
   206n7, 216, 220, 230
Searle, John 3, 6, 12–14, 22, 23n34, 27, 45n6,
   69, 104n7, 108–9, 123–7, 132–3, 138–41,
   165–6, 168, 180, 188n4, 202, 203, 207–8,
   209n8, 219, 228, 231, 306, 317–19, 321,
   328–9, 338–9, 341–2, 346, 349–54, 401n1,
   402, 409–10
Sellars, Wilfrid 13n17, 27n45, 220
Skyrms, Brian 7n8, 19, 27n45, 40, 206n7
Soames, Scott 60, 138n18
Sperber, Dan 3n3, 5n6, 7, 41, 70, 320n2, 328,
   330
Stalnaker, Robert 14–15, 17, 18n25, 19, 21,
   22n31, 24, 40n2, 44, 53, 55, 56, 58–63,
   73n12, 103n6, 104, 151n43, 154nn54, 56,
   167–8, 171, 190n19, 191n22, 202–3,
   211–13, 223, 225, 297n2, 298, 301, 305,
   318, 321, 322, 326–8, 352, 354, 375, 384n2,
   386nn5, 7, 388n9, 393n15, 395n19,
   396n20, 398n20, 400, 402, 403nn4, 5,
   404–7, 413–15, 418, 418–19n25, 420n26,
   421–3
Stanley, Jason 12n15, 28n51, 29, 41n3,
   146nn14, 16, 148, 159n74, 189n12, 351,
   369n10, 373–4, 378, 380–1, 412
Starr, William B. 3n2, 8n9, 14n20, 17–18n24,
   19–20, 21n30, 22, 23n34, 24, 25, 28n51,
   77n18, 78nn21, 22, 86n35, 147n18,
   153n53, 166–8, 169–71, 173, 175n2,
   177n3, 181, 188n4, 195n31, 203, 209n8,
   210, 211, 223–4, 225, 305, 321, 322, 347–8,
   356, 400, 415n20
Stenius, Erik 104n7, 109, 208, 223
Stevenson, Charles L. 1n1, 21n29, 409–10
Stokhof, Martin 19n27, 24n35, 127n4, 134n12,
   225, 305, 403, 404n6
Stone, Matthew 3–4, 16–17, 25, 53–4, 65, 70,
   165–82, 206n6, 222n17, 342n16
Strawson, Peter F. 3n2, 5, 55, 109, 207,
   402
Swanson, Eric 21n30, 67, 93n48, 146n16,
   147n18

Thomason, Richmond H. 14n20, 17–18n24, 150–1, 156, 167, 168, 170, 190n16, 312n12, 324, 342n16

Tirrell, Lynne 13, 28n52, 40n1, 146n16, 204, 206n7, 221, 248, 255, 288n62, 289n63, 382

Turri, John 10, 12n15

Unger, Peter 10n14, 11, 12n15

Vanderveken, Daniel 22n32, 107, 108n15, 123n1, 202–3, 207–8, 209n8, 306, 341, 401n1, 402

Veltman, Frank 14n20, 17–18n24, 21n30, 225, 400, 415n20

Waldron, Jeremy 28, 144n5

West, Caroline 146nn12, 16, 147n18, 148n28, 153nn52, 53, 154n56, 159n74, 160n75, 221

Willer, Malte 21n30, 79, 392, 395, 397, 400, 415

Williamson, Timothy 10n14, 11–12, 220, 247n13, 248, 262, 276–7n48, 400, 415n20

Wilson, Deirdre 3n3, 5n6, 7, 38, 41, 70, 320n2, 328, 330

Witek, Maciej 151, 153n52, 154n56, 155n59, 158

Wittgenstein, Ludwig 1n1, 10n14, 21n29, 58, 205n5, 321

Yalcin, Seth 17–18n24, 21–2, 69n4, 72n10, 79n25, 87n38, 93n48, 204n3, 213, 291, 400–26

Zanuttini, Raffaella 3, 24n35, 320–1, 329–30, 339, 346–9

Zwicky, Arnold M. 69, 223, 262n35, 289, 319

Term Index

accommodation 145, 148–55, 157n65, 160–1,
  192–3, 301–2, 361, 373
ambiguity 55, 100n3, 111–12, 179–81, 208,
  250n19, 259, 341, 363
anaphora 19–21, 23, 58, 60, 337, 385
assertion(s) 4–12, 15, 17, 18n25, 20–2, 23n33,
  25–6, 44, 60, 63, 67, 71–2, 75, 83, 109, 123,
  133, 153–4, 159, 190–1, 212, 229, 246–8,
  266–7, 298–301, 303–4, 318–19, 349–51,
  386, 394, 401–3, 405–7
  and cancellation 136–8
  norms of 11–14, 220

back-door speech acts 146–8, 153–4, 159–61

clause-type 3, 7, 19, 23, 25, 67–75, 78n21, 93,
  94, 169, 300, 302, 313, 319–21, 327–8,
  330–1, 354–5
  embedded 73, 74n13, 89–90, 115–18, 133,
  135–7, 139–40, 169, 320–1, 330, 392
collaborative inquiry 42, 318, 322–3
commitment 13–14, 15–16, 18, 27, 41, 43–4,
  50, 57–61, 63, 76, 106–7, 108n15, 117–18,
  168–9, 203–6, 225–30, 298–313, 323, 343,
  351–2
  slates 226, 298–300, 303
common ground 14n20, 15–17, 19–21, 44,
  52–3, 56–9, 61–3, 72, 75, 103–5, 146n16,
  154–5, 160n75, 190n17, 191–2, 196,
  212n12, 213, 223, 224–5n21, 229, 298,
  301–6, 311–12, 318, 322–3, 325–6, 349,
  351–2, 354–5, 373, 374–8, 386, 394,
  396–8, 406
common knowledge 213, 245, 385, 391,
  394, 406
compositional semantics 8, 52, 60, 72–3,
  77n20, 82, 87, 88n40, 90, 94, 116, 120, 223,
  225, 245n10, 262n35, 264n38, 303, 306,
  313, 319, 328, 347–8, 384, 387–9, 300, 401,
  410–16, 418, 425
conditional(s) 21n30, 24–5, 26, 77n19, 77–9,
  85n34, 90n42, 115–16, 119–20, 137–8,
  175–7, 246, 331–2, 337, 348, 386–7, 393
  antecedent(s) 26, 77, 79, 82, 90, 109, 111,
  117, 120, 136, 138
  cancellation 117, 136–8
  imperatives see imperative(s), 'conditional'
  material 78, 387
  and parentheticals 110–11, 117–18, 136, 138
  preference 166, 169, 170, 175–6, 178–9
  questions 25, 175

context 14–22, 52–63, 74–6, 171, 184–92, 211,
  222–8, 297–306, 322, 324–7, 385–6, 402–4;
  see also common ground; conversational
  record; conversational score;
  conversational state
context–change potential(s) 16–17, 22, 25, 300,
  302, 304–5, 388–90, 392, 395–7, 404,
  407n11, 415, 425
context sensitivity 8, 14, 17, 48–9, 63–4, 74, 84,
  90–1, 91n45, 385, 403–4, 414, 425
  set 14n20, 76, 104–5, 301, 303, 312n12, 323,
  343–4, 385–6, 389–91, 394–5, 397, 402–4,
  406, 424
convention
  Lewis's account of 16–17, 40–1, 53, 58, 155,
  167, 180–1, 204–5, 214, 218, 270–1n44,
  271n45, 234
  linguistic 3–4, 5–6, 8, 14, 19, 21, 27, 41, 63,
  243n8, 258–9, 265, 270n44, 273, 280,
  284, 349
  social 2–3, 16n23, 202, 205, 207, 209–10,
  219, 230
conventionalism 2–4, 7, 12, 16–17, 19, 53
conventional meaning 45n6, 50, 168, 180–1,
  204, 206n6, 209–10, 230–1, 243, 249,
  249n17, 256–7, 260, 265, 273, 289
conversational maxims (Grice) 12, 219, 244,
  260, 266–7, 276–7n48, 324
conversational record 14n20, 21, 52–63,
  167–70, 178, 190, 371
  off–record contributions 20, 43, 55, 58, 61
conversational score 2, 14–20, 21, 29, 53,
  58–62, 153–4, 159, 188n10, 188–91, 204,
  324–7, 332–3, 346, 352–55, 375, 404
conversational state 14n20, 204, 226–30,
  402–6, 414–15, 423–5
Cooperative Principle (Grice) 12, 14, 197, 324
coordination
  problem 40–1, 214–15, 218, 228n24
  games 214, 217, 219–20
counter–speech 144–6, 148n25, 149, 150
  blocking 145–61

declaratives 18n25, 19, 21, 24–6, 67, 71–4, 82,
  93, 126, 127, 133, 135–6, 166, 169, 178,
  202, 210–11, 212n11, 223–9, 297, 300,
  303–7, 312–13, 319–22, 327–9, 338, 346,
  348, 385nn3, 6, 405, 412–15
deniability 44–52, 55, 58–63, 371
deontic modals 19, 21n30, 25n39, 79, 81–6,
  331, 332n7, 333, 337, 344, 384, 395–6, 425

derogatives 28, 237–91, 410n13
direction of fit 123–5, 133–5, 138–9, 208, 318
directive(s) 5, 8, 11, 15, 17–18, 24–5, 26, 43–4,
    55, 60, 70, 76–8, 80, 92, 104, 124, 135, 138,
    141, 150–3, 155, 166, 168–70, 210, 301,
    309–10, 317, 319, 329, 330, 335, 337–9,
    343–7
  see also imperative(s)
dogwhistles 11, 29, 41n3, 43, 55, 146n16, 164,
    201, 360–82
  intentional vs unintentional 29, 361–71
  covert 159n74, 364–5, 369, 371, 373–8
dynamic pragmatics 17, 24, 74–7, 78n21, 93,
    297–306, 311–13, 385–94, 404
dynamic semantics 4, 15n22, 16–17, 25, 175n2,
    204, 225, 298, 302, 305–6, 312, 384–5,
    388–94, 396–8, 404, 415–16

epistemic modals 21n30, 77n20, 93n48,
    331–2n7, 384, 393–8
euphemisms 57, 245, 274, 291, 367n9
exercitives 146, 150n37, 187–201, 373, 375
  covert 13, 15, 146, 194–201, 375
expressionism 9–11, 12, 14
expressivism 1n1, 9n12, 19n26, 21, 26, 87n38,
    275n29, 400–1, 408–25
expressive(s) 28, 102–3, 108n14, 124–5,
    138–41, 241, 243–4, 268, 289n61, 317,
    319, 408
externalism 283–4

felicity condition(s) 2, 10, 12–13, 16, 20, 29,
    103, 147–53, 155–8, 161, 224, 277, 309n8,
    324, 326, 330–1, 334, 341, 346, 350, 354
  see also sincerity
force/content distinction 3, 17, 19, 22–6, 43–4,
    60, 70, 75, 93–4, 123–8, 131–41, 206–12,
    228, 300, 304–5, 320, 332, 347–9
force assignment 24, 75, 78n21, 92–4, 112, 303
free-speech 28, 148n25, 187, 188n5, 258–9n31
functionalism 7–11, 130n9

goals of discourse 15, 19, 41, 46, 179, 211, 318,
    322–8, 334, 343–5, 354, 406
grammar-meaning interface 71, 165–6, 169,
    177, 179, 181, 197, 297–9, 302, 349

hate speech 13, 28, 144, 152–4, 161, 238, 360,
    375, 376nn18, 19
humor 168, 228, 253, 256, 288
hyperplan 400, 414, 417–21, 423–5

illocutionary act(s) 1–14, 19–24, 28, 29, 44,
    55n13, 56, 69–70, 72, 75, 99, 101, 103n6,
    104n7, 105–12, 115, 123–5, 127, 133, 146,
    153–7, 187–8, 206–10, 289n61, 300, 320,

341–2, 347, 353–4, 375, 386, 400–2, 407,
    410–11, 415, 423
disablement 146, 159, 221
illocutionary vs. dynamic force 401–8,
    410–11, 424
locutionary acts 1, 22, 102, 109, 127, 149,
    206–8, 210, 342, 407
  vs. perlocutionary acts 1, 4, 56, 149, 154–5,
    157, 207–10, 289n61
assignment see force assignment
imperative(s) 7, 10, 18–19, 23–5, 76–7, 82, 84,
    86, 94, 305, 313, 321–2, 327, 329–38,
    339–40, 343–9, 353–5, 385n3, 386n6, 404,
    408, 409
  conditional 24–5, 68, 76–9, 81, 84, 89, 91,
    175, 331–2, 336, 348
  embedded 76–81, 82n31, 85–6, 89–90, 321,
    331, 334, 338
  illocutionary variability 18–19, 76, 83, 90–2,
    306, 310, 320–1
  see also directive(s)
implicature
  conventional 20, 28, 110n19, 243, 244,
    247–9, 268, 348
  conversational 48, 115, 165, 244, 246n11,
    249, 360
indexicals 198, 332–3, 338, 386
indirect speech act(s) 4, 8, 17–18, 28, 58, 70,
    92n47, 165–70, 176–81, 208, 268, 313,
    340–3, 354
  normative consequences of 28, 44–5, 48, 51
inference see also rational inference
information structure 14n20, 41, 173, 226, 305,
    322–3, 343, 385, 396, 403
insinuation 4, 11, 16, 20–1, 42–63, 146nn14,
    16, 190n17, 371
intentionalism 4–7, 9, 10, 11, 14–15
  see also Grice, H. P.
interrogative(s) 19, 23–4, 67–9, 72–4, 86, 93,
    104–5, 112, 124, 127, 133–4, 166–7, 174,
    177, 181, 211–12, 223–5, 300, 303, 319–22,
    327–30, 336, 338, 346–7
irony 115–16, 120, 168, 216, 222n17, 269,
    270, 288

linguistic convention 2–8, 12, 14, 16–17,
    19–21, 40–1, 53, 63, 146n12, 300, 317, 324,
    342, 346, 349, 355, 358
  and slurs 243–5, 259–61, 264–8, 270–3,
    276–80, 284–5
Literal Force Hypothesis 208, 300–1, 303,
    306

marriage 1–3, 139, 147, 150n39, 152n48, 153,
    157–8, 186, 207, 230, 274
metaphor 4, 45n6, 147, 206n6, 222n17, 277

misfire 2, 106, 145–8, 151, 152n49, 155, 156, 158–9, 161, 190n18, 194n27
modal(s) 3, 19, 21n30, 25n39, 59, 67–8, 71–3, 77–85, 86n37, 87–9, 90n44, 90, 92–4, 105n10, 175n2, 224, 296, 301–2, 309–10, 328–34, 337, 341, 343–5, 353–4, 384, 393–8, 404, 411, 425
    epistemic, to strong/weak necessity statements 269, 309
mood (grammatical) 7, 23, 104, 108n14, 109n17, 133n11, 134, 135, 204, 209–10, 212n11, 222–5, 298, 300, 302–4, 305n6, 313, 319–22, 322, 327–30, 332, 335–6, 338–9, 346–9, 353, 387n8
    see also declaratives; force/content distinction; imperative(s); interrogative(s)
Moore's paradox 10, 11–12

non-natural meaning see speaker meaning
nonlinguistic communicative acts 7, 8, 17

ordering source 19, 78, 84–5, 86n37, 88–94, 309, 330–5, 337, 341, 353–4, 395

pejorative(s) 28, 238, 240, 249–50, 253, 255–6n26, 264, 279–80, 285, 291, 364–5
    hybrid words 237, 239, 240n6, 244, 247n12, 249–50, 263–4, 275, 279–80, 291
performative(s) 19, 26, 70, 81–5, 94, 109, 111, 151n44, 152–3, 156, 157n65, 169, 309n8, 319, 321–2, 329, 331, 339, 342, 349–52, 355, 402, 404
perlocutionary acts 1, 4, 67, 87, 149, 154–5, 157, 207–10, 289n61, 349, 376–8
    as covert dogwhistles 376–8, 381
possible worlds 88, 93, 104–5, 171–3, 175–6, 191, 223–4, 301, 311–12, 322, 326, 330–1, 333–4, 343–4, 386n6, 387, 389–90, 393–7, 402, 414–24
    accessibility relations 56, 58, 59, 60, 171, 301, 330, 343–4, 404
pragmatic inference see rational, 'inference(s)'
preference 10, 18, 19, 87, 89n41, 166–71, 174–9, 181, 223–4, 226–7, 229–30, 306, 308–9, 311, 351, 373–4, 411, 418–19n25, 420, 424
presupposition(s) 20, 40, 49–50, 58, 60, 91n46, 103, 145–51, 153, 155, 157–60, 189, 193–4, 243, 244, 249n17, 301, 308, 312, 330, 332,
334, 337, 345, 355, 375, 384, 387–93, 402, 406
propositional attitude(s) 14–15, 68, 73–4, 85–7, 105, 127, 130n9, 131–5, 168, 224–5n21, 342, 343, 392, 412, 421

question under discussion (QUD) 15, 58, 302, 322–8, 337–8, 344–5, 352, 354–5

racism 43, 199–200, 238, 252, 256, 264, 278–9, 289–90, 364–5, 381
rational
    constraints 6, 323–4, 326–7, 329
    inference(s) 6, 92n47, 101, 113, 209–10, 212, 243n8, 260, 261, 267, 269, 275, 296, 322, 326, 340–1, 350
relevance 45, 49, 60, 190, 302, 324, 326, 328, 329, 337–8, 342

sarcasm 168, 212, 228, 268, 340
sexism 43, 151, 185, 199, 200, 280
signaling 7–8, 42n4, 55, 107, 209, 211–17, 229
silencing 28, 144, 146, 161
sincerity 12, 50, 72, 124–5, 141, 168, 212, 220, 228, 287, 288, 325, 328–9, 335, 339–41, 350–1
slurs 28–9, 146, 147n18, 160, 220, 237–91, 363n4, 410n13
social norms 161, 187n3, 195, 197, 204–6, 214, 218–22, 229–31, 244, 267, 285
    vs. descriptive norms 218
    enacting 13–15, 153, 155, 185–8, 195–8, 199–201, 375; see also exercitives
    see also felicity condition(s)
speaker meaning 5–6, 44, 53–6, 63, 69n4, 101–3, 107–8, 112, 115, 208, 329
speech acts
    illocutionary see illocutionary act(s)
    indirect see indirect speech act(s)
    perlocutionary see perlocutionary act(s)
successful communication 4–5, 20–1, 45–7, 49, 53, 56, 58–9, 61, 63, 139, 145, 153, 186, 217, 221, 351–52, 371, 373, 386, 391, 402

to-do list 15–16, 18, 75–81, 83, 94, 298, 302–13, 332, 336, 349, 354, 404, 414

underdetermination 3, 209–10, 245, 324
unity of the proposition 128–31, 137n17
uptake see successful communication